AIR TRANSPORT IN THE 21ST CENTURY

We would like to dedicate this book to the memory of Maura O'Connell and to Frances Margaret Williams.
May they rest in peace.

Air Transport in the 21st Century
Key Strategic Developments

Edited by

JOHN F. O'CONNELL

AND

GEORGE WILLIAMS

Routledge
Taylor & Francis Group

LONDON AND NEW YORK

First published 2011 by Ashgate Publishing

Published 2016 by Routledge
2 Park Square, Milton Park, Abingdon, Oxon OX14 4RN
711 Third Avenue, New York, NY 10017, USA

Routledge is an imprint of the Taylor & Francis Group, an informa business

British Library Cataloguing in Publication Data
Air transport in the 21st century : key strategic developments.
1. Airlines--Management. 2. Airlines--Finance.
3. Strategic alliances (Business) 4. Aeronautics,
Commercial--Security measures.
I. O'Connell, John F. II. Williams, George,
387.7'068-dc22

ISBN 9781409400974 (hbk)

Library of Congress Cataloging-in-Publication Data
O'Connell, John F. (John Frankie),
Air transport in the 21st century : key strategic developments / by John F. O'Connell and George Williams.
    p. cm.
Includes index.
ISBN 978-1-4094-0097-4 (hardback)
1. Aeronautics, Commercial--Deregulation. 2. Airlines--Deregulation. 3. Aeronautics, Commercial--Deregulation. 4. Competition, International. I. Williams, George, 1948- II. Title.
HE9777.7.O25 2011
387.7--dc22

2011009550

Contents

PRACTITIONER PIECES

ACADEMIC SECTION

List of Figures

List of Tables

About the Editors

John F. O'Connell (Frankie) is currently an airline lecturer in the department of Air Transport at Cranfield University. He comes from Co. Cork in Ireland and completed an MSc in Air Transport Management from Cranfield University and an MBA (Aviation) from Embry-Riddle Aeronautical University, later returning to Cranfield to complete a PhD on airline management. He is also a certified IATA instructor and holds a pilot's licence. Previously, he has worked for the Boeing commercial aircraft company as an analyst for a number of years and then for Embry-Riddle Aeronautical University (extended campus in California) as an airline lecturer for a further five years. While at Embry-Riddle, he regularly lectured at the NASA Ames research facility at Moffett Field. He has spent a large chunk of his time down through the years travelling to the world's airlines[1] on behalf of IATA, the Arab Air Carriers Organization and Cranfield University in both an advisory and training capacity on areas such as strategy, management, marketing, cost reduction, distribution and low cost carrier operations. He has published papers in the *Journal of Air Transport Management*, *Journal of Transport Geography*, *Journal of Airport Management*, *Journal of Research in Transportation Business & Management*, *Journal of Tourism Economics*, *Journal of World Review of Intermodal Research* and the *Journal of Air Transport Studies*.

George Williams was until September 2009 Reader in Airline Economics at the Department of Air Transport, Cranfield University. He continues to lecture and research in the fields of Air Transport Economics and Regulation, with a particular focus on the provision of air services in remoter regions. George graduated with a BSc in Economics from City University in 1971, an MA in Transport Economics from Leeds University in 1972 and a PhD from Cranfield University in 1991. He joined the Air Transport Department at Cranfield University as a lecturer in 1995. He has extensive international lecturing experience and has written extensively exploring the impact of deregulation on the airline industry. In 1998 he was appointed Special Adviser to the UK House of Lords European Communities Committee enquiry into the Commission's proposals to extend its powers to apply existing competition provisions to air services between the EU and third countries. He has led major studies into airline service provision in Ireland, the

---

1   Air India, Air China, Biman Bangladesh, China Eastern, Egyptair, Etihad Airways, Garuda Indonesia, Gulf Air, Hainan Airlines, Indian Airlines, Qatar Airways, Kuwait Airways, Libyan Airlines, Malaysia Airlines, Mahan Air, Oman Air, Saudi Arabian Airlines, Singapore Airlines, Royal Air Maroc, Royal Jordanian Airlines, Sri Lankan Airlines, Tunisair and Yemenia.

Netherlands, Norway, Spain, Sweden and the UK on behalf of the European Commission, Government departments, regulatory authorities, airlines and airport authorities. Whilst at Cranfield George headed the Centre for Air Transport in Remoter Regions, which organises a biennial international Forum devoted to issues concerning air transport provision in Remoter Regions, the most recent of which took place in Bergen, Norway in April 2009. He is a Fellow of both the Royal Aeronautical Society and the Chartered Institute of Logistics and Transport.

List of Contributors

Dr Sean Barrett is a Senior Lecturer at the Department of Economics and a fellow of Trinity College, Dublin, Ireland. He is a graduate of University College, Dublin, and McMaster University, Canada. He is a Government of Ireland nominee to the National Economic and Social Council of Ireland and a member of the international editorial board of the *Journal of Air Transport Management*. He has participated in international research on airline and airport competition under the auspices of the European Science Foundation, the European Union, the OECD/ECMT and CESifo. He is a board member of the Alfred Beit Foundation and the Kenmare economic policy conference and academic adviser to the FBD Trust.

Graham Braithwaite joined Cranfield in 2003 as Director of the Safety and Accident Investigation Centre and became Head of the Department of Air Transport in 2006. Graham holds a BSc (Hons) in Transport Management and Planning and a PhD in Aviation Safety Management from Loughborough University. He is a Fellow of the Royal Aeronautical Society and Member of the International Society of Air Safety Investigators. Professor Braithwaite has led the development and delivery of investigation, human factors and safety management courses for a range of external clients including the European Aviation Safety Agency, Australian Transport Safety Bureau, Hong Kong Civil Aviation Department, British Midland Airways, SAS, Qantas Airways, Rail Accident Investigation Branch and the Omani Royal Flight. He has also consulted extensively in safety and human factors matters for organizations such as Airservices Australia (ATC teams and supervision; provision of Aviation Rescue and Firefighting), Halcrow (human factors issues of driver vigilance systems), Regional Express (safety health survey), Risk and Reliability Associates (human factors issues of railway worksite signalling), Qantas Airways (design standards for engineering and maintenance task cards), Airplan (third-party risk around aerodromes) and the UK CAA (human factors issues for CPDLC datalink). Graham has also been called upon by various media organizations including the BBC TV and radio, Sky News, ITN, Associated Press to provide expertise on matters of aviation safety. He has also provided testimony to the House of Commons Transport Select Committee review of the CAA and since 2007 has served as a member of the Advisory Board to the Singapore Aviation Academy.

Ben Daley is a Lecturer in Environmental Management at the Centre for Development, Environment and Policy, School of Oriental and African Studies (SOAS), University of London. His work focuses on environmental change and environmental history, including studies of the environmental effects of the air transport industry. He has worked on several projects to investigate potential environmental improvements at airports resulting from revised air traffic management technologies and procedures, as well as from revised operational procedures. He also works on the relationship between air transport and climate change. The Centre for Development, Environment and Policy undertakes research and postgraduate teaching in the fields of applied economics, environment and biodiversity, and sustainability and development.

Peter Forsyth has been Professor of Economics at Monash University since 1997, and prior to this he was at the University of New England, Australian National University and the University of New South Wales. He studied at the University of Sydney and gained a DPhil in Economics from the University of Oxford. Most of his research has been on applied microeconomics, with particular reference to the economics of air transport, tourism economics and the economics of regulation. He has done extensive research on air transport, including on international aviation regulation and Australian domestic air transport. He has published several papers on airport regulation, and is the joint Editor of a book on the subject (*The Economic Regulation of Airports: Recent developments in Australasia, North America and Europe*, Ashgate, 2004). Recently he published, with Larry Dwyer, a jointly edited volume, (*International Handbook on the Economics of Tourism*, Edward Elgar, 2006). In 2003 he was awarded an Australian Research Council Discovery Grant for research on Airport Privatization and Regulation. He has also done substantial research on tourism economics and policy. This has covered measurement of the benefits of tourism, assessment of international price competitiveness of tourism industries, foreign investment in tourism and taxation of tourism. Recent work has involved using Computable General Equilibrium models to assess the economic impacts of tourism, including events, and to analyse tourism and aviation policy issues. Current research includes climate change policies and their impact on aviation, and developing models to assess the implications of climate change policies for the tourism industry. This work has been supported by the Australian Sustainable Tourism Cooperative Research Centre.

Alan Gogbashian is a commercial lawyer and Executive MBA graduate currently working in the public sector. He holds degrees from King's College, University of London, and Imperial College Business School. He has worked as a consultant on airline privatization projects in the former Soviet Union and in the international development and biotechnology sectors.

Dr Anne Graham is a Senior Lecturer in Air Transport and Tourism at the University of Westminster in London, UK. She has a First Class Honours BSc degree in Mathematics from the University of Newcastle, a MSc in Tourism from the University of Surrey and a PhD in Air Transport and Tourism Management from the University of Westminster. Before joining the University, Anne worked in air transport consultancy. Anne has been involved in the teaching, research

and consultancy of air transport and tourism for over 20 years and has developed two key research interests. First is the analysis and forecasting of tourism and aviation demand and the relationship between the tourism and aviation industries. Her other research interest is airport management, economics and regulation. Her latest publication in this area will be the third edition of her key book entitled *Managing Airports: An International Perspective* (published by Elsevier/ Butterworth-Heinemann). She has written many conference papers and articles about these two research areas and is on the Editorial Board of the *Journal of Airport Management*. She is a member of the Tourism Society and the Chartered Institute of Logistics and Transport and Logistics, UK.

Sveinn Vidar Gudmundsson is Senior Professor Strategic Management, Toulouse Business School, France. He is Vice President of the Air Transport Research Society and formerly Senior Visiting Fellow SSEE, Oxford University. He serves an Associate Editor of *Transportation Research E* and European Editor of *World Review* of *Intermodal Transportation Research*. He has been involved with air transport scholarship for over 20 years, having authored more than 70 publications and edited over 20 special issues of academic journals. Sveinn is a frequent speaker in conferences and professional meetings on strategy.

Thomas Lawton is Professor of Strategy and International Business at EMLYON Business School in France and Visiting Professor at the Tuck School of Business at Dartmouth College in the United States. He holds degrees from University College Cork and the London School of Economics and has a doctorate from the European University Institute in Florence, Italy. Thomas consults for and advises leaders and managers on business development and market growth. He has published over 30 papers and book chapters and is the author or editor of 6 books, including *Cleared for Takeoff* (2002), *Breakout Strategy* (2007) and *Strategic Management in Aviation* (2008). His next co-authored book, *Aligning for Advantage: business strategy for the social and political arenas*, will be published by Oxford University Press in 2012.

Professor Peter Morrell graduated in economics from Cambridge University and subsequently gained a Masters in air transportation from the Massachusetts Institute of Technology, where he worked on NASA sponsored research into airline forecasting and profitability. He has a doctorate in airline capital productivity from Cranfield University. He initially worked with merchant bank Lazard Brothers in the City, before joining the Association of European Airlines in Brussels as an economist in 1971. He worked as an air transport consultant from 1978 to 1991, initially with Alistair Tucker Associates and subsequently independently. He is a former head of the Department of Air Transport at the College of Aeronautics at Cranfield University, where he is a Reader and specializes in air transport economics and finance. He is the Department's Director of Research, is the European Editor for the *Journal of Air Transport Management*, on the editorial

board of Tourism Economics, and an aviation adviser to the World Economic Forum on environmental matters. He is the author of the textbook *Airline Finance* (the third edition of which was published in 2007), and has written many articles for both academic and industry journals.

Christian Lechner is Senior Professor Strategic Management and Entrepreneurship, Toulouse Business School, France. He earned his PhD (Management) from University of Regensburg, Germany, MBA from the University of Georgia, USA, BA from the University of Munich, Germany, International Business Studies at the University of Florence, Italy. His current research focuses on networks, business groups, habitual entrepreneurs, entrepreneurial orientation and the resource-based view.

Andreas Papatheodorou is an Assistant Professor in Industrial Economics with emphasis on Tourism at the School of Business Administration, University of the Aegean, Greece. He is also an Honorary Research Fellow at the Nottingham University Business School and a Visiting Senior Fellow at the University of Surrey, UK. Andreas holds a MPhil in Economics from the University of Oxford and a DPhil in Geography from the same university. He started his academic career as a Lecturer in Tourism at the University of Surrey. Dr Papatheodorou is actively engaged in tourism research, focusing on issues related to competition, pricing and corporate strategy in air transport and travel distribution. Most of his work is related to the Mediterranean Region and has been published in international academic journals. He has also edited two books, that is, *Corporate Rivalry and Market Power: Competition Issues in the Tourism Industry* (published by IB Tauris in 2006) and *Managing Tourism Destinations* (published by Edward Elgar in 2006). Andreas has also offered his services as an Advisor to the Greek Government on tourism policymaking, education and development, and conducts air transport and tourism executive courses organized in Africa and the Middle East on behalf of IATF and AACO. He is a Fellow of the Tourism Society, UK and sits on the Executive Board of the Hellenic Aviation Society. He is also a Partner at the Air Consulting Group and presided over the Executive Committee of the 2008 Air Transport Research Society Conference held in Athens, Greece.

Professor Robert Raffel is a graduate of the University of Maryland School of Law. He was a 10-year member of the Maryland state police force serving as a trooper, a criminal investigator, and finally as a member of the legal counsel unit.

In 1985, Robert Raffel joined the US Department of State's Anti-Terrorism Assistance Program (ATAP). While there, he developed and presented training in police and aviation security operations to students from a variety of countries. He later left ATAP for a position as a Special Agent with the FAA's Office of Civil Aviation Security, where he was assigned to FAA Security's Europe, Africa and Middle East Office in Brussels, Belgium. During his tenure in Belgium, Bob

participated in the post-incident investigation of the Pan American Airlines flight 103 tragedy (bomb-caused crash over Lockerbie, Scotland, in 1988).

Following his overseas tour, he was assigned to FAA Headquarters, Office of Foreign Operations, where he developed and managed a foreign airport technical assistance programme. He also acted as a subject-matter expert for the Anti-Terrorism Assistance Program and worked in several countries, notably in Eastern Europe.

Professor Raffel's foreign experience includes work assignments in Asia and East Asia, the Middle East, Near East, West and Central Africa, Eastern and Central Europe and Central and South America. While at FAA Headquarters, he went on to manage foreign airport assessment activity in various areas of the world and helped develop and produce the FAA's first Foreign Airport Assessment Course.

In 2002, Professor Raffel became senior director of public safety with the Greater Orlando Aviation Authority. As senior director, he conducted management oversight of the Orlando Police Department's Airport Division, the Airport Rescue Firefighter Department, and the Security Division at Orlando International Airport. He also managed the FAA-FBI Joint Vulnerability Assessment Program after his transfer to Orlando International Airport as the airports' Federal Security Manager.

Professor Raffel's military career includes: service in the Marine Corps, the Army Reserve (Special Forces, Transportation Command, Airborne Civil Affairs Battalion) and the Maryland National Guard (Tactical Intelligence Officer). He attained the rank of Colonel, USAR (Ret.), with over 31 years of experience. Security Specialist, US Department of State's Anti-Terrorism Assistance Program. 17 years US Government experience with FAA's Office of Civil Aviation Security, Federal Security Manager, programme management at national and international levels. Senior Director of Public Safety, Orlando International Airport. Recipient, Studies in Intelligence Award, Central Intelligence Agency, 2007.

Prior to arriving at Embry-Riddle, **Dr Jim Ramsay** was a professor of health and safety at the University of Wisconsin-Stevens Point, and professor of safety sciences at the Indiana University of Pennsylvania.

With undergraduate training in biology, chemistry, and German, Dr Ramsay completed an MA in business, majoring in health services administration from University of Wisconsin, Madison, in 1988. His doctoral training is in health services research (a combined programme in industrial engineering and preventive medicine) with a doctoral minor in research methods and statistics, also at UW Madison.

Publications and research interests include: the relationships between environmental health, air, land, food and water resources and homeland security; the economic evaluation of health care and occupational safety programmes, and the integration of environmental health, homeland security and occupational safety and health programmes.

Courses taught include environmental security, fundamentals of emergency management, introduction to homeland security, fundamentals of homeland

security systems, business skills for the homeland security professional, senior practicum in homeland security, advanced emergency management, epidemiology, economic evaluation of health and safety programmes, safety management, environmental health, fundamentals of industrial hygiene, research methods and statistics.

Dr Dawna Rhoades received a PhD in management from the University of Houston and a Master in Public Administration with a specialization in Environmental Policy and Natural Resource Management from the University of Washington. In addition to serving as the director of the CBTR, she is the associate dean for Research and Graduate Studies and a Professor of Management in the College of Business at Embry-Riddle. Her research interests include: strategic alliances, regional carrier strategy, service and safety quality at airlines and airports, intermodal transportation, and sustainable transportation. Her work has appeared in such journals as: the *Journal of Air Transport Management*; the *Journal of Air Transport World Wide*; the *Journal of Transportation Management*; the *Journal of Managerial Issues*; *Managing Service Quality*; *World Review of Science, Technology, and Sustainable Development*; and the *Handbook of Airline Strategy*. She is the author of *Evolution of International Aviation: Phoenix Rising*, now in its second edition, and the editor of the *World Review of Intermodal Transportation Research*.

In June 1984, **Dr Manjit Singh** started his career in aviation as an air traffic controller with the Department of Civil Aviation Malaysia accumulating various operational ATC ratings – Area Procedure and Radar, Aerodrome, Approach Procedure and Radar Control. He progressed to increasingly responsible positions such as an OJT Coach, ATCC Supervisor and ATS Check Officer. Later as Assistant Director with DCA Malaysia he was involved in assignments related to modernization of ATM facilities, *project coordination of* – ADS/CPDLC R&D Trials, State Y2K readiness programme, Aviation Frequency Spectrum protection matters and conducting ATS Incident Investigations. From June 2006, as Deputy Director of Malaysia Aviation Academy he was involved in *project managing* the building of a new campus site and subsequent specification/procurement of ATM Simulator Training solutions and courseware. In September 2009, he became the Director of ATS Inspectorate Division responsible for ANS regulatory oversight functions of DCA Malaysia. Incidentally, from June to December 2010, Manjit was seconded to the ICAO Asia Pacific Regional Office in Bangkok as the Regional Officer Technical Cooperation on a special service agreement. Manjit has also attended many international aviation training courses, seminars including ICAO, ASEAN Transport Working Group, CANSO meetings, the World Radio Conference 2000, 9th Air Transport Research Society Conference 2005, World Route Development Forum 2008, and ATC Global Exhibition and Conferences in 2004 and 2009. From an academic perspective, Manjit holds exceptional postgraduate qualifications which include a Master's in Air Transport Management

and a PhD degree, both from Cranfield University, UK which is also testimony to his commitment to *life-long learning*. His wife Manjit Kaur is a Deputy Director with the Malaysian Investment Development Authority and they have two teenage children Pamynder and Bhpyndhar.

John Snow joined the Department of Air Transport of the College of Aeronautics at Cranfield University in 1993 as a Senior Lecturer sponsored by Emirates Airlines. Since 1997, he has continued at Cranfield on a part-time basis. Previously he was employed by Saab Aircraft International Ltd. as V-P Market Development and Engineering. As such, he was deeply involved in the specification of Saab's family of regional airliners and the provision of fleet planning input for prospective customers. Prior to Saab, he performed similar tasks at Hawker Siddeley Aviation and Airbus Industrie. He also worked as an operations and development engineer with supplemental air carriers in Scandinavia. John is a Chartered Engineer and a Fellow of the Royal Aeronautical Society as well as a graduate in engineering from both Southampton University (BSc) and the then Cranfield Institute of Technology (MSc) reading Air Transport Engineering. The Cranfield experience paved the way to a successful and satisfying career in aviation, which has now turned full circle through his providing training for the coming generation of Air Transport management.

Callum Thomas is Professor of Sustainable Aviation in the Centre for Air Transport and the Environment (CATE) at Manchester Metropolitan University. He worked for over 15 years at Manchester Airport where he established the Bird Control Department, Environment Department and Community Relations unit. He has worked on various international and national projects investigating the management of aircraft noise, community affairs and bird control at airports. His main focus is on the sustainable development of aviation – especially in relation to environmental capacity constraints at airports. He is a member of several UK Government, EU and industry working parties and committees.

Acknowledgements

We would like to pay thanks and gratitude to a number of people:

Eugene, Rose, Nina and Jane O'Connell; Paddy, Mary and David Mathews; Billy, Ursula, Julie, Orla, Michael and Aideen O'Conor; Tim and Imelda Collins and family; Andrew and Julia Walsh and family; Quigley family – Mary, you will be a great pilot; Willie Joe and Joan O'Regan and family, June and Nora Turner; Michael, Julie and John Kennedy; Maria Hurly – the nicest person you could ever meet; Roukaia Ajroudi – may you take Tunisair to great heights; Dan Radowicz and family; Dennis O'Donovan and family; Patsy Kelleher; Dennis Kim and family – you are a brilliant and inspiring flight instructor; Ahmed Rihan – thank you so much for everything; Tessa Hilson-Greener; Teresa Bennett – gorgeous personality; Walsh family, Blarney; Andy Hofton – the nicest and most inspiring aviation expert ever; Ruth Rousso; David Warnock Smith and family; Kieran and Noreen O'Sullivan and family; Thomas and Nuala Sheedy and family; Derry and Ann O'Connell and family; William and Aisling O'Callaghan and family; Cliodhna and Donnagh O'Callaghan and families; Elmar Cronin – a person with many great qualities; David Spicer – the village legend; Mike Chapman; Donal Dineen; Siobhan Tiernan; Jim Deegan; Mary Wallace; Niall and Kristen Cullen and family; Capt Alla Ashour; Eudoxios Theodoridis; Ursula O'Donnell; Maria Benson; Fiona Tobin; Dan Radowicz and family; Mohammed Yeahiya and family; Noirin Hourigan and family; Brid Crotty; Sinead O'Leary; O'Sullivan family in Bere Island; Catriona Rolfe and family; Michael and Shelia O'Boyle and family; Paul and Jacinta Walsh and family; Anthon and Jane Coleman and family; Eva Barton – life is fun; Pam Bocci; Michelle Hill – another lovely person; Marjorie Barry; Declan and Anne Dunne and family; Trevor Hussey; Simon Fagan; Peter McDonald and family; Brian O'Donoughou; Joseph Burke; Joan Dugan; Philip Ryan at the aviation dept at Cork College of Commerce; Robert Owns – the young fella; Annela Anger – founder of environmental aviation; Reem Oraby – an alliance expert; Karen Kennedy and family; Deirdre Dunne-Cronin and family; Robert and Jules Barnes and family at Roxhill Manor Farm; John Mangan and family; Colleen and Art Work and family; Dave Ceasar; Sugandhi Jayaraman; Anouchka Mahadawo; Mary Kane, Boeing; and Diane Weatherup from Orbis; Riania Smith, Wissam Hachem, Tracy McGowan and Tasneem Songerwala – four great stars in the airline industry.

We would also like to extend our sincerely thanks to all the staff members at Cranfield's Air Transport department who include Graham Braithwaite; Keith Mason; Ian Stockman; Romano Pagliari; Rodney Fewings; Andy Foster; Simon Place; Richard Moxon; Zheng Lei; Miyoshi, Chikage; Rico Merkert;

Matt Greaves; Saryani Asmayawati; Hamad Rashid; Alan Parmenter; Barbara Mcgowan; Catriona Rolfe; Hayley Thompson; and Teresa Hills.

We would like to conclude our acknowledgments with a special thanks to Guy Loft from Ashgate Publishing who has been an inspiration throughout this long journey.

List of Acronyms

AACO	Arab Air Carriers Organization
AAI	Airport Authority of India
ABN AMRO	Algemene Bank Nederland-Amsterdam Rotterdam Bank
ACARE	Advisory Council for Aeronautics Research in Europe
ACI	Airports Council International
ACMI	Aircraft, Crew, Maintenance and Insurance
ACSA	Airports Company South Africa
ACSSP	Air Carrier Standard Security Program
ADP	Aéroports de Paris
ADR	Aeroporti di Roma
ADS-B	Automatic Dependency Surveillance-Broadcast
AEA	Association of European Airlines
AFCAC	African Civil Aviation Commission
AMAN	Arrival Management
ANA	All Nippon Airways
ANAC	National Civil Aviation Agency (Brazil)
ANC	Air Navigation Conference
ANSPs	Air Navigation Service Providers
AOA	Air Operations Area
APD	Air Passenger Duty (UK)
APEC	Asia-Pacific Economic Cooperation
APUs	Auxiliary Power Units
AQS	Air Quality Standards
ARIMA	Autoregressive Integrated Moving Average
ASAs	Air Service Agreements
ASEAN	Association of South East Asian Nations
ASK/M	Available Seat Kilometres/Miles
ASPA	Association of South Pacific Airlines
ASRS	Air Safety Reporting System
ATA	Air Transport Association
ATAG	Air Transport Action Group
ATC	Air Traffic Control
ATI	Air Transport Intelligence
ATM	Air Traffic Management
ATO	Air Traffic Organization
ATOL	Air Travel Organisers' Licensing (UK)
ATR	Avions de Transport Régional
ATS	Air Traffic Services

BAA	British Airports Authority Ltd
BAE	BAE Systems plc
BAO	Bomb Appraisal Officer
BASA/BATA	(Bilateral) Air Services Agreements/Bilateral Air Transport Agreements
BCBP	Bar Code Boarding Pass
BOT	Build-Operate-Transfer
BSCA	Brussels South Charleroi Airport
CAA	Civil Aviation Authority (UK)
CAAC	Civil Aviation Administration of China
CAAS	Civil Aviation Authority of Singapore
CASK/M	Operating Cost per Available Seat Kilometre/Mile
CASLO	Civil Aviation Security Liaison Officer
CCSP	Certified Cargo Screening Program
CCTV	Closed-Circuit Television
CDAs	Continuous Descent Approaches
CEC	Commission of the European Communities
CEO	Chief Executive Officer
CFR	Code of Federal Regulations
CGE	Computable General Equilibrium
CHiRP	Confidential Human Factors Incident Reporting Programme
CIA	Central Intelligence Agency
CNS	Communication, Navigation and Surveillance
CNTA	China National Tourism Administration
CPI	Consumer Price Index
CRJ	Canadair Regional Jet (Bombardier)
CRM	Cockpit Resource Management
CRP	Carbon Reinforced Plastics
CRS	Computer Reservation System
CRT	Centre for Regional and Tourism Research (Denmark)
CUSS	Common Use Self Service
CWC	Carriers Within Carriers
DAC	Department of Civil Aviation (Brazil)
DCMS	Department for Culture, Media and Sport
DCS	Departure Control System
DEFRA	Department for Environment, Food and Rural Affairs
DETR	Department of the Environment, Transport and the Regions
DfT	Department for Transport (UK)
DHS	Department of Homeland Security
DINK	Double Income No Kids
DMAN	Departure Management
DoT	Department of Transportation (USA)

DRDNI	Department for Regional Development Northern Ireland
DTI	Department of Trade and Industry
DVT	Deep Vein Thrombosis
EAS	Essential Air Service
EASA	European Aviation Safety Agency
EC	European Commission
ECA	Economic Commission for Africa
ECAA	European Common Aviation Area
ECAC	European Civil Aviation Conference
EEA	European Economic Area
EEC	European Economic Community
ELFAA	European Low Fares Airlines Association
ERJ	Embraer Regional Jet
ETS	Emissions Trading Scheme
EU	European Union
EUDGE	European Union Directorate General for the Environment
EUROCONTROL	European Organisation for the Safety of Air Navigation
EWR	Newark Liberty International Airport
F&B	Food & Beverages
FAA	Federal Aviation Administration
FADEC	Full Authority Digital Electronic Control
FAM	Federal Air Marshall
FARs	Federal Aviation Regulations
FAST	Fully Automated Seamless Travel
FBA	Functional Blocks of Airspace
FBI	Federal Bureau of Investigation
FDI	Foreign Direct Investment
FDM	Flight Data Monitoring
FEGP	Fixed Electrical Ground Power
FFP	Frequent Flyer Programme
FIRs	Flight Information Regions
FOQA	Flight Operations Quality Assurance
FSC	Full Service Carrier
FSM	Federal Security Manager
FTKs	Freight Tonnes Kilometres
FTSE	The Financial Times Stock Exchange
GA	General Aviation
GAO	General Accounting Office
GCC	Gulf Cooperation Council
GDP	Gross Domestic Product
GDS	Global Distribution System
GE	General Electric
GFF	Global Futures and Foresight
GNP	Gross National Product

GPS	Global Positioning System
GST	General Sales Tax
HIAL	Highlands and Islands Airports Limited
HSBC	Hong Kong and Shanghai Banking Corporation
IACA	International Air Carrier Association
IACS	Immigration Automated Clearance System
IATA	International Air Transport Association
IATF	International Airline Training Fund (IATA)
IBM	International Business Machines
ICAO	International Civil Aviation Organisation
ICCAIA	International Coordinating Council of Aerospace Industries Associations
IFE	In-flight Entertainment
IFR	Instrument Flying Rules
IMF	International Monetary Fund
IOSA	IATA Operational Safety Audit
IPCC	Intergovernmental Panel on Climate Change
IPS	International Passenger Survey (UK)
IT/ICT	Information Technology/Information and Communication Technologies
JFK	John F Kennedy International Airport
KADCO	Kilimanjaro Airport Development Company (Tanzania)
KLM	Koninklijke Luchtvaart Maatschappij (Royal Dutch Airlines)
Km	Kilometers
LAGs	Liquids, Aerosels and Gels
LAX	Los Angeles International Airport
LCC	Low Cost Carrier
LCY	London City Airport
LD	Low Drag
LGA	LaGuardia Airport
LP	Low Power
MALIAT	Multilateral Agreement on the Liberalization of International Air Transportation
MD	McDonnell Douglas
MIA	Malta International Airport
MICE	Meetings, Incentives, Conferencing, Exhibitions
MIISPA	Managed Integrated Independent South Pacific Airlines
MMS	Multimedia Message Service
MORS	Mandatory Occurrence Reporting System
MSG	Maintenance Steering Group
MTA	Malta Tourism Authority
NADPs	Noise Abatement Departure Procedures
NAS	National Airspace System

NASDAQ	National Association of Securities Dealers Automated Quotation System
NATCA	National Air Traffic Controllers Association
NCAA	Nigerian Civil Aviation Authority
NFC	Near Field Communications
NGATS	Next Generation Air Transportation System
NIA	National Investigation Agency
NIMBY	Not-In-My-Back-Yard
NRPs	Noise Preferential Routes
NTSB	National Transportation Safety Board
OAA	Open Aviation Area
OAG	Official Airline Guide
OECD	Organisation for Economic Co-operation and Development
OEF	Oxford Economic Forecasting
OEW	Operating Empty Weight
OFT	Office of Fair Trading (UK)
ONDA	Office National des Aéroports (Morocco)
OPEC	Organization of the Petroleum Exporting Countries
OTAs	Online Travel Agencies
PATA	Pacific Asia Travel Association
PC	Personal Computer
PFLP	Popular Front for the Liberalisation of Palestine
PM	Particulate Matter
PNR	Passenger Name Records
PPP	Private – Public Partnership
PSI	Principle Security Inspector
PSO	Public Service Obligation
R&D	Research & Development
RASK/M	Passenger Revenue per Available Seat Kilometre/ Mile
RCEP	Royal Commission on Environmental Pollution
REDAC	Research Engineering & Development Advisory Committee
RFID	Radio Frequency ID
RJ	Regional Jet (associated with BAE)
RNP	Required Navigation Precision
RPI	Retail Price Index
RPK/M	Revenue Passenger-Kilometres/Miles
RTIC	Registered Traveller Inter-operability Consortium
RTP	Registered Travellers Programmes
RUCUR	Relative Unit Cost – Unit Revenue
SAA	South African Airlines
SABRE	Semi-Automated Business Research Environment
SARPs	Standards and Recommended Practices

SARS	Severe Acute Respiratory Syndrome
SAS	Scandinavian Airline Systems
SDR	Special Drawing Rights
SE	South-East
SESAR	Single European Sky ATM Research
SITA	Société Internationale de Télécommunications Aéronautiques
SMS	Short Message Service
SMS	Safety Management System
SP1	Standard Provision 1
SPT	Simplifying Passenger Travel
SPTO	South Pacific Tourism Organization
SRA	Strategic Research Agenda (European Union)
ST-EP	Sustainable Tourism – Eliminate Poverty (Africa)
STSM	Structural Time-Series Model
SWIM	System-wide Information Management
T&E	Transport & Environment
T&T	Travel and Tourism
TAAI	Travel Agents Association of India
TDP	Tourism Development Plan (Mauritius)
THY	Turkish Airlines
TINA	The Intelligent Airport (Heathrow, UK)
TSA	Transport Security Administration (USA)
UAE	United Arab Emirates
UDF	UnDucted Fan
UK	United Kingdom
ULD	Unit Load Device
UN	United Nations
UNCSD	United Nations Commission on Sustainable Development
UNCTAD	United Nations Conference on Trade and Development
UNESCO	United Nations Educational, Scientific and Cultural Organization
UNHAS	UN's Humanitarian Air Service
UNWTO	United Nations World Tourism Organization
USA (or US)	Unites States of America
USOAP	Universal Safety Oversight Audit Programme
USPS	US Postal Service
VARIG	Viação Aérea RIo Grandense (Brazil)
VASP	Viação Aérea São Paulo (Brazil)
VAT	Value Added Tax
VFR	Visiting Friends and Relatives
VOC	Volatile Organic Compounds
VWP	Visa Waiver Program (USA)
WAAS	Wide Area Augmentation System

WCED	World Commission on Environment and Development
WFP	World Food Programme
WTO	World Tourism Organization (former name of UNWTO)
WTTC	World Travel and Tourism Council

Glossary:
Definitions of Commonly Used Air Transport Terms

Aircraft hours are the total number of aircraft block hours in revenue service, block hours being calculated from the moment an aircraft moves under its own power for purpose of flight until it comes to rest at the next point of landing.

Aircraft kilometres are the sum of products obtained by multiplying the number of flights performed on each flight stage by the stage distance.

Aircraft utilization is the average number of block hours that each aircraft is in use. This is generally measured on a daily or annual basis.

Ancillary revenue per booked passenger represents the average revenue earned per booked passenger flown from ancillary services.

Available seat kilometres (ASKs) are obtained by multiplying the number of seats available for sale on each flight stage by flight stage distance.

Available tonne kilometres (ATKs) are obtained by multiplying the number of tonnes (2,204 lb) of capacity available for carriage of passengers and cargo on each sector of a flight-by-flight stage distance.

Average aircraft capacity is obtained by dividing available tonne kilometres by aircraft kilometres flown (or available seat/kms by aircraft kms flown).

Average booked passenger fare represents the average fare paid by a scheduled fare-paying passenger who has booked a ticket.

Average fuel cost per US gallon represents the average cost per US gallon of jet fuel for the fleet (including fuelling charges) after giving effect to fuel hedging arrangements.

Average passenger haul is obtained by dividing revenue passenger kilometres flown by the number of passengers.

Average stage length is obtained by dividing aircraft kilometres flown by number of aircraft departures for each airline; it is the weighted average of stage/sector lengths flown by an airline (normally the great circle distances).

Average yield per ASM represents the average scheduled flown passenger fare revenue for each available seat mile (ASM).

Average yield per RPM represents the average scheduled passenger fare revenue for each revenue passenger mile (RPM), or mile each a scheduled revenue passenger is flown.

(Bilateral) Air Services Agreements (BASAs) (also known as **Bilateral Air Transport Agreements**) are agreements between governments which establish the rules for international scheduled air services. There is an increasing number of **Open Skies BASAs** which are much more liberal agreements.

Block time (hours) is the time for each flight stage or sector, measured from when an aircraft leaves the airport gate or stand (chocks off) to when it arrives on the gate or stand at the destination airport (chocks on).

Booked Passenger Load Factor represents the total number of seats sold as a percentage of total seat capacity on all sectors flown.

Breakeven Load Factor (BLF) is the average per cent of seats that must be filled on an average flight at current average fares for the airline's passenger revenue to break even with the airline's operating expenses.

Break-even load factor (per cent) is the load factor required to equate total traffic revenue with operating costs.

Break of gauge is used in air services agreements to allow an airline, which has traffic rights from its own country (A) to country (B) and then fifth freedom rights onto country C, to operate one type of aircraft from A to B and then a different type (usually smaller) from B to C and beyond. This normally involves basing aircraft and crews in country B. United Airlines and American operated such break of gauge flights from London to European points until the mid 1990s.

Cabin Crew refers to stewards and stewardess.

The **Chicago Convention** was a meeting of government officials in 1944 which set up the **International Civil Aviation Organization (ICAO)** and established many rules and standards for air travel.

Cockpit Voice Recorder records the flight crew's voices, as well as other sounds inside the cockpit.

Code sharing is the use of the designation code of one or more airlines on a flight operated by another airline. Code sharing is usually (but not exclusively) implemented in the context of *Strategic Alliances* among airlines.

Combi is an aircraft type in which passengers and freight are carried on the main deck.

Coordinated airport is an airport where an independent coordinator has been appointed to facilitate the allocation of take-off and landing slots (times) to airlines at congested airports in Europe.

Cost per Available Seat Mile (CASM) is the measure of unit cost in the airline industry. CASM is calculated by taking all of an airline's operating expenses and dividing it by the total number of available seat miles produced.

Dry Lease is the lease of an airframe only. Normally only of interest to airlines already operating the aircraft in question.

Damp Lease is the lease of an aircraft together with qualified flight crew but no cabin crew.

Engine pooling happens when airlines, lessors or manufacturers create a pool of spare engines which any member of the pool can use.

Export credit agencies are in countries where aircraft are manufactured and will often guarantee financing to help secure aircraft sales. The Export Import Bank of the United States guarantees Boeing aircraft. France's Coface, Gernamy's Hermes and the UK's Export Credits Guarantee Department support Airbus aircraft. Brazile BNDE's guarantees Embraer aircraft in with Export Development Canda supporting Bombardier. Export credit agencies typically guarantee only 85 per cent of an aircraft's value. There is also a home country rule for Airbus and Boeing where the agencies agree not to finance aircraft in each other's country.

Fleets and subfleet: a fleet is the aggregate of all aircraft operated by an airline, whereas a subfleet is comprised of one particular type (including variants).

Flight Data Recorders on board aircraft record many different operating conditions of a flight. By regulation, newly manufactured transport category aircraft must monitor at least 88 important parameters such as time, altitude, airspeed, heading, and aircraft attitude. In addition, some FDRs can record the status of more than 1,000 other in-flight characteristics that can aid in the investigation. The items monitored can be anything from flap position to auto-pilot mode or even smoke alarms.

Flying time (hours) is the time for each flight stage or sector, measured from when the aircraft leaves the ground or lifts off to when it touches down on the runway on arrival at the destination airport.

Fortress Hub describes a situation in a deregulated market where, an airline seeks to control competition by achieving a high degree of dominance at a particular airport.

Franchising involves an agreement between a large airline (the franchisor) and a smaller airline (franchisee) under which the latter operates a number of or all its services on behalf of the franchisor, usually with the former's aircraft colour scheme, uniforms and product features.

Freight tonne kilometres (FTKs) are obtained by multiplying the number of tonnes of freight carried on each sector of a flight, by flight stage distance.

Freight Yields are obtained by dividing total revenue from scheduled freight by the freight tonne kilometres (FTK) produced (usually expressed in US cents per FTK).

Gateways: under the terms of an air services agreement, the points in each country which can be served in each country by the airline receiving Designation.

Grandfather rights is the convention by which airlines retain the right to take-off and landing slot times at an airport as long as they are used (also used in conjunction with route rights in certain instances).

Hub and spoke system: system of air transportation in which local airports offer air transportation to a central airport where long-distance flights are available. Airlines have found it more cost-effective to consolidate operations at a single airport rather than operate a point-to-point service. For example, consider five airports that could all be connected together either by using one airport as a hub or by flying between each city. Using a hub, all the airports can be connected to each other with a minimum of four flights.

Intergrators are air freight companies offering door-to-door express and small shipment services including surface collection and delivery. Fedex, DHL and UPS are the largest.

Interlining is the acceptance by one airline of travel documents issued by another airline for carriage on the services of the first airline, according to conditions laid down in an interline agreement (which include the allocation of revenues between the two carriers); an interline passenger is one using a through fare for a journey involving two or more separate flights and two or more carriers.

Instrument Flight Rules (IFR) are rules governing flight in certain limited visibility and cloud conditions. Under IFR an aircraft is required to be in contact with air traffic control facilities and is separated by ATC from other IFR aircraft.

Instrument Landing System (ILS) provides radio-based horizontal and vertical guidance to an aircraft approaching a runway. It is used to guide landing aircraft during conditions of low visibility.

Net Margin represents profit after taxation as a percentage of total revenues.

Number of airports served represents the number of airports to/from which the carrier offered scheduled service at the end of the period.

Number of owned aircraft operated represents the number of aircraft owned and operated at the end of a period.

Online passenger is one who transfers from one flight to another but on the same airline.

Operating costs per ATK is a measure obtained by dividing total operating costs by ATKs. It includes flight operating expenses, sales ticketing and promotional costs, ground operations costs and general and administration costs. It usually excludes interest payments, but includes aircraft lease rentals.

Operating Lease is a lease for less than the full operating life of an aircraft, with the lease having no interest in the aircraft residual value.

Operating Margin represents operating profit as a percentage of total revenues.

Operating ratio (per cent) is the operating revenue expressed as a percentage of operating costs.

Part 145 is the European regulatory standard for aircraft maintenance established by the European Aviation Safety Agency.

Passengers carried are obtained by counting each passenger on a particular flight (with one flight number) once only and not repeatedly on each individual stage of that flight (or one ticket coupon equals one passenger), with a single exception that a passenger flying on both the international and domestic stages of the same flight should be counted as both a domestic and an international passenger.

Passenger load factor (per cent) is passenger-kilometres expressed as a percentage of available seat kilometres (on a single sector, this is simplified to the number of passengers carried as a percentage of seats available for sale).

Punctuality is measured as the percentage of flights departing within 15-minutes of schedule, according to the most widely used airline industry standard.

Regularity is the percentage of flights completed to flights scheduled, excluding flights cancelled for commercial reasons.

Regulation refers to the erection of institutional impediments in the way a market functions. The aviation industry is characterized by strict regulations in the areas of safety and security; in the past, there was also heavy economic regulation at both domestic and international levels. Gradually, however, this has been relaxed or entirely lifted in the context of market *deregulation* and *liberalization*. In spite of the existence of a few differences (for example, deregulation may take place within a country whereas liberalization is usually across countries), these last two terms are often used interchangeably. Regulation in tourism is in many cases associated with planning restrictions in terms of infrastructure standards (for example, safety and hygiene), construction and architectural styles. In the past, there was also economic regulation in certain tourism sectors but this has been globally reduced in the last two decades.

Revenue passenger refers to passengers paying 25 per cent or more of the normal applicable fare (for ICAO statistical purposes).

Revenue Passenger Kilometres (RPKs) are obtained by multiplying the number of fare paying passengers on each flight stage by flight stage distance.

Revenue Passenger Miles (RPMs) represents the number of miles flown by booked fare-paying passengers.

Revenue Tonne Kilometres (RTKs) are obtained by multiplying the total number of tonnes of passengers and cargo carried on each flight stage by flight stage distance. Passengers tonne kilometres are normally calculated on a standard basis of 90 kg average weight, including free and excess baggage, although this has been increased recently by some airlines (e.g. British Airways have recently increased the average passenger weight from 75 kg to 80 kg, as a result of a CAA directive, to which the 20 kg free baggage allowance should be added).

Seat factor or passenger load factor on a single sector is obtained by expressing the passengers carried as a per cent of the seats available for sale; on a network of routes it is obtained by expressing the total passenger kms as a per cent of the total seat kms available.

Seat pitch is the standard way of measuring seat density on an aircraft. It is the distance between the back of one seat and the same point on the back of the seat in front.

Scheduled freight yields are obtained by dividing total revenue from scheduled freight by RTK from freight.

Scheduled passenger yields are obtained by dividing the total scheduled passenger revenue by RTK from passengers.

Scheduled services are services provided by flights scheduled and performed for remuneration according to a published timetable, or so regular or frequent as to constitute a recognizably systematic series, which are open to direct booking by members of the public; also extra revenue flights occasioned by overflow traffic from scheduled flights; and preliminary revenue flights on planned new air services.

Slot at an airport is the right to operate one take-off or landing at that airport within a fixed time period. In practice, the slot timings are only nominal and flights often take-off and land at times outside their specified slot period, although airlines must possess the nominal slots to operate air services. Slots are traded between airlines legally in the US, and unofficially in other parts of the world (where only the exchange of slots is officially permitted).

Start-ups and new entrants: 'start-up' is used to refer to a newly launched carrier. 'New entrant' or 'entrant' refers to a carrier entering a market to challenge one or more incumbents; a new entrant might be a start-up, or it might be an established carrier.

Transfer passenger is one who changes planes en-route at an intermediate airport.

Transit passenger is one who continues on the same aircraft after an intermediate stop on a multi-sector flight.

Unducted fan is a kind of engine that uses the basic core of a jet engine to drive large, fan-like blades which produce the major thrust component of the engine. A propfan is one kind of unducted fan.

Unduplicated route kilometres are the lengths in kilometres of all the flight stages operated by an airline, each counted only once, and regardless of frequency or direction.

Unit costs are obtained by dividing total operating costs by ATKs (or ASKs).

Weight load factor is revenue tonne kilometres performed expressed as percentage of available tonne kilometres (also called overall load factor).

Wet lease usually involves the leasing of aircraft with flight crews, and possibly cabin crews and maintenance support as well. A dry lease involves just the aircraft without any additional support.

Wide-bodied aircraft are civil aircraft which have two passenger aisles in normal configuration (e.g. B767); narrow-bodied aircraft, such as the B757 have only one aisle.

Yields are obtained by dividing the total operating revenue by RTKs (or sometimes by ATK); passenger yields are obtained by dividing passenger revenues by RPKs, and cargo yields by dividing cargo revenues by FTKs. Revenues have historically been recorded before the deduction of travel agent commissions, giving gross rather than yields net of commissions.

Yield management: also known as revenue management, the process airlines use to set prices for a flight. The goal is to find the mix of seat prices that produces the most revenue.

Freedoms of the Air[1]

First Freedom of the Air: the right or privilege, in respect of scheduled international air services, granted by one State to another State or States to fly across its territory without landing (also known as a *First Freedom Right*).

Second Freedom of the Air: the right or privilege, in respect of scheduled international air services, granted by one State to another State or States to land in its territory for non-traffic purposes (also known as a *Second Freedom Right*).

Third Freedom of The Air: the right or privilege, in respect of scheduled international air services, granted by one State to another State to put down, in the territory of the first State, traffic coming from the home State of the carrier (also known as a *Third Freedom Right*).

Fourth Freedom of The Air: the right or privilege, in respect of scheduled international air services, granted by one State to another State to take on, in the territory of the first State, traffic destined for the home State of the carrier (also known as a *Fourth Freedom Right*).

Fifth Freedom of The Air: the right or privilege, in respect of scheduled international air services, granted by one State to another State to put down and to take on, in the territory of the first State, traffic coming from or destined to a third State (also known as a *Fifth Freedom Right*).

ICAO characterises all 'freedoms' beyond the Fifth as 'so-called' because only the first five 'freedoms' have been officially recognized as such by international treaty.

Sixth Freedom of The Air: the right or privilege, in respect of scheduled international air services, of transporting, via the home State of the carrier, traffic moving between two other States (also known as a *Sixth Freedom Right*) The so-called Sixth Freedom of the Air, unlike the first five freedoms, is not incorporated as such into any widely recognized air service agreements such as the 'Five Freedoms Agreement'.

Seventh Freedom of The Air: the right or privilege, in respect of scheduled international air services, granted by one State to another State, of transporting traffic between the territory of the granting State and any third State with no requirement to include on such operation any point in the territory of the recipient State, i.e. the service need not connect to or be an extension of any service to/from the home State of the carrier.

---

1   See Chapter 9 by Professor Forsyth.

Eighth Freedom of The Air: the right or privilege, in respect of scheduled international air services, of transporting cabotage traffic between two points in the territory of the granting State on a service which originates or terminates in the home country of the foreign carrier or (in connection with the so-called Seventh Freedom of the Air) outside the territory of the granting State (also known as a *Eighth Freedom Right* or 'consecutive cabotage').

Ninth Freedom of The Air: the right or privilege of transporting cabotage traffic of the granting State on a service performed entirely within the territory of the granting State (also known as a *Ninth Freedom Right* or 'stand alone' cabotage).

Preface

The principle aim of this book is to give a description of the current pulse points that are reshaping air transport today.

This is a unique book comprising two distinct parts. The first presents the views of a number of industry executives at CEO/VP level from airlines, aircraft/ engine manufacturers, airports, safety organisations, navigational provider groups and technology companies who have written short accounts of their views on the industry. The second part contains chapters written by 19 distinguished academics specialising in different aspects of aviation.

We begin with an overview of the turbulent nature of the airline industry by Frankie O'Connell of Cranfield University's Air Transport Department. In Chapter 2, Dawna Rhoades of Embry Riddle Aeronautical University reviews the difficulties faced by US carriers in transforming their business model and assesses to what extent they are likely to succeed. Sean Barrett of Trinity College Dublin explores the phenomenal success of European low-cost carrier Ryanair in Chapter 3. How legacy carriers can face the challenge of the likes of Ryanair forms the subject matter of Chapter 4, which is written by Alan Gogbashian and Thomas Lawton of EMLYON Business School in France. The significance and growing importance of ancillary revenues to airlines is analysed by Frankie O'Connell in Chapter 5, while a number of issues involved in the development of airline alliances are explored by Sveinn Gudmundsson and Christian Lechner of Toulouse Business School in Chapter 6. In the seventh chapter, George Williams of Cranfield University's Air Transport Department assesses the prospects for Europe's charter airlines as the region's low-cost carriers continue to expand, while the link between tourism and air transport in an era of economic liberalisation is explored in Chapter 8 by Andreas Papatheodorou of the University of the Aegean, Greece. Peter Forsyth of Monash University, Australia analyses the economics of 7th Freedom air traffic rights in Chapter 9, while Peter Morrell of Cranfield University's Air Transport Department reviews the air cargo industry in Chapter 10. In Chapter 11, Anne Graham of Westminster University examines the key issues facing the airport industry, while in the following chapter Ben Daley and Callum Thomas of Manchester Metropolitan University outline the many ways in which environmental issues represent an actual or potential constraint to the growth of air transport. Advances in aircraft and engine design are explored in Chapter 13 by John Snow of Cranfield University's Air Transport Department. This is followed by a review of Safety Management Systems in Aviation by Graham Braithwaite, Head of the Air Transport Department at Cranfield University. In Chapter 15, Manjit Singh from the Department of Civil Aviation Malaysia assesses the various attempts that are being made to achieve cooperation in the provision of Air Navigation Services. The latest innovations in Information Technology are reviewed by Frankie O'Connell in Chapter 16. Aviation security experts, Robert Raffel and Jim Ramsey from Embry Riddle Aeronautical University, examine the security issues relating to aviation in the United States in Chapter 17 and the book concludes with an in-depth examination of the world's most profitable airline in 2009/10 by Frankie O'Connell.

Thank You

We are absolutely thrilled to be able to write this book on behalf of the charity 'Orbis', the Flying Hospital which operates to third-world countries to restore people's eyesight. **All** the editors' proceeds from the sale of this book will go to aid this worthy charity, where eye surgeons, pilots, mechanics and a whole host of other personnel have all come together to dedicate their free time to this selfless and uplifting charity.

We are most grateful to all the chief executive officers and vice presidents right across the globe who took their precious time to write about the aviation industry and we are also overwhelmed by those who also dedicated their time to write stimulating chapters about this ever-changing industry that is aviation. Your gracious efforts will touch those less fortunate and we sincerely thank you all very, very much for contributing and we are most humbled by your kind and boundless generosity.

Thank you all very, very much.

Sincerely,

John F. O'Connell

George Williams

ORBIS
saving sight worldwide

In too many countries children who are blind or visually impaired struggle in school, are unable to join the workforce, and are therefore unable to reach their full potential or contribute to their family income and are seen as a burden on families and society. The fact is that up to half of children in developing countries who become blind will die within a year.

ORBIS, an international charity dedicated to the treatment and prevention of blindness in the developing world, is working to change this and since it was founded in 1982 it has, through the generosity of its donors, worked tirelessly to achieve its goal. Our focus is on teaching and training, and since 1982 ORBIS has carried out more than 1,000 sight-saving programmes and treated more than 10 million people worldwide.

This has been achieved through the teaching of sight-saving skills to eye-care professionals in local hospitals and clinics and aboard the ORBIS Flying Eye Hospital. These professionals, in turn, have passed on their expertise to tens of thousands of others. ORBIS also works with communities, governments and hospitals to improve healthcare, facilities and foster awareness of eye-health.

Over the past decades ORBIS has received huge support from the aviation industry, mainly due to the impact of the Flying Eye Hospital on the countries it visits. The ORBIS Flying Eye Hospital is literally a hospital with wings that brings together dedicated eye-care professionals and aviators to give the gift of sight to the visually impaired people of developing countries around the world.

On board the aircraft, local doctors, nurses and technicians work alongside ORBIS's international medical team to exchange knowledge and improve skills. Along with the full-time Flying Eye Hospital team, volunteer doctors and nurses from around the world donate their time.

The Flying Eye Hospital contains a complete ophthalmic operating theatre room, a four-bed pre-operative and recovery room, sub-sterile room and laser-treatment room. In the front of the aircraft is a 48-seat classroom, where doctors gather for lectures, discussions and live broadcasts from the operating room. The mobile teaching hospital truly is a unique tool in the fight against preventable blindness in developing countries.

Prior to the Flying Eye Hospital visit, local doctors select patients whose conditions are relevant to the upcoming programme's specialties. Selected patients are screened by ORBIS volunteer faculty members at the programme site. Priority is given to children, individuals who are bilaterally blind, those who cannot afford to have the surgery and those who represent good teaching cases. Local doctors maintain oversight of patients before, during and after surgery.

As part of ORBIS's commitment to ongoing quality care, an ORBIS ophthalmologist returns to the host country within two months of each programme to examine patients and review cases with the local doctors. When the Flying Eye Hospital leaves, the ORBIS mission continues through the work of local doctors and nurses. In this way, ORBIS is strengthening the capabilities of local healthcare communities in blindness prevention and treatment and therefore ensuring long-lasting effects on the villages, cities and towns it visits.

Since its first programme in 1982, the ORBIS Flying Eye Hospital has travelled to more than 70 countries and saved the sight of millions of people. In addition the high profile of the plane helps to raise awareness of the issues of blindness in the countries it visits. The plane always creates huge interest wherever it goes.

On behalf of the board, staff, volunteers and beneficiaries of ORBIS, I would like to thank everyone involved in creating this book. We are always humbled by the generosity of others and it is through the support of everyone who has contributed to the publication of this book that ORBIS can continue its work with the Flying Eye Hospital in the hope that one day there will be no more avoidable blindness in the world. This is a massive undertaking, but one that not only brings the gift of sight to those who are needlessly blind but is also vital to the social and economic development of the societies in which they live. Through the support of all who have contributed to this book and all who have purchased this book, this goal could become a reality.

Dr Robert F. Walters
Chairman ORBIS International

Introduction to Practitioner Pieces

The interest and concern that air transport provokes is substantial. Air transport is the backbone of economic prosperity as it integrates the global marketplace. Over two billion people travelled by air in 2010 and air travel's relative affordability has allowed it to become an integral part of many people's lifestyles. Those involved in the air transport industry invariably exhibit enormous enthusiasm and dedication in the work that they do. It is particularly pleasing to begin this book with a series of thoughtful insights about recent key developments in air transport from a group of individuals who have played such a key role in shaping today's industry. This commercial input sets the scene for the book, and their views as to the sector's likely future evolution are especially appreciated. A small sample of the practitioners who contributed to this book includes: Willie Walsh (CEO of British Airways) who discusses the ongoing difficulties faced in the industry; Gary Kelly (CEO of Southwest) who discusses the importance of controlling costs; Alan Joyce (CEO of Qantas) who highlights the volatility of the industry; Brian Pearce (Chief Economist at IATA) who explains how the industry is so beneficial to the global economy, but profitability remains elusive; William deCota (Director for John F. Kennedy International, Newark, and LaGuardia Airports) who describes the challenges facing airports; Rigas Doganis (Professor of Air Transport) who describes how the industry remains an inherently unstable industry; while another renowned professor, Kenneth Button, pinpoints the inevitable evolution of aviation. The contributions are listed in alphabetic order using the first name of each author.

Volatility in the Global Airline Industry is Shaping its Future Evolution

Alan Joyce
CEO of Qantas

The global airline industry in 2009 served up unprecedented market volatility that I believe will continue to shake and shape the aviation industry into the next decade.

In 2008 we saw air travel reach new highs throughout the world with new carriers emerging, a global pilot shortage and a struggle to confirm fleet orders in order to meet unprecedented worldwide demand for air travel.

This all changed as the global financial crisis took hold and moving forward I predict a greater level of market consolidation, carrier cost rationalization and a greater focus on innovation in the aviation business.

Consolidation will occur as airlines look to leverage partnerships to extend reach and growth whilst consolidating cost in a new world environment which will struggle with organic demand opportunities in the short to medium term.

Cost rationalization, already part of the fabric of carriers such as Qantas and Jetstar, will become a survival tactic for many carriers struggling to stay afloat and remain profitable. Carriers like Jetstar, who have continued to remain profitable whilst reducing costs year on year, will become key areas of study for many carriers looking at areas of their business which can be adapted to the new world environment. Consolidation and partnership opportunities will allow greater sharing of best practice techniques and cost reduction opportunities.

This environment I also believe will create a greater platform for accelerated investment in innovation, use of the latest technology and state of the art aircraft. It will force creative thinking and a greater reliance on automated technology in terms of self-service booking and airport facilities.

And finally, carbon emissions and an airline's ability to continue to minimize emissions and its carbon footprint will continue to gain momentum as carriers and their home nations head towards legislated emissions targets.

The Future of Air Navigation

Ashley Smout

CEO of the Civil Air Navigation Services Organisation (CANSO)

Air Traffic Management differs from other forms of transportation in that ATM is the only truly global utility or infrastructure in our society. There is no other form of transport – whether it be road or rail – that is as truly global in nature, as air transport. So in the ANS industry, something we term 'interoperability' – the compatibility of airspace infrastructure systems – is of huge significance. Yet our uniquely global natural resource of 'airspace' is fragmented into a patchwork quilt of 190 flight-information regions. Set up after the Second World War, this system is now badly in need of an overhaul. ATM needs to meet the challenges of the twenty-first century – in which a global, seamless airspace is developed, based on cost-effective and efficient services, with sufficient capacity to meet the world's air transport needs.

The Single European Sky is significant in this respect. It seeks a balance between airspace sovereignty and airspace functionality, via the so-called Functional Airspace Blocks, or FABs. Progress is slow but has recently gathered momentum. But it requires a lot more political support if the Single European Sky is to become a reality, and we are to see optimized civil and military airspace, a reduction in the proliferation of ATC facilities, and reduced costs.

But whatever the political outcome, and whatever the results of efforts to reduce ATM centres and costs, what the airlines really need is interoperability between Air Navigation Service providers (ANSPs). ANSPs represent approximately 3–5 per cent of an airline's costs. However, they have a key influence on an airline's fuel costs, which typically amount to 10 times this, or 30–35 per cent. Therefore the ANS industry must deliver the straightest and most direct routes the airlines can use, to help minimize fuel consumption, and as importantly, to minimize emissions.

We are now seeing a range of initiatives aimed at just that. CANSO[†] has developed a checklist of best-practice fuel and emissions initiatives, based on the five sections of flight from taxiing and departure, through the climb and the cruise, to the approach and landing. By 2050 we believe that these initiatives have the potential to deliver 80 million tonnes of CO_2 reductions each year.

Of course we cannot deliver these benefits in isolation, and there is a need to significantly step up the level of collaboration in the industry if we are going to meet the required efficiency and safety targets in a world where traffic has increased significantly. This is at the heart of both the SESAR and NextGen ATM modernization projects in Europe and the USA respectively. In collaboration with airlines, avionics suppliers, airports and regulators, the ANS industry has to deliver on these programmes, or we face the possibility of unacceptable delays, and increased level of incidents. Automation of ATM systems and moving from air traffic 'control' to air traffic management or enabling, will be the path the industry must follow.

Change is coming, but the pace of change is too slow. All aviation participants – including governments- need to act together to speed things up.

†CANSO, the Civil Air Navigation Services Organisation, unites the world's air navigation service providers and their industry partners. CANSO is the global voice of air traffic management (ATM).

Aviation Safety Concern

Bill Voss
CEO of Flight Safety

As aviation enters its second century as a vital global transportation system, the industry's unparalleled safety advances deserve recognition. However, aviation safety experts know that in order to maintain this enviable record and to push to higher levels of safety, the industry must persevere in its efforts to discover and address potential problems before they can become real threats.

One of the most exciting developments in the past several decades is the increasing use of information from normal flight operations to identify these potential problems before a tragedy occurs. This approach developed as accidents became increasingly scarce, reducing the industry's ability to learn lessons from the accident investigation process, coupled with a desire to advance safety without having to wait for a tragedy to point the way.

The gathering of this information is crucial. Some data are gathered electronically through flight operation quality assurance programmes (FOQA), and some come from crews' voluntary reports of flight experiences through aviation safety action programmes (ASAP). The key to this free flow of information between crews, management and regulators is the confidential and the non-punitive nature of these programmes. Humans will always make mistakes; these programmes allow for a full understanding of the factors that allow mistakes to occur and enable the development of corrective actions. Some of the Flight Safety Foundation's most popular technical safety training products, such as the *Approach and Landing Accident Reduction Toolkit*, were created to disseminate to the industry best practices based on what has learned about these mistakes.

In recent years, the aviation community has seen some disturbing trends in the handling of this data. Judicial systems are allowing ASAP data to be released to plaintiffs in legal disputes, and criminal charges based on safety investigation data are being filed against pilots, air traffic controllers and even regulators in the wake of accidents. Some respected ASAP systems are falling to the wayside due to labour/management disputes or concern that this data is now 'discoverable' in court, exposing industry participants to wider damages. These trends are evident all around the world, but are of special concern in regions such as North America or Western Europe that traditionally lead in aviation safety.

The Flight Safety Foundation, along with other aviation groups, is leading the charge to protect this information. Clearly, the states know how to handle sensitive data without compromising an investigation or invading someone's privacy. That is seen every day in the handling of cockpit voice and flight data recorders. It is vital that ASAP, FOQA and accident investigation data are given the same legislative protections.

Despite these very real concerns, the safety record of aviation remains stellar, the envy of other industries. It is gratifying to see safety management systems taking hold throughout the world, expanding even beyond aviation. Aviation safety professionals have the tools and the knowledge to continue to improve the industry's safety record. Now the industry needs the statutory protection to ensure that these tools remain available.

A Beneficial Industry but One With Elusive Profitability

Brian Pearce

Chief Economist at IATA

There are not many industries whose services are in such demand from consumers and business as air transport. The world economy has expanded fourfold in the four decades since 1970. But the number of people travelling by air each year has expanded sixfold. Journey distances are longer, so passenger kilometres flown are up ninefold. Air freight markets are 12 times larger.

This burgeoning demand is unlikely to stop in the next four decades, though its pattern will be different. There are more than three scheduled seats available to fly each year for every person in the US and two for every European citizen. With slowing population growth these markets may be close to saturation. But in China and India there are today only 0.1–0.5 seats per person for a combined population of 2.3 billion. I don't have to do the maths to demonstrate the huge potential demand to fly.

Air transport is already creating tremendous value for its customers. Air fares, adjusted for inflation, have fallen by a half since 1970. Choice, in destinations and frequencies, is up many-fold. With annual airline revenues worldwide of around $500 billion it is not unreasonable to suggest that the value created for consumers, over and above what they pay for the fare or shipment, is in the region of $200–300 billion each year. This 'consumer surplus' would not exist if people were unable to fly and businesses unable to maintain global supply chains and rapid access to markets.

There are also wider economic benefits beyond the value created for customers. These are not the oft-quoted jobs supported in the value chain, but the fact that globalization as we know it today could not exist without the timely connectivity between nations provided by air transport networks. These benefits are hard to quantify but without these intercontinental networks just-in-time global supply chains would be impossible. Skilled labour markets would be far more inflexible and local. Ideas generated from face-to-face contact would be slower to spread. Productivity would suffer.

Rapid growth is not without its problems. Despite having one of the highest rates of fuel efficiency improvements, close to two per cent a year, rapidly expanding demand for travel and goods shipments has meant that the industry's carbon emissions are expanding, impacting the climate. Dealing with this problem is one of today's exciting challenges with a global sector agreement and new fuels being developed.

The environment problem is not solved yet. But applying widely used values for the damage done by emissions to the industry's annual 650 million tonnes of CO_2 emissions suggest an economic cost of around a tenth of the value created for consumers. That's before any wider economic benefits. This does not mean the problem should be dismissed, but clearly air transport creates tremendous value net of any costs for the world.

Yet despite the rapid growth in demand and the creation of substantial consumer value, since 1970 only $5 billion in profits have been generated from $12,000 billion of revenues, a margin of 0.05 per cent. Airlines are notorious for consistently destroying shareholder value at an average rate through the cycle of $11 billion a year. Alliances, joint ventures and code shares are airline innovations that have sought, with varying degrees of success, to overcome the regulatory barriers preventing airlines themselves from globalizing and rationalizing capacity. With increasing liberalization in the past 30 years 75 per cent of airlines are now privately owned. Given the profitable alternatives to the $700 billion currently invested in the industry this is not sustainable.

Further deregulation of markets is necessary to extend the tremendous consumer benefits of air transport to future consumers and business in China, India and elsewhere. Environmental challenges need to be addressed and solved. But sustainability also requires that investors get a reasonable return on their capital. A solution to that problem surely requires some radical change to the structure of the industry. The articles in this excellent book will throw some welcome light on a number of these issues.

The Challenges Faced by Independent Ground Handlers and In-flight Caterers

Clement Woon
CEO of SATS Ltd

The independent ground handling and in-flight catering markets have become sizeable as more and more airlines began to spin off their non-core operations. On average, global airlines have struggled to deliver a fair return on capital. The aviation industry is cyclical and volatile due to its high sensitivity to regional and global events. Legacy processes, labour and fuel costs are examples of other pressures that potentially drive down shareholder value.

Spinning off non-core operations such as ground handling and in-flight catering as subsidiaries or divesting them entirely helps to reduce the total costs of airlines as these spin-off entities are expected to develop differentiated cost structures that hopefully will be comparatively lower than those of the airlines. Ground services costs will also become more variable to airlines than before.

In practice, the spin-off entities have to continue with the airlines' cost structures for some time before they can actually optimize their cost structures. They will also find it challenging to generate revenue growth on their own as only airlines and airports can drive growth directly, and hence they are subject to the same market volatility as the airlines and airports.

Following the divestment of non-core operations, the character of the airlines will change with time and so will be the services they require. Some airlines reduce their ground services requirements while others actually have reasons to increase. Whatever the case, independent ground handlers and in-flight caterers are left on their own to compete and find continuity for their future. Unlike the airlines, there is no global voice for ground handlers and in-flight caterers. IATA has a chapter specifically for ground handling but it is more a voice for the airlines than for ground handlers.

With increasing deregulation in the aviation industry, airlines continue to restructure and may potentially consolidate. Open skies across the Atlantic and within ASEAN, for example, will provide impetus for more strategic moves. The centre of travel demand, traditionally in the US, will first shift to China as 1.5 billion people will soon have the means and reason to travel with growing economic affluence and greater freedom. Will foreign carriers have a piece of this lucrative travel market? Will increasing outsourcing and sale of non-core entities provide the required funding for the required aviation asset expansion?

There is hope that there will be more independent ground handlers and caterers in the future, or alternatively the incumbents may become larger as they acquire more airlines' in-house operations. However, profitability of the industry remains below expectations and investors must have a long-term view and holding power.

Profitability of ground handlers and in-flight caterers is a function of efficiency in the deployment of resources amidst the peaks and troughs of airline schedules. Therefore size will be important at each operating location. Alternatively, the setting up of adjacent businesses to redeploy resources during the lull periods may be a solution. Other methods such as using casual labour will help manage cost but performance and consistency may suffer as a result.

The economics of a pure ground handling and in-flight catering company will be challenging as it is a business-to-business proposition. Its growth and profitability will be largely determined by the airlines and to some extent the airports as the power resides with them to determine the level of competition at each hub or airport.

The civil aviation industry intuitively remains attractive for its promise as an effective mass transportation solution. However, at the moment investors are not getting their fair returns as airlines continue to struggle to remain in the black. The industry needs a total revamp on cost and operating structures but is held back by traditional paradigms. Under this scenario, independent ground handlers and in-flight caterers will have to continue fighting against commoditization of their products and services in order to deliver better returns. They can only succeed through differentiation as well as expansion of their core competencies.

Growth Opportunities in Brazil

Constantino de Oliveira Junior
President and CEO of Gol and Varig

In the first half of 2008 the challenge of the airline industry was to survive in a world with rising costs and stagnated prices. The main concern was the evolution of oil price which overcame the barrier of US$135 per barrel, making fuel costs represent 38 per cent or more of the total costs of an airline.

This scenario represented a special threat to low-cost carriers because their cost gap when compared to legacy carriers – their main competitive advantage – is achieved mainly by better managing indirect costs and operating expenses. Because the direct costs trend was toward representing a growing proportion of total costs, the room for obtaining cost advantage for low-cost carriers was becoming narrower.

Demand was not a problem at all because the world was experiencing a long period of continuous prosperity.

In the second half the scenario changed completely: oil prices dropped dramatically achieving US$30 per barrel, equivalent to the level of five years before. A proportional impact on fuel prices had happened. Demand fell sharply by 10–15 per cent basis in the first world. This new scenario was opposite to the previous one and represented an important opportunity for the healthy low-cost carriers because the room for obtaining competitive advantage was re-established.

Some low-cost carriers like GOL saw an opportunity to adjust their operating model by introducing some attributes that are commonly associated with legacy carriers. The acquisition of VARIG was the chance for GOL to make this repositioning in an easier way. VARIG's frequent-flyer programme was extended to GOL, catering was revised, comfort class was introduced, alliances were developed and several other improvements implemented.

At least three lessons may be learned from these happenings. First, the economic environment is so volatile that being flexible is undoubtedly the best competence an airline can pursue. Second, monitoring the environment in order to detect business opportunities is one of the healthiest activities a firm can perform. Third, having a deep commitment with the organization principles and core competencies –in GOL's case, offering services of high quality at the lowest production costs – is crucial to entrepreneurial success.

On the external side, Brazil continues to grow in spite of the worldwide economic difficulties. Income distribution is improving each day, adding numerous new clients to the airline industry, and GOL continues to be the preferential choice for these new segments.

GOL is evolving, lowering costs, improving services and internal processes, adding to the fleet new and up-to-date aircraft. I have to be optimistic.

Can Gulf Carriers Sustain Their Current Growth Rate?

Professor Fariba Alamdari

Vice President, Marketing and Value Analysis, Boeing, Seattle

The airlines in the Gulf region have expanded dramatically over the last decade driven by the unique combination of economic expansion (Figure 0.1), well-coordinated growth plans, modern air transport infrastructure and a favourable geographic location. The most notable expansion has been in the long-haul market segment, with carriers such as Emirates, Etihad, and Qatar Airways. The LCC business model has also arrived in the region; carriers such as AirArabia, Jazeera and recently Fly Dubai have stimulated traffic in the short and medium-range markets. Another LCC start-up, NAS Air, has recently entered the Saudi Arabian domestic market. A very impressive expansion of capacity looks set to continue, with the Gulf region very well represented in the airplane manufacturers' order books.

Such an expansion by the Gulf carriers raises the following questions:

- Is the current expansion rate sustainable?
- Would it be at the expense of European and Asian carriers' market share?
- Would there be any constraints to this growth?

As illustrated in Figure 0.2, the growth rate of Gulf carriers over the past years has been 20 per cent per year. Our studies of the market indicate that maintaining such a growth rate seems unlikely, whereas a more realistic average annual growth rate of around 10 per cent is more probable for the following reasons:

- It is much more difficult to sustain high levels of growth after a decade of growing at 20 per cent per year.
- Over the years, established European and Asian carriers have ceded some degree of market share to sixth-freedom services of Gulf carriers. Some further market share gain from established European and Asian carriers is likely, but not so much as to support the current growth rate. That said, future growth opportunities remain with future destinations to China, Africa, South and North America, thereby further exploiting the multiplier effect of their already strong networks.
- The regional flows between Europe, Southern Asia and Oceania are growing by nearly six per cent per year, which could potentially support moderate growth of Gulf carriers but not at historic levels.

- The recent LCC start-up carriers in the Gulf also look set to expand vigorously. As of today, the combined in-service fleet and orders of Jazeera, AirArabia, NAS, and flydubai still add up to less seats than a carrier like easyJet or Jetblue puts on the market. Even so, the addressable markets in Europe and the US are over twice that of the Gulf region.

Continued expansion by Gulf airlines is not without its constraints, risks and challenges. Below are the potential main constraints facing the Gulf carriers:

- Comparatively high inflation rates in the Gulf countries are eroding purchasing power, which in turn affects travel patterns, particularly for migrant workers and their families (Figure 0.3). High inflation rates have moderated lately, but the worldwide downturn affects the pace of construction causing fewer movements by migrant workers. This is most notable in Dubai with the collapse of the real-estate market, both for office and tourist construction projects.
- Although the industry and governments are investing in infrastructure to support the economic benefits of aviation's growth, the ground infrastructure that is being built and planned does not match the airspace capacity, reported by IATA.[1]
- Airlines in regions like India are also expanding capacity, offering non-stop services to European destinations on routes that compete directly with the Gulf carriers' more traditional traffic. All of the expansion requires investment in infrastructure and pilots; at times, the resource requirements of rapidly expanding regions may compete with one another.
- Regional stability plays a key role in attracting passenger traffic: in the absence of major events affecting the region adversely, the Gulf countries have been very successful at stimulating tourism and international traffic. We can only hope for a continued environment of stability.

Expansion does not come by itself. Especially in this turbulent industry, management must put successful growth strategies in place and then execute those strategies. To date the Gulf carriers have done exactly that, by providing a price-competitive product at an extremely high level of service and by building a 'one-stop to anywhere' network of destinations that focuses not only on major hubs but on smaller yet equally important destinations in Europe such as Manchester, Birmingham, Hamburg and Milan. Geography is an immense benefit to this strategy with the Gulf positioned ideally between European and Southern Asia gateways. The Gulf carriers are also set to exploit traffic flows in underserved markets by leveraging their geographic positioning for Africa, China, and South and North America.

---

1 Press Release: The MENA Challenge. Coping with Growth, 20 October 2010, No: 48.

Barring any major economic or political calamities, the successful strategies that have been pursued by the Gulf airlines will continue to result in expansion, albeit at a somewhat slower pace than we have seen in the last few years. This expansion will significantly benefit consumers as well as the Gulf economies.

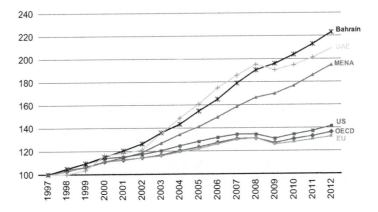

Figure 0.1   Annual real GDP level (Index, 1997 = 100)
Source: IMF WEO (October 2010 database).

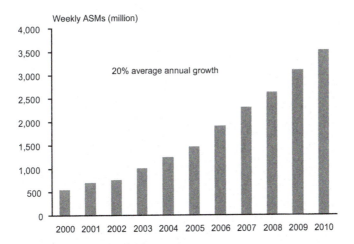

Figure 0.2   Gulf carriers' growth rate
Source: May OAG for respective years. (Includes Emirates, Etihad, Gulf Air and Qatar Airways).

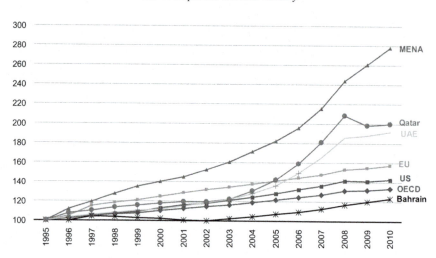

Figure 0.3   Average consumer prices (Index, 1995 = 100)
Source: IMF WEO (October 2010 database).

Forecasting the Fate of the Airline Industry

Gary Kelly

Chairman, CEO, and President Southwest Airlines

Forecasting the fate of the airline industry is chancy in the best of times, and these certainly aren't the best of times. As you can imagine, the airline industry is brutally competitive, and ever-changing. And this past decade has been the most challenging in the history of the industry. The good news is things have improved, and we're in better shape as than we were a year ago. But major challenges still exist, and we are not out of the woods yet.

Of course, no one knows the future, and I will be the first to tell you I had no idea this financial crisis was coming the way it erupted several years ago. But I can tell you emphatically that Southwest Airlines was prepared for it. Just like we were prepared for 9/11, and just like we were prepared for the first Gulf War in 1991. Southwest Airlines is strong; we're well-positioned; and we're healthy; and because of that, we are able to take advantage of opportunities and be bold.

As for the industry today, our situation is much improved versus a year ago. Still, it's a very difficult time for the airline industry. The airline industry is particularly sensitive to recession and it typically takes years for business travel to fully recover, and keep in mind that this is once the economy is in expansion. Additionally, airline economics have fundamentally changed over the last decade because airlines are also particularly sensitive to energy costs.

Fuel costs in the latter half of the decade have more than tripled, compared to the previous 20 years. As a result, our operating cost structures have flipped from being dominated by fixed costs to being dominated by variable costs. That means flying more doesn't drive unit costs lower. Over the last decade, then, fares have been forced up to even much higher operating costs.

As fares go up, some amount of traffic demand is lost, because air travel is so price sensitive and discretionary. We must all recognize cost matters a great deal when it comes to air travel. Keeping costs, and fares, as low as possible continues to be a core philosophy of Southwest.

For the domestic industry, 2010 clearly brought a profit recovery from the energy price crisis and the 2008/2009 recession. But it is purely a result of reduced capacity to match reduced demand. Excluding Southwest, traffic capacity and revenues remain below 2007 levels, primarily due to fewer business travellers. Hotels tell a similar story. It appears that 2011, based on all we know about the US economy, the lack of job growth, and our fiscal and monetary challenges, will be more of the same.

At Southwest, the road travelled has been different. At Southwest, our outlook for next year and next decade is different. While the rest of the domestic industry shrank over the last 10 difficult years, Southwest is setting records: record traffic, record load factors, and record revenues over the decade. Because we offered something different, especially low fares, we could grow. Because we were well prepared for tough times, we had time and resources to plan and adjust to a rapidly changing environment.

As we begin our fifth decade of service in 2011, our momentum is strong. We have thoroughly updated our plan for the next 5–10 years. We have tremendous opportunities ahead.

Changing Global Air Transport

James Hogan
CEO of Etihad Airways

The global airline industry has changed significantly during the past 50 years but the most striking of these changes in recent times is the emergence of the Middle East as the centre for the aviation industry.

Behind the phenomenal growth of airlines from the Middle East is the region's drive towards increasing trade and tourism, along with many other additional factors, providing a multilayered formula for success.

Also at the forefront is the Middle East's ideal global location for the aviation industry – perfectly placed as a convenient air bridge between East and West.

The Middle East region's carriers are also making major investments in terms of aircraft and airport infrastructure. Etihad alone made an order for up to 205 aircraft worth US$43billion at the 2008 Farnborough International Air Show.

Ten airports across the Middle East are also investing US$37 billion in new airport infrastructure and capacity which will provide for an additional 318 million passengers per year by 2012.

Middle East gross domestic product (GDP) is growing year-on-year between five and six per cent and this is leading to the emergence of an economic powerhouse akin to India and China.

There has been tremendous action by the United Arab Emirates towards diversifying its economy away from the traditional oil and gas sectors, which in 1975 accounted for 70 per cent of GDP. This had been reduced to 30 per cent by 2005 as sectors like tourism, real estate, logistics and financial services matured.

Diversification has powered the aviation sector's double digit capacity and traffic growth in the last four years.

Another great plus for Middle East carriers is that their catchment area is not simply the region, it is the whole world, and they have grown to such an extent that they now compete on a global stage.

The region, especially during the recent tough economic times, still needs to ensure that it manages capacity against growth but the signs are that real and lasting change is sustainable.

The UAE's capital city Abu Dhabi is seeing a huge transformation as it looks to become a major global centre. Currently it enjoys a market share of just 2.3 per cent in world travel and tourism with about a million visitors a year, but there are ambitious and realistic targets to increase this to more than 3 million visitors a year by 2015.

Abu Dhabi's development as a major tourism destination will be enhanced by a range of exciting, top-of-the-range attractions including the Formula 1 Grand Prix track on Yas Island, the Guggenheim museum, Warner Brothers theme park and a Louvre museum, the first of its kind outside France.

The future is bright for the region and the Middle East enjoys the perfect launch-point for its airlines. It can fully exploit the range of modern aircraft and there are exciting and expanding business and leisure opportunities.

The global aviation order is changing and the roots of growth and development that will make the Middle East the centre of global aviation can now start to be seen.

The Inevitable Evolution of Aviation

Professor Kenneth Button

*Director of the Center for Transportation, Policy and Operations,
George Mason University, USA*

Economic progress, in capitalist society, means turmoil. And ... in this turmoil competition works in a manner completely different from the way it would work in a stationary process, however perfectly competitive. Possibilities for gains to be reaped by producing old things more cheaply are constantly materializing and calling for new investments. These new products and new methods compete with the old methods not on equal terms but at a decisive advantage that may mean death to the latter.

J. Schumpeter, *Capitalism, Socialism, and Democracy*, 1942.

Schumpeter's quote gives a pretty good description of the modern, deregulated airline industry. There is certainly progress and the legacy suppliers are finding their traditional models of operations under threat. The question now is less whether these forces of creative destruction will change in themselves (this seems unlikely in the near future), but whether governments will allow them to continue. There is always an inevitable tendency to assume that regulators can bring about beneficial change more efficiently and less painfully than competitive forces. In one sense this can be true if one is concerned with minimizing stranded costs and putting a high weight on the welfare of incumbents, rather than the most efficient use of resources over time. The ability of entrenched coalitions has often slanted policy towards a more interventionist approach in aviation: politicians and the like are easier to control than are markets. Added to this, there are pronounced long-term cyclical swings in the general attitude towards markets and economic regulations more generally.

The evidence is that there are pressures for more intervention in aviation markets. The recession from 2007 has clearly brought about more government involvement in markets across the board, and it is difficult to see air transport insulated from this. This has nothing to do with the fact that one of the main reasons for the housing bubble and financial crash in the US was the intervention of government in the mortgage market from 1994 that fostered the excessive lending, but rather that policies are driven by perception and not always by logical considerations. Aviation will just be swept along in the wake of a general regulatory movement.

The move to more, or at least different, specific airline regulation seems probable as scheduled airlines continue to find it difficult to cover their costs in highly competitive conditions. The larger units that are emerging as mergers take place, and as the three global alliances continue to grow, may provide some respite but the absence of a core in markets with free entry and where resources (planes, fuel, crew, slots, and so on) have to be committed well in advance of sales inevitably will push fares down to short-run marginal costs. Bankruptcies (and especially Chapter 11 bankruptcies in the US) have meant that investors have borne the brunt of the costs of this, but it seems unlikely that the industry will remain a sexy bed for investors for much longer with such high levels of risk involved. The airlines may find new, inventive ways to enjoy some monopoly power and avoid this problem but as with frequent flyer programmes, hub dominance and differential fare setting are likely to provide only short-term respites. Inevitably the authorities will feel that they can do better despite the realities of history.

Finally, the air transport industry will be brought more fully under the umbrella of environmental regulation. The challenges this brings are possibly not as great as some imagine; the industry is more flexible than often thought, and doubts about some of the extreme claims regarding such things as damage caused by CO_2 emissions seem likely to result in policies less restrictive than once thought. Nevertheless, the costs of air transport will rise despite new technologies and managerial innovations, and this will impact on markets.

Longer-term Prospects for Air Transport

Laurent Rouaud

Vice President of Research at Airbus

The aviation industry is famously cyclical, with a number of significant down turns in the past linked not only to the world's economic health, but also exacerbated by other significant world events. However, all those involved in the industry are fortunate that the need for air transportation is such that when we have these occasional difficult periods, demand and the fortunes of those involved in the industry have traditionally quickly recovered. During the last cycle that was characterized by 9/11, SARs and the second Gulf War, air traffic recovered from the lows experienced in 2002 to reach levels 36 per cent above those seen in pre-down 2000 by the end of last year.

Although it is a truism to say that aviation is a global industry, it is this that is at the heart of its strength. The need for air transportation between the world's major cities continues to grow, as these major centres of population continue to grow and prosper. In the 1970s there were just four major agglomerations of over 10 million people: today there are 26, with more than 30 forecast by 2015. These cities are located in the relatively mature markets in the US and Europe where passenger traffic growth is forecast to continue, as well as within the economic powerhouses developing in Asia, such as China. As economic wealth develops further in these countries, we can expect to see more and more of the world's population have access to the benefits air transportation brings, further driving traffic growth, which as in the past is expected to double again in the next 15 years.

Facilitating this growth will be the continued deregulation between air transport markets. With much in this area already achieved within and between the US and Europe, the pace is also quickening in Asia, further allowing this region's potential to be realized.

Airlines in the Middle East have been quick to take advantage of their geographical location to develop global hubs to service demand between regions and to facilitate trade within their own. Meanwhile, airlines continue to focus on costs to achieve prices that are within reach of more and more people. A goal the low-cost carriers have championed with more future potential, particularly in Asia, expected to provide another potent driver for growth. However, whilst the demand and benefits air transport brings both economically and socially are evident, in the future it will be necessary to balance these benefits against any costs, particularly environmental. This is a challenge our industry, like many others with greater impact, has taken.

Airline Consolidation in China and the Prospects for China Eastern

Liu Shaoyong

Chairman of China Eastern Airlines

The 'clouds swallow', China Eastern Airlines Corporation Limited (China Eastern or CEA), which is one of China's three major national air transport carriers, is marching gradually onto the path of developing scientifically.

The year of 2009 was another remarkable year in the history of CEA with net profits of $79 million, together with a well-kept safety record. China Eastern has become one of the biggest airlines in China and is ranked the first nationwide in terms of the flight regularity in 2009.

More good news came on July 13, 2009, of the programme of the merger of China Eastern and Shanghai Airlines Co., Ltd, through a shares swap. China Eastern, after the combination of Shanghai Airlines and itself, will have a fleet of 300 and more aircraft. Its flight routes will cover more than 180 cities. The structure of the flights layout will be more optimized and the flights transit network will be more perfect.

Besides, China Eastern has established regular services from many cities of the Mainland to some Taiwan airports from August 31, 2009, which can carry millions of people from the Taiwan Straits back and forth every year.

As we know, 2008 witnessed the financial crisis sweeping the world, and the whole international aviation industry was plunged into serious recession. It is really a long winter season for our China Eastern together with all the airline companies of China and the world.

However, it is predicted that China will take the lead in the recovery of the world economy. The signs show that the world economy, including the aviation industry, will get slightly better in 2010.

2010 is full of hope for us. Expo will be held in Shanghai in this year. China Eastern is its first partner and the only designated carrier. When the event occurs from May to October 2010, some percentage of about 70 million visitors might fly to Shanghai by flights of China Eastern.

In 2010 we will make far-sighted and overall plans for the development of CEA, strictly observing the principle of safety first, continuing to focus on our main business, relying on our motivated and creative staff, and developing our information platform, adapting CEA to the requirement of the nation's economic and social development.

We are proud of what we have achieved as we look back. Ahead of us, there is a bright future. Looking into the future, CEA is now at a new starting point in history. We are shouldering heavy responsibilities while full of confidence. Let us march forward with concerted efforts and courage towards a great nation in civil aviation.

The 'clouds swallow' has swallowed the sorrow suffered so far.

China Eastern from East China will be flying fast and far.

Overcoming the Constraints of Aeropolitics

Maurice Flanagan

Executive Vice Chairman of Emirates

A recent excitable article in *The Times*, repeated in *The Australian*, would lead you to think that international commercial air transport is in terminal decline. Well, we've been there before. Although things are tough, they're not that tough, and the article places undue emphasis on low-cost carriers, and fails to recognize profound regional disparities.

The traditional benchmark for a region's importance in international aviation has been its population size, but this criterion now has less relevance, despite the looming dominance of China and India in total (though not international) traffic.

Singapore and Dubai are two rather good examples – both cities, or rather city-states, have small local populations (approximately 4.3 million, and a fast-growing 2 million respectively); but their airports each process more than 30 million passengers a year (in 2007, SIN: 36.7 million, DXB: 34.3 million). It is interesting that the governments of both Singapore and Dubai operate an Open Skies aeropolitical regime, allowing free entry to foreign airlines, without demanding reciprocity. It means that Singapore Airlines and Emirates have to be smart to survive, let alone prosper, which we both manage to do. Passenger traffic through Dubai is growing at 18 per cent a year, showing no signs of slowing down, is expected to hit 75 million by 2012–2015 and 120 million after completion of the six-runway Al Maktoum International in about 2021.

International air traffic flows are shifting eastwards for a number of reasons. Economic growth in Asia and the Middle East is a big driver, but what has made this shift possible has been the advance, however grudging in many countries, of liberalization, and new ultra long-range aircraft.

Before the 1980s, most international routes trans-pacific, trans-Atlantic, and towards Australia, originated or 'hubbed' in Europe. Europe's dominance in part stemmed from post-colonial trade routes and trade links with the Gulf, Far East and Australasia.

European hubs are still a major force in global aviation, but their relative importance declines as Asian and Middle Eastern hubs become more powerful.

And according to IATA's global air traffic growth forecast for 2007–2011, Asia and the Middle East are in the ascendant.

The Middle East will be the fastest-growing region for international air traffic, and Asia second. Their average annual growth rate outstrips growth in any other region, as well as the global average.

Table 0.1   Average annual growth rate 2007 to 2011 (international)

	Passenger Numbers	Freight Tonnes
Africa	5.6%	4.6%
Asia Pacific	5.9%	5.4%
Europe	5.0%	4.3%
Latin America/ Caribbean	4.4%	4.2%
Middle East	6.8%	5.0%
North America	4.2%	3.9%

Source: IATA.

The regional differences in passenger growth rates will largely reflect differences in regional economic growth and the structure of each regional market. The Middle East, developing economies in Asia and, to a lesser extent Africa, will be boosted by strong GDP growth, along with significant new capacity and new routes.

European growth will be close to the average, though Eastern Europe will see a more rapid expansion. The relatively low Latin American growth reflects lower demand growth in key markets to North America and within the region itself. North America is expected to be the slowest growing region, reflecting both mature markets and cyclically slower growth in the US economy.

The forecast growth in freight traffic closely follows expected growth in regional economies and trade flows. Routes linked with Asia Pacific, and China and India in particular, are forecast to show particular strength. Middle Eastern air-freight is also expected to show strong growth, as the region's carriers take advantage of the current strong purchasing power for the region provided by high oil prices to increase capacity on existing and new routes. However, that does not go for Dubai. Oil contributes less than three per cent to Dubai' GDP, tourism over 20 per cent.

All Airlines Face More or Less the Same Challenges:

Talent and Skilled Staff

Becoming harder to find, particularly as the air industry is booming in the Arabian Gulf and Asia, led by the massive economic development in India, China and the GCC countries.

Oil Prices

At the time of writing this piece, oil prices were hitting US$105 a barrel. Even with the most advanced and fuel-efficient aircraft, oil prices are a huge challenge to profitability. Thus far, demand for travel has been resilient to the rising fuel surcharges and increased fares that airlines have been forced to impose in order to remain solvent. But how elastic will demand for air travel prove to be? A few short years ago fuel represented 13 per cent of a typical full-service airline' total costs. Now it is running at about 34 per cent. That's our largest element of cost – more than our people cost, and more than our aircraft cost.

Environmental Lobby

Another looming thundercloud is the environmental lobby, particularly in Europe. Somehow airlines have been demonized for their part in climate change (as if climate ever did anything else but change), and most of the debate has been more emotional than rational.

But we have to deal with the perception, false though it certainly is, that we are uniquely the global emission villains. As it happens, sound economics coincides with the green agenda. The A380 generates lower global emissions, and lower seat-mile costs, per passenger than any previous aircraft. The Boeing 787 and the Airbus A350 will follow, with their composite wings and airframes and new engines. That same technology will be applied to the Boeing 787–8 series, giving that splendid aircraft another 30 years lease of life.

Aeropolitics

There has been some evidence of progress towards aeropolitical liberalism in recent years. The traditional industry model – closed domestic markets, strong national flag carriers, and bilateral agreements – is the fault of the British, who were behind the Bermuda Agreement in the forties. This was designed when 2.5 million people a year were travelling. There are now over 2.5 billion. The bilateral system is an abomination, and is exploited by national airlines who persuade their governments to protect them against the overall interests of their economies. But some have seen the light. The UAE's Air Services Agreement with the USA allows Emirates to fly to any point in the States, how often we wish, with no capacity restriction, and with rights to carry traffic from intermediate points.

An interesting example is Australia. When Emirates started flights there in 1997 our incursions were bitterly resisted by Qantas, and the Australian government listened to them, until they saw the added economic benefit quickly enjoyed by the places to which we flew. We now have 49 flights a week to Australian cities, and will expand to 80. And, interestingly, Qantas is more profitable than it has ever been.

More and more countries are subscribing to the fact that liberal air access has a multiplier effect on their economies and that protection of their national carriers no longer stacks up in the cost-benefit equation, or serves their national interest.

Things are changing, but not fast enough. There are still some allegedly advanced countries who are still in the aeropolitical dark ages.

In Search of Sustained Profitability 30 Years After Deregulation

Dr Peter P. Belobaba

MIT, Global Airline Industry Programme

The transformation of the world's airline industry is still a work in progress, one that began 30 years ago with the US *Airline Deregulation Act* of 1978. Airline deregulation or at least 'liberalization' has now spread to much of the world, introducing competition to both domestic and international markets.

Overall, the benefits of airline deregulation have outweighed the costs – air travel has grown at unprecedented rates while average fares continue to decline, with no statistical evidence of negative impacts on airline safety. Nonetheless, the shift to market-driven competition has led to losses of airline jobs, deteriorating customer service and increased profit volatility, raising concerns about the required reinvestment to sustain airline operations.

Cost containment and productivity improvement became a focus of US airlines shortly after deregulation, and non-US airlines have more recently been forced by competitive realities to address this challenge as well. The more recent growth of new entrant 'low-cost carriers' (LCCs) redefined the competitive landscape for traditional 'legacy' airlines, as the cost advantages of new LCCs reflected substantial differences in the productivity of both aircraft and employees.

The US legacy carriers were able to use bankruptcy (or the threat thereof) to respond to the LCC challenge, by downsizing, cutting operating costs and improving productivity as part of their restructuring efforts. They realized productivity gains not only by reducing headcount, but also by introducing new technologies and by moving capacity from domestic to international routes in an effort to improve aircraft utilization and increase revenues. At the same time, LCCs have begun to see increasing operating costs, driven by ageing fleets and personnel with increasing seniority. In fact, there is much evidence of recent cost and productivity convergence between the legacy and LCC airlines, changing the competitive landscape yet again.

The airline industry thus continues its dramatic restructuring, involving even more fundamental changes than those imagined by the architects of deregulation. Yet, after three decades of deregulation – and after multiple cycles of financial successes and failures – the industry remains fragile. US airlines may have led the way in this industry transformation, but they have been unable to find a workable strategy to achieve sustained profitability.

The liberalization of airline markets is irreversible in today's global economy, so re-regulation is not a realistic option. The outcome of this remarkable industry transformation will depend on all stakeholders finally accepting the reality that the competitive landscape has been changed forever. No amount of wishful thinking by regulators, labour unions, airline managers or consumers will return us to the 'golden days' of air transportation. Instead, strategies to better manage expectations and costs, to continue to improve productivity, to deal with the cyclicality of both demand and capacity, and to deliver a product for which consumers are willing to pay a compensatory price will ultimately determine which airlines will survive to face inevitable future changes to the competitive landscape.

IT, Airlines and the Recession: What is a Chief Information Officer to Do?

Paul Coby

Chair of SITA and Chief Information Officer of British Airways

After 9/11, the airline industry came back strongly, turning an $11 billion loss in 2002 into a $13 billion profit by 2007. Similarly, in 2010 the industry recovered from the recession to make an estimated net profit of $15 billion. This followed losses of $9.4 billion in 2009 as the world entered the recession. This was, of course, a team effort across airlines and alliances, but I believe smart use of technology played a fundamental part in the recovery on both occasions. I think that SITA, which started online selling, and BA – which led many innovations on the web – can claim to have initiated many of the IT innovations that helped the air transport industry to weather the financial firestorms.

Whether you look at the massive shift to selling airline tickets online, the move to eTickets, the re-creation of the direct relationship with our passengers, or the optimization of every kind of resource, IT has been central to the airline industry's transformation in the twenty-first century. The roughly 2.5 per cent of airline revenues represented by IT have begun to help generate all channels of airline revenues, just as they should address all of airline costs. I believe technology and technologists have made a difference because these days there are no IT projects – only business projects. I feel that this maxim – which I coined back in 2000 – is now being proved true at the heart of the air transport industry.

So, having once again been an engine of the fight-back, what can IT do for the airline industry as the world struggles to come out of recession? Is IT last year's model – or does it still really matter? There seems little doubt that the airline industry will face new challenges in 2011. The situation of airlines and airports in high-growth economies like China, India and Brazil is very different from that in economically troubled Europe. I propose three new imperatives to ensure we make the most of IT in the next decade.

Do Even More for Even Less!

Easy to say but hard to do: if the name of the game in recent years has been 'doing more with less' our strapline for 2011 must be 'doing even more with even less'. This may sound trite, but any company in pretty much any industry – and especially in the air transport industry – which does not get its cash out-flow under control is going to have problems. So, although growth is happening in many parts of the world, the trick is growing the top-line and holding the costs down.

There is going to be caution about investment, so we need to concentrate on the key priorities that really make a difference and stop the rest. This is very relevant to the continuing cost of running our technology platforms. Now that you, as CIO, have made every department in your airline dependent on your technology, you, as CIO, are going to have to find a way to run all of that technology for a great deal less.

The good news is that new technologies can produce step changes – using multiple racks of Linux servers rather than expensive bespoke Unix, for example, is both good for the wallet and good for the environment. And Voice over IP (VOIP) telephony, virtualization across servers and software as a service from the 'Cloud' all have important parts to play. We cut the costs of running BA's IT by more than 50 per cent over the last decade in cash terms. You must keep looking for substantial savings everywhere, whether you are in growth or in recession.

Focus on Customer-facing Systems

Holding onto the customers your airline already has – and winning over those of your competitors – is as vital in growing markets as in shrinking markets. Your selling systems like revenue management and sales force automation, the ease of your online experience, and the attractiveness of your Frequent Flyer Programme, are key tools in any airline's competitive tool-set. Fixing problems here is going to pay fast dividends. However, there are two other areas that are less obvious.

Understanding your customers – really understanding them, using modern data-warehousing to provide real business intelligence – is hard and meticulous work and certainly not cheap. But get it right and you can target your marketing and really up-sell to customers with products and services they really want.

Secondly, the Web 2.0 revolution has transformed many online customers into social net-workers. Not everyone has taken this step – but many people are no longer satisfied any more with simply using the Web to buy tickets or to change their seat or print a boarding pass. Now they want to interact with your airline and with each other. They want to tell you about your product – what works well and what doesn't – to tell you what they think of your company when it messes up, and to recognize great performance and great service from our crew when we do well. Not just that – they also want to tell each other which are the best Italian restaurants in Soho in London and SOHO in New York and Hong Kong – check out BA's metrotwin.com.

Remember IT for the Middle and Back Office Too

Again not obvious, but IT is vitally important for the middle and back offices – that is, for the call centres at the frontline, for customer relations in the middle, and for finance and administration, HR and passenger revenue accounting at the back. Often this is a neglected area for IT in an airline, where concentrations on the customer and the Web have been our twenty-first century priorities. Now, just spending $ millions buying an ERP will not improve matters and will make a serious hole in your investment portfolio. An integrated approach, however, which looks at back office proposition, processes and people *before* looking at the IT can really drive the cost reduction and business control which are so sorely needed in challenging times. Furthermore, cleaning up your back office processes will give you a control environment and analytics that will enable your airline to react to new challenges and take opportunities as they arise.

An Inherently Unstable Industry: Airlines Have Themselves to Blame

Professor Rigas Doganis

The airline industry is cyclical. Historically, 4–5 years of global losses have been followed by 5–6 years of profits, which enabled many airlines to recover financially. Such 10-year cycles can be discerned going back to the 1960s. In the first decade of the twenty-first century that pattern was broken. In the period 2001 to 2009 the airline industry as a whole only made a significant profit of US$12.9 billion in one year 2007. But it lost $26 billion in the following two years. It was not till 2010 and 2011 that profitably returned to the industry. Though several larger airlines and some low-cost carriers operated profitably for much of the decade, most airlines did not enjoy enough profitable years to allow them to recover their financial strength. By 2010, despite the fact that the industry as a whole was doing better, many airlines were in dire straits.

Yet, the IATA DG, Giovanni Bisignani and airline chief executives have rarely accepted any responsibility for their industry's failings. They have been quick to blame external factors – high fuel prices, rising airport charges, health pandemics, terrorist attacks or financial crises. Certainly there were many external shocks during the decade. But there may be a more fundamental structural problem afflicting the industry. Air transport appears to deviate from one of the basic tenets of economics, namely that after periods of instability when weak and/or loss-making companies leave the market, markets tend towards equilibrium. Equilibrium is when supply of a particular good or service matches demand at prices at which suppliers can make an adequate profit or return on their investment.

The problem with the airline industry is that, rather than being in a state of stable or even unstable equilibrium it appears to be in chronic disequilibrium. This is because the industry seems to be in a permanent state of over-supply; in other words, of over-capacity. This is true even though in the short-term, as they did in 2009, airlines may cut capacity by grounding aircraft, reducing frequencies or switching some flights to smaller aircraft. Longer-term capacity growth means constant downward pressure on fares. Passenger load factors have risen but high load factors belie the reality. They are only achieved by collapsing fares to fill empty seats. They do not ensure profitability. While some better managed airlines generate profits most years, very many airlines are profitable only spasmodically. Speaking in May 2009, Glen Tilton, the CEO of United Airlines, stated that the airline industry 'systematically failed to earn its cost of capital'.

The industry's chronic disequilibrium is due primarily to the interplay of two forces. The first is a strong, inherent and, it seems, unstoppable tendency for the provision of too much capacity. The second is that ailing and bankrupt airlines, especially larger ones, like elephants, take a long time to die. In fact, unlike elephants, some airlines, like Alitalia or Japan Airlines, never seem to die no matter how ill they are.

The strong tendency within the airline industry to over-order new capacity is driven by several factors. First, and perhaps most important, is the ease with which airlines can acquire new aircraft. If airlines need debt finance to purchase aircraft directly they can offer the aircraft as security to their lenders. Such asset-based financing is attractive to banks and other financial institutions because aircraft are moveable assets that can, in most cases, be readily repossessed and placed elsewhere. Both lessors and financial institutions lending to airlines have been helped and encouraged by the 2001 'Cape Town Convention on International Interests in Mobile Equipment', which has made repossession of aircraft in the event of default on interest or lease payments very much easier. The reality is that most airlines, even if suffering chronic losses, are still able to acquire new aircraft.

Aircraft financiers may have further security in that loans may be guaranteed by one of the government run export credit agencies (ECAs) such as the Ex-Im Bank in the US, the ECGD in the UK, Hermes in Germany or COFACE in France. These further reduce the risks to lenders. In 2009 when traditional funding institutions were in some difficulties following the banking crisis, the ECAs stepped in to fill the funding gap for new aircraft deliveries. They provided guarantees for loans totalling $23.5 billion which amounted to just over one third of the aircraft finance required that year.

As an alternative to buying aircraft, airlines have the option of acquiring capacity on operating or finance leases from one of the many aircraft leasing companies such as, GECAS or ILFC. The lessors make it easy, even for airlines with weak balance sheets or new-entrant start-ups with only projected balance sheets, to acquire additional capacity.

To further facilitate debt finance or leasing agreements, many governments have themselves been prepared to guarantee the loans raised or the lease payments when the airlines concerned are partially or fully government-owned. Though no longer permitted within the European Union, this happens elsewhere.

The second driver of over-capacity is the manufacturers themselves. They claim that their new aircraft have 'significant' technological improvements – perhaps lower fuel consumption, longer range, higher payload and so on – which will enhance their operational and financial performance. Airline executives often feel that buying such new equipment will ensure future profits. Too frequently it merely enhances their indebtedness and pushes up interest or lease payments.

The pressure from manufacturers to buy new aircraft is reinforced by their willingness, in many cases, to buy back some of the existing aircraft that an airline owns, even if they are aircraft built by a different manufacturer. In cases where airlines may have difficulty raising finance the manufacturers may help. In 2009 the four jet manufacturers between them provided $2.5 billion in finance for new aircraft.

The third driver creating over-capacity in some markets is government policies. Many airlines find themselves being pressurised by their governments to expand services and widen their networks in support of national policies to develop incoming tourism or local business activity. Such airlines tend to order or operate many more aircraft than are required in the markets they are serving. The most recent and vivid example of this is that of the Gulf airlines, Etihad Airways of Abu Dhabi and Qatar Airways, which have been tasked by their governments to match the worldwide network and success of their neighbouring carrier Emirates. Profitability is seen as a long-term objective, not a short-term requirement.

The tendency to over-capacity is reinforced by airline executives' obsession at maintaining or enhancing market share on key routes at almost any price. Adding more capacity is one way of doing this. Too often this leads to falling yields and increasing losses. In too many short-haul markets in Europe, the US and elsewhere, legacy carriers' obsession with market share has pushed them into costly head-on battles with low-cost airlines which they rarely win.

Economic theory suggests that in any industry, firms making losses and unable to cover their cost of capital will collapse and leave the market to those who can operate successfully. In the case of airlines this process has been distorted by the direct and indirect involvement of governments in aviation. Direct involvement has been through majority or minority shareholdings in major national airlines. Indirect involvement has arisen because most governments see their airlines, even if fully or partially privatized, as national assets generating employment and tourism and providing key communication links. As a result, their survival has to be ensured, and governments will do all they can to bring this about. In the mid-1990s European governments provided around $11 billion in so-called 'state aid' to their government-owned airlines. Around the world, many airlines in financial straits, whether government owned or private, have not been allowed to collapse by their governments. Late in 2009 the Japanese government ensured that the Development Bank of Japan offered a $700 million loan to save Japan Airlines, a chronic loser! It was not enough. JAL filed for bankruptcy protection a few months later. In 2010, following further government intervention, $6.1 billion of the airline's debts were waived by its creditors and another $4.1 billion of capital was injected by the newly created Enterprise Turnaround Initiative Corporation (ETIC).

As an alternative to saving collapsing or insolvent airlines themselves, governments will often use heavy political pressure to induce reluctant local companies or investors to take over ailing airlines or resurrect airlines that have collapsed. The Belgian government did this in 2001 after the collapse of Sabena, the Swiss government did this to ensure the creation of the new Swiss Airlines in 2002 and the Italian and Greek airlines used such pressure to ensure the privatization of Alitalia and Olympic in 2009.

The United States, Canada and a few other countries have bankruptcy laws that allow companies on the verge of collapse to seek protection from creditors while they try to restructure their operations and finances. While not specifically aimed at airlines, such laws particularly in North America have enabled carriers such as United, Delta, USAir and Air Canada to survive. Some of the world's largest airlines in the 2000s managed to keep flying by using Chapter 11 when economic theory would have expected them to exit the market. They did not die. Nor was the aircraft capacity sloshing around the markets reduced.

The manufacturers' long lead times for deliveries create pressure on executives to get their orders in early and to over-order in case future demand is even better than anticipated. They tend to forget that the airline industry like the world economy tends to be cyclical. Repeatedly over the last 40 years, aircraft ordered during the boom years are scheduled for delivery during the following downturn when they are least needed. Nearly 1,000 commercial jets were delivered in 2009 at the bottom of the cycle, though some replaced retired aircraft. Another 900 or so were due for delivery in 2010 while the current order backlog for all jet aircraft manufacturers is close to 7,000 aircraft.

While the industry as a whole returned to profit in 2011, profit margins in this and subsequent years are likely to be low and will be insufficient to cover airlines' cost of capital. While some airlines will generate adequate profits, the airline industry as a whole will continue to be inherently unprofitable because of the ease with which airlines can and will continue to add additional capacity and because too many loss-making airlines will not be allowed to exit the market. Instead of blaming others for their problems, airline executives must find ways of reducing the inexorable growth in capacity. If not, they will continue flying off course.

Note: This is based on a chapter in Rigas Doganis' new book *Flying Off Course: Airline Economics and Marketing,* Fourth Edition, Published in 2010 by www.routledge.com.

Engine Makers Can Help Airlines Thrive, Even in a Difficult Environment

Robert J. Keady

Senior Vice President, Pratt & Whitney Commercial Engines & Global Service

With the enormous challenges facing the world's airlines, such as unpredictable oil prices and increased pressure for environmental performance improvements – come exciting opportunities for the aviation industry. There are opportunities to address these challenges head on – with real and exciting new technologies that bring comprehensive solutions to the economic and environmental pressures facing commercial operators. Historically, no significant advancement in aviation has occurred without a step-change in engine technology.

At Pratt & Whitney, we are an industry-leading Original Equipment Manufacturer (OEM) with more than 16,000 engines installed; we also have the largest network of Maintenance, Repair and Overhaul (MRO) centres in the industry. We call ourselves an OEMRO® because we are the only company in the world that offer the capabilities and advanced technology of an OEM and the flexibility and world-class service of an MRO – for our products and our competitor's products.

Today, our commercial customers face unprecedented challenges and the aerospace industry needs to work to ensure the long-term health of commercial aviation.

Consider the economic challenges. Oil costs are unpredictable and account for around 40 per cent of an airline's operating expenses. At the same time, there is growing pressure on our industry to improve the impact of commercial air travel on the environment. There are changing regulations on noise and emissions. There are operational challenges due to noise restraints and curfews. There are more air traffic congestion and routing issues and there are public protests against new airports and growing infrastructure.

In the face of these enormous challenges, airlines have done an excellent job to ensure continued operation in an increasingly difficult environment. Airlines have taken new approaches to cutting costs and increasing revenues. They've maintained high capacities and worked hard to reduce environmental impact.

So what more can be done? In addressing the economic and environmental challenges facing the industry, we believe there are four areas where our industry must focus its efforts.

First, we must work together to implement a next-generation air traffic control infrastructure and enact regulations that will lead to more direct routing and less airport congestion. We strongly support government funding to implement these much needed improvements.

Second, we must increase our efforts into developing and delivering alternative fuels that reduce our dependence on oil while lowering costs and improving environmental performance. These fuels must be developed responsibly and realistically – in a manner that is commercially viable and does not impact the food supply.

Third, we must develop lighter, more efficient aircraft using the latest materials and aerodynamic technologies.

Finally, we must develop quieter, more fuel-efficient jet engines to deliver the step-change in environmental performance and economic value that the industry desperately needs. Better engines are a huge part of the solution.

In fact, from the 1950s through the 1990s, better engines – from all manufacturers – have reduced fuel burn by 50 per cent and noise by 75 per cent. These improvements were due to the ability of manufacturers to design engines that use bigger fans to drive a higher bypass ratio. A higher bypass ratio means we've been able to create thrust more efficiently from more fan airflow.

These improvements are based on simple physics. Thrust is achieved by increasing the velocity of the airflow. The higher the bypass ratio, the more thrust we are able to create by increasing the amount of airflow at a lower velocity. From 1960 to 1990 we were able to increase bypass ratio steadily to improve fuel efficiency and lower engine noise. But over the past 15 years, we reached a point of diminishing returns. As we continue to grow the size of the engine fan, we have to add more turbo-machinery to the engine to drive that larger fan. This adds weight to the engine, which negates any fuel efficiency benefit.

This is because in today's engines, the fan is directly connected to a power turbine, via a shaft, at the back of the engine. Larger fans must turn more slowly to be efficient, while turbines are most efficient when rotating much faster. Because the fan and turbine are directly connected and turning at the same speed, the engine is inherently less efficient.

The laws of physics inhibit a further improvement in bypass ratio – and therefore fuel efficiency – without a change in engine architecture. Pratt & Whitney realized this challenge in 1990, when we began developing Geared Turbofan™ technology. We've spent more than 20 years developing this technology and we believe that it is the best, most comprehensive solution to the challenges facing the airline industry today.

In a Geared Turbofan engine, we can disconnect the fan from the turbine by introducing a reduction gear box. This allows the fan to turn more slowly – its optimum speed for greater efficiency and lower noise – and the turbine to turn much faster – three times the speed of the fan for peak efficiency.

The result is an improvement in engine fuel burn of more than 16 per cent compared to today's engines. That's installed fuel burn, which takes into account weight and drag when in operation on an aircraft. In terms of specific fuel consumption (SFC) in a test stand like others often quote, the improvement is closer to 20 per cent

The PurePower PW1000G engine will also deliver a noise reduction that is 20 dB below Stage 4 requirements, which yields a 75 per cent reduction in audible noise footprint compared with today's aircraft. Aircraft this quiet will open new opportunities for managing air traffic and reducing congestion. Aircraft could fly more direct routes, avoid curfews and fly into more airports without having any additional noise impact to airport communities. The PW1000G engine brings double-digit reductions in CO_2 and NO_x without compromising noise or maintenance costs.

And the best part is that this technology isn't just a concept or proposal. We've launched a new series of products named the PurePower® family of engines. Our PurePower PW1000G engine – using our Geared Turbofan technology – has been selected as exclusive power for the new Mitsubishi Regional Jet, the Bombardier CSeries, the Irkut MC-21, and was just selected to power the Airbus A320 new engine option (neo) family of aircraft. All of these aircraft are available for order now and will enter service as early as 2013. These aircraft can deliver block fuel burn up to 20 per cent better than any aircraft flying today, and almost 40 per cent better than older aircraft in the same class. The majority of this improvement is because of the PW1000G engine.

The industry is excited watching us develop this technology. They are excited because the PurePower family of engines is a complete, comprehensive solution that addresses the changes of fuel efficiency, environmental emissions, engine noise and operating costs without compromise.

In this difficult economic environment, the PW1000G engine offers truly game-changing improvement in fuel efficiency and operating cost savings of up to $1.5 million per aircraft, per year.

All of this is just the beginning. Since introducing the first turbofan engine in the 1970s, we've improved fuel efficiency by one to one and a half per cent per year through technological improvements. By making the step change to the Geared Turbofan architecture, we've opened up decades of opportunity to continue to improve fuel efficiency, lower noise, reduce environmental emissions and lower operating costs – without trade-offs. Pratt & Whitney has detailed technology plans to deliver these benefits well into the next decade.

In summary, with the PurePower PW1000G engine, airlines can have it all: lower fuel burn, lower emissions, lower noise and lower operating costs. More importantly, they can have it all right now.

The Future of Airline Sales Distribution

Scott D. Nason

Vice President of Revenue Management at American Airlines

To paraphrase Mark Twain, the rumours of the death of the travel agent have been greatly exaggerated. By now, most everyone was supposed to be buying directly from the airlines' websites … and many people are. But while the role of the travel agent has changed, and many are now digital (OTAs), they still sell the majority of tickets in many markets, and likely will continue to do so.

I think we will have at least a three-pronged distribution world for many years:

1. Airline websites (and call centres) – This channel will continue to grow in usage and importance. It is the cheapest and most efficient channel for airline and customer alike, if the customer knows pretty much what he or she wants, and has a reasonable sense of the marketplace, or lots of time to comparison shop on multiple sites.
2. Online agencies and meta-search sites – This channel is an improving option for those customers who value the ease with which they accomplish price comparison and/or appreciate their value-added services, for typically nominal fees. Their growth will depend in large measure on their ability to gain and maintain access to content and their ability to offer the full range of services that airlines offer on their own sites, for very little money.
3. Full service travel agencies – Once the only reasonable choice for finding out who was selling what for how much, and the best way to get the necessary paperwork (that is, a ticket), both of those competitive advantages have been eliminated by technology, so travel agents today must rely on their ability to provide certain services that no one else can or will provide. And they are now (mostly) paid by their customers, rather than the airlines. But they still have expertise about travel destinations that benefit a segment of the market and they can provide third-party control mechanisms for businesses to enforce rules and minimize travel costs. Will even these services eventually get overtaken by automation and the Internet? Very possibly, but not very soon.

The relative strength and success of these three channels will, in large measure, by determined by and determine the future of GDSs. Conflicting business models – ranging from airlines' direct sales efforts to direct access software which can connect internet or travel agency customers with airlines' res systems to full service GDSs, vying to continue their booking fee structures – will all compete to be the channel of choice for the most customers. How and when it will play out is anyone's guess. But it will be exciting to watch.

Dynamic Air Transport Industry

Tewolde GebreMariam
CEO of Ethiopian Airlines

Over the past century, the Air Transport Industry has grown from an experimental mode of transportation to a major and main part of the transportation system of our world. The industry was somehow transporting an extensive airmail system in the 1930s until the emergence of DC-3 which revolutionized passenger travel. The industry boomed after that and specifically after World War II which served as engine for the air transport industry.

The deregulation of the US industry in 1978 and the European industry in 1997 allowed airlines to fly in other markets that were once off-limits. It also ignited a fierce competition among airlines that resulted in many mergers and failures.

Up until the 2008/9 recession, air travel had grown by about seven per cent annually over 10 years, with an estimated 1.5 billion passengers taking to the air last year. The Asia/Pacific region has witnessed the fastest growth by climbing nine per cent a year in the last decade which shows that the industry has lots of room for growth in the future and Africa's huge and untapped potential is being noticed by the rest of the world and I strongly believe that Africa plays a pivotal role for the growth of the airline industry in the future.

In fact, there are problems which need to be addressed for the growth of the industry in Africa. Among other things, the main issue is reluctance by many African Governments to implement the Yamoussoukro Decision/Declaration which remains the single most important air transport reform policy initiative by African Governments to date. It was adopted out of the recognition that the restrictive and protectionist intra-African regulatory regime based primarily on Bilateral Air Services Agreements (BASAs) hampered the expansion and improvement of air transport on the continent.

One of the vital parts of the Decision was liberalization, which was viewed as a means to develop air services in Africa and stimulate the flow of private capital in the industry.

While the growth potential is evident in Africa and the rest of the world, the industry is one which runs with stiff competition resulting in razor-thin profit margins and probably the lowest profit margin compared with other industries.

Hence, survival in the industry solely rests upon our ability in managing costs. To put it simply, one who succeeds in managing costs to achieve the lowest unit cost per available seat kilometre (CASK) can lead the market with strong pricing power. It is, therefore, imperative that we need to focus on cost management tools and undertake lots of research in that regard.

The Dilemma Facing Airport Management: Taking Control of the Airport Environment

William deCota

William is the Director of Aviation for the Port Authority of New York and New Jersey. He is responsible for John F. Kennedy International, Newark Liberty International, and LaGuardia Airports.

Imagine earth without the dominance of people; imagine airports without the dominance of strong airport management. In any eusocial society – whether earth or airports – characterized by specialization of task and cooperative care, there has always had to be a strong dominant central force to take control and bring order. That central force may evolve and change during the process of formulation and growth as a product of a society's development. A key example is how airport managers today play a stronger role in guiding and directing all of the entities that operate at airports and coordinating their activities than they did 30 years ago. But evolution of airport management just as evolution of earth is not always easy. Often there is resistance to strong authority even though the outcome can be shown to be more favourable. Nevertheless there is and will continue to be an inevitable and necessary progression to stronger central management of airports by the airport manager.

In ecology where there is an assemblage of many populations of different species occupying the same geographical area, there is great usefulness to dividing the tasks based on function and behaviour. Airports are a microcosm of earth … a world in miniature. Like almost anything – animate objects, inanimate objects, places, concepts, events, properties, relationships and most notably earth – airports are taxonomies. They are part of a society, along with airlines, service providers and others characterized by a taxonomic scheme, which has evolved from airports just being one of the players in the network to airports increasingly becoming more dominant.

There once was a time long ago when nature claimed the planet earth. Then humans became the dominant species the earth had ever known and they managed the flora and fauna, harvested the raw materials and built cities, roads, farms and other infrastructure that supported robust life. Likewise, airports were once just grassy fields, nothing more than a place for the landing and takeoff of planes. There was no order, no development, and no progress. But thanks to careful and thoughtful airport management larger planes evolved and commercial passenger and cargo business evolved thanks to paved runways, terminal buildings, navigational aids and customer services.

At one time, before deregulation of the airline industries in the US and abroad, airports were just part of a network structure interacting with airlines and service providers within their environments by providing infrastructure for the landing and take off of planes, terminals and cargo building for the passage of air travellers and air cargo, and spaces for the provision of fundamental services such as food and beverage and retail, or aircraft handling or parking and ground transportation. This worked fine when the old Civil Aeronautics Board governed capacity and fares in the US airline industry, when airlines remained in business, were profitable and could be counted on always providing appropriate service. The customer knew what to expect and his or her expectations were met.

After deregulation in 1978, and as the task of airport management grew with the demands for air travel by society at large, the role of airport managers also changed from the purveyor of infrastructure to the dominant manager over the process of getting people and goods out of land vehicles into air vehicles. Today, two converging factors have changed the role airports take to being in a greater position of control. First, customers are more demanding ... to them the airport is the airport. They demand that someone take control to provide good and seamless service regardless of who the service provider is. The central player in those demands is the airport – the axle on which all other airport participants depend. In addition, one of the key spokes on that axle – the airline – often comes and goes due to the competitive effects of supply and demand and deregulation. In this type of environment, airport business models have had to evolve to place them in the more dominant position in the taxonomy and take back control of many aspects of the airport service equation.

Over the last 30 years airport control has evolved much like ecological dominance, or the degree to which different species in an ecological community predominate. In most ecology, one or a few species are most numerous, or form the bulk of the biomass and these become the dominant species. At airports, the airport operator may not form the bulk of the biomass, but it must become the most prevalent of the parties, concerned with all aspects of the airport environment. As most ecological communities are defined by their dominant species, likewise, airports are increasingly being defined by the airport operator themselves which has caused a rethinking of the airport business model.

Many years ago, airports leased space or granted permits to those who operated there. Today, airports grant permission to operate but define not only space, metes and bounds and rental rates and fees but also how business will be conducted. Airport agreements address one of the biggest challenges facing airports, which is taking back control. For example, today, airport agreements set service standards for all of the people doing business at their airports to follow.

In the area of concessions, for example, airports set standards for implementing first-class concessions programmes and also define customer service training, providing courteous, knowledgeable and helpful employees who are continuously and rigorously monitored through customer satisfaction surveys, mystery shopping and day-to-day and personal encounters and experience at the airports. In passenger terminals, airports likewise establish standards related to utilization criteria for their facilities and to the services airlines provide. Today airline leases for passenger terminals include maintenance standards, service standards, termination rights, limitations on uses, construction standards, rules and regulations, consumer service standards for everything from in-flight meals to restaurants in the terminals, condition surveys and many others.

The challenge of course is that not everyone agrees with airport dominance. In every eusocial society there is always resistance to control. Plants and animals, for example, often try to fight back against human domination. If left alone, the earth will try to reclaim itself. Similarly, airlines have argued that no one can control customer service standards, not airports and not the US federal government. They argue that at best, they are willing to try to reach consensus that an airport community-developed programme is preferable to a legislatively imposed one. However, they argue that it is neither advisable nor appropriate for airports to establish mandatory rules and procedures for airports to even recommend specific service actions by airlines. For example, in the area of customer service, they argue that the US Department of Transportation has consumer protection authority supported by regulatory framework that obviates independent requirements by others.

Likewise, the US federal government has not allowed airports pricing freedom to manage their proprietary affairs. While airlines were given freedom under the US aviation deregulation act of 1978 to enter markets, exit markets, and price their products, airports still must follow antiquated pricing mechanisms under strict control of the US DOT. For example, all commercial service airports operating in the United States and most other airports that are open to the public have accepted grants for airport development under the Airport Improvement Program. In exchange for receiving grant funds, airport operators must give a variety of assurances regarding the operation of their airports and the implementation of grant funded projects. Among other things, airport operators pledge to make the airport 'available for public use on reasonable conditions and without unjust discrimination'. This obligation purportedly encompasses the obligation to establish reasonable and not unjustly discriminatory fees and charges for aeronautical use of the airfield but the direct effect is to limit airfield pricing to a recovery of cost rather than market pricing like airlines can charge. Likewise, even under the federally enabled Passenger Facility Charge program, airports are limited in the level of fees that can be collected per enplaned passenger and are limited in their use of these fees to fund FAA-approved projects that enhance safety, security, or capacity; reduce noise; or increase air carrier competition. In Canada, airports are allowed to charge airport infrastructure fees that have no such limitations.

It's clear that much progress has been made by airports to take more control, but more has to be done. There is no refuting that the process of eusociality at airports has many benefits, or that the airport operator must achieve more dominance. There are obvious advantages to establishing a common basis by which all parties seamlessly serve the airport customer – utilizing various parts of a logistical distribution chain that is governed by standards which are established and maintained by a single entity, the airport operator. Every symphony needs an orchestra leader to organize and conduct the music, and every airport needs strong central management to lead and direct the ensemble of airport players so that the parts, taken together, are considered only in relation to the whole. The results are proven in terms of a better interpretation for customers and stakeholders.

Surviving the Crisis

Willie Walsh
CEO of British Airways

The global aviation industry has a habit of lurching from crisis to crisis. Its default financial position is in the red, not the black. As Warren Buffett famously remarked, if the original Wright Brothers flight had been shot down, future airline investors would have been much better off. Yet aviation has survived. Confidence that the turn of the business cycle will always come to the rescue in the end seems to be what keeps some airline executives going.

But the past is an unreliable guide to the future. The truth is that the aviation industry has never had to cope with oil prices as high as they are now and look set to remain for the foreseeable future. Let us not forget that between 2003 and 2006, the global industry failed to make a profit – despite oil prices averaging less than $50 a barrel. So the traditional business model of many airlines was failing anyway. And with fuel prices now representing between a third and a half of costs, that model is shattered beyond repair.

This new situation demands a new structure. The historic fragmentation of the industry must end. We need a bonfire of the archaic limits on foreign ownership and control, the nationality restrictions on traffic rights, the unnecessary government interference and the dead hand of subsidy. We do not need 3,000 international treaties to determine which airlines can fly where. We do not need 600 different airlines to meet the world's demand for air travel. What we need is the kind of structure that exists in almost every other global industry. Freedom for companies to merge across national boundaries and to fly wherever they can attract enough customers to make their flights profitable. Customers do not care who owns airlines. They are not interested in governmental imposition of route rights. What they want are safe, secure airlines flying where they want to go at a price they are prepared to pay.

I believe consolidation will happen. The economic pressures on the industry are too great for it to continue in its present form. Governments will be less keen to bail out failing flag carriers if the commitment looks like a financial black hole. Similarly, regulators will be less determined to maintain rules that lack political support. And labour unions too will be less wedded to the status quo if the alternative for their members' jobs is oblivion. We know that deregulation works. The liberalization of domestic airline markets in the US in the 1980s and particularly in the EU since the early 1990s has demonstrated clear benefits for the industry and customers. It brought new operators, new routes, new markets, massive competition, greater efficiency and lower fares. Worldwide liberalization, permitting cross-border consolidation, would be equally successful. With long histories of negligible profit, and now unprecedented fuel costs, many airlines must face the truth that they should consolidate or die.

Introduction to the Academic Section

The second part of the book comprises the work of 19 distinguished academics who have written on their specific areas of expertise.

We begin with an overview of the turbulent nature of the airline industry by John (Frankie) O'Connell of Cranfield University's Air Transport Department. In Chapter 2, Dawna Rhoades of Embry Riddle Aeronautical University reviews the difficulties faced by US carriers in transforming their business model and assesses to what extent they are likely to succeed. Sean Barrett of Trinity College Dublin explores the phenomenal success of European low-cost carrier Ryanair in Chapter 3. How legacy carriers can face the challenge of the likes of Ryanair forms the subject matter of Chapter 4, which is written by Alan Gogbashian and Thomas Lawton of EMLYON Business School in France. The significance and growing importance of ancillary revenues to airlines is analysed by Frankie O'Connell in Chapter 5, while a number of issues involved in the development of airline alliances are explored by Sveinn Gudmundsson and Christian Lechner of Toulouse Business School in Chapter 6. In the seventh chapter, George Williams of Cranfield University's Air Transport Department assesses the prospects for Europe's charter airlines as the region's low-cost carriers continue to expand, while the link between tourism and air transport in an era of economic liberalization is explored in Chapter 8 by Andreas Papatheodorou of the University of the Aegean, Greece. Peter Forsyth of Monash University, Australia, analyses the economics of 7th Freedom air traffic rights in Chapter 9, while Peter Morrell of Cranfield University's Air Transport Department reviews the air cargo industry in Chapter 10. In Chapter 11, Anne Graham of Westminster University examines the key issues facing the airport industry, while in the following chapter Ben Daley and Callum Thomas of Manchester Metropolitan University outline the many ways in which environmental issues represent an actual or potential constraint to the growth of air transport. Advances in aircraft and engine design are explored in Chapter 13 by John Snow of Cranfield University's Air Transport Department. This is followed by a review of Safety Management Systems in Aviation by Graham Braithwaite, Head of the Air Transport Department at Cranfield University. In Chapter 15, Manjit Singh from the Department of Civil Aviation Malaysia assesses the various attempts that are being made to achieve cooperation in the provision of Air Navigation Services. The latest innovations in Information Technology are reviewed by Frankie O'Connell in Chapter 16. Aviation security experts, Robert Raffel and Jim Ramsey from Embry Riddle Aeronautical University, examine the security issues relating to aviation in the United States in Chapter 17 and the book concludes with an in-depth examination of the world's most profitable airline in 2009/10 by Frankie O'Connell.

Chapter 1

Airlines: An Inherently Turbulent Industry

John F. O'Connell

Every day, the airline industry propels the economic takeoff of our world. It is the great enabler, knitting together all corners of the earth, facilitating the movement of people and goods that is the backbone of economic growth. It also firmly embeds us in that striking process of globalisation that is defining the twenty-first century.

Dr Daniel Yergin – Pulitzer Prize winner in 2005.

1.1 Introduction

Commercial aviation has undergone enormous growth over the last few decades as the globalization of industry and commerce has matured, while at the same time air travel's relative affordability has allowed it to become an integral part of many people's lifestyles. With just a few hundred metres of runway, even the most remote corner of the planet has the potential to be integrated into the global economy. Yet the industry remains in a financially distressed state returning only marginal profitability down through the decades which can be directly attributed to its high fixed cost structure, overleveraged balance sheets, low barriers to entry, high barriers to exit, fragmentation, militant unions, cyclical macroeconomics, fluctuating fuel prices, a unique regulatory environment, and monopolistic/oligopolistic suppliers – which are just a small sample of the varying dynamics that reside when managing airlines.

In 2009, there were around 900 airlines globally with a combined fleet of nearly 22,000 aircraft[1] serving some 1,670 airports. Data for 2010 indicates that the global airline industry operated around 2.6 million flights per month and provided 317 million seats per month to travellers around the world (OAG, 2010). The air transport industry is at the epicentre of a very wide and far reaching value chain that encapsulates many industries. The Air Transport Action Group (2010)

---

1   ICAO estimated that the global fleet consisted of 22,000 aircraft in 2009 of which: 60 per cent are narrowbody aircraft, 23 per cent widebody and the remainder are composed of Regional Jets and turboprops (Airfinance Annual report 2009/10). Included in this figure are the 225 airlines that are members of IATA which operated 10,626 aircraft in 2009 comprising: 63 per cent narrowbody; 32 per cent widebody with the remainder composed of Regional Jets and turboprops (World Air Transport Statistics, 2009).

report that the air transport industry generates a total of 29 million jobs globally;[2] is responsible for an estimated US\$2.9 trillion worth of global economic activity, which is equivalent to eight per cent of world Gross Domestic Product (GDP); while 25 per cent of all companies' sales are dependent on air transport. In the United States[3] for example, aviation contributed 5.2 per cent to the GDP in 2009 as almost 704[4] million passengers travelled for business or leisure activities with the associated impact stimulating ongoing economic prosperity (FAA, 2009). Tourism is a very important catalytic enterprise in which aviation plays a key role and it is fast becoming one of the world's most important industries. There were approximately 880 million international tourists in 2009, 52 per cent of whom arrived by air whereas 30 years earlier only one-third travelled by air, which highlights the growing interdependency between aviation and tourism which are becoming more and more interwoven (World Travel and Tourism Council (WTTC), 2009; United Nations World Tourism Organization (UNWTO), 2010). See Chapter 8 for a detailed description of the interrelationship between the tourism and airline industry.

Figure 1.1 shows that 2.3 billion passengers travelled by air worldwide in 2009 – double the number of passengers since the early 1990s. The growth[5] is largely attributed to a number of factors, including deregulation; low entry barriers; strengthening global economies; increased disposable income; falling fares; rise of low-cost carriers (LCCs); tourism development; overseas holidaying; and increased international trade which sparks business travel.[6] Airlines worldwide reacted by adding enormous amounts of capacity in order to capture the increasing traffic. Many different categories of passengers travel by air today

---

2   The airline and airport industry directly employ 4.3 million people; airframe, component and engine manufacturing employs 730,000; *5.8 million indirect jobs* are from companies in the supply chain that service the air transport industry; *2.7 million induced jobs* arise through spending by industry employees; and *15.5 million direct and indirect jobs* result from air transport's catalytic impact on tourism (Air Transport Action Group, 2010).

3   Every day in the US, close to two million people, 50,000 tons of cargo and more than one million bags travel onboard 25,000 US airline flights. Commercial aviation supports nearly 11 million US jobs and contributes \$731.5 billion to the US gross domestic product. The value of US exports transported by air in 2009 was 145 times the value of exports transported by sea (Air Transport Association Economic Report, 2010).

4   The 704 million passengers are broken down as follows: 630.5 million domestic and 73.5 million international passengers (Air Transport Association, 2010).

5   World traffic growth averaged: 6.9 per cent between 1970 and 1990; 4.6 per cent between 1990 and 2002; and 4.2 per cent from 2002 to 2009.

6   Business passengers travel in both the business class compartment of the aircraft as well as in economy class. In 2009, business passengers who travel in the business class compartment typically accounted for 15 per cent of an aircraft's total passenger load, but contribute to between 35 to 40 per cent of the airlines' total revenues – mostly stemming from long-haul flights.

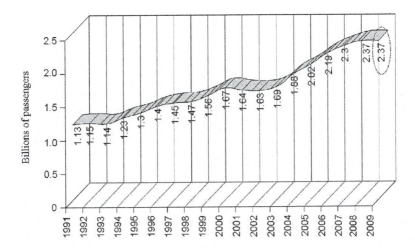

Figure 1.1 Number of passengers carried worldwide 1991–2009

Source: ICAO, AEA, ATA, AAPA, AACO.

and their characteristics and needs are very different from each other. Passenger segmentation[7] data captured by the UNTWO in 2007 found that approximately 50 per cent of passenger boardings arose for 'leisure, recreation and holidays', while 16 per cent were for 'business and professional' purposes, whereas 26 per cent were travelling for 'visiting family and relatives, health and religion' reasons, while the travel purposes of the remaining group of passengers was not specified (United Nations World Tourism Organization, 2007). However this varies significantly from region-to-region and from country-to-country as a 2006 passenger survey conducted at UK[8] airports found that 26 per cent of the passengers were travelling for business, 30 per cent to visit friends and family and 41 per cent were flying for holidays (UK CAA, 2007).

Air travel has a bright future ahead of it with the Airbus Global Market Forecast (2009) predicting that traffic will assume an Annual Average Growth Rate (AAGR) of 4.7 per cent from 2008 to 2028, which will result in global airlines' carrying 5.7 billion passengers[9] by 2028.

---

7 *Passenger segmentation* is the subdivision of a market into discrete customer groups.

8 The UK is Europe's largest air transport market which accounted for 218 million passengers in 2009. From an international perspective, it is a powerful entity as the UK accounts for around 30 per cent of the total US-EU passenger market.

9 Research by Rolls Royce (2009) indicates that airline traffic will triple by 2039, while the number of flights will double. This will significantly pressurise the infrastructure of airport and navigational services. Rolls Royce indicates that this traffic growth will necessitate the doubling of today's airports in order to accommodate the growth or

1.2 The Shifting Dynamics Within Airline Business Models

The 2.3 billion passengers that travelled by air in 2009 were transported by different types of airline business models, each with a different set of structural dimensions, operating characteristics and passenger specifications as shown in Table 1.1.

Full service airlines have a long legacy as they were mostly set up by governments as far back as the 1930s, or even earlier and continue today to be the flag carriers of their respected countries. They have multiple passenger cabins (first, business, premium economy,[10] economy) with cargo remaining an important part of the business model. Around three quarters of air cargo is transported by carriers that combine passenger and cargo divisions, with cargo typically generating up to 10 per cent of the revenues[11] of full service airlines. (See Chapter 10 for an in-depth analysis of the air cargo industry.) A core competency of full service airlines is their network, which facilities the seamless movement of passengers through a central hub[12] from both their own network and from the networks of other carriers via code share agreements or through alliance partnership. The majority

---

alternatively and more realistically trigger a demand for 40 per cent more airports, with each one operating 40 per cent more efficiently than today. See chapter 11 for a detailed description of the key issues facing airports today.

10   Premium Economy is a separate class of seating and service that differs from the standard Economy class product. It offers about 5–7 inches of extra legroom as well as additional amenities, which can include: wider seats; more recline; leg rests, more channels on the In-Flight Entertainment system with larger screens; laptop power ports; and premium food service. Premium economy is generally 35 per cent more expensive than the standard Economy fare. By 2010, there were around 25 airlines worldwide that offered the premium economy product.

11   European carriers such as British Airways and SWISS generated seven per cent and 10 per cent respectively of their transport revenues from cargo in 2009, while US based carriers like American and United each generated three per cent. However, a large number of Asian full service carriers generate as much as 30 per cent of their revenues from cargo. Korean Air, Cathay Pacific and China Airlines for example generated 29 per cent, 26 per cent and 37 per cent respectively of their revenues from cargo in 2009 (Source: airline annual accounts).

12   A hub is a highly efficient means of coordinating incoming 'spoke' traffic with departing flights at a carriers' home base. The strategy involves combining point-to-point traffic with transferring passengers originating from the points at the end of each spoke of the hub. Whereas the point-to-point traffic terminates at the hub, the transferring passengers pass through and depart to other domestic or international destinations on the hub's spoke network. The science involves the synchronization of incoming flights to provide maximum feed for departing aircraft waiting to take-up their multi-origin share of incoming passengers. This form of scheduling creates a bank of many incoming flights arriving almost simultaneously, followed by a wave of departures. This method serves as an effective traffic multiplier. Approximately 40 per cent of all long-haul passengers carried by Lufthansa are directly originating at its hubs in Frankfurt and Munich, while about 60 per cent are transfer passengers.

Table 1.1   Breakdown of the top 200 airlines by airline type in 2009

	Passengers Transported	Load Factors	Yield US$ Cents/RPK
Full Service Airlines	1.57 billion	77.1%	6.81
Low cost carriers	523 million	81.8%	5.97
Regional Airlines	219 million	73.3%	8.86
Charter Airlines	56 million	99.8%	3.62
Total	2.3 billion	-	-

Source: ICAO, AEA, ATA, AAPA, AACO.

of world traffic continues to be carried by these airlines (1.57 billion passengers) and they attract high yield passengers because their business model incorporates the following traits: large networks; interconnectivity via partner airlines; a wide array of distribution channels (for example, travel agents, online travel agents, call centres, websites, and so on); a wide spectrum of business amenities (for example, airport lounges, fast track security, limousine service, and so on); flexible[13] tickets for business passengers; a vast portfolio of in-flight products (for example, flat beds, quality food and beverage, advanced in-flight entertainment systems with multiple channels, internet and mobile phone connectivity, and so forth); convenient airports; frequent flyer programmes; and so forth.

However, full service airlines are now facing major challenges as they have emerged from decades of regulation and remain riddled with high cost structures. Passengers have become more demanding down through the decades and can now select from a large pool of competitors. It is becoming increasingly difficult for network airlines to maintain their high levels of service standards due to their need for widespread cost cutting because of the low returns that the industry generates. The dual effects of high costs and the complexity of the business model are making it very difficult for full service airlines to effectively defend their territory especially in the short-haul market.[14] This vulnerability continues to be vigorously exploited by the LCCs and this effect has been replicated in other parts of the world that have deregulated their markets.

Low-cost carriers have produced the greatest paradigm shift in airline history. They have reshaped the competitive dynamics of the short-haul market and have been largely responsible for increased growth in air transport activity over the last 15 years or so. They operate on a very different operating platform from that of full

---

13   Ticket flexibility is provided for the business class passenger who wishes to change the travel date or time and reserves the right to cancel the trip and receive a full refund.

14   Discussions at airline conferences in Europe show that most of the short-haul operations by full service airlines in Europe are loss making.

service airlines as they enshrine the concept of 'low cost' into their organizational culture and offer low fares in exchange for eliminating many of the traditional passenger services. Southwest Airlines formulated this innovative and robust business model back in 1971 and since then it has been replicated all over the world. The business model engraved a framework of cost leadership[15] that paralleled operational simplicity and high productivity (both aircraft and employee) together with no frills. Table 1.1 previous shows that low-cost carriers transported over 520 million passengers worldwide in 2009, up from 300 million in 2005. Figure 1.2 and Figure 1.3 give a diagrammatical representation of the speed at which these low-cost carriers are growing, as the number of European routes served by low-cost carriers in 2000 is compared against the number of routes operated in 2008. In 2000, the bulk of the routes served by the low-cost carriers were centred in Ireland and the UK, largely because Ryanair and easyJet had set up their initial bases in this region. However, by 2008 there was a paradigm step-change to the landscape of Europe's low-cost carrier route network as they have grown exponentially with around 40 low-cost carriers operating out of 22 EU member states. This effect added enormous volumes of capacity which in turn triggered yields to fall sharply in the short haul market. The member carriers of the Association of European Airlines[16] carried 20 million less passengers in 2009, while the carriers that belong to the European Low Fare Airline Association[17] carried nine per cent more passengers. These budget carriers are growing passenger traffic in two ways: firstly by stimulating new demand; and secondly by diverting passengers from full service airlines in the form of substitute traffic. Skeels (2005) confirms this hypothesis by stating that around 37 per cent of LCCs passengers represented a substitution effect from full service to low-cost carriers, while 59 per cent was for new demand, and of the latter, 71 per cent was stimulated because of the low fare promotions offered by LCCs. O'Connell (2007) researched that low-cost carriers around the world have taken up to 60 per cent of the annual growth from the full service airlines, which partly explains the low growth rates experienced by full service airlines year-over-year. By 2009, low-cost carriers accounted for around 41 per cent of the European market; 27 per cent of North America; 18 per cent of Asia Pacific; 8 per cent of South America; and 1 per cent of the Middle East market (Dunn, Govindasamy and Ranson, 2009; Aviation Strategy, March 2010).

---

15   In 2009, Ryanir's unit costs were 55 per cent lower than Air France/KLM and 63 per cent lower than SAS, while Southwest's unit costs were 53 per cent lower than those of United Airlines. Stage lengths were adjusted for these unit cost calculations.

16   The Association of European Airlines (AEA) brings together 36 European established full service scheduled network carriers. In 2009, these airlines collectively carried 374 million passengers and 7 million tonnes of cargo, operated 11,934 daily flights with 2,689 aircraft which served 662 destinations in 162 countries (Association of European Airlines, 2010).

17   The ELFAA members include: Blue Air, easyJet, flybe, Jet2.com, Norwegian Air Shuttle, Ryanair, Sverige Flyg, transavia.com, Vueling and Wizz Air.

Figure 1.2   European low-cost carrier route network in 2000
Source: UK CAA.

Figure 1.3   European low-cost carrier route network in 2008
Source: UK CAA.

In Asia, a unique development is taking place as nearly every legacy airline has (or is in the process of) establishing a LCC offshoot with Singapore Airlines stake in Tiger Airways; Qantas with Jetstar; Garuda's Citilink; Philippine Airlines' Airphil Express; Korean Air's Jin Air; Asiana Airlines' Air Busan; Thai Airways' Nok Air; Malaysia Airlines' Firefly; and so forth. This strategy is questionable, as nearly all the LLC subsidiaries that were set up by the legacy carriers in the US and Europe has failed. The Asian legacy airlines have been forced to introduce fast retaliatory measures to react to the unprecedented expansion of private budget operators such as Air Asia, Lion Air and Cebu Pacific, which had 250 short-haul aircraft on order by the end of 2010. Similar to what transpired in the US and Europe, the LCCs are increasing capacity on secondary routes, while at the same time increasing their presence on major trunk rotes which have been the domain of the network operator for decades. Many airports in the region have also reacted to the shifting passenger dynamics by building low-cost carrier terminals to accommodate the new growth.

Low-cost carriers have also been synonymous with strong financial performance as many of the best performing budget carriers had operating margins[18] that were on average three times that of the network airlines in 2007. The high financial returns being reaped by the low-cost carriers has attracted investors, which has allowed them to become well capitalized and invest in enlarging their fleets. Low-cost carriers have completely changed the competitive dynamics within the airline industry and have placed enormous pressure on full service airlines as their short haul traffic which acts as a feeder to their long haul operation is being severely threatened. Many business passengers travelling on short sectors (three hours or less) have switched to low-cost carriers, with Moores (2010) confirming that 24 per cent of Ryanair's passengers were travelling for business purposes in 2010. Data from the Association of European Airlines confirmed that the number of business passengers travelling with full service airlines on intra-European routes fell by 36.6 per cent over the period 2005–2009, which reflects the alarming structural change in the marketplace. IATA's chief Economist, Brian Pearce resonated a similar belief that there has been a structural shift in the 'class' of travel that business passengers were using in the short haul market as many have shifted from the premium cabin to economy class and he surmised that it may be a permanent fixture (Pearce, 2010). It is very apparent that the business model of the full service airlines must continue to be restructured or budget carriers could replace them and cause a paradigm shift in the global air transport market. See Chapter 3 for an in-depth discussion on the Ryanair business model.

The fleet type generally differentiates the *regional airlines* from the other types of airline business models as they operate aircraft that generally have less than 90 seats composed of a mix of turboprop and regional jets. Regional airlines normally serve a dual role by feeding passenger traffic into the hubs of full service airlines and by operating on low-density routes from peripheral communities which are unprofitable for the full service carriers. The partnerships between regional airlines[19] and full service carriers differ considerably throughout the world. In the

---

18   Operating margin is a measure of profitability and operating efficiency. An operating margin of five per cent for example implies that for every $1 in sales the company makes $0.05 (before interest and tax) in profit.

19   In the US, the regional carriers now account for more than 50 percent of the nation's commercial scheduled flights and carried 159 million passengers in 2008 (Regional Airline Association, 2010).

US for example, seven[20] regional airlines provide feeder services to United Airlines with a large number of these US regional affiliates also serving a number of other US Majors[21] at the same time. Flint (2010) stated that around 25 per cent of US mainland traffic is outsourced to lower cost regional partners under code share arrangements. The structure is different in Europe and Asia as regional airlines are designed primarily to feed traffic only to their parent company. Lufthansa CityLine for example pledges allegiance solely to Lufthansa, while Australia's Sunstate Airlines serves only Qantas. The financial arrangement between these independent US regional airlines and the US Majors varies depending on the contract with some designed on the fundamentals of 'pass-through costs' which enables the regional airline to earn a fixed fee for each flight, while large costs items such as fuel and maintenance are often provided by the Major airline. More recent provisions include 'pro-rate agreements' where the regional carrier receives a portion of the ticket revenue for the segment that they operate and a portion for the onward connecting journey that is operated by the Major carrier. However, under such arrangements the regional carrier assumes the full cost of operating the aircraft.

Charter airlines usually offer flights as part of a holiday package that also includes transfers and hotel accommodation, most of which are provided by vertically integrated tour operators, which is a key reason why this type of airline business model has such high load factors, but low yields. In some instances, economies of scale derived from the integrated holiday package cross subsidises the economics of operating the aircraft. However, this business model has been under considerable pressure in the past decades as low-cost carriers are increasingly biting into the markets of the charter airlines forcing them to operate on longer and thinner segments (for example, Milwaukee to Puerto Vallarta in Mexico with USA 3000 or from London to Sharm el Sheikh in Egypt with Monarch Airlines). Data from the UK CAA revealed that the overall UK Charter market has declined from 34.5 million passengers in 2001 to 22.1 million in 2009, which clearly indicates that this business model is in decline. Discussions at industry conferences suggest that charters might evolve into scheduled low-cost carriers, similar to Monarch Airlines' strategy.[22] See Chapter 7 for an in-depth analysis of the charter airline industry.

---

20   These include: Shuttle America, Mesa Airlines, GoJet Airlines, Colgan Air, Skywest Airlines, ExpressJet and Trans States Airlines.

21   US Majors are defined as those airlines that generate more than $1 billion in revenues per year and include heavyweights such as United, American and Delta Air Lines.

22   In 2000, less than 10 per cent of Monarch's passengers flew on their scheduled services, but by 2008, it had risen to over 60 per cent.

1.3 The Drivers of Airline Cyclicality

The airline industry has experienced healthy passenger growth rates over the recent decades, despite the fact that it is fully exposed to many external forces which cause its growth to widely fluctuate. Events such as wars, terrorism, diseases, natural catastrophes, recessions, credit tightening, high inflation, and rising oil prices, force downward pressure on economic activity, while the opposite occurs for prolonged stock market gains, rising house prices, high employment, and so on. These characteristics all contribute to the cyclical nature of economic activity, which is intrinsically linked to the demand for air travel. From the 1970s to the present day, there has been a number of major cataclysmic events which have adversely affected economic prosperity and these include: the oil crises of the 1970s and late 1980s; the Gulf War in the early 1990s; the Asian crisis; SARS; 9/11;[23] the Iraq War; and the severe recession that followed in the late 2000s. In between these events, global economies recovered but the cycle of boom years followed by recession is becoming a permanent fixture in the global economic landscape. Consequently, the demand for air transport is also cyclical in nature as it is synchronised with the economic cycles.

A number of studies have identified a direct correlation between Real GDP (inflation adjusted) and the demand for air services and this interlink contributes to the poor financial performance of the industry. Gallagher (1995) showed that since the mid 1960s the US airline industry has experienced five major cycles. Figure 1.4 clearly illustrates the fact that GDP and passenger traffic move in parallel and that air travel is primarily driven by economic growth. The demand for air transport is highly leveraged to the economic cycle, but the fluctuations in airline demand are far more pronounced. There is usually a time lag of around three to six months from when the economy contracts to when traffic falls. Air traffic tends to grow faster than GDP expanding and contracting on average 1.6 times the rate of growth of the economy throughout the cycle. However, Figure 1.4 shows that traffic grew twice as fast as GDP for the good years of the economic cycle: 1971–1979; 1984–1990; 1993–2000; and 2004–2007. In the UK for example, demand for air travel has grown by 130 per cent in the past two decades, whereas GDP has risen by 54 per cent (Davies and Armsworth, 2010). A major fault of the industry is that airlines add large volumes of seat capacity in the boom years to capture market share, but in the down-cycle they are unable to realign capacity to passenger demand fast enough, which significantly impacts profitability.

---

23   Ito and Lee (2005) researched that the events of September 11th led to an ongoing downward shift in the demand for commercial air service in the US of roughly 7.4 per cent, after accounting for factors such as trend, seasonality and general macroeconomic conditions.

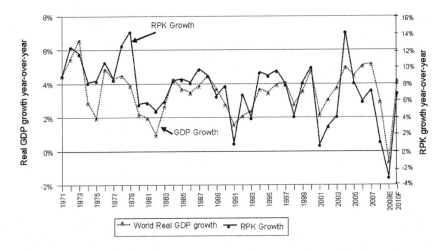

Figure 1.4   Economic activity (real GDP) and the airline demand (RPKs) cycles

Source: ICAO, IATA and International Monetary Fund.

1.4 An Analysis of the Profit-and-Loss-Making Years of the Global Airline Industry

Figure 1.1 above shows that the number of passengers has steadily increased over the last two decades (1.1 billion in 1991 to 2.3 billion today) and that this growth has only been briefly interrupted for short periods (normally 1–2 years) in the early 1990s, early 2000s and late 2000s. Despite this, the airline industry has been incapable of transforming the revenue generated from carrying passengers and cargo into sustained profitability. Figure 1.5 illustrates the financial performance of the world's airlines showing a pendulum like motion of profitable and loss making swings that are getting larger, with the profits in the mid 1990s greater than those in the 1980s and the losses in the early 2000s greater than those a decade earlier. Academics, Chin and Tay (2001) extensively studied the cyclicality of the airline industry over the last 35 years and confirmed that the downturns have been getting more pronounced. The revenues generated by the airline industry have increased nine-fold from around $58.7 billion in 1978 to a forecast of around $545 billion by 2010, yet the airline industry has never generated an overall profit since its inception in the 1920s. Hätty and Hollmeier (2003) reported that a reputed research company had conducted an in-depth analysis of the financial performance of the 11 largest North American airlines' financial performance during the 1990s and concluded that the aggregate losses by far exceeded the sum of aggregated profits. Airlines must manage this cycle and the true challenge is to create value over the whole cycle. Sustained profitability remains a very difficult or close to impossible task, as the industry's overall profit margins are miniscule (normally around 3–4 per cent for full service carriers in good economic times). Many financial analysts have deemed that the airline industry has just not been profitable enough to justify investment, which is part of the reason why some carriers are opting to lease more aircraft instead of self-financing these assets.

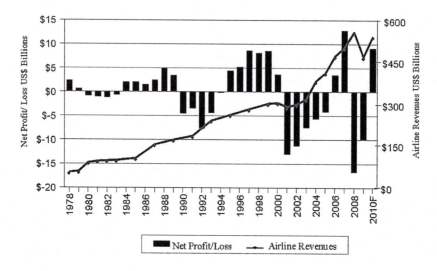

Figure 1.5   Net profit and loss for the world's commercial airlines
Source: ICAO data to 2009, IATA forecast for 2010.

1.4.1 The 1970s to the Mid-1990s

Most of the world's scheduled airlines were founded during a time when global air transport was totally regulated. In 1978 the US was the world's first air transport market to become deregulated with the underlying premise to replace government regulation in determining fares, routes and market entry. In the years between the onset of airline deregulation in 1978 and 1995, 19 airline mergers took place between US carriers and research concluded that few were deemed successful. Deregulation allowed carriers the freedom to serve new and growing markets, to fashion more extensive route networks and to charge low fares. The US Major airlines shifted dramatically from point-to-point linear route networks to hub-and-spoke systems, which provided superior network connectivity and so wider market coverage. The deregulation of the US domestic airline industry in 1978 was the precursor of similar moves by most other developed economies in Europe (1988–1997), Canada (beginning in 1984), Australia (1990) and New Zealand (1986).[24]

---

24   Canada's deregulation did not occur till 1987. Australia and New Zealand signed an open skies agreement in 2000, which created a single Australia–New Zealand air market,

The argument was that the industry was mature and capable of surviving under open market conditions subject to the forces of competition rather than under economic regulation.[25] Up to the late 1980s, many international carriers around the world (excluding the US carriers) remained under the control of their national governments and were the sole flag carrier of their respective country. They were largely inefficient, unproductive and had escalating costs and were accompanied by high fares which in-turn caused less people to travel, thereby producing low load-factors, all of which have contributed to the distressed financial state of the industry. Airlines were riddled with bureaucracy, strong unions, operational inefficiencies, overstaffing, poor service and had frequent changes to senior management.[26] They had expanded their networks by adding new destinations and service frequency in order to gain market share, but invariably they were undercapitalized and had accumulated enormous debts which were largely underwritten by their respective governments. These effects cumulated to produce the poor returns that were witnessed in the early to late 1980s.

Europe's Single European Act of 1986 sought to eliminate barriers in intra-European competition without lowering barriers to competition from non-EU airlines and thus create the platform for deregulation. Three deregulation packages, agreed by the European Council of Ministers in 1987, 1990 and 1992 fully deregulated European air transport. Following the single European Act to unite the European Community by the end of 1992, the rules on licensing of air carriers within the European Union were set out in the Council Regulation Acts. The first two rounds of intra-EU liberalization, which came into effect in 1987 and 1990, allowed European airlines to offer lower fares and to match the prices charged by European charter airlines. They also allowed routes to be served by more than one airline from a single country (double or even multiple designation) and loosened the market-sharing bilateral arrangements among EU nations. Deregulation was introduced in a time-phased manner through three packages but it was the 'Third Package'[27] under the constitution entitled Council Regulation 2409/92 that effectively removed all remaining government-imposed restrictions regarding designation, market access and capacity. In effect it liberalized the

---

including the right of cabotage. Canada and the US signed an open skies agreement in December 2005.

25   In contrast to deregulation within domestic borders, international aviation has been slower to liberalize. Consequently, the degree of regulation (with regard to fares, capacity, commercial agreements, and airline operations) varies across routes depending upon the countries involved. In some cases, however, most notably in Australia/New Zealand and Europe, there have been regional air trade pacts, which have deregulated markets between and within countries.

26   When new management comes to the helm of an airline, they give it a different direction, not allowing the existing strategies that are in-place time to reach their objectives.

27   Note that although the third package effectively created a totally 'open skies' agreement within the European Union, services outside the European Union are still governed by bilateral air services agreements.

licensing of carriers, the routes they fly and the prices they can charge. It also opened up cross border and domestic markets (including cabotage)[28] and removed national ownership restrictions. Europe became the world's first truly deregulated region. Other regions throughout the world may follow Europe's example of staged phases (as opposed to the US, which rapidly introduced deregulation) and this gives the deregulation process time to evolve and airlines the chance to adjust their strategies in order to accommodate for the change and not to be faced by the sudden transition to liberalized skies.

By the early 1990s, another global recession was unfolding helped along by the onset of the first Gulf War when the number of international passengers dropped for the first time in aviation's history. The financial difficulties were exacerbated as airlines over-ordered aircraft in the boom years of the late 1980s, leading to significant excess capacity in the marketplace as these aircraft were delivered in the following recession. In the four years (1990–1993) the world's scheduled airlines made losses of over $20 billion, which was greater than the accumulated net profits generated by the industry over the previous six decades.

1.4.2 The Profitable Years: 1995–2000

During the period 1995 to 2000, the airline industry recaptured profitability as many of the restructuring programmes and cost cutting measures that were introduced in the previous downturn were beginning to take effect. However, there was also a protracted demand for air transport which was fuelled by strong economic growth, high employment, high disposable incomes, the dot.com boom and global stability through the absence of terrorism and wars. Ticketless travel, new interactive entertainment systems, flat beds in business class and revamped frequent flyer programmes were just some of the product enhancements that were introduced to attract and retain passengers. Tactical pricing and yield management systems were also being optimized by running complex algorithms to generate higher yields per sector and enhance profitability. Deregulation continued to dismantle the regulatory shackles that constrained growth as Europe for example had now become a single 'Open Skies' market. Deregulating markets across the globe triggered yields[29] to fall, which reduced profitability but was somewhat counterbalanced by increases in passenger traffic. The late 1990s and early 2000s also saw a wave of consolidations, between, for example, Air Canada and Canadian Airlines,[30] American Airlines and TWA, and Japan Airlines and Japan

---

28   Cabotage occurs when domestic services are operated in one EU Member State by a carrier based in another Member State. This agreement allows Aer Lingus for example to operate between the Italian cities of Milan and Rome.

29   ICAO data indicates that global yields fell from around 115 US cents per ATK in 1995 to around 51 cents per ATK by 2000 (in constant prices).

30   Six carriers merged into Canadian Airlines in the late 1980s, creating a duopolistic domestic market with Air Canada.

Air System. Many Asian carriers were hit by the financial meltdown[31] of several Asian economies in 1997/98 and subsequently posted losses, but overall the global airline industry posted a net profit of around $39 billion during 1995–2000. However, by early 2000, world GDP had reached its cyclical peak and the US economy was beginning to contract, while at the same time oil prices were rising and the US dollar was appreciating in value. Several airlines reported lower profits than in the previous year and it was inevitable that the industry was facing another downturn.

1.4.3 Aviation's Worst Years: 2001–2005

As Figure 1.5 shows, the years from 2001 to 2005 were some of the darkest ever experienced in aviation. The 11th of September, 2001 will be forever engraved as the most catastrophic event, ever witnessed in the history of civil aviation. Security suddenly became aviation's number one criteria. (See Chapter 17 for a detailed description of the changes that were applied to aviation security in the United States.) An economic downturn was already underway prior to 9/11, but this event cascaded the industry into freefall as it triggered the financial meltdown of the US carriers, whose net losses in 2001[32] alone totalled $8 billion. Official Airline Guide (OAG) data showed that worldwide traffic dropped by three per cent in 2001, while high yield international business traffic across the North Atlantic fell by 30 per cent immediately after the attacks and it took a number of years for this traffic to regain traction. The US Majors[33] were facing multiple problems, including the 9/11 attacks; the sudden decline of the dot.com industry (critical component of their business class passenger revenues)[34]; high operating unit

---

31   During the 1990s, each of the four ASEAN economies (Thailand, Indonesia, Malaysia and the Philippines) experienced a credit boom, as the growth of bank and non-bank credit to the private sector far exceeded the rapid growth of the real economy. The credit boom was stoked in part by large net private capital inflows, and much of it was directed to real estate and equities. This overextension and concentration of credit left these four ASEAN economies vulnerable to a shift in credit conditions. When that shift came, induced by a need to control overheating and to defend fixed exchange rates, it brought with it, inter alia, falling property prices and a rising share of non-performing bank loans. Banks in an effort to lower borrowing costs, undertook most of their foreign borrowing at short maturities and in foreign currency. These liquidity and currency mismatches eventually triggered the Asian financial crisis, which is similar to what has happened to the global economy in the late 2000s.

32   These losses would have been significantly higher had the US Congress not quickly passed the Air Transportation Safety and Stabilization Act in September 2001, which provided $5 billion in emergency assistance to US based airlines.

33   These included Alaska, American, Continental, Delta, Northwest, United and US Airways.

34   IBM for example spent nearly US$340 million on domestic US air travel in 2001 (IBM, 2003).

costs;[35] delays;[36] increasing debt;[37] falling yields;[38] and the threat posed by the low-cost carriers which were increasingly encroaching on their domestic markets.[39] In addition, there was overcapacity in the US market as the Majors added 750 mainline and 575 regional jets in the late 1990s, which significantly contributed to their financial problems. Subsequently, from 2001 to 2005 the US carriers posted net losses of almost $35 billion[40] (Air Transport Association, 2006). To give an idea of the severity of the problem facing US carriers in 2005 – 41 per cent of the US domestic seat capacity was provided by airlines in bankruptcy protection. Continuous restructuring programmes that were largely made in Chapter 11 bankruptcy arrangements[41] allowed the US carriers to cut staff numbers by one-third, while also reducing their salaries by 25 to 30 per cent (Doganis, 2010, p. 101) (see Chapter 2 for an in-depth discussion on the state of the US airline industry). Overall, the global airline industry had witnessed its deepest and most prolonged period of crisis during this period (2001 to 2005) as the cumulative net losses for the industry over this period totalled $41.5 billion.

One notable event that transpired during this period was the merger between KLM and Air France in 2004. It represented a significant step in the consolidation of the global airline industry as it was the first true cross-border merger between two major carriers and it created the world's largest airline group with combined revenues of over €18 billion in 2004. The merger proposed to remove almost €500

---

35   The break-even load factor of US Network scheduled airlines was over 85 per cent from late 2001 to late 2002.

36   In 2005, 36 per cent of the flights at major-airports were delayed (Air Transport Association Economic Report, 2010). Johnson and Savage (2006) calculated that the cost for ground delays for a United Airline's flight departing at 18:00, when there were 27 aircraft queuing for take-off, was $5,165 in 2004.

37   By late 2005 the US Air Transport Association stated that US airlines accumulated approximately $100 billion in debt, up 41 per cent since 2000. American Airlines for example repaid $957 million in 2005 to service its debt, which represented five per cent of sales (Air Transport World, July 2006, p30).

38   The yield of the US Majors fell by around 17 per cent from 2000 to 2004. United Airlines for example reported that the proportion of its domestic revenues from its premium passengers (business class and unrestricted economy) fell from 41.0 per cent in 1999 to 19.8 per cent in 2003 (GAO-05–834T; US DOT DB1A database).

39   In a counteractive strategy, the US Majors passed a significant proportion of their unprofitable domestic short-haul network to their Regional based partner airlines. The domestic market share capacity of the legacy carriers fell from 79.5 per cent in 2000 to around 75 per cent by 2004.

40   ATA member airlines lost $8.2 billion in 2001; $11 billion in 2002; $2.3 billon in 2003; $7.6 billion in 2004 and $5.6 billion in 2005.

41   Chapter 11 is a chapter of the United States Bankruptcy Code which governs the process of reorganization under the bankruptcy laws of the country. In contrast, Chapter 7 governs the process of a liquidation bankruptcy.

million[42] in costs within five years and it would also intensify scale and density economies. KLM was a relatively large carrier from a relatively small European state and its single national hub was the focus for its route and traffic network. Amsterdam accounts for less than 50 per cent of all of KLM's departure seating capacity while the dual hubs of Paris CDG and Amsterdam's Schiphol were not capacity constrained, and so they are in a position to compete or cooperate for additional traffic. Baker (2004) stated that the network had little overlap – out of the 104 long-haul routes, only 34 were in competition with each other. Furthermore, in the short-haul market Air France was stronger in southern Europe, while KLM was more dominant in northern Europe. The move also reshuffled the alliance groupings as KLM belonged to Wings, while Air France was affiliated to SkyTeam and it triggered these alliances to also merge, which was another first for the industry.

1.4.4 Two Full Years of Profitability: 2006–2007

By 2007 the global industry had fully recovered and had produced a profit of almost $13 billion[43] which came about as a result of a number of factors, which included the strengthening of global economies which in-turn triggered a seven per cent increase in international traffic; a realignment of capacity and passenger demand which caused load factors to increase by more then seven per cent when compared to 2001; the depreciation in value of US currency against other global currencies;[44] and increased aircraft utilization; while labour productivity had improved by 64 per cent since 2001 largely as a result of the restructuring programmes. The excessive and harsh cost cutting measures that were introduced in the previous downturn were beginning to take effect with unit costs (excluding fuel) falling for the first time in years (IATA, 2008). In addition synergies from alliances[45] were also beginning to positively impact revenues as partner carriers were increasingly feeding high yield traffic to the networks of their members which in-turn also

---

42   The following cost synergies were identified: €100 million from sales distribution; network, revenue management and fleet €195 million; cargo, €35 million; maintenance, €65 million; IT systems, €70 million; while other areas of cost reduction would produce cost savings of some €30 million (Baker, 2004).

43   The breakdown of profits in 2007 were as follows: the US carriers made a net profit of $5.3 billion; the European carriers made a net profit of $5.4 billion; the Asian carriers made a net profit of $2.1 billion; while the Latin American and African carriers each made a profit of $100 million (IATA, 2009).

44   Many airlines around the world (excluding US based carriers) pay as much as 50 per cent of their expenses in US Dollars (e.g. fuel, aircraft financing, etc) and when the US Dollar depreciates in value, it alleviates the cost burden for airlines that operate outside the US.

45   There are three global airline alliances, Oneworld, SkyTeam and Star which collectively carried 1.38 billion passengers in 2008, serving some 2,940 destinations and collectively generating $344 billion worth of revenues in 2008 (Source: Alliance websites).

delivered higher load factors. Alliances were also producing synergies as member airlines were financially benefiting from joint partnership programmes such as: joint purchasing; operational efficiencies (for example, maintenance, ground handling, and so on); common sales offices; reciprocal frequent flyer programmes, and reciprocal use of airport lounges.

1.4.5 Another Challenging Time for the Airline Industry: 2008

Profitability was short lived, as a set of extraordinary economic conditions converged on the global economy in 2008. In metaphorical terms, these events were akin to a hurricane; a typhoon and a tornado, all of which converged at the same time to create a 'perfect storm'. 2008 was one of the worst years in aviation history and this section provides an in-depth analysis to uncover the principle reasons why airlines recorded record losses.

As the US housing bubble peaked, a highly competitive and liquid market had made mortgage money easily available to households which otherwise would not have qualified for underwriting. These low credit mortgages planted the seeds of the eventual subprime mortgage crisis. The onset of financial crisis started after the real estate market peaked in 2007. Mortgage delinquencies and foreclosures rose sharply, which in turn caused huge losses for banks and financial institutions that held large amounts of mortgages and mortgage-backed securities. The tightening of the credit default market and liquidity, and the decline of real estate value, in conjunction with the tremendous loss of wealth in the stock market, finally cut into economic growth, which started the US recession that quickly propagated into a global one. Banks worldwide were being bailed out by governments and loans for businesses were becoming increasingly difficult to secure. Business travel which is closely correlated to economic prosperity fell sharply and data from the IATA's World Air Transport Statistics (2009) indicated that revenues from premium[46] travellers were down by 20 per cent ($15 billion) in December 2008. Many of the passengers that were previously travelling in business class were downgrading to economy and some carriers expedited the introduction of the premium economy cabin onto their long range widebody aircraft as a mechanism to stop business passengers downgrading to economy class in order to capture a higher yield. Leisure travellers were also taking fewer trips as consumers began shifting their disposable income away from air travel and were no longer prioritizing vacations to overseas destinations. Leisure traffic was down by around six per cent by late 2008 and was continuing to deteriorate. Air Cargo is a barometer of economic activity and this plummeted by 25 per cent (in terms of tonne kilometres) during 2008, with yields subsequently falling by 20 per cent.

---

46   Yield for business class passengers is around 19 cents per RPK, while economy class passengers only generate around five cents per RPK. Meanwhile the yield from premium economy is around 8.5 cents per RPK.

Oil prices have always been a major cost component for airlines and their fluctuations have a direct impact on profitability. Bisignani (2008) indicated that for every $1 increase in oil, industry costs increase accordingly by approximately $1.6 billion. Figure 1.6 shows the trend in oil prices from 2003 to 2010 and during the economic crisis crude oil prices unexpectedly doubled from $74/barrel (July 2007) to $147 (July 2008) – abruptly, fuel had become the largest cost element for airlines, representing up to 40 per cent of total operating expenses. Carriers were now in a financially dangerous and treacherous situation as prolonged periods of high oil prices could trigger the meltdown of the industry. Consequently, this forced airlines to endorse hefty fuel surcharges,[47] which inevitably makes tickets more expensive and in turn dissuades some passengers from travelling. Airlines, worldwide paid $167 billion for fuel in 2008, compared to $133 billion the previous year – a 25 per cent increase and fuel had now replaced labour as the industry's most expensive cost item. A unique trait that is characteristic to jet fuel is that it is only refined by a limited number of oil refineries around the world. In recent years airlines had increased capacity (by adding flights and increasing frequencies) and this effect triggered the price between crude oil and refined aviation fuel (known as the crack spread) to increase by an average of $20 per barrel in 2008 because the refineries reached close to their operational capacity for refining jet fuel. Refining jet fuel added around 18 per cent to the cost of crude oil in 2008, with transportation and storage costs also contributing to jet fuel costs.

However, the financial meltdown of the airline industry in 2008 was compounded by mismanaged fuel hedging policies. In order to protect rising fuel costs, airlines hedge fuel to minimize their exposure to adverse price movements based on expected future price levels. If an airline buys 'a future' at $90 per barrel and oil goes up to $133, that contract protects $90 worth of jet fuel purchases from the expected 48 per cent increase in price. Morrell and Swan (2006) researched that most airlines today hedge their fuel, while 15 years ago it was rare to do so. The authors also noted that a wider divergence of jet aviation fuel prices from crude oil prices (crack spread) tends to occur at times of greater volatility in crude prices. Aviation fuel is almost always priced in US dollars, therefore airlines that operate outside the US are also faced with the risk of exchange rate movements.

---

47   British Airways like many other carriers reacted to the increased fuel charges by adding surcharges to tickets. In May 2004, the incumbent had a blanket surcharge (same charge across all classes of travel) of £2.50 per passenger. However by June 2008, a first/business class passenger was charged £133 for a long-haul flight that was more than nine hours in duration. Similarly, Lufthansa charged passengers a fee of €105 per long-haul sector, with surcharges of €35 for short haul flights. Analysis suggests current surcharges can generate only up to 50 per cent of the nominal cost of fuel, while the carriers must absorb the rest of the fuel costs (European Commission, 2008).

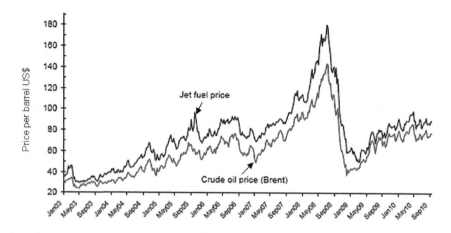

Figure 1.6   Jet fuel and crude oil price ($/barrel)
Source: Platts.

Many of the world's larger airlines also hedge for foreign exchange risks,[48] when they do not have adequate fuel hedge cover.

The fuel hedging procedures of so many of the world's airlines was exacerbated when investment banks such as Goldman Sachs predicted that fuel could escalate to between $150 – $200 per barrel by 2009 because of the following factors: the limited spare capacity of oil refineries; the booming economies of China and India; and concerns over oil producing nations that were in conflict such as Iraq, Nigeria and Venezuela (Association of European Airlines, 2008). This effect[49] instilled 'panic' and triggered airlines to partake in acquiring fuel hedging contracts at excessively high prices.

Figure 1.6 clearly shows the sharp decline in crude oil prices from its high of $147 per barrel in mid 2008 to around $40 per barrel by the end of 2008 and towards the beginning of 2009. Airlines that initiated hedging contracts when fuel was escalating beyond $100 per barrel were severely disadvantaged when fuel cascaded to $40. The sudden oscillation in the price of fuel plunged the industry into financial disarray as carriers incurred massive losses as they had secured fuel supplies for the proceeding 12–18 months at extortionate prices. Many airlines also saw their cash positions decline due to significant cash collateral posting requirements related to their out-of-money fuel hedges. Singapore Airlines – Asia's most profitable airline made a loss of $378 million on fuel hedging for the January–March quarter of 2009 alone, as it had hedged at an average price of

---

48   In order to manage currency risk, airlines implement strategies such as cross-currency swaps, forward foreign exchange contracts, etc.

49   Yet, aviation fuel consumption today corresponds to between two per cent and three per cent of the total fossil fuel use worldwide.

US$131 per barrel, considerably above the $40–50 spot price at that time (Aviation Strategy, May 2010). Merrill Lynch reported that nine Asian carriers reported estimated losses of around $3.8 billion as a result of fuel hedging contracts in 2008 (Bloomberg news, 2009). Dunn (2009) reported that the following airlines incurred fuel hedging losses in 2008: Cathay Pacific, $980 million; Air France/KLM, $370 million (in the 3rd Quarter of 2008 alone); while hedging losses for US based carriers such as Alaska, American, Continental, Delta, United and US Airways collectively totalled over $1.5 billion for the fourth quarter of 2008.

Consolidation in the industry continued to gather momentum with the merger of Delta Air Lines and Northwest Airlines creating the world's largest[50] airline in 2008. Excess capacity and low returns have led many of the world's airlines into consolidating and merging. It provides an instant step-change to a carrier's route network. Delta Air Lines (2008) stated that the merger was expected to generate $2 billion in annual synergies from the following: a more comprehensive and diversified route system; effective aircraft utilization; reduced overheads and improved operational efficiency. The network integration would produce the greatest synergy as only 12 routes overlapped out of about 1,000 routes. The carriers had complementary networks as the merger would combine Delta's domestic network that stretched from the Northeast, South and Mountain West with Northwest Airlines leading positions in the US Midwest. Meanwhile the international network would now combine Delta's strengths in Europe and Latin America to Northwest's strong presence in Canada and Asia. The international position of Delta Air Lines was further enhanced as six members (Delta Air Lines, Northwest Airlines, Air France, Alitalia, Czech Airlines and KLM) of the SkyTeam alliance were granted antitrust immunity[51] rights over the North Atlantic by the US Department of Transportation (DOT) in mid 2008. The move allowed these carriers to capture 30 per cent of the lucrative transatlantic market and triggered other alliances to seek such arrangements with the US Department of Transport. In April 2008, Continental decided not to merge with United Airlines,[52] while a short while later United decided not to pursue a merger with US Airways. See Chapter 6 for an in-depth account alliances and mergers.

---

50   The newly merged airline retained the brand name of Delta Air Lines and operates more than 800 jets, employs around 75,000 personnel and generates about $32 billion in annual revenues. It completed re-organization, integration and rebranding under the Delta banner over a two year time span.

51   Antitrust immunity allows airlines to coordinate schedules, pricing, yield management, and other functions without the risk of antitrust enforcement. A core requirement for US antitrust immunity is that the foreign carrier's homeland must have an open skies agreement with the United States.

52   United and Continental announced plans for a wide range of marketing partnerships, which involved Continental switching from SkyTeam to the Star alliance. This created a synergy whereby both carriers could begin to interlock their fundamental business models that would create an opportunity for a merger at a later timeframe, which has since occurred.

1.4.6 The Continuing Economic Slump: 2009

2009 was a slightly better year as the global airline industry reduced its losses to $9.9 billion, with US airlines losing just $2.7 billion (World Air Transport Statistics, 2010). However, major structural problems in the global economy remained, as consumers who had over-borrowed before the crisis were now saving more and consuming less. Housing booms gave way to housing slumps, with housing investment likely to remain depressed for some time. The fiscal stimulus enacted by the world's governments has not had the desired effect, with weaknesses in the financial system still constraining credit. Net exports were not contributing to growth in advanced economies and their trade deficits remained imbalanced. These economic effects were directly interlinked to the airline industry as around $85 billion was erased from the industry's balance sheets in 2009 (15 per cent down on 2008 figures). Historical financial data showed that the world's carriers lost $49.1 billion between 2000 and 2009, which is an average loss per year of around $5.0 billion (IATA, 2009). Similar problems that were encountered in the previous year continued to loom in 2009. Data from World Air Transport Statistics (2010) showed that revenue from business passengers was down by 30 per cent, when compared to the previous year, while freight revenue was 24 per cent lower in 2009. Similarly revenues from economy class also declined as the number of passengers travelling in this cabin fell by nine per cent. These effects were largely responsible for the industry's $85 billion revenue shortfall in 2009, which knocked the sector back to where it was three years earlier. 2009 was the second time in the industry's history that global airline traffic fell.

However, as 2009 drew to a close, airlines were showing strong signs of recovery and the industry was finally beginning to convert more revenues into higher levels of profit. The five principle reasons for the reduction in losses in 2009 were as follows:

1. Fuel had averaged $71 per barrel and represented 24 per cent of airlines costs – a healthy formula where airlines can regain traction in restoring profitability.
2. Capacity was removed from the market. OAG data (2009) showed that the world's airlines had scheduled 3.3 million fewer seats in July 2009, compared with the same month in the previous year. Around the globe there were numerous cuts to capacity, which included a five per cent reduction in global international markets;[53] 10 per cent reduction in the US; while freight capacity had decreased by 15 per cent (Airline Business, 2010). The reduction in capacity was also achieved by operating aircraft less hours per

---

53   On International markets, the capacity cuts (2009 vs 2008) were as follows: US to EU, -9 per cent; US to Asia, -7.7 per cent; US to Latin America, -0.2 per cent; EU to Asia, -4.9 per cent; Africa to EU, -1 per cent. The only region to experience capacity growth was the Middle East (Airline Business, 2010).

day with average utilization rates declining by six per cent when compared to 2008. This reengineered the shape of the industry because yield and load factors gradually improved as a result of the realignment of capacity and demand.

3. The restructuring programmes, cost cutting measures and productivity enhancements that were earlier introduced were beginning to take effect.

4. Airlines were switching to more innovative and cost reducing IT platforms. (See Chapter 16 for a detailed description of technology innovations.)

5. Ancillary revenues were a sizzling new concept that were quickly gaining importance in airline boardrooms across the world and are an industry game changer. Traditionally, all the flights products have been included in the price of an airline ticket, but lately these products (for example, baggage) have been unwrapped from the fare and sold separately as an add-on. Data from the US Bureau of Transport Statistics (2010) showed that US airlines made $2.7 billion by charging for baggage in 2009, while just two years earlier, they had bundled 'baggage' into the fare and offered it as complementary product, where it produced no revenue. In addition, carriers were also developing ancillary revenues through commission-based web applications that are provided by third parties (for example, sale of hotel rooms, car rental, insurance, and so on). Airlines are cross selling these travel by-products through bolt-on hyperlinks from their websites. Consumers assimilate their individual travel components such as hotel accommodation and car hire from an airline website, as they are obvious products that naturally complement the sale of an airline seat. The process is termed Dynamic Packaging. It integrates tourism related data onto one transparent platform and in effect, consumers build a tailor-made package that suits their specific requirements. Airlines have been leaking huge volumes of revenues to suppliers for decades and dynamic packaging aims to significantly curtail this trend. See Chapter 5 for an in-depth account of the latest trends in ancillary revenue.

Airline mergers continued to occur in 2009, with British Airways and Iberia announcing their joint partnership to create the world's fifth largest airline, with $21 billion in aggregate revenues. BA and Iberia's networks are complementary with the latter holding 26 per cent share in the South Atlantic market (EU to Central and South America), while the British incumbent had around 10 per cent of the North Atlantic market (EU to US) in 2009. Boyle (2010) stated that the merger will generate synergies of around €400 million per year with 63 per cent coming from cost[54] savings with the remaining stemming from revenue synergies. By 2009, the

---

54 Information Technology is expected to generate about 28 per cent of the overall cost savings; maintenance efficiencies to contribute 23 per cent; the joint corporate centre will account for an additional 14 per cent; joint purchasing 11 per cent; fleet savings seven

European landscape was changing fast as large incumbents such as Lufthansa,[55] Air France/KLM and BA/Iberia were expanding their geographical footprint through mergers, while Ryanair[56] and easyJet were organically growing and were a threatening presence in the short-haul market. From a global perspective, excess capacity and low returns were forcing airlines around the world to consolidate.[57]

Liberalization continued to proliferate throughout the world and by 2009, Asia was showing signs of dismantling its regulatory[58] shackles as the coveted Kuala Lumpur-Singapore route had now opened up to competition.[59] It had been dominated by Malaysian Airlines and Singapore Airlines as a near duopoly for many decades. A year earlier the EU and US signed an open skies agreement[60]

---

per cent; savings in sales activities six per cent; and other activities such as airport and cargo will generate the remainder (Boyle, 2010).

55   Lufthansa had changed its strategic direction from the monolithic airline of the 1980s to an aviation powerhouse by 2009 as it has acquired full ownership of a number of European flag carriers that were all members of the Star alliance. These include SWISS, Austrian and bmi, while it also has a 45 per cent equity shareholding in SN Air Holding which owns Brussels Airlines. In addition it was one of the few European flag carriers that capitalized on Europe's open skies policy by setting up a subsidiary in Italy. Lufthansa also has equity in Eurowings (45 per cent), Jetblue (19 per cent) and Luxair (13 per cent).

56   By November 2010, Ryanair was Europe's largest carrier with 10 per cent of the market, while easyJet had six per cent.

57   There has been little cross border consolidation in the Asian market to date, however there has been many instances of domestic consolidation. In China, for example, nine state owned airlines consolidated into three groups by 2005 around Air China, China Eastern and China Southern. In 2009 Shanghai Airlines merged with China Eastern. In India, Air India merged with Indian Airlines, while Air Deccan was absorbed by Kingfisher towards the latter part of the decade. It is expected that there will be increased consolidation in the European market over the next decade, as Europe has a large number of relatively small carriers.

58   In intra-Asia markets there is an array of regulatory constraints and barriers, as Asia has a much more restrictive international regulatory regime than North America or Europe. For example, there is no "open-skies" agreement currently within Southeast Asia although the countries of the Association of South-East Asian Nations (ASEAN) have set up the timetable to gradually move to regional open skies by 2015.

59   In 2001 Singapore Airlines operated 63 flights a week between Kuala Lumpur and Singapore, while Malaysian Airlines had 83 services a week, other foreign airlines operated an additional 10 flights a week and in total the route had 156 flights per week. However, by 2010 the landscape had completely changed as there were 210 services per week between Kuala Lumpur and Singapore with the following breakdown: Malaysian Airlines operated 47 flights/week; Singapore Airlines, 17 services/week; Silk Air 37 per week; Tiger 22 per week; Air Asia 63 flights per week; Jet Star Asia 19 per week; with others operating an additional five flights per week. (Source: Analysis from OAG – data taken for the first week in August 2001 and August 2010).

60   The agreement replaced the individual bi-lateral arrangements of EU Member States with the United States and removed all barriers for airlines of either side wishing to fly between and beyond Europe and the United States. For the first time, European

that liberated the lucrative North Atlantic market. Change was coming fast to the airline industry and carriers were being faced with new challenges with every passing year.

1.4.7 The Beginning of an Upcycle: 2010

2010 was the first year of the new decade and airline managers in boardrooms across the world were hoping that they could put the cataclysmic events of the past decade well behind them. This chapter contains data for the first *6 months of 2010* only as the book was going to print.

Turbulence in the aviation industry is unrelenting, as 2010 started off with the headline news that Asia's largest airline; Japan Airlines was bankrupt after amassing debts of $25.6 billion, making it one of Japan's largest ever bankruptcies. It was delisted from the stock market; over 15,700 jobs were to go; all the B747–400s and MD-90s were to be phased out; 15 international and 30 domestic routes were dropped; 11 overseas bases were to be closed (Air Transport Intelligence, April 2010). Japan Airlines typified the business model of a doomed flag carrier as its problems were deeply rooted and included: high labour costs; a bureaucratic corporate structure; eight militant in-house unions; poor staff morale; an expensive pension scheme; as well as an obligation to operate many unprofitable domestic routes. Some months later Mexico's oldest and largest airline, Mexicana, filed for bankruptcy with accumulated debts of more than $1 billion. Its problems were also deep rooted as unions had pushed salaries beyond the carrier's reach – to endemic proportions. *The Economist* (2010) reported that Mexicana pilots earned 49 per cent more than pilots working for the big American carriers, and 185 per cent more than pilots who work with Mexican low-cost airlines, such as Volaris and Interjet. Meanwhile flight attendants earned 32 per cent more than their American counterparts. In addition, the carrier was exposed to the financial downturn and to the H1N1 (swine flu) that devastated the Mexican travel and tourism industry. To add to the problems facing Mexican aviation, the FAA had downgraded Mexico to category two under the IASA safety assessment programme by mid 2010.[61] See Chapter 14 for a detailed description of Safety Management Systems in Aviation.

---

airlines could operate from bases outside their licensing state, creating the opportunity, for example, for an Irish airline like Aer Lingus to operate flights from Madrid to New York. The agreement significantly disadvantaged British Airways as it opened up Heathrow to all US carriers, which under the old Burmuda II agreement restricted access for two US carriers namely United and American Airlines.

61   The downgrade while only temporary implies that Mexican airlines cannot launch new services to the US or use their aircraft for code shares with US carriers. Meanwhile, in Africa, 110 airlines from 13 countries are on the list of carriers banned from operating to the EU – only 30 per cent of the international traffic to/from the continent is carried by African carriers (Thomas, 2010). The EU ban also includes carriers from four Asia Pacific countries: Indonesia (although the ban against Garuda has been lifted), Cambodia, North Korea, and all airlines based in the Philippines.

Aviation is subjected to so many external factors that are irrelevant to so many other industries, such as the eruption of Mt Eyjafjallajokull in Iceland in April 2010. It was another first for the industry as an ash cloud closed the airspace of 23 European counties for six days, forcing the cancellation of more than 100,000 flights affecting the travel plans of around 10 million passengers. Over 300 airports, representing 75 per cent of the European network was closed (Association of European Airlines, 2010). The US government provided $5 billion in emergency assistance to US-based airlines after the 9/11 attacks as the skies remained closed for 3 days as the Air Transportation Safety and Stabilization Act was immediately enacted. However, European airlines had to assume full liability, without any financial support from their respective governments as losses[62] from the closure of the airspace amounted to €1.4 billion, while airports lost €200 million with air navigation service providers losing out on €175 million in revenues. At the peak of the crisis just under 30 per cent of worldwide scheduled passenger capacity was cancelled (IATA, 2010c; Harbison, 2010).

The ash cloud highlighted the inefficiency of Europe's air space as thousands of aircraft each day navigate through Europe's air corridors. The skies over the 27 member countries of Europe are in-turn controlled by 27 separate airspace authorities that remain under the control of national governments. This fragmentation has negative repercussions in terms of the efficiency of Europe's air travel because airlines have to traverse across numerous air-traffic control systems to reach their destination airports. It also causes safety concerns by creating additional air traffic and causes more carbon to be emitted. According to the EU Commission the fragmented airspace adds as much as €1 billion per year to airline operating costs (Commission of the European Communities, 2007). To address these issues, the Commission launched an initiative aimed at creating a 'Single European Sky' (SES) by reforming the current air traffic management system. It will take a number of airspace blocks and operate them as one single entity. (See Chapter 15 for a detailed insight into Air Traffic Management and the integration of the skies.)

Economic recovery continued to gather pace during the first half of 2010. Global activity expanded at an annual rate of about 5.25 per cent (World Economic Outlook, 2010). A surge in inventory and fixed investment accounted for a dramatic rise in manufacturing and global trade. However, low consumer-confidence and reduced household incomes were holding consumption down in many advanced economies, while the underlying sovereign and banking vulnerabilities remain a significant challenge amid lingering concerns about risks to the global recovery. The extent of economic recovery differed significantly across regions, with Asia in the lead. The World Economic Outlook (2010) indicated that the output

---

62   Regulation (EC) No 261/2004 is an EU enforced law that applies only to passengers flying in European airspace or to/from European airspace. It establishes rules for compensation and assistance to passengers in the event of denied boarding, cancellation and long delay.

of emerging[63] economies will expand at a rate of 6.4 per cent for 2011. For advanced[64] economies, however, growth is projected at only 2.2 per cent for 2011. This cyclical upturn has impacted positively on the airline world as the global industry is forecast to produce a profit of $8.9 billion for 2010. IATA reported an average growth (measured in RPKs) of eight per cent for international traffic for 2010, which has been achieved by 'tight capacity' that has pushed up load factors and yields.

By mid 2010, passenger and freight markets were back above pre-recession levels (IATA, 2010a). Strong business confidence, driven by a recovery in world trade and corporate profits has been a major driver in attracting back premium passengers.[65] The dramatic recovery in global trade in 2010 has impacted positively on the industry. The US majors may have finally turned the corner as the nine largest carriers posted profits of $1.45 billion for the three months ending June 30, 2010, from a net loss of $556 million for the same period in 2009 (Karp, 2010). The four principle reasons that were cited earlier (fuel, capacity,[66] restructuring programmes[67] and ancillary revenues) as well as the rebounding economy were the primary drivers for the resurgence in profits. The 17 member airlines that comprise the Association of Asia Pacific Airlines (AAPA) are a formidable force as they carry a quarter of the world's passenger traffic together with 40 per cent of global freight. Collectively, these carriers are forecasting profits of about $5.2 billion for 2010, much improved from the $3 billion posted during the last industry peak in 2008. This energized region has been the fastest to rebound with air cargo witnessing growth rates of 30 per cent for the first half of 2010, whilst international passenger traffic was up almost 15 per cent (Association of Asia Pacific Aviation, 2010).

---

63   Examples of emerging economies include: Argentina, Brazil, Chile, China, Colombia, Estonia, Hungary, India, Latvia, Lithuania, Malaysia, Mexico, Pakistan, Peru, Poland, Russia, South Africa, Thailand, Turkey, Ukraine and Venezuela.

64   Examples of advanced economies include: Australia, Canada, Euro area, Hong Kong, Israel, Japan, Korea, New Zealand, Norway, Singapore, Sweden, Switzerland, Taiwan, United Kingdom and United States.

65   Credit Suisse banking corporation for example has over 49,000 employees and made $6.8 billion in profits on revenues of $34 billion in 2009. Tarry (2010) reported that its travel and entertainment bill rose from $198 million in the first half of 2009 to $246 million for the corresponding period in 2010.

66   US domestic airline capacity remains below 2000 levels. Analysis from data supplied by the Air Transport Association shows that scheduled capacity for the 2nd quarter of 2010 was about seven per cent below that for the corresponding quarter of 2000. The number of daily departures declined around 18 per cent over the period.

67   Delta Air Lines for example has managed to keep its non-fuel costs stable over the years (2007–2010), while bringing employee salaries up to industry standards, despite a five per cent overall reduction in capacity. The carrier's unit costs continue to be among the lowest in the US Major sector. It is in line to produce between 10–12 per cent annual operating margins, while reducing its net debt by more than $2 billion in 2010.

Meanwhile, the European economy remains in a fragile state. Five countries (Portugal, Ireland, Italy, Greece, and Spain) were facing a sovereign crisis. These countries shared similar financial characteristics – they had significant budget deficits, high debt to GDP, and high unemployment rates relative to the broader EU27. The economic weakness and faltering consumer confidence had a direct impact on passenger traffic. Europe's GDP growth for the first 6–9 months of 2010 remained below one per cent, while the weak Euro has made operating costs for airlines more expensive. IATA (2010b) stated that Europe's carriers are expected to incur losses of $1.3 billion for 2010, which can be attributed to a number of factors, such as economic downturn, volcanic ash crisis, a series of labour strikes and strike threats. However, Dunn (2010) states that European airlines were experiencing a strong business-led recovery in traffic and a sharp bounce in air cargo towards the latter part of 2010 – signs that an upturn is underway?

Consolidation continued to gather pace in 2010 with Continental/United; LAN/TAM; Aegean Airlines/Olympic Air; Avianca/TACA; Southwest/Air Tran agreeing to merge. The $3.3 billion merger between Continental and United created the world's largest airline.[68] Aviation Strategy (2010) researched that the networks of the carriers is a natural fit with only 14 overlapping domestic routes, while the merged entity commands a leadership position in the US domestic market with a 21 per cent share, ahead of Delta's 20 per cent. In total, the merged company will have 10 hubs spread out across the US, with four strategically positioned in the largest cities. Internationally, United is strong in the Pacific rim, while Continental is dominant in transatlantic and Latin American markets. Approximately 40 per cent of United's and 50 per cent of Continental's capacity is deployed on high yield international routes, which on a strategic level is very important as the US has open skies agreements with over 100 countries, many of which are not served directly. Flint (2010) reported that the Continental-United merger will derive synergies of $1–$1.2 billion per year by 2013; this includes incremental annual revenues of $800–$900 and net cost synergies of $200–$300 million.

Meanwhile, two of Latin America's largest airlines, made a surprise announcement in August that they had agreed to merge creating LATAM Airlines. The venture would include Lan Airlines and its affiliates in Peru, Argentina and Ecuador, together with Lan Cargo and its affiliates; while TAM adds its Paraguayan associate TAM Mercosur to the pact. LATAM Airlines will be South America's leading carrier accounting for 35 per cent of the passengers carried by Latin American carriers, while their combined revenues accrued $8.5 billion in 2009. Unlike the earlier mergers which were orchestrated within domestic markets

---

68   The newly merged airline will have a fleet of almost 700 mainline aircraft and a further 550 regional aircraft under capacity agreements serving 370 destinations with 5,800 daily flights and a combined staff of more than 87,000. The combined airlines will have annual revenues of $31.4 billion and an unrestricted cash balance of $9 billion (June, '09) and aggregated, the airlines carried 143 million passengers in 2009 (Air Transport Intelligence, July 2010).

or in unified territories such as the EU, this cross border merger is restricted by national ownership and control rules.[69] Brazil has one of the more restrictive foreign ownership caps, allowing only 20 per cent (likely to increase to 49 per cent in 2011), while in complete contrast Chile has one of the most liberal policies where there is no foreign ownership cap and control. Any airline can operate within Chile provided its place of business is domiciled there. Their networks are highly complementary, with little overlap. LAN has a strong presence in a number of South American countries[70] and operates a formidable cargo operation that generates 34 per cent of its total revenues; while TAM offers the prime European routes and a solid position in the large Brazilian domestic market, where it holds a 42 per cent share, which is similar to GOL's share.

1.4.8 Looking Forward: Beyond 2010

Environmental issues will become a major concern for airlines beyond 2010 as the EU Emissions Trading Scheme (ETS) will become effective in 2012. Aviation is responsible for 2–4 per cent of global Green House Gas (GHG) emissions[71] (Hofer et al., 2010; Zhang et al., 2010). Aircraft and engine technology[72] has

---

69   Cross-border investments and mergers are the norm for many businesses across the global economy. Italy's FIAT owns Chrysler; India's TATA Motors owns UK based Jaguar; Lenovo, a Chinese company owns IBM's PC business; Avaya owns Nortel; Roche pharmaceuticals in Europe owns Genentech in the US; Vodafone owns Verizon, and Deutsche Telekom provides communications services on five continents including 100 per cent ownership of service providers in Brazil, Japan, China, and the United States. Yet, enormous barriers to ownership remain endemic in global aviation. The outdated bilateral system is preventing cross border consolidation, thus keeping the industry financially handicapped. Alliances have been the only other means of meeting the market need for global reach.

70   LAN has around 80 per cent of the Chilean domestic market and 67 per cent of the Peruvian market, while in Ecuador and Argentina it holds about 22 per cent (Analysis from PaxIS data).

71   Of the exhaust emitted from the engine core, 7–8 per cent is composed of carbon dioxide and water vapour, with another 0.5 per cent composed of nitrogen oxides, unburned hydrocarbons, carbon monoxide, and sulphur oxides. Other trace chemical elements in significant abundance include the hydroxyl, nitrogen compounds and carbon-based soot particulates. The balance (>91 per cent) is composed of Oxygen and Nitrogen (Lee, 2010).

72   Engine efficiency in large commercial aircraft, as measured by the cruise specific fuel consumption (SFC) of newly-introduced engines, has improved by approximately 40 per cent over the period 1959–2000, which equates to an average improvement of 1.5 per cent annually. Aerodynamic efficiency in large commercial aircraft has increased by approximately 15 per cent historically, averaging 0.4 per cent per year for the same period. Better wing design and improved propulsion/airframe integration are enabled by improved computational and experimental design tools, and have been the primary drivers (Antoine and Kroo, 2005). See chapter 13 for an in-depth description to the Advances made in Aircraft and Engines down through the decades.

advanced considerably down through the decades while Morrell (2007) confirmed that there was a 70 per cent improvement in the fuel efficiency of airlines over the past 40 years. From 2012 onwards, all CO_2 emissions from flights departing from or arriving at airports within the European Union have to be offset thorough a mechanism known as EU ETS within the Kyoto protocol. It will also include non-EU airlines that land and depart from EU airports. Under the directive, a limit on the amount of CO_2 emissions from aviation activities is preset based on historical carbon emissions. In 2012 the number of carbon allowances allocated to airlines will be capped at 97 per cent of average greenhouse gases emitted during the period 2004–2006. Eighty-five per cent of these allowances are granted for free, while the remaining 15 per cent are to be auctioned. If an airline reaches its cap, it can buy additional emissions credits on an open market. From 2013 onwards, the total quantity of allowances will be reduced to 95 per cent of historic aviation emissions. A report published by aviation consultancy RDC Aviation and energy intelligence specialist Point Carbon, estimated the aviation sector could face a shortfall of 77 million tonnes of CO_2 when it enters the ETS in 2012, which implies that carriers must buy carbon on the open market. This equates to an annual cost of over €1 billion ($1.4 billion) from 2012 based on a spot price of €14.40 per tonnes of CO_2 (Air Transport Intelligence, 2009). However, the scheme is flawed because it applies only to Europe and is not standardized across a global platform as carriers operating within Asia and in the US Domestic market, for example, do not have to conform, unless they operate to the EU. Subsequently it will damage the international competitiveness of European airlines in a number of ways.

1. There is a likely risk of carbon leakage as traffic might be diverted from EU operators to the benefit of non-EU operators. Data from MIDT indicates that around eight per cent of passenger traffic that arrives from non-EU origins into the EU (via a hub such as London Heathrow) is onward connecting to other non-EU destinations. These passengers can bypass the EU and travel to their final destination via a non-EU hub such as Istanbul for example, which would result in a loss of traffic for European carriers. This results in a traffic shift in favour of airlines that are less affected by ETS costs, while at the same time it increases the level of unregulated emissions.
2. On intercontinental markets between the EU and non-EU countries, passenger traffic could be lost to airlines that offer connections outside the periphery of the EU borders like Turkish Airlines which will face lower ETS costs.
3. Cargo airlines can choose to add a stop-over outside the EU (for example, Singapore – Frankfurt via a stopover in Cairo) which will reduce the distance covered by the EU ETS.
4. Those inbound tourists that originate outside the EU may choose to holiday elsewhere due to the additional charge of the emissions scheme.
5. Corporations may ask travelling executives to shift their short-haul journeys to high speed rail and/or to use communication technologies as a substitute

for long-haul travel, as their corporate governance policies may insist that carbon reduction is implemented within their organizations.

The overall scheme is badly flawed and it needs a system in-place that governs the compliance of emissions across a worldwide platform that incorporates all airlines, from all regions of the world – otherwise European Airlines will become competitively disadvantaged as they feed short haul traffic (already loss making) to long haul destinations (becoming more expensive due to ETS charges). (See Chapter 12 for an in-depth analysis on the environmental issues.)

Taxes will continue to plague the industry. In Europe, the German government will introduce a new 'environmental tax' on all passengers departing from German airports starting on 1 January 2011 as part of its 'cost-cutting' measures to shore up its stretched public finances. It is highly unlikely that this tax will be replaced by the EU ETS charge in 2012. Germany is one of the world's largest exporting nations and its exports account for half the national GDP, which is a reflection of the prosperous air transport market which accounted for 182 million passengers in 2009. The measure will raise €1 billion per annum levying a charge of €13 for short-haul flights and €26 for long-haul sectors. In a matching move, the Austrian government will also impose a departure tax on airline passengers, of €8 for short-haul journeys and €40 for long-haul. Aviation remains a soft target for legislating governments to apply taxes. A similar airline passenger tax already exists in Ireland, Belgium and the UK. The Netherlands and Denmark both tried to adopt such taxes but dropped them after seeing travellers bypass their airports in favour of lower-cost alternatives in neighbouring countries. In the US, customers paid $22 tax on a $300 domestic roundtrip ticket in 1972, which represented seven per cent of the fare, which by 2010 had risen significantly to $61 or 20 per cent[73] of the fare. This contributes to the $23 billion in taxes and fees paid annually to airports, the FAA and to the Department of Homeland Security. These excessive costs make travel less affordable, which has further ramifications as the drop in revenue prohibits airlines from making future investments, ultimately harming the people and businesses that rely on the air transport industry (Air Transport Association Office of Economics, 2010).

Low-cost carriers have flourished on short haul markets and a natural progression for the business model would be to expand that success into long-haul operations. Air Asia X, Air Transat and Jetstar Airways are current examples of long-haul low-cost carriers and these may become the template for future generations of this airline model. Some European low-cost carriers have undergone an evolution towards greater geographical diversification and evidence of this can be seen from Norwegian as it now serves Dubai from both Oslo and Stockholm. Ryanair and easyJet have multiple bases across Europe and an extension of this business model would be to position long range aircraft at these bases and operate to the US as the

---

73   Surprisingly, airline taxes are higher than those levied for alcohol and tobacco in the US.

open skies policy between the EU and the US has cleared the regulatory pathway to accommodate this objective. Southwest for example already offers seamless connectivity through its hubs. It is also actively seeking cross-border code share and interline partners, signalling a change of emphasis over its short-haul network (Morrell, 2008). Many LCCs across the world are modifying their business models in a way that is more receptive to 'connectivity' by having code share agreements in place. Virgin Blue, for example, now code shares with Delta Air Lines, while the same applies for Skywest Airlines and Virgin Atlantic. Bipartisan partnerships such as the JetBlue/Aer Lingus linkup, allows the partners to sell combination tickets that funnel two flights into a single itinerary. A peek into the future could reveal the distinct possibility of Ryanair operating across the North Atlantic to connect to a Southwest Airlines flight, similarly Air Asia could cover the transpacific market or indeed Southwest could capitalize and get 'first mover' advantage by operating on both markets. This would be an industry game changer and place the full service airlines in a perilous state as the long-haul market is one of the last frontiers where low-cost carriers have little visibility.

Another major challenge facing the industry are the Arabian Gulf based carriers, which are fast becoming the new power brokers in global aviation. The United Arab Emirates and Qatar have enacted a master plan to simultaneously expand their airline fleets and their airports to unprecedented proportions. Emirates, Qatar and Eithad Airways are altering and reshaping the way that traditional traffic flows are being routed and they are presenting huge threats to the long haul operations of Asian, European and even North American full service airlines. The Gulf carriers are increasingly encroaching on the primary hubs of their competitors' core cities by adding frequencies, while at the same time commencing new routes to secondary cities. By mid 2010, Emirates for example had placed orders for 90 A380s, together with 101 B777–300ER aircraft making it the world's largest operator of such airplanes and sending shock waves through the aviation world when it also ordered 70 new generation A350s. *The Economist* (2010) reported that Emirates expects to have 400 widebody aircraft in operation by 2020, dwarfing the long-haul capacity of any other airline in the world and by which time it will be carrying almost 80 million passengers per year. The airport master plan is equally staggering as Dubai's existing airport has been expanded to accommodate 70 million passengers annually, while the construction of a new airport called Dubai World Central is currently unfolding. This will be comparable (in terms of number of passengers) to the combined size of Chicago O'Hare, New York JFK and Los Angeles International (LAX), handling 160 million passengers per year when fully operational. Similar master plans are also unfolding for Etihad and Qatar Airways. As liberalization increases its footprint across global markets, these Gulf-based airlines are poised to take full advantage and it could be very possible for these carriers to be operating on transpacific routes in the near future by exercising 7th freedom traffic rights. (See Chapter 9 for an in-depth discussion on 7th freedom traffic and Chapter 18 for an-depth discussion of the Emirates business model.)

This chapter concludes with a short insight into how airlines can achieve sustained profitability into the future. It has become an increasingly difficult task with each passing year to sustain profitability as different economic forces continue to reshape the industry that seems to be experiencing near constant turbulence. Airlines must prepare well in advance for the impending cyclicality of downward macroeconomic forces that regularly hit the industry. They must remain armed with agile and responsive strategies to challenge competitive threats. (See Chapter 4 for an in-depth analysis on airline strategy.) Carriers must decide if their core competencies are pivoted on differentiation or low cost, as it is extremely difficult to integrate both elements successfully – being 'stuck in the middle' positions the carrier towards 'Mediocracy' and structural weakness. Full service airlines should rely on producing added value and consumer driven product differentiation beyond the basics of the low-cost carrier product. Airlines need to build up a large cash balance as it has become an essential element in defying the gravitational pull towards bankruptcy. All carriers must continue their resolve to tighten cost and become better negotiators as each link in the supply chain (aircraft manufacturers, airports, navigational service providers, freight forwarders and so on) generates higher margins than the airline industry itself. It is high time that airline alliances merged their bargaining synergies to obtain higher discounts.

Incremental cost efficiencies will be driven by technological developments and carriers must adopt IT applications that peel away cost and drive value – airlines must become innovators and not followers. Check-in procedures are a prime example of how the industry has rapidly evolved in a very short time frame moving from the traditional mechanism of checking-in by agent, to kiosk, to web, to mobile phone, with each pulse point removing cost while adding value. Capacity control is an urgent necessity; unfortunately as airlines envision an economic upturn, capacity is always added which distorts the profitability equation. Open markets will ensure that capacity will never be controlled and carriers will have to manage this difficult imbalance long into the future. Airlines must mastermind the science of fuel and currency hedging, because these practices inflict large collateral damage to profits when mismanaged. Marketing through social media sites is a new sizzling concept that must be adopted by all carriers, as Facebook's 650 million members provides an instant and fertile platform to launch a promotional sales campaign. Presently, such sites are a lifestyle tool for the younger generation and they will become a platform from where airline brands will become indoctrinated into the mindset from a young age. They have the potential to become another distribution channel posing challenges for online travel agents and GDSs. Creating additional revenue streams inside the framework of the conventional business model will be the next game changer, as airline products become un-bolted from the fare and sold off as separate entities, while cross selling third party commission based travel by-products like hotels and travel insurance will reform the mechanism of regenerating profitability. The wider dimension of the frequent flyer programme could serve as a template to the potential revenue that can be generated by integrating its footprint into other industries. Mileage is a loyalty enabler that has spread beyond its vision of intent as it has evolved into a lucrative 'revenue engine' with a vast and unassuming portfolio of businesses purchasing loyalty points.[74] Carriers must continue to find more innovative platforms to convert revenues into profits as today's margins are not enough to support the investment that will be needed for the industry's infrastructure into the future.

References

Airbus Global Market Forecast (2009), Global Market Forecast. Available at: http://www.airbus.com/en/corporate/gmf2009/.

Airfinance Annual report (2009/10), Airfinance Annual Contents, *Euromoney Year Book*, UK.

Airline Business (2010), 2009 in pieces, *Airline Business*, January, pp. 24–25.

Air Transport Action Group (2010), Pressroom, facts and figures. Available at: www.atag.org/content/showfacts.asp?folderid=430&level1=2&level2=430&.

Air Transport Association (2010), Annual Results: US Airlines. Available at: www.airlines.org/Economics/DataAnalysis/Pages/AnnualResultsUSAirlines.aspx.

Air Transport Association Office of Economics (2010), The Economic Climb-Out for US Airlines: Global Competitiveness and Long-Term Viability, November. Available at: www.airlines.org/Economics/ReviewOutlook/Documents/ATAIndustryReview.pdf.

Air Transport Association Economic Report (2010), When America flies it works. Available at: www.airlines.org/Economics/ReviewOutlook/Documents/2010AnnualReport.pdf.

Air Transport Association (2006), Annual Earnings US Airlines. Available at: www.airlines.org/economics/finance/Annual+US+Financial+Results.htm.

Air Transport Intelligence (July, 2010), Intelligence data on United Airlines and Continental Airlines. Available at: rati.com.

Air Transport Intelligence (April, 2010), JAL to drop 45 routes in drastic cuts to network, 28th April. Available at: www.rati.com.

Air Transport Intelligence (2009), Emission scheme to cost airlines over €1bn annually: study, 22 July. Available at: www.rati.com.

Air Transport World (2006), Location, location, location, *Air Transport World*, vol. 43(7), July, pp. 26–33.

Antoine, N.E. and Kroo, I.M. (2005), Framework for aircraft conceptual design and environmental performance studies, *AIAA J.*, 43(10), 2100–9.

Association of Asia Pacific Aviation (2010), Strong recovery in traffic as the region leads the world out of recession. Available at: www.aapairlines.org/resource_centre/AAPA_PR_Issue19_AP54_Outlook_4Nov10.pdf.

---

74   In 2008, American Airlines sold $1billion worth of FFPs to Citibank in 2008, while Delta sold $1 billion worth of Skymiles to American Express (Source: InsideFlyer, 2010).

Association of European Airlines (2010), IATA Legal Forum Washington, September. Available at: http://files.aea.be/Speeches/SG2_IATA_Legal per cent20Forum_0810.pdf.

Association of European Airlines (2010), The new role of the European Parliament in Air Transport Agreements, 5th May. Available at: http://files.aea.be/ Speeches/RELEX per cent20Educ_Tool per cent20UPD_2April.pdf.

Association of European Airlines (2008), State of the Industry, Brussels, 29th May.

Aviation Strategy (2010), The United/Continental deal, Issue 151, May, pp. 1–2.

Aviation Strategy (2010), Tough times ahead for SIA, Issue 139, May, pp. 12–17.

Aviation Strategy (2010), US LCCs: When will they resume growth?, Issue 149, March, pp. 14–19.

Baker (2004), Joint Vision, *Airline Business*, vol. 20(7), July, pp. 33–36.

Bisignani, G. (2008), State of the Air Transport Industry – 64th Annual General Meeting – Istanbul, Turkey, 2nd June.

Bloomberg news (2009), 9 Asian airlines may lose $6 bn on fuel hedging, weak demand. Available at: www.livemint.com/2009/01/22222747/9-Asian-airlines-may-lose-6-b.html.

Boyle, R. (2010), Interview with Airline Fleet Management, entitled Defining Days, *Airline Fleet Management*, Issue 68, July/August, pp. 20–26.

Button, K. and Ison, S. (2008), The economics of low-cost airlines: Introduction, *Research in Transportation Economics*, 24(1), pp. 1–4.

Chin, A. and Tay, J. (2001), Developments in air transport: implications on investment decisions, profitability and survival of Asian airlines, *Journal of Air Transport Management*, vol. 7(5), pp. 319–330.

Commission of the European Communities (2007), Communication from the Commission to the Council and the European Parliament, Brussels, 15th March. Available at: http://eur-lex.europa.eu/LexUriServ/LexUriServ.do?uri= COM:2007:0101:FIN:EN:PDF.

Davies, Z.G. and Armsworth, P.R. (2010), Making an impact: The influence of policies to reduce emissions from aviation on the business travel patterns of individual corporations, *Energy Policy*, vol. 38(12), pp. 7634–7638.

Delta Air Lines (2008), Delta and Northwest Merge, Creating Premier Global Airline, October 29th. Available at: http://news.delta.com/index. php?s=43&item=216.

Dunn, G. (2010), Europe peeks out from the gloom, *Airline Business*, vol. 26(10), October, p. 67.

Dunn, G. (2009), Airlines take another fuel hit, *Airline Business*, vol. 25(3), March, p. 10.

Dunn, G., Govindasamy, S. and Ranson, L. (2009), Asia Leading Low Cost Growth, *Airline Business*, May, p. 56.

Doganis, R. (2010), *Flying Off Course, Airline Economics and Marketing*, 4th Edition, Routledge publishing.

European Commission (2008), Fuel and air transport, a report for the European Commission by Air Transport Department, Cranfield University. Available at: http://ec.europa.eu/transport/air/doc/fuel_report_final.pdf.

FAA (2009), The Economic Impact of Civil Aviation on the US Economy. Available at: www.faa.gov/air_traffic/publications/media/FAA_Economic_Impact_Rpt_2009.pdf.

Flint, P. (2010), Merger of Equals, *Air Transport World*, vol. 47(6), June, p. 47.

Flint, P. (2010), United thinks smaller, *Air Transport World*, vol. 47(1), January, p. 5.

Gallagher (1995), Aircraft finance and airline financial analysis in the fifth cycle of the jet age. In: Jenkins, D., Editor, *Handbook of Airline Economics*, McGraw-Hill, New York.

Harbison, I. (2010), Hit and Myth, *MRO Management*, vol. 12(2), pp. 18–24.

Hätty, H. and Hollmeier, S. (2003), Airline Strategy in the 2001/2002 crisis – the Lufthansa example, *Journal of Air Transport Management*, Vol. 9(1), January 2003, pp. 51–55.

Hofer, C., Dresner, M.E. and Windle, R.J. (2010), The environmental effects of airline carbon emissions taxation in the US Transportation Research Part D, *Transport and Environment*, Vol. 15(1), pp. 37–45.

IATA (2010a), Financial Forecast, Strong Upcycle in 2010 but weaker 2011, September. Available at: www.iata.org/whatwedo/Documents/economics/Industry-Outlook-Sep-10.pdf.

IATA (2010b), Improved Profitability – But Europe Still Lags in the Red, September. Available at: www.iata.org/pressroom/pr/Pages/2010–09–21–02.aspx.

IATA (2010c), IATA Economic Briefing, The impact of Eyjafjallajokull's volcanic Ash Plume. Available at: www.iata.org/whatwedo/Documents/economics/Volcanic-Ash-Plume-May2010.pdf.

IATA (2009), $5.6 Billion Loss in 2010 – Low Yields and Rising Costs Keep Industry in the Red, 15 December. Available at: www.iata.org/pressroom/pr/Pages/2009–12–15–01.aspx.

IATA (2008), IATA Annual Report 2008, 64th Annual General Meeting, June.

IBM (2003), Driving an operational model that integrates customer segmentation with customer management. Available at: www.03.ibm.com/industries/automotive/doc/content/bin/auto_driving_operational.pdf.

InsideFlyer (2010), Buying Your Way to the Top. Available at: www.insideflyer.com/articles/article.php?key=5983.

Ito, H. and Lee, D. (2005), Assessing the impact of the September 11 terrorist attacks on US airline demand, *Journal of Economics and Business*, 57, pp. 75–95.

Johnson, T. and Savage, I. (2006), Departure delays, the pricing of congestion, and expansion proposals at Chicago O'Hare airport, *Journal of Air Transport Management*, 12(4), pp. 182–190.

Karp, A. (2010), Soaring profits, flat capacity, *Air Transport World*, vol. 47(9), September, pp. 75–76.

Lee, J. (2010), Can we accelerate the improvement of energy efficiency in aircraft systems?, *Energy Conversion and Management*, vol. 5(1), pp. 9–196.

Moores, V. (2010), Cabin Sickness, *Airline Business*, vol. 26(5), May, pp. 58–60.

Morrell, P. (2008), Can long-haul low cost airlines be successful?, *Research in Transportation Economics*, 24(1), pp. 61–67.

Morrell, P. (2007), An evaluation of possible EU air transport emissions trading scheme allocation methods, *Energy Policy*, vol. 35(11), pp. 5562–5570.

Morrell, P. and Swan, W. (2006), Airline Jet Fuel Hedging: Theory and Practice, *Transport Reviews*, 26(6), pp. 713–730.

OAG (2010), Healthy Growth in Global Airline Capacity in May Reports OAG. Available at: www.ubmaviation.com/Press-Room/Healthy-Growth-in-Global-Airline-Capacity-in-May-Reports-OAG.

OAG (2009), Global Airline Capacity Shows Marginal Growth After a Year of Decline, 18th August. Available at: www.ubmaviation.com/Press-Room/Global-Airline-Capacity-Shows-Marginal-Growth-After-a-Year-of-Decline-Reports-OAG.

O'Connell, J.F. (2007), The strategic response of full service airlines to the low-cost carrier threat and the perception of passengers to each type of carrier, unpublished PhD thesis, Cranfield University.

Pearce, B. (2010), Forecasting – lessons and pitfalls, Lecture to Air Transport MSc class, Cranfield, March.

Platts (2010), Insight and analysis. Available at: www.platts.com/CommodityHome. aspx?Commodity=Oil.

Rolls Royce (2009), Market Outlook 2009, Forecast 2009 – 2028, Derby, England.

Regional Airline Association (2010), US summary statistics. Available at: www. raa.org/RAAHome/IndustryStatistics/USSummaryStatistics/tabid/81/Default. aspx.

Skeels, J. (2005), Is airport growth a necessity or a luxury? Overall view of market growth. Report Presented to ACI Annual Congress 2005, Munich.

Tarry, C. (2010), Taking shape without form, *Airline Business*, October, vol. 26(10), p. 64.

The Economist (2010), What goes up must come down, 5th August. Available at: www.economist.com/blogs/newsbook/2010/08/mexicanas_bankruptcy.

The Economist (2010), Rulers of the Silk World, 3rd June.

Thomas, G. (2010), Africa's safety travails, *Air Transport World*, vol. 47(10), October, pp. 35–38.

UK CAA (2007), CAA Passenger Survey Report, 2006, Civil Aviation Authority, London.

United Nations World Tourism Organization (2010), *World Tourism Barometer*, vol. 8(1), January, Madrid.

United Nations World Tourism Organization (2007), *Handbook on Tourism Market Segmentation*, World Tourism Organization and European Travel Commission, Calle Capitán Haya, 42, 28020 Madrid, Spain.

US Bureau of Transport Statistics (2010), Table 1C: Baggage Fee Collections, Form 41; Schedule P1.2. Available at: www.bts.gov/press_releases/2010/bts021_10/html/bts021_10.html.

World Air Transport Statistics (2010), Digest and Key Performance Indicators, IATA, 54th edition, Montreal and Geneva.

World Air Transport Statistics (2009), Digest and Key Performance Indicators, IATA, 53rd edition, Montreal and Geneva.

World Economic Outlook (2010), Recovery, risk and rebalancing, International Monetary Fund, October. Available at: www.imf.org/external/pubs/ft/weo/2010/02/index.htm.

World Travel and Tourism Council (2009), Travel and Tourism Economic Impact. Available at: www.wttc.org/bin/pdf/original_pdf_file/exec_summary_2009.pdf.

Zhang, A., Gudmundsson, S.V. and Oum, T.H. (2010), Air Transportation Research Part D, *Transport and Environment*, Vol. 15(1), pp. 1–4.

Chapter 2

State of US Aviation: Clinging to Old Ways in a New Century

Dawna L. Rhoades

2.1 Introduction

In a 2005 report to the US Congress, the US General Accounting Office (GAO) stated that bankruptcies are 'endemic' to the airline industry because of 'longstanding structural issues'. This report noted that since the Airline Deregulation Act of 1978 which freed US carriers to compete in a manner dictated by market forces – price, route structure, service quality levels – there have been 160 airline bankruptcy filings. Further, airlines fail at a higher rate than other types of companies and have the worst financial performance of any US industry sector (USGAO, 2005). Warren Buffet, Chairman of Berkshire Hathaway and one of the worlds' most famous individual investors, has noted that while airlines are one of the industries that has transformed both business processes and individual lifestyles, it seems incapable of making a long-term profit (Loomis and Buffet, 1999). Just as US airlines returned to profitability following the severe post-9/11 downturn, rising fuel prices are placing new pressures on industry profits and appear to be setting off a new wave of bankruptcies as well as renewed talk of consolidation. It also remains to be seen whether the much awaited multilateral Open Skies between the US and EU will herald an era of profitability or place new competitive pressure on US airlines that have not fared as well as their EU cousins (The CalTrade Report, 2008).

These challenges to the US airline industry are highly visible and much discussed; however, there are two other major issues that threaten the future of the industry. The first issue concerns the aviation infrastructure, specifically the air traffic control system. In the US, the Next Generation Air Transportation System (NGATS), commonly referred to as NextGen, is the air transportation solution for the twenty-first century. NextGen is roughly equivalent to the European SESAR programme (Single European Sky ATM Research). NextGen is currently behind schedule, over budget, and a major source of contention between various political and industry groups. The second issue concerns the Federal Aviation Administration which regulates the industry, including overseeing NextGen implementation. The FAA budget has been held up in the US Congress over the change in funding it had proposed to help pay for NextGen technology and implementation. At the same time a series of reports on failures of FAA maintenance oversight have prompted

Congressional hearings into its ability to regulate the safety of the industry itself (Oberstar, 2008).

The purpose of this chapter is to explore what these four challenges – financial stability, liberalization, NextGen funding and implementation, and industry regulation may mean for the US airline industry. These factors have the potential to strengthen the industry by adding capacity, insuring safety, and promoting healthy competition. On the other hand, they may further weaken the airline industry in the US and the many other industries that depend on it for the movement of goods and people. If this weakening occurs, then it is likely that the industry will witness even greater volatility in the coming years.

2.2 Financial Stability

Highly cyclical demand, high fixed costs, and low barriers to entry are some of the reasons cited by the GAO for the 'inherent instability' of the airline industry (USGAO, 2005). They are not the first to observe that the airline industry is subject to a complex set of characteristics that make it exceedingly difficult to generate sustainable profits. Taneja (2003) has cited the following characteristics as contributing to the complexity and financial instability of the industry: excessive government intervention, network-driven structure, organized labour, high labour, capital, and fuel intensity, high fixed costs and low marginal costs, high cyclicality and seasonality, revenue vulnerability, destructive competition, commodity products, vulnerability to weather and infrastructure, uneven playing field, and extremely variable planning horizon. These instability generating characteristics have been exacerbated by what the Air Transport Association (2003) has called a 'Perfect Storm' caused by the confluence of four distinct factors. Two of these factors have plagued the civilian airline industry since its beginning – economic recession and war. Predictions in early 2001 had called for the world airline industry to lose almost US$2 billion that year as a result of economic slowdown. While it is too early to know the final cost of the Iraq War, the ATA has estimated that the first Gulf War cost the airline industry 25,000 jobs and over $13 billion (Air Transport Association, 2003). The other factors in this 'Perfect Storm' dramatically multiplied industry losses – the 9/11 terrorist attacks, Severe Acute Respiratory Syndrome (SARS). Together, these four factors created a crisis that resulted in worldwide airline losses greater than all the profits made in the industry since the 1903 flight at *Kitty Hawk* (Gahan, 2002). By 2009, a whole series of new events transpired that cumulated to produce even more losses for the industry and included: the severe economic down-cycle; the credit crunch; and an outbreak of swine flu which all aggregated to produce enormous net losses for the airline industry. As Table 2.1 shows, these losses were particularly deep and long in the US.

Table 2.1   US and global profits 2000–2009

	2000	2001	2002	2003	2004	2005	2006	2007	2008	2009E
US										
Operating	7.0	(10.3)	(8.6)	(2.1)	(1.5)	0.4	7.5	9.3	(3.7)	2.4
Net[1]	2.5	(8.3)	(11.0)	(2.4)	(7.7)	(5.8)	3.1	5.0	(9.5)	(2.5)
Global										
Operating	10.7	(11.8)	(4.8)	(1.4)	3.3	4.3	15.0	19.9	(8.9)	(1.2)
Net	3.7	(13.0)	(11.3)	(7.5)	(5.6)	(4.1)	3.6	12.9	(16.0)	(9.9)

Note: [1] Adjusted net profit/loss figure for US Carriers.
Source: US figures from Air Transport Association, annual economic reports, www.airlines.org/economics/review_and_outlook.
Global figures from IATA www.iata.org/economics.

These factors also accelerated an industry change that had been gaining momentum in the US since the 1978 deregulation, namely the rise of the low-cost carrier (LCC). The legacy carrier with its hub-and-spoke system, complex fare structure, and multiple classes of service was now facing 'unprecedented pressure on prices, challenges to further cost cutting, the replacement [by LCCs] of turboprops by more comfortable regional jets, and a change in flying habits since September 11' (Costa, Harned, and Lundquist, 2002: 5). Further pressure came from the flight of the high-yield business class passenger who had accounted for the majority of revenue generated by the traditional carriers. Many of these highly valued passengers have apparently decided that it 'is one thing to charge a very high walk-up fare to a last minute business traveler in a hub city where the passenger at least gets a nonstop flight. It is another thing to ask for a fare of an order of magnitude higher than the deep discount fare and still force a passenger to go through a hub with the extra trip time involved, and the possibility of missed connections and lost baggage' (Taneja, 2003: 78–79). In the aftermath of 9/11, the LCCs were the only US carriers expanding service and posting profits (Bond, 2003; Haddad, 2003; Zellner, 2003). In fact, at one point the stock value of Southwest Airlines alone exceeded that of the combined top six, traditional carriers-American, United, Delta, Northwest, Continental, and US Airways.

It had been suggested that this segment could capture 40–50 per cent of the US domestic market in the near future[1] (Haddad and Zellner, 2002; Velocci, 2002). The expansion of Southwest Airlines, the original LCC, has now earned it the top spot as the largest US airline. After significant reductions following 9/11, the legacy US carriers had slowly increased their number of flights while changing the mix of domestic and international flights. Historically, US carriers have relied

---

1   However, by 2009, the low-cost carrier market share in the US (in terms of domestic revenue passenger miles) was around 26 per cent.

on large domestic networks and derived only about 30 per cent of their revenue from international activity, but higher international yields encouraged them to cut less profitable domestic routes and re-deploy aircraft to new international destinations, an action that created further openings for the LCCs. Rising fuel prices are accelerating the trend to shrink operations, particularly small regional jet operations (Reuters, 2008; Taneja, 2003).

The 'Perfect Storm' and the rise of the LCC have both given rise to talk of industry consolidation, a classic response to financial trouble in the airline industry (Rhoades, 2003). US Airways had one of the highest cost structures in the US and a route structure that was heavy in overlapping hubs. It was also very regionally concentrated. The failure of its 2000–2001 attempt to merge with United placed it in an extremely weak position going into 9/11. It became the first major US carrier to file for bankruptcy in 2002, emerged in 2003, re-filed in 2004, and finally merged with America West in 2005. Delta Air Lines and Northwest filed for Chapter 11 in late 2005 and later exited in early 2007. However, both ran into cash shortages that were worsened when oil prices spiked in the wake of Hurricane Katrina. Delta and Northwest agreed to merge in 2008, in a $3.1 billion deal that would create the world's biggest carrier and could trigger other airlines to pursue mergers of their own. Between them, they controlled 17.5 per cent of the US domestic market. United Airlines also tried to merge with Continental Airlines and shortly thereafter with US Airways, but it did not materialize. However, Continental withdrew its membership from SkyTeam and joined the Star alliance signalling that a potential merger between United and Continental could take place in the future,[2] which has since occurred.

Sadly, there is very little evidence that airline consolidation will achieve its hoped for (promised) results. There have been more than 20 major acquisitions in the US since deregulation, but only one has been judged truly successful – Delta and Western (Steffy, 2007). Even this merger was not deemed an unqualified success by all parties. According to Wever (1995), the merger benefited top management and the pilots union, but not the other three unions. Still, Western which was one of the top ten US carriers in the early 1980s and had suffered greatly under deregulation survived under a new name, most of the employees retained their position, labour costs were reduced, and productivity increased, just the sort of things that mergers are supposed to accomplish (Wever, 1995). Most mergers have been far less successful. The Piedmont and US Airways (then called USAir) merger which occurred in 1989 was the largest airline merger at the time and has been judged an abysmal failure. Almost as soon as the merger was completed, US Airways began to post operating losses. The merged airline attempted to avoid employee

---

2   From October 2009 onwards, United and Continental customers are able to purchase flights operated under the carriers' code sharing agreement. Some 400 Continental flights, principally in transatlantic markets and many domestic US markets, are being marketed as United flights, with some 400 United flights being sold with a Continental flight number (United Airlines, 2009).

unrest by raising the salaries of former Piedmont employees to US Airways levels. Eventually US Airways would have the highest cost structure of any major US carrier (Jones and Jones, 1999). The US government will presumably ponder these questions when considering whether to approve future mergers, however, industry critics may be more concerned about the effect of a wave of mergers that might leave the US with significantly fewer carriers (Beebe, 2008).

2.3 Liberalization

The US airlines carried 693 million domestic passengers in 2007 and a further 76 million on international services (Air Transport Association, 2008). The North Atlantic is a high yield market and the US carriers transported 24.6 million passengers across the Atlantic in 2007. On the 30th April 2007, EU and US leaders signed the Open Skies Agreement at a summit in Washington. This came into force on 30th March 2008 and superseded the individual EU country Open Sky Agreements that many EU countries had with the US, commencing with the Netherlands in 1992. However, some observers see the Europeans invading a market 'with weakened US airlines and a currency that makes buying into the US market a bargain at almost any price' (Centre for Asia Pacific Aviation, 2008). Of course, this is not the outcome that the US envisioned when it began to pursue an Open Skies strategy after its domestic deregulation. In 1979, the US passed the International Air Transportation Competition Act setting out three goals for future US aviation policy: (1) multiple carrier designations, permissive route authority, and no operational restrictions on capacity and frequency; (2) market determined air fares; and (3) elimination of discriminatory practices such as foreign computer reservation systems that favoured other national carriers, government user fees at international airports, and exclusive contracts for ground handling and other service (Toh, 1998). By 2008, US airlines carried around 652 million domestic passengers and a further 91.6 million on international services (Air Transport Association, 2009a).

The US pursued its new policy through the application of two levers. The so-called Encirclement Strategy was designed to bring pressure on smaller market countries to sign Open Skies agreements as a means of diverting traffic from larger aviation markets and was based on the assumption that Open Skies would lower fares causing passengers to change their travelling patterns in pursuit of these lower fares. The primary targets for encirclement were Japan and the United Kingdom because they represented the key entry ports for US travellers to Asia and Europe respectively (Levine, 1979). There was never any question of exchanging domestic opportunities (cabotage) with these nations since they had little or no domestic markets to exchange for the sizable US domestic market (Rhoades, 2003).

The second lever to open skies was the decision to tie it to alliance approval on the theory that alliances in the Open Skies context would prove beneficial to the US consumers (Gellman Research Associates, 1994). Furthermore, the US Department of Transportation was empowered to grant immunity from anti-trust enforcement to alliances between carriers from open skies countries. Anti-trust immunity allows competitors to coordinate on issues of pricing, capacity, and scheduling. Thus, they are able to achieve greater levels of operational integration, cut costing, and improve quality through coordination (Oum and Park, 1997). According to Williams (2002), Open Skies and anti-trust did allow the carriers involved to double frequency, re-route flights, and provide online connections to more destinations.

Still, the latest agreement does not grant the cabotage or foreign ownership rights that the EU was seeking. In fact, the EU insisted on a 'suspension clause' if the US does not change its position on foreign ownership[3] by mid-2010 which made it harder for US carriers to invest in EU airlines. In May 2008 second stage negotiations were launched with an aim of achieving an Open Aviation Area (OAA) by mid-2010 that will have considerable implications for factor mobility and airline ownership if it is achieved. London Heathrow is Europe's most important gateway as over 20 per cent of all the North Atlantic seat capacity from the US converges on Heathrow and the Open Skies agreement has favoured US carriers enormously as it now allows all US carriers to enter the airport, provided they can obtain a slot.[4] Previously, under the old agreement only American Airlines and United had access to Heathrow. Evidence does appear to indicate that consumers on both sides of the Atlantic are likely to benefit from lower fares (Williams, 2002). Button (2008; 2009) stated that consumers will benefit by about €5.2 billion a year from lower fares, brought about by greater competition and increased travel across the Atlantic and that there would be between 4.1 and 11.0 million additional passengers. However, few US airlines have commented on the new Open Skies agreement (*Air Cargo World*, 2008).

2.4 Next Generation Air Transportation System (NextGen)

The Federal Aviation Administration (FAA) is predicting that traffic levels will rise by a factor of two to three by 2025 (FAA Fact Sheet, 2007). In order to accommodate this level of air traffic, the US must make some very significant investments in aviation infrastructure otherwise the current capacity shortfall will grow to critical

---

3   Foreign investment policy in US airlines is subject to the following restrictions: 25 per cent legislated cap on voting equity, 25 per cent – minus-one-share regulatory cap on non-voting equity. US companies can own 49 per cent of the voting rights in European Airlines.

4   Slots at London Heathrow are very expensive with Continental Airlines paying $209 million for four pairs of slots in 2008 (Air Transport Intelligence, 2008).

levels, threatening growth and the safety of the system. The current system of ground-based radar, voice communication, and positive control dates from the period just after World War II. While the system has been modernized over the decades, it is essentially based on the same general technology and framework. There are two broad ways to address capacity constraints – control demand or increase supply. Increasing supply can be achieved by the addition of physical infrastructure or improving the utilization (productivity) of existing infrastructure. Although North America has the space to construct more basic infrastructure, that is, airports and runways, doing so raises environmental concerns as well as the more general not-in-my-backyard (NIMBY) reaction. The closing of a number of US military bases had raised the hope that some of these facilities could be converted to civilian use, but in many cases local opposition halted these plans (Department of Defense, 2005). The last major airport constructed in the US was Denver International Airport (DIA) which opened in 1995. The FAA Annual Service Volume plan calls for the construction of eight new runways through 2008 to increase capacity at other airports (FAA, 2008). The FAA has projected that an additional 14 airports and eight metropolitan areas will require new capacity to meet air traffic growth projections for 2025 including Atlanta, Philadelphia, Los Angeles, San Diego, and Las Vegas (Wilson, 2007). Atlanta, the busiest airport in the US, facilitated around 88 million passengers[5] in 2009 and recently added a fifth runway to deal with chronic delays. The new runway is predicted to increase airport arrival capacity by almost 30 percent. A new airport is in the early stages of planning for the Las Vegas area (Yu, 2007). The Air Transport Association (2009b) pointed out that there was an estimated 129 million system delay minutes in 2008, which cost the scheduled US passenger airlines nearly $10 billion in direct aircraft operating costs.

The NextGen answer to capacity constraints is a totally new architecture that will allow information integration, combining new technologies on the ground and in the sky to create a more efficient system. This new architecture is expected to 'create' new capacity by allowing air traffic to more efficiently utilize the existing airspace. These new systems will also help the industry address many of the economic and environmental concerns that have arisen over fossil fuels and carbon emissions. More efficient, direct continuous descents[6] and ascents use less fuel, thus contributing less carbon and other greenhouse gases to the environment and reducing the national dependence on petroleum. Improvements in air space utilization are expected to relieve some of the need for more airport construction. According to the FAA Research, Engineering and Development Advisory Committee (REDAC), the NextGen system will require the development

---

5   Atlanta handled over 79 million domestic passengers and 8.8 million international passengers in 2009.

6   Global navigation satellite systems provide guidance to fly the aircraft on optimized flight paths into an airport using a continuous descent. Emirates and Air New Zealand have undertaken this activity at San Francisco.

and implementation of nine capabilities: network enabled information access, performance based services, advanced air traffic automation services, aircraft trajectory-based operations, weather assimilation into decision loops, broad-area precision navigation, equivalent visual operations, super density operations, and layered adaptive security (NGATS, 2005). There are at least two key technologies:

- *Automatic Dependency Surveillance-Broadcast* (ADS-B) is a satellite-based system that allows aircraft to broadcast their position to others. ADS-B *out* will replace many ground radars with ground-based transceivers. ADS-B *in* would allow aircraft to receive signals from the ground-based transceivers as well as from ADS-B equipment onboard other aircraft. ADS-B is an important element in implementing Required Navigation Precision (RNP) procedures. It is believed that these procedures will help to eliminate en route and terminal inefficiencies.
- *System-wide Information Management* (SWIM) is a new system architecture that would allow airspace users to access a wide array of data on the National Airspace System (NAS) and weather. SWIM is a net-centric link between air traffic management, customers, and the departments of Homeland Security and Defense which would provide full automation and data convergence across all authorized users on a common platform.

Two problems currently plague the NextGen programme. The first is funding. In 1981, the FAA began what it initially envisioned as a 10-year modernization programme to upgrade and replace the National Airspace System's facilities and equipment to meet projected increases in traffic volumes, enhance the system's margin of safety, and increase the efficiency of the air traffic control system. Yet, there is almost universal agreement that the 'FAA's funding structure is obsolete and unpredictable' (May, 2006; Oster and Strong, 2006). However, there is no agreement on a new means of funding the FAA or NextGen. Most of the FAA funding comes from the Airports and Airways Trust Fund whose revenues are generated through excise taxes. In fact, roughly 70 per cent of the 2004 revenues came from the passenger ticket tax, flight segment tax, rural airport tax, and frequent flyer tax (Oster and Strong, 2006). The growth in LCCs has driven down average fares and threatened the viability of the Trust Fund (Cordle and Poole, 2005). The 2004 uncommitted balance in the Trust Fund was US$7.3 billion and is expected to drop to US$1.2 billion by 2006 (May, 2006). To date, FAA has spent $43.5 billion for its NAS modernization effort and plans to spend an additional $9.6 billion through fiscal year 2009, primarily to upgrade and replace ATC systems and facilities (GAO, 2005). The FAA 2007 Reauthorization bill proposed moving from the current system of excise taxes to a cost-based user fee system in which the aircraft operator would pay for the air traffic services they used, however, the bill ran into early trouble over contract talks with the National Air Traffic Controllers Association (NATCA) who were angered by the FAA imposed contract in 2006. Further opposition came from the general aviation community who has argued that they should not be included in the new funding structure because many General Aviation (GA) flights operate in uncongested airspace under visual flight rules and hence do not use significant air traffic services. In fact, several studies have estimated that the GA share of ATC costs is between 10 and 25 percent, well above their three per cent contribution to the Trust Fund (Oster and Strong, 2006).

The issue of cost and utilization is the second problem facing NextGen. The FAA can account for its inputs – labour, facilities, equipment and supplies – and it can provide a broad list of outputs from its activities – aircraft movements, departures, but the connection between the cost of inputs to cost of specific outputs has never been clearly presented. The FAA's (1996) report, 'A Cost Allocation Study of FAA's 1995 Costs (CAS)', assigned costs to various services, but this study has been criticized at a number of levels. First, it fails to demonstrate that an aircraft of a given type (B-737) on a flight from point A to B generates X costs to the FAA air traffic system. Second, there is a question of how it allocates usage between commercial and GA aircraft. It has been suggested that the estimates of cost are based more on the ability to pay than on the actual cost of the services provided. This inability to clearly identify the usage and cost of service has seriously hampered the FAA's ability to make an argument for user fee charges.

2.5 Industry Regulation

The industry and its chief regulator, the FAA, have been the subject of a number of 'complaints', most are long standing and recurring. The list includes NextGen spending and management, safety oversight, and airline performance. These issues have given rise to calls for re-regulation of some aspects of the industry as well as more radical calls to privatize or corporatize some of the FAA responsibilities. Critics of the FAAs performance on NextGen have raised the following problems: (1) promising more capability than they ultimately deliver, (2) being completed later than promised, and (3) costing far more by the time they are completed than the initial cost 'estimates' (Oster and Strong, 2006). A US GAO inspector general noted 'that cost growth, schedule delays, and performance shortfalls with major acquisitions continue to stall air traffic modernization' (US GAO, 2005).

This review noted that eleven of the 16 projects appeared to be experiencing total cost growth while over half were experiencing schedule slips from 2–12 years. Such reports raise serious doubt about the ability to deploy any of the main elements of NextGen. One example of the overall problem is the development and implementation of the Wide Area Augmentation System (WAAS). WAAS was projected in 1994 to cost $509 million. The Inspector General testified before Congress in 2004 that the projected cost of the yet-to-be implemented programme had risen to over $2.9 billion, a 227 per cent increase in the cost the programme whose implementation had been extended by 13 year (NATCA, 2008). Further, the National Air Traffic Controllers Association (NATCA) has charged that the FAA is neglecting existing facilities maintenance, creating unsafe conditions, and wasting money in Air Traffic Organization (ATO) reorganization and modernization efforts (NATCA, 2008). Oster and Strong (2006) suggested that there are really only two options for advancing the NextGen vision: (1) leave air traffic services with FAA under a user fee structure (essentially the approach of the most recent FAA reauthorization bill), or (2) remove the system from the FAA and establish an autonomous agency similar to NAV CANADA and NATS. Option one does not resolve the fact that the FAA has yet to determine the cost of its services, has a poor record of performance, and lacks the organizational independence to pursue a market-based rather than politically based strategy. Option two avoids these problems but faces opposition because of the user fee issue as well as more generalized opposition to privatization.

The FAA has been challenged for a number of years over its safety oversight function. In the most recent challenge, Congressman Jim Oberstar, chairman of the Transportation and Infrastructure Committee of the US House of Representatives, has said that 'many FAA inspectors have given up reporting failures by the carriers because there is such a cozy relationship between FAA management and airline management' (Oberstar, 2008). This comment was prompted by the grounding of a number of US aircraft following CNN investigations into maintenance irregularities at Southwest Airlines. Subsequently, three other US airlines were forced to ground aircraft for inspection when it was revealed that they had failed to comply with various airworthiness directives (Bronstein, 2008; Griffin and Bronstein, 2008; Koenig, 2008). The outsourcing of maintenance, particularly to foreign FAA-certified repair facilities, has also raised concern. The FAA is responsible for inspecting almost 5,000 certificated domestic and foreign repair stations. There are currently only 103 FAA inspectors for the 692 foreign stations. In addition, the FAA permits air carriers to use non-certified facilities as long as the work is approved by an FAA-certified mechanic. In 2005, the Department of Transportation Inspector General's Office concluded that neither the FAA nor the airlines provided adequate oversight of the 1,400 non-certificated facilities (Business Travel Coalition, 2008).

A third area that has provoked concern is related to airline service quality. Consumer complaints overall are up almost 60 per cent from 2006 to 2007. Figures for January 2008 indicate that complaints were up 75.6 per cent from the prior January. For all of 2008, 24.4 per cent of US commercial flights were late (Department of Transport, 2008). At key hub airport in the New York metropolitan area (JFK, EWR and LGA) only 51 per cent of departures left on time in 2008, While US carriers have showed a slight improvement in mishandled baggage in 2007, this was not enough to compensate for the complaints, delays,[7] and cancellations that occurred (Associated Press, 2008; Air Transport Association, 2009c). In a review of 20 years of US airline service quality, Rhoades and Waguespack (2008)

---

7   ATA estimates that delays in 2007 cost airline customers more than $4 billion in lost productivity and wages (Air Transport Association, 2008).

concluded that 'the airline industry in the US is back where it started from in terms of quality. In fact, in some respects the industry is set to post its worst year since the US Department of Transportation began public reporting' (p. 26). In addition to LCC competition and general financial pressure, both of which led many carriers to reduce service quality levels, the periods of improved quality performance appear to correspond to downturns in the economy and the industry. The explanation for this finding may lie in the fact that airlines tend to reduce the number of flights during times of economic downturn which improves on time performance as there are fewer planes trying to land at congested airports. There are also 'fewer passengers flying, fewer bags to lose, fewer people to complain' (p. 26). Schedule reduction or expansion is an airline issue. Typically, airlines race to add more flights to meet demand when times are good. Unfortunately, as mentioned above, the US aviation system is constrained by the air traffic control system and the available landing slots and runways at airports. When too many planes try to fly into a congested system, the inevitable result is flight delay. Weather problems in a tightly constrained, full capacity network system create a ripple effect throughout the system. JetBlue experienced this phenomena first hand during a Valentine Day weekend in 2007 that resulted in stranded passengers and lost holiday luggage. Tired of waiting for the federal government to act, the State of New York passed its own bill, but this was struck down by a Federal Appeals Court that ruled that this kind of regulation was the responsibility of the federal government (Abrams, 2008). These types of events have forced the DOT to act and they introduced new measures by issuing a ruling[8] which stipulates that carriers must adopt contingency plans for lengthy tarmac delays and to publish those plans on their websites.

2.6 Conclusion

After finally digging out from under the post-9/11 financial crisis, US airlines and the aviation system that support them are facing a series of challenges – financial stability, liberalization, NextGen funding and implementation, and industry regulation – that threaten the future growth and prosperity of the industry. Whether the second decade of the twenty-first century will herald a new era of prosperity or a capacity-constrained decline in quality and service levels depends on resolving these issues. Unfortunately, the US industry seems intent on clinging to the old responses to crisis, the old technology, the old labour-management battles, and the old ways of managing and regulating the industry. The change in US political leadership in January 2009 may also be the catalyst for change in aviation and it is likely that there will be increased calls for regulatory change and oversight. These might also begin to focus on carbon constraint since the issue of climate change

---

8 Code of Federal Regulations, which is published under 50 titles pursuant to 44 U.S.C. 1510.

is gaining attention in the US. While the airlines are unlikely to see increased regulation as a positive outcome, they might welcome a new focus on the issues surrounding the implementation of NextGen. This system is a key to providing the level of capacity needed to meet predicted demand for air travel. The future of a fragile industry depends on finding new solutions to old problems.

References

Abrams, J. (2008), 'Congress Debates Air Passenger Rights', The Associated Press. Available at: http://abcnews.go.com/print?id=4529479.

Air Cargo World (2008), 'Terminal Velocity', April, pp. 14–15.

Air Transport Association (2009a), December 2009 Airline Traffic Data. Available at: www.bts.gov/press_releases/2010/bts012_10/html/bts012_10.html.

Air Transport Association (2009b), Cost of Delays. Available at: www.airlines.org/economics.

Air Transport Association (2009c), 2009 Economic Report. Available at: www.airlines.org/Economics/ReviewOutlook/Documents/2009AnnualReport.pdf.

Air Transport Association (2008), 2008 Economic Report. Available at: www.airlines.org/Economics/ReviewOutlook/Documents/2008AnnualReport.pdf.

Air Transport Association (2003), *Airlines in Crisis: The Perfect Economic Storm,* Air Transport Association of America, Washington, D.C.

Air Transport Intelligence (2008), Continental's Heathrow slots carry a $209 million price tag, 4th March. Available at: rati.com.

Associated Press (2008), 'Complaints Soar at US Airlines', CNN online. Available at: http://www.cnn.com.

Beebe, P. (2008), 'Feds will now mull Delta, Northwest airlines merger deal', The Salt Lake Tribune, May 15. Available at: http:// www.sltrib.com/portlet/article.html.

Bond, D. (2003), 'Traffic on the treadmill', *Aviation Week and Space Technology*, August 11, pp. 42–43.

Bronstein, S. (2008), 'FAA Takes Risks with Shoddy Oversight, Experts Say,' CNN online. Available at: http://www.cnn.com.

Business Travel Coalition (2008), 'Aircraft Maintenance Outsourcing Issue Analysis'. Available at: info@btcnewswire.com.

Button, K. (2009), The impact of US-EU 'Open Skies' agreement on airline market structures and airline networks, *Journal of Air Transport Management*, vol. 15(2), pp. 59–71.

Button, K.J. (2008), The impact of EU-US 'Open Skies2 Agreement on airline market structures and airline networks'. Paper presented to Airneth workshop on the implications of the EU-US Open Sky Agreement, The Hague.

Centre for Asia Pacific Aviation (2008), 'A Changing Aviation World Balance – It Will Happen Faster than you Think' *Air Transport News*. Available at:http://www.airtransportmews.aero.

Cordle, V. and Poole, V. (2005), Resolving the crisis in Air Traffic Control Funding, May. Available at: http://reason.org/files/acab6b7b89b6bcd943b6fdef8231fe82.pdf.

Costa, P.R., Harned, D.S. and Lundquist, J.T. (2002), 'Rethinking the aviation industry', *McKinsey Quarterly*, online edition, www.mckinseyquarterly.com.

Department of Defense (2005), Converting military airfields to Civil Airports, Office of economic adjustment, 3000 Defense Pentagon, Washington, D.C. 20301–3000, September.

Department of Transport (2008), Aviation consumer protection and enforcement. Available at: www.airconsumer.ost.dot.gov/reports/atcr08.htm.

FAA (2008), 'Capacity: Annual Service Volume'. Available at: www.faa.gov/about/plans_reports/portfolio_2008/media/annaul per cent20service per cent20volume.pdf.

FAA (2007), 'Fact Sheet'. Available at: http://www.faa.gov/news/fact_sheets/news_story.cfm?newsId=8807.

FAA (1996), 'A cost allocation study of FAA's 1995 costs', UD Department of Transportation, Washington, D.C.

GAO (2005). National Airspace System, FAA has made progress but continues to face challenges in acquiring major air traffic control systems, GAO-05-331, June. Available at: www.gao.gov/new.items/d05331.pdf.

Gahan, M. (2002), 'Aviation's Continuing Crisis,' BBC News Online, August 13.

Gellman Research Associates (1994), 'A Study of International Airline Codesharing', report submitted to Office of Aviation and International Economics (Office of the Secretary of Transportation, US Department of Transportation, Washington, D.C.).

Griffin, D. and Bronstein, S. (2008), 'FAA Inspectors: Southwest Tried to Hide Safety Problems,' CNN online. Available at: http://www.cnn.com.

Haddad, C. (2003), 'Catch him if you can', *Business Week*, September 15, pp. 93–94.

Haddad, C. and Zellner, W. (2002), 'Getting down and dirty with the discounters', *Business Week*, October 28, pp. 76–77.

Jones, G. and Jones, G.P. (1999), *US Airways* (Ian Allan: Shepperton, UK).

Koenig, D. (2008), 'American Expects More Cancellations', *The Associated Press*. Available at: http://abcnews.go.com.

Levine, M.E. (1979), 'Civil Aeronautics Memo by Michael E. Levine', *Aviation Daily*, March 8, pp. 1–7.

Loomis, C. and Buffet, W. (1999), 'Mr Buffet on the Stock Market', *Fortune*, Special Issue, vol. 140(10), pp. 212–220.

May, J.C. (2006), 'Speech by James C. May: Smart – and Fair – Skies: Blueprint for the Future', International Aviation Club, Washington, D.C., March. Available at: www.airlines.org/news/speeches/speech_4-18-06.htm.

National Air Traffic Controllers Association (2008), Press Releases. Available at: www.natca.org/index.aspx.

Next Generation Air Transportation System (NGATS) (2005), 2005 Progress Report to the Next Generation Air Transportation System Integrated Plan. Available at: www.dtic.mil/cgi-bin/GetTRDoc?Location=U2&doc=GetTRD oc.pdf&AD=ADA508134.

Oberstar (2008), 'Oberstar Puts FAA on the Hot Seat', March 7. Available at: http://www.oberstar.house.gov/index.asp?Type=B_PR&SEC=(C2C6D65E-F1A2-4540-a7.

Oster, C.V. and Strong, J.S. (2006), *Reforming the Federal Aviation Administration: Lessons from Canada and the United Kingdom*, IBM Center for the Business of Government, Virginia.

Oum, T.H. and Park, J. (1997), 'Airline Alliances: Current Status, Policy Issues, and Future Directions', *Journal of Air Transport Management*, vol. 3, pp. 133–144.

Reuters (2008), 'Big US Airlines Look to Shrink to Save Money,' CNBC, March 17. Available at: http://www.cnbc.com/id/23680667/for/cnbc.

Rhoades, D.L. and Waguespack, B. Jr. (2008), 'Twenty Years of Service Quality Performance in the US Airline Industry', *Managing Service Quality*, 18(1), pp. 20–33.

Rhoades, D.L. (2003), *Evolution of International Aviation: Phoenix Rising* (Ashgate Publishing, Aldershot, UK).

Steffy, L. (2007), 'Airline Mergers Usually Don't Fly', Houston Chronicle online edition. Available at: http://www.chron.com/disp/story.mpl/bussiness/steffy/5309876.html.

Taneja, N.K. (2003), *Airline Survival Kit: Breaking out of the Zero Profit Game* (Ashgate Publishing Ltd., Aldershot, UK).

The CalTrade Report (2008), Pressure on US Airlines as Skies open. Available at: www.caltradereport.com.

Toh, R.S. (1998), 'Towards an International Open Skies Regime: Advances, Impediments, and Impacts', *Journal of Air Transportation World Wide*, vol. 3, pp. 61–70.

United Airlines (2009), United Airlines Welcomes Continental Airlines to Star Alliance, United Airlines website. Available at: www.united.com/press/detail/0,7056,61210-1,00.html.

USGAO Report (2005), Commercial Aviation, Structural Costs Continue to Challenge Legacy Airlines' Financial Performance, GAO-05–834T, 13 July. Available at: www.gao.gov/new.items/d05834t.pdf.

US GAO (2005), National Airspace System: FAA Has Made Progress but Continues to Face Challenges in Acquiring Major Air Traffic Control Systems, GAO-05–331, June. Available at: www.gao.gov/new.items/d05331.pdf.

Velocci, A.L. (2002), 'Can majors shift focus fast enough to survive?' *Aviation Week and Space Technology*, November 18, pp. 52–54.

Wever, K.S. (1995), 'Revisiting the Labor-Management Partnership at Western Airlines' in Peter Cappelli (ed.) *Airline Labor Relations in the Global Era: The New Frontier* (Cornell University Press, Ithaca, NY).

Williams, G. (2002), *Airline Competition: Deregulation's Mixed Legacy* (Ashgate Publishing, Aldershot, UK).

Wilson, B. (2007), 'Flight delays top the list of pax complaints new study finds', *Aviation Daily*, Washington, D.C., vol. 369(35), p. 4.

Yu, R. (2007), 'Flight delays worst in 13 years', *USA Today* online edition. Available at: www.usatoday.com/travel/flights/2007–06–04-airline-delays_N.htm.

Zellner, W. (2003), 'Strafing the big boys-again', *Business Week*, June 23, p. 36.

Chapter 3

Ryanair and the Low-cost Revolution

Sean D. Barrett

3.1 Ryanair's Market Entry

Ryanair carried over 66 million passengers in 2009/10. It is the world's largest international airline and the innovative leader in the European low-cost sector despite having its home base in Ireland with a population of only 4.2 million. In its first year of operation in 1985 it carried 15,000 passengers on one route from Waterford to London Gatwick. Its market capitalization at the end of FY 2009/10 was €7.5 billion, more than twice that of British Airways.

Features of the rapid growth of Ryanair include very low air fares and an even lower cost base which yielded an operating margin of 13.5 per cent in the 12 months ending March 31, 2010. Staff productivity is extremely high due to 25-minute airport turnaround times, high seat-density per aircraft, a single aircraft-type fleet, the single-class configuration of aircraft cabins, the provision of in-flight services on a pay per item basis, the use of secondary airports, and the retailing of tickets on the internet rather than in airline offices or travel agents.

Ryanair commenced services in July 1985 with a 15-seat *Bandeirante* aircraft operating between Waterford and Gatwick. In May 1986 it began service on the Dublin–London Luton route with two 46-seater BAe 748 aircraft. The fare charged was £Ir94.99 or €121 compared to the Aer Lingus/British Airways fare of £208 or €264, a 54 per cent reduction. Ryanair had 15,000 passengers in 1985 and 82,000 in 1986.

The background to the launch of Ryanair was public indignation in Ireland at the high level of fares charged by Aer Lingus, the Irish national airline, and its colluding partner national airlines. Particular consumer irritation was caused by the Dublin–London fare charged by Aer Lingus and British Airways. In hindsight it can be seen that Ireland as an outer offshore island was a likely loser from policies which restricted competition in aviation. The surface travel alternatives were a nine-hour boat and train journey to London and a 22-hour boat journey to the European mainland.

Aer Lingus enjoyed protection by the Irish government from before it started services in 1936 through to the 1980s. In the official history of Aer Lingus, Share (1986) notes the refusal in 1935 of an application by Crilly Airways to operate air services between Britain and Ireland. 'The reason given was the government intention to set up a national airline at the earliest possible date.' In 1949 a proposal for a service from Cork to Britain by Cambrian was vetoed 'on the grounds that air transport policy did not contemplate that airlines other than Aer Lingus would operate a scheduled service between the two countries' (Share, 1986). In 1950 a proposal for a car-carrying service from Liverpool to Dublin by Silver City was refused because Aer Lingus was 'considering the opening of a similar service on the route' (Share, 1986). All attempts by other airlines to serve Ireland were refused by the Government and the Department of Transport became known as a downtown office of Aer Lingus.

A study by the Civil Aviation Authority in 1987 of 11 short-haul routes from London to six internal UK destinations plus Amsterdam, Paris, Dublin, Frankfurt and Brussels found that the Dublin route had the highest rate of fare increase at 72.6 per cent and the lowest rate of passenger increase at 2.8 per cent. The White Paper on Tourism Policy (1985) found that the number of air tourists to Ireland fell by 50 per cent between 1975 and 1983 (Share, 1986). Public opinion in the early 1980s, a time of economic depression in Ireland, swung sharply against colluding national airlines and in favour of deregulation. Share stated that 'as consumerist and monetarist attitudes became fashionable in the early and mid-1980s, the social role of Aer Lingus came increasingly under scrutiny' (Share, 1986). Share also notes Sean Barrett 'conducting a sustained campaign in favour of de-regulation of air fares with particular reference to Irish Sea routes'.

The crucial swing in parliamentary opinion in May 1984 saw the refusal of the Dail (the lower house of the Irish Parliament) to pass The Air Transport Bill as an emergency measure. Following an unsuccessful High Court case against travel agents who sold TransAmerica tickets for less than the Minister for Transport's authorized price emergency legislation was introduced which sought to imprison and fine heavily such travel agents. Following this rare parliamentary revolt the Government changed its policy and the Ryanair licences soon followed.

Ryanair's first route was from Waterford to Gatwick launched in July 1985 some 14 months after the parliamentary revolt against the Air Transport Bill. The route was served by a 15-seat *Bandeirante* aircraft and had 15,000 passengers in 1985. The second Ryanair route was launched in May 1986 from Dublin to London–Luton using two BAe 748 aircraft with 46 seats. In August 1987, the first full year of deregulation passenger numbers on the Dublin–London route were 91.7 per cent greater than in August 1985, the last full year of pre-deregulation policies.

3.2 The Development of Ryanair

Table 3.1 shows the numbers of passengers and staff of Ryanair since 1985. Between 1985 and 1990 Ryanair lost €25 million while growing to 745,000 passengers. In addressing this unsustainable situation the company abolished business class and the frequent flyer club in 1989 and ceased turboprop operations in May 1991 when it also switched its London based operations from Luton to Stansted. Ryanair cut its network from 19 to 6 routes in 1992. These were Stansted to Dublin, Cork, Shannon and Knock and Dublin to Luton and Liverpool. The adoption of the Southwest model in 1990 brought changes such as abolition of free meals and drinks on board, charging the lowest fares in each market and moving to a single aircraft type. Passenger numbers fell by 13 per cent in 1991 but Ryanair made its first profit of €372,000. In 1992 passenger numbers increased by 45 per cent to 945,000 and grew every succeeding year to 66.5 million in 2009/10.

Table 3.1   Ryanair passenger traffic and employees 1985–2009

	Passengers (thousands)	Employees
1985	5	51
1986	82	151
1987	322	212
1988	592	379
1989	644	477
1990	745	493
1991	651	477
1992	945	507
1993	1,220	503
1994	1,666	523
1995	2,260	523
1996	2,950	605
1997	3,730	659
1998	4,629	892
1999	5,358	1,094
2000	7,002	1,262
2001	9,335	1,467
2002	13,419	1,547
2003	19,490	1,746
2004	24,635	2,288
2005	30,946	2,700
2006	34,800	3,300
2007	42,500	3,744
2008	50,900	5,262
2009	66,500	7,032

Source: Ryanair.

In 1993 the first new route for five years was opened from Dublin to Birmingham and passenger numbers exceeded 1 million for the first time; Manchester, Glasgow Prestwick and London Gatwick being added in 1994. In 1995 Ryanair became the market leader over Aer Lingus on the Dublin-London route and entered the internal UK market on the London-Glasgow Prestwick route.

In 1997 Ryanair was floated on the Dublin and NASDAQ stock exchanges. The flotation price of €11 rose to €25.5 on the first day of trading. Ryanair entered the mainland Europe market with services to Stockholm Skavsta, Paris Beauvais and Brussels Charleroi. In 1999 passenger numbers exceeded 5 million for the first time and in 2000 it carried more passengers than its home national airline, Aer Lingus. In 2000 Ryanair launched its website with large efficiency gains in its sales and ticketing. By 2004 it handled 98 per cent of Ryanair bookings. In 2001and 2002 new bases were opened in Glasgow Prestwick (2000), Brussels Charleroi (2001) and Frankfurt Hahn (2002). Buzz was acquired from KLM in 2003. Passenger numbers were almost 20 million in 2003 and exceeded 30 million in 2005. At the time of its first takeover bid for Aer Lingus in late 2006 Ryanair carried five times as many passengers as the former national airline.

Ryanair is the first European airline to avail of the single EU market opportunities. In 2009 Ryanair had around 1,000 routes across Europe and Morocco from its 40 bases, only three of which were in its home country, Ireland. Its fleet comprised of over 200 aircraft of which only 23 were based in Ireland. By contrast legacy national airlines in Europe were identified with their home nation and have yet to avail of the new market opportunities opened up by the abolition of previously restricted fifth freedom services between third countries and cabotage services within other countries.

3.3 The Ryanair Product

The Ryanair product is the lowest fare with a lower cost base. The average Ryanair fare in 2009/10 was €35 compared to €52 on easyJet and €77 on Aer Lingus, the major competitors of Ryanair. The Goldman Sachs estimates in 2004 were €83 for Aer Lingus Europe, €62 for easyJet and €39 for Ryanair (Davy, 2006a). The low cost-base makes Ryanair the most profitable airline in Europe with a net margin in FY 2009/10 of 10.2 per cent compared to -5.3 per cent for British Airways, 2.7 per cent for easyJet and 0.9 per cent for Southwest.

The Ryanair low average fare is the main market attraction of the airline. There are also some customer service benefits from the Ryanair product such as punctuality, higher flight completion rates, lower rates of lost bags, no overbooking, and for some passengers there are benefits from service at local airports and the avoidance of hub airports. Smaller airports with less congestion improve timekeeping. The simple point to point airline product reduces check-in times. Fewer bags are lost on point to point trips compared to journeys with onward connections through hubs and there no delays waiting for connecting aircraft. Local airports may be more convenient for some passengers at least and save them journeys to hub airports.

Ryanair's booking policy penalizes no-show passengers who are not given refunds. In contrast traditional airlines addressed the problem of no-show passengers was by overbooking. When the number of no-show passengers was lower than that assumed in the overbooking policy the overbooked passengers were denied travel. The Ryanair policy is to penalize the no-show passengers rather than passengers overbooked by the traditional airline.

In comparing the Ryanair lower fares and the above service improvements with the product and services of the traditional full service airline, the Ryanair passenger has to consider the loss of many services associated with the traditional full service airline. Table 3.2 lists these items which were bundled into the full-service airline product rather than sold separately. Seventeen examples of service deletions and restrictions facing Ryanair passengers and not traditionally faced by passengers on full-service airline are shown.

A measure of the public's reaction to the new price-product trade-off is that since its relaunch as a low-cost airline in 1990 Ryanair has increased from 745,000 to 66.5 million passengers and from 18 routes in 1990 to 1,100 routes in 2009/10. Some of the service deletions listed in Table 3.2 have over time been seen as attractions. For example, those with origins and destinations close to secondary airports no longer have to transit through hub airports and enjoy both fare and time savings on their trips. In addition, point-to-point service has fewer lost bags, late flights and cancellations than flights through hubs.

Table 3.2   **The Ryanair customer product contrasted against the full service airline product**

Customer service items dropped from the traditional European airline product by Ryanair		
Inflight service items:	**Airport service items:**	**Ticket restrictions:**
No sweets, newspapers, free food or beverage service.	Secondary airports are typically served.	Tickets are not sold through travel agents nor through company retail ticket outlets.
No seat allocation.	No interlining or connecting journey tickets are issued.	No frequent flyer programme.
No business class service.	Passengers and baggage must be checked in at each airport on a multi-sector journey.	Stricter penalties for "no show" passengers.
More seats per aircraft and a higher load factor.	No airport lounge service.	

Source: Barrett (2004).

Some of the elements of the changes in airline product shown in Table 3.2 were the results of the previous structure and organization of the air transport market rather than a first option by Ryanair. The grandfather rights allocation of capacity at hub airports made large-scale hub airport entry by new airlines difficult. The payment of travel agent commission as a percentage of the ticket price made their sale of low-cost airline tickets less remunerative than sales of full service airline tickets. Cityjet, a full-service airline which entered the market at the same time as Ryanair, paid travel agents 15 per cent commission in order to secure more support for their product from the retailers (Byrne, 2004). In addition, the owners of global distribution systems in travel agents offices charged some 10 per cent of the ticket price.

The Skytrax passenger rankings of airlines place Ryanair in the two-star category with BMI Baby. Easyjet is ranked as three-star with Aer Lingus, KLM, SAS, Hapag Lloyd, British Midland and Alitalia. British Airways, Air France and Lufthansa are rated four-star. Singapore, Malaysia, Cathay Pacific and Qatar Airways are rated in the highest five-star category. On short-haul flights such as performed by Ryanair the value to consumers of services provided by five-star airlines is open to question. Davy (2006a) found that 83 per cent of Ryanair passengers had flown with the airline before. The growth of Ryanair has significantly exceeded the growth of the three-star and four-star European airlines. The Skytrax surveys have a response rate of less than four per million Ryanair passengers. The Ryanair annual report for 2009/10 shows that the airline achieved both the best on-time performance of large European carriers (93 per cent on-time) and the least number of missed bags (0.4 per 1,000 passengers).

3.4 The Ryanair Cost Base

In combining the lowest average fare charged in Europe, €49, and the highest net margin, 18 per cent, requires a strategy of cost reduction by Ryanair both within the airline and across all its suppliers, in addition to the product cost savings shown in Table 3.2. The scope for these cost reductions was significant. Goldman Sachs (2004) note that 'with the exception of Ryanair, no other European airline has outperformed the FTSE Eurotop 300 index over the past ten years, highlighting the varying degrees of market underperformance by the sector as a whole'.

Labour productivity in Ryanair is significantly higher than among its competitors. This is achieved by outsourcing maintenance and handling, fleet standardization, the 25-minute airport turnaround thus increasing the flying time per working day, better crew-to-aircraft ratios, eliminating overnighting costs by recruiting locally the crews at each base airport, reducing sales and distribution costs by use of the Internet, and by having a general start-up corporate culture quite different from the inherited corporate culture of legacy airlines from the era of non-competing national carriers.

In a report on a large strike at Dublin Airport in 1998 Flynn and McAuley (1998) found that staff at Ryanair considered that they worked harder than those at other airport companies. As a commercial airline rather than a legacy national carrier Ryanair did not face political pressures to become a job-creation agency. As a start-up airline Ryanair had younger staff that did not have the rent-seeking opportunities open to staff in the legacy airlines. This combination of rent-seeking opportunities due to lack of competition in European aviation and political control of national airlines has been described by Doganis (2001) as 'distressed state airline syndrome'. The elements of the syndrome are substantial losses, over-politicization, strong unions, overstaffing, no clear development strategy, bureaucratic management and poor service-quality (Doganis, 2001).

Ryanair did not have the adaptation costs of replacing the traditional sales and distribution of tickets through expensive downtown airline offices and travel agents but was able to move immediately to online booking. The carrier did not have an advertising and public relations cost base from the era of non-price competition between airlines but competed on price. Table 3.3 shows the number of passengers per staff member in Ryanair and competing airlines in 2008. Ryanair carried 66.5 million passengers in 2009/10 with 7,032 staff, equal to 9,457 passengers per staff member. By contrast the full-service network airlines had a much lower number of passengers per staff member with British Airways producing around 758 passengers per staff member.

In the era of price coordination between airlines the suppliers of services to the sector all earned profits which were higher than earned by the airlines. These higher profit suppliers included airports, aircraft manufacturers and leasing companies and airline catering companies. Ryanair has been a staunch opponent of European airport charges, both in opposing expensive construction proposals at Stansted and Dublin, seeking lower cost secondary airports, and developing competition between airports serving the same catchment areas. Examples of airport competition stimulated by Ryanair include Luton v. Stansted, Birmingham v. East Midlands, Manchester v. Liverpool and Leeds-Bradford, Prestwick v. Glasgow, and Bristol v. Cardiff in the UK and a wide range of airport competition in mainland Europe, including that across national borders.

With 66 million passengers in 2009/10 Ryanair is the largest international airline in the world. The Ryanair fleet has more than doubled from 100 to over 200 aircraft between 2006 and 2010. This gives the airline leverage in its fleet purchasing. After 9/11 it negotiated a very favourable deal from Boeing at a time when other airlines were postponing or cancelling orders. The first Ryanair offer document for Aer Lingus (in November 2006) estimates that Aer Lingus costs of narrowbody aircraft were 40 per cent greater than the Ryanair cost for equivalent aircraft.

Table 3.3   Passengers per employee 2008

Airline	Number of passengers per staff member
Ryanair	9,679
easyJet	6,152
Aer Lingus	2,478
Alitalia[†]	2,197
Brussels Airlines	1,700
Austrian	1,372
TAP	1,251
Czech	1,210
Lufthansa	1,172
LOT	1,102
Iberia	1,080
British Midland	1,048
Finnair	862
British Airways	798
KLM/Air France	690
AEA Members (31)[†]	915

Sources: Air Transport Intelligence; Association of European Airlines (2007); the data for Ryanair is from the company report.

[†]Alitalia and Association of European Airlines (AEA) data is for 2007.

There is a huge difference in the corporate culture of low-cost and legacy airlines in their approach to both internal and external cost savings. The low-cost airlines have outsourced and increased their own staff productivity and extracted price reductions from aircraft suppliers and airport operators resulting in both low fares and high profit margins. The colluding legacy airlines in the past could avoid cost pressures by jointly raising their fares thus avoiding difficult cost confrontations with either airline staff or suppliers of goods and services. The knowledge that their customer airlines did not engage in price competition reduced cost pressures in sectors supplying services to airlines, in particular in the airport sector. The staff of legacy airlines also enjoyed the economic rent from employment in a sector in which there was no price competition between the incumbent national airlines and from which new entrants were excluded.

3.5 The Ryanair Takeover Bids for Aer Lingus in 2006 and 2008/9

On 5 October 2006 Ryanair announced a cash offer of €2.80 per share for Aer Lingus. This valued Aer Lingus at €1.48 billion, 27 per cent above the flotation value eight days earlier with a flotation price of €2.20. By February 2007 Ryanair held 25.2 per cent of Aer Lingus acquired for an average of €2.54 per share. The stated object of the takeover bid was to build a strong Irish airline group with over 50 million passengers capable of competing with other European and world airline groups such as Lufthansa/Austrian/Swiss with 79 million passengers, Air France/KLM with 70 million passengers and British Airways/Iberia with 63 million passengers. Ryanair promised to cut Aer Lingus costs, lower short-haul fares by 2.5 per cent a year, improve service delivery and retain the Aer Lingus brand and its 23 Heathrow slots. The offer was opposed by the Government of Ireland and the employee share ownership trust which owned Aer Lingus and was rejected by the EU on competition grounds in June 2007.

Ryanair launched a second bid for Aer Lingus in December 2008 when it already owned 29.8 per cent of the company. The offer was rejected by Aer Lingus in January 2009. The shareholders opposed to the Ryanair bid are the Government of Ireland which owns 25.1 per cent of the company, and the Aer Lingus staff share ownership trust which owns 14.2 per cent. Those opposed to the takeover thus held 39.3 per cent of the company. 30.8 per cent of shares are held by other shareholders.

The Aer Lingus case against the takeover was that the success of its IPO gave it capital, and that its return on capital and operating margin were second only to Ryanair in Europe. It had fleet utilization in line with Ryanair despite offering seat allocation and serving primary airports, and was uniquely positioned to benefit from the expected relaxation in the bilateral air agreement with the United States. The Aer Lingus management team was targeting significant unit cost reductions in 12 key areas which would benefit its shareholders. Six of these concern staff costs including new employee contracts, simplified grading and improved productivity on long haul routes. The other six refer to operating cost reductions being sought by Aer Lingus from its suppliers such as handlers, maintenance contractors, airports, and distribution and marketing costs. The Aer Lingus returns justify a premium rating and the airline has excellent prospects as an independent company. Table 3.4 contrasts the two companies in 2006/07. The acquisition of Aer Lingus would be a relatively small matter for Ryanair since its passenger number was due to grow by 8 million in 2007 without a takeover of Aer Lingus. Acquiring Aer Lingus would add only one year's growth to the Ryanair passenger numbers.

The promised gains for passengers from the 2006 proposed Ryanair acquisition of Aer Lingus were fare reductions of 2.5 per cent per year for four years and the removal of fuel surcharges. Based on the Aer Lingus prospectus estimate of an average short haul fare of €87.55 for 6.875 million passengers this promises fare savings worth some €175 million over four years to Aer Lingus passengers following the Ryanair takeover. On the other hand Aer Lingus has warned strongly that the takeover is not in the consumer interest and that the acquisition would secure for Ryanair a dominant position in the markets shown in Table 3.5. In the open EU market since 1 April 1997 the high market shares shown in Table 3.5 may be a sign of 'virtue, not vice' (Baumol, 1981).

The 2009 Ryanair offer price for Aer Lingus was a 28 per cent premium on the average closing price of an Aer Lingus share for the previous 30 days.

Table 3.4   Ryanair and Aer Lingus contrasted

	Ryanair	Aer Lingus	Date
Market Capitalization (€bn)	9.3	1.5	Feb 2007
Revenue (€m)	1693	1116	2006
Passengers (m)	43	9	2007
Average Fare (€)	49	88[†]	2006
Employees	3063	3556	2006
Fleet	113	35	2006
Profit after tax (€m)	301	77.3	2006
Assets (€bn)	5.76	1.88	2007

[†]Aer Lingus short haul average fare.

Table 3.5   Market shares of a Ryanair/Aer Lingus combined airline on Irish routes

	per cent
Austria	100
Belgium	100
France	75
Germany	80
Italy	92
Netherlands	100
Portugal	92
Spain	81
UK	77

Source: Aer Lingus, 1 December 2006.

The offer was worth €188 million to the Irish Government and €137 million to the employees of Aer Lingus. The Ryanair goal was to create a Ryanair/Aer Lingus combined airline able to challenge the three other major airline groups emerging in Europe. These were Air France-KLM, British Airways-Iberia, and Lufthansa-Swiss-Austrian-SAS-British Midland. Ryanair undertook to reinstate the Shannon–Heathrow route, to hand control over the Aer Lingus Heathrow slots to the Irish Government and to recognize trade unions in Aer Lingus. Ryanair undertook to grow the Aer Lingus brand with a promise of 1,000 extra jobs in the airline. Ryanair also claimed that the future of small independent airlines such as Aer Lingus was bleak and that Ryanair offered it and Ireland a better link than any of the other three emerging large airline groups in Europe. In response Aer Lingus stressed its role as an independent airline. It removed fuel surcharges and also promised to restore the Shannon–Heathrow service.

The Ryanair takeover bid for Aer Lingus is the first takeover attempt by a low-cost airline to acquire a former national airline. The changes in Aer Lingus in converting its short haul routes to low-cost operation since 2001 have made the takeover less dramatic than might be the case in other possible cases of a low-cost airline acquiring a legacy airline. The Aer Lingus product is substantially a low-cost product with the retention of seat allocation and the use of hub airports. Aer Lingus left the oneworld alliance in 2007 thus moving its focus to the low-cost point-to-point model. Goldman Sachs (2004) noted that 'the change in the Aer Lingus business model may have made it a less complimentary acquisition for the traditional airlines such as British Airways. The demise of Go and Buzz as low-cost sections of British Airways and KLM reflected the view that "Go was cannibalising British Airways routes" ' rather than the view that 'the low-cost revolution was an unstoppable force and that British Airways needed to be fighting in that market' (Cassani, 2003). The passengers per employee data in Table 3.3 also indicate that Aer Lingus has made considerable progress in increasing its productivity. Industrial relations costs and redundancy payments made would be at risk of being in vain if the airline were to revert to a legacy airline model.

While the first choice of Aer Lingus management is to remain an independent airline, its business model made it a more likely takeover target for a low-cost rather than full service airline. Given Ryanair's profitability it was the most likely bidder for the privatized Aer Lingus.

3.6 Ryanair and Low-cost Rivals

Table 3.6 shows the estimated market shares of the European low-cost airlines in 2009. Ryanair is the market leader at just under 33 per cent and easyJet is its closest rival at just over 23 per cent. Together they have 56 per cent of the market. Air Berlin is next at 14 per cent, followed by Norwegian with 5.4 per cent. The remaining 14 low-cost airlines each had a market share of less than five per cent.

Ryanair's advantages over the smaller low-cost airlines in Table 3.6 include first mover advantage due to the political change in Ireland in favour of low-cost airlines in 1984/6. The widespread brand recognition of Ryanair gives it the advantage in being the first website visited by passengers making bookings.

Ryanair's start-up mistakes in the period between 1985 and 1991 were financed by the Ryan family with funds from Guinness Peat Aviation dividends; there is high demand for low-cost aviation in island economies such as Ireland, Ryanair's first home base; Ryanair has gained from its use of regional and less congested airports neglected by legacy airlines in both reducing its airport costs and generating good will in the cities and regions now served.

Ryanair's low-costs make it difficult for the smaller low-cost airlines to enter Ryanair's markets. Ryanair's scale economies give it more leverage in negotiating with aircraft manufacturers and airport authorities than the smaller low-cost start-up airlines can exert. Ryanair's main rival in the low-cost aviation market in Europe therefore is easyJet. The two tend not to compete head to head and have a different market emphasis. easyJet's product includes flying to main airports, flexibility to take earlier or later flights and seeking business travellers in its marketing campaigns. The easyJet service has a Skytrax rating of three stars compared to the Ryanair two-star rating. Table 3.7 contrasts the two airlines. The accounting year for easyJet ends in September and for Ryanair it ends in March. The accounting periods overlap by only six months per year and both companies are growing rapidly, but the data indicates that Ryanair is the better performing airline.

Table 3.6   European low-cost airlines passenger numbers and market shares, 2009

	Passengers (millions)	Low cost market share (%)
Ryanair	65.3	32.8
easyJet	46.1	23.1
Air Berlin	27.9	14.0
Norwegian	10.8	5.4
Vueling	8.2	4.1
Wizz Air	7.8	3.9
Germanwings	7.2	3.6
Flybe	6.7	3.4
Monarch	3.7	1.9
Jet2	3.1	1.6
Wind Jet	3.0	1.5
bmibaby	2.9	1.5
Niki	2.6	1.3
Transavia France	1.3	0.7
Flyglobespan	1.2	0.6
Iceland Express	0.6	0.3
Blu-Express	0.4	0.2
Smart Wings	0.4	0.2
Total	199.2	

Sources: ATI, easyJet, Ryanair, UK CAA.

Note: Flyglobespan ceased trading in December 2009.

Table 3.7   easyJet and Ryanair contrasted, 2009/10

	easyJet Year end 30 September 09	Ryanair Year end March 10
Passengers (m)	45.2	66.5
Growth in passengers (%)	3.4%	13.5%
Average fare (€)	52	35
Total operating revenues (€bn)	3,040	2,988
Profit after tax (€m)	206	319
Fleet	181	247
Employees	5,563	7,032
Routes	422	1,100

Sources: easyJet annual results for year ended September 2008; Ryanair annual results for year ended March 2009.

3.7 The Future of Ryanair

The future of Ryanair depends on three factors: the views of passengers, how Ryanair organizes its production of air transport services, and the external operating environment's impact on the airline. The consumer assessment of Ryanair is positive in terms of the rapid increase in its passenger numbers. There is a high level of repeat business and passenger numbers increased 4.6 fold between 2003 and 2009 from 13 million to 60 million passengers. There is little evidence that air passengers wish to revert to the full-fare, full-service legacy airline product and hub airports. A crucial factor for passengers is an airline's safety record and Ryanair has completed 21 years of safe operations.

On the production side Ryanair might face problems due to labour unionization and wage claims, increases in airport charges or if the airline's management failed to control costs. In February 2007 Ryanair won a Supreme Court case in Ireland against both a trade union and the Labour Court concerning its industrial relations procedures and the use of legislation to secure union negotiating rights where a large majority of the staff were not union members. Ryanair's criticisms of airport charges remain strong at Stansted and Dublin and it promotes inter-airport competition. In December 2008, it won a European Court of First Instance case against the European Commission fine arising from its hub at Charleroi airport. In early 2009 Ryanair also won its case at the Aviation Appeals Panel in Dublin against the Commission for Aviation Regulation in relation to the high cost and large size of Terminal 2 at Dublin Airport.

The Ryanair fleet has an average age of 2.5 years and its new aircraft produce 50 per cent less emissions, 45 per cent less fuel burn and 45 per cent less noise per seat mile thus reducing its exposure both to fuel price rises and environmental levies. However, since Ryanair fares are lower than charged by other airlines the impact of fuel prices and flat environmental taxes on fares is likely to be greater, other things being equal. Environmental taxes based on actual emissions reflect the lower environmental costs of Ryanair compared to airlines with fleets of older aircraft serving congested airports. In 2008/9 fuel accounted for 45 per cent of Ryanair's operating costs, but as a result of lower fuel prices, this fell to 34.6 per cent in 2009/10. The high fuel prices, however, have not reduced the competitiveness of Ryanair.

The current projections are for passenger traffic to grow to 85 million in 2013 with a fleet by then of 299 aircraft. Doganis (1992) attributed the phenomenal growth of Ireland–Britain air services after deregulation in 1986 to 'the special characteristics of this market, notably the large Irish population in the UK and a very substantial volume of seaborne ferry traffic which was ripe for diversion as fare levels fell. It is unlikely that deregulation elsewhere will have such a profound effect of doubling traffic in two years.' Doganis, inventor of 'distressed state airline syndrome' and, sometime chief executive of Olympic Airways which exemplified distressed state airline syndrome, joined the board of easyJet in 2006.

Ryanair is the largest scheduled international airline with 66 million passengers in 2009/10 and a 14 per cent growth rate in passenger numbers. This phenomenal growth in passenger numbers has had a profound effect far beyond the initial international deregulation between Dublin and London in 1986. The Ryanair model has been most successfully exported.

References

Aer Lingus (2006a), Initial Public Offering Prospectus, Dublin, September.
Aer Lingus (2006b), Fly High with Aer Lingus, Chairman's Statement, December.
Aer Lingus (2008), Rejection by Aer Lingus of Ryanair Proposal, 1 December.
Association of European Airlines Yearbook (2005), Brussels.
Association of European Airlines Yearbook (2007), Brussels.
Barrett, S. (1997), The implications of the Ireland-UK airline deregulation for an EU internal market, *Journal of Air Transport Management*, vol. 3, no. 2, pp. 67–73.
Barrett, S. (1999), Peripheral market entry, product differentiation, supplier rents and sustainability on the deregulated European aviation market- a case study, *Journal of Air Transport Management*, no. 5, pp. 21–30.
Barrett, S. (2000), Airport competition in the deregulated European aviation market, *Journal of Air Transport Management*, no. 6, pp. 13–27.
Barrett, S. (2004), The sustainability of the Ryanair model, *International Journal of Transport Management*, no. 2, pp. 89–98.
Barrett, S. (2006), Commercialising a national airline- the Aer Lingus case study, *Journal of Air Transport Management*, no. 12, pp. 159–167.
Baumol, W. (1982), Contestable Markets: An Uprising in the theory of industrial structure, *American Economic Review*, vol. 72, pp. 1–15.
Byrne, P. (2004), *Fuelled by belief, The Cityjet Story*, Dublin, Liffey Press.

Cassani, B. (2003), *Go, An Airline Adventure*, London, Time Warner.

Davy Securities (2006a), Ryanair as a consumer growth company, Dublin, March.

Davy Securities (2006b), Aer Lingus, Dublin, June.

Doganis, R. (1992), *The Airport Business*, London, Routledge.

Doganis, R. (2002), *Flying Off Course, the Economics of International Airlines*, Third Edition, London, Routledge.

easyJet (2006), Preliminary Results, November.

Flynn, P. and McAuley, D. (1998), Report of Enquiry into the Industrial Dispute at Dublin Airport, Dublin, Government Publications.

Goldman Sachs (2004), Evaluation of ownership options regarding Aer Lingus plc, Dublin, Department of Transport.

Government of Ireland (1985), White Paper on Tourism Policy.

Insead (2003), Note on the European Airline Industry, Fontainebleau.

O'Leary, M. (2007), Ryanair roadshow presentation, Trinity College Dublin, January 29.

Ryanair Holdings (2006a), Annual Report and Financial Statement 2005/6.

Ryanair Holdings (2006b), Proposed Acquisition of Aer Lingus Group plc, October 23.

Ryanair Holdings (2008a), Half Year Results.

Ryanair Holdings (2008b), Ryanair Offers to Merge with Aer Lingus, December.

Share, B. (1986), *The Flight of the Iolar, The Aer Lingus Experience 1936–1986*, Dublin, Gill and Macmillan.

Skytrax Passenger Opinions (2007), January.

Williams, G., Mason, K. and Turner, S. (2003), Market Analysis of Europe's Low Cost Airlines, Air Transport Research Report 9, Cranfield.

Chapter 4

Airline Strategy: Keeping the Legacy Carrier Competitive. How Can Mature Airlines Stay Ahead in the Low-fare Airline Era?

Alan Gogbashian and Thomas Lawton

4.1 Introduction

Air France, British Airways, PanAm, Qantas, Swissair, Lufthansa, KLM, Aer Lingus, Olympic, Iberia, Aeroflot, Alitalia – these are just a few of the brands which, for decades, represented passenger air travel around the world. Not long ago, many of these airlines were state-owned, had entrenched monopolistic route rights and enjoyed quasi-diplomatic status by 'flying the flag' for the country with which their brand name was synonymous. Today the industry looks radically different. Of those same airlines, PanAm and Swissair no longer exist, Alitalia and Olympic teeter on the verge of collapse, and Air France has merged with KLM. Aer Lingus has reinvented itself as a low-cost carrier and the remainder, with varying degrees of success, have sought to remain significant players in an increasingly liberalized industry. Market deregulation, the privatization of state-owned carriers and the onslaught of new competitors, especially in the form of low-fare airlines, have caused the former flag carriers to rethink their business models. Cost efficiencies, service restructuring and profit maximization have come to the fore, as the 'flag carrier' has been superseded by the 'legacy carrier', a label used to differentiate mature airlines from the myriad of new carriers launched since deregulation began in the US in the late 1970s.

Most recent industry success stories have tended to involve start-up low-fare airlines (LFAs) rather than legacy carriers. The nimble, ultra-lean business models of the LFAs often make the legacy carriers look cumbersome, anachronistic and financially unappealing. This raises legitimate questions: is there a future for the mature legacy carrier in an industry which is undergoing rapid change and where further consolidation is predicted by some as the only way mature airlines can hope to survive? Can the legacy carrier survive by organic growth alone? If so, what strategy can they adopt, not only to survive, but to once again be forerunners in a very crowded market?

In this chapter, we answer these questions by identifying mature airlines that have recently transitioned from disappointing financial performance to consistent financial growth and, in doing so, have managed to remain powerful competitive forces in liberalized markets. Having identified the standout airlines within this category, we proceed to discuss strategies and models that have been successfully developed and implemented by these airlines to achieve financial success. This highlights existing trends and potential directions for other legacy carriers attempting to respond to changing competitive dynamics around the globe.

4.2 Identifying Turnaround

The airlines examined in this chapter were selected according to a number of criteria. First, in order to qualify as 'mature' companies, they had to have been in existence before deregulation of the airline industry began under the Airline Deregulation Act of 1978 in the United States. The 1978 Act was chosen for this purpose as it was very much an historical turning point. It paved the way for international liberalization of the industry, ushered in an era of new competition for legacy carriers and was subsequently emulated in Australia, the European Union, Japan and many other airline markets around the world.

Second, in order to discount very small airlines and now-defunct airlines from the scope of the project, only those airlines that have featured in the top 150 revenue-earners in the industry every year since 1997 were included. The year 1997 was chosen as the first one for financial data collection as archived financial data on the top 150 revenue-earners was only available from the trade magazine *Airline Business* from 1997 onwards. Commencing in 1997 offered the additional benefit of providing an arc of data spanning the last decade.

Third, airlines that have merged or were acquired by another company since 1997 were not considered (for example, Air France and KLM were not considered since they have now fully merged and operate as Air France-KLM).

Some 70 airlines qualified according to these criteria. 'Net results' (profit after all costs, tax, exceptional items and contributions from subsidiaries) for a decade from 1997 to 2007 in respect of each of these airlines were then analysed in order to ascertain which had successfully experienced 'turnaround'. 'Net results' were chosen over possible alternative financial indictors, such as revenue, as changes in airline revenue can be very much dependent on economic and regulatory factors beyond management's control. In contrast, net result also takes into account how successfully management controls costs. Also, increased revenue may indicate market growth but not necessarily profitability. It is therefore a more appropriate indicator for identifying those airlines which have improved performance through deliberate management strategies.

In order to qualify as a successful 'turnaround', the airline had to have experienced unremarkable, poor or declining financial performance for the former part of the 1997–2007 period, and at least three years of consistent growth leading up to 2007. Airlines with wildly and consistently oscillating profits and losses were discounted (for example, Lufthansa), as were airlines that seemingly had experienced turnaround but then dramatically slumped towards the end of our time frame (for example, British Airways and Iberia). Consistently outstanding performers without periods of major stagnation or decline were also discounted (for example, Singapore Airlines and Emirates Airlines). The aim was to pinpoint companies that had emerged from *consistent underperformance* to *consistent growth*. No objective statistical formula was applied to measure turnaround. Rather, curves were drawn to help visualize downward and upward trends in performance.

Applying the methodology just outlined, eight airlines were identified as achieving turnaround:

- Aeroflot Russian Airlines
- Air Canada
- ANA All Nippon Airways
- LAN Airlines
- Qantas
- TAM Brazilian Airlines
- Thai Airways International
- Turkish Airlines.

Figures 4.1–4.8 below depict the turnaround trajectory of each of these airlines during our chosen timeframe.

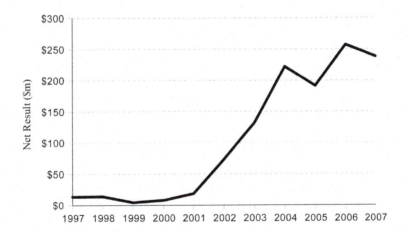

Figure 4.1   Financial performance of Aeroflot 1997–2007

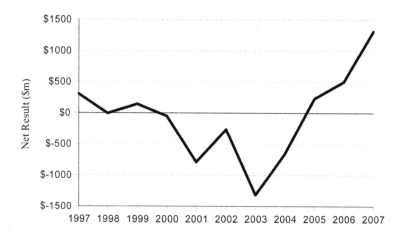

Figure 4.2   Financial performance of Air Canada 1997–2007

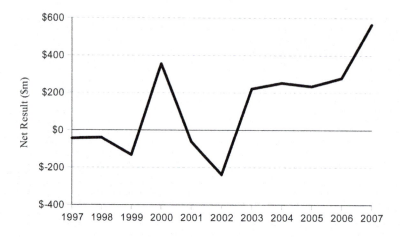

Figure 4.3   Financial performance of ANA 1997–2007

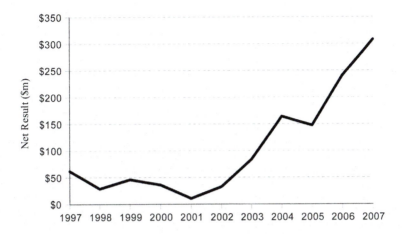

Figure 4.4   Financial performance of LAN 1997–2007

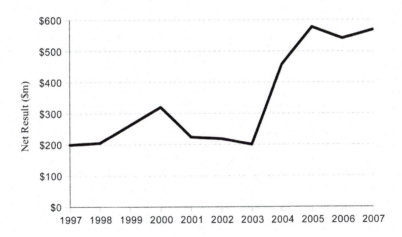

Figure 4.5   Financial performance of Qantas 1997–2007

Air Transport in the 21st Century

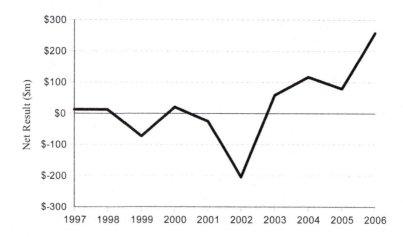

Figure 4.6   Financial performance of TAM 1997–2006

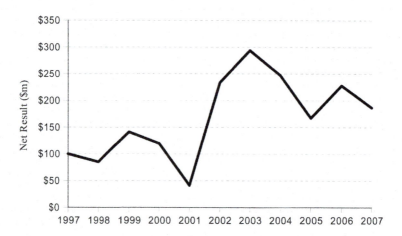

Figure 4.7   Financial performance of Thai 1997–2007

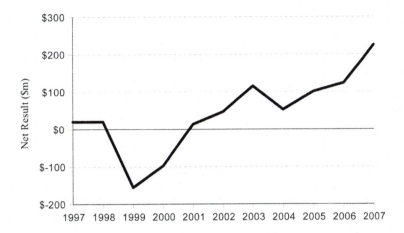

Figure 4.8   Financial performance of THY 1997–2007

Coincidentally, the eight turnaround airlines listed above represent a geographical mix spanning North America, South America, Europe, the Middle East, Asia and Australasia. Each of these airlines was contacted to request interviews with senior management and access to internal data. Six agreed to cooperate with our study[1] and ultimately case studies were developed around five of these: Aeroflot, Air Canada, ANA, LAN and TAM. Our findings were compared and contrasted in order to identify key commonalities and differences between the five case airlines. This comparative data analysis fed directly into our key conclusions and recommendations for legacy airline leaders.

4.3 Global Turnaround at Aeroflot, Air Canada and ANA

Of the five turnaround airlines studied, three –Air Canada, ANA and Aeroflot – can be best described as 'big improvers' (companies that introduce a compelling new value proposition or significantly more efficient business model, enabling them to refashion and recapture established markets).[2] Air Canada has gone from losses of $809 million six years ago to a net profit of $1.3 billion by 2007 and ANA has gone

---

1   Interviews were also conducted with managers at a sixth company, Thai Airways, but insufficient data was collected overall to construct a comprehensive case study of this airline's turnaround.

2   For a more detailed explanation of big improver turnaround strategy, see Finkelstein, Harvey and Lawton (2007) *Breakout Strategy: meeting the challenge of double-digit growth* (McGraw-Hill, New York).

from chronic loss making to net profits of $565 million in 2007, while Aeroflot has seen its net profit rise from US$4.5 million in 1999 to $238 million in 2007. In doing so, these airlines and the managers who run them, have gone on to receive a variety of industry awards and recognition. These are airlines that successfully deploy a compelling new value proposition to existing and potential customers, sustained by a significantly more innovative and efficient business model. By 'value proposition' we mean 'the offer of a product or a set of related products that a company makes to a customer, including all the experiences that go with making the purchase – before, during and after the purchase itself' (Finkelstein et al., 2007, p. 180). Some examples of improvement include Air Canada's radical reworking of its fare structures to provide customers with an à la carte approach to pricing, allowing them to pick from five branded fares each with its own price points and attributes. By purchasing a slightly higher fare bracket, it increased the flexibility. Its success sparked the airline to extend this fare mechanism to its international operations by early 2006. All tickets were sold as on a one-way basis and it did not require a Saturday night stay or advanced purchase. The transparent pricing structure had no hidden rules or restrictions and customers felt confident using the aircanada.com website to purchase their seats and subsequently more than 60 per cent of its domestic sales was generated by this channel (Flint, 2006; Hampton, 2006).

The term 'business model' is best defined as: 'The unique configuration of resources and processes that enables the organization to deliver its value proposition, synchronizing market perception and corporate reality' (Finkelstein et al., 2007, p. 20). Instances of re-engineering and enhanced business models for Air Canada included installing new seats in all of its aircraft, with lie-flat beds in business as well as audio/video on demand on every seat on every aircraft with more than 70 seats, while it also included innovative design features like Air Canada's mood lighting (Flint, 2006; Atkinson, 2007). Instances of re-engineered and enhanced business models at ANA included the seat covers being treated by using a photo-semiconductor technique that gives the fabric more resistance to bacteria and to odours. The seats are also made of lighter carbon fibre saving 40,000 litres of fuel a year for a 777. It also uses 2-D bar code technology allied with mobile phone telephony and the internet to replace the traditional airport check-in. Its improved reliability is evident as it has only a one-minute tolerance for flight delays (Japan Transportation Scan, 2002; Thomas, 2006).

Aeroflot's aggressive new service standards, improved fleet utilization, increased flight frequencies and better connection with Skyteam partners has attracted many high-yield passengers to its carrier as its unit yield increased from six USc/RPK in 2003 to around 8.25 by 2006 (*Aviation Strategy*, 2007). Its enhanced business model includes a Sabre reservation system which gives it an immediate international presence and the introduction of self-service check-in kiosks.

All three of these airlines invested in improving their reputation by boosting their brand equity. Aeroflot has been the most radical in this regard as its share of the domestic market has increased from 13 per cent in 2006 to 18 per cent by the following year (Aeroflot Annual Report, 2005; Endres, 2007), but ANA also implemented a very intentional programme to consolidate its brand (Ionides, 2004). Air Canada sought to reposition its brand in line with its new efforts for improved customer service as well as modernizing its livery (Knibb, 2006). Behind all of these initiatives is the basic assumption that the 'old way of the airline industry' is dead, with Robert Atkinson, head of Sales for Air Canada in the UK and Ireland, unequivocally asserting the new ethos underpinning turnaround success: 'The legacy model was broken and beyond repair. We are not going back to where we were.'

Air Canada, ANA and Aeroflot have also challenged existing business model assumptions and radically overhauled the way they make money. Routes and fleet have been simplified at all three airlines, with special care being taken at Aeroflot and Air Canada to strengthen possibilities for transit traffic through Moscow (Sakhnova and Melnikova, 2006) and Toronto (Atkinson, 2007) respectively. Aeroflot financed the building of a new $430 million terminal at Moscow's Sheremetyevo airport which will allow it to transfer domestic and international traffic more efficiently boosting its profits by around $20 million per annum (Aviation Strategy, 2007). Aeroflot's new route strategy, implemented in 2000, saw its network cut back to 90 streamlined high margin destinations. Extra high margin routes, such as those to and from European capitals, saw daily frequencies increase from one to three as international passengers account for 62 per cent of Aeroflot's revenues (Ivanov, 2001; *Aviation Strategy*, 2007). Staffing cuts have been made at all three airlines and ancillary businesses have been spun off at Air Canada[3] (Field, 2006) and ANA (*Japan Times*, 2007) in order to achieve a leaner, more focused group structure. For instance, the spinning-off of Air Canada's frequent flier programme, Aeroplan, brought US$200 million into the group and created a valuation worth around US$1.4 billion – showing how value may be surfaced in less obvious aspects of the business (Michaels and Chipello, 2006). In all three cases, new leadership was introduced to radically rework the business model and, most importantly, to oversee the unlearning of poor practices and establish a new corporate culture committed to delivering the revised business model. All those interviewed credit the new leadership with introducing and managing the changes needed to achieve turnaround.

Although patterns and trends among these three airlines are remarkably consistent considering the different continents they represent, there are also some noteworthy differences between them. Unlike Air Canada and Aeroflot, ANA is not a major network carrier, in that the majority of its business is domestic – 5,887 weekly domestic flights – and it holds 47 per cent of this market in 2006. Its

---

3　Air Canada was the pioneer of selling 'extras' along with 'up selling', as ancillary revenues grew by 17 per cent in 2007 when compared to the previous year. This additional $210 million reflects the carrier's success in persuading 45 per cent of its passengers to purchase extras or to 'buy up' to a higher fare category (Field, 2008).

international operations are currently secondary, although that is about to change as ANA consolidates its presence at Tokyo Haneda and focuses on expanding its Chinese network[4] (Thomas, 2006). Secondly, the airlines differ in their vision statements. ANA's vision ('To become Asia's number one airline in terms of quality, customer satisfaction and value creation') is both external and internal in scope and is clearly articulated throughout its marketing and sales materials. Aeroflot's vision ('To be a top five European airline in terms of service') is more regionally focused, while Air Canada does not appear to have a clear, publicly available vision laid out in written form. This is perhaps surprising considering how strategic and successful Air Canada has been in executing its new business model and raises the question as to how significant a role vision statements make in facilitating big improvement turnaround. Finally, Air Canada is the only airline of the three to have radically leveraged up its value proposition on price. Although ANA carries out domestic promotions on fares, this falls short of Air Canada's simple, transparent, sub-branded series of fares, the lowest of which matches WestJet, its low-fare domestic rival (Merrill Lynch, 2007).

4.4 Latin American Turnaround at LAN and TAM

LAN and TAM are also turnaround success stories but they have followed a different path to Aeroflot, Air Canada and ANA. LAN has increased in size 10 times since 1995, while TAM has gone from a loss of $24 million in 2001 to net profits of $256 million in 2006.[5] Both are fully committed to a strong customer-focused value proposition and stand apart from competitors in the region because of the strength of their service-oriented culture. However, neither appears to have gone through a radical market overhaul and corporate restructuring in the way our other three case companies did. In the case of LAN, growth appears to have been achieved by exploiting the airline's strength in the cargo sector to offset any unexpected downturns in the passenger market (Dempsey, 2004). 40 per cent of LAN's revenues come from cargo, compared to six per cent at British Airways and three per cent at American Airlines. This gives LAN the unique ability to breakeven with a load factor of 56 per cent compared to one of 73 per cent if it was relying on a more orthodox passenger-cargo mix (Selman, 2007). In addition, LAN has grown organically by aggressively accessing new Latin American markets and setting up airlines beyond its home country of Chile – in Peru, Ecuador and Argentina (Knibb, 2002). LAN Peru has a domestic share of 85 per cent, while LAN Ecuador has a 24 per cent international share and LAN Argentina

---

4   Ionides (2008) states that Air China and All Nippon Airways are expanding their codeshare arrangements to cover 532 international and 233 domestic one-way flights per week by September 2008.

5   TAM had an accident in July 2007 that claimed 199 lives – to avoid distortion, data was taken from 1997 to 2006.

has a market share of about 27 per cent (Field, 2008). In this sense LAN has been successful through international expansion, premised on what Finkelstein, Harvey and Lawton (2007) call a 'boundary breaker' strategy. This is where a company carries a winning business formula from one geographically defined market space into others. In LAN's case, this was enabled through a leadership team that knew how to expand and promote the LAN brand for quality and reliability from a domestic into a regional force (Selman, 2007).[6] LAN CEO Enrique Cueto sees the airline's rigorous commitment to customer service as the secret to making LAN's regional expansion a success: 'If you ask someone going to Asia what airline they want to fly, even if it's someone who's never been to Asia, they'll say Singapore Airlines. They know that airline is famous and what is the basis of that fame: Service. In this industry, the image is everything and that image is created by the service that is given.' (Dempsey, 2004)

Similar to our earlier case examples, TAM's turnaround was 'big improver' in nature but unlike the other companies looked at, this was prompted mainly by a combination of three external events: strong growth in the Brazilian economy (Regalado, 2007), the decline of former market leader Varig and the spur of increased competition provided by low-fare competitor, Gol. Although Gol had initially impacted negatively on TAM's profits, it forced the airline to adopt a more cost-efficient business model and ultimately improve performance (Adese, 2006). The airline successfully leveraged its reputation for customer-service (it has a 97 per cent average on-time record (Patrick, 2007)) and strong brand identity in Brazil to position itself as a more reliable, high quality alternative to Gol. It offers a different set of flight products to that of Gol such as: stronger network; more direct flights; high frequency; loyalty program; in-flight entertainment; and a meal service. This made it particularly attractive to the business segment of the market and by 2008, TAM accounted for more than half the air traffic in Brazil (Pereira, 2006; Endres, 2007; Uphoff, 2008). It was also able to improve its proposition on price, bringing prices down to make them competitive with Gol's, but still allowing a small price premium in recognition of additional service value by customers (Shifrin, 2005).

Both LAN and TAM have clear visions. LAN's vision is to be one of the 10 best airlines in the world, while TAM's is to be the largest and most lucrative airline in Latin America (TAM Annual Report, 2006). Interestingly, of our five case airlines, TAM's is the only vision statement that makes no reference to quality – it is purely about size of operations and profits. This seems at odds with the airline's strategy of differentiating itself from competitors through customer service, suggesting that the airline's stated and actual strategy may not be aligned. This perhaps reinforces the argument that TAM's turnaround is primarily due to a fortuitous combination of external events rather than to an intentional, organic strategy for improvement and growth.

---

6   On a much smaller scale, Aeroflot is, like LAN, seeking to expand its market by consolidation.

4.5 Common Turnaround Determinants

All of the turnaround airlines we looked at shared certain additional characteristics. All five had engaged in simplifying their businesses by reducing costs as much as possible across all aspects of the airline (Duffy, 2004; Thomas, 2006; Betts, 2006; Atkinson, 2007; Selman, 2007). This appears to have been a universal approach in response to high oil prices and increased industry rivalry from low-fare airlines. For example, ANA implemented an action plan to cut ¥30 billion from its cost base annually to April 2006, with ¥20 billion coming from personnel and the remainder from operations (Ionides, 2004). However, none of the airlines studied had chosen to reposition themselves as a low-fare carrier. All five continue to operate as full-service airlines known primarily for quality of service over bargain basement pricing. This is particularly evident in the special attention the turnaround airlines give to servicing the business traveller market (Ruggia, 2003; Duffy, 2004; Barroso, 2006) which, in TAM's case for example, makes up 65 per cent of the passenger market. Cost reductions have focused on non-customer facing aspects of the business, with the customer value proposition remaining central. Atkinson (2007) points out: 'We had to put on products which customers actually wanted to buy, not what we thought we ought to sell'. It is this commitment to customer focus which Air Canada sees as the key to moving from legacy carrier to 'loyalty carrier' (Knibb, 2006). All five airlines mention heavy investments in information technology as being a key part of ensuring long-term cost efficiencies (Dempsey, 2004; Aeroflot Annual Report, 2005; Patrick, 2007; Atkinson, 2007; ANA Annual Report, 2007). Moreover, all five clearly claim that they have no desire to be flag carriers for their country, with the pursuit of profit being the primary motivation for their existence.

Determined and focused leadership was also a defining characteristic of all the airlines we examined. All interviewees mentioned that their airline's leadership had played a key role in the airline's turnaround (albeit with TAM the association was more in relation to former CEO Rolim Amaro than the present incumbent). CEO Valery Okulov at Aeroflot, CEO Enrique Cueto at LAN and former CEO Robert Milton at Air Canada acquired almost celebrity-status through their efforts in driving turnaround. An emphasis on staff training and human resource development initiatives were also a consistent feature of each turnaround airline, with notable features including the opening of the LAN Corporate University in 2006 and the consolidation of TAM's Training Academy (Skrin, 2005; LAN Annual Report, 2006; Patrick, 2007).

Except for TAM, all the turnaround airlines in our study are members of a global airline alliance,[7] each giving credit to the alliance for contributing in some form to the airline's turnaround. Air Canada and ANA credit Star Alliance with helping to reduce cost, focus revenue streams and maximize profits (Atkinson, 2007; Endo and Nakamura, 2007), with ANA stating that Star brings a net benefit

---

7   TAM was accepted to become a Star alliance member in October 2008.

of ¥15bn to the company annually (Thomas, 2006). Aeroflot estimates that the revenue impact of joining SkyTeam is worth around $20 million per year and it also credits SkyTeam with helping to catalyse improvements in its customer service and overall value proposition through the alliance's emphasis on improvements in 20 different areas of Aeroflot's business (Concil, 2007; Aviation Strategy 2007). LAN points out how Oneworld gives it 'global reach' (Selman, 2007). It is worth noting here that successfully leveraging alliance membership can bring benefits to airlines across all dimensions of a value proposition:[8] *price* is potentially made more competitive through joint activity cost savings and revenue connectivity; product *features* are improved through sharing of innovative practices and know-how; *quality* is augmented as customers have access to a global network with integrated interlining facilities and coordinated schedules; *support* improves as customers can receive assistance from all alliance members around the world and are not solely reliant on representatives of the airline in their country of origin; *availability* improves through multiple access points and integrated route networks provided by the combined presence of all member airlines of the alliance; and *reputation* improves as lesser-known airlines are given a boost to their credibility because of the company they keep. ANA is an excellent example of this last point, as the number of its non-Japanese customers grew significantly after joining Star, due to Western business people trusting the Star brand, despite not necessarily having heard of ANA (Endo and Nakamura, 2007). LAN also notes that Oneworld alliance membership helped Western passengers perceive the airline more positively in terms of safety and reliability compared to other Latin American carriers (Selman, 2007).

4.6 Observations and Conclusions

The practices and trends we noted in the case studies leads us to make six common observations. From these, management recommendations can be generated about the strategies and structures employed to revive the performance of mature legacy carrier airlines.

First, a focus on profit maximization is the foundation of turnaround. This may seem like a simplistic conclusion and a business 'no-brainer' but it has often been rather neglected by legacy carriers in favour of political and social concerns. The airlines we consider do not act like flag carriers. Flag carriers typically behave as unofficial representatives of their home countries and maintain loss-making routes for political reasons. The airlines we studied are motivated by generating as much profit as possible. This involves aggressive cost-cutting exercises (referred to by some of the airlines as 'simplifying the business'), revenue-maximizing initiatives and strategic investment in information technology.

---

8   The six pillars of a value proposition are detailed in Finkelstein et al., 2007.

Second, quality of service should not be compromised. All of the turnaround airlines considered in our study are committed to high service standards and place reliability and quality as central to their brand's identity. Although cost-cutting has taken place at all of these airlines, this has not usually directly affected the level of service offered to customers. The cost-cutting is limited to 'behind the scenes' activities not directly facing the customer. Indeed, rather than cutting back on service, the airlines studied are constantly trying to raise their standards through innovation and greater customer focus. Clearly, morphing into a low-fare carrier has not been the preferred turnaround strategy of the airlines studied.

Third, new leadership plays a key role in achieving big improver turnaround. All the airline improvements we studied were shaped by strong and effective leadership. For *big improvers* (four out of five of our cases), new leadership was brought in to turn around the whole organization and impacted the airline in respect of both technical and cultural aspects of the business. For the other turnaround airline (LAN), focused, innovative leadership helped define its success. Most of the airlines' leadership teams have adopted clear vision statements that help define and embed their strategic objectives right across the company. The leadership teams of the airlines studied are noted for excellent communication and people skills. This is not 'ivory tower' leadership conducted from a distance and in a very hierarchical fashion, as has often been the case at legacy airlines.

Fourth, membership of an alliance network acts as a turnaround catalyst. Four out of the five airlines studied were members of one of the three big global alliances and spoke of membership in very positive terms. Membership of an alliance has the potential to assist turnaround by increasing revenues through code-sharing or other commercial partnerships, cutting costs through economies of scale generated by the alliance's purchasing power and the sharing of good practices and IT, boosting the customer value proposition by providing increased routes and global service, speeding up the increase of service standards in order to meet alliance criteria and boosting the reputation of member airlines' brands through association. It should be noted of course that joining an alliance is not in and of itself a guarantee of business success.

Fifth, regional consolidation can contribute to turnaround. Two of the airlines studied (LAN and Aeroflot) claimed that regional consolidation was a key aspect of their strategy – overwhelmingly so in the case of LAN. New markets can be served and therefore new revenues generated by pursuing liberalization of the regional industry and moving into lucrative but poorly served territories.

Finally, investment in staff development and management-employee relations underpins turnaround. All of the turnaround airlines studied invested in improving relations with their staff and in providing comprehensive training for employees in technical skills, customer service and change management, especially revised corporate culture and strategic aims. Several have dedicated training academies, exclusively devoted to training and staff development. Excellent communication between airline management and staff during times of strategic change within the airline also characterize the turnaround airlines.

When taken together, these six observations provide a powerful set of principles and practices that can be weaved together into a successful turnaround strategy. As is illustrated throughout this book, aviation competition is intense across the world and legacy carriers have struggled to adapt to increased customer expectations and new competitor threats. Our study provides a ray of hope for legacy airline managers everywhere, illustrating how not only to keep pace with but move ahead of low-fare airlines and other new entrants in the struggle for passengers, markets and profits.

References

Adese, C. (2006), 'TAM and Gol fill Varig's vacuum', *Airline Business*, vol. 22, Issue 8, p. 16.

Aeroflot Annual Report (2005), <www.aeroflot.ru/eng/company.

AK&M (Russia) Information Agency (2007), 6 June 2007.

ANA Annual Report (2007), <www.ana.co.jp>.

Atkinson, R. (2007), Interview with Alan Gogbashian, MBA Project, Tanaka Business School, 7 December.

Aviation Strategy (2007), Aeroflot battles through chaotic times in Russia, Issue 11, April, pp. 11–20.

Barroso, L. (2006), 'Strategic Overview Presentation', TAM Day 2006, 8 December.

Betts, C. (2006), 'Financial Overview Presentation', TAM Day 2006, 8 December.

Concil, A. (2007), 'Interview with Aeroflot CEO Valery Okulov', *REA Oreanda*, 17 August.

Dempsey, M. (2004), 'Flying High,' *Latin Finance*, October, Issue 161, p. 35.

Duffy, P. (2004), 'A Decade of Change', *Air Transport World*, vol. 41, Issue 4, pp. 28–30.

Endres, G. (2007), Arranged marriages, *Airline Business*, March, pp. 54–56.

Endres, G. (2007), Staying power, *Airline Business*, November, pp. 26–29.

Endo, T. and Nakamura, Y. (2007), Interview with Alan Gogbashian, MBA Project, Tanaka Business School, 7 December.

Field, D. (2006), 'ACEs high: Robert Milton', *Airline Business*, 22 August.

Field, D. (2008), Barrier Buster, *Airline Business*, November, pp. 48–52.

Field, D. (2008), Drive for more ancillaries picks up, *Airline Business*, March, p. 15.

Finkelstein, S., Harvey, C. and Lawton, T. (2007), *Breakout Strategy: meeting the challenge of double-digit growth*, McGraw-Hill, New York.

Flint, P. (2006), A different flight path, *Air Transport World*, April, 24–28.

Hampton, M. (2006), 'Flag carrier fights back', *Travel Weekly*, 24 February, p. 60.

Ionides, N. (2004), A Grand Plan, *Airline Business*, September, pp. 35–38.

Ionides, N. (2004), 'Yoji Ohashi's grand plan at ANA', *Airline Business*, 1 September.

Ionides, N. (2008), ANA, Air China add more flights to codeshare deal, *Air Transport Intelligence*, 15 September.

Ivanov, A. (2001), 'Aeroflot: New crew, new destinations', *Troika Dialog Research*, 12 March, p. 8.

The Japan Times (2007), 'ANA to sell 13 domestic hotels', 14 April.

Japan Transportation Scan (2002), 'ANA unveils group strategy to counter JAL-JAS alliance', 13 May.

Knibb, D. (2002), 'Winner Takes All', *Airline Business*, 1 October.

Knibb, D. (2006), 'Air Canada tweaks model', *Airline Business*, February, vol. 22, Issue 2, p. 14.

LAN Annual Report (2006), www.lan.com.

Merrill Lynch Global Transportation Conference Presentation (2007), 'Air Canada: Changing the Game', 13 June, p. 12.

Michaels, D. and Chipello, C. (2006), 'ACE in the hole', *The Wall Street Journal*, 27 April.

Patrick, K. (2007), Interview with Alan Gogbashian, MBA Project, Tanaka Business School, 7th December.

Pereira, E. (2006), 'Brazil's New Leader', *Air Transport World*, vol. 43 Issue 12, 1 December.

Regalado, A. (2007), 'Boss Talk: Flying High', *Wall Street Journal*, 22 January.

Ruggia, J. (2003), 'Nippon at your heels', *Travel Agent*, 5 May.

Sakhnova, E. and Melnikova, A. (2006), 'Aeroflot: A bird of prey?', *Deutsche UFG Company Research*, 16 March, p. 8.

Selman, J-C. (2007), Interview with Alan Gogbashian, MBA Project, Tanaka Business School, 7 December.

Shifrin, C. (2005), 'Wake-up call', *Airline Business*, 1 November.

Skrin (2005), 'Aeroflot Personnel Department Declared Best in Russia,' 19 July.

TAM Annual Report (2006), www.tam.com.br.

Thomas, G. (2006), 'ANA: All New Airline', *Air Transport World*, October, p. 32.

Uphoff, R. (2008), TAM boosts market share as Brazilian traffic jumps, Air *Transport Intelligence*, 11th September.

Chapter 5

Ancillary Revenues: The New Trend in Strategic Airline Marketing

John F. O'Connell

5.1 Introduction

Achieving profitability in the airline industry is becoming an increasingly difficult task with each passing year. Around $85 billion was erased from the industry balance sheets in 2009 (15 per cent down on 2008 figures) because of the recession, while historical financial data shows that the world carriers lost $49.1 billion between 2000 and 2009, which is an average loss per year of around $5.0 billion (IATA, 2009). Ancillary revenue[1] can go some way to clawing back those lost earnings. One of the oldest forms of ancillary revenue is in-flight sales of duty-free products, and for decades this was the solitary mechanism by which airlines could capture additional revenues from passengers while on-board. It proved lucrative despite the fact that many passengers had passed through airport duty-free shops prior to boarding their flight, as Generation Research (2009) pointed out that airlines were generating around $3 per passenger on in-flight retail in 2008 – a figure that has little changed since the mid 1990s. The indications are clear that passengers are willing to purchase products on board, as Korean Air and British Airways, for example, generated over $180 million and $140 million respectively from selling duty free items in 2008 (Generation Research, 2009). History suggests that airlines may have mismanaged the expectations of passengers as they have received all the perks of the trade (such as free baggage, meals, in-flight entertainment, and so on),[2] which were all encapsulated within the 'fare'. The industry operates in a hypercompetitive environment where the rivalry between carriers is very intense, and this forces airlines to set fares close to marginal costs or lower, which is a primary reason for the poor returns that this industry generates. Cargo was another area through which airlines made additional revenue from the flight, and this is an important component of the industry as it facilitates the transportation of perishable and high value goods that interlink

---

1 Ancillary revenues are incremental revenues that an airline earns after the fare has been paid and are generated either through the website or during the travel experience.

2 Ferry companies for example charge for meals, drinks, sleeping quarters, access the cinema, etc., yet airlines have bundled it all together and offer it as part of the fare.

the global supply chain. Traditional full service airlines that carry belly freight[3] are also subjected to excess competition from a large number of similar players, such as integrators (for example, FedEx), cargo divisions of scheduled airlines (for example, Korean Air)[4] and from other intermodal transport systems, such as shipping companies, trains and road transport. IATA (2010) reported that cargo produced $64 billion in revenues for the airline industry in 2008, dipping to $49 billion in 2009 as the result of the severe global recession, but is estimated to recover by 2010 reaching $61 billion in sales. Operating margins[5] for air cargo are discouraging as they averaged just over three per cent for 2008 (See Chapter 10 for an in-depth discussion on the air cargo industry). The cargo unit of Air France-KLM accounted for more than a third of the airline's losses ($614 million) for the fiscal year 2009/2010 (Barnard, 2010). Clearly, air cargo also struggles to generate adequate returns.

Airline yields[6] have continued to deteriorate over the last few decades as more entrants have joined the foray, and today, airline companies operate in fiercely competitive 'electronic markets' which have made fares very transparent – while this has also forced the archaic fare rules to be dismantled. This results in more 'Y fare' (unrestricted economy) passengers dropping down to lower fare buckets. In turn, the revenue management system encounters less demand for higher fares and so makes less available, leading to high load factors, but low yields. It is becoming more apparent that the traditional revenue management systems can no longer maximize revenues. Clearly, the industry needs to 'think outside the box' and devise new types of ideologies if it is to generate additional revenue streams. Starbucks, for example, has become a huge success story, yet its core product is concentric around the basic 'coffee bean'. The company has horizontally and vertically stretched that coffee bean by brewing multiple variations of different types of coffee, and has also added a whole array of associated products for sale, such as cakes, panini, salads, pastries, yoghurts, brewing equipment, tumblers, cups, and so on.

The 2009 SITA/Airline Business survey cited that the top two reasons why airlines are investing in Information Technology (IT) is to reduce costs, followed closely by its ability to increase revenues (Jenner, 2009). IT allows new business opportunities to be spawned from within the airlines' existing operations. One of the key areas that airlines are targeting today is ancillary revenue, as this has become an engine in which to drive revenues and is gaining much traction in airline boardrooms throughout the world. Its increasing importance to the industry

---

3   Cargo that is transported in the lower freight compartments of passenger aircraft.
4   Cargo generates up to 30 per cent of Korean Air's total revenues.
5   Operating margin is a measurement of what proportion of a company's revenue is left over after paying for both fixed and variable costs of production such as salaries, fuel, landing charges, etc. An airline with an operating margin of three per cent indicates that it makes $0.03 (before interest and taxes) for every dollar of sales.
6   The yield is the average fare per seat mile.

is evident – there have been numerous conferences and seminars dedicated to the subject all around the world, yet surprisingly, there is no academic research into the topic to date. IdeaWorks, a leading authority on the research of ancillary revenue, stated that airlines had generated around US$2.3 billion in ancillary revenues in 2006, but by 2008 this had jumped by 345 per cent to $10.2 billion (IdeaWorks, 2009). In fact, IATA expects that non-ticket revenue will make up 12 per cent of airline turnover[7] in 2010 (Moores et al. 2010). Ancillary revenues[8] are fast becoming the cornerstone of the new airline business model.

The mechanism that is driving the growth of ancillary revenue is the Internet: over the last 15 years, this has changed the landscape of airline distribution as more than a third of all sales globally have shifted to the Internet (Sobie, 2010). PhoCusWright is an authority on travel ecommerce and it completed such a study on the European market in 2009, which revealed that 69 per cent of the online sales stem from airline websites, while the remainder is derived from the online travel agents (PhoCusWright, 2009). It is evident that the proportion of travel booked online will continue to escalate: research from Yu (2008) estimated that 42 per cent of the revenues from Asia-Pacific based airlines will be Internet-based by 2010. Airline websites are applying increasing pressure on the major reservation platform suppliers or Global Distribution Systems (GDS). For decades, the GDS's have monopolised the distribution of airline seat inventory, which also captures the sale of hotel rooms and car hires – these are travel products that naturally complement the sale of an airline seat. In 2010, the three major GDS companies comprised of Amadeus, Sabre and Travelport, and collectively they supplied the global reservation platforms of: over 550 airlines; 90,000 hotel properties; and 30,000 car rental locations to almost half a million travel agencies. The total revenues that accrued from these transactions amounted to more than $268 billion in 2008 – clearly, the GDSs control a mammoth proportion of the world's global travel industry (PhoCusWright, 2010). However, there is a fertile opportunity for airlines to capture a chunk of this enormous market by encouraging passengers to book through the carriers' website, which appears to be gaining in momentum as the data quantifies that carriers are now beginning to impact the dominance of these intermediaries. Customer surveys by EzRez software discovered that 87 per cent of people who searched airline websites believed that airlines have the best travel deals (on items such as flights, hotels, insurance, car rental companies) on their sites (McDonald, 2009).

Unquestionably, ancillary revenue is fast becoming the next milestone for the industry as it has become a core competency within the marketing mix. Sabre Airline Solutions confirms the argument – it administered surveys across 90 airlines worldwide where a large proportion of the respondents believed that

---

7   This includes air cargo.

8   Ancillary Revenues can add more than $0.75 cents per RASM (Revenue per Available Seat Mile) to a mid-sized carrier if they adopt many of the ancillary components that are available today.

ancillary revenue will positively contribute to their bottom line results. Baggage fees, travel insurance and vacation packaging were rated among the highest revenue producers[9] (Sabre, 2009). A similar theme is echoed by the CEO of British Airways who also reiterated that ancillary revenues will be the next big paradigm shift in the industry (Walsh, 2009). The profit margins from ancillaries are much higher than the commodity based sale of airline seats, with estimates of gross profit margins up to 40 per cent, largely because of the low costs associated by selling through the web. It is clear that ancillary revenues will become a game changer for the industry. They fall into two categories:

1. Unbundle or à la carte products.
2. Commission-based ancillaries that are provided by third parties.

5.2 Unbundled Flight Products

This is the revenue that is generated from selling products or services separately, which traditionally have been included in the price of the airline ticket. Innovation in today's airline industry has stemmed from the low-cost carrier business model, and many concepts associated with budget airlines are gradually finding their way onto traditional network airlines – one of these pioneering developments has been ancillary revenues. The low-cost carriers began to disassemble the fare into various individual components, known as 'unbundled flight products', which included separate charges for items such as checked baggage, priority boarding in the case of unassigned seating, premium seating; onboard sales of drinks and food, and so forth. Allegiant Airlines is a low-cost carrier based in Las Vegas which has recorded 29 consecutive quarters of profitability to June 2009, and its net income for 2009 increased by 115 per cent over the previous year. It has become the global leader in turning ancillary revenues into profits, as this accounted for 30 per cent of its total revenues in 2009. Passengers travelling on Allegiant Airlines pay $5–25 per assigned seat per segment, $5-$8.50 for priority boarding, $15–20 per checked bag per segment, and $14 convenience fee to book a seat via the website.

Traditionally, airlines did not charge for the first two pieces of checked luggage unless they exceeded the overall weight limitation. Now baggage fees are one of the fastest growing items in a portfolio of unbundled products which were initiated by the low-cost carriers. Ryanair introduced the trend of charging for checked baggage back in 2005, and prior to this 80 per cent of its passengers were checking in luggage, but by 2010 less than 40 per cent did so – this allowed the carrier to remove a whole series of costs, while at the same time reducing the rate

---

9   Frequent Flyer Programmes are also an important revenue producing entity as American Airlines for example sold $1 billion worth of miles to Citibank, its credit card partner in September 2009. Frequent Flyer Programmes are a marketing tool, designed to enhance brand loyalty.

of mishandled baggage (Moores et al. 2010). This concept quickly spread across the globe, and baggage fees were introduced in the US in 2008 when oil prices soared, reaching $147 per barrel. Air fares around the world, particularly in the US, have fallen sharply since the onset of the recession, making baggage fees an increasing lifeline for the airline sector. IATA (2010) reported that the US airline industry lost $2.7 billion in 2009 (down considerably from its 2008 losses of $9.6 billion). However, there is a noticeable change to the financials of the US airline industry in recent years as profitability has strikingly improved. A new 'ethos' of generating more revenues without the cost of having to operate additional flights has evolved – ancillary revenues are quickly becoming a permanent fixture in the airline landscape.

Table 5.1 shows that the US airline industry collected a staggering $2.7 billion from checked baggage fees in 2009, up from $1.1 billion a year earlier. Delta Air Lines has amassed $481million, while American and United Airlines took in $475 million and $269 million respectively[10] in 2009. The US-based airlines are continuously earning more revenues quarter by quarter by charging for baggage – and have recorded an average increase of almost 48 per cent from the end of 2008 to the end of 2009.

Table 5.2 shows the pace at which Delta Air Lines has increased its bag charges, with the carrier extracting $9.44 per passenger in 2010, while three years earlier the carrier was only charging for bags that exceeded their weight limitation (which averaged out at $1.49 per passenger). In contrast, Southwest Airlines does not charge for baggage, but could potentially earn between $450 to $500 million per year if it implemented such a charge for the first and second checked bags. However, the carrier chooses to keep this as a differentiation strategy. Data by the Nielsen Co indicated that Southwest boosted its advertising spend by 20 per cent to $112.6 million during the first six months of 2009 in order to differentiate itself from its competitors through a 'bags fly free' campaign. Passenger traffic increased at Southwest by about five per cent during the third quarter of 2009 when compared with the same period one year earlier – it is highly speculated that passengers are switching from carriers that are charging for baggage, and also because the advertising campaign was positively impacting the public's awareness of baggage charges between rivals (*Seattle Times*, 2009). However, some operational and financial implications still remain as the IT platforms between carriers are not fully standardized to accommodate seamless interline baggage. For example, when passengers and their baggage interline between Egyptair (which does not charge for baggage) and United Airlines (which does charge for baggage), and then onto TAM (which does not charge for baggage), some IT systems are incompatible and not fully integrated, even from carriers within the same alliance.

---

10   Delta, United, Continental and US Airways all are charging $25 for the first bag and $35 for the second bag checked-in at the airport. Passengers who check in online on those four airlines will pay $23 for the first bag and $32 for the second as of 10 February 2010.

Table 5.1   Revenues (in $US millions) from baggage fees collected by US major airlines

4th Quarter 2009 Rank	Airline	4th Q 2008	1st Q 2009	2nd Q 2009	3rd Q 2009	4th Q 2009	Percentage change 4thQ 2008 to 4thQ 2009	Total 2009 revenue from baggage fees (US$ millions)
1	Delta	60.5	102.2	118.4	129.5	131.1	116.7 %	481.7
2	American	113.9	108.1	118.4	119.5	129.2	13.4 &	475.2
3	US Airways	93.8	94.2	104.1	111.4	122.5	30.6 %	432.3
4	Northwest	63.6	59.8	67.2	78.9	79.9	25.6 %	285.8
5	Continental	49.3	55.6	63.2	66.0	67.9	41.4 %	254.5
6	United	58.8	59.1	67.4	77.9	64.6	9.9 %	269.0
7	AirTran	12.7	30.9	40.5	40.2	34.3	170.1 %	146.0
8	Alaska	5.5	5.4	6.2	25.2	21.8	296.4 %	58.7
9	Frontier	10.0	12.5	13.5	14.9	14.4	44.0 %	55.2
10	Spirit	N/A	N/A	16.2	16.4	14.3	N/A	46.8
Industry Total[†]		498.6	577.9	669.6	739.8	736.1	47.6 %	$2,723.4

[†]A total of 21 carriers reporting their revenues from baggage fees.

Source: Bureau of Transport Statistics, Form 41; Schedule P1.2.

Table 5.2   The increasing charges for baggage issued by Delta Air Lines 2007–2010

Time period	Charges per passenger	Baggage criteria
3rd Quarter 2007	$1.49	Overweight and excess baggage fees
1st Quarter 2009	$7.59[†]	1st and 2nd bag fees
3rd Quarter 2009	$8.81[†]	1st and 2nd bag at-airport fees increased
2010 estimate	$9.44[†]	More increases in fees

[†]Figures include 2007 baseline charges of $1.49 from earlier overweight and excess bag charges.

Source: IdeaWorks and Delta Air Lines.

Airlines are continuing to push the boundaries of producing revenues from baggage: Spirit Airlines is evolving the concept one step further as it will charge $45 at the gate for carry-on baggage, or $30[11] if it is prepaid on the website, from August 1st, 2010 (Air Transport Intelligence, 2010). United Airlines has customized the travel experience by offering door-to-door baggage facilities (including skis or golf clubs), which enables customers in the continental US to conveniently ship their suitcases, while charges for using the service range from

---

11   Spirit's Fare Club members pre-reserving their carry-on bags in advance online also receive a $10 discount.

$149 to $179 depending on the length of the trip. Meanwhile, Air France-KLM passengers can receive a 30 per cent discount on standard excess baggage fees when booked through the website, which gives passengers the flexibility to add additional weight to their luggage, while it is probable that some passengers may not exceed the higher weight threshold – which is a gain for the carrier.

Price competition among carriers has become very aggressive and it is highly unlikely that baggage will become a component of the fare again, as otherwise it will make the carrier become disadvantaged on price based Internet searches. There has been commercial and academic research conducted on the willingness of passengers to pay for additional products or services that add convenience, comfort and value. Leflein Associates is an independent US-based market research company whose survey of over 1,000 US based travellers revealed that many would pay for extra perks (Alexander, 2006). Balcombe et al. (2009) conducted a survey of 568 passengers which focused on the in-flight experience on journeys of between 4.5 to 5.5 hours in duration, which is the approximate travelling time between the UK and Egypt or Turkey. Bayesian methods were applied to estimate a mixed logit specification, and the results indicated that passengers were willing to pay €22 for additional seat pitch (leg space). Over the past 10–15 years, leisure passengers have become more knowledgeable about air travel and ask more frequently for window, aisle or emergency exit row seats. It is only in recent years that airlines throughout the world have begun to capitalize on this, by charging for the privilege of acquiring these unique seats that hold value for the passenger. Espino et al. (2008) and Martin et al. (2008) also undertook research in this area by conducting a passenger survey of two virtual airlines that were operating between the Spanish domestic points of Gran Canaria and Madrid, where the flying time between the two destinations is 2.5 hours. The authors applied an economic model which calculated that passengers would be willing to pay between €15 and €33 for additional legroom in economy class. Premium carriers were paying close attention to the changing parameters of seat 'valuation', and airlines such as Air France[12] and Singapore Airlines, for example, began reacting to the market conditions by charging €50 and $50 respectively for exit-row seats in economy class on long-haul flights in 2008. Barcelona-based Vueling Airlines has unbundled the economy class seating configuration by offering passengers the choice of purchasing a middle seat for €30 and also provides an option to procure an extra large seat for €13, while Air Berlin soon thereafter introduced a fee for XL seats, based on sector distance. US Airways adopted a similar methodology by introducing a 'Choice Seat'[13] and allocated 16 per cent of its seat capacity to

---

12   Air France-KLM is optimizing all elements of its in-flight business. It is introducing a new, lighter short-haul seat on its single-aisle Airbus fleet from January 2010, which will increase fuel efficiency. The seat is jointly developed by the carrier and interiors specialist Recaro and it will weigh 9.1kg, which is a 40 per cent reduction when compared to its pre-existing seats.

13   Choice Seats are located in the aisle or window of the Coach cabin.

this preferred sales pool, which generated sales worth $5.3 million in 2008 (Air Transport Intelligence, 2009). JetBlue has also been very successful in developing new ancillary revenue streams through key initiatives such as 'Even More Legroom', with a 38-inch seat pitch on rows two to five and in emergency exit rows on their A320 cabins. JetBlue's 2nd Quarter 2008 earnings call to Wall Street reported that it will charge passengers $10 for the enlarged seat pitch on short-haul flights, $20 for medium-haul and $30 for long-haul trips, and the carrier expects to generate $40 million in incremental revenue in 2008 as a result of the unbundling (Seeking Alpha, 2008). Traditionally, airlines have also included seat assignments as part of the bundled travel package, but low-cost carriers pioneered the change in this aspect of the business. Asia's largest low-cost carrier, AirAsia, charges around $1.30 to pre-select a seat, and passengers who choose not to purchase an assigned seat will be designated one at random. Air Asia also introduced a new programme called 'Pick a Seat' in early 2009, which is an ensemble of assigned seating, pre-boarding, and extra legroom for $6.93 per segment. In addition, AirTran Airways offers several advance seat assignment options, which is generating around $30 million on an annual basis (Field, 2009). Low-cost carriers who do not assign seats offer priority boarding, as some customers value early boarding where they can choose their own seating arrangements – which is popular among families and for business travellers that want overhead bin space for their carry-on luggage. At easyJet, around 11 passengers per flight typically select Speedy Boarding, which averages out at €0.50 per passenger throughout the year. United Airlines sells 'Premier Line' which allows non-regular flying leisure passengers the opportunity to purchase a bundled package for $19. This grants priority to check-in, access to dedicated security lanes and priority to board, all of which are normally reserved for business or for members of a high-tiered frequent flyer programme. Legacy airlines remain entrenched in their ideologies that strong revenues can only be extracted from the top yielding 30 per cent of their passengers, and they need to refocus their strategic marketing direction and begin capturing additional revenues from the remaining 70 per cent of passengers. Mason (2005) showed that the revenue from leisure passengers has fluctuated from a high of 70 per cent in 1992 to a low of 63 per cent in 1997, but overall it averaged 67 per cent throughout the last decade. This indicates that airlines have found it very difficult to increase the revenue stream from leisure passengers – United's Premier Line is an excellent indication of how this concept could evolve that ideology.

Reservation change fees are another revenue reaper for the industry. Passengers are charged for any changes to the date and/or time of the flight, as well as to any changes to the destination (per one-way basis), while passengers must also pay the fare difference between the newly booked flight and the previously reserved one – even if the available fare is lower on the new flight, no refund will be made. Ryanair, for example, charges a €35 administration fee to change any part of the schedule and €100 fee to change the passenger name. Both Delta Air Lines and American Airlines charged $150 to change an itinerary for a domestic service and much more for an international flight in 2010, while the difference must be also paid between the original price and the new price at the time the change is applied. Iliescu et al. (2008) researched the passenger behaviour of airline cancellations (as measured by refund and exchanges) together with no-shows[14] in the US market, and found that higher cancellations rates were generally observed for recently purchased tickets and for tickets whose associated flight departure dates are near. Their study used data from the Airline Reporting Corporation[15] and found that around eight per cent of bookings were cancelled (as measured by refunds and exchanges), but emphasized that cancellations of 30 per cent or more are not uncommon today. Table 5.3 illustrates that the US carriers have collected $2.3 billion in reservation change fees in 2009, and it shows that American Airlines earned $450 million from reservation changes in 2009 – which is a welcome earner when fares continue to spiral downwards.

Table 5.3   Reservation change fees (in $US millions) collected by US major airlines

4th Quarter 2009 Rank	Airline	4th Q 2008	1st Q 2009	2nd Q 2009	3rd Q 2009	4th Q 2009	Total 2009 reservation change fees (US$ millions)
1	Delta	4.5	86.9	100.7	112.0	106.5	406.0
2	American	114.5	115.9	109.6	120.4	104.0	449.9
3	Northwest	107.1	101.2	105.0	100.5	91.2	397.9
4	United	81.9	78.1	81.1	79.4	71.2	309.9
5	US Airways	68.3	66.5	64.0	61.0	57.3	248.8
6	Continental	N/A	59.6	59.8	56.0	52.6	227.9
7	JetBlue	34.3	32.2	30.0	28.7	30.4	121.3
8	AirTran	5.8	4.8	12.3	12.2	13.5	42.8
9	Alaska	17.1	16.3	15.3	15.6	13.4	60.6
10	Spirit	5.6	5.8	5.9	5.9	5.9	23.6
Industry Total[†]		459.9	587.5	606.5	613.5	563.7	2,371.1

[†] A total of 19 carriers reporting their revenues from baggage fees.

Source: Bureau of Transport Statistics, Form 41; Schedule P1.2.

---

14   No-shows are passengers that do not turn up for their flights. Klophaus and Pölt (2007) stated that 4.9 million passengers did not show up for flights operated by Lufthansa in 2005, which corresponds to 12,500 fully loaded Boeing 747s. Since all customers who request seats do not actually travel, airlines overbook to reduce the expected number of empty seats on flights when there is demand for those seats. Overbooking serves as a hedge against cancellations and no-shows.

15   The Airline Reporting Corporation is an airline-owned company where more than 170 airlines and railroads from around the world distribute, process and settle ticketing data.

5.2.1 Passenger Segmentation and its Impact on the Unbundling Process: A Case Study on Air Canada

Full service network airlines today are facing a marketing dilemma as they are trying to offer a range of flight products to cater for time sensitive business travellers, while concurrently offering a different set of attributes to fare sensitive leisure passengers. Doganis (2010, p228) states that passengers are influenced by five key product features, which include price, schedule, convenience, a comfortable and relaxing cabin, and the carrier's image. A carrier must then decide how to combine these various product features in order to meet the different needs of customers. O'Connell (2007) researched that those leisure travellers who pay for their own travel can be segmented into three distinct passenger categories. 'Price seeking' customers accounted for about 77 per cent of this leisure group, and this group envisions ticket price as the most important product dimension, followed by schedule. The second category is composed of 'service seekers', which make up around 14 per cent of all private travellers – they require comfort and convenience, but consider fare as a measured necessity. The remaining group are 'flexibility seeking' customers who want the opportunity to interchange travel schedules without penalties and get refunds, but consider fare to be a binding influence on their purchase decision. The customer group travelling in the business class cabin is not uniform. A segmentation of the population within the business class cabin is essential to understand consumer demands. The literature explicitly declares that price is not necessarily the most important variable to all business travellers, as the convenience of schedule and the attractiveness of frequent flyer programmes are often of higher importance. Trying to brand the leisure and business class elements of the marketing mix is becoming a major problem for the full service airlines. This has resulted in a mismatch between the expectations of passengers and the airline promise, which may frustrate passengers and make them question the integrity and competence of the brand. The airline business models between network and low-cost carriers are becoming increasingly blurred, and in some instances are converging.

Air Canada is the world's eighth largest passenger airline by fleet size and is a founding member of Star Alliance, but it needed a radical reform if it was to regain profitability and challenge Canada's leading low-cost carrier, WestJet which had been pricing aggressively and taking market share from the Canadian incumbent. Air Canada surprised airline strategists around the world by completely overhauling its vast portfolio of flight products by segmenting them into specific categories based on price. The fare structure was transformed into an innovative and dynamic platform that was customer friendly. It offers three different fare levels within its economy cabins that were branded as Tango, Tango Plus and Latitude, and two business class divisions entitled Executive Class Lowest and Executive Class Flexible (as outlined in Table 5.4).

Table 5.4 Air Canada fare unbundling product (domestic market, 2010)

Fare components	Tango	Tango Plus	Latitude	Executive class lowest	Executive class flexible
Refundability	Non-refundable	Non-refundable	Refundable	Non-refundable	☑ Refundable
Any-time change fee	$75 + fare difference	$50 + fare difference	fare difference	$50 + fare difference	fare difference
Fee to change to an earlier flight (at the airport)	$150	$75	☑	$75	☑
Same-day airport standby			☑	☑	☑
Frequent Flyer Mileage (FFP) accrual and top tier benefits	Tango	Tango Plus	Latitude	Executive class lowest	Executive class flexible
Air Canada status Miles accumulated	25 per cent	100 per cent	100 per cent	150 per cent	150 per cent
Eligibility for upgrade to executive class cabin		Available	Available		
Bonus FFP for every dollar spent at aircanada.com	Earn 1 mile per $3 spent	Earn 1 mile per $2 spent	Earn 1 mile per $1 spent	Earn 1 mile per $1 spent	Earn 1 mile per $1 spent
Travel Experience	Tango	Tango Plus	Latitude	Executive class lowest	Executive class flexible
Priority check-in, baggage handling, and boarding			☑	☑	☑
Access to business lounge	+$45	+35	+30	☑	☑
Complementary checked-bags	2	2	2	3	3
Advanced seat selection	+$15 or +$25 for Exit row seat	☑ +$25 (Exit row)	☑ +$25 Exit row	☑	☑
Complementary meal				☑	☑
Onboard Cafe ($9 value)	+$7	+$7	☑	☑	☑
Savings if you earn no FFPs	-$3				
No baggage	-$3	-$3	-$3		

Source: Air Canada.

Note: ☑ Already included as part of air fare.

It bears a strong correlation to the segmentation theory proposed by O'Connell (2007), as described earlier. Tango had the lowest registered fare level[16] on the Air Canada website, but consequently had a rigid set of restrictions attached to it, whereby passengers could not get a refund, had no opportunity to select a seat in advance, where fees were levied when passengers made any changes to their itinerary, where passengers received 25 per cent of Frequent Flier Miles, where additional charges were levied for phone calls made to the airline call centre, and so forth. The pricing mechanism in the Tango fare category is especially innovative as it allows customers the choice to personalize their flight products, which in turn allows Air Canada to upsell these products to its lowest yield passengers. For an extra C$15, passengers can reserve a seat, and for C$25 they can avail of a more spacious seat in an exit row. If passengers wish to opt out of the Frequent Flier Programme, then the system deducts C$3 from the fare bucket, and previously there was also a discount for not checking a bag. At the mid-range level, Tango Plus offers more benefits, including lower charges to change and cancel a reservation, option to select a seat in advance, 100 per cent mileage, and so forth. The highest fare level in economy is termed latitude, and it offers an even greater range of benefits and lower fees. The business fare is divided into two divisions, each with a set of different attributes that are aimed at different segments of the business passenger, and are entitled Executive Class Lowest and Executive Class Flexible. The lower fare level retains some restrictions, such as a non-refundable ticket together with a C$50 penalty for changing the ticket and a C$75 fee if the passenger wishes to change his/her reservation to an earlier flight. The highest fare level is executive class, which is typical of a business class product which has a full range of flexible entities that are synonymous with the demands of pressurised business travellers. Throughout the process, passengers have the opportunity to 'buy-up' into the next fare category (for example, Tango to Tango Plus) for a fee, which gives access to a wider range of flight products and greater flexibility – the fare will be recalculated accordingly to reflect the higher tier level. From a revenue management perspective, seats have always been sold from the bottom up – from the lowest qualified fare. However, with the introduction of branded products, an airline has the capability to sell from the middle or the top, based on a consumer's preference for the privileges associated with a branded product. Air Canada (2008) reported that 47 per cent of its passengers chose a higher branded fare because of the additional attributes, while Straus (2008) stated that Air Canada's unit revenues have risen by 22 per cent since it launched its branded fares. By implementing this type of tiered fare structure, the consumer is able to purchase these additional products as part of the base ticket price, thus enabling the buy-up option, which in turn generates additional revenue for the airline. These multi-fare

---

16   The GDS had no way of differentiating between the Tango fare and the Tango Plus fare and it also lacked the technical standards to include the individual flight products that have been unbundled. However the GDSs have indicated that they will release a fully integrated platform that will accommodate these unbundled flight products by 2010.

offerings support an airline's ability to segment demand based on the desirability of various features. However, carriers that offer multiple products under the umbrella of a bundled package are becoming increasingly disadvantaged, as this will cause them to slip down the rankings in price based web searches. As low-cost carriers continue to increase their presence in the market, consumers will come to expect ever-lower fares.

Table 5.5 demonstrates how much the landscape of ancillary revenues has changed over the two-year time span from 2006 to 2008. The data clearly indicates that legacy airlines are increasingly unbundling their fares to produce new revenue streams, while low-cost carriers continue to extract more revenue by implementing newer, innovative ways[17] to generate revenues by ancillary means – which prove to be a testbed that other carriers can adopt if they prove to be successful.

Table 5.5   Ancillary revenues of top five Airlines in 2008 and 2006

2008		2006	
American Airlines	€1,650,000,000	United Airlines	€416,116,752
United Airlines	€1,200,000,000	Ryanair	€362,104,000
Delta Air Lines	€1,125,000,000	easyJet	€189,476,508
Ryanair	€625,350,240	Alaska Airlines	€134,662,086
Qantas	€458,622,000	Aer Lingus	€63,407,000

Source: IdeaWorks.

5.2.2 On-Board Connectivity: The Newest Leap in Producing Ancillary Revenues

Charging for onboard email and mobile phone services is a more recent trend that has enormous potential to generate ancillary revenues. Kirby (2010) stated that over 800 aircraft have been fitted with in-flight connectivity platforms by early 2010, and projections indicate that over 4,500 aircraft will have such installations by 2013. Guidon (2009) researched that 50 per cent of passengers aged between 18 and 51 required internet access on-board, while revenues from in-flight Broadband are anticipated to reach almost $1 billion worldwide by 2010. Installation costs for on-board Broadband are estimated at around $100,000 per aircraft, and by 2010 carriers such as American Airlines are charging $12.95 for flights over three hours in duration and $9.95 for shorter flights, while Qantas charges $8 per flight. Christodoulidou (2008) studied the topic through focus groups and concluded that US business passengers were willing to pay $10 to use the Internet for flights lasting three hours, $20 for five hours and $25 for more than five hours – which clearly indicates that customers value this product, while carriers are undercharging for it.

---

17 Ryanair is introducing two new ancillary products each year.

WiFi Certified is a global, non-profit organization that certifies the brands of wireless networks. It released the details of its 2009 survey which confirmed the marketing hypothesis that access to in-flight Broadband is fast becoming a highly valued product among frequent flyers and business travellers who valued it more than meal service, free movies and other perks. The study also pointed out that business travellers would be willing to make significant sacrifices or change travel plans to ensure WiFi access while in the air: 76 per cent would choose an airline based on the availability of in-flight WiFi; 55 per cent would shift their flight by one day if it meant having in-flight WiFi; and 71 per cent would opt for a flight with WiFi access over one that provided meal service (Wi-Fi, 2009). In time, Broadband connectivity may become an integral part of the core competencies of in-flight services. Saudi Arabian Airlines, Libya's Afriqiyah Airways and China's Shenzhen Airlines are carriers that are not generally associated with technological pioneering, but all offer in-flight internet connectivity – which signifies that this product will become a dominant feature across the world's carriers. Passengers travelling on Virgin America[18] can access the Internet through the seat-back In-Flight Entertainment (IFE) system. Its passengers can order food, beverages and movies over the IFE via a new technological platform which allows the passenger to have more control and flexibility over the flight service – a proven marketing concept that drives sales. The IFE-Internet platform can also facilitate online gambling, which is another activity that is being widely discussed at industry forums and conferences: The online gambling industry was valued at $16.7 billion in 2007 and is set to reach $26.5 billion by 2012. The activity already has roots – for example, Ryanair sells scratch cards on-board for €2. The airline industry must constantly adapt as passengers are bringing an increasing range of personal devices on-board, such as iPods, smart phones, portable media players and so on, which suggests that the next technological step-change will be to interface these devices through the onboard IFE system. This will produce an interactive platform that can extract revenues, while at the same time sell advertising. Frost and Sullivan, an independent market research company, pointed out that the market for IFE and connectivity in Asia Pacific was estimated at US$464.7 million in 2009, and is expected to expand rapidly, recording annual growth rates of 12.6 per cent till 2012 (Yee, 2010).

Using mobile phones on board is another enormous revenue generating opportunity for airlines, yet it remains prohibited on US flights.[19] According to the United Nations, there are 4 billion mobile phone subscribers, while there are around 2.3 billion people travelling by air (International Telecommunications

---

18   Virgin America's ancillary revenues are up 40 per cent year-on-year.

19   Congressman Peter DeFazio introduced the HANG UP Act in 2008. It states that an individual may not engage in voice communications using a mobile communications device in an aircraft during a US domestic flight. The law does not attempt to restrict all mobile phone use, just 'voice communications'. According to the bill passengers could still use their mobile phones to access the Internet, e-mail and send text messages.

Union, 2008). This suggests that the penetration rate of mobile phone users may be close to 100 per cent. Arabian Gulf based Oman Air carried 2.3 million passengers in 2009, and has installed both Internet and mobile connectivity on its five new A330 aircraft. Emirates began offering mobile phone connectivity in March 2008, and one year later it had equipped 50 aircraft with the service. The carrier confirmed that the penetration rate is growing rapidly – as 35 per cent of usage occurs on routes to Europe, 16 per cent to the Middle East, 15 per cent to North Asia, four per cent to South Asia, 21 per cent to Africa and nine per cent on Australasian routes (Air Transport Intelligence, 2009). In-flight mobile connectivity provider, AeroMobile confirmed that the operating system is being widely adopted by users across the globe, as almost one-third of passengers are using the service in 2010. Call rates are set by individual mobile operators and are in line with EU international roaming rates, which typically range from €2–3 per minute for voice calls, emails more than €1.25, and texts costing at least €0.50.

5.2.3 Unbundling is the New Unstoppable Force

To conclude this section, unbundling the product is growing in popularity and is fast becoming a new unstoppable force. A 2008 survey of 113 airline executives conducted by IdeaWorks revealed that more and more airlines are turning to à la carte pricing in order to provide a revenue boost, as shown in Figure 5.1.

A comparison of the 2008 IdeaWorks survey with the previous year found a number of services whose popularity rose more than 10 points, which included

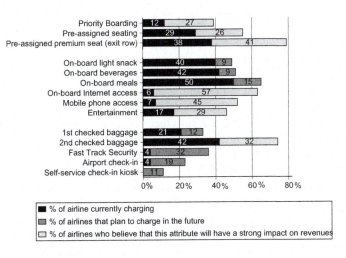

Figure 5.1   Current and future a-la-carte airline fee landscape in 2008 (survey from 113 airline executives)

Source: IdeaWorks and Airbus.

onboard meals or sandwiches (50 per cent from 36 per cent), onboard beverages (42 per cent from 25 per cent), onboard snacks (40 per cent from 24 per cent), pre-assigned premium or exit row seats (38 per cent from 20 per cent), pre-assigned seats (29 per cent from 11 per cent), and the first piece of checked luggage (21 per cent from eight per cent). Forecasts for passengers who plan to use the Internet and mobile phone onboard are expected to grow exponentially, as the six per cent who now charge for onboard internet is expected to rise to 63 per cent into the future, with mobile phones expected to do the same. Airlines have a captive audience onboard, and it is only in recent years that carriers have been pioneering new methods to generate additional revenue streams from their passengers. There is a greater willingness on the part of consumers to pay for an ancillary offering than to absorb a base fare increase. The next generation of onboard ancillaries may very well take the form of an annual membership fee, whereby a passenger will purchase a set bundle of specific flight products for an annual fee, similar to the banking industry. Undoubtedly, the disassembly of the flight products, along with the myriad of permutations stemming from the connectivity platforms like Broadband and mobile phones, has the likelihood of becoming a very promising enterprise with solid rates of return as the airline industry remains saddled with high costs and low yields.

5.3 Commission-Based Ancillaries That are Provided by Third Parties

Commission-based ancillaries that are provided by third parties are another important component of how airlines are generating revenues today and the concept is known as dynamic packaging. It is dynamic because pricing, constraints and ultimate choice are determined online based on a real-time inventory. Consumers assimilate their individual travel components such as hotel accommodation and car hire from an airline website, as they are obvious products that naturally complement the sale of an airline seat. It integrates tourism related data onto one transparent platform and in effect, consumers become their own travel agents by building a tailor-made package that suits their specific requirements. Airlines have been leaking huge volumes of revenues to suppliers for decades and dynamic packaging aims to significantly curtail this trend.

Travel, tourism and hospitality represent the world's largest industry as it accounts for eight per cent of worldwide employment, nine per cent of invested capital and 10 per cent of global GDP. From 1950 to 2007, international tourist arrivals grew from 25 million to 908 million. The overall income (international tourism receipts and passenger transport) exceeded US$1 trillion in 2007, or almost US$3 billion per day. In 1950, the top 15 destinations absorbed 98 per cent of all international tourist arrivals, while in 1970 the proportion was 75 per cent, but this fell to 57 per cent by 2007, reflecting the emergence of new destinations, many of them in developing countries (World Trade Organization, 2009). The Centre for Regional and Tourism Research in Denmark is a leading authority on the European travel market and calculated that Europe's total travel market for 2008 was €260 billion, while the online component accounted for €58.4 billion[20] or 22.5 per cent of the total European travel market, which has been steadily capturing market share year-after-year as shown in Figure 5.2.

A breakdown of the €58.4 billion worth of online travel sales reveals that air travel accounted for 54 per cent, hotels (and other accommodations) 19.5 per cent, package tours 15 per cent, rail 7.5 per cent, and rental cars four per cent (Centre for Tourism Research, 2009). Since the Internet's inception, there has been a decisive shift from supplier power to consumer power. In realization of this enhanced consumer sovereignty of the Internet age, carriers have come to accept the empowered consumer as a permanent market condition. Further research by IPK International (2009) outlined the extent of the number of vacations taken by Europeans as they undertook 395 million outbound trips in 2009, which in turn accounted for 3.5 billion overnight stays at hotels. Meanwhile, the UK CAA found that UK residents travelling by air to Europe for leisure purposes spent an average of £560 on their holiday in 2004, of which only 27 per cent was accounted for by the air fare (UK CAA, 2005). The central theme resonating from these research centres (that is, Centre for Regional and Tourism Research, IPK International and UK CAA) is that there is an enormous opportunity awaiting carriers to penetrate the holiday-package and short-break market as airlines can by cross sell these travel by-products such as car hire and hotel rooms through bolt-on hyperlinks from their website.

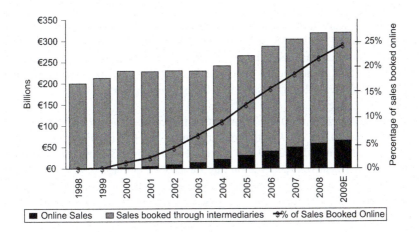

Figure 5.2   Breakdown of the European travel market by traditional and online sales measures

Source: Centre for Tourism Research.

20   In 2008, the UK accounted for €17.5 billion of the European online travel market, with Germany in second place at €10.5 billion.

Dynamic packaging could well become the key to sustained airline profitability and become the next game changer in producing revenues for the airline industry. Consider the following case study where by a customer travels to London on business for two days and books a hotel and car through the airline's website. The hotel will charge $200 per night where a commission rate of around 10 per cent is paid generating $40 which is then split between the travel portal company (a software company that horizontally integrates the third party suppliers across a common platform)[21] and the airline. The commission is similar for car hire where contributions can range from between $20–$50 per passenger booking. Therefore for a mid-sized airline with five million annual passenger segments per year and where the look-to-book ratio[22] is one in 10 – this has the potential to generate 500,000 cross selling opportunities. If the average spend per ancillary sale is $200 per hotel stay and $100 per car hire, then the total incremental ancillary revenue is $15 million and if the look-to-book ratio is doubled this then rises to $30 million. The travel portal is essential as it makes sharing data easy across applications – by transferring data from the airline reservation system, the dates for staying at the hotel become instantaneously populated as they are synchronized with the travel dates. This reduces the complexity and duplication for the traveller and enriches the customer-relationship management process.

Lobbenberg et al. (2007) at ABN AMRO banking conducted an in-depth study of Ryanair's ancillary revenues from 2002 to 2007 which is detailed in Table 5.6.

The analysis shows that the revenues on all 17 products increased year after year and in 2007 ancillaries represented 16.5 per cent of total revenues. Ryanair continued to capitalize on this revenue stream as it had amassed over €663 million by 2010, with ancillary revenues representing 22 per cent of total revenues. Malighetti et al. (2010) who completed an in-depth analysis of Ryanair's pricing strategy confirmed that its ancillary revenues have been outpacing passenger growth over the last number of years and forecasts that it will continue to do so. Table 5.7 provides a deeper insight into the partnership between Ryanair and the car hire companies.

Lobbenberg et al. (2007) estimated that the carrier sold around €76 million worth of car rentals in 2007, with Ryanair earning over €26 million from the joint-venture agreement and by 2009 this had increased to over €32 million. There is a only a four per cent web-penetration rate for car hire among Ryanair passengers, which is characteristic of the industry at present, but this is expected to increase considerably as passengers become more comfortable and familiar in cross-

---

21   This is an Application Service Provider that uses XML as a transaction standard and web services as the integration platform. The application uses Microsoft's.NET which is an industry wide standard.

22   In this case the look-to-book ratio is the number of people who visit an airline web site and look at the hotel and car deals on offer which is compared to the number who actually makes a purchase.

Table 5.6   Ryanair ancillary revenue model (millions of €Euros)

	2002	2003	2004	2005	2006	2007E
Car Hire – adjusted to net pre 2005	6.59	9.62	12.23	15.71	19.75	26.51
Food – adjusted to net	0.39	0.49	0.69	0.81	1.02	1.83
Beverages – adjusted to net	0.80	1.03	1.27	1.35	1.75	2.62
Merchandise (net)	0.16	0.17	0.20	0.27	0.36	0.81
Internet income	4.83	12.16	17.72	24.36	27.30	39.42
Sale of rail tickets (net)	0.63	0.94	1.62	2.05	3.00	3.67
Sale of bus tickets (net)	0.17	0.25	0.39	0.59	0.78	1.28
Hotel accommodation (net)	1.72	3.20	5.47	7.40	11.41	19.27
Insurance (net)	0.29	0.58	0.96	3.73	7.30	9.29
Priority boarding/ Online check-in	0.00	0.00	0.00	9.93	18.78	53.59
Visa card partnership	0.00	0.11	0.28	0.46	0.76	1.23
Flight change fee	2.03	3.49	5.74	6.55	8.81	11.62
Name change fee	2.08	4.43	6.51	8.28	11.08	15.95
Credit/Debit card fee	7.07	15.66	31.29	60.43	76.14	93.15
Infant fee	0.00	0.00	1.27	1.87	2.27	3.30
Excess baggage	2.20	5.37	11.27	13.33	25.31	17.01[†]
Sports/music equipment	0.90	2.08	3.09	3.37	5.46	8.63
Total Ancillary Revenue	29.86	59.58	100	160.49	221.28	309.18
Revenue from Ticket Sales	551	732	925	1,128	1,433	1,875
Ancillary revenue as a per cent of total revenues	5.4 %	8.1 %	10.8 %	14.2 %	15.4 %	16.5 %

Source: Lobbenberg et al. (2007).

Note: Up until the year ending March 2005, Ryanair reported gross car hire revenues, logging the full revenue paid by passengers for car hire. In 2006, the carrier switched to reporting net car hire revenues. ABN AMRO recalculated the historical data.

[†]By 2007, Ryanair had begun charging for checked baggage and these revenues were part of passenger revenues.

Table 5.7   Ryanair car hire model

	2002	2003	2004	2005	2006	2007E
Car Hire (gross, €millions)	18.91	27.62	35.11	45.09	56.70	76.10
Car Hire (net, €millions)	6.59	9.62	12.23	15.71	19.75	26.51
Passenger penetration%				3.5%	3.5%	3.8%
Revenue per flown passenger (€)	0.59	0.61	0.52	0.56	0.56	0.62
Average value of car hire (€)				107	110	110
Average price per day (€)				34	35	35
Average number of days				3.15	3.15	3.15

Source: Lobbenberg et al. (2007).

purchasing more travel products[23] from airline websites. The academic marketing literature supports this claim by enunciating that if the core brand is trusted, then customers will trust the other brands that are associated with it. It is important to have marketing relationships to multiple car suppliers to choose from (for example, Avis, Hertz, Enterprise, Thrifty, and so on) because a distinct segment of today's passengers is loyalty driven and if a carrier neglects to offer a particular supplier (with a large customer base) it will risk losing the customer to a substitute carrier that hold this preferred supplier. Healy (2008) confirms the importance of having multiple suppliers by referencing an example from Hawaiian Airlines who opted to transgress from one car supplier on its website to three, which had an immediate positive impact on the number of bookings. The global car rental market is a €28 billion industry but is very concentrated with 55 per cent of the revenues coming from North America and 32 per cent from Europe. Surprisingly, 60 per cent of car hires occur at the airport and airlines need to reduce this leakage by incentivizing passengers (through discounts) to hire a vehicle while inside the booking path of a website. Pilling (2007) reiterated the significance of such a positioning strategy by reporting that the penetration rate of Ryanair's travel insurance had increased fivefold from two per cent to 10 per cent, when it was offered inside the booking path rather than at the end. Travel insurance is another element of the travel supply chain that is financially lucrative as the US Travel Insurance Association (2009) noted that US consumers spent more than $1.3 billion on travel insurance (for trip cancellation, equipment insurance, medical travel insurance) in 2006, up 20 per cent over 2004 figures, while AirSavings (2009) noted that a similar amount (£670 million) was being spent in the UK each year. Low cost carriers again pioneered the horizontal integration between both parties and are reaping the rewards as easyJet earned $48.6 million on travel insurance commission in 2008, averaging $1.15 per passenger.

5.3.1 Pioneering New Commission-Based Ancillaries

Airlines are embarking on ways to look beyond the traditional travel bi-products and spawn into products that are unaligned to air travel. Ryanair has 18 million visitors to its website each month and it continues to 'think outside the box' where it cross-sells a whole array of products that are not affiliated to air travel such as cruises, bingo, third party advertising,[24] and so on. FBD, an Irish car insurance company received 16,500 insurance quotes within six days by positioning itself on the carriers' website (Straus, 2008). However, most carriers sell ancillary products that are aligned to air travel, but are getting more innovative in their commercialization as UK based Monarch Airlines for example provides a hyperlink

---

23   Lobbenberg et al. (2007) also indicated that Ryanair had over a three per cent penetration rate from hotel bookings.

24   A diverse portfolio of companies advertises on Ryanair's website such as Microsoft and Boots which is an international pharmacy-led health and beauty group.

to airport car parking from its website, which has a four per cent penetration among the passengers who book an airline ticket and it receives a 20 per cent commission for each booked car space (Jeans, 2008). Lufthansa has pioneered a tool called 'Trip Finder' which gives customers the flexibility to search for destinations based on a predetermined budget. The destination contains a portfolio of tourist activities (for example, golf, diving, beach, museum visits, historical sites, and so on) that the passenger can partake in and this type of cross fertilization will be an important building block for developing regional tourism offshoots.

Currently, dynamic packaging is in an embryonic stage but there are countless ways to expand its dimensions. For a peek into the future, consider the following scenario where a frequent flyer enjoys the sport of diving and is travelling to Florida on business – data mining algorithms initiated by the CRM could interpret this as an opportunity and offer the passenger a discounted two-day diving excursion to nearby Bahamas. The carrier generates multiple revenue streams from the arrangement as the passenger takes an additional flight, overnights at a hotel, and generates commission from the diving centre. The process in turn builds a value-laden relationship with the passenger.

5.4 Conclusion

Airlines are facing excessive competition, overcapacity, falling yields as the industry remains eclipsed with high cost structures and low barriers to entry. These characteristics are largely accountable for the industry's shortfall in generating profits. Airline marketing departments are beginning to reinvent themselves as their core strategic flight products are changing their integrative shape by pioneering new methodologies to generate additional income. Ancillary revenues are a sizzling new concept that will represent a paradigm leap to produce more revenues, while the profit margins from ancillaries are much higher than the commodity based sale of airline seats, which is undoubtedly, a game changer for the industry. Its success can be measured by the fact that it has contributed over $10 billion to the balance sheets of the world's airlines in 2008, up 345 per cent from two years earlier. It produces revenues through two unique practices. The first is by dismantling the fare mechanism, which allows the carrier to charge for each individual flight product and secondly by cross-selling third party travel by-products through bolt-on hyperlinks from an airlines' website. Figure 5.3 summarizes the chapter by dividing the flight products into three distinct categories.

Firstly, the core products (that is, safety, schedule and reliability) are pivotal elements to a successful carrier because they are an integral component of the overall flight. Each of these cannot be fragmented further and do not have the potential to generate revenues on a stand-alone basis. The second category represents a vast array of products that are unbundled or separated from the fare in all instances of the flight (that is, pre-flight, in-flight and post) and each unbundled product has the potential to generate revenue. Not all customers are equal and each

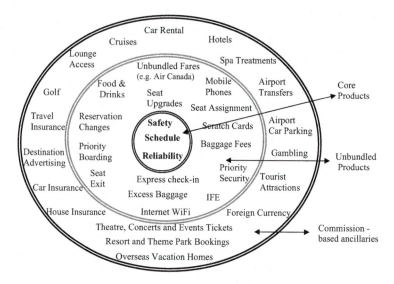

Figure 5.3   Map of core airline products (non-revenue) and revenue producing products

Source: O'Connell.

of these products offers a different value proposition and a different price, with a stripped-down product definition. US-based network airlines for example have generated billions of dollars by charging for items such as baggage, which was previously incorporated in the fare. Many full service airlines around the world are now following the innovative practices of Air Canada which optimized its marketing activities by bundling a distinct set of product and service attributes with individual 'fare families' for the customer, which offer minimal privileges at the lowest fares, and highly flexible and feature-rich products at higher fares. Many carriers throughout the world are now imitating this practice. Thirdly, commission-based ancillary revenue represents a paradigm leap to produce more income as customers assimilate their individual travel components such as hotel accommodation from an airline website. It integrates tourism related data onto one transparent platform in a collaborative manner where in effect, the consumer becomes their own travel agent by building a tailor-made package that suits their specific requirements. This concept is now evolving to embrace products that are unaligned to air travel such as car insurance, for example, which could be sold on airline's ecommerce website. In concluding, the core competencies of airline marketing are being remoulded whereby each product is transformed into a revenue generator which is being horizontally extended to capture additional revenue streams from third party based enterprises. It's apparent that changes to the fundamentals of airline strategic marketing were long overdue – ancillary revenue is reinventing new ideologies to produce income and is a game changer.

References

Air Canada (2008), Fourth Quarter Overview. Available at: www.aircanada.com/en/about/investor/documents/2008_q4_release.pdf.

AirSavings (2009), The ancillary evolution. Available at: www.airsavings.net/.

Air Transport Intelligence (2010), Spirit to charge for carry on bags in tandem with lowering fares, 6 April. Available at: www.rati.com.

Air Transport Intelligence (2009), US Airways aims for continued expansion of preferred seat sales, 17 March. Available at: www.rati.com.

Air Transport Intelligence (2009), AeroMobile now installed on 40 per cent of Emirates fleet, 17 August. Available at: www.rati.com.

Alexander, K.L. (2006), Paying More for Small Extras, *Washington Post*, 31 January.

Balcombe, K., Fraser, I. and Harris, L. (2009), Consumer willingness to pay for in-flight service and comfort levels: A choice experiment, *Journal of Air Transport Management*, 15(5), pp. 221–226.

Barnard, B. (2010), Air France-KLM to report $617 cargo loss, *Journal of Commerce*, 8 June. Available at: www.joc.com/air-expedited/air-france-klm-report-614-million-cargo-loss.

Centre for tourism research (2009), Trends in European Internet Distribution – of Travel and Tourism Services, 2 March. Available at: www.crt.dk/UK/staff/chm/trends.htm.

Christodoulidou, N. (2008), Which ancillary revenue products best complement the travel purchasing corridor and deliver maximum profits, Ancillary Revenue in Travel conference, Las Vegas, Nevada, October 1–2.

Espino, R., Martin, J.C. and Roman, C. (2008), Analyzing the effect of preference heterogeneity on willingness to pay for improving service quality in an airline choice context, *Transportation Research E* 44, 593–606.

Doganis, R. (2010), *Flying Off Course, Airline Economics and Marketing*, 4th Edition, Routledge.

Field, D. (2009), Interview: AirTran chief executive Bob Fornaro, *Airline Business*, February, pp. 20–23.

Generation Research (2009), Travel retail statistical reference. Available at: www.generation.se/About/default.aspx?pageId=3.

Guidon, J. (2009), Ancillary revenues from a connected aircraft, Row 44, Airline Channel Sales Forum, Miami, 12 May.

Healy, B. (2008), Understanding the ancillary proposition, The Ancillary Revenue Summit, Radisson SAS, 1 December, London.

IATA (2010), Fact Sheets: Industry Statistics, August. Available at: www.iata.org/pressroom/facts_figures/fact_sheets/Documents/Fact per cent20Sheet per cent20Industry per cent20Facts per cent20- per cent20AUG per cent2010.pdf.

IATA (2010), Financial Forecast, March. Available at: www.iata.org/whatwedo/economics/Documents/IndustryOutlookMar10.pdf.

IATA (2009), $5.6 Billion Loss in 2010 – Low Yields & Rising Costs Keep Industry in the Red, 15 December. Available at: www.iata.org/pressroom/pr/Pages/2009–12–15–01.aspx.

IdeaWorks (2009), Airlines All Over the Globe Post Ancillary Revenue Gains. Available at: www.ideaworkscompany.com/press/2009/PressRelease47AncillaryRevenueReport.pdf.

IPK International (2009), Global Travel Trends 2009, ITB Berlin Future Day, 10 March. Available at: www.ipkinternational.com/uploads/media/ITB_Press_Release_IPK_2010.pdf.

International Telecommunications Union (2008), Worldwide mobile cellular subscribers to reach 4 billion mark late 2008. Available at: www.itu.int/newsroom/press_release/2008/29.html.

Iliescu, D.C., Garrow, L.A. and Parker, R.A. (2008), A hazard model of US airline passengers' refund and exchange behavior, *Journal of Transportation Research Part B: Methodological*, 42(3), pp. 229–242.

Jeans, T. (2008), The Ancillary Revenue Summit, Radisson SAS Portman, London, 1 December.

Jenner, G. (2009), IT Trends Overview – Early Returns, *Airline Business*, July, pp. 42–57.

Kirby, M. (2010), Making the connection, *Airline Business*, January, pp. 38–41.

Klophaus, R. and Pölt, S. (2007), Airline overbooking with dynamic spoilage costs, *Journal of Revenue & Pricing Management*, 6(1), pp. 9–18.

Lobbenberg, A., Cowley, C. and Burke, N. (2007), *Ancillary Revenues, ABN AMRO Bank*, 23 July, 250 Bishopsgate, London, EC2M 4AA, London, pp. 1–40.

Malighetti, P., Paleari, S. and Redondi, R. (2010), Has Ryanair's pricing strategy changed over time? An empirical analysis of its 2006–2007 flights, *Tourism Management*, 31(1), pp. 36–44.

Mason, K. (2005), Observations of fundamental changes in the demand for aviation services, *Journal of Air Transport Management*, 11(1), pp. 19–25.

Martin, J.C., Roman, C. and Espino, R. (2008), Willingness to pay for airline service quality. *Transport Reviews*, 28, pp. 199–217.

McDonald, M. (2009), Tapping the ancillary revenue wall, *Air Transport World*, March, pp. 59–61.

Moores, V., Ranson, L. and Yeo, G.L. (2010), The Last Drop, *Airline Business*, January, pp. 34–37.

O'Connell, J.F. (2007), The strategic response of full service airlines to the low-cost carrier threat and the perception of passengers to each type of carrier, PhD thesis, Cranfield University, UK.

PhoCusWright (2010), The role and value of the gds in travel distribution, 8 February. Available at: www.phocuswright.com/free_downloads.

PhoCusWright (2009), PhoCusWright's European Online Travel Overview Fifth Edition, October. Available at: www.phocuswright.com/store/918.

Pilling, M. (2007), Flat out, *Airline Business*, January, pp. 46–48.

Sabre (2009), How will airlines survive? Results of a Sabre Airline Solutions survey of global carriers may be surprising. Available at: www.sabreairlinesolutions.com/images/uploads/releases/AS2009AirlineTrendsSurveyRELEASEFINAL101309.pdf.

Seattle Times (2009), Southwest's 'bags fly free' policy is landing new customers, 13 November. Available at: http://seattletimes.nwsource.com/html/travel/2010269091_websouthwest13.html.

Seeking Alpha (2008), JetBlue Airways Corporation Q2 2008 Earnings Call Transcript, 22 July. Available at: http://seekingalpha.com/article/86285-jetblue-airways-corporation-q2–2008-earnings-call-transcript?page=-1&find=par.

Sobie, B. (2010), Attention Deficit, *Airline Business*, March, pp. 36–38.

Straus, B. (2008), Revenue window of opportunity, *Air Transport World*, April, pp. 37–40.

UK CAA (2005), Demand for outbound leisure air travel and its key drivers, December, UK Civil Aviation Authority.

US Travel Insurance Association (2009), Americans Spend More Than $1.3 Billion On Travel Insurance. Available at: www.ustia.org/news/articles/2007survey-reveals-growth.htm.

Walsh, W. (2009), A discussion on British Airways, Air Transport Department, Cranfield University, Bedfordshire, UK, October.

Wi-Fi (2009), In-flight Wi-Fi® takes off; Frequent flyers, business travelers say it tops other airline amenities, Austin, Texas – September 1. Available at: www.wi-fi.org/news_articles.php?f=media_news&news_id=847.

World Trade Organization (2009), Tourism and travel-related services. Available at: www.wto.org/english/tratop_e/serv_e/tourism_e/tourism_e.htm.

Yee, L.H. (2010), More airlines expected to offer WiFi services, Asia News Network, 8 March. Available at: www.asianewsnet.net/news.php?id=10597&sec=2.

Yu, S-F. (2008), Price perception of online airline ticket shoppers, *Journal of Air Transport Management*, 14(2), pp. 66–69.

Chapter 6

Multilateral Airline Alliances: The Fallacy of the Alliances to Mergers Proposition[1]

Sveinn Vidar Gudmundsson and Christian Lechner

6.1 Introduction

Over the past decades, bilateral alliances and multilateral alliances have blurred the borders between airline companies worldwide. Competition between airlines is less a matter of individual firms competing against individual firms but of airline groups against airline groups, or to be more precise – networks against networks (Gomes-Cassares, 1994). General studies on alliances and networks have largely focused on the benefits of alliances and many have listed some sort of a management check list of how to make alliances work (Child and Faulkner, 1998). For airline alliances the literature has covered formation of benefits (Park and Zhang, 2000; Brueckner and Whalen, 2000; Oum and Yu, 1998; Park, 1997), alliance typologies (Hsu and Shih, 2008; Wang and Evans, 2002; Rhoades and Lush, 1997) and duration (Holmberg and Cummings, 2009; Gudmundsson and Rhoades, 2001).

Parkhe (1991) defined alliances as *enduring inter-firm cooperations that include governance structures*. Multilateral alliances are multilateral dyads that have some form of authority. In the airline industry we have three such alliances *Star* (28 members), *oneworld* (11 members) and *SkyTeam* (13 members).[2] Bilateral alliances with only two partners constitute low governance complexity, while multilateral alliances encompass greater complexity and many possible governance forms.

Being part of a multilateral alliance allows airlines to exploit scope and density economies across geographical boundaries, in other words, to access resources otherwise not attainable. Such alliances are horizontal and therefore co-opetition relationships where airlines are competing on some aspects and cooperating on other. While the value of these arrangements is well understood, alliance processes, stability and evolution are less well understood. We can draw parallels between the social structural theory of competition (Gwilliam, 2008; Burt, 1992; and Coleman, 1988, 1990) and airline networking opportunities and constraints to explain the link between alliance processes, stability and evolution in the airline industry.

---

1   A previous version of this chapter was published in the *Journal of Air Transport Management* under the title 'Multilateral airline alliances: balancing strategic constraints and opportunities', 12 (2006): pp. 153–158.

2   Members as at mid 2010.

6.2 Network Competition

6.2.1 Networks

A network is defined as 'any collection of actors (n > 2) that pursue repeated, enduring exchange relations with each other, and at the same time lack a legitimate organizational authority to arbitrate and resolve disputes that may arise during exchange' (Podolny and Page, 1998: 59). The network approach considers market opportunities to be determined by the structure of networks and correspondingly network redundancy is a state induced by strategic constraints in exploiting further ties, that is, lack of opportunities. The main question is how competition is determined by the relations that market players possess. Some airlines have trust relations with some airlines, switch between others,[3] and engage in affiliation relations with others (for example, being members of an association).

6.2.2 Structural Holes and Network Closure

Competition of firms can be viewed as search for means to be different, or in the language of social networks, competing for *structural holes*. A structural hole is an opportunity, an un-served space that can be exploited as a result of brokering connections between disconnected segments generating capital. Bourdieu and Wacquant (1992: 119) define social capital as '... the sum of the resources, actual or virtual, that accrue to an individual or group by virtue of processing a durable network of more or less institutionalized relationships of mutual acquaintance and recognition.' However, there is an ongoing debate as to whether the open perspective we just mentioned is superior to the closed perspective. The opposing side (Coleman, 1988, 1990) holds that network closure creates social capital. Coleman argues that network closure facilitates trust between partners in honouring obligations and cooperative behaviour due to the cost of inappropriate behaviour. Thus, the concept tells us that closed highly cohesive networks would generate higher 'social capital' and thus superior 'economic rent' as we would have more trust, reputation and cooperation within a closed group with strong internal ties. The third perspective argued in this chapter for multilateral airline alliances, actually bridges the two and reflects recent work by Burt (2001), allowing us to state that in multilateral airline alliances a combination of opportunities to bridge 'structural holes' as well as achieving a degree of cohesiveness are important in combination but not exclusive of each other.

6.2.3 Network Perspective of Competition

Competition is a relational phenomenon and market opportunities are a matter of airline's network of relations. Thus, to be the first to establish a relation (with

---

3   Continental Airlines switched from SkyTeam to the Star Alliance in 2009.

a client) or to try to end another player's relation is what is usually understood as competition. The former tends to be the situation in young and growing markets, the latter in mature and declining markets (Grant, 1991). The lack of structural holes in mature markets is translated into lack of new opportunities and interchangeability of sellers by buyers; thus the buyers' bargaining power is increased, margins shrink, and the competitive arena as a whole becomes less attractive. Competition is not a visible relation since competitors are supposedly not connected with each other. Competition for structural holes is characterized by absence of ties or ties to be established. The competitive relation is time and space dependent. Only if a firm fights for a structural hole at the same time in the same place does it enter into a competitive relationship with another firm. The attribute 'competitor' might be misleading. Two airlines usually have competitive relations but if a serious new player moves into the market, they may act as allies to drive the new actor out, we use the term co-opetition for this phenomenon.

6.2.4 Competition Among Networks

It is increasingly acknowledged that cooperation is more than a two-party alliance (Holmberg and Cummings, 2009; Weber and Chathoth, 2008; Child and Faulkner, 1998). Airlines are embedded in not only formal relations such as multilateral alliances (Star, Oneworld, SkyTeam), but also formal one-on-one alliances (that is, KLM exclusive relations with Delta on the North Atlantic routes)[4], and informal relations with suppliers and value-chain partners such as car rentals and hotels. This extension of the cooperation view brings up new considerations about the competitive behaviour of firms. The 'new' cooperation view focuses on networks of alliances. Extending this view to several partners in an alliance, new competition arises: 'group versus group' or 'networks against networks' (Gomes-Casseres, 1994: 62; Nohria, Garcia and Pont, 1991). The various branded airline alliances (*Star, oneworld, SkyTeam*) are examples of this group versus group competition.

6.2.5 Competition Within a Network

Competition within a network depends on the creation and filling of structural holes. An airline that possesses a structural hole between two other airlines sits structurally above them. The creation of structural holes therefore leads to the hierarchical structuring process of a network. In this sense, airlines which bring in their own networks can influence their own position within a multilateral airline alliance but also other airlines' position to the better or the worse. Smaller airlines with fewer partners (that is, a smaller network) might find it more attractive to join multilateral alliances where the overall network is smaller because they might gain a more prominent position within the network by working actively on building

---

4   This exclusive bilateral agreement was signed between Air France and Delta on 17 October, 2007.

more bilateral partnerships. However, larger airlines might find it more attractive to group many smaller airlines to increase their power within the multilateral alliance through the size of the network they bring into the alliance.

6.3 Competing for Structural Holes

6.3.1 Airline Alliances as Resource Races

Airline alliances are resource races as opposed to learning races characterizing many technology alliances. The airline industry seeks scope and density economies (Levine, 1987) as opposed to scale economies in manufacturing industries.[5] The primary benefits of alliance cooperation in the airline industry are network rooted, that is, schedule convenience (frequency), connectivity (joining carriers over nodes) and flow improvement (reducing total travel time between any nodes in the network). The resource based view (Teece, 1982; Wernefelt, 1984) emphasizes the importance of unique resources, or low network density position, enabling alliance partners the exploitation of a large number of structural holes (*see* Obstfeld, 2005). Thus, airlines in a dominant position within a multilateral alliance should continuously seek new partners and new opportunities. Likewise partners with a high number of redundant ties[6] without a central position should seek opportunities where their resource is more unique in a competing multilateral alliance, for example, Finnair joining *oneworld* as opposed to *Star* that includes SAS its geographic neighbour.[7]

6.3.2 Alliances as a Struggle for Position

A partner can build strength from within the alliance if in a central position. Hamel, Doz and Prahalad (1989), suggested that the primary success indicator of an alliance was if a partner emerged out of an alliance stronger than when it entered. However, this may not hold well for multilateral airline alliances due to their services orientation as opposed to technology or manufacturing orientation. High sunk costs and inseparability of alliance benefits from the partner make it difficult to exit on strength. Exit is therefore an act of measuring up costs and benefits of switching alliance groups. A notable example was when KLM joined Air France, necessitating Northwest and Continental to join SkyTeam as severance of the alliance with Northwest would have proved costly for KLM. Thus, two levels of alliance relationships (KLM allied with Northwest, which was allied

---

5   This does not mean, however, that multilateral alliances should not seek cost savings through scale economies.

6   Reduntant tie = non-unique tie.

7   Finnair did join the European Quality Alliance with SAS, but left it after a short period.

with Continental) were brought into SkyTeam, demonstrating the notion of being 'stuck in your own net', in lieu of strategically planned alliance development.

The notion that multilateral alliance benefits can be distributed evenly and that they can be stable is misplaced. Participation in a multilateral alliance is a strategic contest for position and resources both internal and external to the alliance. Multilateral alliances will and should persistently have partners entering and exiting: a revolving cycle of opening up and covering structural holes by attracting non-redundant and emitting redundant partners, starting and terminating bilateral ties (see Figure 6.1). The alliances can do this in different ways through a relaxed entry of new members, through a formal annex programme such as the *SkyTeam Associate Members*,[8] or retain a relatively closed structure but allowing bilateral agreements with external partners.[9] Partners can certainly maintain external stability at the same time that internal bilateral relationships influenced by the external competitive environment, are entered into and shed without necessarily destabilizing the overall alliance.

The failure of the *European Quality Alliance*[10] (in 1990) and *Qualiflyer* (in 1998)[11] can be explained from the structural-hole concept as both being alliances

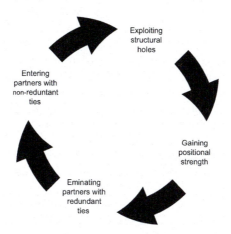

Entering
partners with
non-reduntant
ties

Exploiting
structural
holes

Gaining
positional
strength

Eminating
partners with
redundant
ties

Figure 6.1   Multilateral alliance positional cycle

---

8   *SkyTeam* has started an Associate Programme that contains two airlines in December 2009 (Air Europa and Kenya Airways) each sponsored by a different 'full' member of SkyTeam.

9   British Airways (oneworld) had a bilateral relationship with KLM to the Middle East; Iberia (*oneworld*) had connections with Air France (*SkyTeam*) to a number of destinations, etc.

10   Swissair, Austrian and SAS and Qualiflyer.

11   Sabena, Swissair, TAP, Turkish Airlines, AOM, Air Liberté, Air Littoral, Crossair, Volaré and Air Europe.

with many redundant ties. First, the limited geographical scope of partners in both alliances (all European based) made the exploitation of structural holes limited. Second, the closeness of the *Qualiflyer* alliance, with Swissair having equity shares in most of the partners, caused strategic constraints for the alliance in terms of entering new and emitting redundant partners. We can theorize that *Qualiflyer* had high degree of network closure as well as high density, that is, many redundant ties. Hence, economic rent in an alliance with limited scope, high density and many redundant ties will be low and coordination costs high due to overlapping territories.[12]

6.3.3 Cohesion, Scope and Centres of Gravity

Multilateral alliances with a combination of high scope and multiple centres of gravity create maximum perceived value for customers and opportunities for partners. The reason is that partners can exploit various bilateral ties enabled by each partner's uniqueness rather than having to focus on one or few centres of gravity. This, among other factors, explains the success of large multilateral alliances like *Star* (*see* Brueckner and Whalen, 2000). The ability to move within a multi-centre alliance and exploit not only commonalities but also bilateral relationships is more likely to contain somewhat the inherent instability within multilateral alliances as partners seek new opportunities – structural holes. Thus, partners can enter and exit internal bilateral relations to explore opportunities and respond to competitive dynamics.

Partners need also to be able to enter and exit bilateral relationships external to the alliance when the external competitive pressures and opportunities cannot be resolved within. Consequently, multilateral alliances' processes that aim at maximum control of partner's through lock-in (for example, *Qualiflyer*) and exclusive relations will reduce strategic flexibility and reduce derived alliance benefits, since high performance multilateral alliances are dynamic co-opetition relationships.

Potentially high exit cost in a highly cooperative alliance hinders progression of alliance processes beyond alliance features that have low sunk costs. This is natural from the standpoint of the structural holes concept although it may limit the extraction of some alliance benefits enabled by full closure. Airlines may for example resist intensive IT link-ups involving proprietary strategic assets (*see* Feldman, 2002) such as common customer data-bases, common yield management systems and exclusive platforms with high resource tie-up, unless proprietary

---

12   Although it is difficult to furnish evidence for this assumption due to the few alliance groupings that exist, we can point out that the largest multilateral alliance *Star* with 28 members had a turnover in 2009 of $372,697per employee opposed to about $332,018 for Oneworld and $348,828 for SkyTeam. Star had about 1,315 passengers per employee, opposed to 1,084 for Oneworld and 1,213 for SkyTeam (based on Airline Business, 2009 and alliance websites).

assets can be ring-fenced and potential exit costs kept acceptable.[13] Thus, high performance is characterized by processes that are limited to flow improvement (for example, seamlessness and low intensity IT integration), cost-saving cooperation (for example, joint procurement) and revenue-generating network opportunities (structural holes) rather than partners' full cohesion through control and centrally dictated standards (strategic constraints).

6.3.4 Maximizing Resource Opportunities

Lindquist (1996) argued that as alliances proliferate, the relative benefits will decline, and in an environment characterized by shifting priorities, finding partners who share objectives and have similar long-term goals will become increasingly difficult. However, the concept of structural holes applied to multilateral airline alliances leads us to question the necessity for rigid common long-term goals and shared objectives of all partners. What really matters in a successful alliance is the maximization of resource opportunities (tapping value) to realize strategy leading to higher economic rent than if remaining alone. Each partner may have different strategic motives when taping into different resources within the boundaries of the alliance. For multilateral airline alliances we can argue that there could be many 'central' positions for partners depending on which resource we are looking at: frequent flyer programme, airport access, network connection, distribution network, maintenance capabilities, and so on.

One of the earliest multilateral alliances (established in 1975) – the KSSU (KLM, Swissair, SAS and UTA) revolved around cost savings achieved by partners' specialization in different aspects of aircraft maintenance and joint fleet purchasing: SAS and Swissair maintained airframes, while KLM concentrated on engines and UTA on landing gears. So far as all partners operated similar fleets of aircraft the alliance worked. In the 1980s the partners changed directions and the fleets became no longer compatible leading to the dissolving of the alliance in the early 1990s. This example demonstrates that similar strategies and objectives are unlikely to remain, and should certainly not be stifled by an alliance relationship: partners need to reshuffle the cards as strategic direction changes. An alliance that imposes specific aircraft types on partners is bound to enter and shed partners more rapidly than an alliance not setting such standards. Alliances are not strategy but means to realize strategy.

6.3.5 Alliance Over-embeddedness

The idea of structural holes is also linked to the idea of effective networks and a firm's autonomy of action. Structural holes are an opportunity to coordinate action and access valuable resources. An absence of non-redundant ties, however,

---

13   This is usually accomplished through general standards that allow uncomplicated transfer of assets back to the airline or some other multilateral alliance when exit occurs.

would mean that the autonomy of the firm is heavily restricted, since each decision taken by a firm is subject to the acceptance and influence of all the interconnected firms. Networks that have predominantly redundant ties restrict therefore a firm's autonomy and lead to a phenomenon that is called over-embeddedness: firm trapped in it own net (Gargiulo and Benassi, 2000). Countering this phenomenon, associated with full closure, existing multilateral alliances in the airline industry do allow flexibility for bilateral agreements external to the alliance as discussed before.[14]

A push towards cohesion or high level of 'cooperation' and reduced 'competition' within the alliance increases strategic constraints of partners. The constraining of partners will either cause departure of weaker partners or lead to increased emphasis on control and common processes as a tool to achieve the strategic and decision-making flexibility of a single firm and ultimately a merger as soon as exit costs surmount the financial viability of independence.

Multilateral alliances evolving to a high cooperation level will still retain the 'looseness' of an independent organization and potential agent's self-serving behaviour. These traits retained in an alliance will cause individual partners to depart from 'what is good for the alliance' to 'what is good for me' not a particular threat in a singular firm, but a potential cause for alliance break-up. The increasing exit costs of closer cooperation will further stimulate increasing need for formal contracts, eventually pushing for the transformation of the 'alliance structure' into a hierarchy (merger/acquisition). Actors having a clear vision to this effect can use the alliance to establish a comfortable relationship[15] and a slow progress towards a merger (Bleeke and Ernst, 1993; Haspeslagh and Jemison, 1991). However, a larger merged entity would still need to generate opportunities at the same time that network rationalization generates opportunities for competitors – structural holes. Thus, one can question if the merged larger entity would be in a better position to create opportunities although it may enhance market-power.

---

14   Multilateral alliances have stipulated a closed regime regarding partners cooperation with other multilateral alliances, but do allow external bilateral agreements to serve markets not accessible through the existing multilateral network (Ott, 2002).

15   The KLM-Air France merger could indicate the opposite, i.e. a fear that an alliance relationship preceding a merger could jeopardize the unification. For this reason 'two airlines' and single holding company may have its advantages and circumvent the apparent difficulties of cross-border mergers. An example from the automotive industry was the case of Volvo and Renault in the early 1990s, wanting to progress slowly towards a merger, but actually broke up during the alliance phase.

6.4 Multiplexity of Networks

6.4.1 Customer, Route and Rights Networks

Airline networks are characterized by multiplexity. The relations of an airline with other airlines might fulfil different functions and might lead to different values. Airlines possess: a customer base which can be defined as a *customer network*; routes that can be defined as a *route network*; access to exclusive geographical territories and international air services agreements that can be defined as a *rights network*. The value of these three different networks can be independent: an airline can be an attractive new member to a multilateral alliance because it has a large customer base and/or because it possesses a monopoly on some routes or exclusive geographical access (for example, US airlines within the USA). There are also indirect network resources: an airline might in theory possess neither a lot of customers nor fly on a lot of routes but be geographically well positioned. In this sense, we distinguish between three network resources of airlines and postulate that the motive for tapping into each of these may differ from one partner to another stimulating various bilateral ties within the boundaries of the multilateral alliance.

6.4.2 Partner Variety

Large size differences of customer, routes and/or rights networks will be a barrier to harmonization due to customer and supplier loyalty being regarded as a proprietary asset. Thus, the larger the transaction sets[16] and transaction networks,[17] the larger the proprietary assets retained by partners.

One of the most important assets of airlines is their customer base. Joining an alliance could mean that airlines lose some control over their most important assets by making them accessible to the other members of the alliance. For example, when Austrian Airlines left the *Qualiflyer* alliance, that ran a joint frequent flyer programme, it became an issue how to segregate the customers of the exiting partner from the remaining partners' customers (Gudmundsson, de Boer and Lechner, 2002). The more important the direct and the indirect customer networks through other partners, the less incentive an airline may have to join an alliance unless there are some mechanisms that allow for the protection of the customer base brought into the alliance and this instrument should also facilitate the theoretical exit of the firm without losing this exclusive and valuable asset. Such a mechanism could allow individual partners to build positional strength within the alliance through exploiting opportunities.

However, this might pose a problem: a small airline with a high proportion of non-redundant routes could gain a lot of influence within the alliance even if the customer base of this airline is small. The trade-off between a customer

---

16 Network of relationships with external parties (arms length).
17 A fixed network of relationships with external parties (permanent).

network with little value and a route network of high value might hinder the strengthening of alliance processes since large airlines might not be willing to share their large customer base, and a smaller airline possessing an important connecting node might consequently decide not to share access. Multiplexity of networks can therefore negatively influence alliance processes. Having in mind the different network resources we already mentioned, both parties have strong arguments for their position. In this sense, alliance partners have to develop some form of 'internal currency' to exchange diverse resources. Diverse complimentary resources are a facilitator for derived alliance benefits, since hard to replicate combinations of diverse resources can be a source of competitive advantage (Porter, 1980). If partners are willing to accept complimentary resources that firms bring into the alliance, partner variety can lead to the strengthening of alliance processes. In other words, in the presence of complementary resources and weak ties (Granovetter, 1973) the alliance grouping is more likely to explore new opportunities due to less strategic constraints and lower coordination costs when adding or shedding partners.

6.5 Conclusion

In this chapter multilateral airline alliances have been explored through the lenses of the structural-holes and network-closure views. One can conclude that airlines need to keep options open in order to generate opportunities, yet alliance cohesion provides important building blocks for realizing alliance value based on process trust and consequently lower coordination costs. Hence, the structural-holes view, advances our understanding on airline alliance behaviour by emphasizing strategic flexibility and opportunities. Using the balanced lenses of these views we are driven towards a combination of modest cohesion and generation of opportunities and value for partners. Lower emphasis on cohesion and common standards leads to more emphasis on inter-alliance bilateral relations within a closed group that generates opportunities through growth and renewal.

In multilateral airline alliances the trust benefit of alliance closure is clearly attractive to partners, whilst sufficient opportunities, structural holes, can only be maintained through adding partners with many non-reduntant ties and shedding partners with many redundant ties. However, this can be accomplished both internally and externally to the airline through bilateral ties. Consequently, highly distributed multilateral alliances such as *Star* should be better positioned to exploit opportunities than smaller (in members) higher density alliances such as *Skyteam* and *oneworld*.[18] In other words strategic constraints associated with alliance cohesion (closure) are offset by a greater set of within alliance opportunities

---

18   The Star alliance has the highest market share on three key transcontinental corridors out of four in 2010: Europe – Asia Pacific (37.4 per cent); North America – Asia (37.9 per cent); Europe – North America (39.3 per cent); (*Airline Business*, 2010).

stemming from greater scope and multiple network centres. What is more, strategic realignment causing the departure of an individual partner in a large multi-centre alliance is less likely to threaten the existence of the alliance itself or the remaining partner(s) if compared to an alliance composed of fewer members with greater density (for example, the former Qualiflyer and 'Wings' KLM-Northwest, and so on).

Turning alliances into hierarchies remains an interesting option for a highly cohesive closed multilateral alliance with locked-in partners. However, one must question whether large size per se in a hierarchy bears better fruit than the opportunities generated by a balanced multilateral alliance. We argued that a larger merged entity would rationalize its network generating opportunities for competitors. Furthermore, the enlarged hierarchy would search for alliance relationships to take advantage of structural holes and the story repeats itself.

All in all, airlines are strategically better off, balancing the benefits of openness and closure perspectives, that is, by remaining in an alliance and seeking mergers in a bilateral independent fashion rather than to engage in multilateral alliances to build a larger hierarchy. The alliances to mergers logic is by no means a natural process and especially not in the airline industry where large size is not necessarily associated with superior economic rents. The airline industry is much rather characterized by resource races where various new combinations of resources, opportunities, spell out the ability of individual airlines and group of airlines to achieve superior rents. Burt (2001) argued that firms should focus on the value added generated by structural holes, but exercise a degree of closure to realize the value buried in the holes, this is perhaps nowhere as true as for the airlines.

References

Airline Business (2010), Alliance survey, September, pp. 32–44.

Airline Business (2009), Alliance survey, September, pp. 43–60.

Airline Business (1998), Euro challenger, August, pp. 48–51.

Bleeke, E. and Ernst, D. (Eds) (1993), *Collaborating to compete: using strategic alliances and acquisitions in the global marketplace*. New York: John Wiley.

Bourdieu, P. and Wacquant, L.J.D. (1992), *An Invitation to Reflexive Sociology*, Chicago, IL: University of Chicago Press.

Brueckner, J.K. and Whalen, T.W. (2000), The price effects of international airline alliances. *Journal of Law and Economics*, 43(2), pp. 503–545.

Burt, R.S. (1992), *Structural holes*. Cambridge: Harvard University Press.

Burt, R.S. (2000), The network structure of social capital. In: Sutton, R.I. and Staw, B.M. (Eds), *Research in Organizational Behavior*, 22, Greenwich, CT: JAI Press.

Burt, R.S. (2001), Structural holes versus network closure as social capital. In: Lin, N., Cook, K.S. and Burt, R.S. (Eds), *Social Capital: Theory and Research*. New York: Aldine de Gruyter, pp. 31–56.

Child, J. and Faulkner, D. (1998), *Strategies of co-operation*. New York: Oxford University Press.

Coleman, J.S. (1988), Social capital in the creation of human capital. American *Journal of Sociology*, 94, pp. 95–120.

Coleman, J.S. (1990), *Foundations of social theory*. Cambridge, MA: Harvard University.

Feldman, J. (2002), Common connections. *Air Transport World*, November, pp. 56–59.

Gargiulo, M. and Benassi, M. (2000), Trapped in your own net? Network cohesion, structural holes, and the adaptation of social capital, *Organization Science*, 11(2), pp. 183–196.

Gomes-Cassares, B. (1994), Group versus group: how alliance networks compete, *Harvard Business Review* (July-August), pp. 62–74.

Granovetter, M. (1973), The strength of weak ties. *American Journal of Sociology*, 78, pp. 1360–1380.

Grant, R.M. (1991), The resource-based theory of competitive advantage: implications for strategy formulation. *California Management Review* (Spring), pp. 114–135.

Gudmundsson, S.V. and Rhoades, D. (2001), Airline Alliance Survival Analysis: Typology, Strategy and Duration, *Transport Policy*, 8(3), pp. 209–218.

Gudmundsson, S.V., de Boer, E.R. and Lechner, C. (2002), Integrating frequent flyer programs in multilateral airline alliances, *Journal of Air Transport Management*, 8, pp. 409–417.

Gwilliam, K. (2008). A review of issues in transit economics, *Research in Transportation Economics*, 23(1), pp. 4–22.

Hamel, G., Doz, Y.L. and Prahalad, C.K. (1989), Collaborate with your competitors- and win, *Harvard Business Review*, 67(1), pp. 133–139.

Haspeslagh, P. and Jemison, D. (1991), Relative standing: a framework for understanding departures of acquired executives, *Academy of Management Journal*, 36, pp. 733–762.

Holmberg, S. and Cummings, J. (2009), Building Successful Strategic Alliances: Strategic Process and Analytical Tool for Selecting Partner Industries and Firms, *Long Range Planning*, 42(2), pp. 164–193.

Hsu, C-I. and Shih, H-H. (2008), Small-world network theory in the study of network connectivity and efficiency of complementary international airline alliances, *Journal of Air Transport Management*, 14(3), pp. 123–129.

Levine, M.E. (1987), Airline competition in deregulated markets: theory, firm strategy and public policy, *Yale Journal of Regulation*, 4, Spring, pp. 393–494.

Lindquist, J. (1996), Alliances – Marriages made in heaven? *The Avmark Aviation Economist* (January/February), pp. 12–14.

Obstfeld, D. (2005), Social networks, the Tertius Iungens orientation, and involvement in innovation. *Administrative Science Quarterly*, 50, pp. 100–130.

Ott, J. (2002), Alliances may be fewer, but savings will improve. *Aviation Week & Space Technology*, 157(21), pp. 65–67.

Oum, T.H. and Yu, C. (1998), *Winning airlines: productivity and cost competitiveness of the world's major airlines.* Boston: Kluwer Academic Publishers.

Park, J-H. and Zhang, A. (2000), An empirical analysis of global airline alliances: Cases in North Atlantic Markets. *Review of Industrial Organization,* 16(4), pp. 367–384.

Park, J-H. (1997), The Effects of airline alliances on markets and economic welfare. *Transportation Research Part E: Logistics and Transportation Review,* 33(3), pp. 181–195.

Parkhe, A. (1991), Interfirm diversity, organizational learning and longevity in global strategic alliances, *Journal of International Business Studies,* 22, pp. 579–601.

Parkhe, A. (1998), Current issues in international alliances. *Business Horizons,* 4(6), pp. 2–3.

Podolny, J. and Page, K. (1998), Network forms of organization. *Annual Review of Sociology,* 24, pp. 57–76.

Porter, M. (1980), *Competitive Strategy: Techniques for analyzing industries and competitors,* New York: The Free Press.

Rhoades, D.L. and Lush, H. (1997), A typology of strategic alliances in the airline industry: Propositions for stability and duration, *Journal of Air Transport Management,* 3, pp. 109–114.

Teece, D.J. (1982), Towards an economic theory of the multiproduct firm, *Journal of Economic Behaviour and Organization,* 3(1), 39–63.

Wang, Z.H. and Evans, M. (2002), Strategic classification and examination of the developments of current airline alliance activities, *Journal of Air Transport Management,* 7(3), 73–101.

Chapter 7

Comparing the Economic and Operating Characteristics of Charter and Low-cost Scheduled Airlines

George Williams

Charter airlines in the past were always able to carry their passengers at significantly lower unit costs than scheduled carriers. The emergence of low-cost scheduled carriers, however, has radically altered this situation and produced major challenges for the charter operators (Williams, 2001). The operating costs of charter airlines and low-cost carriers are little different when adjusted for stage length and aircraft size. The greater flexibility offered to the traveller by low-cost scheduled carriers has seen the demise of many short haul charter services. More recently, low-cost operators have been turning their attentions to charter sectors of more than three hours. Charter airlines have responded to the decline in their traditional markets in different ways, some opting to reduce their shorter haul operations to concentrate on developing longer haul markets, while others have sought to emulate the low-cost scheduled business model either by introducing scheduled services along side their charter activities or by establishing scheduled subsidiaries (Williams, 2008). Not all of these latter strategic responses have proved to be successful, which has resulted in the disappearance of some well-known charter airlines.

The majority of charter services in Europe are provided by airlines that form part of vertically integrated tour operating organizations. The volatility of the charter market and its poor image with travellers had led tour operators to set up their own airlines. Typically, in-house charter airlines have provided between 70 per cent and 90 per cent of their parents' flight requirements (*Airfinance Journal*, 2005). In the face of a declining inclusive tour market in Europe, it is likely that not all tour operators will wish to continue to operate their own charter airlines. Kuoni has already sold off Edelweiss to Swiss International Airlines and indicated that it wishes to dispose of its other airline subsidiary Novair. The rapid expansion of Air Berlin with its acquisition of Belair, dba, LTU and Niki, and its planned purchase of Condor has led to possible further consolidation involving the larger German-owned tour operator TUI Travel (*Aviation Strategy*, 2008). In January 2009 Lufthansa and TUI Travel signed a memorandum of understanding covering plans to merge TUIfly with Germanwings and Eurowings. TUIfly itself was formed in 2007 by the combination of charter airline Hapagfly (known as Hapag-Lloyd until 2005) and low-cost scheduled carrier HLX.

There are just over 100 charter carriers operating commercial aircraft seating over 80 passengers in Europe.[1] These range in size from TUI with an aircraft fleet of 45 to a group of very small airlines with between one and five aircraft in operation. By contrast there are at the time of writing close to 30 low-cost scheduled carriers in existence in Europe, the largest of which easyJet and Ryanair operate fleets of 169 and 215 respectively. Table 7.1 shows the largest low-cost carriers that currently operate in Europe.

With many former charter only airlines now providing large numbers of scheduled services, it has become increasingly difficult to separate charter operations and the economics thereof from their overall operating performance. Hybrid leisure carriers providing both types of service are continuing to grow, representing a flexible response to the changes in traditional charter markets resulting from the rapid growth of LCC.

Table 7.1   Europe's largest low-cost scheduled airlines at January 2010

Airline	Country	Established as an LCC	Fleet	Comments
Air Berlin	Germany	2006	100	Charter operations began in 1979
Blue Air	Romania	2004	12	
Blu-Express	Italy	2005	2	Owned 100% by Blue Panorama
Bmibaby	UK	2002	19	Owned 100% by bmi
Cimber Sterling	Denmark	1999	26	Charter operations began in 1962
EasyJet	UK	1995	169	Acquired GB Airways in 2008
Flybe	UK	2002	75	Low cost regional
Germanwings	Germany	2002	27	Owned 100% by Lufthansa
Helvetic	Switzerland	2001	4	
Iceland Express	Iceland	2003	3	
Jet2.com	UK	2003	32	
Monarch	UK	2002	32	Charter operations began in 1967
Niki	Austria	2003	11	Owned 49.9% by Air Berlin
Norwegian	Norway	2002	47	Acquired FlyNordic in 2007
Ryanair	Ireland	1991	215	
Smart Wings	Czech Republic	2004	2	Owned 100% by Travel Service Airlines
Thomson	UK	2004	51	Owned 100% by TUI Travel. Charter operations began in 1962

1 Europe here includes the 27 EU Member States, Croatia, Iceland, Norway, Switzerland and Turkey.

Table 7.1   *Continued*

Transavia	Netherlands	2000	27	Owned 100% by KLM. Charter operations began in 1966.
Transavia France	France	2007	7	Owned 60% by Air France, 40% by Transavia
TUIfly.com	Germany	2002	30	TUI acquired 19.9% of Air Berlin and Air Berlin acquired a 19.9% equity in TUIfly in 2009
Vueling	Spain	2004	37	Vueling and Clickair merged. Iberia has a 45.9% equity in Vueling
Windjet	Italy	2003	13	
Wizz	Hungary	2004	24	

Note: Over the last year, the following European low-cost carriers have ceased trading: Centralwings, FlyGlobespan, MyAir, SkyEurope and Volareweb.

7.1 Key Characteristics of Charter and Low-cost Scheduled Airline Business Models

When considering the operating performances of charter and low-cost scheduled carriers, it is important to bear in mind the differences that exist between the various types of business model in terms of their operating characteristics (see Table 7.2). Variations in these operating features significantly affect the economics of an airline (Williams and Mason, 2004). Table 7.3 provides a summary of the sources of cost advantage for three types of business model, namely: charter, low-cost scheduled and leisure hybrid (essentially a combination of the two).

Table 7.2   Key features of charter, low-cost scheduled and leisure hybrid business models

Features	Charter	Low cost	Leisure hybrid
Direct sell	✗	✓	✓
Extensive outsourcing	(✓)	✓	(✓)
High-density seating	✓	✓	✓
High public awareness	✗	✓	✓
No in-flight catering	✗	✓	(✓)
Pre-bookable seats	✓	(✓)	✓
Point-to-point traffic only	✓	✓	✓
Seat assignment	✓	(✓)	(✓)
Secondary airports	(✓)	✓	(✓)

Table 7.2   *Continued*

Short-haul focus	✗	(✓)	(✓)
Short turnarounds	✗	✓	(✓)
Single aircraft-type	✗	✓	✗
Single-class cabin	(✓)	✓	(✓)
24-hour operation	✓	✗	(✓)

Note: Brackets indicate that the advantage does not apply to all carriers in the category.

Table 7.3   Sources of cost advantage

Characteristic	Low-cost scheduled	Integrated charter	Leisure hybrid
Larger aircraft > 200 seats		✈	(✈)
Longer sectors > 1500 kms		✈	(✈)
Load factor > 85%		✈	(✈)
High aircraft-utilization	✈	✈	✈
High labour-productivity	✈	✈	✈
Low distribution costs	✈	(✈)	(✈)
Low passenger-service costs	✈	(✈)	(✈)
Low landing-fees	(✈)	✈	(✈)
Low admin & finance costs	✈	✈	✈

Note: Brackets indicate that the advantage does not apply to all carriers in the category.

7.2 Cost Differences Between Charter and 'No-Frills' Scheduled Carriers

The combination of large aircraft, long-flight sectors, high aircraft-and-crew utilization, and high load-factors has provided charter airlines with low operating costs per passenger. The average sector flown by Europe's charter airlines is around 2,500 kms, over double the average distance flown by the low-cost scheduled companies (Figure 7.1). It is invariably the case that unit costs fall as sector distance and aircraft carrying capacity increases.

While it is undoubtedly the case that charter carriers achieve the lowest unit operating costs of all, when adjustments are made to take into consideration the differences in average stage length and average aircraft capacity between low-cost 'no-frills' airlines and charter carriers the LCC Ryanair is the clear winner in the lowest operating cost stakes. Figure 7.2 shows the influence of stage length in 2006 on the unit costs of five LCC (easyJet, Germanwings, Jet 2, Ryanair, Vueling), five charter airlines (Astraeus, Excel, First Choice, MyTravel, Thomas Cook) and two leisure hybrid companies (Air Berlin, Monarch). Ryanair's unit cost is more than

40 per cent lower than the unit cost trend curve indicates would be the equivalent figure for the five charter carriers and two hybrid leisure companies at an average stage length of 1,000 kms. By contrast, the other four LCC shown in Figure 7.2 have unit costs either equivalent to or higher than the levels achieved by the five charter and two hybrid leisure carriers when these are adjusted for average stage length.

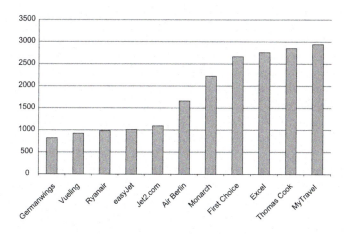

Figure 7.1   Average sector distance flown (kms) in 2006
Sources: ICAO and UK CAA.

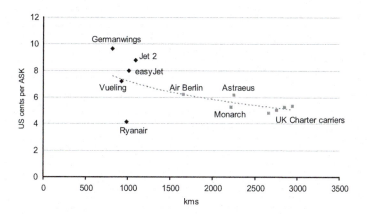

Figure 7.2   Influence of stage length on unit operating costs (2006 data)
Sources: UK CAA, ICAO, ATI.

7.3 Operating Cost Implications of the Hybrid Leisure Carrier Business Model

In response to the loss of many of their traditional short haul markets charter operators have acted in different ways. First Choice and Thomas Cook have steered clear of operating scheduled services,[2] while Monarch, MyTravel and Thomson[3] have done so with varying degrees of success (Air Transport World, 2005). Monarch has undergone the greatest transformation, however, with 60 per cent of its passengers carried on its scheduled services by early 2008 (up from 17 per cent in 2002). The airline began operating scheduled services to a small number of its traditional holiday charter destinations in Spain and Portugal back in 1983, but since 2000 has considerably expanded its scheduled operations. Figure 7.3 traces the relationship between Monarch's unit operating costs and its scheduled/charter traffic mix between 1999 and 2008. Between 2001 and 2008 the carrier's unit cost has risen by around 90 per cent to almost 6.5 US cents per ASK, while the proportion of its ASKs devoted to scheduled operations has grown from nine per cent to almost 50 per cent over the same period. Judging by the increases in unit costs experienced by other UK carriers that have continued to focus primarily on charter operations, Monarch appears to have been able to manage this transformation in its business model in a relatively cost effective manner (see Figures 7.4, 7.5 and 7.6).

Between 2001 and 2007 First Choice's unit cost rose by 63 per cent to 5.88 US cents per ASK, while the proportion of its ASKs devoted to scheduled operations fell from 22 per cent to zero over the same period (Figure 7.4). Between 2002 and 2006, Excel's unit cost rose by 35 per cent to 5.01 US cents per ASK. Only four per cent of the carrier's capacity was devoted to scheduled operations in 2001 and none in 2006 (Figure 7.5). Thomas Cook Airlines (UK) experienced a 34 per cent increase in unit operating cost between 2001 and 2007 from 3.95 to 5.3 US cents per ASK, while the proportion of its ASKs devoted to scheduled operations rose from zero to 10 per cent over the same period (Figure 7.6).

---

2   Aside, that is, from operating to a small number of destinations for regulatory reasons.

3   The charter airline Britannia adopted the Thomsonfly name in 2005. From May 2008, Thomsonfly and First Choice Airways began operating under a single AOC and by mid 2009, the two carriers were combined as Thomson Airways.

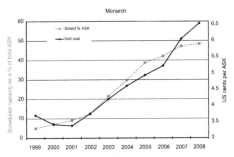

Figure 7.3   Relation between Monarch's unit cost and its scheduled/charter mix

Sources: UK CAA, ATI.

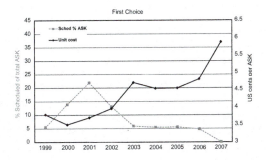

Figure 7.4   Relation between First Choice's unit cost and its scheduled/ charter mix

Sources: UK CAA.

Note: First Choice merged with Thomson Airways in November 2008.

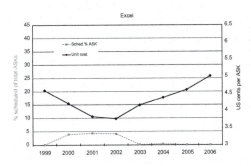

Figure 7.5   Relation between Excel's unit cost and its scheduled/charter mix

Sources: UK CAA.

Note: XL Airways (UK), known as Excel until 2006, ceased trading in September 2008.

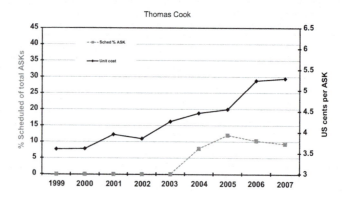

Figure 7.6   Relationship between Thomas Cook's unit cost and its schedule/charter mix

Sources: UK CAA, ATI.

Note: MyTravel Airways merged with homas Cook Airlines in March 2008.

7.4 Financial Performance Comparison of the Different Business Models

In terms of financial performance, it is apparent that Ryanair has achieved by far the best results of Europe's LCCs. Figure 7.7 depicts the operating ratios[4] of four of Europe's no frills scheduled carriers (easyJet, Jet2, Ryanair, Vueling) from 2000 to 2008. Vueling, which began operations in 2004, has yet to return a profit, while Jet2, which commenced services in 2003, has achieved only very modest returns in 2007. By contrast, easyJet has performed to a similar level as the best performing of the charter airlines, First Choice (see Figure 7.8). It is apparent from available data and anecdotal evidence in respect of other European LCCs, that many purveyors of this business model are not profitable.

Figure 7.8 depicts the operating ratios of five UK charter carriers (Excel, First Choice,[5] Monarch, MyTravel,[6] Thomas Cook)[7] from 2000 to 2008. Charter operators responded in different ways to the growth of low-cost scheduled carriers, with Excel, First Choice and Thomas Cook steering clear of operating scheduled services.[8] MyTravel's entry to the low-cost scheduled market began in October 2002 in the form of its subsidiary MyTravelLite and lasted three years before being subsumed into the charter airline, at a time when the MyTravel Group was experiencing severe financial difficulties. It would appear that First Choice's

---

4   The operating ratio is a financial term defined as a company's operating expenses as a percentage of revenue.

5   First Choice changed its name from Air 2000 in 2004.

6   MyTravel was known as Airtours until 2002.

7   Thomas Cook changed its name from jmc in 2003.

8   Apart from operating to a small number of destinations for regulatory reasons.

strategy of reducing its dependence on short haul mainstream holiday destinations, developing a better quality long haul product and acquiring specialist niche market tour operators has proved to be the most successful strategic response. Ryanair however, has clearly achieved the best financial performance of all the lower cost carriers, whether scheduled or charter (Figure 7.9).

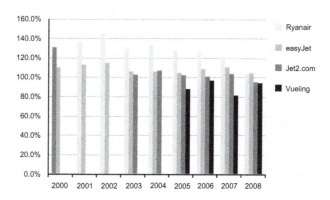

Figure 7.7   Operating ratios of four European LCCs from 2000 to 2008
Sources: UK CAA, ICAO, ATI.
Note: Jet 2 commenced operations in February 2003 and Vueling in July 2004.

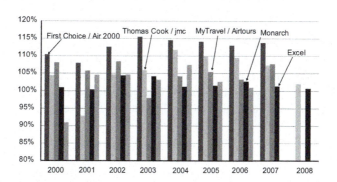

Figure 7.8   Operating ratios of five European charter carriers from 2000 to 2008
Sources: UK CAA, ICAO, ATI.
Note: First Choice merged with Thomson Airways in November 2008. MyTravel Airways merged with Thomas Cook Airlines in March 2008.

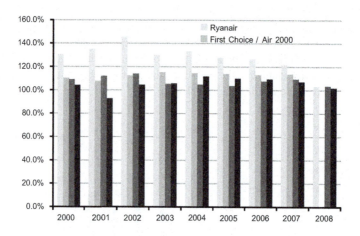

Figure 7.9   Operating ratios of best performing European LCC and charter airlines

Sources: UK CAA, ICAO, ATI. Note: First Choice merged with Thomson Airways in November 2008.

7.5 What Next?

Most European countries have experienced a significant decline in charter traffic. Over the next decade it would seem probable that in most short haul markets the services provided by LCC will replace package tour charter flights. Further market liberalization (for example, EU–North Africa) and the accession of additional countries to the EU (particularly, Turkey) will lead to further contraction of the charter sector. Overall, Europe's charter sector is likely to contract to only half its present size within 10 years. Its focus will be increasingly on medium to long haul operations, with much emphasis on seeking out niche markets.

References

Airfinance Journal (2005), Charting the Future, March, pp. 31–33.

Air Transport World (2005), First Choice Airways goes after the upper end of the leisure market, May, p. 48.

Aviation Strategy (2008), Europe's charter industry consolidates into two giants, January/February, pp. 2–8.

UK Airlines (1999–2008), Civil Aviation Authority, London.

UK Airline Financial Tables (2000–2008), Civil Aviation Authority, London.

Williams, G. (2001), Will Europe's charter airlines be replaced by 'no-frills' scheduled airlines?, *Journal of Air Transport Management*, vol. 7, pp. 277–286.

Williams, G. (2008), *The Future of Charter Operations* in *Aviation and Tourism*, Edited by Graham, A., Papatheodorou, A. and Forsyth, P., Ashgate.

Williams, G. and Mason, K. (2004), *Market Analysis of Europe's Low Cost Airlines (2nd Edition)*, Air Transport Group Research Report 9, Cranfield University.

Chapter 8

Airlines and Tourism: Interrelations and Trends

Andreas Papatheodorou

8.1 Introduction

Tourism is one of the largest sectors in the modern service economy. According to the United Nations World Tourism Organization, 880 million international tourism arrivals were recorded in 2009; this constitutes a sharp increase since 1990 when 436 million were recorded or even 2000 when 682 million arrivals were reported (UNWTO, 2008; 2010). International tourism receipts in 2009 accounted for US$852 billion, that is, US$970 per arrival (UNWTO, 2010). The above statistics do not incorporate the impact of domestic tourism, which may be of even greater importance. In 2009, the global travel and tourism industry contributed with 3.2 per cent into the world GDP (that is, US$1,870 billion) supporting 77.3 million jobs (that is, 2.7 per cent of total employment) (WTTC, 2009). Moreover, when the total (that is, direct, indirect and induced) economic effects of the travel and tourism industry are considered, its GDP share rises to 9.4 per cent (that is, US$5,474 billion) and job generation to 219.8 million (that is, 7.6 per cent of total employment) (WTTC, 2009). Although the footprint of the recent financial crisis on the short run tourism forecasts is still apparent, the long-term future of the travel and tourism industry looks brighter (UNWTO, 2010; WTTC, 2009). Economic contribution of tourism is also expected to rise accordingly.

Air transport is structurally interrelated to tourism. The demand for air transport is essentially derived, that is, very few people fly for the sake of flying, as the great majority flies to go somewhere and do something. Given that tourism comprises not only leisure but also business, health, sport and other activities (according to the UNWTO definition), it is not a coincidence that the business patterns of the two sectors move in parallel: both are highly cyclical and are strongly affected by external factors including recession and political instability. In fact, the airline industry may be termed as a tourist one, since its 'tourism ratio' is often over 90 per cent. The latter refers to tourism related receipts of a specific sector expressed as a percentage of its total turnover (Smith, 1998). When the ratio is over 15 per cent, then the existence and survival of the sector in question would face serious difficulties in the absence of tourism; for this reason, the sector is regarded as part of the wider tourism industry. In fact, about 50 per cent of international tourists travel by air today compared to 35 per cent in 1980 (Kester, 2009), while the direct employment effect of air transport on tourism is estimated at 7.7 million jobs (ATAG, 2008).

This chapter studies the relationship between tourism and air transport. Section 8.2 assesses the implications of airline deregulation for tourism whereas Section 8.3 studies vertical integration between air transport and the distribution system. Sections 8.4 and 8.5 then focus on two major trends, that is, dynamic packaging and short-breaks. Finally, Section 8.6 summarizes and concludes.

8.2 Implications of Airline Deregulation for Tourism: An Assessment

The deregulation of the airline industry in the European Economic Area (completed with the full implementation of the Third Package in April 1997) had important implications for tourism. The intensification of competition has often resulted in lower fares and occasionally in improved service quality (in terms of higher flight frequency, punctuality and better services on board) in the last decade. Thick routes benefited largely from these developments, as the traditional market incumbents had to fight the newly established low-fare airlines when the latter introduced scheduled and cheap point-to-point services to a large number of destinations (Papatheodorou, 2002). This new breed of carriers also initiated flights to previously un-serviced areas in continental Europe empowering the regions and enhancing accessibility. To survive in this changing business environment, charter airlines had to restructure their model adopting practices from both the traditional scheduled and the low-fare carriers (Papatheodorou and Lei, 2006). In particular, they tried to resemble the former in terms of service reliability and quality and the latter by relaxing or even removing existing constraints in holiday packages, for example, by enabling passengers to buy seat-only, single ticket packages instead of a bundle of services including accommodation, transfers, and so on. The impact of these changes on the tourism product is significant as cost reduction in one of its major components (that is, transport) encouraged people to travel more. Ryanair[1] is a prominent example of an airline, which generates traffic and complementary tourism expenditure mainly in the hospitality sector of the serviced destinations. For this reason, many small secondary airports and local authorities across Europe are prepared to offer large subsidies to attract the Irish carrier (Papatheodorou, 2003; Papatheodorou and Arvanitis, 2009).

In addition to the above-mentioned positive impacts, air transport deregulation is associated with negative implications for tourism. In particular, the market has experienced instability as many carriers incurred losses while some of them have declared bankruptcy over the last decade. Over the period of 2008–09 some traditional airlines that have ceased trading include: Aloha Airlines and Skybus in the US; Oasis in Asia, while Europe's Sabena and Swissair have been taken over

---

1   Ryanair carried around 66 million passengers in the financial year ending 31 March 2010.

by Lufthansa. Some examples of European low-fare carriers that no longer operate include Debonair, Air Polonia, MyAir, Duo Airlines and SkyEurope. In fact, deregulation may effectively lead to dramatic market concentration; the 10 largest airlines in the US have a domestic market share exceeding 80 per cent (Bureau of Transportation Statistics, 2009), while some analysts believe that the end-market configuration in Europe may involve consolidation and survival of only three major network carriers (that is, British Airways, Air France and Lufthansa) and three low-fare ones (that is, Ryanair, easyJet and Air Berlin). Increasing concentration may result in restricted market conduct (behaviour) or even tacit collusion; the few remaining carriers may then generate super-profits at the expense of the tourists' welfare; for this reason, policymakers should be attentive to face the emerging problems in competition (O'Connell, 2006).

Another important topic to consider is the relationship between deregulation, air safety and perceptions of tourists (Papatheodorou and Platis, 2007). According to the available accident statistics, the aeroplane is the safest transport mode (ICAO, 2005); yet, there is always a popular argument that cost reduction in air services is achieved to the detriment of safety standards. Early studies using US deregulation data suggested that such fears are unfounded (Rose, 1992; Borenstein and Zimmermann, 1988). More recent evidence, however, supports mixed results (Raghavan and Rhoades, 2005). Major low-fare airlines operating in countries with a transparent institutional framework are unlikely to be negligent on safety issues; nonetheless, the outcome may be different in countries where regulation constraints are not fully enforced. In any case, it is expected that persisting airline accidents could have a very negative effect on tourism, especially in destinations serviced predominantly by unreliable carriers and/or in long-haul areas where transport mode substitutability is effectively impossible.

Deregulation may also be associated with negative social and environmental effects. Although accessibility enhancement is often regarded as highly important by local authorities, plans for airport construction or expansion may occasionally raise tensions among local people; this resistance is often termed NIMBY (Not In My Back Yard) and is often associated with the negative impact that airports may have on noise levels, neighbouring road congestion, the possible contamination of underground water sources and the overall landscape of an area (Daley et. al. 2003). Still, NIMBY tension may emergence as a way to express resentment against further tourism development. The case of Chios Island in Greece is a good example, where in the 1980s and 1990s the local population was against the island's airport expansion as this would bring unwelcome tourism flows; illustratively, the locals once greeted a prime-ministerial visit with black flags to deter the prime minister from referring to a runway expansion, whereas in other cases the locals entered the runway to prevent aircraft from landing!

NIMBY protests may have recently escalated in certain areas as a result of deregulation since increased demand for travel and higher schedule frequency put pressure on existing airport capacity (Graham and Guyer, 1999). In this context, NIMBY may also be related to the possible negative impact of aviation on the environment. Rising polluting gas emissions from aircraft may lead to a deterioration of air quality and facilitate the conditions for global warming. Although contemporary aircraft are more fuel efficient and less noisy than in the past (ATAG, 2008), the scale effects of deregulation may overshadow any possible technological improvements. As a result, certain tourism areas may become victims of their own success. Reduced fares in a deregulated market may generate additional tourism flows that exceed a destination's carrying capacity with devastating consequences for the physical and built environment. Such development is clearly unsustainable. Moreover, lower fares may induce some poorer people to fly for the first time and engage in mass tourism activities. Despite the social benefits of this tourism democratization, certain area may experience a reduction of tourism receipts in per capita terms and subsequently suffer from a low-quality image (Papatheodorou and Song, 2005).

Islands and small states may be particularly susceptible to these negative connotations because of their limited territorial scale and fragile bio-environment. To validate this argument, Papatheodorou and Liasidou (2006) undertook primary research in Cyprus. They interviewed business and government executives on the possible role of airline deregulation in Cypriot tourism; to enable comparison, interviews took place in 2003 and 2005, that is, one year before and one year after the accession of Cyprus into the European Union.

According to Figure 8.1, respondents seem to be supportive of the view that air transport deregulation will lead to an increase of tourism arrivals in Cyprus. Nonetheless, respondents are rather sceptical in 2005 compared to 2003 realizing the increasing competition for market share in the Mediterranean tourism. Moreover, Figure 8.2 produces evidence that respondents have become more cautious about the environmental impacts of deregulation; whereas in 2003 the great majority of interviewees were neutral, in 2005 there is a shift of opinion towards pessimism.

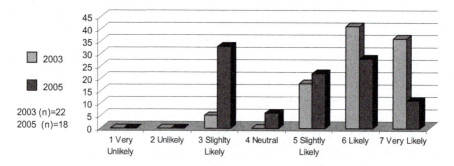

Figure 8.1   Will air transport deregulation lead to an increase of tourism arrivals in Cyprus? (per cent respondents)

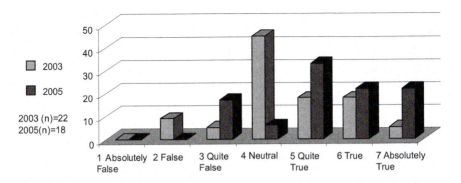

Figure 8.2   Will air transport deregulation have negative environmental impacts in Cyprus? (per cent respondents)

8.3 Air Transport, Leisure Travel and the Distribution System

Leisure travel has been traditionally associated with the concept of a holiday package. According to the European Commission Package Travel Regulations (currently under review) a package may be defined as 'the pre-arranged combination of at least two of the following components when sold or offered for sale at an inclusive price and when the service covers a period of more than 24 hours or includes overnight accommodation: a) transport, b) accommodation, c) other tourist services not ancillary to transport or accommodation and accounting for a significant proportion of the package' (Yale, 1995: 1). Holiday packages are put together by tour operators who can then either sell the product directly to the customer or through a travel agent. In this context, the tour operator acts as the wholesaler and the travel agent as the retailer in the holiday package market: in the financial year ending June 2008, 23 million British travelled overseas having booked a package with a tour operator (Starmer-Smith, 2009).

    To sell their packages effectively, a number of large tour operators have engaged in vertical integration practices with the air transport sector. In this context, they bought or established charter carriers, which operate on a seasonal basis to leisure destinations (see Chapter 7 which discusses the charter airline industry). Typical examples in Britain included Thomson with Britannia Airways and First Choice with Air2000, which are now all part of the TUI Group, the largest travel conglomerate in Europe. Vertical integration allows the tour operator to control and better manage the airline seat inventory; in its absence, the operator may be unable to secure sufficient number of air seats to meet potential seasonal hikes in demand. On the other hand, in case of a recession a tour operator may ask its affiliated airline to redirect or lease its aircraft to more profitable destinations. This is in sharp contrast with vertical integration involving hotels, which are spatially fixed by definition. Moreover, a tour operator may vertically integrate with a charter airline to avoid double marginalization and offer its package at a more competitive price: had the tour operator and the airline been independent, they would charge a separate price mark-up adding to the final travel cost at the expense of the customer. Conversely, the avoidance of double marginalization allows the operator to enhance its profitability by entering into a complementary market.

Vertical integration may also be used to erect barriers to market entry (Papatheodorou, 2006). In particular, a tour operator may ask its affiliated airline to sign an exclusivity contract denying seats to its rival operators; alternatively, the airline may be asked to offer such seats only at a very high cost. As a result, to survive and prosper in the marketplace the other tour operators will have to follow suit, that is, to buy or establish their own charter carriers. Such a strategy, however, is very expensive and few operators can afford it. Hence vertical integration may turn the tour operations market into a highly concentrated oligopoly. Such practices, though, are clearly anti-competitive and may draw the attention of the competition authorities. Moreover, a tour operator may abstain from constraining its affiliated carrier to such a degree fearing that some of its seats may remain unsold and lost forever. In fact, a tour operator may prefer to exercise its bargaining power and sign exclusivity contracts with non-affiliated airlines to avoid internalizing the cost of unsold seats.

In addition to vertical integration practices stemming from the tour operator's side (upstream integration), downstream business strategies are also apparent, that is, scheduled airlines establishing their own tour operators. Typical examples include British Airways with British Airways Holidays, Virgin Atlantic with Virgin Holidays and Emirates with Emirates Holidays. These carriers offer holiday packages to their home consumers based on scheduled flights from conveniently located airports. Moreover, they generate business from inbound tourists, wishing to travel, for example, to Britain or Dubai. Increasingly, such tour operators also address the global market using sixth-freedom rights of their carriers. For example, Emirates Holidays offers honeymoon holiday packages to Mauritius to customers residing in Greece; the idea is that the customer would fly from Athens to Port Louis via Dubai with Emirates.

The rationale behind such integration moves is similar to the arguments presented earlier; major emphasis is put onto securing a marketplace to sell spare seat capacity. In this context, the business of tour operations provides a complementary service to yield management techniques utilized extensively by scheduled airlines. Although leisure travel tends to be more price elastic than business trips (hence commanding lower price premia), at least some people are willing to spend extra money to celebrate a special occasion, for example, their honeymoon to a remote destination. By offering such integrated services through an affiliated tour operator, the airline may secure additional premium passengers, who, if properly served, may become loyal customers for a lifetime. Moreover, by introducing special offers and building on the power of their frequent flyer schemes, scheduled airlines can generate further business for their tour operations and subsequent profitability for their entire group of companies.

Will such vertical relationships continue to prosper in the future? As argued earlier, the airline marketplace has become increasingly unstable since the introduction of airline deregulation. To survive in a competitive environment such portfolio activities should be combined with inherent flexibility to better match the changing consumer preferences. In this context, dynamic packaging may become the way forward despite a number of caveats as now argued in Section 8.4.

8.4 Air Transport and Dynamic Packaging in Tourism

The popularity of packaged holidays has been recently questioned primarily due to the emergence of dynamic or DIY packaging. In fact, one of the major advancements of the Internet revolution was disintermediation, that is, the possibility for the consumer to transact directly with the service producer without the middleman. Dynamic packaging is inherently flexible as it allows the customer to build their own holiday package by assimilating individual components such as flight, accommodation and car hire. It is dynamic because pricing, constraints and ultimate choice are determined online based on a real-time inventory. In this way, consumers become travel agents of their own selves and derive satisfaction by building a tailor-made package, which better suits their individual needs. Moreover, consumers feel that they are in control as pricing is transparent in contrast to the obscure deals of the past (Stabler et al., 2010).

Mounting competitive pressures and subsequent cost reduction efforts have made the airlines think about possible ways to reduce commission to traditional travel agencies. The way ahead was e-ticketing, which allows disintermediation as passengers can now buy their tickets on the websites of the airline and its associates (web portals, online travel agencies). More recently, airlines stepped forward by engaging into dynamic packaging activities themselves, offering hotel bookings, excursions and car hire. In fact, generating additional revenue through ancillary revenues has become a major issue especially among low-fare airlines,[2] which have joined forces with various other service providers to start replicating the business of tour operators; for example, by visiting the Ryanair website (www. ryanair.com) potential customers may not only book tickets (through Ryanair itself), hotel rooms (through booking.com) and car hire (through Hertz) but they may even buy gift vouchers and play Bingo online (offered by jackpotjoy.com)! In other words, Ryanair has not only fully embedded the derived nature of the airline product in its business model but it has also gone beyond this to fully capitalize on the huge popularity of its website.

It seems, therefore, that dynamic packaging may be the way forward both for airlines and consumers. Still, there are a number of potential caveats that should be carefully assessed. From an airline's perspective, temptations to boost revenue

---

2   Ancillary revenues made up over 25 per cent of Allegiant Airlines (US-based) total revenues in 2009 and 20 per cent of Ryanair's revenues (Murphy, 2009).

from ancillary services may damage the value as well as the proper marketing of the core product. In fact, an airline may decide to cross-subsidise its products by selling its flights cheaply hoping to raise profits through complimentary products sold at high margins. Such a strategy may prove risky, however, as the airline is legally prohibited from making certain conditional offers. As a result, the customer may first buy a cheap ticket from the carrier and then visit the website of other service providers to continue their online purchases on an independent basis. Moreover, an airline may become too obsessed with increasing ancillary revenue and devote many of its marketing and other resources towards this aim. As a result, airlines may pay less attention to the core airline product, which may subsequently deteriorate in terms of service quality thus leading to lower customer satisfaction and brand dilution. Finally, airlines should be careful to use dynamic packaging in a way that does not cannibalize existing partnerships and/or integrated relationships with the travel distribution system. For this very reason, British Airways performs dynamic packaging through British Airways Holidays, which also continues selling traditional holidays packages.

Dynamic packaging may also bear risks for passengers too, essentially due to inadequate consumer protection. This is particularly applicable to Britain but similar issues are also faced by other countries. In particular, the United Kingdom operates a system of air insolvency protection organized by the Civil Aviation Authority (CAA), which is based on Air Travel Organizers' Licensing (ATOL) (Yale, 1995). The relevant regulations '... require companies selling air travel to hold ATOL licences unless they operate the flights themselves, or provide an airline ticket or ATOL holder's confirmation straight away' (CAA, 2005: A1). Until 2008, ATOL applications were accompanied by bonding funded by the applicant's own capital. In that year, the bonding system was largely replaced by the ATOL Protection Contribution (APC) scheme, which enables the Air Travel Trust of the CAA '... to collect contributions from ATOL holders, based on £1 for every passenger booked under an ATOL' (CAA, 2008: 6). The scheme is financially backed by a credit facility with Barclays Bank, a British government guarantee and an insurance policy with AIG UK (CAA, 2008). Outgoing tour operators and travel agents are the main ATOL holders, whereas scheduled or charter carriers selling ticket-only services are not covered by the scheme. Because of ATOL protection, the CAA is able to offer substantial help to customers of collapsing travel companies, including cover of repatriation fees for those stranded abroad and refunding for those who have paid a deposit against future travel. Illustratively, between 1986 and 2005, ATOL funds were used to repatriate over 200,000 customers at the end of their holidays, while more than 1,000,000 were refunded (CAA, 2005); moreover, in 2008 and thanks to ATOL protection, 1,650 passengers managed to complete their holidays and be safely repatriated, while 20,771 received back their advance payments (CAA, 2008).

The original rationale behind the exclusion of scheduled carriers from the ATOL scheme was twofold. First, the great majority of scheduled airlines were state-owned in the past hence the probability of bankruptcy was regarded as extremely low. Second, holiday-making was essentially associated with an inclusive package combining at least a charter flight with accommodation; scheduled flights were predominantly reserved to business passengers (CAA, 2005). Nonetheless, the emergence of low-fare airlines and the subsequent advancements in dynamic packaging have radically changed the market scene. In fact, none of these DIY packages are ATOL-protected simply because they are not covered by the legal EC definition of a holiday package. Illustratively, ATOL covered about 98 per cent of leisure air passengers in 1997; this percentage has fallen, however, down to 66 per cent in 2004 and 57 per cent in 2006 (CAA, 2005; Department for Transport, 2007). This means that a significant number of air passengers are not protected in sharp contrast to the previous decade. Interestingly, these passengers are not only carried by scheduled airlines (traditional and low fare) but also by charter carriers, which now sell ticket-only packages.

Had the passengers realized the lack of protection, they could have reacted accordingly. Nonetheless, most surveys reveal that the great majority of customers are unaware of the fact that dynamic packages are not protected by ATOL (CAA, 2005). To make things worse, few travel insurance policies cover against airline insolvency. As a result, ATOL holders are found at a competitive disadvantage: due to the financial obligations of the scheme their average cost and prices are higher compared to those of dynamic packaging service providers; on the other hand, ignorance of the legal framework means that customers are unable to appreciate the added value of the protection offered by the former. To deal with this problem, tour operators and travel agents may actively seek ways to sell their products out of the ATOL undermining the very existence of this protection mechanism. Nonetheless, the widely publicized airline failures in 2008 (including the collapse of the XL Leisure Group) made the risks involved in uninsured DIY travelling become more apparent supporting indirectly bookings with tour operators and travel agents (Association of British Travel Agents, 2008). In fact, and possibly also due to the effect of the economic recession and the subsequent need to carefully manage their travel budget, consumers seem to have recently rediscovered the virtues of all-inclusive package holidays (Starmer-Smith, 2009).

8.5 Air Transport, Tourism and Short Breaks

Vacation habits and patterns have changed dramatically over the last 25 years. Whereas in the past, most people would opt for a 2–4 week holiday in the summer followed by 1–2 week break in the winter, travel behaviour is now characterized by shorter though more frequent breaks. This is largely related to changes in work requirements, as it is becoming increasingly difficult to be away from the office over prolonged periods of time; for certain business executives, terms like 'working holiday' and 'stay connected' are part of their everyday life. Moreover, an increasing part of the population is becoming DINK (Double Income No Kids); these cash-rich, time-poor professional couples find it difficult to take long vacations at the same time, whereas on the other hand they can afford short breaks on a regular basis even off-season as they have no children obligations. A short break may also provide an excellent opportunity for a get-together of friends and family; in this context, it is also related to Visiting Friends and Relatives (VFR) traffic.

One of the often noted consequences of low-fare airlines was the introduction of short breaks involving air travel. These first appeared between the UK and Ireland following the market deregulation in the mid 1980s. Increasingly, however, low-fare airlines have managed to service a multitude of destinations within a two-hour flight range from major cities in Britain, Germany and Italy. As a result, a Londoner may now spend a long weekend flying to Prague, Milan or Barcelona at an affordable price. It may even prove cheaper to spend a long weekend abroad than partying at home! According to anecdotal evidence, Go introduced the London–Prague route in the late 1990s with great success not only because of wanderlust tourists who wanted to visit the famous monuments of this Central European city but also thanks to British boozers who had the opportunity to taste the cheaper but excellent Czech beer.

In fact, short breaks involving air travel have become so popular in Western Europe that an increasing number of people decide to buy a second home abroad for holiday and/or investment. According to a study undertaken by Mintel, 800,000 households in Britain owned a second home abroad in 2006; this constitutes a rise of about 45 per cent in comparison with June 2004 (Kirby, 2006). Such consumer decisions are welcomed by low-fare airlines as they establish a captured, spatially locked-in clientele for their services. Conversely, however, short-break travellers lose their bargaining power against the airlines as their price elasticity is reduced. In fact, this may have devastating effects in case an airline operates a monopoly service, as with Ryanair to a number of secondary airports around Europe. If such an airline decides to drop a destination in favour of another one (as Ryanair did with Strasbourg in favour of Karlsruhe Baden), then people who have bought property at the dumped destination may suffer not only for major inconvenience but also from capital loss; this is likely to be the case when the majority of real estate transactions in the local market comes from other foreign second-home seekers. Similar though of potentially wider scale may be the results of a low-fare airline becoming insolvent, which is not unusual these days.

Finally, this short break frenzy may be curbed in the future by plans of the European Commission to introduce certain policy instruments in order to internalize the impact of air travel on the environment. Such economic instruments may include aircraft fuel taxes, inclusion of air transport in the EU emissions trading scheme (see for example the relevant Directive 2008/101/EC published in the Official Journal of the EU in January 2009), en-route charges or taxes on aircraft emissions and impacts, departure and/or arrival taxes as well as VAT on air transport. According to a 2005 survey undertaken by the European Union Directorate General for the Environment (EUDGE), 68 per cent of the respondents fully agree and a further 17 per cent rather agree that the cost of climate change should be included in the price of air transport (Cairns and Newson, 2006). If the airline industry fails to convince policymakers of its substantial contribution to the economy compared to its light use of infrastructure, then the introduction of some sort of taxation may be unavoidable in the near future. Similarly to the case of levies for protection against airline insolvency, if such taxation is imposed in a specific rather than in ad valorem way, it will predominantly hurt the low-fare airlines as relative prices will change in favour of the higher fare carriers. As a result, short breaks involving air travel may also be hit. Ironically perhaps, some UK hotels consider joining forces with the environmental lobby to persuade people taking short breaks at home rather than abroad (Milmo, 2007).

8.6 Conclusions

Air transport and tourism are inextricably interlinked. Demand for air transport is essentially derived by tourism activities. Nonetheless, the paradigm shift in airline operations caused by deregulation has also led to new tourism practices (that is, dynamic packaging) and activities (that is, short breaks by air). This chapter aimed at highlighting these important issues stressing not only the positive and synergistic but also the negative and confrontational aspects of the air transport – tourism relationship. As in every symbiosis, however, what matters is to understand the common future and pave the way based on the principles of sustainable development: air transport may help tourist destinations grow and prosper, however, the latter should be careful not to become victims of their own success. Likewise, consumers may benefit substantially from the new opportunities in air travel; nonetheless, they should always be aware of risks such as lack of protection and spatial lock-in. Flexibility and modesty seem the best way to deal with complexity.

References

Air Transport Action Group (2008), *The Economic and Social Benefits of Air Transport*, Geneva: ATAG.

Association of British Travel Agents (2008), *Annual Report and Financial Highlights for the Year Ended 30 June 2008*, London: ABTA.

Borenstein, S. and Zimmermann, M. B. (1988), Market Incentives for Safe Commercial Airline Operation, *American Economic Review*, 78(5), pp. 913–935.

Bureau of Transportation Statistics (2009), Airline Domestic Market Share, January–December 2008, available from: http://www.transtats.bts.gov.

Cairns, S. and Newson, C. (2006), *Predict and Decide (II): The potential of economic policy to address aviation-related climate change*, Oxford: UK Energy Research Centre, University of Oxford.

Civil Aviation Authority (2005), *Financial Protection for Air Travellers and Package Holidaymakers in the Future, CAA Advice to the Government, September 2005*. CAP 759, London: CAA.

Civil Aviation Authority (2008), *Air Travel Trust: Report and Accounts*, London: CAA.

Daley, B., Dimitriou, D. and Thomas, C. (2008), *The Environmental Sustainability of Aviation and Tourism*, in Graham, A., Papatheodorou, A., and Forsyth, P. *Aviation and Tourism: Implications for Leisure Travel*, Aldershot: Ashgate, pp. 239–253.

Department for Transport (2007), *Reform of Air Travel Organizer's Licence (ATOL) Bonding: Final RIA*, London: Department for Transport.

Graham, B. and Guyer, C. (1999), Environmental Sustainability, Airport Capacity and European Air Transport Liberalization: Irreconcilable Goals? *Journal of Transport Geography*, 7, pp. 65–180.

International Civil Aviation Organization (2005), *The World of Civil Aviation 2003–2006*, Circular 307-AT/129, ICAO, Montreal.

Kester, J. (2009), Short and Long-Term Trends in International Tourism: the UNWTO Perspective. 4th International Scientific Conference of the University of the Aegean – Planning for the Future – Learning from the Past: Contemporary Developments in Travel, Tourism Hospitality, Rhodes Island, Greece, 3–5 April.

Kirby, T. (2006), Britons with Second Home Abroad Up 45 per cent in Two Years, *The Independent*, 22nd November. Available at: news.independent.co.uk/uk/this_britain/article2004223.ece.

Milmo, D. (2007), British Hotels attack Budget Airlines, *The Guardian*, 22 January. Available at: travel.guardian.co.uk/article/2007/jan/22/travelnews.theairlineindustry.hotels.

Murphy, P. (2009), Exploring the future for ancillary revenues, The Future of Air Transport, IEA 17th annual conference, 2–4 December, London.

O' Connell, J. (2006), Corporate Rivalry and Competition Issues in the Airline Industry. In Papatheodorou, A. (ed.) *Corporate Rivalry and Market Power: Competition Issues in the Tourism Industry*, pp. 54–75, London: IB Tauris.

Papatheodorou, A. (2002), Civil Aviation Regimes and Leisure Tourism in Europe, *Journal of Air Transport Management*, 8(6), pp. 381–388.

Papatheodorou, A. (2003), Do we Need Airport Regulation? *Utilities Journal*, 6(10), pp. 35–37.

Papatheodorou, A. (2006), *Corporate Rivalry, Market Power and Competition Issues in Tourism: an Introduction*. In Papatheodorou, A. (ed.) *Corporate Rivalry and Market Power: Competition Issues in the Tourism Industry*, London: IB Tauris, pp. 1–19.

Papatheodorou, A. and Song, H. (2005), International Tourism Forecasts: A Time Series Analysis of World and Regional Data, *Tourism Economics*, 11(1), pp. 11–24.

Papatheodorou, A. and Lei, Z. (2006), Leisure travel in Europe and airline business models: A study of regional airports in Great Britain, *Journal of Air Transport Management*, 12(1), pp. 47–52.

Papatheodorou, A. and Liasidou, S. (2006), Aviation Deregulation and Tourism in Cyprus following EU Accession, *Cutting Edge Research in Tourism Conference*, organized by the University of Surrey in Guildford, United Kingdom.

Papatheodorou, A. and Platis, N. (2007), Airline Deregulation, Competitive Environment and Safety, *Rivista di Politica Economica*, 97(I-II), pp. 221–242.

Papatheodorou, A. and Arvanitis, P. (2009), Spatial Evolution of Airport Traffic and Air Transport Liberalization: The Case of Greece, *Journal of Transport Geography*, 17(5), pp. 402–412.

Raghavan, S. and Rhoades, D. (2005), Revisiting the relationship between profitability and air carrier safety in the US airline industry, *Journal of Air Transport Management*, 11, pp. 283–290.

Rose, N. (1992), Fear of Flying? Economic Analyses of Airline Safety, *Journal of Economic Perspectives*, 6(2), pp. 75–94.

Smith, S. (1998), Tourism as an Industry – Debate and Concepts. In Ioannides, D. and Debbage, K.G. (eds) *The Economic Geography of the Tourism Industry – A Supply Side Analysis*, pp. 31–52, London: Routledge.

Starmer-Smith, C. (2009), Return of the Package Holiday, *The Telegraph*, 15th April. Available at: www.telegraph.co.uk/travel/budgettravel/5130485/Return-of-the-package-holiday.html.

Stabler, M., Papatheodorou, A. and Sinclair, M.T. (2010), *The Economics of Tourism*, second edition, Routledge: London.

United Nations World Tourism Organization (2008), *Tourism Highlights, 2008 Edition*. Madrid: UNWTO.

United Nations World Tourism Organization (2010), *World Tourism Barometer*, vol. 8(2), Madrid: UNWTO.

World Travel and Tourism Council (2009), *Travel and Tourism Economic Impact 2009*, London: WTTC.

Yale, P. (1995), *The Business of Tour Operations*, Harlow: Longman.

Chapter 9

The Economics of 7th Freedom

Peter Forsyth

9.1 Introduction

While international aviation markets have been extensively liberalized over the last three decades, this liberalization process remains incomplete. In particular, the opportunities for airlines to operate on a 7th Freedom basis remain tightly restricted. 7th Freedom flights are those operated between two countries by airlines from third countries, which are not operated through the third countries nor are extensions for flights to or from those third countries. Nearly all the traffic directly between two countries is reserved for the airlines of those two countries. The limits on 7th Freedom operations has the effect that competition on many international routes is not as strong as it could be, and there is little scope for trade in airline services. This means that it is not possible for the airlines best suited to serving a route, whether they are from the countries at the ends of the route or not, to actually serve the route. The result is that costs are higher than they need be, and the gains from international air transport are smaller than they need be.

This chapter focuses on 7th Freedom traffic and why it has been slow to develop. The bilateral system, which still forms the framework of international aviation regulation, does not of itself rule out 7th Freedom operations, but it does make it difficult for them to come about. Many countries take an 'exchange of rights' approach to international negotiations, and this severely limits the ability of countries to negotiate 7th Freedom rights for their airlines. Other countries have moved away from this, and have emphasized liberalization of their air transport markets. These countries have opened up their markets to their own airlines and the airlines of their partner countries. However, pro-competition policies do not necessarily imply pro-trade policies, and the same countries which are keen to promote competition on their routes are unwilling to allow airlines from third countries to participate in that competition.

Other countries have been taking a more pragmatic approach to air transport negotiations, and these countries are willing to liberalize only when they perceive gains from doing so. Parallel to this, economists have been developing models for measuring the benefits and costs of air transport policy changes, such as liberalization options or allowing mergers or alliances between airlines. The same approach can be used to explore whether, and under what circumstances, allowing 7th Freedom rights to other countries' airlines will be beneficial to them.

The opening up of routes to 7th Freedom operations can be to the benefit of a country, though this is not always the case. The factors that determine whether it is beneficial can be identified. The issue is illustrated by means of a case study of the trans-Pacific US–Australia route, on which Australia has rejected a request from Singapore Airlines to operate on a 7th Freedom basis.

The analysis indicates that granting 7th Freedom rights to other countries can be in a country's interest, even where it gains no rights in return. However, it also shows that doing so is not always in a country's interest. Thus a country might reject requests for 7th Freedom rights because doing so is against its interests, even though such rights would lead to more efficient international air transport markets overall.

The chapter begins with a review of international air transport traffic rights, with a particular emphasis on 7th Freedom rights. It then looks at old and new approaches to negotiating air transport rights. The economic model by which the benefits and costs of policy options can be assessed is outlined, and the granting of 7th Freedom rights is evaluated using this framework. The key points which emerge from this are illustrated by application to the trans-Pacific US–Australia market. Finally, some conclusions are drawn.

9.2 Open Skies, Competition and Trade

Recent years have seen extensive air transport liberalization, especially in the markets of Europe and North America. Within the bilateral framework of international air transport regulation, countries have opened up their air routes, by allowing in more airlines to compete, and relaxing or abolishing capacity restrictions. The result has been more competition and lower costs and air fares, and new types of carriers, such as the low-cost carriers, stimulating air travel (for a discussion of international aviation changes, see Doganis, 2002; Doganis 2010).

However, it is notable that liberalization has only gone so far – it has rarely been complete. Most liberal bilateral agreements only allow airlines from the two partner countries to participate in the market on an unrestricted basis. A typical US 'Open Skies' agreement will be liberal in that it has no limits on the number of airlines from the US and its partner country which are permitted to compete on routes between the two countries, and that it does not restrict capacity. However, it does not permit airlines from third countries to serve the route, except perhaps on a very limited basis, and it will impose strict controls on the ownership and control of the airlines which are regarded the US or the partner country's airlines. The recent US–Europe open skies agreements opens the market up somewhat, in that it allows for all European airlines to fly US–Europe – for example, a British airline can fly from France to the US. However, it does not permit non-US or non-European airlines to fly the route.

Thus these liberal agreements have typically allowed competition to develop, but not trade. By trade is meant the ability of an airline, regardless of which country it is based in or owned by, to participate in a route market between other countries. Thus the US to Japan market would be served by US and Japanese carriers, but Indian or Thai carriers are not permitted to offer services in it. Even otherwise-liberal air services agreements will be very prescriptive about which countries airlines can serve the market. These restrictions limit the gains from trade – airlines from one country which could be very competitive in serving a market between two other countries are not allowed to enter. While it is natural to expect that airlines from two countries at either end of a route will wish to serve the route, there needs presumption that they would be the most competitive airlines on the route.

In this respect, air transport is very different from most other goods and services. With manufactured goods there is no restriction normally on which countries can supply a particular product. Thus, there is no restriction which states that only Korea and the UK can supply the Korean and UK markets with motor vehicles. These types of restrictions are absent in the industry which is most similar to air transport – shipping. Shipping lines from any country can carry cargo between any other pairs of countries. Thus shipping lines from Denmark or Singapore or China can carry goods from Australia to the US or Japan to Canada. In many cases, the shipping markets of pairs of countries are dominated by shipping lines which are from neither of the countries. The shipping lines which are most competitive in serving a particular market are the ones which serve it – in this way, the costs of shipping is minimized.

Traffic Rights and the 'Freedoms of the Air'

The regulatory framework which governs international aviation is based on bilateral agreements between the two end countries. The sets of rights which describe what traffic each countries airlines are able to access are described, somewhat oddly, as the 'Freedoms of the Air' (these are outlined in Appendix 9.1). The agreement, say between the US and Japan, will specify what Freedoms are present in the market. Typically they will grant 3rd and 4th Freedom – the rights for airlines of the two countries to carry passengers or cargo between the countries. Thus, some or any US and Japanese carriers will be permitted to carry passengers and cargo between the US and Japan. Many air routes are dominated by airlines operating on a 3rd/4th Freedom basis.

An agreement may permit an airline from a third country to pick up passengers or cargo and carry them between the two countries as part of a longer trip from or to the third country. This is described as 5th Freedom traffic. Thus a Thai airline might be permitted to carry passengers from Japan to the US as part of a longer Thailand – US service via Japan. US airlines have extensive 5th Freedom rights beyond Japan to other parts of Asia and Australia. These rights were negotiated in the early post war period, and many countries did not expect them to be exercised. Thus the US airline Northwest flew from the US to Australia via Japan, and was permitted to pick up passengers from Japan to Australia, though the Australian government attempted, unsuccessfully, to restrict Northwest's ability to do this. 5th Freedom rights must be negotiated by the three countries, and many countries are not willing to make them too extensive. Depending on the rights they gain from their partner countries, they may be prepared to allow some 5th Freedom traffic on longer routes to enable their partner countries' airlines to fill up their flights on sectors to and from the country in question. The expectation is that most of the traffic on a flight will be 3rd and 4th Freedom traffic.

6th Freedom is rather different. It comes about when an airline of one country, which serves routes to two other countries, serves the route between these countries through its home base. Thus a Singapore based airline can serve routes from Singapore to Australia and to France – this means that, in effect, it can serve the Australia – France market through Singapore. 6th Freedom comes about because of geographical location rather than negotiation between countries. As such, it is difficult for countries to prevent 6th Freedom operations even when they do not approve of them. Thus Singapore might have rights for its airlines to fly between Australia and Singapore, and France and Singapore, and if so, its airlines can effectively operate from Australia to France via Singapore. Some airlines have built up their market on the basis of 6th Freedom traffic – an early example was Singapore Airlines, and more recent examples have included the Middle Eastern airlines such as Emirates.

7th Freedom

7th Freedom is where an airline from one country is permitted to serve a route between two other countries, other than on a 5th or 6th Freedom basis. An example would be a Singaporean airline serving the route between the US and Chile, not through Singapore or as a sector of a Singapore–Chile service via the US. Very few air services agreements, other than those involving multiple countries, allow for genuine 7th Freedom traffic.

7th Freedom flights can come about as a result of multilateral agreements between a group of countries. Some multiple country agreements are regional – the best example of this is within Europe. Airlines from one country can fly between two other counties. Thus an Irish airline, Ryanair, is permitted to fly between the UK and Germany on flights which do not involve Ireland. The European regional grouping is the largest and most comprehensive group, though others do exist. Thus Australia has a single aviation market with New Zealand, and a New Zealand airline can operate between Australia and the US. Airline groupings need not be based on a region – any group of countries could agree to liberalize air transport amongst them. A grouping which is only partly regionally based is MALIAT, which includes the US, Singapore, Brunei and Chile. These are all countries which are members of the Asia Pacific Economic Cooperation grouping, APEC, though most countries in APEC are not members of MALIAT. Airlines which are owned by countries which are members of MALIAT are permitted to fly between the member countries – thus a Singaporean airline can fly between the US and Chile.

The existence of 7th Freedom rights is a factor which discourages some countries from being members of MALIAT.

The lack of 7th Freedom rights means that international air transport traffic has a very restricted pattern. Even after many years of liberalization, most of the flights operated between two countries are flown by airlines of those two countries. This is especially true for direct flights. Some traffic between two countries will be carried on a 5th Freedom basis, but this is usually restricted to a small proportion of the traffic. On some, mainly longer routes, 6th Freedom operations will be feasible, and sometimes airlines operating on a 6th Freedom basis will have a majority of the traffic (as is the case between Australia and Europe). Within regional groupings, such as within Europe, airlines will operate on a 7th Freedom basis, but only airlines from the region will be permitted to do this. Thus, while Ryanair can fly between the UK and Germany, the Malaysian airline Air Asia cannot.

Restrictions on 7th Freedom operations mean that trade in airline services is still quite restricted. An airline from one country will normally not be permitted to sell its services on a route between two other countries. Most countries are essentially quite protectionist when it comes to their international air transport services – these will be more or less reserved for their own airlines, or the airlines of their direct partner countries. Even the US, which is normally pro competition, is restrictive when it comes to allowing third countries to operate services between it and other countries (though it is a member of MALIAT, which permits 7th Freedom services between members).

The Ownership and Nationality of Airlines

The discussion of 7th Freedom above presupposes that the nationality and ownership of airlines is clear. In practice it is not, and the notion of the nationality of an airline is becoming cloudier over time. Until two or so decades ago, the nationality of an international airline was clear. An airline would be owned by interests in a country, probably the national government, and it would be based in that country and would have the core of its operations in that country. Over time, this is ceasing to be the case. With privatization, and the quotation of airlines on stock exchanges, it has become possible for interests outside the country to part own the airline. Partly because most international air services agreements specify that airlines from a country be substantially owned and controlled by that country's interests, governments have put limits on the ownership of their international airlines. Thus the US limits foreign ownership of its airlines to 25 per cent or less, and other countries put a limit of just less than 50 per cent.

For many airlines, there is strong pressure to relax these limits. Some airlines have financial structures such that they are more than 50 per cent owned by foreign interests, but control remains in the home country. In some countries, airlines are not owned by home country interests, but their principal place of business is in the country – other countries with which the country has aviation agreements may be prepared to accept a 'principal place of business' test rather than a substantial ownership and control test. An example of this is Cathay Pacific, which is owned by non-Hong Kong interests, but which has its principal place of business in Hong Kong. It is possible that there will be a shift by countries. Some countries are becoming willing to allow more than 50 per cent foreign ownership of their airlines, along with foreign control, and moving more to a principal place of business test in their international air services agreements, but they cannot do this unilaterally, since they have to convince their partners in these agreements to accept their airlines on this basis.

Apart from the ownership aspect, airlines are becoming more internationalized in other respects. Airlines are employing more of their staff on international rather than just domestic labour markets. They may contract out maintenance in other countries, and they may outsource services, especially IT services, abroad. They sometimes operate hubs in foreign countries. A substantial proportion of the economic activity associated with operating an airline may take place outside the airline's home country.

Ownership of airlines is important in the context of the 7th Freedom issue for two reasons. The first is that ownership and aviation rights are to an extent, substitutes. If ownership conditions are liberalized, but air services agreements are not (and do not allow 7th Freedom operations), an airline from one country may be able to operate airline services between two other countries by setting up a subsidiary in one of these countries (assuming that both of those countries are willing to accept a principal place of business test of nationality). Thus, Singapore Airlines might not be permitted to operate between Canada and New Zealand on a 7th Freedom basis, it might be able to set up a subsidiary in New Zealand which could fly to Canada. If this begins to happen in a big way, countries may be prepared to permit 7th Freedom operations directly.

The second reason concerns the benefits and costs which accrue to countries as a result of their air services. Profits accrue to airline owners, not countries, though countries may tax some of the profits. If an airline is part foreign owned, less of the profits it earns on a route will be retained by its home country. This country may be less prepared than before to protect it by refusing competitor airlines 7th Freedom rights. If a foreign airline sets up a subsidiary to be able to access a route from a country, that country will share some of the profits it earns. The economic activity associated with an airline will occur, at least to a large extent, in the airline's home country. If countries perceive that there are benefits to be gained from airline economic activity, they will be favourable to options which encourage such activity. In short, the benefits and costs of permitting 7th Freedom operations will depend on who owns the home and foreign airlines, and whether foreign subsidiaries give rise to benefits from greater profits and greater economic activity to the home country. These benefits and costs will be explored further in Section 9.4.

9.3 Trading Rights

The international air transport market is regulated through a system of bilateral agreements between countries. Thus two countries, such as the US and China, come to an agreement which governs air transport between the two countries – most international air services are governed by bilateral air services agreements (ASAs). The main exception to the bilateral approach is where there are regional agreements, such as applies within Europe. While there have been attempts to establish a multilateral approach to air transport, these have not got very far – indeed even regional agreements are difficult to achieve and most agreements are not very far reaching. This bilateral structure has an important effect in making 7th Freedom services difficult to achieve.

When countries negotiate ASAs with their bilateral partners, the focus will be on their own airlines. Historically, with the exception of limited 5th Freedom rights and 6th Freedom rights (which are difficult to prevent), most or all traffic between two countries will be reserved for the airlines of those countries. In earlier years, there was normally only one airline from each country which was permitted to operate on any international route. Bilateral agreements were typically very restrictive, specifying which airlines could fly, which cities they could operate to and how much capacity they were permitted to offer. Over time, many of them have become more liberal – for example, the 'open skies' agreements that the US prefers to enter into do not specify the number of airlines, or the capacity they are permitted to offer, or the cities they are allowed to fly to. This bilateral structure is not conducive to the development of 7th Freedom services. For these to come about, a country must conclude agreements with two other countries to induce them to permit its airlines to fly between them.

While the bilateral *structure* of ASAs is not helpful to the development of 7th Freedom services, it does not necessarily prevent them. Perhaps a more significant barrier has been the *content* of ASAs, and the ways in which countries have gone about negotiating them. Traditionally, air services negotiations have been undertaken on a strictly legalistic basis, with countries seeking to exchange 'rights'. These rights are rights for airlines to access markets. Thus country A may grant country B the right for its airline to service an additional city, or may grant the right for the airline to operate additional services. In return for granting these rights, country A will expect to be granted rights by country B, for example, the right for its airlines to fly through B and then on to third countries. Each opportunity for an airline to access a new market, or to expand its access to its existing markets, is regarded as a right which has to be negotiated from the partner country. Rights are regarded as valuable and countries are unwilling to grant them unless they gain additional rights for their own airlines. In addition, it is typically the case that aviation rights can only be traded for other aviation rights – agreements which trade aviation for non-aviation rights (for example, greater access for a country's manufactured goods) are frowned upon, though in practice implicit trade offs are often made between aviation and non-aviation rights.

The values of rights depend on airline strategies and the ability of airlines to make use of them. Airlines from country B may be able to gain from having more flights into A, but As airlines may not be able to gain from having more flights into B. Unless there are some other rights that A's airlines want, it will be difficult for B to negotiate for more capacity into A. This may be a particular problem for a country, such as Singapore, which already has liberal agreements with most of its aviation partner countries – there are few rights of value which it can grant in return for being granted rights which it wants. Since most original ASAs are quite restrictive, it can be difficult and slow for countries to negotiate less restrictive agreements – hence the slow pace of international air transport liberalization.

In this scenario, a country which wishes to secure 7th Freedom rights so that its airlines can operate between two other countries must obtain this right from both these other countries. It will need to offer each of them something which they value, and often this will not be possible. If either or both the potential partner countries is satisfied with the existing arrangements, they will not agree to grant the right to operate 7th Freedom flights. Thus, under the 'exchange of rights' approach to international air transport negotiations, achieving 7th Freedom services is problematic, though not impossible.

The Gains from 7th Freedom Operations

Thus the bilateral system as it is operated makes for very limited use of 7th Freedom flights. Does this matter – is there a need for 7th Freedom flights?

There is no strong reason why airlines from two countries, A and B, should be dominant in serving a route between them. These airlines could have a locational advantage, though this could be quite small as compared to airlines from nearby countries. An airline from country C, which operates services to A and B, could have effective operational bases in A and B, and also have a strong marketing presence in these countries. Such an airline would easily be able to operate between A and B. Airlines from other countries can have other advantages – perhaps the most important of these might be a lower cost base. Airlines from Asian countries may be as technically efficient as European airlines, yet pay lower input prices – such airlines could be competitive in the Europe – North America markets. Overall performance of the industry will be best if the airlines most suited to serving routes are permitted to do so. Potentially, all countries which are involved can gain, though this may not happen in particular cases. The contrast between aviation and shipping is strong – international shipping is now globalized and shipping lines from origin and destination countries do not seem to have much advantage in serving the origin–destination markets.

Perhaps the strongest evidence on the gains from permitting 7th Freedom operations comes from markets which have been opened up to them. When 7th Freedom flights are permitted, they happen. This is clearly evident from the European experience, where many of the new low-cost carriers operate a high proportion of flights between countries other than their home country. As soon as the transatlantic market between Europe and the US was opened up, European airlines moved to start flights to the US from countries other than their home country – for example, a British Airways subsidiary has commenced flights from France to the US. Some countries and their airlines, such as Singapore Airlines, have actively sought 7th Freedom rights. The recognition that obtaining such rights is very difficult is probably the main reason why most airlines are not actively pursuing them.

The exchange of rights approach is essentially producer oriented – countries seek to expand market access for their carriers. Airlines seek additional market access, because they can expand their business, and potentially earn more profits. In negotiations, governments seek to satisfy their requests. Agreements they conclude will usually have to involve granting rights to partner countries, and this will impact negatively on the home airlines business and profits. Governments will thus try to conclude agreements which result in a net increase in market access, business and profits for their airlines.

Many countries have now moved beyond the exchange of rights approach, and this has facilitated liberalization. Several countries, such as the US, have been actively seeking to liberalize their international air transport markets. Doing this could also be motivated by producer interests – perhaps they believe that their own carriers will do well in a liberalized context. However, it is likely that governments which have been promoting liberalization have broader interests, and in particular, are willing to take account of consumer interests. Such countries will be willing to encourage competition on a route, through more airlines competing, and fewer restrictions on the ability of these airlines to compete (for example, through the removal of capacity limits). Such governments may be prepared to liberalize even where it is not in the interests of their carriers, as long as the gains to their consumers/travellers outweigh any losses to the carriers.

Countries may be pro competition, though not pro trade. They may be willing to have their international air transport routes being competitive, but they may not wish to open up these routes to foreign airlines (except perhaps on a limited 5th Freedom basis). Such countries may not be concerned about the division of the benefits from operating the route between travellers and carriers, but may still wish to ensure home production of air transport services. This policy stance has parallels elsewhere. Many countries promote competition in their domestic air transport markets, but they do not permit foreign airlines to enter. The US promotes competition in its coastal shipping, but does not permit foreign vessels to enter the trade. Thus, in international air transport, the US is pro competitive, and seeks to conclude open skies agreements with other countries which facilitate competition between the airlines of the US and its partner countries. However, it is not willing to open up routes to airlines from third countries (though it is open to this possibility in the context of multilateral agreements, such as in MALIAT).

Economic and Pragmatic Approaches to Negotiations

A contrast with the 'rights' approach to air services negotiations is what can be termed the 'economic' approach. This approach poses the question of what are the benefits and costs of some option, such as one to liberalize, and what the balance of these benefits and costs is. This approach would indicate liberalization when the overall net benefits from doing so are positive, though it should be recognized that government decision-makers might chose to give different weights to different groups (for example, they might put more emphasis on airline profits than consumer or traveller benefits). The two primary stakeholders in air transport policy changes are consumers/travellers, and producers, such as the airlines, though other stakeholders can be identified, such as the nation's tourism industry, and its government, which can be affected through its tax collections. Furthermore, a country will be mainly concerned about the benefits and costs to its own citizens, through the fares they pay for air travel and the profits its airlines make, though it will also be interested in how its partner country fares, since this will affect its willingness to enter agreements.

Agreements which have the effect of liberalizing air transport are more likely than not to provide net benefits to a country. Typically, there will be an efficiency or welfare gain from increased competition, with benefits to travellers outweighing reductions in profits to the airlines. This does not imply that all liberalization options are positive for a country, however. A country's airlines might have a high market-share on a high fare, high profit route, but its share of passengers might be small. Liberalization which leads to increased competition would lead to lower fares on the route, and benefits for travellers. These could well exceed the reduction in airline profits. However, the country only gains a little from the increased traveller benefits, but it loses a lot from the reduction in airline profits – overall, it would lose from liberalization. This was a real possibility for Australia in the context of the Australia–Japan route. Fares and profits were high, and the Australian airlines had about half the traffic. However, most of the travellers were Japanese, and these would be the main beneficiaries from liberalization (Yamauchi, 1997). Liberalization could be negative overall for Australia, and while Australia was generally favourably disposed to liberalization, it was ambivalent about applying such a policy to the Australia–Japan route.

The economic, or cost benefit approach to evaluating air transport policy options has developed over the last 20 or so years. The objective has been to quantify the benefits and costs of an option. An early study was that of Morrison and Winston (1986) which retrospectively evaluated the benefits and costs of US domestic airline deregulation. The approach has been used to set out a framework for international ASA negotiations (Department of Transport, 1988). A number of authors have used the approach to examine specific liberalization options (Street and Smith, 1994; Gillen, Harris and Oum, 1996; Productivity Commission, 1998; Gregan and Johnson, 1999 and Gillen et al. 2001; Duval, 2008). This approach was employed by competition authorities and consultants for the airlines in evaluating the economic effects of a proposed alliance between Qantas and Air New Zealand (now abandoned) (Air New Zealand Limited and Qantas Airways Limited, 2002; Australian Competition and Consumer Commission, 2003; Commerce Commission, New Zealand, 2003;). These studies identify the benefits and costs of policy changes and quantify them. The main direct benefits and costs are those which accrue to travellers and airlines, though there can be other benefits and costs, such as those stemming from additional foreign exchange receipts (relevant for some developing countries), and employment (perhaps relevant when unemployment is present).

One type of benefit which has been receiving more attention of late is tourism benefits. When aviation policy changes lead to more inbound tourism to a country, that country may gain. Additional exports of any service such as tourism do not necessarily lead to a gain for the exporting country. However, there can be positive effects, in particular, due to the presence of tax distortions, and terms of trade effects (see Dwyer and Forsyth, 1993; Dwyer et al. 2003; Forsyth, 2006; Forsyth, 2008). When a country experiences increased inbound tourism expenditure, the cost of providing goods and services to the tourists may be less than the revenues gained, because tourism is a relatively highly taxed export industry in many countries. Additional demand for tourism resources also can push up their prices and the home country can enjoy a terms of trade increase. These possibilities are discussed in Forsyth (2006). Tourism benefits have been recognized as something of relevance for international aviation policy (Department of Transport, 1988; Productivity Commission, 1998) and they were discussed in the context of the Qantas–Air New Zealand alliance proposal (Commerce Commission, 2003). Estimates suggest that tourism benefits are moderately significant but they are not likely to be as large as the direct benefits and costs to travellers and airlines (Forsyth, 2006). Tourism benefits are of distinct relevance in assessing the benefits and costs of proposals to permit 7th Freedom operations.

The economic approach to ASA negotiations is being implicitly, and sometimes explicitly, recognized in countries' aviation policies. Probably most countries around the world still adhere to the 'exchange of rights' approach, though others are now taking an explicit pro competition approach, such as that of the US and its promotion of open skies. However, there are other countries which can be described as taking a pragmatic approach to their ASA negotiations – the UK and Australia are cases in point. Such countries are neither inherently restrictive nor liberal – rather they adopt a case by case approach to each proposal. When considering whether to grant 7th Freedom rights to Singapore, Australia undertook an explicit economic evaluation of the costs and benefits of doing so. While such explicit use of an economic approach is not yet common, countries are becoming more systematic about what economic and other benefits and costs they expect from proposals.

This approach needs to be qualified by the recognition that the assessment of benefits and costs is something which informs a negotiation strategy, and that other aspects may also be critical in these negotiations. A country may be seeking to gain the most it can from negotiations with a partner country, and that country will typically have its own objectives for the negotiations (and these may not be similar to those of the home country). The home country may see itself as gaining from a proposal to liberalize, but it may hold back from agreeing, in order to attempt to gain larger benefits in the longer run. It will seek to keep a negotiating coin. If it liberalizes completely now, which may be its preferred option, it will not have any negotiating levers to use with the other country in the future. For example, Singapore has concluded liberal aviation agreements with Australia – this means that there is little that Australia wants from Singapore, and thus Singapore has little leverage with Australia if it seeks additional rights, such as 7th Freedom rights.

9.4 Air Transport Policy Changes: Benefits and Costs

The economic or cost benefit approach to evaluating air transport policy options, as discussed above, involves identifying the possible impacts that a change might have, and evaluating them. It also identifies who is affected by the impacts – whether they are home or foreign interests. This approach can be (and has been) used to evaluate a wide range of options, from domestic deregulation, opening up international markets to more airlines and freeing up capacity, evaluating the effects of alliances between airlines, and benefits and costs to a region of a major shift, such as a move to open skies. It can also be used to determine how a country will fare if it permits airlines from other countries to operate on a 7th Freedom basis on its routes.

Policy changes can have a range of impacts, though some are likely to be much larger than others, except in special cases. In Table 9.1, the main types of impacts are identified, along with other impacts which are likely to be less significant. This Table supposes that the change consists of liberalization on a route, leading to more competition and lower fares – other policy changes would have similar types of impacts, though the pattern of benefits and costs would be different.

The main gain to travellers is likely to be lower fares. Travellers may also be affected by changes in frequency, by changes in the number of direct flights, and possibly by more convenient routings. Airlines will be negatively affected, through lower fares, and possibly, profits. They will enjoy a larger market, and this will partly (and sometimes completely) counteract the effects of lower fares on profits. A more competitive environment may lead the airlines to lower their costs through improving their productivity. This too will moderate the impact on airline profits, though it could mean that airline workforces will enjoy less attractive working conditions. All of these are impacts which are potentially central to any evaluation of a liberalization option. In addition, the production of the home air transport industry could change, and employment in it could also change. These aspects may be of interest to a government.

Table 9.1   Liberalization: sources of benefits and costs

Source	Main impacts	Other impacts
Passenger benefits	Lower air fares	Greater frequency Direct flights Network changes
Airline benefits and costs	Changes in profits Possible impacts on costs	Production by the air transport industry Employment changes
Tourism benefits	Changes in tourism benefits from changes in expenditure	
Government revenues	Changes in taxes on airline profits	Changes on taxes on tourism
General economic effects		Foreign exchange changes Regional economic impacts
Environmental effects	Environmental externalities (e.g. greenhouse gas emissions)	Other environmental impacts, such as airport noise impacts

Liberalization will lead to changes in tourism flows. Lower fares will increase inbound and outbound tourism. If the effect on inbound tourism is greater than outbound (discussed below) the country will face a net increase in tourism expenditure, and as noted above, it can gain from this. Government revenue could change, as taxes on airline profits will change. In addition, taxes on tourism could change (though these may have already been counted as part of tourism benefits). There will be environmental impacts – if air transport increases, as it is likely to do so under liberalization, there will be increased environmental externalities. In particular, greenhouse gas emissions will increase – this could be a moderately significant impact, and airport noise will increase. Beyond these aviation specific impacts, there can be other impacts which will be of interest to some governments, including foreign exchange impacts and impacts on regional economies.

These impacts will affect both home and foreign stakeholders. Thus both home and foreign travellers will gain from lower fares. Governments can be presumed to be interested in those benefits and costs which accrue to their own citizens. In most models of aviation policy changes, it is implicitly assumed that all of the profits of home country airlines accrue to home country citizens. While this *was* a realistic assumption, it is becoming increasingly less so, with large foreign shareholdings in home country airlines. In evaluating policy changes, it is now necessary to allow for this, and only count the changes in airline profit which accrue locally. A proportion of airline profit will be taxed and will accrue to the home government, some will accrue to home citizens, and some will accrue to foreign citizens.

Both inbound and outbound tourism will be affected by a change such as more competition on a route. There is an asymmetry, however, and it is likely that lower fares will have a greater impact on inbound than outbound travel. When air fares fall on a route, travel on that route will increase. Some of this will be at the expense of other routes. In the case of outbound travel, some of the increase in outbound travel on the route will be at the expense of outbound travel on other routes – the change in outbound travel overall will be smaller than the change on the liberalized route. Inbound tourism will also increase, and some of this will be at the expense of travel on other routes – to other countries. Thus the net gain in inbound tourism will be the same as the gain on the route. If the impacts of the lower fares on inbound and outbound tourism on the route are similar, there will be a net gain in inbound tourism to the home country as a whole, after the fall in outbound tourism on other routes has been allowed for.

Evaluating 7th Freedom Operations

When 7th Freedom rights are granted to the airlines of a country the market between two countries is opened up to more competition. Assuming that this competition comes about, it will generally lead to lower fares. In this respect the outcomes will be similar to those when a market is opened up to more competition from the 3rd/4th Freedom carriers. However, there are some important differences.

Firstly, when a 7th Freedom carrier enters, it will gain some market share at the expense of the home and foreign carriers already serving the route. The home carriers will face lower fares and a smaller market share, and even with expansion of the market, they will experience a fall in profits. This will be a particular issue if the profit margin on the route is high, and the new competition does not bring fares down by much.

Secondly, it is possible that the 7th Freedom carriers will have different cost bases. It is possible that they will have a similar cost base to those of the existing carriers, in which case they will have no particularly strong competitive advantage. If they have a higher cost base they are unlikely to enter. If the 7th Freedom carriers have a cost advantage, this could lead them to be strong competitors, and entry might be followed by substantial fare reductions. This will be positive for travellers, but negative for the home airlines. If profit margins were not high before entry, they could become negative, and the home carriers will exit. This is not unlikely – almost all city pairs on the Europe to Australia route which used to be served by European and Australian carriers are now served solely by 6th Freedom carriers, which have been able to exploit their cost advantages on the route.

As with any situation of increased competition, the exact outcome is uncertain. Two areas of uncertainty involve the strength of competition and the cost response of the incumbents. New entry might be accompanied by much stronger competition amongst the airlines, with significant falls in fares, or it could be accompanied with a small fare reduction, with the entrant obtaining a modest market share and the incumbent carriers accommodating it. In the latter case, profitability in the market will be maintained. The outcome depends on the strategies of the incumbents and entrants – most entrants prefer not to start price wars, but sometimes incumbents defend their market shares strongly.

Another uncertainty concerns the ability of the incumbents to reduce their costs. If they have allowed their costs to be higher than the minimum, during a period of weak competition, they may be able to respond to stronger competition by reducing their costs. One of the advantages of competition is that it forces firms to pay more attention to their costs. If incumbents are already quite efficient, they will have little scope to reduce their costs.

The impacts that 7th Freedom entry will have, and the benefits and costs for the home country, will also depend on the initial competitive environment. The market could be relatively uncompetitive, with a small number of airlines enjoying high profit margins. This could come about because competition is limited by the ASA for the route – if so, the origin and destination countries should not just contemplate allowing 7th Freedom entry, but they should also permit more entry from their own carriers. Alternatively, the route could already be moderately competitive, with fares close to costs – if a 7th Freedom entrant were to be successful, it would need to have a lower cost base than the incumbents.

Some key impacts on the market, and the resultant benefits and costs to the home country, are as follows. 7th Freedom entry on profitable routes:

- The market share and profitability of the home carriers would be reduced.
- The reduction in home carrier profits would be greater than if competition had been increased as a result of entry by a new home carrier.
- If a 7th Freedom entrant has lower costs than a home based entrant, there will be more pressure on fares and costs.
- Entry by a 7th Freedom carrier could be either positive or negative for the home economy.
- If there is weak price competition, it is more likely that the home economy will lose from entry, since benefits to home travellers and tourism will be small, but the loss of home carrier profits could be significant.
- If there are only small cost savings, little foreign ownership of the home carrier, and moderate to large loss of market share by the home carrier, the outcome is likely to be negative for the home country.

Entry by the 7th Freedom carrier results in the following benefits and costs:

- An efficiency gain by through fares being closer to costs, which the home country shares.
- Possible cost reductions, which the home country shares.
- A gain to the home country from lower airline profits paid to foreign shareholders.
- Tourism benefits.
- A loss of profits for the home country airline.

Thus, depending on the circumstances, the home country could either gain or lose from permitting 7th Freedom operations on a route. 7th Freedom entry on marginal routes:

- Lower air fares reduce the profitability of incumbent carriers and induce exit by them.
- The loss of profits is limited by exit.
- If the market is strongly competitive and air fares fall considerably, there are substantial gains to home country travellers, through greater reliance on trade in airline services.
- In this situation, extensive rather than limited and restricted entry by 7th Freedom carriers is in the interest of the home country.
- In some situations, incumbents may be able to reduce costs and survive.

Overall, in this second case, the home country is likely to benefit from allowing 7th Freedom operations, since the gains to its travellers will exceed profit reductions to airlines, and tourism benefits will be positive. Production by the home air transport industry will be reduced, and the country will be relying more on imports of air transport services – in short, it will be taking advantage of the gains from trade.

9.5 Case Study: The Trans-Pacific Route

The trans-Pacific US–Australia route provides a useful case study of the benefits and costs of 7th Freedom operations. For several years, Singapore Airlines has wanted to fly on the US–Australia route, and the Singapore Government has supported it in its request. The US, which like Singapore is a member of the MALIAT group, is willing to allow 7th Freedom operations on the route by Singapore Airlines. In 2005–06, in response to repeated requests by Singapore Airlines, the Australian Government conducted a review of the issue, and in 2006 announced that it would not grant the request. At the same time, it agreed to facilitate the entry on to the route of a new Australian carrier, V Australia, a subsidiary of the domestic carrier, Virgin Blue. Singapore Airlines is still seeking to enter the market.

For a number of years, the US to Australia route has been dominated by United Airlines from the US and Qantas from Australia. Knibb (2009) reported that Qantas was the bigger player with about 75 per cent of the capacity prior to open skies and it generated 15 per cent of Qantas' total profit. Its only other competition came from the one-stop carriers – Air New Zealand, Hawaiian, and Fiji's Air Pacific, plus the round-about routing offered by several Asian carriers. Of all these, only Air New Zealand provided any serious challenge in terms of seats and schedules. In 2007 there were 1.73 million passengers travelling between the US and Australia. In April 2008, Australia signed an open-skies agreement with the US which allowed other US and Australian airlines to challenge the duopoly and commence flights between the two countries. By 2009 there were almost 2 million passengers travelling between the US and Australia (Bureau of Transport and Regional Economics, 2009). Knibb (2009) calculated the market share of the key airlines that operated between the US and Australia in 2009, and were as follows: Qantas, 56.7 per cent; United Airlines, 21.0 per cent; V Australia, 15.0 per cent; and Delta Air Lines, 8.4 per cent. The Sydney–Los Angeles route has the largest share of the US Australia market with around 1.4 million passengers in 2009, with Qantas operating double-daily; while both United Airlines and V Australia had a daily service; while Delta Air Lines served the city pair six times a week. Duval (2008) stated that Air Canada applied to operate on the Toronto–Los Angeles–Sydney route if both the Canadian and Australian governments agree to amend the existing ASA between the two countries, which currently does not allow such a routing.

Singapore Airlines has mounted a strong campaign to enter the route. It has argued that stronger competition would bring down fares, to the benefit of Australian travellers and to the benefit of the Australian tourism industry. Tourism interests in Australia support the Singapore Airlines case. Singapore Airlines has commissioned modelling to illustrate economic benefits from its entry, and the Australian Government also undertook economic modelling of the proposal, though it has not released the results of its studies. This is a 7th Freedom proposal which has been subjected to detailed scrutiny, especially of its economic aspects.

It is possible to evaluate the benefits and costs to Australia from permitting 7th Freedom operations on the trans-Pacific route. A range of possible outcomes is summarized in Table 9.2 and this study was undertaken prior to the deregulation of the US to Australian market. These estimates are not definitive, though they are illustrative of possible orders of magnitude. In the base case (not necessarily the most probable scenario), it is assumed that Singapore Airlines is permitted to enter the market, and that it is quite competitive. Its entry results in a 10 per cent reduction in average fare per passenger, and it is assumed to result in the Australian carrier's market share falling by 15 per cent, from around 56 per cent to 41 per cent (it will also win market share from US carriers, though this is not relevant for these calculations). Passenger flows increase, as does net inbound tourism expenditure. The full assumptions are listed in Appendix 9.2 and the calculations are discussed in detail in Forsyth (2005).

In the base case, there is a net gain to Australia from allowing access by Singapore Airlines. The gains to home country travellers exceed the loss to home airlines profits mainly because some of these profits accrue overseas, due to approximately 50 per cent foreign ownership (allowing for profits tax, it is assumed that 70 per cent of Qantas profits accrue to Australia). In addition there are benefits from additional tourism, giving rise to an overall net benefit for Australia. The benefits would be larger if the home carrier were able to reduce its costs to moderate the loss of profits.

Table 9.2   Benefits and costs of 7th Freedom entry (Australian dollar in millions)

	Home travellers benefits	Change in carrier profits accruing to Australia	Net tourism benefits	Net benefits to Australia
Base case	124.2	-95.53	51.28	71.95
With cost reduction	124.2	-65.74	51.28	109.74
Entry by Australian subsidiary	124.2	-80.97	51.28	94.51
Entry with no impact on fares	0.0	-16.8	0.0	-16.8
Smaller-scale entry	58.05	-56.18	25.64	27.52
Lower demand elasticity	118.8	-97.89	29.72	50.63

Note: Calculations as described in text.

Another possibility is that, instead of a 7th Freedom entrant, an Australian based airline which is part foreign owned enters. Such an airline could be a subsidiary of an existing Australian airline, such as Virgin Blue's subsidiary, V Australia, or it could be a subsidiary of Singapore Airlines. Such an entry could have the same benefits in terms of reduced fares to Australian travellers, and the same impacts on tourism expenditures, but it would lead to a smaller reduction in airline profits accruing to Australia. This option would be superior to a 7th Freedom entry if the two are mutually inconsistent, but this need not be the case, and entry by both could be feasible.

If entry by the 7th Freedom carrier led to smaller reductions in fares, the negative impact on home airline profits would be smaller, but so would the positive impacts on home traveller benefits and on tourism. Overall, the net gain would be smaller. The net benefits to Australia would be smaller if demand elasticities are lower, and the positive effect of entry on tourism is smaller. In the extreme, it might be possible for the 7th Freedom entrant to gain some market share without reducing prices, if it has a strong reputation in the market (this could be the case for Singapore Airlines which is well regarded on both sides of the Pacific). In this case, there would be no benefits to home travellers or through increased tourism, and only a loss of profits by the home carrier – Australia would lose from granting 7th Freedom rights.

These numbers are the result of a set of simulations, and do not constitute a forecast of what would happen if Singapore Airlines were permitted to operate on the US–Australia route. They do indicate how the benefits and costs to a country of permitting 7th Freedom operations depend on various key factors. Granting

7th Freedom flights can be positive or negative for a country; however, it is more likely to be positive. The following represent the effects:

- The lower the current profit margin.
- The higher the home country share of traffic.
- The lower the home country airlines market share.
- The greater the demand elasticity.
- The greater the net benefits from tourism.
- The greater the scope for home carriers to reduce costs in the face of increased competition.
- The greater the foreign ownership share of the home airlines.
- The larger the impact of entry on competition and fares.

9.6 Conclusions

If international air transport markets are to become as efficient as is feasible, individual markets between two countries need to be open to all airlines, so that those which are best suited to serving the markets are actually permitted to do so. For this to be the case, 7th Freedom rights would have to become freely available. In reality, this is not the situation, and the extensive use of 7th Freedom rights, outside the context of regional groupings, is rare. This is not surprising given the bilateral structure of air transport regulation along with the preference of many countries for a producer oriented 'exchange of rights" approach to air transport negotiations. However, many countries espouse liberalization and competition in their international air transport policies, while others have become more pragmatic, seeking to assess the benefits and costs to them of liberalization options. In spite of this, few of the liberal or pragmatic countries have been willing to allow 7th Freedom operations.

When the benefits and costs, to a specific country, of allowing 7th Freedom operations is assessed in terms of a rigorous economic model, there is no general result. Granting 7th Freedom rights can be in a country's interest, though it may not be. On the positive side, this suggests that the widespread aversion to granting 7th Freedom rights may be misinformed, and that such countries may be rejecting options they can gain from. At the very least, countries should be taking a pragmatic view, and assessing what the benefits and costs to them might be. The factors which determine whether granting 7th Freedom rights will be favourable for a country can be identified, and tested against actual conditions on a route market. Broadly, if granting 7th Freedom rights results in little additional competition or fare reductions on a route, but mainly involves sharing of profits with foreign airlines, it is unlikely to be beneficial. However, if it results in fare reductions, to the benefit of home country travellers and the tourism industry, it is probable that the benefits will outweigh the costs. This is especially likely to be so if the airlines which operate on a 7th Freedom basis possess cost or other advantages, which result in lower transport costs for the home country.

In a number of cases, countries will lose if they grant 7th Freedom rights – this will be so even though granting such rights increases the efficiency of the route market overall. Countries with pragmatic approaches to international air transport policy will reject such options, and this will make achieving comprehensive international air transport liberalization more difficult to achieve. Efficient solutions will only come about if there is some means of compensating those countries which lose. In this way, as in other ways, air transport differs from other trades. Apart from cases where the optimal tariff argument applies, unilateral opening up of markets is in a country's interest. In the air transport case, countries can lose from unilateral liberalization, and this can be so when the liberalization option being considered is that of granting 7th Freedom rights.

9.7 Appendix 1: Freedoms of the Air

First Freedom of the Air – the right or privilege, in respect of scheduled international air services, granted by one State to another State or States to fly across its territory without landing (also known as a *First Freedom Right*).

Second Freedom of the Air – the right or privilege, in respect of scheduled international air services, granted by one State to another State or States to land in its territory for non-traffic purposes (also known as a *Second Freedom Right*).

Third Freedom of The Air – the right or privilege, in respect of scheduled international air services, granted by one State to another State to put down, in the territory of the first State, traffic coming from the home State of the carrier (also known as a *Third Freedom Right*).

Fourth Freedom of The Air – the right or privilege, in respect of scheduled international air services, granted by one State to another State to take on, in the territory of the first State, traffic destined for the home State of the carrier (also known as a *Fourth Freedom Right*).

Fifth Freedom of The Air – the right or privilege, in respect of scheduled international air services, granted by one State to another State to put down and to take on, in the territory of the first State, traffic coming from or destined to a third State (also known as a *Fifth Freedom Right*).

ICAO characterizes all 'Freedoms' beyond the Fifth as 'so-called' because only the first five 'Freedoms' have been officially recognized as such by international treaty.

Sixth Freedom of The Air – the right or privilege, in respect of scheduled international air services, of transporting, via the home State of the carrier, traffic moving between two other States (also known as a *Sixth Freedom Right*). The so-called Sixth Freedom of the Air, unlike the first five Freedoms, is not incorporated as such into any widely recognized air service agreements such as the 'Five Freedoms Agreement'.

Seventh Freedom of The Air – the right or privilege, in respect of scheduled international air services, granted by one State to another State, of transporting traffic between the territory of the granting State and any third State with no requirement to include on such operation any point in the territory of the recipient State, that is, the service need not connect to or be an extension of any service to/ from the home State of the carrier.

Eighth Freedom of The Air – the right or privilege, in respect of scheduled international air services, of transporting cabotage traffic between two points in the territory of the granting State on a service which originates or terminates in the home country of the foreign carrier or (in connection with the so-called Seventh Freedom of the Air) outside the territory of the granting State (also known as a *Eighth Freedom Right or 'consecutive cabotage'*).

Ninth Freedom of The Air – the right or privilege of transporting cabotage traffic of the granting State on a service performed entirely within the territory of the granting State (also known as a *Ninth Freedom Right* or '*stand alone*' *cabotage*).

Source: International Civil Aviation Organization (ICAO), Manual on the Regulation of International Air Transport (Doc 9626, Part 4).

9.8 Appendix 2: Assumptions for Simulations

Base Case

> Size of market (Passengers PA): 800,000
> Australian carrier share 56 per cent
> Australian share of passengers 45 per cent
> Tourism demand elasticity 3.0
> Air Fare $A3,000
> Average total trip cost $A6,000
> Profit per passenger $A400
> Tourism benefits – proportion of inbound expenditure 0.1
> Tourism cost – proportion of outbound expenditure
> (part spent in Australia) 0.05
> Reduction in fares $300

New Australian carrier market share 40 per cent
Share of home carrier profits accruing to Australia 70 per cent

Alternative Cases

Reduction in costs by Australian carrier $A100
Fare reduction under smaller scale entry $A150
Australian carrier share under smaller scale entry 48.5 per cent
Share of profits from home based entrant accruing in Australia 70 per cent
Lower demand elasticity 2.0

References

Air New Zealand Limited and Qantas Airways Limited (2002), Submission to the Australian Competition and Consumer Commission in Support of the Application for Authorization, 9 December.

Australian Competition and Consumer Commission (2003), Draft Determination Applications for Authorization, Qantas and Air New Zealand, 10 April.

Bureau of Transport and Regional Economics (2009), International Airline Activity annual publications. Available at: http://www.bitre.gov.au/publications/04/Files/CY09.pdf.

Commerce Commission (New Zealand) (2003), Final Determination: Qantas Air New Zealand Application, 23 October.

Department of Transport and Communications (Australia) (1988), Negotiating International Aviation Rights, Consultants' Report, June.

Doganis, R. (2010), *Flying Off Course: Airline Economics and Marketing*, 4th edition, London, Routledge.

Doganis, R. (2002), *Flying Off Course: The Economics of International Airlines*, 3rd edition, London, Routledge.

Duval, D. (2008), Regulation, competition and the politics of air access across the Pacific, *Journal of Air Transport Management*, 14(5), pp. 237–242.

Dwyer, L. and Forsyth, P. (1993), Assessing the Benefits and Costs of Inbound Tourism, *Annals of Tourism Research*, vol. 20, No. 4, pp. 751–768.

Dwyer, L., Forsyth, P., Spurr, R. and Ho, T. (2003), The Contribution of Tourism to a State and National Economy: A Multi-regional General Equilibrium Analysis, *Tourism Economics*, vol. 9, No.4, pp. 431–448.

Forsyth, P. (2006), Tourism Benefits and Aviation Policy, *Journal of Air Transport Management*, vol. 12, pp. 3–13.

Forsyth, P. (2008), *Tourism and Aviation Policy: Exploring the Links*, in Graham, A., Papatheodorou, A. and Forsyth, P. *Aviation and Tourism: Implications for Leisure Travel*, Aldershot, Ashgate, pp. 73–82.

Gillen, D., Harris, R. and Oum, T. (1996), *Assessing the Benefits and Costs of International Air Transport Liberalization*, Ottawa, Transport Canada.

Gillen, D., Hinsch, H., Mandel, B. and Wolf, H. (2001), *The Impact of Liberalizing International Aviation Bilaterals: The Case of the North German Region*, Aldershot, Ashgate.

Gregan, T. and Johnson, M. (1999), Impacts of Competition Enhancing Air Services Agreements: A Network Modelling Approach, Productivity Commission, Staff Research Paper, AusInfo, Canberra.

Knibb, D. (2009), Pacific Splash, *Airline Business*, July, p36–38.

Morrison, S. and Winston, C. (1986), *The Economic Effects of Airline Deregulation*, Washington, DC, Brookings Institution.

Productivity Commission (1998), International Air Services: Report No 2, Ausinfo, Canberra, September.

Street, J., Smith, J.D. and Savage, S. (1994), An Analysis of the Trade-offs in International Aviation Rights, *Australasian Transport Research Forum*, vol. 19, Transport Research Centre, University of Melbourne, pp. 183–206.

Yamauchi, H. (1997), *Air transport policy in Japan: limited competition under regulation*, in Findlay, C., Sien, L. and Singh, K., *Asia Pacific Air Transport Challenges and Policy Reforms*, Singapore, Institute of Southeast Asian Studies, pp. 106–122.

Chapter 10

The Air Cargo Industry

Peter S. Morrell

10.1 Introduction

The air cargo industry includes the movement of freight, express packages, mail and courier bags by air. The term 'air cargo' is often used for the combination of freight and mail, but the emergence of the express package sector and the decline of courier bags has led to a blurring of types of traffic carried. The demand for air cargo is for a door-to-door product, whether from manufacturer to final user, or between the various intermediaries in the supply chain. This will involve trucking and flights and possible a part of the trip by rail. Integrated carriers such as FedEx and DHL offer a door-to-door service while airlines generally only offer an airport to airport service, with other parties providing delivery to the airport and collection at the destination airport. Air cargo is a key ingredient of the trade in goods, whether internationally or between different regions of the same country, although the latter tends to be carried by truck or rail. Air cargo accounts for 34.6 per cent of the value of non-land international trade in goods, but only six per cent of the weight (Kararda, 2006). The average value to weight ratio of air shipped goods is 31 times as that of vessel shipped goods. This enables such items to bear the higher cost of shipment by air. Air cargo can thus be described as a derived industrial product. Some countries such as India have been very successful in developing services industries which are much less dependent on air transport. China on the other hand has a substantial manufacturing base and generates substantial air cargo flows both to North America and Europe. Air cargo rates tend to be significantly higher than those for surface transport. Thus high value-to-weight ratio products tend to be better able to support such rates. Companies do not want high value inventory in transit and take advantage of air cargo's shorter transit times.

Urgent items such as medical supplies or spare parts also tend to use air freight. Similarly, perishable goods demand a rapid mode of transport otherwise they lose their market either through physical spoilage or through being out-of-date. One segment of air freighted perishables is newspapers and magazines. These need a quick mode of delivery but their final price on the news stand will not support a high charge. They thus are generally offered an especially low rate, especially as a means of filling space that would not otherwise be filled in the lower deck of passenger flights. Fashion goods are also 'perishable' in that their market might only last for a limited period, but these are able to pay higher rates. Another example of perishables going by air is the annual shipment of 'Beaujolais

Nouveau' wine from France, whose market lasts only for a number of days. The other perishables segment are fresh produce that might be spoiled using surface transport, even using temperature controlled containers. Examples of these are fruit, vegetables and flowers. Perishables are described as being part of the cool chain sector with imports into Europe (by all modes of transport) estimated at 858,000 tonnes in 2005 with an eight per cent average growth 2000–2005. The US imported 523,000 tonnes in 2005, and Asia 501,000 tonnes in 2005, while Africa–Europe is the world's biggest intercontinental lane for perishables by air, making up around 360,000 tonnes (*International Freighting Weekly*, 2006). Many of the fresh produce imports by air come from developing countries where they provide much-needed jobs and export earnings. This is underlined by large differences in income between rich and poor countries; for example, Kenya's average income per head in 2008 was US$1,600 compared to $37,100 for the UK. Many of the poorer countries are in Africa, and it is estimated that over 1 million people are supported by fresh fruit and vegetables exports from rural Africa just to the UK, most these going by air (CIA Factbook, 2008; MacGregor and Vorley, 2006). Successful examples of this are Kenya and Peru. Peru's exports by air of fresh asparagus are currently 64,000 tonnes a year, and fresh flowers, fruit and vegetables make up 65 per cent of all exports from Kenya to the European Union (EU), with most of this going by air. Flowers/plants are the fastest growing segment, although there has been some switch from air to surface transport, especially by sea, with better control facilities. The Peru to US asparagus market changed in the past 10 years from 80 per cent by air to 80 per cent by sea (*International Freighting Weekly*, 2006).

The air cargo industry provides a ready source of lift for emergency food aid and medical supplies. Governments and aid agencies, such as USAID, EuropeAid, and Oxfam, charter freighter aircraft from the industry at short notice to meet emergencies, and some have their own aircraft. Without a flourishing air freight industry these flights would cause much greater disruption to scheduled flights and international commerce. One of the largest agencies, the World Food Agency, through its World Food Programme (WFP), relies heavily on airlifts to get food into some of the world's most hostile and inaccessible places, or to remote areas where much of the infrastructure has been damaged or destroyed, for example in the wake of the December 2004 Indian Ocean tsunami and the 2008 Sichuan earthquake. One of the WFP partnerships is with the integrator TNT which provides in-kind services and knowledge transfer, enabling the WFP to respond to emergencies more effectively. In 2006 TNT contributed to WFP's response to emergencies in Pakistan, Indonesia, Lebanon and Togo by offering transport services, warehousing and specialized personnel deployed in direct support of the WFP. In 2008 the WFP/UNHAS (the UN's Humanitarian Air Service) was itself operating some 100 aircraft on missions ranging from food airdrops to transporting relief workers to remote and dangerous locations. The WFP-UNHAS chartered aircraft carried 361,000 passengers and 15,200 metric tons of cargo in 2008 (World Food Program, 2008).

However, air cargo is more generally associated with the carriage of high value items and these goods are required within a specific time limit. Table 10.1 shows the tonnage breakdown by commodity for one of the major air cargo inter-regional flows. Other regional flows are likely to be less dominated by apparel (clothing), machinery and electrical goods as is the case for Asia and more by leather goods, flowers and other fresh produce (for example, South America to the US).

Traditionally a higher percentage of air freight is shipped using agents than for the passenger side of the business. Air cargo agents are called 'forwarders', and the larger ones are involved in combining shipments from different shippers to the same destination. These are called 'consolidators'. Gadola (2008) indicated the power of forwarders by stating that such freight forwarders control up to 90 per cent of the global air cargo capacity of airlines. In Europe, forwarders account for a higher share than in North America which is influenced by a strong integrator presence. It is notable that the percentage of shippers using only direct contacts with airlines is very low, and much lower than on the passenger side. While this might increase in the future, the forwarder will still retain the important consolidation role that passenger agents do not have; second, airlines still depend on others for airport collection and delivery of air freight shipments. For these reasons the direct share may not expand as much as for some passenger airlines.

Table 10.1   Air cargo traffic by commodity, Europe to/from Asia, 2007

	Europe to Asia	Europe to Asia
	%	Tonnes (000)
General/industrial machinery	20	286
Documents/small packages	10	149
Electrical machinery/apparatus	5	74
Miscellaneous manufactured	3	46
Other	62	889
Total	100	1,443
	Europe from Asia	Europe from Asia
	%	Tonnes (000)
Apparel (for example, clothing)	17	436
Miscellaneous manufactured	15	383
Office machines	14	346
Electrical machinery/apparatus	10	251
Documents/small packages	10	248
Other	34	842
Total	100	2,506

Source: Boeing World Air Cargo Forecasts, 2008.

The largest four of the world's forwarders or consolidators accounted for around 30 per cent of the total air cargo agent[1] turnover in 2006. DHL Global was the leader with US$2.92 billion in turnover, followed by Nippon Express with $1.02bn, Kühne & Nagel with $759 m and Schenker (more recently merged with BAX) with $606m. Computerized air cargo booking had a much later start than the passenger Global Distribution Systems, and there are now three major players: Cargo Portal Services, GF-X and EzyCargo. The first is more North America focused, the second has major airlines in both Europe and the US signed up, while the third was set up by Cathay Pacific, Singapore Airlines, Japan Airlines and Qantas Airways.

10.2 Air Cargo Traffic

World schedule air freight traffic increased at an average rate of 7.4 per cent a year between 1970 and 2008 to reach 156 billion freight tonne/kms (ICAO, 2008). This growth rate was around 1 per cent a year higher than the growth in air passenger/ kms. The largest share of this traffic is carried by airlines based in the Asia/Pacific region (35 per cent) followed by 28 per cent for North America and 27 per cent for Europe.

Figure 10.1 compares the growth rates for both air passengers and cargo for international air services. Cargo increased at an average rate of 5.5 per cent a year over the period from 1993 to 2007, compared to passenger growth of 5.6 per cent a year. Thus more recent rapid growth in the low-cost airline passenger sector has brought the two outputs closer together in terms of rate of growth. Both types of traffic also display some cyclicality, with a freight downturn in 2000 as a result of the collapse of the IT and high tech bubble following 'the year 2000'. This preceded the passenger downturn in 2001/02 following the events of 9/11. However, a strong air cargo recovery was underway in 2004 especially in Asia; with IT/PC replacement needed again (3–4 years after Y2K), but this appears to have stalled in 2005/06. Some industry analysts believe that a downturn in the air cargo industry is often followed by a downturn on the passenger side around six months later. A previous downturn was evident in 1991, but this was more marked for passengers with many trips by air cancelled through fear of flying during the aftermath of the Gulf War.

Difficult market conditions that began in May 2008 led to a contraction in cargo traffic of about six per cent for the year, in comparison to 2007 levels which was due to the slowing world industrial production and international trade (Boeing Current Market Outlook, 2009).

One of air freight's characteristics, and one that differentiates it from the passenger business, is directionality. This is usually because of an underlying imbalance in the trade of goods. As mentioned above, China's exports exceed their

---

    1   IATA registered air cargo agents.

imports by a wide margin. This is also evident in their air trade with substantially higher outbound flows compared to inbound. On the other hand some Middle Eastern or African countries export very little by air, but need to import such commodities as pharmaceuticals and industrial machinery by air. This leads to a similar imbalance. Figure 10.2 gives an idea of the extent of the imbalance for the three key region pairs, with an almost 2:1 ratio for exports by air from Asia/Pacific to North America.

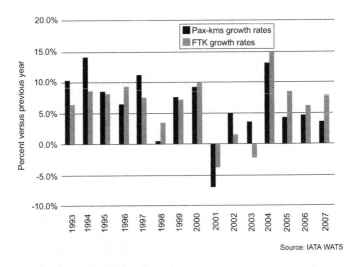

Source: IATA WATS

Figure 10.1 Annual growth rates by traffic type for IATA International Scheduled Service

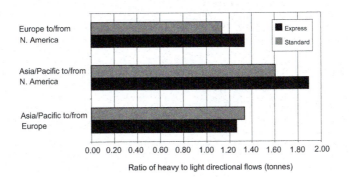

Ratio of heavy to light directional flows (tonnes)

Figure 10.2 Air freight directionality by major flows
Source: MergeGlobal Inc. in Aviation Strategy, October 2005.

The proportion of air cargo on freighter flights has been increasing since the early 1990s, but has tended to flatten out over the past five years (see Figure 10.3). One reason for the increase was the reduced capacity on some long-haul passenger flights. This was because of the trend towards operating longer non-stop sectors, requiring more fuel and less payload available for passengers and cargo, resulting in less cargo space in the lower deck compartments. Long-haul flights account for quite a large part of total flown cargo, since shorter sectors are often operated by truck. A second reason was that over the past 10–20 years, the integrated carriers such as FedEx and DHL have tended to grow faster than the average and these carriers tend to use their own freighter aircraft on some routes. FedEx is the world's largest cargo airline transporting around 16 billion FTKs in 2007, up by around four per cent from a year earlier.

The Boeing Current Market Outlook (2009) predicts that world air cargo will almost triple over the next 20 years and the number of freighters in the world fleet will grow by more than two-thirds. An earlier forecast predicted that there will be an increase in the share of freight traffic that is carried on freighters and this is set to increase by six per cent between 2005 and 2025.

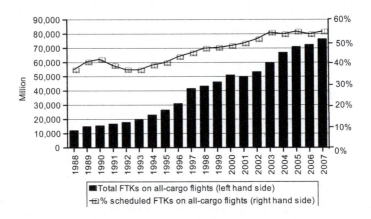

Figure 10.3   Air cargo share on freighter aircraft (IATA International Scheduled Services)

Source: IATA WATS, 53rd Edition.

10.3 Air Cargo Trucking

Flying cargo in freighters over short sectors is inherently uneconomic due in part to the high fuel burn in the take-off phase of the flight that could not be spread over a long sector and thus more tonne/km traffic. Second, passenger aircraft used on shorter sectors are usually narrow-bodied and offer very little space for air cargo. As a result these sectors are mostly operated by truck at lower unit cost with little speed or time disadvantage. This occurs mostly in Europe and North America where airlines feed cargo into hub airports for carriage over long-haul sectors. In these regions the feeder part of the trip can easily be operated by truck, and airlines do this on an airport to airport basis even using flight numbers and air cargo pricing.

Integrated carriers also use smaller tucks to collect and deliver packages in addition to using the larger trucks described above to feed their hubs. UPS for example operated 107,000 vehicles together with a fleet of around 570 aircraft in 2008 (UPS annual Report, 2008). Figure 10.4 shows the percentage of packages moved by air and surface transport within the US for the main operators. These are the US Postal Service (USPS) and the three largest integrators (which fly much of the USPS priority packages by air on a contract basis).

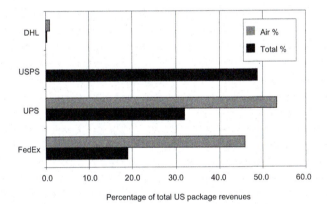

Percentage of total US package revenues

Figure 10.4   Share of US air and ground package revenues by carrier, 2008/09

Source: Company accounts.

10.4 Air Cargo Carriers

Around three quarters of air cargo is carried by carriers that combine passenger and cargo transport. They have the advantage, at least on longer sectors, of having a considerable space in the lower deck of the aircraft for air cargo. Aircraft Commerce (2006) analysed the revenue potential of carrying belly cargo on flights between London and Chicago (October 2006 fuel prices) and indicated that a 777–200 and/or A340–300 would burn around 500–900 US gallons more from carrying such belly hold freight. Overall the additional belly freight will generate a gross margin of between $4,500–5,000, provided the yield is set to $0.35 per lb. Similarly a 777–300/777–300ER will generate up to $7,600 from the belly freight that it carries. An A330–200 and A340–300 passenger aircraft has an available cargo capacity of 2,336 cubic feet, which provides 18,688 lbs of belly freight capacity when packed at 8 lbs per cubic feet. Table 10.2 below shows the payload that is available for air cargo after allowing for sufficient space in the hold for a full load of passengers' checked bags.

Table 10.2   Percentage of total payload available for cargo by aircraft type

	Total payload (tonne)[†]	Cargo tonnes @ 167 kg/ cu.m	% total payload
B767–200	29	10	35.4
B767–300	36	14	38.2
B787–8	42	17	40.6
A330–200	43	17	39.0
B777–200	51	20	38.7
A340–300	51	20	39.9
B747–400	64	20	32.2
B777–300	65	27	41.5
B747–8	71	22	31.5
A380–800	73	16	21.3

[†]five-hour sector.

Source: Cranfield and aircraft manufacturers.

Around half of the combination carriers'[2] cargo traffic is carried on passenger flights and the other half on freighters. Specialist air cargo carriers only carry just above seven per cent of world international traffic, with the European based Cargolux the largest. Polar of the US (itself now 49 per cent owned by DHL) is part of a group that includes Atlas Air, a company that leases freighter aircraft to the other operators in Table 10.3.

Table 10.3   World international air cargo traffic by carrier in 2007

	RTK (m)	% total
Cargolux	5,482	
Nippon Cargo	1,873	
Polar Air	1,817	
Volga-Dnepr	123	
CAL Israel	383	
Astar (USA)	47	
Cielos Peru	44	
Total all cargo carriers	*10,532*	**7.1**
FedEx	6,507	
UPS	5,077	
DHL (incl. EAT)	590	
TNT Belgium	433	
Total Integrators	*10,997*	**7.4**
IATA all-cargo (not in above)	*57,759*	**38.9**
IATA passenger flights	*69,014*	**46.5**
World total	**148,302**	**100.0**

Source: IATA WATS 2008, 53rd Edition.

2   Combination carriers are those airlines that carry freight in the belly hold and also have a dedicated freighter fleet such as Northwest Airlines (now merged with Delta Air Lines), Lufthansa, Emirates, Korean Air, Singapore Airlines, All Nippon Airways, etc.

Integrator traffic reported to IATA amounted to just over seven per cent of the world total in 2007. This would increase substantially if US domestic traffic were included. Internationally, the major integrators use their own aircraft to carry traffic between their main regional hubs, with international feeder routes often contracted out to local operators, and thus appear under other categories in the table. Integrators also make use of other scheduled airlines to reach other points on their network. For example, DHL is a significant customer of British Airways. DHL has also joined up with Lufthansa to form a 50:50 air cargo operator, AeroLogic, which will operate at least 14 B777–200F freighters from a Leipzig Airport base from summer 2009.

The so-called 'wet leasing' of freighter aircraft by operators such as Atlas and ABX to mainly combination carriers has expanded rapidly from the early 1990s. This market is commonly called the ACMI sector, since the lessor provides aircraft, crew, maintenance and insurance, leaving the lessee to market, handle and administer the flights without the high costs of owning and operating a small freighter fleet. Boeing estimated that this market carried around 10.8 billion freight tonne/kms in 2007 and that ACMI operators were responsible for transporting around six per cent of the world's total air cargo traffic (Boeing, 2008). An example of this was the ACMI agreement in 2008 between ABX Air and All Nippon Airways for the wet lease of two B767–200F aircraft. This extended a short-term arrangement to a two-year contract, which was the first time a foreign carrier was approved by the Japanese Civil Aviation Bureau to conduct cargo aircraft operations on behalf of a Japanese airline.

With the high growth of air cargo traffic from China, some airlines have taken the opportunity to set up joint ventures there: Lufthansa and Shenzhen Airlines formed Jade Airlines in 2004 to operate A300 freighter services from Guangzhou base (Shenzhen Airlines taking 51 per cent, Lufthansa 25 per cent and a German government agency, KfW, 24 per cent). In May 2005 SIA Cargo took a 25 per cent stake in Great Wall Airlines, based in Shanghai, with a Singapore government subsidiary holding 24 per cent and China Great Wall Industry with 51 per cent. Finally, Air China has a 29.9 per cent stake in Cathay Pacific, while the Hong Kong flag carrier will take a 25 per cent interest in Air China Cargo in early 2010. Air China Cargo, was operating seven B747 freighters by mid 2009 and also handles the allocation of cargo hold space on other Air China flights.

10.5 Freighter Aircraft

In addition to the considerable space and payload available on passenger flights, many combination carriers have sizeable freighter fleets, as well as the integrators and other cargo specialists. Table 10.4 shows that 26 per cent of the world jet freighter fleet is composed of large widebodies, defined as greater than 80 tonnes payload. This would include MD11s, B747s and Antonov 124s, and in the future A380Fs.

Boeing forecast an increase in the world freighter fleet from 1,940 in 2008 to 3,892 aircraft by 2027, with only 873 of the additional fleet required new of which 60 per cent will be for in the widebody category (Boeing 2008). In addition around 40 per cent of the future freighter capacity will be based in Asia. New aircraft will include B777F and B747–800F from Boeing and A330F, A350F and A380F from Airbus. Conversions will tend to focus on B767 and B747 and some Airbus aircraft.

Table 10.5 shows the major larger commercial jet freighter aircraft by payload. The table excludes smaller jet, turbo-prop and piston-engined types used to feed integrator's hubs. For example, FedEx had, at the end of October 2009, 13 ATR-72 freighters with a payload of eight tonnes, 26 ATR-42s with 5.5 tonnes, and 252 Cessna 208s with a payload of around 1.5 tonnes.

Table 10.4   World freighter fleet by size category at end 2008

	Aircraft	%
Standard body (< 45t)	760	39.2
Medium widebody (45–80t)	680	35.1
Large widebody (> 80t)	500	25.7
Total aircraft	1,940	100.0

Source: Boeing Current Market Outlook, 2009.

Table 10.5   Jet freighters by maximum payload

Aircraft type	Payload (tonnes)
A310–300F	40
A300–600F	51–55
A330–200F	64
A350–900F	90
A380–800F	152
B757–200F	40
B767–300F	54
MD-11F	88
B777F	104
B747–200F	112
B747–400F	113
B747–8F	134
Antonov 124 Russian	150

Source: *Flight International*.

'Combi' aircraft are passenger aircraft with main deck cargo capacity (as well as passengers). They differ from the passenger aircraft of the same type in having a higher operating empty weight (OEW) due to a strengthened main floor, handling equipment and a cargo door. They can be used on routes with low passenger traffic and also have the advantage of varying the number of seats and cargo space on the main deck to suit seasonal flows. However, a major accident and the resulting need for changes to the aircraft imposed by the authorities led to their decline in popularity. However, KLM still operated 17 B747–400 combis by late 2009, configured with 278 seats (compared to the passenger version having around 430 seats) and some Asian airlines still operate combi types.

Another type of aircraft used both for passengers and cargo is the 'quick change' aircraft. These tend to be short/medium haul aircraft that can be converted from all the main deck for passengers to all this space for air cargo. This again needs a strengthened floor, handling equipment, a large cargo door and palletized seats. The seats are removed on pallets after the aircraft has completed its daily schedule, say at 10–11pm. The aircraft is then operated through the night as a freighter and converted back at 4–5am in readiness for the first passenger aircraft. Examples of this in Europe were both with the B737–300 aircraft, with Lufthansa operating cargo flights for the German Post Office and Aéropostale in France for the French Post Office. In the USA, UPS operated cargo flights during the week with a B727–200 aircraft and passenger charters at week-ends with 113 seats, but it was discontinued at the end of 2001.

10.6 Cargo Financial Results and Economics

Of the airlines carrying air cargo, only the cargo specialists publish detailed financial statements including a balance sheet, especially when they are publicly owned. Integrators also publish such information but it is for all their operations including a sizeable ground transport component. It is thus not comparable with the air cargo airlines. The combination carriers that carry both air cargo and passengers have sometimes established separate cargo subsidiaries (for example, Lufthansa) and thus required to report profitability. However, where a passenger airline has a cargo division, profits are rarely broken down into the passenger and cargo business. Figure 10.5 shows the air cargo specialist operating margin for 2006/07 and 2007/08, maintained at between 3–4 per cent. Singapore Airlines Cargo recorded an operating loss in 2006/07 due to higher fuel costs and a fall in yield which was only partially offset by fuel surcharges. However, this was turned into a net profit the following year by the sale of two B747–400F aircraft for a profit of S$46 million.

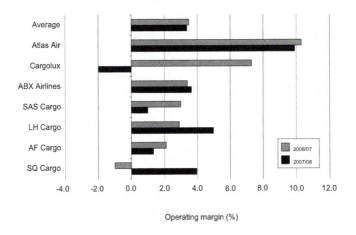

Figure 10.5   Air cargo operator operating margins
Source: Air Transport Intelligence and airline annual reports.

Air cargo charging has evolved from a complex system of special commodity rates to contract and ULD rates. The former offered various reductions from general cargo rates depending on the commodity category that the shipment fitted. There were many hundreds of different categories, which led to simplified FAK (Freight All Kinds) rates, and significant reductions for pre-containerised shipments and volume contracts.

Air cargo yields for Europe's flag carriers for all regions have been declining by 1.4 per cent a year between 1991 and 2005 (AEA, 2006). These were expressed in current US dollars, and should be compared to the US consumer price index increase of 2.5 per cent a year over the same period. The main reasons for the decline were:

- A small increase in average length of haul.
- Competition, especially for premium products, from integrators.
- Productivity improvements and unit cost reductions.

In the past few years rates actually went up somewhat, helped by fuel surcharges on international services. These were imposed using an agreed formula, which triggered increases and decreases:

Fuel price index: 100 = 53.35 US cents per US gallon
Fuel price average of five most important spot aviation kerosene markets
For example, fuel price index (3 June 2005): 291
Fuel surcharge = 0 for fuel price index of 100, then for example:
Fuel price index exceeds 240 for a period of two consecutive weeks:
Fuel surcharge adjusted to €0.30 per kg
Fuel price index exceeds 265 for a period of two consecutive weeks:
Fuel surcharge adjusted to €0.35 per kg
Fuel price index exceeds 290 for a period of two consecutive weeks:
Fuel surcharge adjusted to €0.40 per kg
and so on
Two weeks' notice for all changes

However, in 2006 competition authorities in the UK, US and EU started investigations against many of the airlines implementing the above on the basis of collusion over price or rate increases. In September 2007, British Airways were fined US$200 million and Korean Air $100 million by the US Department of Justice for price fixing, followed by a fine for Qantas of $61 million two months later. The European Commission sent letters to at least 15 airlines in December 2007 alleging that they took part in cargo price-fixing.

More recently the global freight yields have declined by 21 per cent from mid 2008 to mid 2009 due to the global recession which has significantly impacted the industry, but it is expected to flatten out by mid 2010 (IATA Economics, 2009).

The share of fuel costs for air cargo tends to be higher than for passenger operations, partly because of its long-haul nature and partly because cargo avoids some operating costs such as cabin crew and passenger services (for example, lounges, delay and overbooking costs, insurance and so on). In addition to fuel, freighter aircraft services incur separately identifiable costs such as aircraft capital (lease rentals, depreciation and interest), maintenance and overhaul, hull insurance, cockpit crew and landing and navigation charges. The carriage of cargo on passenger flights leads to costs that can be attributed to each product:

Cargo Specific/Related Costs:

- Handling (loading/unloading/transhipment).
- Sales, promotion and commissions.
- Cargo insurance and other.
- Additional fuel (due to cargo payload).

Passenger Specific/Related Costs:

- Handling (check-in, baggage, ramp, lounges).
- Cabin crew and in-flight catering.

- Airport passenger departure fees.
- Sales, ticketing, promotion and commissions.
- Passenger third party liability insurance.
- Passenger airport services, delay costs, and so on.
- Additional fuel (due to passenger/bags payload).

Joint costs will include basic (or all if not included in the above) fuel costs, aircraft capital (lease rentals, depreciation and interest), maintenance and overhaul, hull insurance, cockpit crew and landing and navigation charges. These can be allocated to each product according to the volume occupied by each, or based on the weight payload available to each. Volume allocation is preferred by many combination carriers with a significant air cargo business, and has been the recommended method for the IATA cost committee. Alternatively, no allocation is made and the profit for the flight as a whole is shared between each product according to their revenue shares. This can be improved by first deducting the specific costs listed above and sharing profit according to each product's contribution. Finally, some airlines make sure cargo covers its specific costs, and any surplus goes towards covering some joint costs, with all the profit recorded by the passenger side of the business (cargo break-even method). An example of the volume based allocation was provided by Boeing for the B747–300 combi aircraft with six main deck pallet positions. In this example, the revenue from passengers was $52,200, and the revenue from cargo $23,700, and their specific costs $20,400 and $10,300 respectively. Joint costs were $35,200:

Effective volume of passenger cabin: 360 passengers @ 36.1 cu.ft/passenger	= 12,996 cu.ft (65.4 per cent)
Cargo cabin volume: 6 pallets + lower deck (ex passenger bags)	= 6,867 cu.ft (34.6 per cent)
Total volume	= 19,863 cu.ft (100 per cent)
Costs allocated to passengers (65.4 per cent × $35,200)	= $23,000
Costs allocated to cargo (34.6 per cent × $35,200)	= $12,200
Passenger profit = [$52,200 – 20,400] – 23,000	= $8,800
Cargo profit = [$23,700 – 10,300] – 12,200	= $1,200

Source: Boeing

Establishing a separate air cargo subsidiary is an option that has been chosen by a number of combination carriers. Lufthansa was one of the first, followed by SAS, Singapore Airlines, LAN and Varig. Lufthansa split their cargo subsidiary into three divisions:

- Global Cargo Net.
- Global Cargo Handling Services.
- Global Freighter Operations.

The first (Global Cargo Net) was responsible for marketing their air cargo services across the network, the second focused on airport cargo handling while the third covered the operation of the freighter aircraft fleet. The main benefits came from making their own planning and investment decisions, greater cost and profit transparency, and better customer focus. On the negative side, they lost some economies of scale (for example, from the additional overheads such as HR and finance departments) and still needed to negotiate rates for lower deck capacity with the passenger business. In theory they could decide not to buy any lower deck capacity from Lufthansa's passenger flights, especially if they considered it too expensive. In practice this would be unthinkable, since Lufthansa would then have to market this separately with all their expertise now in the cargo company. In practice, the volume allocation would still be used for pricing the lower deck space, and it was agreed that the cargo company would not need to purchase space on some flights (for example, all German domestic services).

The cargo company owned by the Brazilian carrier Varig was named Varig Log, and with Varig's effective bankruptcy was sold to a Brazilian logistics company Volo do Brasil together with the much reduced passenger business of Varig. This passenger business (VRG Linhas Aéreas, trading as Varig) was subsequently sold to the low-cost carrier, Gol, but by that time its fleet consisted mainly of narrow-bodied aircraft with little lower deck space for cargo. Volo kept Varig Log and its freighter fleet which included three DC10–30F and two MD-11Fs. This example suggests that the cargo subsidiaries such as Lufthansa could perhaps in the future be sold to logistics specialists, leaving the passenger side to find new customers for the lower deck space.

10.7 Conclusion

Continuing profit challenges at passenger airlines have focused airline attention on opportunities for lower-hold cargo revenue. On average, cargo revenue represents 15 per cent of total traffic revenue, with some airlines earning well over half their revenue from this source. World schedule air freight traffic increased at an average rate of 7.4 per cent a year between 1970 and 2008. This growth rate was around one per cent a year higher than the growth in air passenger/kms. The Boeing Current Market Outlook (2009) predicts that world air cargo will almost triple over the next 20 years and the number of freighters in the world fleet will grow by more than two-thirds. However, one of air freight's characteristics, and one that differentiates it from the passenger business, is directionality and this is attributable to an underlying imbalance in the trade of goods. Integrated carriers will continue to become an important component of the air cargo industry and the combination carriers are increasingly focusing on acquiring widebody freighters. The air cargo business models based on combi aircraft and quick change aircraft are quickly becoming obsolete. Freight yields continue to be problematic but fuel and security surcharges appear to be keeping the air cargo industry financially afloat in more recent years. It remains a difficult industry in which to make substantial returns.

References

AEA (2006), Yearbook 06, Avenue Louise 350 B - 1050 Brussels.

Aircraft Commerce (2006), What is the value of bellyfreight?, *Aircraft Commerce*, Issue 48, October/November, pp. 33–39.

Boeing Current Market Outlook (2009), Long-term market future freight 2009 – 2028, Boeing, Seattle.

Boeing (2008), Boeing World Air Cargo Forecast 2008–2009, p. 9. Available at: www.boeing.com/commercial/cargo/wacf.pdf.

Gadola, M. (2009), Navigating through stormy waters, Panalpina Investor Day, 18 June, Luxemburg, Panalpina.

IATA Economics (2009), 3 September, Cargo e-Chartbook, Montreal-Geneva.

ICAO (2008), World total traffic, ICAO database.

International Freighting Weekly (2006), Air Freight Focus - Fresh challenge for carriers, 11th December. Available at: www.ifw-net.com.

Kararda, J. (2006), The impact of the air cargo industry on the global economy, the International Air Cargo Association, Air Cargo Forum Calgary, Canada, 13 September.

MacGregor, J. and Vorley, B. (2006), Fair miles?, The concept of 'food miles' through a sustainable development lens, International Institute for Environment and Development, London. Available at: www.iied.org/pubs/pdfs/11064IIED. pdf.

UPS annual Report (2008), UPS Investor Relations, 2008 annual report. Available at: www.investors.ups.com/phoenix.zhtml?c=62900&p=irol-reportsannual.

World Food Program (2008), World Food Program Aviation, Annual Report. Available at: www.wfp.org/sites/default/files/Aviation%20Annual%20 Report%202008.pdf.

Chapter 11

Key Issues Facing the Airport Industry

Anne Graham

11.1 Introduction

In recent years the airport industry has gone through a period of unparalleled change. A growing number of airports have been privatized and new global airport companies have emerged. At the same time airline deregulation and the evolution of new types of airline models, most notably low-cost carriers (LCCs), has altered the airport's relationship with its airline customers and has increased the competitive pressures which airports face. Technology is also changing the way that passengers check-in at airports and is having a major impact on security and border control processes which have come under unprecedented scrutiny because of the modern day risks and threats which the air transport industry faces.

The last few years have without doubt been the most volatile and uncertain ever for both the airline and airport industries and it is unlikely that this will change in the future. The current high fuel prices, 'credit crunch' and economic slump have added to these problems. However, whilst traffic growth may now be more uncertain in the short-term and also may be slowing down in mature markets, such as Western Europe and North America, in many other areas, most notably India and China, buoyant high growth rates are expected. This all means that there will continue to be pressure on airport capacity and the need for new investment, at a time when increasing concerns for the environment are making expansion at airports ever more challenging. As a consequence, all options to alleviate this capacity problem, particularly improvements in the current slot allocation process, are likely to receive even more attention in the future.

Therefore it is the aim of this chapter to provide an overview of these key issues facing the airport industry. Firstly airport privatization developments and the consequences for airport regulation and competition are discussed. This is followed by an assessment of the changing nature of the airport product and the influence of technology. Lastly capacity problems are considered.

11.2 Airport Privatization, Regulation and Competition

The first airport privatization occurred in 1987 when the state-owned organization British Airports Authority (which at the time controlled London Heathrow, London Gatwick, London Stansted, Glasgow, Prestwick, Edinburgh and Aberdeen airports) was floated on the London Stock Exchange. Since then, a significant number of airports from most corners of the world have been privatized using an increasingly diverse range of privatization models (see Table 11.1).

Privatization within the airport industry is assumed to be a broader development than just the sale of shares to investors through an initial public offering (IPO) (Graham, 2008a; Carney and Mew, 2003). Whilst such privatization has been used for a number of airports, a more popular option has been a trade sale when some or all of the airport is sold to a trade partner or consortium of investors, usually through a public tender. In these cases the investors will often become strategic partners and subsequently their management and technological expertise will be taken into account as well as their financial capabilities when a winning bidder is being selected.

Many governments are reluctant to hand over total control to the private sector because of the key strategic role that airports play within a country or region and so in this case a concession type of privatization has taken place. Here airport management, but importantly not ownership, will be handed over to another organization or consortium that will operate the airport for a fixed period of time (typically between 20–30 years) and pay the government a regular concession fee.

Table 11.1   Examples of different types of full or partial airport privatizations[†]

Type of privatization	Examples
Share flotation or IPO	BAA (1987), Vienna (1992), Copenhagen (1994), Rome (1997), Auckland (1998), Malaysia Airports (1999), Beijing (2000), Frankfurt (2001), Paris (2006); Incheon (2010)
Trade sale	Liverpool (1990), East Midlands (1993), Belfast International (1996), Birmingham (1997), Naples (1997), Brisbane/Melbourne/Perth (1997), Dusseldorf (1998), South Africa (1998), Wellington (1998), Hamburg (2000), Sydney (2002), Malta (2002), Budapest (2005), Luebeck (2005), Kosice (2006), Xi'an (2007), Mukhino (2007)
Concession	Barranquilla (1997), Caratagena (1998), La Paz/Santa Cruz/Cochabamba (1997), Luton (1998), South East Mexican airports (1998), Pacific Mexican airports (1999), Argentinean airports (1998), main Dominican republic airports (1999) Montevideo (1999), San Jose (1999), North Central Mexican airports (2000), Lima (2001), Montega Bay (2003), Delhi/Mumbai (2006), Antayla (2007), St Petersburg (2009)
Project finance	Athens (1996), JFK international arrivals terminal (1997), Ankara (2003), Hyderabad/Bangalore (2004), Tirana (2005), Larnaca/Paphos (2005), Varna/Burgas (2006), Amman (2007)

[†]Excluding management contracts.

Source: Author.

A similar approach exists with various other project finance privatizations such as build-operate-transfer (BOT) models or private-public partnerships but the key difference here will be that relatively large investments will be needed – often for totally new airports or perhaps for new passenger terminals or other major facilities. The least radical of all privatization models is a management contract, where again ownership remains with the government and the contractors take responsibility for the day-to-day operation of the airport (usually for a period of 5–10 years) with longer-term decisions and investment responsibility remaining, at least in part, with the government owners. There have been management contracts within the airport industry for many years and because of the limited control granted to the new operators, some argue that they should not be considered as a formal privatization model.

As more and more airports have come up for sale, a growing number of different organizations have become interested in airport purchases (Table 11.2). In the so-called early 'gold rush' days of the mid/late 1990s, many of the potential investors were well-established airport companies, such as BAA, Amsterdam Schiphol, Aer Rianta Irish Airports (now Dublin Airport Authority) and Copenhagen airport, that were interested in expanding beyond previously well-defined national barriers. However there were also new players such as property, utility, infrastructure and construction organizations that saw some potential synergies with airport operations. A number of these companies, most notably the German construction company Hochtief and the Spanish infrastructure company Ferrovial, are now major airport operators. In 2009, Global Infrastructure Partners, an energy, transport and water waste company purchased London Gatwick, the UK's second largest airport for $2.5 billion (Global Infrastructure Partners, 2009).

Table 11.2   Examples of international airport owners and operators

Type of operator	Examples
Traditional airport operators	Aéroports de Paris, Fraport, Schiphol, Dublin Airport Authority, BAA, Manchester, Zurich, Copenhagen, Vancouver, Vienna, Singapore Changi, Malaysia Airports
Property companies	TBI (now Abertis), Peel Holdings
Utility and infrastructure companies	Infratil, Ferrovial
Construction companies	Hochtief, Balfour Beatty
Financial investors	Macquarie, Credit Suisse
Energy company	Global Infrastructure Partners

Source: Author.

In more recent years, financial investors have also become major airport investors through private equity and infrastructure funds. The first and largest organization of this type to get involved was the Macquarie Group which now has an interest in airports such as Brussels, Copenhagen and Sydney. At the same time the more volatile aviation industry environment, coupled with more experience of international operations, has meant that a number of traditional airport companies have become more cautious and have reassessed their international expansion ambitions to ensure that they make strategic sense or really add value. For example BAA has sold off nearly all its international investments (primarily to help solve debt problems of the company) and in addition Aéroports de Paris, Copenhagen airport, Aeroporti di Roma and Dublin Airport Authority have also pulled out of some of their international ventures. However, in spite of the current global economic difficulties, all indications are that there will be more privatizations in the future perhaps at airports such as Amsterdam, Lisbon, Bucharest, Milan, Munich, Hong Kong, Narita, Kansai, Incheon or Abu Dhabi. Moreover, secondary sales which have began to occur at a number of airports such as Rome, Copenhagen, BAA, Budapest, East Midlands and Birmingham are likely to become more popular. However, the privatized airport industry is still relatively immature and questions remain as to what are the key factors that will determine the most successful type of airport management in the long run in this new global environment, or which will bring the greatest value added. Hence in 10 years time it is still uncertain as to whether there will be an industry which will still be dominated by the traditional airport operators or whether the financial investors or other new operators will have taken more of a leading role.

When private airports come under common ownership, competition may be inhibited, particularly if the airports have overlapping catchment areas. When the Australian airports were privatized with long-term leases the major airports had to be sold to separate operators whereas with BAA the company remained intact when it was sold off. To counteract the arguments for greater competition, it is claimed that group ownership can bring economies of scale, can make the best use of resources and expertise, and can enable a more strategic and coordinated approach to airport development to be adopted. Ever since the British Airports Authority was privatized way back in 1987, there have been a number of governmental reviews investigating whether the group should be split up but these have generally concluded that the additional benefits of competition would be more than offset by the disadvantages of loss of scale and other factors (Graham, 2008b). However the largest and most wide-ranging review that has ever been undertaken was carried out by the Competition Commission in the UK in 2008 and there was convincing evidence that BAA should sell off some airports in the group. In early 2009, the UK Competition Commission formally ordered BAA to sell both London Gatwick[1] and London Stansted, plus a major Scottish airport,

----

1   Gatwick airport was already on the market.

within two years (Air Transport Intelligence, 2009a; Competition Commission, 2008).

There is also a broader competition issue, which has been relevant to many of the airports which have been privatized, when it is feared that these airports will abuse their market power and will not always operate with the best interests of the airport users in mind by rising charges, by reducing the quality of service, and by under- or over-investing in facilities (Graham, 2006). In a number of cases this has led to a new system of economic regulation being introduced (for examples, see Forsyth et al. 2004). Whilst economic regulation is not just limited to privatized airports it tends to be with these airports where there are more prescribed systems, as opposed to less formal government approval of charges.

The most common form of economic regulation is a price cap on airport charges, commonly determined by a RPI-X formula where RPI is the retail price index and X is an efficiency factor. It is also known as incentive regulation as it provides incentives to reduce costs while simultaneously controlling price increases. The BAA airports of London Heathrow, London Gatwick, London Stansted and the publicly owned Manchester have been subject to this type of regulation as has the state owned Dublin airport and the partially private Airport Company of South Africa (ACSA). Some airports have a more complicated formula, for example at Hamburg and Vienna airports where traffic growth also has an impact on the price cap (Table 11.3).

One of the trends of recent years at some airports has been more light handed regulation which in some cases is complemented with more direct negotiation between the airport operator and its airlines. For example, when the Australian airports were first privatized in the late 1990s they were subject to a formal price cap regime. However, five years on this was replaced with just price monitoring – but with the threat of the re-introduction of the price control should the airports abuse their pricing freedom (Forsyth, 2008). The airports have consequently negotiated airport charges directly with the airlines. Elsewhere in Europe, Copenhagen negotiates charges for three year periods with its airlines and both Frankfurt and Düsseldorf airports have gone one stage further by establishing revenue sharing charges agreements with their airlines. Even within the UK

Table 11.3   Examples of formal airport regulation

Type of regulation	Examples
Price cap	BAA London airports, Dublin, Budapest, Malta, South Africa
Price cap with sliding scale related to traffic growth	Hamburg, Vienna
Light-handed ('reserve')	Australian airports, BAA Scottish airports, Copenhagen
Light-handed with profit sharing with airlines	Frankfurt, Dusseldorf

where a more heavy handed regulatory system currently exists, there was an attempt during the review for the latest setting of the price cap for 2008–2013 to encourage the airport operator and airlines to enter into more direct dialogue. This so-called 'Constructive Engagement' met with some success in some areas but not everywhere.

These shifts away from a heavy-handed approach reflect a more general belief by some that formal regulation is becoming less necessary as the competitive forces within the industry become stronger, through the combined effect of a more deregulated airline industry and a more commercialized airport industry (Starkie, 2005). It has been argued that most of the current regulatory systems are time-consuming, bureaucratic, and costly and that in most cases litigation or national competition law can cope with any abuses of market power. Within this context it is worth noting that the two-price regulated airports (since 1987) of Stansted and Manchester in the UK have recently been investigated by the government with a view to possibly having the price control removed. After considerable debate it was concluded than Manchester did not have a position of substantial market power and was subsequently de-designated for formal regulation but this was not considered to be the case at Stansted (Department for Transport, 2008a; 2008b). Interestingly the whole economic regulatory system in the UK, which has been in existence for 20 years, is also now under review.

Understandably most airlines tend to be more in favour of formal systems of economic regulation and have generally been much more supportive (although with certain criticisms) of the European Commission's proposal to introduce a directive related to airport charges. The proposals are based on the International Civil Aviation Organization's airport charging principles of non-discrimination, consultation and transparency but go further by suggesting specific regulations for all EU airports of over 5 million passengers. The proposals recommend the setting up of an independent national regulator in each country, and propose that airports should supply financial information to the airlines concerning the method of calculation of charges and the cost structure of the airport, whilst the airlines should provide the airports with information on their traffic forecasts and requirements at the airport. The major concern of the airports and some regulatory bodies such as the UK CAA, is that the 5 million passenger threshold (which will affect 70 airports in 2011) means that too many airports, which do not necessarily have substantial market power, will be regulated unnecessarily (ACI Europe, 2008). The final legislation has yet to be approved but clearly this may have a major effect on the airline-airport relationship within Europe.

11.3 Airport Product Developments

The deregulated airline industry alongside the commercialized and expanding privatized airport industry has also had a very significant impact on the airport product which is offered to the airlines and their customers. Firstly airports have had to place more focus on service quality with pressure from airlines that are anxious to get value for money from the airport charges, and from passengers who are becoming more experienced and more demanding customers of the airport product. This had been particularly challenging at a time when more stringent security regulations have been introduced, notably after 9/11 and then the liquids, aerosols and gels (LAGs) terrorist scare of August 2006 and the 2009 Christmas Day threat when explosives were strapped to a passenger on a flight between Amsterdam and Detroit. See Chapter 17 on airline and airport security.

Moreover, some airports are finding that their service quality has been the subject of increased scrutiny by the regulators. For example the regulatory system for both the London and Paris airports allows for rebates of charges for the airlines or bonuses for the airports depending on the level of service which is provided. More generally the EC is proposing that service level agreements between the airports and their airlines should be decided every two years in its charges directive.

Airports are also differentiating their product much more than they used to meet the more diverse needs of their modern day airline customers. Traditionally, product differentiation was limited and mostly confined to airlines providing separate check-in to business and first-class passengers and dedicated airline lounges. Now airline alliance members want to share and get cost economies and brand benefits from operating joint facilities at airports. This requires a different approach from the traditional design when airlines were grouped together according to traffic type – such as domestic and international. A few airports have also been designed with premium passengers in mind such as London City[2] airport and a number of private jet airports. Elsewhere there are a small number of airports where dedicated terminals have been developed for premium passengers alongside other terminals. For example in 2004, a premium terminal for Lufthansa passengers was opened. There are now similar facilities for Lufthansa at Munich and for Qatar Airways at Doha (Sobie, 2007).

At the other extreme LCCs have different needs. For example to ensure that they maintain quick turnaround times, they do not like having airbridges or airport buses. Moreover, they do not require airline lounges or transfer passenger and baggage facilities. Hence some airports have developed a specialized low-cost facility or terminal which has a simpler design with lower service standards than expected in conventional terminals (Jacobs Consultancy, 2007; Rowe, 2007). For example, Amsterdam airport has built Pier H&M (H for non-Schengen[3] traffic, M for Schengen traffic) which has no airbridges and functions with a 20-minute turnaround. Marseilles has a separate low-cost terminal (MP2) which was converted from an old cargo facility and at Lyon the low-cost facility used to be the charter terminal. Budapest and Warsaw have also converted old buildings into low-cost terminals. Copenhagen and Brussels Airports are both developing new

---

2 British Airways now operates a double daily A318 service from London City to JFK, with an all-business class configuration with 32 business seats.

3 Non-Schengen means International and Schengen means Domestic.

low-cost terminals aimed specifically at budget carriers, while France's regional Bordeaux Airport is opening a dedicated budget terminal in the summer of 2010 costing €5.5 million (Air Transport Intelligence, 2009b). Elsewhere in South East Asia, new low-cost terminals have been built at Kuala Lumpur and Singapore, both of which opened in 2006. There has been discussions about providing similar facilities in Bangkok (maybe on the site of Old Don Muang airport), the Philippines, Indonesia, Dubai and Delhi (Centre for Asia Pacific Aviation, 2007). Usually the LCCs will pay the same landing charges at these airports but reduced passenger charges to reflect the lower level of service provided in these low-cost terminals. However, whilst such facilities may meet the needs of the LCCs, they are not always popular with other airlines serving the airports who are fearful that the airport operators may discriminate against them and that they may end up subsidizing the LCC operations (International Air Transport Association, 2007). Indeed this has led to several legal challenges, most notably by Air France-KLM at Geneva and Marseilles airports.

The airport product must also be designed to optimize the commercial or non-aeronautical revenue which can be generated. This has been much more difficult in recent years because of the heightened security measures at airports – especially as regards liquids, aerosols and gels (LAGs). The limits of the LAGs in hand luggage has created confusion amongst passengers as to what they can buy from shops and has led to many unsuspecting passengers from outside the EU having their LAG purchases being confiscated at EU airports if they are transferring onto a different flight. Moreover, the more stringent and more time-consuming security measures have caused congestion and taken up space. This not only has an impact on airport operations but also on commercial revenue generation by reducing the available retail and F&B space and by shortening the dwell time for shopping – unless the passengers are pre-warned and arrive earlier at the airport.

As airports have become more commercially minded they have increased their dependence on non-aeronautical revenue sources. However, these security issues and other challenges such as the abolition of intra-EU duty and tax free in 1999 plus increased competition particularly from the internet has made it that much more difficult to grow these revenues and in fact the relative share of the world non-aeronautical revenues has declined from 1998 to 2005 and then levelling off by 2008 (Table 11.4). This is at the same time as when airlines that are very anxious to control their costs are putting greater pressure on airports to not increase their charges and Table 11.4 shows that the Aeronautical share of the revenues of the worlds airports have remained constant from 2005 to 2008. Moreover, the widespread use of airport discounts on aeronautical charges to encourage traffic growth has put additional pressure on aeronautical revenues. It is argued by some in the case of LCCs that the increased non-aeronautical revenues due to the greater passenger throughput will compensate for lower charges revenue as larger airports can generally offer a wider range of commercial facilities. Also passengers on LCCs are not necessarily budget spenders and are particularly good users of food and beverage (F&B) facilities at airports because of the lack of free in-flight refreshments. The flights offered by low-cost carriers are more evenly spread throughout the day as opposed to network carriers that have concentrated waves of flights at specific intervals and this keeps the food and beverage facilities full throughout the day. However, if there is a specific low-cost terminal, the more limited space and more basic facilities often make it difficult to offer a wide range of facilities, which in turn may prohibit the right atmosphere to encourage travellers to shop. The Amsterdam H&M gate facility is a half-way solution because the passengers use the normal departure lounge with all the commercial facilities before proceeding to the more basic gate facilities.

Whatever type of airport is under consideration, airports have to work harder than before to grow their commercial revenues. In some cases this may involve trying to improve customer satisfaction and penetration levels and a notable example here is so-called walk through shops which require passengers to walk through them to get to the departure lounge or gates as is the case, for example, in Terminal 3 at London Heathrow, Copenhagen, Oslo and Berlin Tegel airports. Other airports may opt for more diversification with the aim of becoming an airport city or 'aerotropolis' and offering services and facilities to many other customers over than just passengers (Reiss, 2007). Amsterdam airport has done this for many years. All indications are that there will be continuing pressures on the aeronautical sources of revenues at the airports in the future and so optimizing revenues from the commercial area is likely to remain a key challenge for airport management in the future.

Table 11.4   Revenue shares (per cent) at world and at European airports 1993–2008

%	1993	1998	2002	2005	2006	2008
WORLD						
Aeronautical	54	46	46	53	52	54
Non-aeronautical	46	54	54	47	48	46
Total	100	100	100	100	100	100
EUROPE						
Aeronautical	54	50	52	52	52	56
Non-aeronautical	46	50	46	48	48	44
Total	100	100	100	100	100	100

Sources: Airports Council International Economic Surveys and Airport Annual Reports.

11.4 Technological Enhancements

Technology has always played a major role in the development of the airport industry and innovations in the airfield and airspace infrastructure are likely to continue to improve the efficiency of operations and help to reduce the negative environmental impacts. Whilst there are many advancements which have occurred, worthy of special consideration here are the developments associated with the essential processes such as check-in, security and border control because of the potential impacts that these can have on space allocation, efficiency and service quality as well as on both aeronautical and non-aeronautical revenue generation – even though in many cases the airport operator will not be directly involved itself in the provision of these processes.

It was about 10 years ago when self-service check-in kiosks started appearing at airports being primarily installed by airlines for their own use. However, whilst these were seen as providing the airlines with competitive advantage it was an expensive venture and so this was followed by the development of common-use self service (CUSS) check-in with the earliest CUSS kiosks being installed at Vancouver and Narita airports in 2002. Around 51 per cent of all passengers used some type of self-service kiosk in 2009 and this is expected to rise to 76 per cent by the end of 2010 (Jenner, 2009). Kiosk usage throughout the world differs greatly. SITA conducted a Passenger Self Service Survey[4] on 2,193 passengers in early 2009 and the results concluded that almost 46 per cent of passengers checked-in via kiosk in 2009 at Atlanta International airport, whereas a relatively small numbers of airlines use such technology in Africa and Russia as only 8.1 per cent did so at Johannesburg International with 2.6 per cent at Moscow International (SITA, 2009). A big step-change within the check-in arena is the use of remote check-in methods such as mobile phones and through the Internet, which are far less costly than using the traditional check-in agent located at the airport. Jenner (2010) announced that survey data had established that around 2.4 per cent of passengers checked in by mobile phone in 2010 and this is expect to grow to 12 per cent by 2013. Close to 90 per cent of global airlines will allow their passengers to check-in via the Internet by 2010 and this platform will become an increasingly important channel into the future (Jenner, 2009). Bruyere (2008) reported that IATA's corporate travel survey revealed that 56 per cent of passengers have used the Internet check-in as opposed to 69 per cent who had used self-service kiosks.

Since checking-in remotely using PCs or mobiles is cheaper for airlines and generally more convenient for passengers, a key issue is whether self-service kiosks are only an interim solution to improving the check-in process and that

---

4   The 4th annual SITA / Air Transport World Passenger Self-Service (PSS) survey conducted in 2009 is an in-depth look at the attitudes and habits of a representative sample of the 232 million passengers who use six leading international airports: Hartsfield-Jackson, Atlanta; Mumbai International; Charles de Gaulle, Paris; Moscow Domodedovo; Sao Paulo Guarulhos, Brazil; and OR Tambo Airport, Johannesburg.

eventually they will not be needed (Jarrell, 2007). However there is a considerable potential to streamline passenger processes to integrating check-in with the other passenger processing technologies involved with the security and border control activities – which could not be fully achieved with the remote methods (Sigala, 2008). For example the kiosks could scan biometric data to check the traveller's identity against the data which is stored on travel documents or secure databases (Airports Council International, 2005). This has the potential of reducing costs and being more efficient for the airports whilst at the same time improving the passenger experience. Within this context, in 2000 the 'Simplifying Passenger Travel (SPT)' programme was set up jointly by the airlines, airports, handling agents, government authorities and technology providers with the aim of developing the current passenger processing model from a series of discrete processes to an integrated model by focusing on the end-to-end journey rather than the individual stages. Ultimately the success of such initiatives will depend on many factors such as the cost of the technology, the capacity of governments to reach agreements on very sensitive and important matters concerning national security and immigration, and more generally the ability of all the stakeholders to effectively work together and coordinate their efforts.

11.5 Capacity Shortages

The more uncertain airport environment and the current economic difficulties make it increasingly difficult to accurately predict short-term demand trends at airports. However, in the longer term, most of the industry is in agreement that traffic will continue to increase, rapidly in some developing areas (especially India and China) and more slowly on more mature routes in Europe and North America. For example, the Airport Council International (ACI)'s latest forecasts predict an average annual growth rate of around four per cent for passengers and 5.4 per cent for freight (see Table 11.5).

This predicted rise in air traffic means that more capacity at many airports is needed at a time when providing new infrastructure is becoming increasingly difficult. This is partly because of the stronger environmental pressures and shortage of available and suitable physical sites, and but also since the public sector which has traditionally been a major investment source is increasingly unable or unwilling to provide such support. This is a key reason for the growing interest in airport privatization. In Europe alone it is predicted that €82.6 billion will be needed for capital expenditure over the next 10 years (SH&E, 2006).

These growing difficulties associated with new capacity helps explain why the industry is placing increasing emphasis on ensuring that the current capacity is used as effectively as possible – particularly through the allocation of airport slots. The current scheduling system, based on 'grandfather rights' when any airline that has operated a slot in the previous similar season has the right to operate it again, is widely accepted and has succeeded in providing a stable environment

Table 11.5   Passenger and freight throughput by continent for 2009 and long-term forecasts for the airport industry

	Passengers (millions) 2009	Freight Tonnes (000s) 2009	Average annual passenger growth to 2025 (%)	Average annual freight growth to 2025 (%)
Africa	150	1,944	5.8	5.4
Asia/Pacific	1,217	27,691	5.8	6.5
Europe	1,408	15,445	3.6	4.8
Latin America/ Caribbean	368	4,178	4.5	4.9
Middle East	184	5,153	4.6	5.3
North America	1,466	25,403	2.7	4.4
World	4,793	79,814	4.0	5.4

Source: Airport Council International (2008; 2009).

for allocating slots. However, critics claim that its gives no guarantee that the scarce airport capacity is used by the airlines that value it most highly, it provides no guide to future investment requirements and is administratively burdensome. Moreover, many new entrants are prevented from competing at major airports. This has meant that a number of alternative market based mechanisms have been explored for both primary allocation, when the slots are initially allocated, and for secondary allocation, when the use of slots may be changed at some later stage (for example see Czerny et al. 2008).

The simplest primary trading method would be to maintain the airport charging mechanism and to price slots at the market clearing level in order to match demand and supply. However, the prices would have to be considerably higher than they are currently, to influence demand. Alternatively the auction mechanism could be introduced – there is experience of this with mobile telecommunications and radio frequencies. This could cause considerable upheaval and disruption for both airlines and passengers depending on the frequency of use and could be costly to implement. There could also be slot lotteries which are likely to be even more disruptive although they could encourage more airline competition. The European Commission has commissioned a number of studies related to some of these market based options (d'Huart, 2009; DotEcon, 2006; Mott MacDonald, 2006; NERA Economic Consulting, 2004) and has consulted relevant stakeholders widely on these issues. However, whilst it has introduced some amendments to the current system with the aim of improving its effectiveness it has yet to make any more radical suggestions that would actually change the primary slot allocation system.

As regards secondary trading, there have recently been some more significant developments. Within the EU, buying and selling slots has officially been illegal although a simple exchange of slots has not been. However, a substantial 'grey market' in slots has developed in recent years – particularly in the UK since the High Court ruled in 1999 that slot exchanges with 'compensation' for less attractive slots was possible. For example capacity at Heathrow has become very scarce as its two runways facilitated 4,331 weekly departing flights in February 2009, opposed to Paris' Charles De Gaulle Airport which accommodated a similar amount of flights (4,382) but with four runways. Consequently the price for a peak slot has risen sharply over the years. In 2002, British Airways bought seven pairs of daily slots from SN Brussels for $62.5 million, and then in 2003 it bought eight pairs from Swiss at a cost of $55.2 million and two pairs from United for $20 million. This shows that a pair of slots in peak time used to reach up to $10 million and indications are that the prices have increased very significantly since 2007 when airlines became very keen to acquire slots at Heathrow to take advantage of the new route opportunities that had arisen because of the EU–US open skies agreement which came into effect in April 2008 (Pilling, 2007). Continental Airlines who were restricted to operating into London Gatwick because of the limiting bilateral that was in place prior to the new EU–US open skies agreement purchased four slots at London Heathrow[5] for $115 million in 2008 and a further $93 million for the slots that Winter (Air Transport Intelligence, 2008). Moores and Kaminski-Morrow (2009) reported that British Midland's[6] slots at Heathrow were valued at $916 million by late 2009 and some of these slots may very well be traded by Lufthansa into the near future.

Such widespread slot-trading has been confined to the UK although there has been some limited practice elsewhere in Europe. However in April 2008 the European Commission made the important step of officially allowing such secondary trading. It is too early to assess the impact of this but it should improve the efficiency of the slot allocation process – albeit that the key issue, namely the shortage of slots, will still remain.

11.6 Conclusion

This chapter has focused on a number of issues which are considered to be very important for the future development of the airport industry. Undoubtedly the greatest challenge that the airport and indeed the whole of the air transport industry faces is how to cope with the huge environmental pressures which now exist – particularly at a time when demand is growing and additional capacity is needed. See Chapter 12 on environmental issues. There will be much more pressure on airports to make the best use of existing capacity. Airports will have to investigate

---

5   The EU–US open skies agreement opened up London Heathrow to all US carriers – prior to this only American Airlines and United Airlines were allowed access to Heathrow.

6   BMI is the second largest airline at London Heathrow with around 12 per cent of the slots. It was 100 per cent owned by Lufthansa by the end of 2009.

the feasibility of introducing alternative slot mechanisms – particularly in Europe, which has already made the first step by allowing secondary trading.

Experience has shown that at a number of airports, the privatization process has enabled much needed investment to take place as well as providing a more business-like and commercial focus to airport operations. This shift to private sector ownership and management seems set to continue into the future and indeed it is claimed that there are over 60 leading (active and potential) global airport investors eager to further develop their international interests in airports (Centre for Asia Pacific Aviation, 2007). Of greater uncertainty, however, is the exact role that the current diverse collection of different airport operators and investors will play in the future and who will be the key players.

Greater competitive pressures in both the airline and airport industry are also likely to have a significant impact on airport operations in the future. This will not only affect the amount of control that governments think is necessary through economic regulation but also the design and quality of the product which the airport offers to its customers and the balance between aeronautical and commercial activities. Finally technological enhancements, as in the past, are likely to have a major influence.

References

ACI Europe (2008), Legislative process for EU Directive on airport charges: European airports still concerned following European Parliament vote, Press release, 15 January.

ACI Economics Survey (2009), Airport Council International, Geneva, PO Box 16, Geneva airport 1215, Switzerland.

Airports Council International (ACI) (2009), World Airport Traffic Report 2009, ACI.

Airports Council International (ACI) (2008), World Airport Traffic Report 2008, ACI.

Airports Council International (ACI) (2007), Global traffic forecast 2006–2025, ACI.

Airports Council International (ACI) (2005), The application of biometrics at airports, position paper, ACI.

Air Transport Intelligence (2009a), BAA skeptical as UK regulator orders it to sell three airports, 19th March.

Air Transport Intelligence (2009b), Bordeaux Airport to establish low-cost airline terminal, 8th September.

Air Transport Intelligence (2008), Continental to bolster Newark-Heathrow service, exit Gatwick, 9th September.

Bruyere, P. (2008), Extending self-service, *International Airport Review*, 1, pp. 53–55.

Carney, M. and Mew, K. (2003), Airport governance reform: a strategic management perspective, *Journal of Air Transport Management*, 9, pp. 221–232.

Centre for Asia Pacific Aviation (2007), *Global airport privatization report*, second edition, CAPA.

Competition Commission (2008), BAA market investigation: Emerging thinking, Competition Commission, 22nd April.

Czerny, A., Forsyth, P. Gillen, D. and Neimeier, H-M (2008), *Airport slots: International experiences and options for reform*, Ashgate.

Department for Transport (2008a), Decision on the regulation status of Manchester airport. Available at: www.dft.gov.uk.

Department for Transport (2008b), Decision on the regulation status of Stansted airport. Available at: www.dft.gov.uk.

d'Huart, O. (2009), Airport Slot Allocations in the European Union: Current Regulation and Perspectives, December.

DotEcon (2006), *Alternative allocation mechanisms for slots created by new airport capacity*, DotEcon.

Forsyth, P. (2008), *Airport policy in Australia and New Zealand: Privatization, light-handed regulation and performance*, Winston, C. and de Rus, G. (Eds) (2008) *Aviation infrastructure performance*, Brookings Institution Press.

Forsyth P., Gillen D., Knorr A., Mayer, O. Niemeier H. and Starkie D. (Eds) (2004), *The economic regulation of airports*, Ashgate.

Global Infrastructure Partners (2009), Our Portfolio, Gatwick Airport limited. Available at: www.global-infra.com/ourportfolio.html.

Graham, A. (2006), *Competition in airports*, Papatheodorou, A. (Ed) *Corporate rivalry and market power: Competition issues in the tourism industry*, I.B.Tauris.

Graham, A. (2008a), *Managing airports: An international perspective*, third edition, Elsevier/Butterworth-Heinemann.

Graham, A. (2008b), *Airport planning and regulation in the UK*, Winston, C. and de Rus, G. (Eds) (2008) *Aviation infrastructure performance*, Brookings Institution Press.

International Air Transport Association (IATA) (2007), Low cost facilities and services, position statement.

Jacobs Consultancy (2007), Review of dedicated low-cost airport passenger facilities, Jacobs.

Jarrell, J. (2007), Self-service kiosks: Museum pieces or here to stay? *Journal of Airport Management*, 2(1), pp. 23–29.

Jenner, G. (2010), Mobile Working, *Airline Business*, July, pp. 48–49.

Jenner, G. (2009), Getting Mobile, *Airline Business*, July, pp. 48–50.

Jenner, G. (2008), Mobilised change, *Airline Business*, July, pp. 48–51.

Jenner, G. (2007), Airport IT trends 07, *Airline Business*, December, pp. 60–61.

Mott MacDonald (2006), Study of the impact of the introduction of secondary trading at Community airports, Mott MacDonald.

Moores and Kaminski-Morrow (2009), Heathrow slot values under pressure? *Airline Business*, December, pp. 12–13.

NERA Economic Consulting (2004), Study to assess the effects of different slot allocation schemes, NERA.

Pilling, M. (2007), Slot machines, *Airline Business*, October, pp. 70–74.

Reiss, B. (2007), Maximising non-aviation revenue for airports: Developing airport cities to optimize real estate and capitalize on land development opportunities. *Journal of Airport Management*, 1(3), pp. 284–293.

Rowe, R. (2007), Budget buildings, *Airline Business*, pp. 40–44.

SH&E (2006), Capital needs and regulatory oversight arrangement: A survey of European airports. SH&E.

Sigala, M. (2008), *Applications and implications of information and communication technology for airports and leisure travellers*, in Graham, A., Papatheodorou, A. and Forsyth, P. (Eds) *Aviation and tourism: Implications for leisure travel*, Ashgate.

SITA (2009), Air Transport World Passenger Self-Service Survey – Highlights. Available at: www.sita.aero/pss2009.

Starkie, D. (2005), Making airport regulation less imperfect, *Journal of Air Transport Management*, 11, pp. 3–8.

Sobie, B. (2007), Stress free, *Airline Business*, December, p. 47.

Chapter 12

Challenges to Growth: Environmental Issues and the Development of the Air Transport Industry

Ben Daley and Callum Thomas

12.1 Introduction

Air transport generates many economic benefits including employment, trade, tourism, investment, knowledge transfer, increased productivity and competitiveness, greater mobility and a wide range of multiplier effects. Air transport also offers important social benefits: faster and easier access to relatives and friends, to a wider range of leisure experiences, to international educational opportunities, and to cultural and sporting events. Hence air transport is regarded as an important 'engine' of economic development and has become a popular, rapidly growing industry (Bishop and Grayling 2003; Boon and Wit 2005; OEF 1999, 2002, 2006; DfT 2003a, 2003b). Yet the benefits of air transport are accompanied by a range of environmental impacts; this fact, together with increasing public awareness of environmental issues in general, means that there are now unprecedented levels of popular and scientific concern about the environmental impacts of flying. Aircraft emissions contribute to climate change and to local air pollution, and aircraft noise affects communities near to airports. In addition, airports have a range of environmental impacts including air pollution, ecological modification, water use and pollution, and the production of other wastes. Concerns about aviation environmental impacts are already acute and are likely to become yet more pressing as demand for air transport grows. Consequently, environmental issues in general – and the issue of climate change in particular – increasingly constitute a significant business risk to aviation and could drastically affect the growth and development of the industry.

This chapter provides an overview of the environmental impacts of the air transport industry, focusing on how those impacts will potentially influence its growth and development. First, we consider the significance of aviation for economic and social development, including its relation to globalization and to tourism, and we discuss the projected rapid growth of demand for air transport over the period until at least 2030. Next, we outline the main environmental impacts of aviation – including the impacts of aircraft on global climate and on local air quality, and the issue of aircraft noise. Whilst technological innovations have been made and the aviation industry has improved its environmental performance, those improvements have been outpaced by the rate of growth of the industry (Åkerman 2005; IPCC 1999: 3; RCEP 2002). Hence we argue that the environmental impacts of air transport – coupled with increasing levels of public environmental concern – have the potential to constrain the growth of the industry. Yet access to international air transport markets is an important aspect of many national and regional development strategies, and environmental constraints of air transport growth could have the unintended effect of blighting development, especially in developing countries. In this chapter, we emphasize the sustainable development dilemma faced by the air transport industry: the need to balance economic, social and environmental considerations – with both current and future generations in mind. That task presents a formidable challenge to policymakers, industry representatives and researchers. In the subsequent section, we discuss a range of responses to that challenge including various technological, operational and policy approaches. In particular, we consider the regulatory, market-based and voluntary measures that can be used to mitigate the environmental impacts of aviation, and we conclude with an assessment of the likely direction of future policy approaches.

12.2 Air Transport and the Challenge of Sustainable Development

Several key studies have indicated that air transport makes a significant contribution to economic development, to the extent that aviation is regarded as a strong driver of economic growth (OEF 1999, 2002, 2006; Button and Taylor 2000; DfT 2003a: 5; Boon and Wit 2005; Rodrigue et al., 2009). In their review of policies for sustainable aviation, Bishop and Grayling (2003: 5) stated that there are 'sizeable economic and social benefits associated with air transport' including the contributions to economic prosperity made by business travel and air freight operations. Bishop and Grayling (2003: 18) summarized the economic benefits of aviation in terms of access to markets, specialization, economies of scale and foreign direct investment (FDI). In another study, Boon and Wit (2005: 1) acknowledged that the continued growth of environmental impacts in the vicinity of European airports has generally been justified 'largely on economic grounds'. In another, authoritative series of analyses of the contribution of aviation to the UK economy, Oxford Economic Forecasting (OEF 1999, 2002, 2006) found that the air transport industry makes a substantial economic contribution to the UK – primarily through its impact on the performance of other industries and through supporting their growth. Given that the UK is an island nation located at the edge of Europe, the study argued that the economic contribution of its aviation industry is probably larger than those of other countries (OEF 1999: 5). Nevertheless, the study found that aviation also makes a substantial economic contribution in its own right: by contributing to GDP, by providing direct and indirect employment, by promoting high productivity, by exporting goods and services, by contributing taxes, and through investment. Hence the OEF (1999, 2002, 2006) studies demonstrated that aviation is a key component of the UK transport infrastructure on which other parts of the economy depend; that investments in that infrastructure boost productivity growth across the rest of the economy; and that air services are vital for the growth sectors on which future economic success is believed to depend.

The substantial economic benefits of air transport are accompanied by numerous social benefits, although these can be difficult to quantify. Bishop and Grayling (2003: 18) summarized the social benefits of aviation in terms of employment, leisure travel, cultural exchange, consumer choice, and visiting family and friends. In particular, air transport offers increased personal mobility to an increasing population of consumers, which can in turn facilitate a range of opportunities: increased contact with relatives and friends who may be widely dispersed, education and research, leisure and recreation, cultural and sporting events, cultural exchange and development, and social inclusion (see DCMS 1999; Horak and Weber 2000; Hoyer and Noess 2001; Caves 2002; Graham 2002; Grieco 2002; Urry 2002; Lethbridge 2002; Shaw and Thomas 2006; Papatheodorou and Zheng 2006; Bieger et al. 2007). As Caves (2003: 39) has acknowledged, 'the social advantages of aviation are more readily apparent in developing countries, in promoting cultural unity within a country and allowing cultural, ethnic and educational links with the industrialized world'. Other social benefits provided by aviation include increased capacity to support disaster relief, medical evacuation, law enforcement, international diplomacy and environmental monitoring (Caves 2003: 39). Given such potential benefits, the UN has acknowledged that air transport has a vital role to play in promoting sustainable development, and that air services should be affordable and accessible in order to ensure mobility on an equitable basis to all sectors of society (UNCTAD 1999a, 1999b, 1999c; UNCSD 2001). In particular, UNCTAD (1999a: 10–16, 1999b: 4, 1999c: 3–4, 7) emphasized the importance of aviation for developing countries, highlighting their need for greater and more equitable participation in air transport markets (see Campling and Rosalie, 2006). Air transport is therefore regarded as an important tool for social – as well as economic – development (see Goldstein, 2001; Rhoades, 2004; Raguraman, 1995; Miller and Clarke, 2007; Hjalager, 2007).

Given the importance of air transport for economic and social development – and the increasing popularity of air travel – the aviation industry has experienced a consistently high level of growth over the last 60 years (Bailey 2007: 249). The sustained growth of demand for air transport has been reinforced by two trends: globalization and the growth of tourism. Globalization is now acknowledged to be a complex process that is responsible for profound economic, environmental and social transformations worldwide (Adey et al., 2007; Hettne, 2008). Communications between some places are now almost instantaneous; global transport is commonplace; the world economy has become increasingly integrated; the influence of multinational organizations has expanded; and the autonomy of most nation-states has diminished. Air transport has been important in facilitating the process of globalization, although globalization has in turn increased demand for air travel (Young 1997: 38). The growth of demand for air transport has also been stimulated by demand for tourism, an industry that is highly dependent upon the availability of rapid, long-distance air services (Cabrini 2005). Globally, tourism, like aviation, is an important economic driver and is projected to expand rapidly – at an average rate of four per cent per year until at least 2020. Projections by the United Nations World Tourism Organization (UNWTO) indicate that international tourist arrivals will double between 2005 and 2020 and are expected to reach 1.6 billion by the latter year (UNWTO, 2007). All of these factors combine to suggest that sustained growth in demand for air transport – of around five per cent per year – is likely to continue until at least 2030 (IPCC 1999: DfT 2003b: 9; 4–6; Bows et al. 2005, Bows et al. 2006: 15–18; see also Bieger et al. 2007).

However, in addition to its substantial economic and social benefits, air transport has considerable environmental impacts, which form the subject of the following section. A range of aviation environmental impacts are local to airports, whilst others are of global concern. Aircraft noise has long been a source of nuisance for communities living in the vicinity of airports and beneath flight paths. Aircraft and airports are sources of local air pollution – in particular, by emitting oxides of nitrogen (NO_x), oxides of sulphur (SO_x), and particles. Airports also have other local environmental impacts including habitat modification and destruction, water use and pollution, and waste production. At the global scale, concern about aviation environmental impacts has focused on two issues: stratospheric ozone depletion and climate change. Aircraft cruising at high altitudes contribute to the destruction of stratospheric ozone by their emissions of NO_x, although that effect is associated with supersonic aircraft flying in the mid-stratosphere – not with contemporary civil air transport. In contrast, the impact of civil air transport on climate is significant and growing: aircraft release greenhouse gases – especially carbon dioxide (CO_2) – that contribute to the radiative forcing of climate. In addition, aircraft emissions of NO_x in the lower stratosphere and upper troposphere (the levels at which civil aircraft generally cruise) cause the catalytic production of ozone (O_3), which acts as a powerful greenhouse gas at those levels. The effects of those emissions are partially offset by other atmospheric impacts of aviation, including the destruction of another greenhouse gas, methane (CH_4), by NO_x, and the production of sulphate and soot particles (which have a relatively small, cooling effect on climate). In addition, aircraft produce contrails (condensation trails) and cirrus clouds, although their impact on climate is not yet fully understood (Lee, 2004; see also Goodman, 2009).

The environmental impacts of air transport are discussed in more detail in the following section. Here, we note simply that those environmental impacts are compounded by the sustained, rapid growth of the industry. Whilst technological and operational improvements have been made – such as advances in fuel combustor technology, the introduction of low sulphur-content fuels, the development of more aerodynamically efficient airframes, and the use of noise abatement procedures – the growth of the industry has outpaced those improvements (IPCC 1999: 3). Consequently, although greater efficiencies have been achieved, the absolute environmental impacts of air transport are projected to increase. Even in scenarios containing very optimistic assumptions about the rate of technological progress, air transport is projected to produce almost twice as much CO_2 in 2030 as in 2002, and in some scenarios CO_2 emissions are projected to more than treble over the same period (Lee, 2004: 13; see also Horton, 2006: 11, 13;). By 2050, in the UK, given the commitments made under the Kyoto Protocol to achieve CO_2 reductions, air transport emissions could consume the entire national carbon budget unless mitigation measures are taken (Bows et al. 2006: 2). Furthermore, whilst the impact of air transport on climate is likely to represent an increasing challenge to growth, local environmental constraints may be even more acute: airport infrastructure development is already significantly curtailed by local agreements to limit aircraft noise nuisance and by local air quality standards. Those environmental standards are likely to become more – not less – stringent as affluence and expectations increase and tolerance levels decrease. Thus the air transport industry experiences constraints to its growth due to increasingly limited environmental capacity (Upham 2001; Upham et al. 2003; Upham et al. 2004).

Hence the air transport industry faces a sustainable development dilemma: how to deliver vital economic and social benefits whilst limiting, mitigating or even reducing its environmental impacts. Addressing that dilemma presents policymakers, industry representatives and researchers with a formidable challenge – a task that is made more difficult by the projected rapid growth of demand for air travel and tourism, the strong links between air transport service provision and economic growth, the high abatement costs of the sector, and the limited potential for radical technological solutions to be found in the short to medium term (DfT, 2004). Success in meeting this challenge depends upon the formulation and implementation of effective policy, although progress has been limited by the complexity of managing the impacts of an international activity that is governed by a multitude of bilateral air services agreements (ASAs). In addition, policy measures to mitigate the environmental impacts of air transport must negotiate sensitive issues of equity – both intra-generational and inter-generational – in balancing a range of economic, social and other environmental considerations. We will return to the subject of policy approaches in a subsequent section; first, however, we present a more detailed account of the various environmental impacts of air transport.

12.3 The Environmental Impacts of Air Transport

In this section, we first discuss the global impact on air transport of climate before considering the localized impacts of air pollution, aircraft noise, ecological modification, water use and pollution, and waste production.

Climate Change

The impacts of aviation on climate have received scrutiny from a range of commentators (IPCC, 1999; Lee and Sausen 2000; RCEP, 2002; Bishop and Grayling, 2003; Lee, 2004; Sausen et al. 2005; Stordal et al. 2005; Forster et al. 2006; Cairns and Newson, 2006; Chapman, 2007; Peeters, 2007; Goodman, 2009; Macintosh and Wallace, 2009). Those impacts include the effects of aircraft and airports. Aircraft emit carbon dioxide (CO_2), a greenhouse gas, in direct proportion to the quantity of fuel burned; CO_2 emissions can also be attributed to airports as a result of the operation of stationary plant, ground support vehicles and passenger surface transport vehicles. Since CO_2 has a long residence time and is well mixed in the atmosphere, the radiative effects of CO_2 emissions persist for many decades at least. Aviation currently generates around 2 per cent of all anthropogenic CO_2 emissions, but that proportion could potentially increase to around 10 per cent by 2050, depending on the scenario adopted; in the UK, aviation could account for much a higher share of national CO_2 emissions by that year (RCEP, 2002; Rogers et al. 2002; DfT, 2004; Lee, 2004: 13). Since aviation CO_2 emissions scale linearly with fuel consumption, they depend upon the fuel efficiencies achieved by aircraft operators, which in turn depend upon aircraft type, aircraft loading, atmospheric conditions, cruising levels, flight duration, cost index, aircraft maintenance history, and a variety of other technological and operational factors.

Aircraft have additional, non-CO_2, effects on climate. Emissions of oxides of nitrogen (NO_x) lead to the catalytic production of tropospheric ozone (O_3) and the destruction of methane (CH_4) – both of which act as powerful greenhouse gases at cruising levels. Therefore, the radiative effect of aircraft NOx emissions are variously positive (due to tropospheric O_3 formation) and negative (due to CH_4 destruction); however, the former effect does not cancel the latter because tropospheric O_3 has a much shorter residence time than CH_4, with the result that its radiative influence is concentrated in the northern hemisphere whilst that of methane occurs globally (Lee 2004: 14). In addition to NO_x, aircraft also emit sulphate and soot particles, both of which have distinct but relatively small effects on climate. Sulphate particles are aerosols that reflect incoming solar radiation, producing a cooling effect on the atmosphere; in contrast, soot particles absorb solar radiation and cause a local heating effect. Sulphate and soot particles also facilitate the formation of contrails and cirrus clouds by acting as condensation nuclei.

A further, direct impact of aircraft on climate occurs through the formation of contrails and cirrus clouds, although scientific uncertainty about these phenomena remains substantial. Contrails form in very cold conditions (typically –35 to –60°C) where air is supersaturated with respect to ice; they may persist for periods ranging from seconds to hours, and they can spread to produce cirrus clouds that are indistinguishable from naturally occurring cirrus (Lee, 2004: 15–16; Stordal et al. 2005). An increase in cirrus cloud cover of approximately 1–2 per cent per decade due to aircraft traffic has been identified, and the net radiative effect of contrails and aircraft-induced cirrus clouds is positive (causing atmospheric warming) – especially at the regional scale (Stordal et al. 2005: 2155–2156). Further research is in progress to quantify the climate impacts of contrails and cirrus clouds with greater precision (Amanatidis and Friedl, 2004; De Leon and Haigh, 2007; Goodman 2009). Overall, the non-CO_2 effects climate of aviation were estimated by the IPCC (1999: 8–9) to be greater than of those CO_2 emissions alone by a factor of 2–4, although that 'radiative forcing factor' has since been revised to approximately 1.9 times the effect of aviation CO_2 emissions alone (Sausen et al. 2005).

Local Air Pollution

Aircraft and airport emissions represent significant sources of local air pollution. Concerns about local air pollution due to aviation have focused primarily on emissions of NO_x and particles, although other pollutants are also emitted in relatively small quantities, including oxides of sulphur (SO_x), carbon monoxide (CO) and volatile organic compounds (VOCs). Aircraft NO_x emissions predominantly comprise nitric oxide (NO), which is rapidly converted to nitrogen dioxide (NO_2) in the atmosphere, although some emissions of primary NO_2 occur (Lee and Raper, 2003: 84); NO_2 is regarded as a critical local air pollutant due to its effects on human health – especially in people with asthma – and on vegetation (DETR, 2000: 44–48, 61). In addition, NO_x is responsible for the catalytic production of tropospheric O_3 – another critical local air pollutant due to its effects as a respiratory irritant (DETR, 2000: 48–51). In relation to air transport, NO_x emissions are greatest in the vicinity of the runways, taxiways and aprons of airports, as well as close to major roads, and recent work has demonstrated that exhaust pollutants may be transported to the ground far more effectively by aircraft wakes than by ambient atmospheric dispersion alone (Underwood et al. 2001; Graham and Raper, 2006a, 2006b; Peace et al. 2006; Schürmann et al. 2007;). Consequently, questions about whether airport expansion could result in local air quality standards for NO_2 being exceeded have generated considerable concern, for instance, in relation to the development of London Heathrow Airport (DfT, 2006).

Aircraft, airport stationary plant, ground support vehicles and passenger surface transport vehicles also emit particles, which are typically defined by their aerodynamic diameter (PM_{10} refers to particulate matter of 10 microns or less in diameter; $PM_{2.5}$ refers to smaller particles of 2.5 microns or less in diameter). Particles (defined as PM_{10}) are regarded as a critical air pollutant of concern due to their impact on human respiratory and cardiovascular systems, asthma and mortality (DETR, 2000: 51–57). Aircraft particle emissions are relatively diverse: particles are emitted from (carbon) brake and tyre wear as well as from main engines and auxiliary power units (APUs) (Underwood et al. 2001: 6–7). In fact, most particles emitted by aircraft are $PM_{2.5}$, which are of greater concern than larger particles in terms of their effects on human health. Highest concentrations of particles occur close to runways, taxiways, aprons and major roads; furthermore, as with NO_x, particles can be effectively transported to the surface by aircraft wakes (Graham and Raper, 2006a, 2006b; Peace et al. 2006). Again, airport infrastructure development can potentially be constrained if airport expansion could result in local air quality standards for PM_{10} being exceeded (DfT, 2006). However, given that measures can be taken to ensure that particle emissions are minimized from many airport sources – for example, by the conversion of ground support vehicles to use liquefied petroleum gas (LPG) fuel instead of diesel – the air quality standards for particles may represent less of a constraint than those for NO_x.

Other local air pollutants emitted by aircraft include SO_x, CO and VOCs, and they are also emitted by other airport sources. Whilst these are significant pollutants in general terms, they are not regarded as major outputs of aircraft operations and they do not represent issues that currently constrain aviation growth – nor can the health impacts of aviation-derived emissions of these pollutants be readily distinguished from those occurring under ambient conditions (Hume and Watson, 2003: 67). Overall, concerns about local air pollution due to aircraft and airport operations are focused on emissions of NO_x and particles; of the local air pollutants discussed here, those are the species most likely to constrain the expansion of major airports – and of smaller airports located in major urban areas (where air quality standards are already likely to be exceeded at times). However, local air pollutants are relatively complex to manage, especially given that many technological and operational factors affect emission levels from aircraft, including the aircraft type, the extent of engine deterioration, the power setting used during take-off, the actual times in mode, the use of reverse thrust, the use of APUs, the condition of brakes and tyres, and the ambient conditions (DfT, 2006: 94; see also Schürmann et al. 2007). Levels of many pollutants are projected to decrease in the short-term (to around 2010), mainly due to reductions in emissions from surface transport. Thereafter, however, the projected high growth rates of aviation mean that emissions of local air pollutants are likely to increase, especially since the growing demand for air travel will prompt greater demand for surface transport to and from airports.

Aircraft Noise

Aircraft noise is generated by main engines, APUs and airframes; however, it is a complex phenomenon involving the interaction of multiple physical, biological, psychological and sociological processes. The relevant physical factors include those associated with noise generation: aircraft type, the timing and mode of operation, and the resulting noise levels. Other critical factors are human factors, which include the basic biological processes of audition and the psychological processes involved in the interpretation of those signals. The latter can interact with factors such as health status, annoyance and stress (Hume et al. 2003; Hume and Watson, 2003: 99). The perceived noise nuisance is influenced by social factors including socio-economic status, cultural differences and lifestyle. Furthermore, although individuals may complain about the 'noise' of aircraft, a variety of other factors – such as fear of air accidents or nuisance caused by other airport-related activities – may also contribute to the underlying annoyance (Moss et al. 1997). The level of perceived noise nuisance is, therefore, only partly a function of the noisiness and frequency of aircraft movements. Consequently, it is important to differentiate between the issues of noise exposure and noise nuisance or intolerance.

Exposure to aircraft noise can create a range of problems: by causing or exacerbating sleep deprivation, by generating stress, by interfering with speech communication, by disrupting learning, and by other cognitive and performance effects. Exposure to aircraft noise thus degrades physical, mental and social well-being (Hume and Watson, 2003: 99). Aircraft noise exposure is a function of both the sound generated by individual movements and the total number of noise events, and the balance of these factors varies with time. Over several decades, numerous technological and operational measures have been taken in an attempt to reduce the sound associated with individual aircraft movements; those measures have resulted in the phasing out of older, noisier aircraft types and their replacement with significantly quieter models; the use of noise abatement departure procedures (NADPs) and noise preferential routes (NPRs); and the development of low power, low drag (LP/LD) approaches (Connor, 1996; Ollerhead and Sharp, 2001; Depitre, 2001; Clarke, 2003; ICCAIA, 2004; Thomas, 2008; Girvin, 2009). Such efforts have led to dramatic improvements in the noise performance of aircraft and to a decline in the number of people exposed to significant noise around many airports over several decades, despite the growth in air traffic. However, this trend is projected to reverse because the anticipated rate of fleet renewal and of technological and operational improvements is likely to be exceeded by the rate of projected air traffic growth (Skogö, 2001; Smith, 1992). The increased exposure to aircraft noise that is projected to accompany increased air traffic levels will probably be compounded by decreasing levels of tolerance: levels of noise that were considered acceptable in the past may not be so in the future. In turn, reduced tolerance of aircraft noise is likely to prompt increasing levels of community opposition to airport development and growth. Consequently, aircraft noise is likely to continue to present a considerable challenge to aviation growth for at least several decades (Collins et al. 2006; May and Hill, 2006; Nero and Black, 2000).

Ecological Modification

By their nature, airports require large areas of land and create zones which are either hostile to wildlife (paved and built) or are ecological monocultures (mown grassland). On the other hand, areas surrounding airports may be of considerable ecological value, particularly if the airport is located in a green belt surrounding a major urban area – as is often the case. The ability of an airport operator to extend the airport boundaries or even to build on parts of its own land may be curtailed by the ecological value of the habitats threatened. This problem is most acute in parts of Europe, where sites protected by national or international conventions have often prevented or restricted airport development. Given the commitments to protect biodiversity made in 1992 by nations at the UN Conference on Environment and Development (the Earth Summit) in Rio de Janeiro, such constraints are likely to become more stringent in the future, even in developing countries (Baker, 2006: 55–59; Grubb et al. 1993). New technologies and operating practices that enable more passengers and freight to be handled using existing infrastructure may be required at some airports to overcome the constraints to growth presented by the ecological value of adjacent habitats.

Water Use and Pollution

Another potential constraint of airport growth arises from the resources needed to deliver adequate customer services and to provide for the normal operation of the airport and the maintenance of its infrastructure. Some European airport operators have expressed concerns that they will be unable to ensure adequate and secure supplies of water – including potable water – in the medium to long-term future. A further environmental issue of concern is the pollution of water that occurs as a result of airport operations, including the use of de-icing fluids.

Waste Production

Forecasts of waste generated by airport activities indicate that significant additional infrastructure will probably be required for the handling, processing and transport of waste from and within major airport sites. Insufficient waste management capacity, therefore, has also been identified as a potential constraint of airport growth at some airports.

12.4 Responding to the Challenge of Sustainable Aviation Growth

The environmental issues described above have the potential to curtail the growth of the air transport industry; indeed, the development of many airports is already significantly constrained for environmental reasons (Upham, 2001, Upham et al. 2003; Upham et al. 2004). In this section, we consider some industry responses to the challenge of ensuring that the growth of the air transport industry is compatible with the requirements of sustainable development; a range of technological, operational and policy responses is considered in turn below. Technological responses include improvements in aircraft design and performance as well as the development of alternative fuels. Operational responses involve different methods of loading, manoeuvring and maintaining aircraft in addition to the use of revised Air Traffic Management (ATM) procedures. Policy responses embrace regulatory measures (standards), market-based measures (such as fuel taxes, emissions charges, subsidies and tradable permits) and voluntary measures (such as carbon offsetting). Given the high abatement costs of the sector and long lead-times involved in developing aviation infrastructure, there is limited potential for radical technological progress to be made in the short to medium term – although those options may be far more promising in the long-term (DfT, 2004). Operational measures, similarly, require considerable investment to be made – including major revisions of airspace and of ATM systems and procedures – if they are to drive substantial improvements in environmental performance, although some improvements in efficiency can be achieved in the short to medium term. The limitations of technological and operational options implies that success in meeting the challenge of sustainable aviation growth depends upon the formulation and development of effective policy – although progress in this area has hitherto been limited (for example, see Pastowski, 2003: 180).

Technological responses have focused on making improvements in aircraft design and performance, and on developing alternative fuels (Thomas and Raper, 2000; Girvin, 2009) Efforts to achieve the former have centred on maximizing the fuel efficiency of aircraft, both by reducing the weight and drag of airframes and by maximizing the energy conversion efficiency of engines. Over the last 40 years, aircraft fuel efficiency has improved by around 70 per cent due to improvements in airframe design and engine technology, and due to increased load factors. Further improvements in airframe performance are anticipated as a result of increases in aerodynamic efficiency, the use of advanced materials, innovation in control and handling systems, and the development of radical aircraft designs (such as the blended-wing body). Improvements in engine technology appear to be less promising: currently, the most efficient aircraft engines are high bypass, high pressure ratio gas turbine engines, and viable alternatives remain elusive. Significantly, current engines are optimized for fuel efficiency (and thus, inadvertently, for CO_2 reduction) rather than for minimizing NO_x emissions (IPCC, 1999: 219). Technological improvements in aviation fuels have resulted in the development of low-sulphur fuels (which, in turn, have reduced aviation SO_x emissions) and work is in progress to investigate the potential for biofuels or hydrogen to supplement or replace kerosene. Overall, however, technological responses – both those relating to aircraft design and performance and to fuels – require substantial investment and are likely to yield benefits only in the long-term; limited potential exists for radical technological solutions to be found in the short to medium term.

Operational responses are based on the principle of maximizing fuel efficiency by a variety of means: reducing aircraft weight, increasing load factors, ensuring high levels of aircraft maintenance, minimizing route distances, optimizing cruising speeds and levels, and manoeuvring aircraft efficiently (IPCC, 1999). Loading aircraft efficiently involves a combination of (a) minimizing the weight of the aircraft before its payload is stowed (for instance, by minimizing the carriage of unusable fuel) and (b) maximizing the payload. High levels of aircraft maintenance – especially engine maintenance – ensure that acceptable fuel efficiency is maintained throughout the service life of the airframe and engine. The remaining operational improvements are generally achieved through the use of revised ATM procedures: improved communications, navigation and surveillance and air traffic management (CNS/ATM) systems; hub-bypass route planning; arrival management (AMAN) and departure management (DMAN) systems; continuous descent approaches (CDAs) and low power, low drag (LP/ LD) approaches, which are designed to minimize aircraft emissions and/or noise during descent; noise abatement departure procedures (NADPs) and noise preferential routes (NPRs), which are intended to reduce noise exposure in the vicinity of airports; expedited climb departure procedures, which are designed to allow aircraft to climb rapidly to their optimal cruising levels; and the use of fixed electrical ground power (FEGP) in preference to auxiliary power units (APUs) (Dobbie and Eran-Tasker, 2001; ICAO, 2004; Morrell and Lu, 2006). However, despite the many ways in which operational procedures could be revised, they have limited potential to reduce the environmental impacts of aircraft; 'these kinds of operational measures will not offset the impact of the forecast growth in air travel' (DTI, 1996: 10).

Due to the high abatement costs of the sector, and the limited potential for radical technological or operational solutions to be found in the short to medium term, success in meeting the challenge of sustainable aviation growth thus depends upon the formulation and development of effective policy. Numerous policy instruments are available to policymakers, many of which have received scrutiny from a wide range of stakeholders; those instruments may be categorized as regulatory, market-based and voluntary approaches. Proposals to cap aviation emissions, to impose taxes and emissions charges, to use or remove subsidies, to issue tradable permits for aviation emissions and to encourage the use of voluntary agreements have received scrutiny from commentators (IPCC, 1999; Bishop and Grayling, 2003; Pastowski, 2003). Such proposals have individual strengths but they are also problematic for a variety of reasons. Regulatory approaches face the problem that air transport is an international industry that spans national jurisdictions – and nations have varying capacity to monitor and enforce environmental standards. Market-based approaches must negotiate difficult issues related to the varying competitiveness of air transport service providers – including the need to internalize differing costs of pollution whilst facilitating access to international air transport markets on an equitable basis between nations. Voluntary approaches – such as carbon offsetting and voluntary codes of conduct – face the criticism that they are too weak to catalyse the profound behavioural change that is required to ensure that air transport is compatible with the requirements of sustainable development.

Regulatory approaches involve the imposition of standards; this approach is frequently used in environmental management, especially where pollutants pose a risk to human health. International aviation is subject to regulatory standards during the ICAO engine certification process, in which emissions of hydrocarbons, CO, NO_x and smoke must not exceed specified values, which provides a starting point for the management of aviation impacts on local air quality (IPCC, 1999: 343). Aircraft noise is also regulated by ICAO, which has defined standards for aircraft noise performance which, if exceeded, preclude aircraft from operating in many airports; the most recent noise certification standard (known as 'Chapter 4', referring to the definition of the standard in Annex 16, Volume I to the Chicago Convention) was adopted by ICAO in 2001 and was introduced on 1 January 2006. In relation to the issue of climate change, international aviation is currently exempted from any fixed limits or caps of its greenhouse gas emissions under the Kyoto Protocol; consequently, limited progress has been made in managing the greenhouse gas emissions of the sector since the Kyoto Protocol was signed (Faber et al. 2007: 13). Article 2.2 of the Kyoto Protocol states that Annex I nations should 'pursue limitation or reduction of emissions of greenhouse gases not controlled by the Montreal Protocol from aviation [.] bunker fuels, working through the International Civil Aviation Organization [.]' (UN, 1998: 2; see also Yamin and Depledge, 2004: 85–87). Discussions are in progress to determine the potential for aviation to be subject to emissions limits in an international post-2012 climate agreement, although it is unclear whether such an approach will be politically acceptable, given the importance of growing demand for international air transport for the economic development of nations (*The Economist*, 10 June 2006: 10).

Market-based approaches are based on the principle of creating economic incentives and disincentives for particular activities. Under such approaches, polluters are not prohibited from causing environmental damage, but they incur financial penalties for doing so and hence are encouraged to bring environmental impacts within the scope of their decision-making. Conversely, market-based approaches may be used to make environmentally desirable courses of action more advantageous to polluters. Market-based policy instruments include a range of incentives and disincentives; the main types used in environmental management are taxes, charges, subsidies and tradable (or marketable) permits. All of these types of policy instrument are either already in use or under consideration as a response to the environmental impacts of aviation, and some will almost certainly form part of future policy frameworks. Yet implementing market-based mechanisms is not easy: complex issues must be negotiated such as the varying competitiveness of air transport service providers and the need to internalize varying costs of pollution whilst facilitating access to international air transport markets on an equitable basis between nations.

The idea of fuel taxation has prompted fierce debate within the aviation industry, given the sensitivity of air transport to kerosene prices. The Chicago Convention precludes the taxation of fuel in transit; whilst individual nations may implement their own environmental fuel charges, few have done so for domestic aviation, and the fuel used in international aviation remains untaxed (IPCC, 1999: 345; Pearce and Pearce, 2000: 3; Seidel and Rossell, 2001: 28–29; Carlsson and Hammar, 2002: 366; Wit et al. 2004; Cairns and Newson, 2006; Mendes and Santos, 2008). The introduction of a tax on fuel used for international flights is hindered by the complexities involved in creating the necessary legal framework: fuel taxation is precluded by the several thousand existing bilateral air services agreements (ASAs) between nations. Further issues might also emerge if aviation fuel taxes were not implemented widely and consistently, as economic distortions could create an incentive for airlines to uplift cheaper fuel – by tankering – in countries where the tax did not apply, with the net effect that aviation emissions could increase and the original purpose of the tax would be negated (Wit et al. 2004: 43). Other forms of taxation could be used to restrain demand for air travel and thereby curb emissions: for instance, imposing Value Added Tax (VAT) on air international tickets, which are currently VAT-free (although this option is regarded as logistically complex) or through increases to the Air Passenger Duty (APD) (an option that is regarded as a 'blunt instrument'; Cairns and Newson, 2006: 78, 83). The level of any tax is critical: Cairns and Newson (2006: 53) acknowledged that 'very large increases in fares would be needed to make a difference to demand' and that such increases would be politically unacceptable. Emissions charges offer an alternative to fuel taxation and represent a straightforward means of increasing the cost of environmentally destructive practices. Emissions charges face fewer legal obstacles than fuel taxes as they not explicitly precluded by legally binding agreements; additionally, if emissions charges were introduced on an en route basis, there would be a smaller likelihood that tankering would occur in response (IPCC, 1999: 346; Wit et al. 2004).

Subsidies are another type of market-based instrument that are designed to provide direct incentives for environmental protection. Subsidies have been widely used in attempts to control pollution and to mitigate the financial impacts of regulations by helping polluters to meet the costs of compliance; they may take the form of grants, loans or tax allowances. In aviation, subsidies could be used to accelerate fleet replacement or to promote the development and use of alternative fuels (as well as other technologies) to reduce the environmental impacts of aircraft (RCEP, 2002; Lambert, 2008). However, aviation already benefits from a range of economic incentives that have allowed the industry to avoid paying the full environmental costs of its activities. Aircraft manufacturers, airlines and airports are subsidized and receive major tax exemptions; jet fuel for international flights has historically been exempted from taxation; international air tickets are exempted from VAT; airlines and new regional airports receive direct aid; the industry receives investment grants, government loans, infrastructure improvement subsidies and launch aid; aircraft landing fees are cross-subsidized with parking and retail revenues at airports; and the manufacture of aircraft is exempted from VAT (EC, 2006; Peeters et al. 2006: 192–193; T&E, 2006: 4, 12–13). Several countries levy ticket or fuel taxes on domestic flights, but those measures do not compensate for the general tax exemption of the sector (T&E 2006: 12). In general, the trend in aviation and environmental policy should ideally be towards the removal of current subsidies and privileges within the sector rather than the creation of new ones (Peeters et al. 2006: 195).

Tradable (or marketable) permit schemes represent another market-based policy instrument; they provide polluters with incentives to reduce pollution by creating a new market with defined property rights (Gander and Helme, 1999; Seidel and Rossell, 2001: 29). Tradable permit schemes operate on a simple principle: (a) a total level of pollution is defined for a specific region; (b) permits equalling that level are subsequently distributed among polluters in the region; (c) those permits can then be traded, either among polluters or between the operational sites of individual polluters. Hence tradable property rights to pollute the environment are assigned to polluters. The overall level of emissions for the industry is fixed (as with a regulatory standard) but, once the market is operating, the distribution of permits – and thus of emissions – is determined by the polluters trading in the market. The trade in permits should in theory result in a concentration of emissions reductions at those sources where they can be achieved at least cost. On the other hand, polluters faced with high abatement costs can purchase permits from polluters who have achieved emissions reductions, as that course of action is cheaper than incurring abatement costs. For aviation, which would incur high abatement costs for its impacts on climate, the possibility of buying additional emissions permits from other sectors could offer a way of continuing to operate despite increasing constraints on emissions at national or international levels (assuming that sufficient emissions reductions can be achieved by other sectors; DfT, 2004).

Under the Kyoto Protocol, the use of tradable permits within emissions trading schemes is evolving as an important element of international climate policy. The largest scheme in the world is the EU Emissions Trading Scheme (EU ETS), now in its second trading period. Aviation was not included in the first round of the EU ETS, but, in December 2006, the EC adopted a proposal to include aviation within the EU ETS. That proposal brings aviation into the trading scheme in two stages, commencing in 2011 with intra-EU flights (domestic and international flights between EU airports) and then expanding in 2012 to include all international flights arriving or departing from EU airports (CEC 2006; Anger, 2010; Anger and Köhler 2010). A range of logistical issues remains to be resolved, particularly in relation to trade rights, the initial allocation of permits, the avoidance of 'windfall' benefits due to the over-allocation of permits, the possible use of a factor to account for the non-CO_2 climate effects of aviation, and the geographical coverage of the scheme (IPCC, 1999: 346–347; Lee and Sausen, 2000; Karmali and Harris, 2004; Lee, 2004; DfT, 2004; Wit et al. 2005: 60; Forster et al. 2006; Mendes and Santos, 2008).

Policy approaches based on voluntary measures rely upon organizations and individuals making decisions that take account of environmental concerns even in the absence of direct regulatory requirements or economic incentives. Such voluntary decisions may be motivated by a variety of concerns. Polluters may believe that working cooperatively with regulators is more likely to lead to sympathetic regulation of their operations, and polluters may perceive greater opportunities to influence the regulatory process if they can demonstrate substantial voluntary efforts to improve their environmental performance. Polluters may adopt voluntary measures in anticipation of stricter regulation in the future, especially if early adoption offers them a competitive advantage; they may voluntarily adopt cleaner processes in order to standardize their operations across countries or regions; and they may seek to maximize their access to worldwide markets by adopting processes that would comply with the environmental regulations of the strictest country. Ultimately, organizations may voluntarily improve their environmental performance if they believe that consumer expectations require such action. Hence companies can improve their consumer relations and brand images by demonstrating corporate responsibility, either environmentally or socially. In relation to aviation and climate policy, voluntary measures currently focus on the use of carbon offsetting, on commitments to achieve carbon neutrality, and on the adoption of a range of broader corporate responsibility initiatives.

Carbon offsetting has become a widespread response to the challenge of climate change; in 2006, an estimated 1.5 million people in the UK paid to offset the emissions of a flight (Jardine, 2005; *New Scientist*, 24 February 2007: 35; Bayon et al. 2007; Gössling et al. 2007; Rousse, 2008). Many issues are associated with carbon offsetting, especially in relation to aviation; those issues relate mainly to the measurement of emissions and to the permanence and credibility of offsets. The main areas of concern are that offsetting is not a sufficient measure to address climate change, as it does not address all of the climate impacts of aviation; it requires accurate measures of the emissions generated and those saved elsewhere; it requires an appropriate price to be put on one tonne of CO_2; it requires demonstrating additionality, which represents a considerable challenge; offsetting schemes are unregulated, may be overpriced and are vulnerable to fraud; schemes can be inefficient; offsets may not be permanent; schemes may create problems of leakage; projects may have mixed sustainable development co-benefits; and schemes may be a distraction from the real challenge of reducing emissions, and so could delay the transition to a low-carbon economy. Given those issues, offsetting is now acknowledged to be a highly problematic response to the challenge of climate change (see Friends of the Earth, 2006; Brouwer et al. 2007; DEFRA 2007; *The Guardian*, 16 June 2007: 15).

Nevertheless, the use of carbon offsetting increasingly forms an element of corporate commitments to achieve carbon neutrality. Within the aviation industry, such commitments are now being made by some airport operators; however, those commitments involve subtle issues of definition and coverage. Airport operators define their spheres of responsibility and influence in various ways, and in particular they differ in their 'ownership' of aircraft emissions in the vicinity of the airport. Some airport operators accept responsibility for aviation emissions produced throughout the aircraft landing and take-off cycle, whilst others restrict their responsibility to those emissions generated while aircraft are parked at the gate or are manoeuvring on the apron and taxiways. Such differences in coverage have potentially major implications for the magnitude of the carbon burden to be mitigated, and for the possibility that some emissions may not be apportioned to any particular polluter. However a given airport's sphere of responsibility may be defined, airport operators have a much larger sphere of influence over airlines and, in addition to demonstrating carbon neutrality for their own operations, could focus greater efforts on encouraging airlines to achieve emissions reductions – for example, by accelerating their fleet renewal processes.

12.5 Conclusion

In this chapter, we have attempted to outline the many ways in which environmental issues represent an actual or potential constraint to the development of the air transport industry. We have emphasized the sustainable dilemma for aviation: the need to address the environmental impacts of aircraft and airport operations without blighting the economies and societies that depend upon the industry. That task presents a formidable challenge to policymakers, air transport industry representatives and researchers – especially because of the projected rapid growth of demand for air transport, the high abatement costs of the sector, and the limited potential for radical technological or operational solutions to be found in the short to medium term. In this chapter, we have outlined the most pressing environmental issues: the fact that the impacts of aircraft on climate may well negate all of the emissions reductions achieved by other sectors of national economies; the fact that NO_x and particle emissions from aircraft could prevent infrastructure development at major airports, or close to major urban areas; and the fact that aircraft noise exposure in the vicinity of airports is increasing due to the growth of air traffic, even though the sound levels of individual aircraft movements have generally decreased. Added to these is a range of other environmental issues – such as ecological modification, water use and pollution, and waste production – that could present acute management difficulties at particular airports, depending upon local circumstances. For all of these reasons, we argue that the development and implementation of effective aviation environmental policy is urgently required. Above, we have considered various policy approaches; but variations in the complexity and political acceptability of those options means that no single policy instrument appears to be ideal, and a combination of regulatory, market-based and voluntary approaches will probably be adopted in future aviation environmental policy.

Specifically, we suggest that – whilst local responses are required to the management of local environmental issues (local air pollution, noise, ecological modification, water use and pollution, and waste production) in the vicinity of airports – the global issue of climate change is likely to dominate debates about aviation environmental impacts and about the growth of the industry. National commitments to achieve reductions in greenhouse gas emissions (in the case of the UK, a 60 per cent reduction in CO_2 emissions by 2050) are likely to have profound implications for entire economies and societies (Stern, 2007). Meeting such commitments may require fundamental changes in the distribution and use of energy; in the development and availability of fuels; in infrastructure, business models, technologies and operating practices; and in the ways in which services are delivered. The air transport industry faces an immense challenge in adapting its activities to this changing context. In the short to medium term, policy approaches focus on the inclusion of international aviation within emissions trading schemes (initially, for instance, in the EU ETS) and on encouraging voluntary agreements within the industry (involving carbon offsetting and commitments to achieve carbon neutrality). However, subsequent measures to limit the environmental impacts of aviation could mean the imposition of more stringent emissions limits; the removal of existing privileges and subsidies of the industry; the wider use of emissions charges, fuel taxes and other levies; and, ultimately, the use of severe demand restraint measures. Such measures would be extremely unpopular; hence, in the long-term, the development of the air transport industry depends above all on finding technological solutions to mitigate the impact of aircraft on climate.

References

Adey, P., Budd, L. and Hubbard, P. (2007), 'Flying lessons: exploring the social and cultural geographies of global air travel', *Progress in Human Geography*, 31(6): 773–791.

Åkerman, J. (2005), 'Sustainable air transport – on track in 2050', *Transportation Research Part D*, 10: 111–126.

Amanatidis, G. and Friedl, R. (2004), 'Science related to atmospheric effects of aircraft emissions continues to mature', *ICAO Journal*, 59(5): 14–15, 26.

Anger, A. (2010), 'Including aviation in the EU ETS: impacts on the industry, CO_2 emissions and macroeconomic activity in the EU', *Journal of Air Transport Management*, 16: 100–105.

Anger, A. and J. Köhler (2010), 'Including aviation emissions in the EU ETS: much ado about nothing?', *Transport Policy*, 17(1): 38–46.

Bailey, J.W. (2007), 'An assessment of UK Government aviation policies and their implications', *Journal of Airport Management*, 1(3): 249–261.

Baker, S. (2006), *Sustainable Development*, Routledge Introductions to Environment Series, London, Routledge.

Bayon, R., Hawn, A. and Hamilton, K. (2007), *Voluntary Carbon Markets: An International Business Guide to What They Are and How They Work*, London, Earthscan.

Beiger, T., Wittmer, A. and Laesser, C. (2007), 'What is driving the continued growth in demand for air travel? Customer value of air transport', *Journal of Air Transport Management*, 13: 31–36.

Bishop, S. and Grayling, T. (2003), *The Sky's the Limit: Policies for Sustainable Aviation*, London, Institute for Public Policy Research.

Boon, B.H. and Wit, R.C.N. (2005), *The Contribution of Aviation to the Economy: Assessment of Arguments put Forward*, Delft, CE.

Bows, A., Anderson, K. and Upham, P. (2006), *Contraction and Convergence: UK Carbon Emissions and the Implications for UK Air Traffic*, Manchester, Tyndall Centre for Climate Change Research (North).

Bows, A., Upham, P. and Anderson, K. (2005), *Growth Scenarios for EU and UK Aviation: Contradictions with Climate Policy*, Summary of research by the Tyndall Centre for Climate Change Research for Friends of the Earth Trust Ltd, 16 April 2005, Manchester, Tyndall Centre for Climate Change Research (North).

Brouwer, R., Brander, L. and van Beukering, P. (2007), 'A convenient truth: air travel passengers willingness to pay to offset their CO_2 emissions', Amsterdam: Institute for Environmental Studies, Vrije Universiteit.

Button, K. and Taylor, S. (2000), 'International air transportation and economic development', *Journal of Air Transport Management*, 6(4): 209–222.

Cabrini, L. (2005), International and European tourism: recent trends and outlook, Public-Private Partnerships in Tourism Seminar, Moscow, Russian Federation, 22 March 2005.

Cairns, S. and Newson, C. (2006), *Predict and Decide: Aviation, Climate Change and UK Policy*, Oxford, Environmental Change Institute.

Carlsson, F. and Hammar, H. (2002), 'Incentive based regulation of CO_2 emissions from international aviation', *Journal of Air Transport Management*, 8: 365–372.

Caves, R.E. (2002), 'The role of aviation in the UK socio-economy', Paper presented at The Social Impacts of the UK Air Transport Industry, ESRC Mobile Network Seminar, Imperial College London, 24 July 2002.

Caves, R.E. (2003), The social and economic benefits of aviation, in *Towards Sustainable Aviation*, ed. P. Upham, J.A. Maughan, D.W. Raper and C.S. Thomas, London, Earthscan: 36–47.

CEC (Commission of the European Communities) (2006), Proposal for a Directive of the European Parliament and of the Council Amending Directive 2003/87/EC so as to Include Aviation Activities in the Scheme for Greenhouse Gas Emission Allowance Trading within the Community, http://europa.eu/scadplus/leg/en/lvb/l28012.htm.

Chapman, L. (2007), Transport and climate change: a review, *Journal of Transport Geography*, 15(5): 354–367.

Clarke, J.-P. (2003), 'The role of advanced air traffic management in reducing the impact of aircraft noise and enabling aviation growth', *Journal of Air Transport Management*, 9: 161–165.

Collins, P., Dowling, A. and Greitzer, E. (2006), 'Academic exploring innovative approaches to achieving 'silent' flight', *ICAO Journal*, 61(1): 24–25, 31.

Connor, T.L. (1996), 'Proposed take-off noise abatement procedures demonstrate potential to mitigate problem', *ICAO Journal*, 51(2): 19–20.

DCMS (Department for Culture, Media and Sport) (1999), *Tomorrow's Tourism: A Growth Industry for the New Millennium*, London: DCMS.

DEFRA (Department for Environment, Food and Rural Affairs) (2007), 'Climate change: carbon offsetting – Code of Best Practice', www.defra.gov.uk/environment/ climatechange/uk/carbonoffset/codeofpractice.htm.

De Leon, R.R. and Haigh, J.D. (2007), 'Infrared properties of cirrus clouds in climate models', *The Quarterly Journal of the Royal Meteorological Society*, 133(623): 273–282.

Depitre, A. (2001), 'Re-certification of aircraft to new noise standards remains an important issue', *ICAO Journal*, 56(4): 14–16, 32.

DETR (Department of the Environment, Transport and the Regions) (2000), The Air Quality Strategy for England, Scotland, Wales and Northern Ireland: Working Together for Clean Air, London, DETR.

DfT (Department for Transport) (2003a), *Aviation, Core Cities and Regional Economic Development*, London, DfT.

DfT (2003b), *The Future of Air Transport*, Presented to Parliament by the Secretary of State for Transport by Command of Her Majesty, December 2003, London, DfT.

DfT (2004), *Aviation and Global Warming*, London, DfT.

DfT (2006), *Project for the Sustainable Development of Heathrow: Air Quality Technical Report*, Report of the PSDH Technical Panels to the DfT, www.dft.gov.uk/stellent/groups/dft_aviation/documents/divisionhomepage/612123.

Dobbie, L. and Eran-Tasker, M. (2001), 'Measures to minimise fuel consumption appear to be of greatest importance to airlines', *ICAO Journal*, 56(4): 24–25, 31–32.

DTI (Department of Trade and Industry) (1996), 'Experts consider operational measures as means to reduce emissions and their environmental impact', *ICAO Journal*, 51(2): 9–10.

EC (European Commission) (2006), Climate change: Commission proposes bringing air transport into EU Emissions Trading Scheme, Press Release, IP/06/1862, 20 December 2006, Brussels, EC.

Faber, J., Boon, B., Berk, M., den Elzen, M., Olivier, J. and Lee, D. (2007), *Climate Change Scientific Assessment and Policy Analysis: Aviation and Maritime Transport in a Post 2012 Climate Policy Regime*, Delft, CE.

Forster, P.M. de F., Shine, K.P. and Stuber, N. (2006), 'It is premature to include non-CO_2 effects of aviation in emission trading schemes', *Atmospheric Environment*, 40: 1117–1121.

Friends of the Earth (2006), 'Joint statement on offsetting carbon emissions', London, Friends of the Earth, Greenpeace and WWF-UK.

Gander, S. and Helme, N. (1999), 'Emissions trading is an effective, proven policy tool for solving air pollution problems', *ICAO Journal*, 54(7): 12–14, 28–29.

Girvin, R. (2009), Aircraft noise-abatement and mitigation strategies, *Journal of Air Transport Management*, 15(1): 14–22.

Goldstein, A. (2001), 'Infrastructure development and regulatory reform in sub-Saharan Africa: the case of air transport', *World Economy*, 24: 221–223.

Goodman, J.C. (ed.) (2007), *Aviation and the Environment*, New York, Nova.

Gössling, S., Broderick, J., Upham, P., Ceron, J.-P., Dubois, G., Peeters, P. and Strasdas, W. (2007), 'Voluntary carbon offsetting schemes for aviation: efficiency, credibility and sustainable tourism', *Journal of Sustainable Tourism*, 15(3): 223–248.

Graham, A. and Raper, D.W. (2006a), 'Transport to ground of emissions in aircraft wakes: Part I: processes', *Atmospheric Environment*, 40: 5574–5585.

Graham, A. and Raper, D.W. (2006b), 'Transport to ground of emissions in aircraft wakes: Part II: effect on NO_x concentrations in airport approaches', *Atmospheric Environment*, 40: 5824–5836.

Graham, B. (2002), 'The role of air transport in a regional economy', Paper presented at *The Social Impacts of the UK Air Transport Industry*, ESRC Mobile Network Seminar, Imperial College London, 24 July 2002.

Grieco, M. (2002), 'The Scottish aviation gateway – problems, prospects and policy possibilities', Paper presented at *The Social Impacts of the UK Air Transport Industry*, ESRC Mobile Network Seminar, Imperial College London, 24 July 2002.

Grubb, M., Koch, M., Munson, A., Sullivan, F. and Thomson, K. (1993), *The Earth Summit Agreements: A Guide and Assessment*, London, Earthscan.

Hettne, B. (ed.) (2008), *Sustainable Development in a Globalized World*, Studies in Development, Security and Culture, Volume 1, Basingstoke and New York: Palgrave Macmillan.

Hjalager, A.H. (2007), Stages in the economic globalization of tourism, Annals of Tourism Research, 34(2): 437–457.

Horak S. and Weber S. (2000), 'Youth tourism in Europe: problems and prospects', *Tourism Recreation Research*, 25(3): 37–44.

Horton, G. (2006), *Forecasts of CO_2 Emissions from Civil Aircraft for IPCC*, DTI Unique Reference No. 06/2178, November 2006, Farnborough, QinetiQ.

Hoyer, K. and Noess, P. (2001), 'Conference tourism: a problem for the environment, as well as for research?', *Journal of Sustainable Tourism*, 9(6): 451–470.

Hume, K., Gregg, M., Thomas, C.S. and Terranova, D. (2003), 'Complaints caused by aircraft operations: an assessment of annoyance by noise level and time of day', *Journal of Air Transport Management*, 9: 153–160.

Hume, K. and Watson, A. (2003), The human health impacts of aviation, in *Towards Sustainable Aviation*, ed. P. Upham, J.A. Maughan, D.W. Raper and C.S. Thomas, London, Earthscan: 48–76.

ICAO (International Civil Aviation Organization) (2004), 'ICAO circular examines ways to minimize aircraft fuel use and reduce emissions', *ICAO Journal*, 59 (2): 23–24, 30.

ICCAIA (International Coordinating Council of Aerospace Industries Associations) (2004), 'Technology continues to play important role in reducing noise around airports', *ICAO Journal*, 59(2): 4–7, 27–28.

IPCC (Intergovernmental Panel on Climate Change) (1999), *Aviation and the Global Atmosphere*, A Special Report of IPCC Working Groups I and III in collaboration with the Scientific Assessment Panel to the Montreal Protocol on Substance that Deplete the Ozone Layer, ed. J.E. Penner, D.H. Lister, D.J. Griggs, D.J. Dokken and M. McFarland, Cambridge, Cambridge University Press for the IPCC.

Jardine, C. (2005), *Calculating the Environmental Impact of Aviation Emissions*, Report commissioned for Climate Care, June 2005, Oxford, Environmental Change Institute.

Karmali, A. and Harris, M. (2004), 'ICAO exploring development of a trading scheme for emissions from aviation', *ICAO Journal*, 59(5): 11–13, 25.

Lambert, C. (2008), Alternative Aviation Fuels, SBAC Aviation and Environment Briefing Papers, No. 4, www.sbac.co.uk/pages/92567080.asp.

Lee, D.S. (2004), The impact of aviation on climate, in *Transport and the Environment*, Issues in Environmental Science and Technology, No. 2, ed. R.E. Hester and R.M. Harrison, Cambridge, The Royal Society of Chemistry.

Lee, D.S. and Raper, D.W. (2003), The global atmospheric impacts of aviation, in *Towards Sustainable Aviation*, ed. P. Upham, J.A. Maughan, D.W. Raper and C.S. Thomas, London, Earthscan: 77–96.

Lee, D.S. and Sausen, R. (2000), 'New directions: assessing the real impact of CO_2 emissions trading by the aviation industry', *Atmospheric Environment*, 34: 5337–5338.

Lethbridge, N. (2002), *Attitudes to Air Travel*, London, Office of National Statistics.

Macintosh, A. and Wallace, L. (2009), International aviation emissions to 2025: Can emissions be stabilized without restricting demand? Energy Policy, 37: 264–273.

May, M. and Hill, S.B. (2006), 'Questioning airport expansion – A case study of Canberra International Airport', *Journal of Transport Geography*, 14: 437–450.

Mendes, L.M.Z. and Santos, G. (2008), 'Using economic instruments to address emissions from air transport in the European Union', *Environment and Planning*, 40: 189–209.

Miller, B. and Clarke, J.-P. (2007), 'The hidden value of air transportation infrastructure', *Technological Forecasting and Social Change*, 74: 18–35.

Morrell, P. and Lu, C. (2006), *The Environmental Cost Implications of Hub-Hub Versus Hub-Bypass Flight Networks*, Research Report 10, January 2006, Department of Air Transport, School of Engineering, Cranfield University.

Moss, D., Warnaby, G., Sykes, S. and Thomas, C.S. (1997), 'Manchester Airport's second runway campaign: the boundary spanning role of public relations in managing environmental organizational interaction', *Journal of Communication Management*, 2(4): 320–334.

Nero, G. and Black, J.A. (2000), 'A critical examination of an airport noise mitigation scheme and an aircraft noise charge: the case of capacity expansion and externalities at Sydney (Kingsford Smith) airport', *Transportation Research*, Part D 5: 433–461.

OEF (Oxford Economic Forecasting) (1999), *The Contribution of the Aviation Industry to the UK Economy*, Final Report, November 1999, Oxford, OEF.

OEF (2002), *The Economic Contribution of the Aviation Industry to the UK: Part 2 – Assessment of Regional Impact*, May 2002, Oxford, OEF.

OEF (2006), *The Economic Contribution of the Aviation Industry in the UK*, October 2006, Oxford, OEF.

Ollerhead, J. and Sharp, B. (2001), 'Computer model highlights the benefits of various noise reduction measures', *ICAO Journal*, 56(4): 18–19, 32–33.

Papatheodorou, A. and Zheng, L. (2006), Leisure travel in Europe and airline business models: A study of regional airports in Great Britain, *Journal of Air Transport Management*, 12(1): 47–52.

Pastowski, A. (2003), Climate policy for civil aviation: actors, policy instruments and the potential for emissions reductions, in *Towards Sustainable Aviation*, ed. P. Upham, J. Maughan, D. Raper and C. Thomas, London, Earthscan, pp. 179–195.

Peace, H., Maughan, J., Owen, B. and Raper, D. (2006), 'Identifying the contribution of different airport related sources to local urban air quality', *Environmental Modelling and Software*, 21: 532–538.

Pearce, B. and Pearce, D. (2000), *Setting Environmental Taxes for Aircraft: A Case Study of the UK*, CSERGE Working Paper GEC 2000–26, www.uea.ac.uk/env/cserge/pub/wp/gec/gec_2000_26.htm.

Peeters, P. (2007), *Tourism and Climate Change Mitigation*, NHTV, Breda, Netherlands.

Peeters, P., Gössling, S. and Becken, S. (2006), 'Innovation towards tourism sustainability: climate change and aviation', *International Journal of Innovation and Sustainable Development*, 1(3): 184–200.

Raguraman, K. (1995), 'The role of air transportation in tourism development: a case study of the Philippines and Thailand', *Transportation Quarterly*, 49: 113–124.

RCEP (Royal Commission on Environmental Pollution) (2002), *The Environmental Effects of Civil Aircraft in Flight*, London, RCEP.

Rhoades, D.L. (2004), 'Sustainable development in African civil aviation: problems and policies', *International Journal of Technology, Policy and Management*, 4: 28.

Rodrigue, J.-P., Comtois, C. and Slack, B (2009), *The Geography of Transport Systems*, 2nd edition, New York, Routledge.

Rogers, H.L., Lee, D.S., Raper, D.W., Forster, P.M. de F., Wilson, C.W. and Newton, P. (2002), 'The impacts of aviation on the global atmosphere', *The Aeronautical Journal*, October 2002, 521–546.

Rousse, O. (2008), 'Environmental and economic benefits resulting from citizens' participation in CO_2 emissions trading: an efficient alternative solution to the voluntary compensation of CO_2 emissions', *Energy Policy*, 35: 388–397.

Sausen, R., Isaksen, I., Grewe, V., Hauglustaine, D., Lee, D.S., Myhre, G., Köhler, M.O., Pitari, G., Schumann, U., Stordal, F. and Zerefos, C. (2005), 'Aviation radiative forcing in 2000: an update on IPCC (1999)', *Meteorologische Zeitschrift*, 14(1): 555–561.

Schürmann, G., Schäfer, K., Jahn, C., Hoffmann, H., Bauerfeind, M., Fleuti, E. and Rappenglück, B. (2007), 'The impact of NO_x, CO and VOC emissions on the air quality of Zurich airport', *Atmospheric Environment*, 41: 103–118.

Seidel, S. and Rossell, M. (2001), 'Potential policy tools for reducing emissions shift emphasis to economic incentives', *ICAO Journal*, 56(4): 27–29, 34.

Shaw, S. and Thomas, C.S. (2006), 'Social and cultural dimensions of air travel demand: hyper-mobility in the UK?', *Journal of Sustainable Tourism*, 14(2): 209–215.

Skogö, I. (2001), 'Public opposition to air transport development underscores importance of tackling noise issue', *ICAO Journal*, 56(4): 22–23.

Smith, M.J.T. (1992), 'Evolving noise issue could persist into the next century', *ICAO Journal*, 47(8): 11–13.

Stern, N. (2007), *The Economics of Climate Change: The Stern Review*, Cambridge, Cambridge University Press.

Stordal, F., Myhre, G., Stordal, E.J.G., Rossow, W.B., Lee, D.S., Arlander, D.W. and Svendby, T. (2005), 'Is there a trend in cirrus cloud cover due to aircraft traffic?', *Atmospheric Chemistry and Physics*, 5: 2155–2162.

T&E (European Federation for Transport and Environment) (2006), *Clearing the Air: The Myth and Reality of Aviation and Climate Change*, Brussels, T&E and CAN-Europe (Climate Action Network Europe).

Thomas, C.S. and Raper, D.W. (2000), 'The role of aero engineering in the sustainable development of the aviation industry', *The Aeronautical Journal*, 1037: 331–333.

Thomas, G. (2008), 'Greening ATW', *Air Transport World*, 45(9): 68–72.

UN (United Nations) (1998), *Kyoto Protocol to the United Nations Framework Convention on Climate Change*. Available at: http://unfccc.int/resource/docs/convkp/kpeng.pdf.

UNCSD (United Nations Commission on Sustainable Development) (2001), *Report of the Inter-sessional Ad Hoc Working Group on Transport and Atmosphere, New York, 6–9 March 2001*, E/CN/17/2001/16, New York, UNCSD.

UNCTAD (United Nations Conference on Trade and Development) (1999a), *Air Transport Services: The Positive Agenda for Developing Countries*, Report by the UNCTAD Secretariat, TD/B/COM.1/EM.9/2, 16 April 1999, Geneva, UNCTAD.

UNCTAD (1999b), Clarifying issues on air transport services to define the elements of the positive agenda of developing countries as regards both the GATS and specific sector negotiations of interest to them: agreed conclusions, TD/B/COM.1/EM.9/L.1, 25 June 1999, Geneva, UNCTAD.

UNCTAD (1999c), *Report of the Expert Meeting on Air Transport Services: Clarifying Issues to Define the Elements of the Positive Agenda of Developing Countries as Regards both the GATS and Specific Sector Negotiations of Interest to Them*, Held at the Palais des Nations, Geneva, from 21 to 23 June 1999, TD/B/COM.1/25, TD/B/COM/EM.9/3. 23 August 1999, Geneva, UNCTAD.

Underwood, B.Y., Brightwell, S.M., Peirce, M.J. and Walker, C.T. (2001), *Air Quality at UK Regional Airports in 2005 and 2010*: A Report Produced for DETR, February 2001, Warrington, AEA Technology plc.

UN (United Nations) (2002), *World Summit on Sustainable Development: Johannesburg, 2002*, New York, UN Department of Economic and Social Affairs, Division for Sustainable Development.

UNWTO (United Nations World Tourism Organization) (2007), 'International tourists 1995–2006 (millions)', www.world-tourism.org.

Upham, P. (2001), 'Environmental capacity of aviation: theoretical issues and basic research directions', *Journal of Environmental Planning and Management*, 44 (5): 721–734.

Upham, P., Raper, D.W., Thomas, C.S., McLellan, M., Lever, M. and Lieuwen, A. (2004), 'Environmental capacity and European air transport: stakeholder opinion and implications for modelling', *Journal of Air Transport Management*, 10: 199–205.

Upham, P., Thomas, C.S., Gillingwater, D. and Raper, D.W. (2003), 'Environmental capacity and airport operations: current issues and future prospects', *Journal of Air Transport Management*, 9: 145–151.

Urry, J. (2002), 'Small worlds and large distances', paper presented at the *The Social Impacts of the UK Air Transport Industry*, ESRC Mobile Network Seminar, Imperial College London, 24 July 2002.

Wit, R.C.N, Kampman, B. and Boon, B.H. (2004), *Climate Impacts from International Aviation and Shipping: State-of-the-Art on Climatic Impacts, Allocation and Mitigation Policies*, Report for the Netherlands Research Programme on Climate Change, Scientific Assessments and Policy Analysis (NRP-CC), Delft, CE.

Wit, R.C.N., Boon, B.H., van Velzen, A., Cames, M., Deuber, O. and Lee, D.S. (2005), *Giving Wings to Emissions Trading: Inclusion of Aviation Under the European Emission Trading System (ETS): Design and Impacts*, Report for the European Commission, DG Environment, Delft, CE.

Yamin, F. and Depledge, J. (2004), *The International Climate Change Regime: A Guide to Rules, Institutions and Procedures*, Cambridge, Cambridge University Press.

Young, E.M. (1997), *World Hunger*, Routledge Introductions to Development Series, London, Routledge.

Chapter 13

Advances in Transport Aircraft and Engines

John Snow

13.1 Introduction

This book concentrates on the aviation industry and is essentially commercial in content. It therefore seems appropriate that this chapter follows suit. While being, to many eyes, intrinsically valuable in its own right, a civil transport aircraft, or airliner, only has value to the industry it serves if it does its job well. This is to fly as much payload as quickly, as far and as efficiently as possible. Thus the developments in aviation covered in this chapter, while all possessing admirable technological virtues, will be primarily considered in relation to the above goal.

The chapter has four chronological subsections. The first, *Early Days – from Railway Carriage to Airliner Cabin,* covers how the first civil aircraft evolved into the post-World War II airliner. Topics include the stressed all-metal structure, the use of the wing as a fuel tank, variable pitch propellers, engine supercharging, cabin pressurization and indirect navigation (radar and so on). The second subsection is entitled '*Giant Steps – The inventions that galvanized the air transport industry*'. This covers the basic jet engine and swept wing plus the significant developments of these – the high bypass fan for the Boeing 747 and the supercritical 'flat-top' wing developed for the Airbus A300 in the early 1970s. The third section, '*1970 Onwards – The Evolutionary Era*', which is the bulk of the chapter, describes how we have arrived at today's products in the light of increasing technology costs, coupled with declining payload yields. Clearly *Concorde* was a warning against unbridled performance, so the airliner has matured cautiously with the use of composite materials, fly-by-wire and artificially intelligent monitoring systems as well as the emphasis on 'ecological' fuel burn. Within this section, another emerging issue, operations management or the rules of civil aviation, is raised. Aircraft scheduling is dominated by pilot work hours and maintenance requirements. A move toward automation could change all that. Long-applied by the military, civil in-flight refuelling could completely revolutionize not only the manner in which aircraft are operated, but also designed. Finally, there is a brief review of some of the technology *'Waiting in the wings'*. On the propulsion side, this looks at non-standard devices and fuels, while airframe areas include the laminar flow blended wing plus swing-wing aircraft with the potential to alleviate the sonic boom.

13.2 Early Days: From Airborne Railway Carriage to Airliner Cabin

The airliner did not emerge in isolation from a clean sheet of paper. The period between the World Wars was one where both sea and rail travel had reached new levels of service and become very popular. If air transport was to succeed, it would have to improve upon the competition which was already capable of 100 mph on land and trans-oceanic range at sea. The earliest passenger aircraft were only marginally faster and struggled to reach Rome from London.

A typical product of the time was the *Handley-Page HP42* (see Figure 13.1 below) which was clearly inspired by the Wright Brothers' design. The structure was primarily organic (wood and cotton) while the cabin had distinct traces of the Great Western Railway in its design. By the time the dust had settled after World War II, a series of developments would change the appearance of the airliner to a very close representation of the contemporary. None of these developments was particularly earth-shattering nor, in some cases, even new. All that was happening was that the civil aircraft was becoming fit for purpose.

Structurally, the aircraft became metallic and primarily aluminium; by using an alloyed microscopic lattice of copper, the easily torn aluminium became as strong as steel at one third of the specific weight so long as the operating temperatures are below 150°C. Both the skeletal elements and the aircraft skin contributed to the overall strength and this enabled further use to be made of the aircraft's volume.

Figure 13.1   The *Handley-Page HP42*

Source: Courtesy of A V Pettit at Airliners.net. This picture is dedicated to A.V. Pettit, who cycled from Hackney to Croydon to take this photograph.

The prime mechanism of aircraft range is the amount of fuel that may be loaded. Hitherto, fuel had been stored in the fuselage, where it had to compete for space with the cabin, the cockpit and other systems. By using the large vacant volume in the wing as fuel tanks, it was possible to increase range significantly, even allowing for the extra structural weight of the light alloy.

The need for ground manoeuvres required the installation of a reusable landing gear. Once in the air, this becomes a penalty in terms of drag. By providing the volumetric space to retract and stow the undercarriage, the energy required to fly at a given speed is reduced by around 15–20 per cent. Loading and unloading during ground stops was made easier by the adoption of the tricycle undercarriage, featuring a nose wheel rather than a tail skid. Not only did the take-off run become shorter, but ground staff no longer had to operate in a fuselage with a 15 per cent gradient, saving time on the ground so that more could be spent in the air.

The aircraft requires thrust for flight and historically there has always been pressure on the engine manufacturers for increased and more efficient power. Flight efficiency improves with altitude, but the same mechanism depletes engine power as air density decreases. The mechanism of supercharging – compressing inlet air before admitting it to the combustion process – became standard to compensate for this, allowing the aircraft to fly higher and/or faster.

Varying demands for power in a changing operating environment benefit from rapidly adaptable power management. Until the arrival of the variable pitch propeller, power variation was only possible by changing rotational speed, which normally meant that at best either the engine or the propeller were at optimal speed, but rarely both. The variable pitch propeller provided rapid thrust response resulting in more control (for safety), shorter take-off and landing distances as well as improved fuel efficiency.

With the improvements in performance mentioned above, the powered flying machine became capable of high-speed, high altitude, long-range flight. To enable the airliner to follow suit and fly above the clouds, two further developments were demanded. The first was the availability of reliable indirect navigation (Instrument Flying Rules or IFR) involving radar and automatic direction finding to complement dead reckoning and celestial aids. From the passenger comfort aspect, the air quality in the cabin was literally vital. Cabin pressurization is a little like being in a submarine, but with the internal air pressure greater than the atmospheric pressure. Without pressurization, breathing becomes uncomfortable at around 10,000–12,000 ft altitude, which is where much air-sickness-inducing turbulence occurs due to cloud formation. By maintaining a cabin environment just below the discomfort zone (8,000ft, say) the airliner could cruise at up to 25,000ft. In addition to the increased comfort afforded, for the same power, a 50 per cent increase in speed results. DC-6 aircraft were indicative of such behaviour and a picture of the aircraft is shown in Figure 13.2.

Figure 13.2   The DC-6

Source: Courtesy of Sascha Foerster at Airliners.net.

So by the gradual application of a series of developments, not all of which had been primarily intended for (civil) aviation, the airliner had evolved into a globe-trotting comfortable means of high-speed (300 mph) transport. The cost of providing this service restricted it to the comfortably well-off. What were needed now were some developments specific to air transport to bring the industry alive and make it more affordable.

13.3 Giant Steps: The Inventions That Galvanized the Air Transport Industry

If we want to travel more economically, we can employ two mechanisms – speed and energy. By travelling faster, less time is wasted and the vehicle can be used more frequently. By using less energy, fuel costs are reduced and we can use a more efficient vehicle carrying more people, because less of the overall weight is fuel. Also, depending on the relationship between time and energy, we can even accept, say, an increase in fuel burn if the time saving is worthwhile. For the 30 years following the arrival of the airliner, a series of purpose-built improvements set the scene for air travel as we now enjoy it.

If one invention has caused the expansion of air travel it has to be the jet engine. Its predecessor, the reciprocating internal combustion engine, while so successful on land had several limiting factors associated with powered flight. The industry wants to fly larger aeroplanes further, faster and higher. Assuming a limit of four engines per aircraft, the piston engine is limited to transatlantic travel with

100 passengers at 300 mph and 20,000 ft altitude. Any *faster* and the propeller tips encounter supersonic shock waves analogous to those on the wing. Any *larger* and the engines become so complex with multiple banks of cylinders that reliability is impacted, while propeller diameter would increase to cause installation problems. Any *further* would demand more engines and thus a larger wing to install them leading to a spiral of diminishing returns. Any *higher* and the aircraft would fly more slowly as power drops off.

The basic jet aero engine is very simple. It sucks air in at the front, compresses it, then mixes it with kerosene in the middle, sets light to the mixture and exhausts it at high speed at the back. The only motion is a rotor which drives the compressor. The engine is self-accelerating as (ram) air piles up at the inlet and will happily accelerate up to Mach 3 (2,000 mph). Size per se is not a problem as turbojets have been developed which are at least an order of magnitude more powerful than the largest piston engine.

In order to accommodate this potential, the DC-6 type of airframe requires modification, in particular regarding the wing. Birds (especially hawks) apply wing sweep to reduce resistance to flight and dive to catch their prey. This also benefits aircraft, although the main purpose for aeroplanes is to delay compressibility (sound barrier) by presenting an apparently more slender wing to the airflow. Inevitably parts of the aircraft surface will become supersonic and this typically occurs at around 85 per cent of the local speed of sound. The typical first generation jetliner was the Boeing 707 carrying around 150 passengers over the North Atlantic at 600 mph. The excess power of the four engines allowed the aircraft to cruise at about 35,000 ft and while fuel burn was still on the extravagant side, the benefits of speed, size, reliability and comfort more than compensated.

The next step came as a result of a demand from the military (nothing new here), but in terms of logistics rather than combat capability. In the 1960s the US Air force demanded an aircraft with three times the payload capability of the C141/B707 product. The winner was the Lockheed C5 *Galaxy* while what became the Boeing 747 came second. Either way, current jet engines were inadequate and so a new approach was required. By developing the current twin-shaft turbojet into a hybrid with a ducted fan (similar to a fixed pitch propeller) driven by the outer turbine it was possible to more than double thrust at a modest 25 per cent fuel burn increase for the same size of core engine hardware. The key was the mixing of the fan and jet exhausts which resulted in a quieter engine better balanced for sub-sonic cruise. This was named the High By-Pass turbofan (since most of the thrust comes from the fan exhaust which bypasses the hot section) and this has been applied to all large civil transport aircraft since.

So the bypass engine compensated for the extravagances of the pure turbojet. Likewise a development in wing design would restore some of the loss of aerodynamic efficiency caused by wing sweep. Early jetliners used wing cross-sections developed decades earlier. These typically had a rounded upper surface with a flatter underside and this would generate suction on the upper surface and hence lift. However, the wing is unevenly loaded as well as exhibiting a strong shock wave at the onset of compressibility. By essentially inverting the wing and setting it at a slightly higher angle of incidence to the fuselage, lift can still be generated while the intense shock is spread and the loading is equalised. This has two useful outcomes – a smaller wing can do the same amount of work, while the wing sweep can be reduced for the same cruise Mach number increasing efficiency and allowing an even smaller wing leading to a positive design spiral of reduced fuel burn and aircraft weight. This together with the high bypass engine was enough enabling technology to launch the Airbus A300B, give it a significant advantage over any conventional competitor and cause the renaissance of the European airliner manufacturing industry. Again this wing technology has persisted more or less as is until the present day.

13.4 1970 Onwards: The Evolutionary Era

The period between the HP42 and the A300B saw rapid change, particularly regarding the capabilities and outward appearance of the aircraft. Subsequent to that, changes in performance and appearance have been far less obvious. The Airbus A340 looks very similar in planform to the Boeing 707. Figure 13.3 illustrates a transatlantic 707 used by Pan Am, while Figure 13.4 shows an A340 operated by China Eastern Airlines.

Figure 13.3   The 707
Source: Courtesy of George Hamlin at Airliners.net.

Figure 13.4   The A340
Source: Courtesy of Vivek Manvi at Airliners.net.

The A380 resembles the B747 and the B787 looks a bit like an air-smoothed A300. All travel at roughly the same altitude and speed, have the same type of propulsion system burning the same kind of fuel and, until very recently, are made out of the same material. So what has happened (or not happened) in the interim and how different are the more recent aircraft under the skin?

The main attraction of air transport is high speed and once supersonic aviation had been explored and understood it was natural to offer this to the travelling public. The resultant vehicle was *Concorde* (incidentally, industrially a forerunner to the Airbus consortium). The design was optimized to cruise at Mach 2.2 – more than double that of anything else – as this represented the highest speed at which the light alloy structure would remain stable under the heating effect of aerodynamic abrasion. Figure 13.5 illustrates a British Airways *Concorde*.

Two main issues plagued the initial euphoria of *Concorde*. The first was the amount of energy required (using afterburning turbojets rather than high bypass fans) and this put a high price on the time saving which would have to compensate for this. The development of *Concorde* took well over a decade, during which time the subsonic goalposts had been moved. While the SST could probably compete economically with the early B707 of the early 1960s, it had no chance against the B747 or the A300.

The second issue was environmental. While, even with afterburners operating at take off, *Concorde* was little louder than the early jets (Vickers VC-10, Convair CV880 *et al*) again the high bypass fans were considerably quieter. Also once the subsonics had left the airport area, the noise went away, while *Concorde* shared its sonic boom with all below. Over land it was restricted to subsonic cruise where, due to its delta wing design, it had only the same range as when supersonic.

Figure 13.5   The *Concorde*

Source: Courtesy of Ed Groenendijk at Airliners.net.

In summary, we might conclude that *Concorde* was designed ahead of its time, but arrived after the party was over. Henceforth, the air transport industry would choose to balance efficiency against effectiveness.

So what does this mean? The relationship between time and energy remains, but with an upper limit on time, we concentrate on *reducing fuel burn*. Aircraft weight strongly affects fuel burn and the airliner has three weight elements – flying machine, fuel and payload of which only the last provides a payback. So to further reduce fuel burn, we can also try to *make the aircraft lighter*.

The aircraft only pays for itself when it is airborne with its payload. At all other times it is only a cost, so we should try to *minimize these unproductive periods*. We cannot eliminate 'waste' totally since the aircraft has to make air and ground manoeuvres, board and discharge payload as well as requiring refuelling and maintenance.

A fleet of aircraft undergoes three stages in its *life cycle*. It must first be designed and tested, then produced in hopefully large numbers of copies and finally exploited so as to pay its way. Each of these stages is demanding in time and *resources*, not the least of which latter is *manpower*. So there should be attention paid here.

The mass acceptance of air transport has been as a result of *affordable reliable* travel. Reliability has two main elements – safety (will I get there in one piece?) and punctuality (will I get there when I was promised?). Neither element will achieve 100 per cent success and there can be a compromise between the two. However, both benefit if the air transport process is logical and straightforward, rather than convoluted and complex. In simple terms, if it can be made acceptably safe a twin-engine aircraft should be more reliable than a four-engine one because there is less to go wrong.

Finally, it is obvious that we match supply (of aircraft) with demand, not just in terms of aircraft numbers, but also in the capacity of the aircraft itself. *Size matters*, but biggest is not always best. We will look at all of the above issues as we trace the development of the airliner to the present day.

13.5 Fuel Matters

While the basic architecture of the high bypass engine has been retained in the original two- or three-spool layouts of the Pratt & Whitney JT9-D of the B747 and the Rolls-Royce RB-211 of the Lockheed L-1011 Tri-Star, there has been significant improvement in virtually all aspects of the basic design, such that their descendants which will power the B787 and A350XWB are far more reliable, less thirsty and quieter. By-pass ratio has been optimized for performance and environmental impact. Higher internal operating temperatures result from cooled ceramic single-crystal turbine blades coupled with improved compressor ratios. The combustion process is now much more complete and leaner. Fans have wider chord blades giving improved aerodynamics from a less complex assembly, while the whole engine operation is controlled electronically (FADEC, for Full Authority Digital Electronic Control) rather than hydro-mechanically.

There are signs that the reasonable limits of all this endeavour are being approached and that significant improvement beyond the state-of-the-art may only be achieved by a departure from the established powerplant architecture and process. As mentioned earlier, the arrival of the variable pitch propeller was the most significant advance in power management at the time. Applied to the gas turbine engine as the turboprop, it is still the best solution for fuel efficiency and thrust management, albeit restricted to short range low traffic operations where cruise speed is less significant. Today's turbofan is essentially a fixed pitch propeller in a cowling, so there exists great potential reward if the pitch could be unfixed, so to speak.

Engine manufacturers (particularly Pratt & Whitney) have struggled to develop a ducted variable-pitch fan. To achieve maximum thrust, the clearance between the blade tips and the inside of the cowling should be as low as possible. Varying pitch will cause inevitable gouging or require unacceptable clearances to avoid this. Durable compliant flexible casings have yet to be demonstrated.

One compromise in the search for efficiency is to retain the fixed-pitch fan, but try to optimize its rotational speed compared with that of the low pressure compressor with which it shares a shaft. The Rolls-Royce solution (RB-211 onwards) has been to separate the fan onto a third shaft with its own turbine. The twin spoolers, notably Pratt & Whitney, are opting for a geared fan, which has always been the solution for the turboprop. While this was a feature of the Avco Lycoming ALF502 engine for the 1970s regional jet, the Hawker Siddeley HS146, it has remained without further application until the arrival of the Bombardier

C-Series 100+ seaters, which will be powered by the Pratt & Whitney PW1000G. Very useful improvements in fuel efficiency of around 10–15 per cent are predicted.

The only realistic way to achieve a variable-pitch fan[1] is to remove the cowling. Varying the pitch more than compensates for the aerodynamic leakage around the blade tips and it is reasonable to expect around 25–35 per cent fuel savings as a result. This was certainly the case when in the late 1980s, GE in particular, explored the possibilities of this approach. Development prototypes were tested and demonstrated to the industry of which an adapted MD-80 using the contra-rotating GE/Dowty UnDucted Fan (UDF) was the most impressive, particularly in fuel burn and thrust response. However, the delivery of this design to the operating industry would hardly be a free lunch. The aircraft flies at normal turbofan speeds and so the blade helical speed would be well supersonic, increasing noise on both sides of the fuselage wall. Even more restricting was the issue of detached blade containment (normally managed by the cowling) and this essentially put the project on hold, where it has remained until quite recently. Figure 13.6 illustrates a picture of the MD-80 attached with the contra-rotating GE/Dowty UnDucted Fan.

However, there are indications that the UnDucted Fan design may rise again spurred on by the recent history of fuel price and the pressure to de-carbonise the environment. The indications are that it may be under consideration for the next generation of single-aisle mainliners. Certainly it is something that airlines would welcome. Figure 13.7 shows an environmentally friendly aircraft design that was proposed by easyJet.[2]

Figure 13.6   MD-80 with the contra-rotating GE/Dowty UnDucted Fan
Source: Courtesy of Frank C. Duarte Jr. at Airliners.net.

---

1   It alters the volume and direction of the induced airflow.
2   EasyJet has stated that this would be 25 percent quieter and would emit 50 per cent less carbon dioxide (CO_2) and 75 per cent less nitrous oxide (NO_x) than today's newest short-haul airliners.

Figure 13.7   easyJet's proposed ecoJet
Source: Courtesy of easyJet.

13.6 Toward the Plastic Aeroplane

The light alloy structure has endured due to a number of factors key to air transport in terms of effectiveness and efficiency. In no particular order it is safe to handle, predictable, electrically conductive, inspectable, repeatable, repairable, light, durable, relatively cheap to extract and produce as well as being easily recyclable and/or disposable. Its weaknesses are that it is susceptible to corrosion (particularly in a salty environment) and cyclic stress-related cracking (fatigue). In addition to structural instability at moderate temperatures, it can be made to burn ferociously. However, we have learned how to manage its use to an acceptable level.

Any alternative to this has to exhibit a better profit-and-loss account, given that its characteristics will be different. Lighter metals such as boron, beryllium and magnesium have had at best limited application (magnesium alloys are used for items such as gearbox casings). Heavier metals, particularly stainless steels and titanium are used where light alloys are inappropriate (typically engine components and landing gears). Titanium is particularly attractive due to heat-, corrosion- and fatigue-resistance, but is very expensive to extract and a challenge to fabricate. Lithium, which is less dense (but more expensive) than the copper of conventional light alloys is steadily finding application in aircraft secondary structures when alloyed with aluminium.

The development of the use of plastics (non-metallic composite materials) generally represents a good opportunity for weight savings in the aircraft structure. In the extreme, plywood demonstrates the principle of bonding different materials (an oak outer laminate for hardness and pine or balsa inner layers for lightness and flexibility) in different orientations. Probably the most famous application of this to an aircraft structure was the *de Havilland Mosquito*, by any standards of the day, a high-performance aircraft.

Carbon Reinforced Plastics (CRP) have been gradually applied to many areas of the airliner from cabin floors to propellers (Saab 340) as well as secondary structures such as fairings and control surfaces. Their main advantages (in addition to a 30 per cent weight saving) is that they neither corrode nor fatigue in the manner of duralumins. They can also be manufactured in quite complex (and aerodynamically efficient) shapes such as the hulls of power boats and luxury yachts. However, they do not retain all of the advantages of light alloys and have a few challenges of their own, including moisture absorption and a tendency to de-laminate, both of which are hastened by ultra-violet radiation (sunlight).

The industry has been understandably cautious in the application of composites to the primary structure of civil aircraft (the first was in the fin box of the Airbus A310 and then the wing box of later versions of the ATR42/72 family of regional airliners), although military applications are well established (Northrop F-18, Saab JA-39 Gripen, for example). The main issues have been damage detection, repair and other effects of the hard-driven airline operations environment. Now it seems that one manufacturer is ready to take the plunge in the elegant shape of the Boeing 787 *Dreamliner*, of which 50 per cent of the structural weight is composite, as opposed to the 7 per cent of the B777. Airbus has yet to make such a dramatic step, still making extensive use of Carbon Reinforced Plastics, but also introducing Glass-Reinforced Fibre Metal Laminate which is composed of several very thin layers of metal (usually aluminium) interspersed with layers of glass-fibre known as GLARE. This is now used in areas of the A380 and it will also be used on the forthcoming A350(XWB) together with lithium alloys. Clearly the world will be watching the progress of each design.

13.7 The Available Aircraft

By virtue of the need to assure maximum technical safety, the engineering function within an airline is essentially the custodian of its aircraft and only *releases* them for operation when it is deemed fit to do so. Aircraft can be withdrawn from service by engineering at any time and in any case at predetermined times irrespective of the operational condition. The purpose of aircraft maintenance is obvious because everything made by man will eventually return to nature, coupled with the conditions that machines are not inherently self-repairing, nor generally self-diagnosing.

However, the more we can understand the way in which things fail and the symptoms they exhibit before failure, the more we can prepare for and react to failure in a timely manner in order to, amongst other advantages, increase the availability of the flying machine. Starting with the B747, a method of designing for maintenance and availability has been applied to all public transport aircraft. It is known as Maintenance Steering Group (MSG) and literally examines every way in which any part of an aircraft design can fail and only approves the design if it can be operated and maintained safely and effectively. MSG is naturally evolving as new designs emerge. Thus new procedures had to be introduced to consider, say, the effect of impact damage on GLARE (see above) on the A380 as well as dealing with lightning strikes and damage inspection on the non-conducting composite structure of the B787.

Operationally, the first breakthrough was the Centralised Maintenance System, featured typically on designs from the 1980s, such as the A320. The ground engineer no longer has to explore the length and breadth of the aircraft to diagnose a fault. Instead, a central cockpit display/keyboard allows him to locate the problem before setting out to deal with it.

One area in which electronics has contributed immensely is *health monitoring*. Pioneered by Rolls-Royce, every one of its modern engines has all of its safety and performance-related parameters monitored in operation online. This gives tremendous savings in removing guesswork and allowing timely restoration. Although still in its infancy, this process will likely be expanded to include the remainder of the aircraft, including the structure, where the current procedure is a lengthy strip down of the aircraft to gain access to potentially ageing parts.

We should not expect the machines to take over yet and become self-repairing, but there is evidence of artificial intelligence in more recent designs. The Boeing 777 introduced the capability of electronic systems to 'regroup' automatically following a component failure, advising the pilot, but not exposing him to the risk of a faulty action.

So we should expect a trend toward the self-maintaining aircraft, but there is other potential for time savings. Currently the most significant cause of delay is in Air Traffic Management (See Chapter 15) but this relates far more to the aviation infrastructure than the actual aircraft. However, there are two areas where aircraft design can improve revenue-generating availability.

Short-range aircraft can spend as much time *in operation* on the ground as in flight. Flight times tend to be predictable (subject to ATM), while it takes very little to make things go wrong on a busy ground stop and the resulting delay cannot be caught up *en route*. Aircraft design practice is normally to only install enough fuselage doors as are required to evacuate the maximum likely number of occupants in an emergency. Additional doors add weight and maintenance cost, but can avoid bottlenecks. The Saab 340 had only one main cabin door and was not particularly ergonomic in turnround. The Saab 2000 had the same cabin cross-section and was 50 per cent longer, but the additional service door gave it a brisker ground stop. Here aviation may actually have something to learn from railway carriage design.

Even when the doors are shut, no money is earned until the aircraft is *en route*. At major airports, such as London Heathrow or Paris Charles de Gaulle, the process of getting airborne can take up to half an hour at busy times. The advent of the tilt-rotor could – at least for short-range flights – allow very worthwhile gains in utilization. What are now typical turboprop flights could avoid runways,

Figure 13.8   Bell *Agusta* BA609
Source: Courtesy of Jon Webb at Airliners.net.

thus also saving a lengthy approach while being chased by a much faster and larger jet. At take-off there would be no need to delay due to the wake vortices of larger aircraft and this would free up the runways for those that really need them. The Boeing-Bell V-22 *Osprey* had a rather chequered development, but is now in operational service with the US Marine Corps, while more commercially adapted prototypes are emerging – see Figure 13.8.

13.8 Life Cycle Resource Management

With the best will in the world, the designers of the early civil aircraft could only make an informed guess as to how their drawing board dreams would perform in reality. The mathematical theories of flight and supporting structure are too complicated to be solved by hand, while man is not particularly good at three-dimensional visualization. Thus the design process was largely hit-and-miss with many iterations during development and flight test.

The advent of high-speed computers over the last 40 years has changed all that. By reinforcing disciplines such as Computational Fluid Dynamics and introducing design tools like Dassault Systemes' CATIA, much of the unnecessary waste is removed and more reliable products are brought to market sooner. When the Boeing 787 and Airbus A350XWB enter service they will likely perform very closely to original predictions. The aircrafts' control laws will have been input directly into the fly-by-wire flight management systems and these will have been reproduced in time for installation into the full-flight simulators used for pilot training. So the flight crew will already be familiar with the aircraft's behaviour before they enter the cockpit, rather than literally taking a trip into the unknown. At present, there seems to be very little to halt the increase in computing power apart from, possibly, our ability to exploit it fully.

When, in 1962, the Vickers VC-10 took to the skies it was watched and applauded by most of the 10,000 employees who worked there. Three decades later, the Saab 2000 attracted an in-house crowd not much greater than its name implied. The production rate of the VC-10 was around 15 aircraft per year, while Saab was delivering more like 50. Even allowing for the size differences, there had clearly been a dramatic change in productivity per head.

The manufacturing challenge is the small production run. There have been over 1,800 Boeing 727s produced before the production ended in 1984, while there have been over 6,200 737s manufactured together with around 4,000 Airbus A320 series aircraft by the end of 2009. Rather than being copies, each is subject to variation, either by customer demand, rectification of design shortfalls or production expediency, so the economies of scale enjoyed by the Sony TV production manager are likely to remain a dream. Still, improvements have been made from the hand-built series of prototypes of 50 years ago. The industrial case for the B777 is that it has around 90 per cent of the capability of the B747, but only about half of the production cost. Robot-produced aircraft are still a way off, but with air travel becoming a commodity, rather than a once-in-a-lifetime experience, as well as the ever-powerful leasing companies ordering in bulk and demanding standardized simpler aircraft, there is still scope for improved production efficiency.

Early airliners typically had a flight crew of at least four – the captain, plus a co-pilot (in case either became ill), a flight engineer (in case the aircraft became ill) and a navigator/radio operator. Gradually this number has been reduced so that even the A380 requires only two. With much of the workload mechanized or automated, their roles have changed from drivers to monitors of an information system.

With the advent of indirect control (fly-by-wire), it has been possible to make the handling characteristics of various aircraft types appear similar to the pilots. Additionally, the cockpit layouts and the presentation of information can be standardized so that the working environment is similar. Thus cockpit crews are no longer restricted to flying only one type (for example, B727) because the B777 would appear, feel and behave rather differently. *Common Cockpit Ratings* – the ability of pilots to operate several aircraft types has given considerable savings in crew recruitment, rostering and particularly training. Here Airbus has been the industry leader with the potential for a common rating for all of its aircraft types currently in production.

The question then arises as to whether the flight crew can be reduced further. From a systems reliability viewpoint there would be little sense in reducing the cockpit to a single pilot. Pilots are also subject to heart-attack, just like any other human and there is a case for a redundant path to assure a successful mission. Of far more interest and relevance is the issue of pilotless airliners.

For many years now, unmanned remotely controlled aircraft have been used by the military (see Figure 13.9 for an illustration of a *Global Hawk*) and certain industries. In particular the 'dull and dirty' missions are appropriate. These include surveillance and counter-insurgency operations, where it is highly undesirable for flight crew to fall into enemy hands, and crop-spraying, where the pilot may become affected by his load. The technology is mature – a 10-year-old can operate a radio controlled model aircraft with impressive ease, while a camera is much lighter, cheaper and mechanically reliable than a dedicated cockpit.

Even though modern airliners can perform a completely hands-off flight, there is still likely to be a need to manage it. A flight plan is at best a statement of what we hope will happen and even on the most benign mission, there is still much that can change or go wrong, requiring in-course adjustments based on judgement. The current management process is a dialogue between a ground-based traffic controller and the pilot, who also has contact with the airline's ground operations. If the pilot is removed, there still has to be ground-based management by the airline, who would now lose direct awareness of what is happening on or near the aircraft. It is not obvious that costs and safety would both benefit at present, so it does look like the airliner pilot still has a career to look forward to, in contrast to the elevator operator.

Figure 13.9   *Global Hawk*
Source: Courtesy of Max Bryansky at Airliners.net.

13.9 Do We Need to Carry Everything at Once?

If reduction in the size and weight of the cockpit is unlikely, are there other ways in which the proportion of the payload to the whole aircraft may be increased? Currently all civil aircraft are designed around a limiting mission (payload and distance) where everything required has to be carried from pushback, but more critically, at take-off. Here the aircraft has to be able to sustain an engine failure which, for a two-engined aircraft, implies that it is provided with double the power required to operate safely. Given that it is impractical to add either aircraft hardware or payload *en route* the issue centres around *in-flight refuelling*.

Again, the military have been refuelling very large jet-engined aircraft for half a century. Despite the apparent hazards, the safety record (Western Air Frces) has been quite remarkable, with only four fatal accidents reported. In most cases, the tanker aircraft is a civil design or derivative (current programmes include the A330 and the B767) and often the recipient can be a cargo aircraft.

The main benefit would be the removal of the trade-off between fuel and payload on a given mission due to take-off weight restrictions. It may well be that the first ventures into civil in-flight refuelling would be cargo aircraft as these tend to have greater payloads, but which have slightly less urgency or concern than passengers. If used in passenger operations, far more direct flights would be possible and much smaller capacity aircraft could be used. British Airways is currently operating a double daily service with an Airbus A318 (typically with 100 seats) from London City airport[3] (LCY) to New York, but with a restricted load of 32 all business class seats, mainly due to the short runway at LCY, but the aircraft is forced to make a technical stop at Shannon, Ireland for refuelling. In-flight refuelling could allow for a full cabin and the rendezvous delay would still be much shorter than the commute across London to Heathrow. If applied generally, in-flight refuelling would completely alter the way in which long-range aircraft are specified. The technology is mature – all that is required is the safety and commercial cases to be made.

13.10 Keep it Simple

As mentioned earlier, reliability encompasses two elements – safety and punctuality. Safety can always be improved, but until there is systematic passenger refusal to board aircraft on safety grounds, it may be argued that the current level of safety is acceptable at the current levels of traffic and cost. Punctuality is in need of improvement, not just because of ATM delays, but more important to the aircraft cancellations and diversions.

At the time of the introduction of the B747, virtually everything large and airborne had four engines. Historically, four were *required* to give sufficient power for a commercially worthwhile mission and were *desired* in order to have a good chance of completing it. While the aerodynamic contribution to air travel has been significant over the past 40 years, it is dwarfed by the developments in electronics and engine power and efficiency. Electronics have miniaturized many airborne systems, while engines are now only limited in growth by the operating scale of

---

3   This airport is right in the heart of London.

the aircraft. Thus we have the Boeing 777 largely capable of replacing the B747 from day one of service.

The key to the move to simplicity came from the realization that the twin-jet wide-body aircraft (A310 and B767) were far more reliable than expected and anything else that had preceded them. The compromise three-engine configuration was of limited success (only the B727 had really worked – the centre engine always being the 'difficult' one) and has essentially been discarded now.

The reliability of the twin-engined aircraft introduced the concept of Extended range Twin-engine Oporations (ETOPS). It enabled twin-engined aircraft to operate over vast tracks of ocean or desert, provided there were sufficient accessible alternate airports *en route*. Within a few years the majority of aircraft flying the Atlantic were B767s and A310s albeit with tracks offset from the great circle minimum.[4] Twenty years on and the B777 can fly virtually any track while the next generation long-range twins will have the freedom of the skies.[5]

So the choice is normally two engines or four, with the latter only applied where two are inadequate in size (A380), special airfield performance is required (the Avro RJ85 at Lhasa near the Himalayas) or military freighters (C17/A400M).

13.11 Size Matters

Deregulation changed the competitive landscape and it established the principle that anyone could start an airline anywhere. While the suppliers might favour the economy of air travel in large lumps, as individual travellers, we want to travel as conveniently as possible. This means when you want and from your back yard. The effect on aircraft was to launch a myriad of regional airlines operating series of new small efficient airliners.

Initially, the majority of these were propeller-powered and between 30 and 50 seats in capacity. They were supplied by high-tech minor league manufacturers based typically in Canada, Sweden, Brazil and the Netherlands rather than by Airbus or from the US West Coast. These latter would not have been able to produce a 50-seater much more cheaply than a mainliner due to their industrial scale. Traffic growth at regional level was such that although a 30-seater was more than adequate in the early eighties, in less than 10 years, a 50-seater was looking a bit on the small side.

There has been extensive consolidation in regional aircraft manufacturing, but those who remained, particularly Embraer and Bombardier, have concentrated on larger aircraft, typically 70–120 seats which are jet-powered. Ironically, these

---

4   The regulations allow an airliner to have 120 minute ETOPS rating on its entry into service. ETOPS-180 is only possible after 1 year of trouble-free 120-minute ETOPS experience.

5   Most of the world's operators of B777s now carry an ETOPS rating of 180 minutes and an ETOPS-180/207 rating covers 95 per cent of the earth's surface.

suppliers have scaled up and can no longer produce the type of aircraft they cut their teeth on. Thus the 19-seat *de Havilland Twin Otter* is being recreated by Viking Air, also of Canada a relative cottage industry compared to Bombardier. At present, the regional jet suppliers are proposing aircraft which encroach on the market for the single aisle mainliners of Airbus and Boeing, while Japan, Russia and China are joining the party, so as usual, interesting times are ahead.

13.12 Waiting in the Wings

Lest we become complacent and expect everything to finish up looking like the A320, it might be worthwhile looking at some non-standard projects and evaluating their chances of appearing in the next 30 years or so. All aerospace development organizations have future project teams and their job is to evaluate new technology and propose applications to aircraft. Clearly the UnDucted Fan concept (discussed above) is an example, but there are many others.

One aerodynamic development which has been in the spotlight for some time is the blended wing aircraft (see Figure 13.10). Conventional aircraft gain virtually no lift from the fuselage and there is even an interference with the wing which delivers a performance penalty. By blending the fuselage into the wing it contributes towards lift, the airflow is more predictable and everything is more efficient. Engines are typically mounted above the wing which alleviates their noise, at least on the ground, although not helping accessibility.

Passengers are accommodated throughout the interior so the cabin will resemble a theatre rather than a bus. Clearly the aircraft will have to be very large if people are to stand up in outer reaches of the wing. The potential gains are fuel efficiency and utilization if the aircraft is quiet enough to beat noise curfews. These will have to outweigh manufacturing complexity, particularly if stretched versions are contemplated, as well as a reduction in utilization due to protracted ground handling and maintenance access.

We have not yet done with wing design. Sweep reduces drag and allows faster speeds, but at take-off and landing an unswept wing performs better requiring a shorter runway due to its lower stalling speed. An adaptable swing-wing has had ready application on aircraft carriers (Grumman F-14 *Tomcat*) and to improve the loading of land-based strike aircraft (BAe *Tornado*). On the North American B-1 bomber, the swing wing allows low *supersonic* cruise without the subsonic inefficiencies of *Concorde* (mentioned above). This aircraft also features the waisted fuselage desirable to minimize drag at trans-sonic speeds. Before concentrating on the B787, Boeing was offering the Sonic Cruiser (see Figure 13.11), which might be described as having all the penalties of supersonic design (complexity, inefficient wing, high fuel burn) without the prime advantage of speed. Once again the technology is there, but at present the numbers are a challenge.

Will we see alternative engines to the gas turbine and/or use fuels other than kerosene? Rockets have been used to boost take-off capability (B727's out of

Mexico City, for example), but have not found favour on their own. Even the military has been cautious after the challenging Me163 of the early 1940s. Fuel choices are between kerosene substitutes from organic sources which are feasible, provided the world does not stop growing wheat instead. Again there is a balance to be dealt with no carbon emissions, but production methods have significant carbon content, storage is not easy and the wing volume will not be adequate while the prime failure mode has been demonstrated as early as the *Hindenburg* and the *R101*.

There is no shortage of proposed aerospace technologies. The main challenge for civil application is to incorporate them in a reliable and economic manner. We have now reached such mature excellence in aircraft design, manufacture, operation and maintenance that current practice will be highly resistant to any revolutionary changes. Certainly the developments of the past 40 years outlined in this chapter will continue as long as they make sense, but how much novelty will be seen is anyone's guess and this author's estimate is a fairly conservative one.

Figure 13.10 The X-48 development by Boeing, NASA and Cranfield University

Source: Courtesy of Boeing.

Figure 13.11 The Boeing Sonic Cruiser
Source: Courtesy of Boeing.

Bibliography

Modern Air Transport, Putnam's Aeronautical Books 2000, ISBN 0 851 77 877 1.
Faster, Further, Higher, Putnam's Aeronautical Books 2002, ISBN 0 851 77 876 3.
Janes' All the World's Aircraft (various years), Janes Information Group.
MSG-3 (editions from 2004), Air Transport Association of America.

Further Reading

Boeing 787 Dreamliner Represents Composites Revolution, Design News June 4, 2007.
Boeing 787 Dreamliner Composite Success, New Designs, Alloys Boost Aluminium in Aircraft, Design News October 8, 2007.
SMR Dominates Hydrogen Production, But There's Many Ways to Make it, Design News July 15 2008.
NASA Awards Future Commercial Aircraft Research Contracts, Green Car Congress, July 11 2009.
Future Technology and Aircraft Types, http://adg.stanford/aa241/intro/futureac.html.
Aircraft and Engine Manufacturers' websites.

Chapter 14

Safety Management Systems in Aviation

Graham Braithwaite

14.1 Introduction

With the publication of the Safety Management Manual in 2006, ICAO signalled its intent that member states should require operators to establish a formal safety management system (SMS) by 1 January 2009. ICAO was realistic about the likelihood that member states would meet the 1 January 2009 deadline, but made a conscious decision to aim for such a difficult target. The flurry of activity during 2008 confirmed the view that most effort would be put in during the immediate period prior to the deadline.

Whilst many of the components that form an SMS are well established, it is their interaction within a well-designed system that promises a tangible improvement in safety. Ultimately, the facilitation of an SMS depends on the shared beliefs and attitudes or 'safety culture' of the organization if it is to go beyond the theoretical framework. There are still many aviation organizations missing the potential of a sound SMS, both in terms of maintaining a safe operation and in terms of the tangible, financial benefit that it can also bring.

14.2 Built on Management Commitment

The statement '… without management commitment, a safety management system will fail' is often spoken and remains at the heart of a successful SMS. For most organizations, the move towards an SMS approach comes from someone other than the Chief Executive or Chairman. This does not mean that they cannot be committed, but as with all other business decisions, they will need to be convinced of the need and/or benefits of such an approach. As safety has focused more on a risk-based approach, so too it has become discussed in terms that are more familiar to those who discuss financial and business risks. This has been an important shift in changing mindsets away from safety being a purely operational issue.

Management commitment defines priorities for safety – in terms of financial and human capital, and in terms of inspirational leadership. This may be in very visible, tangible ways such as the Chief Executive making the time to speak on company safety courses, or less visible ways such as ensuring that Board decisions are made with safety effects in mind. The structure of an organization may also reflect management's approach. Does the Head of Safety report to the Chief

Executive or are there tiers of management in between? Is safety part of another department or merged with an activity such as quality assurance? Independence is important for a safety department, as is the ability to report directly to the Chief Executive.

Even apparently simple things may carry deeper meaning – for example, does the company's mission statement record its commitment to safety? Cathay Pacific states 'Our vision is to make Cathay Pacific the most admired airline in the world – Ensuring safety comes first ...' before then going on to make commitments to service quality, product leadership, financial returns and career opportunities. This is a good clue, but ultimately commitment is evidenced through actions. If senior management does not value the benefits of a safety management system, then it is unlikely that a proactive safety culture will ever develop. Assuming senior staff are committed, then the next step is to ensure that implementation is supported by appropriate staff.

14.3 Competent, Well-trained Staff

Whilst human error may seem to be omnipresent in incidents and accidents, a deeper understanding of the types of errors and violations that are being committed helps to give an appreciation for the best mitigations. Where certain types of errors may be made as a result of poor or incomplete training, others may be made because a lack of currency. In turn, violations (which are normally associated with motivational issues) may reveal that employees are deliberately circumventing procedure either because it is the only way to get the job done, has become routine, or is some way of shortcutting or optimizing. Clearly there is a difference between violations caused by an unworkable procedure and those that are the result of deliberate acts of sabotage or flagrant disregarding of the rules.

Whilst flight deck crew, air traffic controllers and licensed aircraft engineers will need to demonstrate that they have achieved a level of competence set by the regulator prior to licensing, and then will have to undergo a variety of currency checks, many working within the air transport system have no formal training requirements, especially in relation to their role within the safety management system. Indeed, even basic qualifications for recruitment vary depending on the need for staff and the availability of candidates.

Safety training takes many forms from basic occupational health and safety requirements through to specific, targeted training interventions aimed at addressing specific problems. For example, the rise of Cockpit Resource Management (CRM) which later transformed into Crew Resource Management was due to a series of accidents in which individual flight deck crew members held vital information, but did not share it with their colleagues leading to serious errors or oversights. Other training programmes may address specific emergency procedures such as the periodic emergency procedures training that all aircraft crew undertake to familiarize them with everything from how to open doors and evacuate an aircraft through to dealing with a potential hijack.

A fully enlightened SMS looks beyond specific safety training to assure that safety is a core value which pervades all aspects of selection, training and competency assessment. This may be something as simple as ensuring language competence for those being recruited to areas such as ground handling or as strategic as ensuring that all management recruits are inducted into the safety culture of the organization.

When assessing whether an individual has committed a violation, the first point to establish is whether they were appropriately skilled to conduct the task. Poor or incomplete training has lain behind some of the most serious accidents, even when the media subsequently focused on the failings of an individual. The conversion training from B737–300 to -400 series was one factor that influenced the crew's use of a fallible procedure to diagnose an engine failure, which in turn led to the crew shutting down the wrong engine. The aircraft crashed on approach to East Midland Airport in 1989 with the loss of 47 lives.

14.4 Clearly Defined Responsibilities

Although at the broadest level, it is the State that carries the responsibility to ensure safety amongst its air operators, the SMS approach reminds all organizations that they carry a broad duty of care towards their staff and customers alike. This is an important philosophical step in widening the level of responsibility beyond the flight safety officer or occupation health and safety manager. This notwithstanding, a safety management system depends on safety critical tasks and processes having defined 'owners' who fully understand the implications of their role.

Accountable executives need to be identified so that they can take ownership for initiatives in safety. With this come accountabilities and responsibilities that should be clearly documented, communicated and trained for. It is not enough to assign broad, undefined responsibilities to an individual and expect them to cover all eventualities, or for such responsibilities to remain mapped in the corporate memory. Related to this is a need for a defined system for identifying current and future hazards to the operation and for evaluation their potential consequence or risk.

14.5 Hazard Identification and Risk Management

Risk management is not a new concept either within safety or within other parts of the aviation business – in particular, finance. The identification, analysis and management (either through elimination or mitigation, as far as reasonably practicable) of hazards and their related risks is a cornerstone of a safety management system. However, the process of hazard identification is dependent upon the quality and completeness of the data going into it. In particular, a safety management system is dependent on both formal audit-type systems as well as less formal reporting systems to identify existing and emerging risks.

Hazards are then assessed for their likely frequency and severity and measured against the organization's acceptable levels of risk. Where the risk is considered to be unacceptable then this may be recorded on a risk register and an individual or department assigned the responsibility of implementing a strategy to reduce the risk or mitigate its consequences. ICAO (2006) highlights the need for particular care to be taken during high-risk periods of an organization's existence, such as when major operational changes are planned (for example, people, systems or equipment); during a period of significant growth or contraction of an organization; following a corporate merger, acquisition or downsizing.

A formal risk management process can help to identify threats to the operation well before an incident or accident occurs. However, it should also be noted that a risk assessment is only as good as the assumptions made during the process and will not guarantee a successful outcome. If the hazard is improperly measured then the likelihood of a bad outcome may be significant.

14.6 Trusted Reporting Systems

An SMS is dependent upon up-to-date and accurate information if it is to adequately manage risk. Such safety data can come from myriad sources and be presented in numerous forms. Examples of safety data include:

Automated Reporting

This may include technologies such as Flight Data Monitoring (FDM) or Flight Operations Quality Assurance (FOQA) as it is known in North America. FDM collects flight data via an on-board quick-access flight data recorder, which is downloaded at the end of a flight and matched against predetermined performance criteria. The identity of crews is protected via a trusted agent system so that the data are presented in a de-identified form to the various departments who may learn lessons from either an individual event or, more commonly, system-wide trends. An un-stabilized approach, for example, may highlight issues arising from an individual crewmember, a difficult approach procedure, or perhaps a late runway change. In the latter case, several events may point to an issue involving ATC, whereas the former may highlight a training issue that can be resolved via the trusted agent or relevant pilot union in a non-punitive way.

Engineering data may also be collected in a similar way using real-time data that can be downloaded using telemetry. It is not unheard of for a problem with an engine, for example, to be notified to maintenance control even before the flight crew have detected the issue. Such data provide trends across fleets as well as an early warning about impending technical failures.

Mandatory Event Reporting

Accidents and serious incidents involving aircraft must by, international convention, be reported to the national investigation agency (NIA) or state regulatory authority. Whilst accidents, particularly those involving loss of life or serious injury, generally receive widespread publicity, certain mandatory events may not be quite as high profile. The UK CAA requires airlines to report events of a certain level of severity through its mandatory occurrence reporting system – MORS. Serious incidents and accidents should be investigated by the State of Occurrence under the standards and operating practices laid out in ICAO Annex 13. For European states, this is also the formal requirement of EU Directive 94/56/EC.

Voluntary Reporting

There are numerous voluntary reporting schemes in existence within the air transport business with different aims and different levels of success. A recognition that many human errors are either inconsequential or get trapped before a serious effect occurs meant that voluntary reporting schemes were designed to encourage individuals to report their own errors without fear of reprisal. By necessity, some early schemes were set up that preserved full anonymity of the reporter. Such an approach is only really warranted in an environment where employees are untrusting or fearful of their employers. Anonymous reports mean that investigators cannot follow up on a report for clarification, but also can mean that several reports can come from the same person – perhaps someone with a particular agenda or grievance.

A better reporting system approach is to assure confidentiality of the reporter. This generally works through a trusted employee within the safety department who will securely catalogue the origin of a report, providing the possibility for follow-up and feedback without fear of being named. Successful confidential reporting systems include the US Air Safety Reporting System (ASRS) administered by NASA for the US FAA which has received over 723,000 reports since it was established in 1976, leading to over 4,000 safety alerts. Another example is the UK Confidential Human Factors Incident Reporting Programme (CHiRP) which was established in 1982, distributes its findings in a de-identified form through a magazine called *Feedback* which is distributed to UK pilot licence holders and cabin crew.

In-company schemes also provide similar information and can ideally be found in all areas of the operation and not just limited to the flight deck crew.

The ideal reporting system is an 'open' one where employees feel confident that the organization is sufficiently mature in its approach to safety data as to perceive all reports as carrying the potential to increase safety rather than an opportunity to pursue punitive action. No de-identification is necessary and the reporter is happy for the relevant managers to approach them for more information or perhaps to develop a solution. Such systems are rare as they are indicative of a very mature safety culture and of the key ingredient – trust.

14.7 Emergency Response Plan

Disruptions within the air transport system can come from a variety of causes ranging from weather and disease through to aircraft accidents, building fires or acts of sabotage or terrorism. Whilst such events, by their very nature are difficult to predict, contingency planning for such emergencies should be sufficiently flexible as to cope with a range of emergencies. A well executed emergency response can not only assist in the direct welfare of passengers and staff, but also their friends and relatives, and the wider business continuity process.

An emergency response plan should document the actions to be taken by staff in the event of an unexpected event. This may include procedures for notifications, protocols for working with other organizations and even down to specific details about what people should say. For example, staff at easyJet carry cards with a prepared statement that they can use in the event of an occurrence which explains that they are not authorized to speak on behalf of the company and provides contact details for such enquiries.

Any emergency plan is only as good as the last time it was tested. Full-scale simulation of emergency plans can be expensive, requires a great deal of planning and can occasionally become 'public' by accident. However, without such testing, it is likely that notifications will be missed, phone numbers become out of date, and some of the problems that may occur in the real event may not be identified in time. Tabletop exercise can be exceptionally valuable, but will not capture certain things such as the effects of weather, time of day or availability of facilities or communications. How many organizations would be brave enough to run a full-scale test of their emergency response on, say, New Year's Day?

The speed at which an organization responds to an event will have a direct effect on the level of emotional and reputational damage that may be done. This can make the difference between staying in business or not, regardless of the cause of the initial event.

14.8 Systems for Audit and Occurrence Investigation

Safety needs to be continuously monitored and whilst reporting systems provide some information, other processes will provide more detailed information. A formal internal auditing process provides regular checks of compliance. ICAO (2006) describes the function of safety audits as ensuring that:

a. the structure of the SMS is sound in terms of appropriate levels of staff; compliance with approved procedures and instructions; and a satisfactory level of competency and training to operate equipment and facilities and to maintain their levels of performance;

b. equipment performance is adequate for the safety levels of the service provided;

c. effective arrangements exist for promoting safety, monitoring safety performance and processing safety issues; and

d. adequate arrangements exist to handle foreseeable emergencies.

External audits complement this process, but in recent years had become a major burden for airlines, especially those who were members of large alliances (such as Star or Oneworld) where each partner airline would be conducting audits throughout the year. This provided the impetus for the International Air Transport Association (IATA) to develop its own safety audit process; the IATA Operational Safety Audit (IOSA), meaning that a recognized audit standard could replace duplicate audits. Indeed, IATA embraced the concept so firmly that by the end of 2008, all IATA members had to become IOSA registered in order to achieve or maintain IATA membership. The programme has been sufficiently successful that some regulators are even recommending it to non-IATA members as a method for demonstrating suitable safety compliance.

However, ICAO is keen to point out that the regulatory accountability rests with the relevant civil aviation authority including responsibility for monitoring compliance through relevant audit processes. The IOSA process is designed to complement, not replace such oversight and ICAO continues to monitor the conformance of States through its Universal Safety Oversight Audit Programme (USOAP).

In addition to a scheduled audit programme, operators (whether of airlines, airports, maintenance or other aviation organizations) should have the capacity to investigate incidents and accidents. Although serious incidents and accidents will normally be investigated by the State of occurrence, this does not exclude an operator from also investigating these events and other incidents of lower severity. The way in which investigations are conducted will determine both the quality of lessons learned and will also have a significant effect on the safety climate within that organization. If occurrence investigation is considered to be punitive or unfair, then this is likely to reduce the level of reporting and co-operation.

14.9 Regular Fine-tuning of the Programme

An SMS will need to continuously evolve if it is to be able to stay aligned with emerging threats. Like any management system, it will need adjustments over time and regular fine-tuning of the various aspects of SMS if it is to work effectively. Surveys of staff will identify concerns and threats and regular meeting of the safety representatives of the various parts of the business will provide invaluable information. Organizations who find that occurrence reports have dropped significantly may be either benefiting from a genuine reduction in incidents, or may be suffering from a loss of confidence in the reporting system. Any safety meeting that yields the feedback 'no problems' should be especially concerned that the channels of communication have become blocked.

To avoid such problems, the final and most critical component of an SMS should be established as the 'DNA' of a particular organization – that is a positive or generative safety culture.

14.10 Positive Safety Culture

The term safety culture first appeared after the catastrophic reactor fire at Chernobyl nuclear power station in 1986. Since then, the term has been widely discussed by industry and academia alike, although as Reason (1997) points out 'few phrases are so widely used yet so hard to define as safety culture'. Whilst the term itself is just over 20 years old, the role of an organization's way of doing things as a factor in accidents has been known for rather longer.

Seminal investigations including the Royal Commission that followed the fatal accident at Mount Erebus in which an Air New Zealand aircraft collided with terrain with the loss of 257 lives in 1979; the Commission of Inquiry into the fatal takeoff accident involving an F28 at Dryden, Ontario in 1989; and the serious incident investigation in the UK where the pilot of a BAC1–11 was nearly sucked out of his aircraft after the windscreen failed (AAIB, 1992), all played a pivotal role in changing the industry's understanding of the way that organizational factors may influence the likelihood of an accident. With the work of system safety specialists such as Rasmussen (1983 and so on), Reason (1990, 1997b and so on) and Perrow (1996), the understanding of how systems and organizations rather than individuals fail to cause an accident has grown.

In describing the varying levels of safety culture, Hudson (2001) describes the evolution of safety culture from 'pathological organizations' (*who cares as long as we're not caught?*) to the ideal 'generative culture' (*safety is how we do business around here*). Such stages of evolution are useful markers, but identifying where a particular organization finds itself on the scale is a little harder. Several questionnaire-based tools exist, but even these depend on the organization first being sufficiently open to the idea of collecting such data and secondly on their staff giving an objective assessment. The American Institute of Chemical Engineers' (2005) definition highlights why measurement is difficult: 'Safety culture is how the organization behaves when no one is watching'. As such, assessing regulatory compliance in an area such as safety culture is not only difficult, but almost contradictory. Safety culture is not just about how an organization meets its regulatory or legal obligations, but rather what attitude it takes to try and exceed them and to recognize safety as a key feature of business success.

14.11 Ideals for Safety Culture

An *informed culture* comprehends the hazards that it faces and the risk that each faces. Where a *no-blame* approach was once advocated by many in the industry, there is now strong support for a *just culture* to be at the heart of an SMS. It remains appropriate for accident investigations conducted through processes such as ICAO *Annex 13* to be no-blame in order to preserve the integrity and independence of the process. However, modern thinking on SMS highlights the need to make a clear distinction between what is acceptable behaviour and what is not. Where resources and training support the employee to make the right decision, a just culture will treat genuinely unintentional errors quite differently from wilful violations. Indeed when an incident or accident occurs, employees will look for fair treatment of themselves and their colleagues, or behaviours will start to modify accordingly. Misapplication of either no-blame or just culture will undermine the core value of a mature safety culture – trust.

A *reporting culture* wants to know what is happening within the organization – both good and bad. Negative feedback is problematic, but a complete absence is arguably worse. In the airline environment where serious incidents are rare, there can be a natural reluctance to be the bearer of bad news. In one airline, the accident investigation agency commented that they thought it was unusual for the safety manager not to turn out to an incident which had occurred two days previously. For the safety manager, this was the first news of an incident that no-one had wanted to 'trouble him' with. When reviewing the role of reporting following an occurrence, the investigator must consider whether the message was able to get through, whether it was welcomed, or whether its presence was indicative that a problem had been identified, but not dealt with.

A *learning or proactive culture* is one that recognizes that incidents, near-misses and voluntary reports can provide vital lessons before the onset of an accident. Indeed, there is a process in place to collate and do something with the information. All too often, the collection of data has become the focus and with limited resources, there is little time to do anything with it other than present trend data. Several options exist for safety promotion, ranging from publications and presentations to training design and procedural changes. However, it should be borne in mind that no safety improvements can exist in isolation from the financial health of an organization. Budgets are not limitless and choices need to be made in order to prioritize initiatives.

When an accident occurs, it is all too easy for disgruntled employees, or perhaps those who have been affected, to point to missed opportunities for the organization to learn. However, it is possible that the decision that was made at the time was the best one, based on available evidence. A learning culture tries to understand the context of failures. In other words, as Dekker (2002) remarks 'the point of an investigation is not to find where people went wrong. It is to understand why their assessments and actions made sense at the time.'

Finally, a *flexible culture* is adaptable to evolving threats and crises. It is this aspect that can often be overlooked when reactive investigations focus on what went wrong, rather than looking for things that reduced the potential consequences of an event. Whilst safety policies, processes and responsibilities need to be defined clearly as part of an SMS, the way in which an organization responds to new situations is perhaps the greatest test of a safety culture. Encompassing all of the preceding elements, the ability to trap or mitigate against the *impossible accident* is the real test.

14.12 Interpreting Safety Culture

Mandating that organizations implement an SMS will not guarantee a sound safety culture. Regulators are faced with the unenviable task of attempting to measure and assess compliance using elements of a system that are not easy to measure, especially after an event. Although ICAO is clear that the intent of SMS is not something that can be achieved through a 'tick in the box' solution, the challenge of establishing what to measure and how to do it remains. ICAO (2006) acknowledges that 'safety culture is ... difficult to measure, especially when the principal criterion for measuring safety is the absence of accidents and incidents.' Does this mean that the occurrence of an accident suggests a poor safety culture?

Culture is easily misinterpreted, especially if it crosses organizational, professional or national boundaries. Spoken and body language, etiquette and customs are all examples of the variables that can be reflected across the culture of an organization. Different combinations of cultural traits can be assembled to produce the same successful outcome – for example, a culture where questioning of authority does not come easily, can be balanced with strict adherence to standard operating procedures which include cross-checking.

The interpretation of data from certain elements of an SMS needs care to avoid false generalizations or false correlations. For example, an increase in incident reports may be symptomatic of either an increase in incidents or perhaps a greater willingness to report, or increased ease of reporting. Similarly, the operational requirements or conditions placed upon a certain group may yield results which can be misinterpreted. In the case of one major airline, the Boeing 737 fleet appeared to yield a higher proportion of unstable or rushed approaches than the other aircraft types. Was this symptomatic of the way the fleet was being managed or the crew trained? In fact, one of the influences was the type of flying that the 737 fleet was often being required to do, which involved short-notice replacement of aircraft types on sectors where the schedule needed making up – something that by definition was placing increased pressure on crews and even encouraging them to fly 'enthusiastically'. A blame-oriented view was to see the managers as failing whereas a more enlightened view might be that business imperatives were creating risks that needed managing.

14.13 Conclusion

ICAO's Safety Management Manual (1996) states 'safety has always been the overriding consideration in all aviation activities'. Indeed the recent fatal accident rate for most of the aviation industry has been impressively low. The US, for example suffered no fatal commercial jet aircraft accidents in 2007 and 2008 – the first time in the jet age that there have been no fatalities in two consecutive years. Recent accidents such as the crash landing of a B777 at Heathrow in January 2008 and the ditching of an A320 in the Hudson River, New York, in January 2009 may have given false optimism about the survivability of such events. However, several other crashes highlight the fact that no airline or airport is immune from catastrophic events and such crashes include the Spanair MD-83 aircraft at Madrid in August 2008 that resulted in the loss of 153 lives; the Air France A330 operating on a transatlantic flight from Rio de Janeiro to its home base in June 2009, resulted in 228 fatalities; the Ethiopian Airlines 737–800 which crashed into the sea shortly after takeoff from Beirut International Airport in January 2010 with the loss of 82 passengers and eight crew; an Afriqiyah Airways A330 accident at Tripoli International Airport in May 2010, where 103 people perished; and an Airblue A321, accident north-east of Islamabad in July 2010, that took the lives of 146 passengers together with six crew members, which was recorded as Pakistan's worst air disaster.

Finally, ICAO notes 'The air transportation industry's future viability may well be predicated on its ability to sustain the public's perceived safety while travelling. The management of safety is therefore a prerequisite for a sustainable aviation business.' Safety Management is here to stay and should be a priority for all air transport managers.

References

Air Accidents Investigation Branch (1992), *Report on the accident on BAC 1–11, GBJRT over Didcot, Oxfordshire on 10 June 1990*, UK Department of Transport, London.

American Institute of Chemical Engineers (2005), *Building Process Safety Culture: Tools to Enhance Process Safety Performance*, Centre for Chemical Process Safety, New York.

Dekker, S.W.A. (2002), *The Field Guide to Human Error Investigations*, Ashgate, Aldershot.

Hudson, P. (2001), Safety Culture: The Ultimate Goal, *Flight Safety Australia*, September–October, CASA, Canberra.

ICAO (2006), Safety Management Manual, Doc 9859/460, International Civil Aviation Organization, Montreal.

Perrow, C. (1999), *Normal Accidents*, Princeton University Press.

Rasmussen, J. (1983), Skills, Rules, and Knowledge: Signals, signs, symbols and other distinctions in human performance models, *IEEE Transactions on Systems: Man and cybernetics*, 13.

Reason, J. (1990), *Human Error*, Cambridge University Press.

Reason, J. (1997), Corporate Culture and Safety, Paper presented at the National Transportation Safety Board Corporate Culture and Transportation Safety Symposium, 24–25 April, Arlington, Virginia.

Reason, J. (1997b), *Managing the Risks of Organizational Accidents*, Ashgate, Aldershot.

Chapter 15

Cooperation in Air Navigation Services: Is Globalization Arriving in the World of ANS?

Manjit Singh

15.1 Introduction

Cooperation has been identified as an essential requirement for the strategic performance of air transport organizations. It has been noted that cooperation in the form of networks and alliances is essential for the strategic performance of *air transport* organizations, where they are built on the principle that extension of network coverage and coordination of operations among organizations, even without anti-competitive mergers, creates far greater value for the individual organization compared to if the partners pursue an insular strategy (Gudmundsson and Oum, 2005).

While various aspects of airline alliances have been extensively covered in literature, cooperation involving air navigation service providers (ANSPs) is a relationship ignored, probably on the assumption that *sensitivity of 'national sovereignty' precludes air navigation service providers from pushing the envelope of cooperation*. In a provocative address to the *ATC Maastricht Conference* in February 2003, Ashley Smout the CEO of Airways New Zealand, drew a picture of the way in which the air traffic management (ATM) industry will look like in 2030 (see Figure 15.1) where national borders disappear. This raises a crucial question, whether governments can create a market, whereby the national ANS businesses will be permitted to merge with or acquire each other to create regional and ultimately *global* ANS service providers.

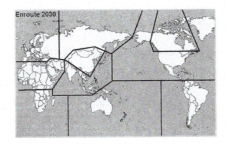

Figure 15.1   Enroute ATM 2030

There are clear developments in the Air Navigation Services (ANS) industry, which require ANSPs to respond to change. Does the key to addressing these serious challenges lie in shifting away to a more regional approach to airspace management, in line with the latest in global ATM thinking? Considering the potential that cooperation involving ANSPs has to improve ANS service provision and reduce costs in the future, brings us to the objective of this chapter which is to enquire whether globalization is finally arriving in the world of ANS?

This chapter follows a conceptual path, first by providing some provocative theses of the current situation of ANS, and then proceeding to discuss various incentives to cooperate, that is, lessons from other air transport cooperation particularly airline alliances, before international and regional regulatory developments, including user expectations. Some insights into the future ANS business model are provided, before exploring the drivers of cooperation in ANS. Based on the findings of an exploratory global survey of ANSPs, a section of the chapter is devoted to the typology of existing and possible ANSP–ANSP cooperation. Having confirmed that there are signs of globalization in ANS provision, this chapter towards the end, proposes strategies in the form of recommendations (to stakeholders) to enhance cooperation in air navigation services.

15.2 Current Situation of ANS

Traditionally provision of air traffic services (ATS) has been based on government ownership and operation of ATS facilities. The model now accepted as the most appropriate substitute for government control is the 'commercial' model which has been in existence for over 20 years. This section lists salient characteristics of the ANS business through the presentation of some provocative theses on the current situation.

ANS: A Complex 'Persona'?

ANS is a product of decades of evolution and a very complex system consisting of the interaction of man, technology and procedures. The ATC objectives of safety and efficiency almost seem contradictory. The interaction of the humans (that is, controllers and pilots) and the interactions between people and equipment (radios, radars, avionics and so on), deliver the objectives of ATC. The objectives are delivered through a system of airspace sectorization using a concept of 'controlled airspace' and internationally agreed procedures.

Brooker (2002) uses the Greek metaphor of '*The Ship of Theseus*'[1] to illustrate the uniqueness of ATM as a type of industry and to suggest that ATM

---

1   Theseus was the mythical hero of Athens, said to have been alive during the Minoan period in Crete.

decision-making processes can be very different from those in other industries. The ATM technology meets the *Ship of Theseus* principles in that new technology is normally added on in a 'step-by-step' fashion to the previous systems and the system is '*backwards compatible*', that is, new functionality is able to carry out both the tasks of the previous generation plus some new ones. The complexity of ATM gives rise to technical issues of interoperability and presents economic and operational challenges of phasing out 'legacy systems'.

The International Dimension of ANS

By its very nature, air transport does not end at state borders (that is, national boundaries are crossed and aircraft are subject to different authorities) and flight safety must be maintained for the whole duration of a flight. For this to happen there are a few prerequisites: the exchange of data (for example, flight plan) relevant for a particular flight, continuous air traffic control (ATC) service across borders through the interoperability of ground and airborne components and an airways structure that links airports and countries together. In spite of the international dimension of ANS there is a resistance by states to recognize ANS as a business whose customers operate in regional and global markets and to relinquish any part of their national sovereignty as recognized by the Chicago Convention.

Fragmented Nature of ANS

Indeed, fragmentation in ANS covers a wide range of issues: airspace fragmentation, institutional fragmentation, technical diversity of the ATM systems and interfaces and so on. While ANS serves an international business, the provision of the service is largely organized on the basis of national systems strongly linked to national interests. The Air Transport Action Group (2009) stated that there were approximately 160 ANSPs employing almost 200,000 staff in hundreds of locations around the world in 2009. Figure 15.2 shows the *patchwork* of Flight Information Regions (FIRs) organized mainly according to geographical national boundaries, each served by an Air Traffic Control Centre (ATCC), in fact some countries may have a few FIRs and similar number of ATCCs.

The existence of diverse legal, political and regulatory frameworks have created a variation in ANSP ownership from 100 per cent state-owned – government department, to 100 per cent state shareholding – corporatized, 100 per cent privatized shareholding – no state control, mixed shareholding – public private partnership. These *institutional variations* in turn result in varying levels of efficiency, equipage, customer focus and governance models.

Financial fragmentation of the current ATM system is characterized through the existence of the many different business models: *for-profit/not-for-profit, charges/no-charges, and government budget/privatized.* Service provision within national borders using national systems has perpetuated a diversity of operational

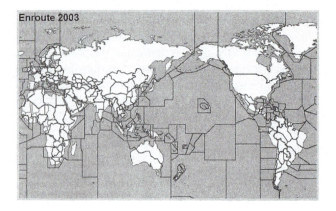

Figure 15.2   Current enroute ATM
Source: Airports International, August 2003.

concepts and relationships with the airspace users and technology suppliers. The *operational fragmentation* reduces efficiency and introduces safety risks.

On the technical perspective, a *diversity of user requirements* and unique operational specifications in adjacent regions, together with uncoordinated R&D, equipment development and deployment has resulted in interoperability issues. The ICAO process relies upon a state's own initiatives for implementation of Standards and Recommended Practices (SARPs) and facilities/services required by international civil aviation, which results in differences in infrastructure capabilities, and provision of services in various Flight Information Regions (FIRs). A lack of political will to cooperate between neighbouring ANSPs, when introducing new systems, has resulted in a sporadic implementation scenario. Thus the advantage to be gained from the envisaged coordinated, seamless and advanced systems across regions is lost.

Different priorities, management and governance structures of neighbouring ANSPs prevent the organizations from 'talking' with one another, and system compatibility with neighbouring ATC equipment is not a priority. The multiplicity of coordination procedures among the various ATS units as a result of *airspace fragmentation* considerably increases the pilot and controller workload and contributes negatively to overall ATM safety and productivity, also duplication of organizations and technology increases the fixed costs and operating costs of ATM.

IATA (2010) stated that European ATM cost airlines €11.6 billion per year, while a 2006 report commissioned by the Eurocontrol Performance Review Unit (PRU), to investigate the impact of fragmentation, quantified the costs of fragmentation in the European en-route ATM/CNS system at some €880 m – €1,400 m (Eurocontrol, 2006). This is undoubtedly a significant amount as it represents around 20–30 per cent of the annual en-route costs. Europe has achieved a single currency, yet there are 36 ANSPs and fragmentation is making the continent's air corridors highly inefficient with IATA estimating that these route inefficiencies cost the industry €3.5 billion (out of the total €11.6 billion) (IATA, 2010). This finding supports the suggestion that fragmentation is an important contributing factor to the performance gap between Europe and the USA.[2] The main components of the cost of fragmentation listed are: (1) many ACCs are below the optimum economic size, (2) duplication of bespoke ATM systems (including piecemeal procurement and sub-optimal scale in maintenance and in-service development), and (3) duplication of associated support training, administration, and R&D. Duplication of ATS units, facilities and systems increases the fixed costs of ATM[3] as well as the operating costs comprising overheads, depreciation and maintenance. By 2020, it is estimated that 20 per cent of flights will continue to be delayed if there is no modernization of the system.

Conservative Governance System

A high standard of safety performance has always been of vital importance to an air navigation service organization as safety is their business. Consequently this has resulted in the development of a strong industry safety culture and a *conservative* governance system as fundamental elements of an overall regulatory framework, which complements the need for either self or even external safety regulation.

Outdated Cost-recovery Mechanism

Traditionally the ANSPs are operating on a full cost-recovery financial system making charges to customers for their services based on a formula mandated by national authorities and backed by the ICAO's policies.

By nature, ATC infrastructure has high fixed capacity costs and low variable costs. ATC operations and facilities are difficult to rescale and reduce costs in the short-term. In state-owned organizations the staff being part of the civil service cannot be laid off when traffic figures fall. Also, in general ATC operates on cost recovery principles and small operating margins, with very little surpluses being accrued. The services are provided on a 24h a day/ 7days a week basis and thus the majority of operating costs are incurred regardless of the traffic serviced. ATC Sectors have to be staffed and equipment maintained even if traffic operating in a particular sector declines. Since the ICAO aeronautical cost recovery system is directly related to traffic numbers the fiscal impact of traffic declines is felt immediately through declining revenues.

---

2   The US controls 13.8 million km2 of airspace with one ANSP and 21 en-route centres. Meanwhile, Europe controls 10.8 million km2 of airspace with 36 ANSPs and 58 en-route centres (IATA, 2010).
3   The abbreviation of ATM covers air traffic control (ATC) and wider issues such as airspace design.

Slow Uptake of New Technology

The airline industry is expecting air passenger traffic to double by 2030 and this is extremely likely as traffic in Europe[4] grew by 27 per cent from 2003 to 2009, signalling that new technologies must be sourced if traffic is expected to reach such growth. However, Klooster (2009) accessed the inefficiencies of the current system and investigated that the Single European Sky ATM Research (SESAR) found that only 77 per cent of short-haul flights were on time in 2007 and by 2009 Eurocontrol (2010) recorded that this had reduced to 75 per cent. Considering the congestion problems, delays and inadequate facilities being experienced in many areas of the world, ICAO has mandated the implementation of new technologies known as the CNS/ATM[5] systems. Whelan (2001) in his evaluation of CNS/ATM and its worldwide implementation status drew the following conclusion: stakeholders are frustrated with the fact that the progression with the implementation of CNS/ATM systems has not progressed as far or as quickly, as originally envisaged. The explanation lies in the fact that the investments required in many instances are of such magnitude that it is not possible for the large majority of service providers to finance them alone.

Concerns Over the Autonomous Trends

Many states are shifting the responsibility of ANS provision to independent entities that operate as a business. As of March 2005, 38 countries worldwide had commercialized their ANS resulting in the formation of independent commercial authorities (US GAO, 2005). Commercial ANSPs are unencumbered by the bureaucracy of government departments, as their sole objective is to ensure the safe and efficient provision of ANS. There is supposedly a greater understanding of airspace users through better customer consultation. Efficiency gains translate to reduced charges and improved levels of service to airspace users. However, it has to be noted that autonomy has also raised the concerns of users ranging from – fear of overcharging of services, lack of transparency with regard to revenues and expenses, inadequate standards, denial of access, inequitable allocation of fixed costs among the different categories of users and safety concerns of the travelling public with regard to safe passage at the lower cost.

15.3 Incentives to Cooperate

Assorted domains of air transportation cooperation have been noted in existing literature, for example, alliances among airlines, cooperation between airports and

---

4   There were 9.4 million flights through European airspace in 2009, up considerably from about 5 million flights in 1990 (Eurocontrol, 2010).

5   Communication, Navigation, Surveillance/Air Traffic Management.

strategic alliances between airlines and airports. The most progressive form of air transport cooperation is the horizontal cooperation or alliances formed by the airlines. Such alliances are seen as the response of airlines to changing economic and regulatory conditions. *Are there any lessons (for ANSPs) from existing cooperation in the air transport industry especially airline alliances?*

15.3.1 Motives for the Formation of Airline Alliances

Various researchers (Burton and Hanlon, 1994; Oum and Park, 1997; Gudmundsson and Rhoades, 2001; Morrish and Hamiltion, 2002; Iatrou and Alamdari 2005; Gudmundsson and Lechner 2006; Pitfield 2007; Holmberg and Cummings, 2009) have offered the following reasons for the formation of airline alliances:

- Expansion of seamless service network.
- Traffic feed between partners.
- Cost efficiency.
- Economics of scale and scope.
- Improved service quality.
- Increased itinerary choices for passengers.
- Exploitation of Computer Reservation System (CRS) display.
- Strategy for growth.
- Technological motives.

Airlines, being an international and service business industry, have always been naturally interested in extending their networks beyond the markets they serve, improving revenues, reducing costs and enhancing customer services. Generally, legislation aimed at protecting national interests has prohibited the acquisition of a controlling stake in airlines in countries or trading blocks outside those in which an airline is owned or operated. Thus, an airline can only grow naturally if it can overcome restrictions such as the normal business limitations to growing in home markets, obtain the regulatory approval to access foreign markets, and acquire the slots at airports to which it wants to operate. As a result of the reasons outlined above and also due to air services agreement restrictions on market access, ownership and control, have forced the airlines to seek other solutions to growth by formation of alliances.

Doganis (2006) offers insights into airline alliance strategy, which involves *three* distinct phases in building long-lasting alliances. The *first phase* is orientated towards revenue generation through network expansion and joint marketing, which generate the marketing benefits of large scale and scope. The partners '*each maintain their separate brand and identity*' which explains why '*abandoning the alliance is relatively easy*'. Doganis calls the *second phase* in alliance building as commercial and focuses on cost saving while continuing and reinforcing the revenue aspects. The second stage will involve establishing separate agreements in specific areas where joint operations can reduce costs. While the number and the scope of the agreements may make it difficult to exit from the alliance, it is still possible. The *third phase* in cementing an alliance is when partners begin to co-mingle their assets and use them jointly, which may involve joint product development and the creation of joint entities to manage different aspects of their operations. Since this phase involves the adoption of single alliance brands, breaking away from the alliance at this stage becomes almost impossible. Only when nationality and ownership rules are fully relaxed, is a full operational merger foreseen.

15.3.2 Lessons (for ANSPs) From Airline Alliances

Most aviation experts continue to predict that airline alliances and air transportation cooperation in general, being a positive sum arrangement will remain a permanent feature of the aviation industry because, they create values to customers while enhancing the profit opportunities for the partners.

On closer scrutiny clear parallels exist between restrictive airline and ANS regulatory environments. To extend their network the airlines and their trade organizations have had to interact or lobby with their regulatory authorities where the evolution of the US deregulation and open skies policies and the European liberalization packages are worthy examples. IATA has been for years calling for stronger political will, with some degree of success, to harmonize aviation's increasingly outdated regulatory framework which include the existing international bilateral agreements, airline ownership rules and national regulations. While the regulatory framework (nationality provisions, traffic rights regime, cabotage rules) have acted as a disincentive to the physical absorption, merger or consolidation of the airlines, it has also provoked airlines to create global alliances as an alternative way to integrate markets and operate domestic services in a foreign market – possibly providing a valuable lesson for the ANSPs.

Learning from the existing areas of airline cooperation, cooperation involving ANSPs has the potential to improve ANS service provision and reduce costs especially through regionalizing airspace, standardizing equipment, training and procedures, joint procurement and avoiding duplication of infrastructure. The biggest hurdle between recognizing benefits and actually able to cooperate is the regulatory framework both international and national, within which the ANSPs operate.

There exist many reasons for formation of airline alliances, which are relevant and applicable to the ANS business. These include the need to share costs and risks, to create critical mass necessary to strike better deals with equipment suppliers, for system standardization and creating systems that could better service their customers.

15.3.3 ICAO Policy Support to Cooperation

Responding to the need for an effective gate-to-gate operation and to support cross-border cooperation in ANS provision, the ICAO Global ATM Operational Concept was endorsed at the ICAO 11th Air Navigation Conference (ANC), in October 2003. The Global ATM operational concept essentially describes how an integrated global ATM configuration should operate, thus providing ANSPs and industry with stated objectives for designing and implementing future air traffic management and supporting systems. This vision of a global harmonized ATM system is an indication of how the future ANS service delivery is going to evolve. Essentially, the key changes to the existing ANS structure and systems as foreseen by Howell (2003) are:

- All airspace would be a useable resource, where its management would be dynamic, with only transitory restrictions allowed. As airspace will be managed flexibly, airspace boundaries would not be constrained by national boundaries but will be adjusted to allow for efficiency of traffic flows.
- Also the vision of a Global ATM takes cognizance of collaborative decision-making, harmonization, homogeneous and traffic-routing areas, which automatically requires all stakeholders including the ANSPs to work collaboratively in order to realize a global ATM. Towards this end, ANSPs would be required to actively seek cooperative regional solutions to ANS, reduce duplication, harmonize and integrate their technology.
- In the area of conflict management the ATM system of the future will require the existence of very large sectors, complete integration of the ATC systems, minimum crossing of airspace boundaries and so on.
- Considering that the ICAO operational concept endorses that all airspace will be managed dynamically and flexibly, this will entail airspace boundaries to be adjusted to particular traffic flows and the removal of national boundary constraints. Consequently the concept promotes institutional restructuring in support of regional service provision, which will ultimately result in ANSPs consolidation. The understanding is that regional service providers will ensure cost effective services.
- From a technical perspective, the concept requires ANSPs to harmonize their equipment specifications to permit an integrated, interoperable, and flexible functionality to provide a global seamless airspace. To achieve interoperability, the ANSPs are expected to cooperate, to develop common functional and interface specifications.
- The global ATM concept seeks to increase capacity by harnessing the capability of new technology while taking into consideration the need to reduce service provision costs. Decisions cannot be taken in isolation and also the ANSPs have to forgo their traditional way of providing proprietary CNS infrastructure to a new concept which would entail the use of regional and global CNS elements.

- The Global ATM also decrees future solutions should be focused towards an optimum use of resources across the entire ATM system thus requiring strategic collaboration among the members of the ATM community. The use of information on system-wide traffic flows and infrastructure would provide the basis for centralization and optimization of assets. The reasoning here is that regional cooperation will assist ANSPs in reducing their operational costs, whilst ensuring sufficient capacity and improving safety.

15.3.4 The Single European Sky (SES) Model

From an European perspective, the formal adoption of the 'Single European Sky' (SES) legal framework by the European Commission (EC) in 2002, would lead to fundamental reform and seriously challenge the way ANS has been organized, regulated and provided thus far, especially impacting the perspective of cross border service provision (Schubert, 2003). This EC legislation contains provisions to enhance cooperation of the European ANSPs, inter alia through regulations governing:

- Development of harmonized rules on ANS provision.
- Restructuring and management of airspace based on operational efficiency irrespective of national borders (that is, Functional Blocks of Airspace or FBA).
- The creation of one EUIR (European Upper Flight Information Region) encompassing the upper airspace above the European Community.
- Mutual recognition of authorizations of ANSPs within the Community.
- Interoperability requirements for equipment (standardization of systems and procedures).
- Increased cooperation between civil and military.

On the institutional perspective, states derive their responsibility for the provision of ANS provision in accordance with the Chicago Convention. The SES raises key institutional issues relating to the foreign ownership of ANS and infrastructure assets and the need to relinquish state boundaries for ATM to appropriate 'functional blocks of airspace' designed for greater operational efficiency. This imposes serious and significant organizational changes to a state's ANS bodies. Another structural change, which the legislation will bring about, is the creation of a Single European Upper Airspace resulting in operational efficiency and seamless airspace.

With the FBA component and the cross recognition of certification, the SES also means that airspace will no longer be designed according to national borders and the state can make a decision on its preferred ANS provider on cost efficiency terms. Thus, from the perspective of a service provider one of the implications would be individual states allowing foreign organizations to provide ANS over at least parts of their territory.

As a result of the interoperability requirement, the SES would result in growing uniformity and standardization in the operations, procedures and technological systems of the ANSPs across Europe. This would also increase the opportunities for joint procurement and reduce the inefficiencies associated with the duplicated use of diverse technologies and systems. Growing uniformity of the ATC systems used across Europe will help reduce equipment cost.

An indication that there is some encouragement to cooperate in the SES is that partnerships between ANSPs are beginning to deepen and broaden as relationships are being constructed in Europe to prepare for business within a 'Single European Sky' market. Notwithstanding the progress so far, there are some essential prerequisites which will determine the success or failure of the SES initiative:

- Mindsets must adapt to the radical changes in ATM, and ANSPs have to accept the fact that cross-border cooperation is an essential aspect of SES, as some of the main activities enshrined in the SES legislation (for example, design of a FBA, establishment of a EUIR) cannot otherwise be carried out.
- Need for an ANS industry body (possibly Eurocontrol) that would facilitate the cooperative efforts of the ANSPs in achieving common standards, harmonization of operating procedures, joint projects and common airspace design.
- Also national level legal frameworks and particularly ownership and management structures must be adapted to permit cross-border cooperation, alliances, joint ventures, outsourcing of supporting functions and so on.
- Mechanisms of financial incentives could stimulate ANSPs to participate positively in SES activities.
- Need to assure the travelling public that safety is not being compromised by devolving regulation to a central non-state body.
- Drawing the rules of implementation in consultation with and support of stakeholders is equally important.

15.3.5 User Expectations: IATA's 'One Sky ... Global ATM' Vision

Worldwide airlines and their passengers paid around US$48.8 billion to airports and Air Navigational Service Providers in 2009 (IATA, 2009b). For all regions of the world, landing and airport charges plus en-route charges represent about seven per cent of the total operating costs of an airline but vary considerably from continent to continent. For example, navigation charges represented about five per cent of an airline's total costs in Europe; while in Africa/Middle East it constitutes around 5.5 per cent; whereas in Asia Pacific it represents around 2.75 per cent; and in North America it only accounts for just 1.25 per cent of total costs (IATA, 2009). Data at Eurocontrol indicated that landing and associated airport charges combined with en-route route facility charges in Europe increased by 10.1 per cent in 2007, compared to the previous year. IATA (2010b) states that 19 European states have proposed increases in 2010 over 2009 levels which will increase the cost by some $360 million. From the users' perspective, having pioneered strategic alliances to become cost efficient, it is only natural that airlines expect ANSPs to cooperate among themselves in order to realize cost efficiencies and rationalization of resources. From their perspective, cross-border cooperation would ideally result in seamless ANS sectors. Showing growing dissatisfaction with the current fragmented national focus of the ATM system, the International Air Transport Association (IATA) in 2003, launched the 'One Sky ... global ATM Vision'.

The views expressed within the IATA 'One Sky' vision have important implications for ANSPs, especially in the way their airspace needs to be structured and managed in the future. Many of the user expected service improvements contained in the document need to be implemented in contiguous regions and include:

- Business-driven approach to ANS service provision.
- Increased reliance on global infrastructure outside ANSPs immediate control.
- Global harmonization and interoperability of ground and on-board systems.
- Reorganization and simplification of airspace guided by commercial traffic flows.
- Integration of civil and military operations to optimize airspace allocation.
- Rationalization of Flight Information Regions (FIRs).

15.4 The Future ANS Business Model

There are clear developments in the industry, which require the ANSPs to respond to change. The benefits of the current 'corporatized' ANS service models seem to be tapering off. Relief from *fragmentation* and its negative impact *will require a new organizational philosophy for service provision*. The *nature of demand for service* from the airlines that operate on a regional and global basis now requires high levels of cost-efficient customer service and *safety on a regional basis across entire routes*. The introduction of *CNS/ATM technologies with regional capability* requires substantial resources and expertise that cannot be sourced within a single ANSP.

On the *regulatory* point of view, the ICAO *Global ATM Operational Concept*, fortifies ICAO's vision for an interoperable, seamless and global ATM system. Clearly each region has its own distinct cultural, economic and political conditions. The SES package has been delivered within the context of the EU (European Union) but it is also an invaluable model for other regions keen to enhance cooperation of their ANSPs. After all its main priority is reducing air traffic delays and improving cost efficiency whilst reinforcing safety. In fact, the endorsement of the ICAO Global ATM Operational concept and the adoption of the Single European Sky concept are two steps indicating that *a more holistic global or cooperative approach* needs to be taken to address the ATM sectors underperformance in the aviation value chain.

Additionally, IATA's *Global ATM Implementation Roadmap* urges governments and the air transport industry to work together, from an international perspective, to address the issue of state sovereignty over airspace and put in place measures that will effectively remove existing 'borders' in the sky.

From another aspect, taking into consideration the developments in Europe especially in the context of the Single European Sky initiative, the consequence of the separation of service provision from regulation at the national level would involve the establishment of regulators independent of the state. These independent regulators ease the way for a future centralised regional level regulator. Centralised regulation could be complemented in the future by the removal of state service provider monopolies and the creation of regional ATM service providers.

A future ANS business model would probably include schemes, which provide greater incentives to ANSPs to pursue cost efficiencies strategies including generating alternative sources of income. Also as a service provider, ANS performance in the future would be measured by its ability to meet and satisfy the needs of its customers.

It should be noted that, even in commercialized environments, the ANS service provision has retained two important characteristics, that is, it remains a monopoly service and secondly ANS remains an integrated bundle of services. Mistry and Fairbanks (2003) have advanced the idea of 'unbundling' the support operations or services from the monopoly Air Traffic Service (ATS) operations. The functions needed to support ATS include CNS infrastructure, aeronautical information services (AIS), meteorological services, training, and so on. This vertical disintegration of the ANS service provision value chain would open the opportunity for competition among new market entrants providing the ancillary services. Over a period of time it would not be hard to envisage that there would be prospects for cross-border integration of the unbundled supporting services themselves, resulting in reduced fragmentation, for example, a regional CNS provider providing the infrastructure needs of ANS.

Air Traffic Control centres of a state generally use propriety CNS infrastructure except for some cases of radar data exchange in Europe. The transition from conventional ATC to CNS/ATM requires a transition from analogue to digital CNS infrastructure. The implementation of satellite-based systems with regional capability gives the ANSPs an opportunity to test the value of merging their CNS operations into regional organizations. Future deployment will have to be managed within a regional environment context with a clear business case made and agreed by all stakeholders. One idea that has been floated involves the merging of national CNS networks into regional CNS organizations, which according to Clinch (2003) has the potential to accelerate the deployment of the new technology and create savings from the rationalization of the systems.

International cooperative ventures in the provision of air navigation services/ facilities and in the collection of related charges have proven to be cost effective for providers and users alike. Also in some instances multinational cooperation constitutes the only means for implementing costly services and facilities, which offer capacity that exceeds the requirements of individual countries. It has been confirmed by ICAO that by cooperating in such facility or service provision, states have been able to provide more cost efficient services and at a lower cost (ICAO, 2000). It is expected that in future ANSPs will give more emphasis to and appreciate the potential value of joint ventures in the provision of ANS.

The central theme of the latest developments and a main element of any future ANS business model would have to incorporate the concept of *'international cooperation'* or *'cross-border cooperation'* in the provision of ANS, hinting at a reduced role of individual nation states in the provision of ANS. Regional partnerships amongst ANSPs is a prerequisite in order to achieve the full potential in safe, cost effective service delivery within the industry. The trends and developments in ANS are pointing towards an underlying philosophical shift (illustrated in Figure 15.3) in ANS service provision, resulting in the formation of 'regional ATM systems', through the disappearance of national borders.

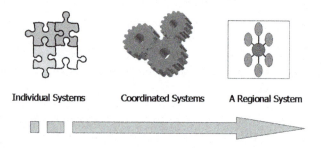

Individual Systems   Coordinated Systems   A Regional System

Figure 15.3   ANS philosophy evolution

15.5 ANSP-ANSP Collaboration

Theoretical wisdom indicates that in the Air Navigation Service (ANS) business, cooperation is part and parcel of managing air traffic flows across national boundaries through mutually maintained route networks linking airports. In fact cross border cooperation seems obvious and a must, especially since efficient flow and capacity management will be even more important in the future when air traffic figures increase dramatically within the same airspace resource. With renewed growth in air traffic the limitations of the current ATM system – scarce airspace, diverse technical systems and fragmented airspace – will become obvious challenges.

Why should two or more ANSPs cooperate? Going by the experiences of airline alliance formation, Figure 15.4 summarizes the possible reasons that could drive cooperation between ANSPs.

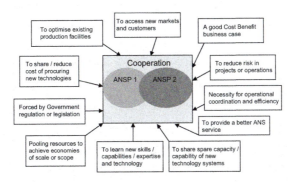

Figure 15.4   Drivers for ANSP-ANSP cooperation

Typology of ANSP–ANSP cooperation Traditionally, cooperation in ANS is constituted within the framework the ICAO and various regional organizations like EUROCONTROL, where it is not initiated and governed by the ANSPs. Singh (2006), through an exploratory global survey of ANSPs, discovered evidence that there exists a spectrum of direct ANSP–ANSP cooperation, ranging from easily implemented offers-of-training, fairly challenging activities like radar data exchanges, as well as efforts towards complex activities linked to integrated airspace and service provision (for example, the Nordic Upper Area Control or NUAC Project) . It is now possible to come across a new breed of direct ANSP–ANSP engagements outside the boundaries of the traditional government or ICAO initiated cooperation.

Commercially minded ANSPs in Europe are taking the lead in finding solutions through collaboration *relating to technology applications* (for example, cooperative development and procurement of Mode-S mono-pulse secondary surveillance radars systems, common definition, development and procurement of a next generation Flight Data Processing System, joint harmonization programmes to ensure system upgrade requirements converge). There are also some radically new direct bi-/tri-lateral agreements and projects between corporatized ANSPs to reduce cost and avoid duplication, for example, in R&D, programmes capitalizing on the cost-benefits of joint procurements, relocation of air traffic controllers, sales of technology/systems, development of common programmes to integrate and harmonize ATM services within their locale and so on. Table 15.1 is an attempt at tabulating *existing and possible* areas of cooperation among ANSPs into four different categories, distinguishing cooperative arrangements based on the associated goals of the cooperation.

Table 15.1   Categories (and areas) of cooperation in ANS

Category I: Non-operational support	Category II: Operational	Category III: Technical	Category IV: Integrated service provision
Goal: focus towards unidirectional gain, image building, voluntary commitment.	**Goal:** focus towards optimization of processes, improving traffic management, improved interoperability, achieving operational efficiency.	**Goal:** focus towards developing a commonly agreed future global ATM technology, minimizing system obsolete risk, technology integration aspects, and efficient use of resources.	**Goal:** focus on long-term commitments and buy-in of partners, institutional defragmentation, integration of airspace and ATS service provision, customer-driven service-delivery.
AREAS OF COOPERATION			
<ul><li>Membership of, and sharing information through, trade organization (CANSO).</li><li>Offering training capability.</li><li>Business consulting.</li><li>Exchange of benchmarking information.</li></ul>	<ul><li>Delegation of ATS services.</li><li>Contingency arrangements.</li><li>Common licensing.</li><li>Establishment of better airspace routings.</li><li>Harmonization of procedures.</li><li>Joint recruitment.</li><li>Operational cooperation on procedures and technical matters.</li><li>Staff exchange.</li><li>Centralised flow management.</li><li>Sharing of Met services.</li><li>Centralised billing.</li></ul>	<ul><li>Radar data exchange.</li><li>Joint R & D.</li><li>Joint procurement.</li><li>Collaboration in CNS planning.</li><li>Technology Integration.</li><li>Joint flight calibration.</li><li>Common Aeronautical Information System (AIS).</li><li>Joint development of software/equipment specifications.</li><li>Sales of operational ATM systems among ANSPs.</li><li>Sharing of CNS infrastructure.</li></ul>	<ul><li>Multinational services/facilities.</li><li>Creation of FBA'a.</li><li>Regional regulatory system.</li><li>Rationalization of maintenance and engineering services.</li><li>Joint ATC training.</li><li>Regional ATM Organization.</li><li>Joint airspace management.</li><li>Establishing joint enterprises /ventures/ financing projects.</li></ul>
TACTICAL COOPERATION		**STRATEGIC COOPERATION**	

Source: Singh, 2006.

What makes some cooperation initiatives 'tactical' and others 'strategic'? The answer lies in the objectives or goals of the cooperation. Tactical cooperation is driven by operational requirements to improve operational efficiency (for example, improved traffic management) and ANSPs generally cooperate on operational issues in one way or another, either directly or through the ICAO forum.

In the ANS business, strategic objectives for ANS cooperation will include: 'rationalization benefits', 'efficient use of resources', and 'economic benefits'. Taking into account this definition of strategic cooperation, Category III and Category IV types of cooperation (in Table 15.1) can be considered as strategic in nature as these forms of cooperation require stronger commitments, some degree of integration that produce interface reduction, efficient use of resources, enable economic benefits and allude to technical or institutional rationalization.

Essentially, environments wherein there is political and economic integration including an element of political compulsion through a regional ATM regulatory framework, commercial ATC and pressure from stakeholders/customers, will drive and create the imperative for strategic ANSP-ANSP cooperation. The lessons from Europe clearly amplify that strategic cooperation does not come 'naturally' but is now being driven by commercialization objectives and is supported by changes in the regulatory framework.

15.6 Strategies to Enhance Cooperation in ANS

Although, there is evidence to suggest that some form of 'globalization' is finally arriving in the world of ANS, strictly speaking, successful ANS cooperation activity around the world is focused more on peripheral ANS functions. What is needed is a fundamental structural change in the industry requiring a strong commitment from stakeholders. Considering that a coherent lobbying strategy to educate and influence stakeholders is critically lacking, this section proceeds to put forward a framework strategy in the form of *recommendations to the various stakeholders* on how to enhance cooperation in ANS.

The International Civil Aviation Organization (ICAO)

There is an urgent need to institutionalize a new understanding of national sovereignty at the ICAO level, which can bypass any limitations of current airspace management practices without negatively impacting upon the essence of state sovereignty. The desirable international regulatory structures on Global ATM should include guidance for convergence of national laws to achieve a common view and cooperation supporting process.

Also it is recommended that ICAO actively formulate and promote the concept of 'ATM Region' as the new way of delineating airspace based on operational requirements, encompassing major traffic flows and homogeneous areas, instead of the present concept of Flight Information Region (FIR) which is associated with the geographical national boundaries.

ANS Trade Organization (CANSO)

It is recommended that CANSO as the relevant trade organization, establish a central databank of existing ANS cooperation initiatives to provide a mechanism for tracking and demonstrating the economic and operational benefits of cooperation. The databank would provide the coordinated platform to highlight 'success stories' of cooperation and serve to communicate 'best practice' models. Strong economic evidence, existing business cases that make sense and success stories will in turn support and justify the strategies which are needed to address institutional and legal barriers to cooperation. Ensuring that successful cooperation initiatives are documented and made visible to all stakeholders will enable CANSO to demonstrate the benefits of and also develop the case for further cooperative projects.

Joint forums and working groups are required to develop a process to support a common approach to the selection and application of future technology for ATM systems. It is suggested that CANSO actively bring the cooperation partners (that is, ANSPs, airlines and their technology providers) together, where the participation of the technical staff in international working groups would improve the will to adopt solutions and working methods from each other.

Considering that major regulatory and institutional barriers to cross-border cooperation will require joint lobbying (with trade organizations of industry partners for example, IATA), to influence governments and other stakeholders, CANSO could initiate a coordinated plan of joint actions agreed upon between the partners.

Air Navigation Service Providers

To assist ANSPs to embark on the path of active cooperation, it is recommended that:

- Top-level management of ANSPs must actively support and communicate the objectives of any cooperation project. It would be essential to develop actions and processes that abolish the fear of loss of control, jobs and influence among key personnel such as air traffic controllers and unions. A phased approach would have to be pursued in contrast to a 'big bang' approach, towards any cooperation plans particularly those that require some rationalization of resources.
- ANSPs will need to commit some level of resource to follow through on cooperation programmes and not undertake this on an ad hoc basis as at the moment. This will include committing a dedicated team to set up meetings, research the value of cooperation and devise action plans.

- Strong relationships, participation and interaction with the regulatory and military authorities are needed to ensure acceptance and approval of cooperation plans.

Strategies for En-route Airspace Cooperation

It is recommended that neighbouring ANSPs meet and agree on common action plans and undertake joint cost benefit studies for cross-border airspace consolidation projects. When dealing with political masters, lobbying support from airlines and airports is also essential especially to overcome the 'sovereignty' sensitivities.

Strategies for Approach Airspace Cooperation

It is recommended that any cost benefit analysis undertaken for upper airspace consolidation should include the scenario to merge both the upper and lower airspace in the calculations and scenario definition phase. Linking en-route and lower airspace consolidation would ultimately reduce fragmentation of airspace.

Strategies for 'ATC Training' Cooperation

It is recommended that regional (SES type) legislation be developed in all regions to harmonize ATC training standards and products (including equipment) as this will create an environment that will encourage opportunities for cooperation. Another strategy would be to develop a rationalization programme on a regional basis, that is, starting with a survey of training approaches and capabilities by each identified region, a rationalization programme could be developed, which could include (i) identification of those who are willing to outsource, (ii) agreement on common licence recognition and standardization of training content with agreed global standards, (iii) allocation to specific ATC training establishments the responsibility for particular types of training, (iv) sharing of personnel and equipment, (v) joint procurement of simulators and/or (vi) establishment of a regional ATC training centre.

Strategies for 'Safety Management' Cooperation

One suggestion for the ANSPs would be to emulate the IATA Operational Safety Audit (IOSA) scheme, which provides an industry 'standard' for assessing operational management and control systems of airlines. The programme aims to improve safety, save money and time by cutting down on redundant audits. Opportunities may exist for harmonization of ANSP operational management when the principles of an IOSA-style audit are applied to safety audits of ANSPs.

Strategies for 'Joint ATM System Development and Procurement' Cooperation

It is recommended that, as a first step, neighbouring ANSPs sit down and identify the key differences in operational procedures and systems. In order to achieve significant cost savings, it is necessary to coordinate requirements and equipment specifications between a critical mass of ANSPs. One suggestion of undertaking this is through a unified effort to agree on and publish functional and technical requirements. A coordinated plan needs to be agreed between ANSPs for replacement of legacy systems and migration to standard protocols. It is envisaged that joint procurement of complex ATM systems would occur naturally as a downstream activity after the creation of a common base system, or through a shared view for ANS system development between the ANSPs. To promote joint procurement, the ANSPs would also have to develop unified procedures and rules for procurement. Also purchasing commercial-off-the-shelf (COTS) products with the potential of continued development should be given priority over customized alternatives.

Strategies for 'Equipment Standardization'

It is recommended that ANSPs jointly adopt standardized requirements for their high specification ATM equipment (which are also the high expenditure items). Cooperation in the technology dimension appears to be a two-step process. Considering the ANSPs have near identical functional requirements for the majority of their systems, cooperation between the ANSPs to create common functional specifications is the first step. Once the functionality and standardization has been agreed, the actual technical specification can be left to a consortium of Technology Suppliers and ANSPs, where the presence of the ANSPs will ensure there is no room for misinterpretation of the functionality. The focus should be on developing a standardized product in order to eliminate duplication and waste in the supply chain.

Strategies for Satisfying 'Customer Expectations'

Cooperation between the ANSPs and airlines will allow optimized allocation of resources focused on the needs of the customer (airlines). It is recommended for the ANSPs and customers to consult effectively prior to major investments.

ANS Technology Providers

It is recommended that Technology Providers must recognize the contribution ANSP operational experts can make in the development of new better quality solutions. Technology Providers can gain valuable feedback from *joint developments* and should pass on some of the benefits derived from such cooperation, by striving to offer more realistic cost for future enhancements and upgrades to participating

ANSPs, giving due consideration to the fact that such products can be further developed to suit new customers with limited customization.

Technology Providers by adopting a wider industry view and understanding the pressures coming down the supply chain (that is, especially the demands the airspace users may put on the ANSPs), should cooperate with the ANSPs to deliver solutions in a cost-effective way.

It is also suggested that the Technology Providers have to play an active role in *standardization of system solutions*. The Technology Providers role includes avoiding unnecessary development of new products while promoting off the shelf products tailored for evolutionary development. By adopting open systems architecture, relying less on company standards to protect their product lines and developing standard module based systems, the technology providers can contribute towards the overall standardization and interoperability of ANS technology.

ANS Customers (Airlines)

It is recommended that the airlines make an effort to understand the long-term nature of ANS infrastructure planning and development and especially to take cognizance of the fact that ANS infrastructure *'does not materialize instantly just when you need it'*. Airlines have to be more specific and clearer about their requirements in terms of *'the definition, planning and development of the future ANS system'* and also *'reconcile the different needs of the airspace users'*. Overall a close consultation process including an *understanding of each other's limitations and constraints* could allow a better and quicker response to airlines requirements.

It is also recommended that the airlines support and allow for the establishment of rate stabilization funds and a fairer cost recovery system for ANSPs.

Regional Organizations and Regulators

It is recommended that regional political organizations take a more proactive role in steering ATM policy including rule-making authority to advance cooperation on a regional basis. It is also natural that support and funding from regional organizations can be effective in promoting cooperation in ANS.

The regulatory framework, in which an ANSP operates, influences its ability to adopt certain technologies it needs, to achieve efficiencies. For example, harmonization of technical regulations will in turn support the introduction of harmonized systems and encourage cooperation. It is the role of regulators to push and create such win/win situations.

15.7 Concluding Remarks

The idea of an ICAO Global ATM concept is ahead of the political, technological and operational reality on the ground. There is inconsistency between international policies with the current nature of national laws with their inherent concept of 'national sovereignty'. Probably one weakness of the ICAO endorsed Global ATM Concept is the fact that it does not specifically address the national-level legal, regulatory and political environment.

Equipment standardization is a strategic issue for the ANS industry. More intense cooperation initiatives can be expected from (systems) technology standardization. Unnecessary cost can be driven out of the supply chain through the agreement of all ANSPs on standardized or global user requirements and a *jointly* (that is, ANSP and Technology Provider) *agreed development roadmap for future technology and systems*, would ultimately bring about the full benefits of cooperation.

Finally, if one wishes to offer a prescription for success of 'cooperation in ANS' in the future, then the conclusion this chapter offers is that: 'there are signs that globalization is arriving in ANS, but in the face of the institutional barriers, further progress is dependent on the scale and dynamics of the ANS industry itself, including the strategies ANSPs employ to interact with the regulatory/public bodies and other stakeholders, as this alone will result in the abandonment of those aspects of the regulatory regime that curtails cooperation in ANS'.

References

Air Transport Action Group (2009), facts and figures. Available at: www.atag.org/content/showfacts.asp?folderid=430&level1=2&level2=430&.

Brooker, P. (2002), Future air traffic management systems and financial decision-making constraints, Research Report CU/SOE/RR/PB/3/1/02, 25 March, Cranfield University, UK.

Burton, J. and Hanlon, P. (1994), Airline alliances: cooperating to compete?, *Journal of Air Transport Management*, vol. 1, no. 4, pp. 209–227.

Clinch, P. (2003), *Benefits of Regional CNS Operations*. CANSO News, Edition 13, April.

Doganis, R. (2006), *The Airline Business*, 2nd Edition, Routledge, Oxon, UK.

Eurocontrol (2010), Performance Review Report, an assessment of Air Traffic Management in Europe during the Calendar Year 2009, May, Brussels, Belgium.

Eurocontrol (2006), The impact of fragmentation in European ATM/CNS – report prepared by Helios Economics and Policy Services, Report commissioned by the Eurocontrol Performance Review Commission, April.

Gudmundsson, S.V. and Lechner, C. (2006). Multilateral airline alliances: Balancing strategic constraints and opportunities, *Journal of Air Transport Management*, 1(3), pp. 153–158.

Gudmundsson, S.V. and Oum, T.H. (2005), Airline networks and alliances for strategic performance, *Journal of Air Transport Management*, 11(3), pp. 125–126.

Gudmundsson, S.V. and Rhoades, D.L. (2001), Airline alliance survival analysis: typology, strategy and duration, *Transport Policy*, 8, pp. 209–218.

Holmberg, S.R. and Cummings, J.L. (2009), Building Successful Strategic Alliances, Strategic Process and Analytical Tool for Selecting Partner Industries and Firms, *Long Range Planning*, 42(2), pp. 164–193.

Howell, J. (2003), Groundbreaking initiative in spotlight at pivotal conference, *ICAO Journal*, vol. 58, no. 5, pp. 8–9, International Civil Aviation Organization, Montreal.

IATA (2010), Fact Sheet: Single European Sky (SES). Available at: www.iata.org/pressroom/facts_figures/fact_sheets/Pages/ses.aspx.

IATA (2010b), Air Navigation Service Providers Increase Prices in Europe. Available at: www.iata.org/pressroom/airlines-international/february-2010/pages/07.aspx.

IATA (2009). Economic Briefing Infrastructure Costs, July. Available at: www.iata.org/NR/rdonlyres/4929507D-5B4B-430B-A52C-A201BBE1A434/0/Infrastructure_Costs_Jul09.pdf.

IATA (2009b), Annual Report, 65th Annual General Meeting, Kuala Lumpur, Malaysia, June.

IATA (2008). All for one, *Air Traffic Technology International*, UKiP, Surrey, pp. 22–23.

Iatrou, K. and Alamdari, F. (2005). The empirical analysis of the impact of alliances on airline operations, *Journal of Air Transport Management*, 11(3), pp. 127–134.

ICAO (2000), WP/5 – International Cooperative Ventures, In: Conference on the economics of airports and air navigation services, Montreal, 19–28 June.

Klooster, J. (2009). Improving air traffic efficiency, *Aircraft Technology*, Issue 103, December, pp. 20–25.

Mistry, H. and Fairbanks, M. (2003), ANS providers place strong emphasis on implementing best practices, *ICAO Journal*, vol. 58, no. 3, pp. 12–14, International Civil Aviation Organization, Montreal.

Morrish, S.C. and Hamilton, R.T. (2002), Airline alliances – who benefits?, *Journal of Air Transport Management*, 8, pp. 401–407.

Oum, T.H. and Park, J.H. (1997), Airline alliances: current status, policy issues, and future directions, *Journal of Air Transport Management*, 3(3), pp. 133–144.

Pitfield, D.E. (2007), The impact on traffic, market shares and concentration of airline alliances on selected European-US routes, *Journal of Air Transport Management*, 1(4), pp. 192–202.

Schubert, F. (2003), The single European sky controversial aspects of cross-border service provision, *Air and Space Law*, vol. XXVIII/1, February, pp. 32–49.

Singh, M. (2006), Aspects of cooperation in air navigation services: Current status and future directions, PhD Thesis, Cranfield University, United Kingdom.

US GAO (2005), Air Traffic Control: Characteristics and performance of selected international air navigation service providers and lessons learned from their commercialization, United States Government Accountability Office Report to Congressional Requesters, GAO-05-769, July, Washington DC.

Whelan, C. (2001), Evaluating and improving worldwide implementation of future air navigation systems, PhD Thesis, Cranfield University, United Kingdom.

Chapter 16

IT Innovations in Passenger Services

John F. O'Connell

16.1 The Early Days

Investment in Information Technology (IT) within the airline industry did not really begin in earnest until the late 1950s. In the early days the reservation systems were at the forefront of technology within the aviation industry. American Airlines, an early pioneer in the use of commercial computer technology, had developed a semi-automated customer reservation system called Reservisor by 1960. The system's original core purpose was to minimize the clerical costs of managing and booking inventory which at that time was characterized by a two-hour process to complete a booking and reservation that could only be made 30 days in advance. Recognizing that semi-automatic systems would not be capable of handling the rapidly increasing demand for air travel, American Airlines had already begun working with IBM to develop the first automated, online, real-time Computerized Reservation System (CRS) called the Semi-Automated Business Research Environment (SABRE). The joint project would use interactive, real-time computing technology developed for a US government air defence project referred to as Semi-Automatic Ground Environment (Eklund, 1994). Most of the computing systems that existed in the 1960s were batch processing systems, but SABRE was an early example of a transaction processing system. It modified the content of the large databases containing flight and passenger information as a direct result of information entered directly from data terminals. Information that was available in a single repository offered an invaluable source of data to assist in other critical functions associated with the planning of capacity and the organization and planning of logistics and supply chain elements such as baggage handling, food and fuel planning. *Fortune Magazine* (1985) reported that American Airlines invested $350 million into SABRE in the mid 1960s, which was enough to purchase seven DC-10 jets.[1] Within five years 8,000 travel agents across the US had leased Sabre terminals. Meanwhile United Airlines, the largest US airline,

---

1   The McDonnell Douglas DC-10 was a three-engined widebody aircraft that had a typical load range of 6,220 miles (10,010 km) and it carried around 250 passengers in a 2-class seating configuration. The DC-10 was succeeded by the related MD-11 which entered service in 1990. The Orbis Flying eye hospital has chosen to replace their ageing DC-10 with a MD-10, which has an upgraded avionics package similar to the MD-11 glass cockpit, which eliminates the need for a flight engineer.

captured 6,000 travel agents with its competing Apollo terminals. Three other airlines TWA, Eastern and Delta followed with weak, belated systems of their own. These reservation systems had revolutionized the travel agency business.

Over the next two decades, airlines continued to learn how investments in information technology could deliver tangible benefits across the full passenger management process. Reservation systems gradually evolved into more sophisticated GDSs which were able to process large amounts of data and to connect more and more industry stakeholders.

Some airlines, notably American and United, eventually established leadership positions through IT innovation – but what is key is where IT innovation was applied. In the case of American and United it was the innovativeness of applying Information Technology to airline pricing and distribution, which at the time was beyond their organizational boundaries, which warranted such leadership and ingenuity. Neither organization at the time was considered a particular IT leader in the industry, yet both of these airlines specifically carved out significant competitive advantages through the application of IT (Segars and Grover, 1995). While deregulation of the industry created an opportunity for radical innovation, both American and United rapidly evolved a core competency in business led technology innovation which enabled them to both identify and rapidly exploit these opportunities much more effectively than the competition. In essence, technology is a crucial driver of innovation, which in turn is a driver of progress (Hooper, 1990; Franke, 2007).

16.2 Technology Has Become the Industry's Game Changer

Buhalis and Law (2008) have stated that the Internet is one of the most influential technologies that has certainly changed the behaviour of travellers. The world's airlines have built up a dependency on information technology, needing it to optimize their competitiveness, while balancing the level of investment to avoid IT costs undermining their profitability. The interconnectivity between passengers, aircraft, airports and staff through an IT system is essential to make the air transport process work.[2] Passengers interface with airline IT systems all the way from buying tickets through flying safely and securely with their bags from the departure to arrival airport. The passenger interfaces directly with

---

2   A host of passenger service systems for example are connected to flight inventory and schedules systems together with pricing and revenue management tools which enable carriers to maximise their yields. There are also multiple connections into all the sales channels such as the website, call centres, travel agents, corporate accounts and GDSs. In addition loyalty programs are interlinked to customer relationship management systems, while the host reservation system communicates to the departure control module that may also include a ground handling company. The IT functionality also needs to download flown revenue into the revenue accounting system. The complexity is apparent.

some of the systems, such as the airline website, but does not see the complex jigsaw of underground IT systems linking airlines to an ecosystem of suppliers and regulators. IT systems ensure high quality and have optimized the efficiency of airside and landside services (Zhang and Zhang, 2003; Sigala, 2004; Suzuki et al., 2004). The three major airline alliances (Oneworld, SkyTeam and STAR) carried over 52 per cent of global traffic in 2009 but the complexity that existed between the different airline IT platforms made it very difficult to interconnect their various database systems.[3] Air France and KLM merged in 2004 and Airline Business (2010) reported that the carriers immediately began combining their IT infrastructures, but it would take eight years (to 2012) before 95 per cent of Air France and KLM passenger commercial IT activities would have a standardized platform. The Air France-KLM group has to manage relationships with more than 70 million passengers, many of them travelling on multiple connections, with multiple airlines throughout the SkyTeam alliance network. However, single systems[4] built on state-of-the-art technological infrastructure and software, are now enhancing customer service functionalities, specifically for sales and airport environments, including such transactions as schedule, seat availability, inventory, reservations, fare quotations and ticketing, as well as passenger check-in. The improvement in customer service will come through ease of use as well as through the provision of better quality and common data for airline service agents when dealing with alliance customers.

Each year for the last 11 years, SITA co-sponsored by Airline Business, conducts a major global survey of the world's airlines[5] to track the key technology trends in the airline industry and for the last six years it has also surveyed the world's airports.[6] Figure 16.1 reveals that 57 per cent of the surveyed airlines cited that the principle reason why they invest in IT was because it decreased their overall costs. Fuel costs are largely outside the control of the carrier and

---

3 Each airline in an alliance has its own back-end check-in, passenger handling and baggage control system and applications. Industry data indicates that it can take up to five years to create a common IT platform for check-in and passenger handling systems that can interface seamlessly with other carriers. However, these systems require a significant investment in technology and IT departments struggle to secure adequate budgets to finance such projects, which undermines their profitability and competitiveness.

4 A typical example of an incompatible IT system is as follows: the rock band U2 is playing their last concert for 2010 in Dublin and there is a booking spike, so the revenue manager closes out the low-fare booking classes. The schedule manager visualises the booking spike and decides to operate a larger aircraft. A common commercial single platform will prevent the revenue and schedule manager from working at cross-purposes.

5 SITA has surveyed 116 airlines from around the world in its 2009 annual survey. This represented about half the airlines in the 2008 Airline Business top 100 financial rankings.

6 SITA has surveyed 172 airports from around the world in its 2009 annual survey. This represented about 69 per cent of the revenues and 60 per cent of the traffic among the top 100 airports financial and traffic rankings for 2009.

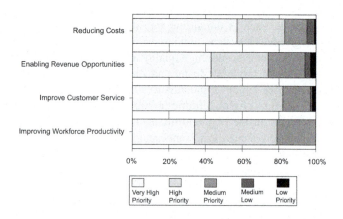

Figure 16.1   The key reasons why airlines are investing in IT (2009 data)
Source: SITA/Airline Business IT Survey July 2009.

have fluctuated greatly over the past decade as they represented just 12–13 per cent of an airline's operating costs in 2003,[7] but by 2008 fuel costs had escalated to around 32 per cent (IATA, 2010). However, IT is a mechanism that can reduce the cost burden for airlines in a relatively short period and its effect is often visible within one year after the IT system is implemented. Table 16.1 shows the cost of labour and distribution[8] for British Airways from 2000/01 to 2008/09 and the table clearly shows the sharp fall in distribution costs as around 67.5 per cent of these expenses have been removed, which is directly attributed to IT. Labour continues to be a difficult expense to reduce and IATA's research on labour costs pertaining to European airlines from 2000/01 to 2008/09 also showed that it had only marginally reduced, which is similar to the British Airways example as shown in Table 16.1 – thus highlighting the difficulty in controlling some of costs associated with the airline industry.

A second area where airlines have prioritized IT investment is in enabling revenue opportunities (see Figure 16.1 above) such as ancillary revenues (See Chapter 5 for a detailed account of ancillary revenues). IT has played a fundamental role in enabling airlines to leverage additional revenues that would have been difficult through the traditional travel agent route. IdeaWorks, a leading authority on the research of ancillary revenue, stated that airlines had generated around €1.7 billion in ancillary revenues in 2006, but by 2008 this had jumped by 345 per cent to €7.6 billion (Straus, 2008; IdeaWorks 2009). Table 16.2 shows that ancillary revenues have become a dominant mechanism by which to produce additional

---

7   The average price of a barrel of oil in 2003 was US$34.7, while in 2008 it rocketed to an *average* price of US$126 (IATA, 2010). Fuel hedging is now a commonplace strategy for controlling costs, but very costly if it is miscalculated.

8   Distribution costs are the costs incurred in selling tickets.

Table 16.1   British Airways cost structure (labour and fuel) from 2000/01 to 2008/09

	2000/01	2003/04	2008/09	% Difference 2001 v 2008
Labour Costs	£2,376	£2,180	£2,193	–8%
Distribution	£1,135	£554	£369	–67.5%

Note: Year ends 31 March.
Source: British Airways Investor Relations Annual Reports (2001; 2004, 2009).

Table 16.2   Ancillary revenue as a per cent of total revenues 2006 and 2008

2006		2008	
Ryanair	16.2%	Allegiant	22.7%
Vueling	14.2%	Ryanair	19.3%
Allegiant	12.8%	easyJet	15.5%
Air Deccan	9.0%	Jet2.com	14.8%
easyJet	8.8%	Vueling	14.1%

Source: IdeaWorks (2009) and Moores (2010).

revenues as it made up almost 23 per cent of Allegiant Airlines total revenues and over 19 per cent of Ryanair's[9] in 2008. Chandler (2010) states that passengers travelling on Allegiant Airlines pay: $5–25 per assigned seat per segment; $5–8.50 for priority boarding; $15–20 per checked bag per segment; and $14 convenience fee to book a seat via the website, and analysis reveals that ancillary revenue per passenger amounted to $33.35 in its 2009 third quarter results. Ryanair's direct link from its website to hotels, car rental companies, insurance companies, and so on, allows customers to build a tailor-made package which suits their individual needs in a flexible and interactive way. Each time a customer selects a hotel for example – a commission or kick-back is paid to the carrier. Network airlines also now capitalize on ancillary revenues as American Airlines for example generated over €1.6 billion from a combination of: à la carte pricing; commission based services; and frequent flyer activities in 2008. In fact IATA expects that non-ticket revenue will make up 12 per cent of airline turnover in 2010 (Moores, 2010). Indeed, the new technology applied to airline websites has produced a paradigm shift in the way that airlines are generating income.

---

9   Ancillary revenue accounted for 23 per cent of Ryanair's total revenues for the first quarter of 2010.

Despite the obvious savings and innovative platforms that IT produces, both airlines and airports have been reducing their IT spend over the last number of years. Figure 16.2 shows that airline spending on information technology and telecommunications dropped to 1.8 per cent of revenue in 2010, the lowest level since 2002, when there was an aviation-industry crisis after 9/11. Research indicates that airlines worldwide are focusing on supporting and rebuilding older IT systems rather than on investing in new systems which keeps carriers locked in 'legacy' processes and behind the technology curve. Meanwhile, Airport spending on IT has also sharply declined reaching three per cent of revenues by 2009, but overall there has been a 35 per cent decrease since 2005 – which is a significant reduction. This overall trend in cutting the IT spend is a direct reflection of the difficult trading environment that aviation faces as the airline industry lost $28 billion over the last two years (2008 and 2009), but is expected to post a $2.5 billion profit in 2010. Many airports cannot afford to expand their airport terminals either because of environmental concerns or budget limitations, so an increasing number are turning to technology to ensure that they are equipped to meet future demand. IT solutions are a way to increase the passenger handling capacity of their existing infrastructure and reduce the need to erect expensive terminals and concourses.

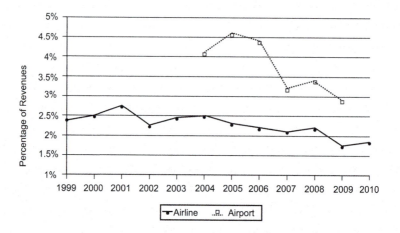

Figure 16.2   IT investment as a percentage of revenues – 1999 to 2010
Source: SITA/*Airline Business*, IT Survey Trends, July 2009.

16.3 Technology's Impact on Passenger Services

Technology has generated a new paradigm shift in the way that business is being conducted in the aviation world. Over the past decade, airlines increasingly have encouraged passengers to use their websites to book tickets and check-in for flights, as well as to use self-service kiosks in airports. At the same time, online commerce has expanded rapidly, with consumers becoming more accustomed to making high-value purchases from the comfort of home. Airlines with distinctive competencies in IT have an outright competitive advantage. Premium services such as 'Off-airport check-in' facilities are now being offered by airlines as a differentiating strategy, which enables passengers to check-in baggage from the hotel reception desk.[10]

16.3.1 The Impact of the Internet on the Airline Industry

Once on the Internet, all companies are global, and many companies are looking at e-commerce options. The emergence of the Internet has empowered individuals and organizations to access a plethora of multimedia information and knowledge sources, regardless of their location for a very low cost or in many cases, free of charge. It is estimated that around 1.9 billion people were using the Internet worldwide in June 2010, which represents 28.7 per cent of the world's population (Internet World Stats, 2010). Over the last 15 years, the Internet has produced a dramatic change in airline distribution as globally more than a third of all sales have shifted to the Internet (Sobie, 2010). There has been a rapid rise in number of consumers that use the Internet for travel purposes and travel-related products have become the largest category of goods sold on the Internet (Yu, 2008). KLM's website for example received approximately 3,000 visitors per week in 1997, while 10 years later the website attracted more than 1 million weekly visitors. In 2001, the site raised average monthly revenues of €0.5 million, whereas the monthly online revenues in 2007 were approximately €156 million (Harison and Boonstra, 2008).

The potential to sell online is enormous as people have become more comfortable at giving their credit and debit card details to airline e-commerce websites because the customers' trust in the security of the airlines' payment settlement systems has matured over the years. Research into the subject area of how people accept IT technologies has been ongoing for a number of years under the auspices of the Technology Acceptance Model (TAM). This was proposed initially by Davis (1986) and has been extensively utilized by researchers[11] and practitioners in order to predict and explain users' acceptance of Information

---

10   Research has indicated that 29 per cent of passengers would like to use remote check-in *and* baggage drop off facilities into the future (*Air Transport World*, 2009).

11   See research work by Davis, Bagozzi and Warshaw (1989); Lam et al. (2007); and Kim et al. (2008).

Technology or IT-related applications. The theory suggests that when users are presented with a new technology – there are two principle factors that influence their decision about how and when they will use it, which include:

- The perceived usefulness.
- Perceived ease-of-use.

Airline websites are becoming more user friendly by using more service orientated architecture together with interactive graphical user interfaces and are an important tool, whereby customers can compare fares, schedules, in-flight products, and so on, in the comfort of their homes without the bias from travel agents which could sway a passenger's decision about choosing a particular carrier. Jupiter Research (2007) estimated that over 60 million users in Europe will buy their travel online by 2010, while Ruiz-Mafé et al. (2009) stated that airline tickets are the most popular item sold on the Internet in Spain in 2007 – amounting to 36.5 per cent of the total e-commerce volume. In the US, UAPT (2010) reported that sales through airline websites have continued to prosper, capturing 65 per cent of sales in 2010. It also estimates that online sales in the US will grow to $355 billion by 2012 – this clearly indicates that the website will become 'the financial engine' of the airline as more and more revenues will be generated from this channel.

Ryanair attracts around 18 million visitors to its website every month in 2010, while 99 per cent of its sales are conducted through the Internet. In particular, low-cost carriers around the world now use the Internet as the primary driver for selling tickets as: Southwest Airlines presently sells 80 per cent through southwest.com; Virgin America sells 75 per cent; Virgin Blue and Air Asia both sell 65 per cent (Sobie, 2010 and Pilling 2008). Lufthansa currently sells 25 per cent online and this is largely because the full service airlines rely more heavily on travel agents, which are widely dispersed across all the major towns and cities throughout the world and this wider scope of distribution channels allows network airlines to capture both the business and leisure traveller market. Thus distribution is generally the third largest operating cost for full service airlines after fuel and labour. Indirect distribution costs use a third party such as a travel agent to sell tickets and include the following expense elements: commissions to travel agents;[12] override commissions;[13] administration costs; transaction fees for the computerized reservation systems that facilitated the transactions, and so on. Doganis (2006, p. 204) estimated that 67 per cent of these distribution costs could be saved by booking directly online via the airline's own website, and Jarach's

---

12   Commissions to travel agents in the US and Europe have largely been eliminated, but commissions are still paid in parts of Asia, and in most countries in the Middle East and Africa.

13   Override commission is an additional commission percentage paid when a certain volume of sales is achieved.

(2002) research suggested that sales through an airline website are four times cheaper than through travel agencies and computer reservation systems.

The rapid development of the Internet has also triggered the development of major Online Travel Agencies (OTAs) such as Expedia, Travelocity, and Orbitz. OTAs act as global portals providing a one-stop travel-shopping facility to consumers, allowing them to gather information and book all their travel needs on a single site. These distribution channels, which are referred to as OTA platforms, quickly became a popular mechanism to book air travel and they comprise a significant proportion of today's online travel transactions. For example, an estimated 15 per cent of the US$40 billion air travel market in the United States flows through OTAs (Offutt, 2007), with an even higher percentage in Asia where the overall online travel market is growing rapidly (Burka et al., 2008). Castillo-Manzano and López-Valpuesta (2010) researched the distribution patterns of the Spanish travel market and uncovered that customers were increasingly switching from using the traditional travel agencies to online travel agencies – in a random sample of 15,000 travellers, they found that 27 per cent of the bookings were through airline websites, 36 per cent were with online travel agencies and the remaining 37 per cent with traditional travel agencies. This signals the importance of the online distribution channel, which is rapidly increasing and is only made possible because of the Internet.

16.3.2 Self-Service Check-in and Kiosk

The traditional check-in process consisted of a passenger handing their ticket to an airline check-in agent who then inputted the ticket details into a computer system which in-turn issued the passenger's boarding pass. However, recent technological advances in the service industry has led to the transformation of this service delivery, from face-to-face service encounters to self-service. Paperless travel has now become a key component of IATA's 'simplifying the business' initiative. SITA conducted a Passenger Self-Service Survey[14] on 2,193 passengers in early 2009 and found that almost half of the respondents would prefer to have an electronic boarding version of their boarding pass (SITA, 2009). The check-in service has been revolutionized by having multiple check-in options such as through a home PC, through self-service kiosks or via a mobile phone. This allows passengers to cut down on time wasted by standing in queues. Kiosks are being increasingly shared by several airlines (that is, Common User Self-Service kiosks), during different times of the day, depending on flight schedules. This process helps both airlines and airports to lower costs and improve operational

---

14   The 4th annual SITA / Air Transport World Passenger Self-Service (PSS) survey conducted in 2009 is an in-depth look at the attitudes and habits of a representative sample of the 232 million passengers who use six leading international airports: Hartsfield-Jackson, Atlanta; Mumbai International; Charles de Gaulle, Paris; Moscow Domodedovo; Sao Paulo Guarulhos, Brazil; and OR Tambo Airport, Johannesburg.

efficiencies. Jenner (2009) stated that around a quarter of all airports are already monitoring passenger wait times by using video analytics[15] and they wish to create value for the passenger by shortening the wait time. Research has shown that many passengers are now prepared to give confidential data in order to speed their way through airport terminals as security is a bottleneck as it's frequently creates a backlog of frustrated passengers. The 2009 SITA/Airline Business survey shown in Figure 16.3 reveals that that around half of the world's airlines today use kiosks and it also illustrates that 60 per cent of surveyed airlines already use web check-in, while nearly all the carriers will have implemented it by 2010. Web check-in came later than self-service kiosks, so the application has not had the same uptake by passengers. To increase the penetration of web check-in, all carriers should have embedded applications that send reminder emails 24 hours prior to departure. Travelport's 'Viewtrip' for example offers such a web check-in product and it is used by some of the US majors such as United and Delta. Figure 16.3 also shows that an increasing number of carriers (25 per cent) are offering mobile or cellular phones to check-in.

Both airlines and airports are aiming for paperless check-in as the traditional boarding document that includes a magnetic stripe (ATB2) that will be replaced by an IATA industry-standard 2-D barcode known as a Bar Code Boarding Pass (BCBP). This allows passengers to check in via the web or a mobile phone. The IATA Board has mandated that all its member carriers should migrate from magnetic stripe to the 2-D bar-code standard by the end of 2010. Leopold (2009) indicates that the incentive will save the industry around US$1.5 billion a year in costs. Some airports throughout the world are already 2-D bar code compliant such as Canada's Montreal-Trudeau Airport. However, there are many challenges facing the initiative as the Transportation Security Administration in the United States for example requires that the 2-D barcode contains a digital signature. Elsewhere in the world the Singaporean government requires that the BCBP be validated against the airline Departure Control System (DCS). Another major challenge is ensuring the compatibility of 2-D BCBPs on a global scale. Tickets are issued all over the world on many different systems, but they all need to interoperate with airport equipment regardless of which airport the passenger is travelling to and from. Figure 16.3 above shows that over 75 per cent of airlines will enable passengers to check-in by Kiosk by 2010. Kiosks use a smaller surface area footprint than a traditional check-in desk, which ultimately results in a more efficient use of space as well as a reduction in costs in the long term. The cost savings are enormous as a traditional check-in agent costs about $3.65 per passenger, while a self-service

---

15   These cameras operate in real time and utilise software algorithms to detect specific activities and scan for suspicious individuals. For instance, cameras with facial recognition technology work to help authorities find terrorist threats and marked individuals on government watch lists. Using behavioural recognition technology, cameras can be programmed to detect incidents such as left objects, congestion, and reverse movement of passengers through checkpoints.

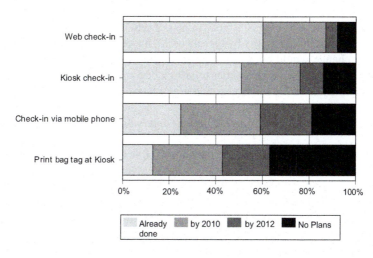

Figure 16.3   Implementation of self service functionality (2009 data)
Source: SITA/Airline Business IT Survey.

kiosk reduces this to 52 cents, with the cost for checking in using a 2-D Bar Code
Boarding Pass just 16 cents (Hooke, 2005; Croft, 2006). Ryanair for example
has indicated that it will eliminate all airport check-in desks, which would
save the carrier €50 million overall (Air Transport Intelligence, 2009). Like all
technological innovations such as kiosks, the cost reduces over time. In 2004, the
cost of purchasing a kiosk hovered around $40,000, but by 2007 it had reduced to
around $10,000 (Jane's Airport Review, 2004; Sobie, 2007). This allowed airlines
to install numerous kiosks at airports across their entire networks. Jonas (2005)
reported that United Airlines deployed 1,200 kiosks at 35 major US airports, while
America West, Continental, Delta Air Lines and other major US airlines installed
between 200 and 1,000 check-in kiosks at several major US airports. However,
the growth and popularity of web and mobile applications look set to overshadow
kiosks as a check-in channel – indeed, airlines in some regions that have yet to
implement kiosks may simply leapfrog this evolutionary stage and go straight to
web/mobile phone check-in.

However, there is plenty of life left in the kiosk as a self-service channel, as
an increasing number of airlines are seeking ways to evolve it further. They could
be used as an effective platform to sell ancillary products while passengers are
waiting in the departure hall prior to boarding their flight. Here, the airline has a
collective audience and passengers could use the kiosk to purchase an upgrade to
business class, or to buy a preferred seat such as a window or aisle seat. Another
evolutionary trend of kiosks that is gaining traction is the printing of baggage tags.
Presently, if a passenger checks-in online but also wants to check-in a bag, there is
a problem as travellers cannot print a bag tag at home, so kiosks may increasingly

be used for printing bag tags[16] – close to 45 per cent of airlines will have adopted this type of kiosk functionality by the end of 2010 (see Figure 16.3). However, the next step change would be for multiple airlines to use the same kiosk[17] (that is, Common Use Self-Service) in order to print a bag tag – it seems the next logical extension to enhance the robustness and use of kiosks.

16.3.3 Mobile Phones and Their Expanding Application to the Aviation Industry

According to the United Nations, there are 4 billion mobile phone subscribers, while there are around 2.3 billion people travelling by air (International Telecommunications Union, 2008). This suggests that the penetration rate of mobile phone users may be close to 100 per cent. Paul Coby, SITA's chairman and British Airway's Chief Information Officer, stated that more people have access to mobile telephones than to personal computers; estimates show that saturation coverage of PCs in Scandinavia is around 60 per cent, compared with more than 95 per cent for mobile phones (Baker, 2007). Thus, it is very possible that mobile phones may be used as the principle medium for storing or holding a boarding pass, thus signalling a trend that paperless travel could be fast approaching. SITA's Passenger Self-Service Survey in early 2009 concluded that almost half of the respondents would prefer to have an electronic boarding version of their boarding pass (SITA, 2009). The boarding pass would be an image of an encrypted bar code displayed on the phone's screen, which can be scanned by gate agents and security personnel. Japan Airlines started the nation's first mobile-based boarding procedure[18] back in 2003 whereby passengers can select a seat and request that an electronic boarding pass be transmitted to their mobile phone from their home PC. Sobie (2007) explained that this type of boarding process was growing in momentum in Japan as between 10,000 – 15,000 All Nippon Airways (ANA) customers used this type of device to check-in every day back in 2006. Jenner (2010) stated that ANA sold 15 per cent of all its internet sales through mobile phones in 2010, which equates to around $438 million in sales. Air Canada, has

---

16   Some technology companies (e.g. BagDrop) are now providing self-service check-in with an automated bag drop facility. The system identifies passengers via a multi-interface platform by scanning their: passport; or the bar code from their web check-in paper print out; or from the barcode on their mobile phone. The system then retrieves the booking and reservation to verify the passenger's flight details and then takes the passenger through various security questions. Thereafter the baggage tag is printed and is attached by the passenger where it is then placed on a receptacle which has the hardware and capability to read the bag tag where it is also weighted and measured for size. Any overweight and oversized bags must be manually dealt with. The system then prints a baggage receipt for the passenger.

17   Airlines remain reluctant to share facilities. This can be the case even within alliances. For example, Madrid's terminal 4 has over 50 CUSS kiosks, but only Iberia uses them despite oneworld partners (BA and AA) operating from the same terminal.

18   This procedure can only be used on Japanese domestic flights.

been using electronic boarding passes with its mobile check-in service since 2007, for flights to both domestic and international destinations except to those in the United States and by mid 2010 it was issuing 25,000 mobile boarding passes each week. Australia's Virgin Blue now offers bookings, flight changes, cancellations, check-in and 2-D boarding passes by mobile phone. It has also proposed additional functionality that will allow its passengers to add in-flight tracking, timetables, loyalty programs and mobile marketing services, which will enable them to manage their entire journey's through a single platform and for it to become a lifestyle tool.

Multiple different types of mobile web platforms, which are in the form of smart phones[19] such as the iPhone, Blackberry, Android, Symbian and Windows Mobile, exist but they had no commonality between them when connecting to an airline's mobile website; however, innovative inbuilt technology now contains device-specific recognition which automatically adjusts the website depending on the device being used, without the need to download an application or make changes to the handset. Research shows that 3.7 per cent of global passengers frequently checked-in by mobile phone in 2009, while only 10 per cent checked-in intermittently and this is expected to grow significantly[20] (*Air Transport World*, 2009). Incheon International Airport in South Korea is focusing on self-service type applications through both e-passports and mobile phones whereby a passenger will pass through immigration and security to board an aircraft without a traditional boarding card. Mobile phones have also been allowed for use on-board aircraft, as many airlines[21] in Europe, the Middle East and Asia are now generating additional revenues from passengers using their phones during the flight. Current indications are that the price of on-board phone services start from approximately €1.60 per minute for a voice call and around €0.43 for a text message.

Figure 16.4 shows the various applications that mobile phones are currently used for in the airline world and indicates that 50 per cent of airlines will have already incorporated the added functionality which will allow passengers to check-in via mobile phone by 2010, jumping to over 80 per cent by 2012.

The next technological advancement of the mobile phone is to integrate the science of Near Field Communication (NFC). It is a short-range wireless connectivity technology that provides a communication linkup when two NFC-compatible devices (that is, mobile and a scanner) are brought within four

---

19 A smart phone is a mobile phone offering advanced capabilities, often with PC-like functionality (PC-mobile handset convergence). These types of phones are now the fast selling mobile phones worldwide and by mid 2010 they represented 17 per cent of the global total mobile phone sales (Jenner, 2010).

20 SITA's comprehensive 2009 survey of 2,193 persons from across the world revealed that around one-quarter of the passengers carried a smart phone (*Air Transport World*, 2009).

21 Mobile phones are banned from use in the US by the Federal Aviation Agency (FAA) under the regulation C.F.R § 91.21.

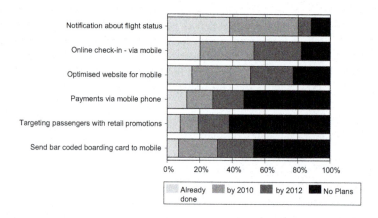

Figure 16.4   Mobile based services to passengers mobile phones (2009)
Source: SITA/Airline Business IT Survey July 2009.

centimetres of one another. Compared with 2-D barcode mobile boarding passes, NFC-enabled mobile phones could even be switched-off or be out of battery power when communicating with a reader. At security inspection, the traveller swipes their mobile phone across a second NFC reader, which displays their boarding pass to the security staff. The data between the mobile phone and NFC reader is linked electronically to the departure control system so that the passenger can be cleared to board the flight. Finally, at the boarding gate, the airline staff only need to check the travellers' identification documents. The NFC reader then prints a coupon with the seat information, enabling quick boarding. In mid 2010, the corporate giant Apple filed a patent for an application called iTravel that books flights, hotels and car reservations, as well as providing ticketless check-in using Near Field Communications. The application could be used to wirelessly check in the traveller at the ticket counter, pass through security, to check themselves in at the boarding gate and help them find their RFID-tagged luggage at the other end.[22] This should stimulate a much more paperless experience.

Mobile phones are also a medium to pay for transactions. A large number of people throughout the world do not have a credit card[23] and this has become a distinct barrier to booking travel online. However, a new converging technology known as mobile payments (or m-payments) enables an airline to extract money from the mobile phone and in turn passengers receive a text message with their e-ticket information. This could open travel to tens of millions of people in third

22   The NFC interface may enable the iPhone to communicate with RFID tags and/or other NFC-enabled electronic devices. For example, the NFC interface may enable transmission of electronic travel documents to transportation and/or security personnel.

23   In 2007, credit cards garnered 60 per cent of online retail purchases (i.e. travel, food, clothing, etc.) in the US (UATP, 2010).

world countries who are unable to secure credit cards. Air Canada is currently initiating an interlinking platform between a customer profile database and an e-banking process that will allow passengers to download money to mobile phones which can then be used to purchase Air Canada products (Jenner, 2010). Juniper Research (2008) stated that over $600 billion worth of goods/services will be purchased using mobile phones by 2013 – indicating the vast potential that underpins this technology. Figure 16.4 shows that almost 50 per cent of airlines will offer such a technological platform by 2012 – indicating that this could be a game changer for the industry into the future. The survey data also clearly indicates that airlines will use mobile messaging to communicate with passengers about items such as: changes to the departure time; rebooking options; on-board services; baggage pickup; wayfinding at the airport gate; checking standby status or acquiring an upgrade status.

16.3.4 Technological Breakthroughs in Baggage Processing

What airlines sell are not physical objects, but rather they are performances and experiences. Every positive interaction between customers and an airline is likely to influence customers' perceptions and therefore the positioning of the airline in their mind. An essential component of a successful positioning strategy is gaining a better understanding of customers' perceptions of the quality of service provided by airlines. An airline with a good service quality has a distinctive competitive advantage over rivals. Many authors such as: Bhadra (2009); Surovitskikh and Lubbe (2008); Pakdil and Aydın (2007); Liou and Tzeng (2007); and Gursoy et al. (2005) have all emphasized that baggage handling is an important service quality attribute. The importance of a good baggage handling service is further illustrated by the fact that the US Department of Transportation (DOT) publishes the results of airline complaints which are collected through a series of different metrics such as mishandled baggage, flight delays, and so on. These complaints are collected from passengers on a monthly basis (see http://airconsumer.ost.dot.gov/) and an Airline Quality Rating (AQR)[24] is used as an objective method of comparing airline quality on combined multiple performance criteria (see http://www.aqr. aero/). The DOT provides the data on mishandled baggage in order to benchmark the performance of the airlines. SITA's own global passenger survey on 2,193 passengers conducted in early 2009, found that over 60 per cent of passengers associated a pleasant trip with having their 'check-in baggage arrive promptly and safely', a score second only to flights being on time (SITA, 2009).

Baggage handling is one of the industry's great unsolved problems and airlines spend about $3 billion annually compensating passengers and reuniting

---

24 The Airline Quality Rating system consists of weighted averages and monthly performance data in the areas of on-time arrivals, involuntary denied boardings, mishandled baggage, and a combination of 12 customer-complaint categories, covering airlines' comparative performance for the 12-month period.

passengers with their baggage[25] (*Wall Street Journal*, 2009). SITA estimated that there were almost 33 million mishandled bags in 2008 (around 1.4 per cent of all checked luggage) down by over 20 per cent from a year earlier, with this reduction resulting in savings of around $800 million to the industry (SITA, 2009). Some of the reasons for this reduction in mishandled baggage can be attributed to the following reasons:

- Fewer bags checked-in per passenger.
- Improvements in baggage handling processes and/or management.
- Increases in number of staff that handle baggage.
- Improvements in tracking and tracing technology.
- Increased separation times between connecting flights and de-peaking at hub airports.

Airlines are beginning to change how passengers perceive checked-in baggage as they are now charging for the privilege of transporting such luggage,[26] particularly in Europe and North America. Some airlines have also relaxed their bag-size policies concerning carry-on baggage. In addition, baggage processing initiatives, such as IATA's Baggage Improvement Programme (BIP) and SITA's Integrated Baggage Management Solutions are now delivering positive results which are helping both the industry and passengers alike. IATA's BIP proposed solutions aim to cut baggage mishandling in half by 2012 – generating annual savings to the industry of around US$1.9 billion dollars each year.

SITA operates WorldTracer which is an automated system for tracing missing bags which is used by over 440 airlines and ground handling companies worldwide. WorldTracer has investigated the various areas where baggage is mishandled and found that bags are mismanaged at the following points (SITA, 2009):

- During aircraft transfers – 52 per cent.
- Failed to load bags – 16 per cent.
- Ticketing error/bag switch/security/other – 13 per cent.
- Airport/customs/weather/space-weight restriction – six per cent.
- Loading/offloading error – seven per cent.
- Arrival station mishandling – three per cent.
- Tagging error – three per cent.

---

25   It costs about $100 to reunite a passenger with their luggage.

26   Ryanair stated that when it started charging for checked baggage, 80 per cent of passengers were checking in bags and by 2010 it was less than 40 per cent. Baggage has now become a revenue generator as Continental Airlines for example has indicated that it generates around $200 million each year in additional revenue for charging for baggage (Moores, 2010).

Bags travel down long belts at around seven feet per second as lasers try to read the tag destination from matchbox-size bar codes affixed at check-in. However, these bar codes can not be automatically scanned without direct line-of-sight and are also unable to decipher damaged print. This has forced the industry to begin to adopt radio-frequency identification (RFID) chips that are embedded into the tags. RFID is a wireless technology, which allows transmission of information without the physical connection or line of sight that is required by optical technologies such as bar codes. In its most basic form, an RFID system has two components: tags and readers. A tag (also known as a transponder) consists of a microchip that stores identification data of the item to which it is attached and an antenna to transmit this data via radio waves. A reader sends out a radio signal and prompts the tag to broadcast the data contained on its chip. The reader then converts the radio waves returned from the tag into digital data and forwards them to a computer system. The possibilities are endless with Singh et al. (2006) reporting that 40 per cent of the participating US-based libraries in their study were considering a RFID system in order to simplify the process of borrowing and returning books. Libraries with a properly tuned RFID-based security system reported a 50–75 per cent reduction in false alarms at exit gates as compared to previous Radio Frequency (RF) or Electromagnetic (EM) strip systems. Masters and Michael (2007) researched that RFID readers were placed at McDonalds drive-through restaurants in New York where consumers could pay their bill by holding their mobile phone near a reader. The reader contacted a wireless banking network and payment was deducted from a credit or debit account. This technology is already being applied to the aviation industry as SITA (2009) reported that the number of airlines using RFID for baggage handling has grown sharply – rising from two per cent in 2007 to 11 per cent in 2008, with a further 32 per cent of airlines expecting to use this technology by 2010. Airports also expect RFID to play a major role, with 51 per cent of airports expecting to use such a device in their baggage management systems by 2013. Replacing traditional baggage systems with RFID can bring about a reduction in processing time of transfer bags by more than 60 per cent (reduced by 66 per cent at Lisbon airport). The average time to process a transfer bag at Lisbon for example is approximately 10 minutes with RFID technology and the associated errors are reduced by 50 per cent. Previously, the process could take 30 minutes or more (Wessel, 2009). The read rates for RFID are about 99 per cent successful, which is far higher than the barcode read rates, which are about 80–90 per cent (Svendsen, 2010). Sigala (2008) reported that IATA researched the concept of replacing bar codes with RFID and found that the latter will mishandle 20 fewer bags per 1000 passengers each year and if full RFID implementation was implemented across the system, it would save the industry US$760 million per year (based on US$0.10/tag cost). However, a major constraint of implementing an RFID is its associated high cost as the average cost of an RFID unit ranges between US$0.20 to US$0.50 (Proctor, 2005). However, the industry consensus is that a unit cost of US$0.05 per tag would justify a mass production of tags, and thus a sign of widespread adoption of RFID (*The Economist*, 2005; Sullivan and Dunn, 2004). As economies of scale begin to take hold and as technology evolves the cost of RFID tags will decrease over time and may very well be the next paradigm step change in how baggage is managed throughout the entire air transport chain.

16.4 Conclusion

This chapter has clearly indicated that IT can reduce costs while at the same time create competitive advantage. The world's leading airlines have optimized their competitiveness by developing leading edge IT chains that integrate the systems all along the business process chain and have automated interfaces to suppliers and partners. Technology has indeed changed the rules of the game, as online booking has empowered airlines to become less reliant on expensive indirect distribution channels that use intermediaries such as GDSs and travel agents which have in effect, dominated the industry since air travel began. IT has allowed carriers to sell tickets through a more cost efficient platform by direct selling to customers through online booking. Technology has also enabled airlines to leverage additional revenues by harnessing their websites to sell additional products such as hotels, car rentals and the like.

Technology has generated a new paradigm shift in the way that business is being conducted in the aviation world as check-in processes are fast becoming self-service with passengers increasingly using platforms such as kiosks and mobile phones. Boarding passes of the near future will be 100 per cent electronic and mobile phones will become an integral part of air travel as they will become the interface between the passenger and the airline/airport technology which will allow the passenger to be quickly processed to board an aircraft. The annual $3 billion baggage conundrum that has plagued the industry for decades is gradually taking a new positive direction as RFID wireless technology is optimizing the efficiency of the baggage process and has the potential to significantly reduce the annual cost burden.

In conclusion, IT provides tools to make an airline and airport more agile and technology delivers a difference to the bottom line in the fastest possible timescale. The profitability of the global airline industry is highly cyclical with years of losses followed by years of profits. The recession in 2008 and 2009 triggered a $28 billion loss, however in spite of the dark clouds, there is a silver lining as IT will be at the heart of the upcoming recovery as it strips away inefficiencies and cost. IT may even be that magic ingredient that will forever transform these cyclical losses into permanent profits, which is something that this industry has struggled with since air travel commenced.

16.5 Acknowledgements

The author is very, very grateful to both Fergal Kelly and Philip Clinch from SITA who provided valuable insights into this chapter. The section entitled 'The Early Days' was entirely written by Fergal Kelly and was an excellent introduction to this chapter. In addition, Sugandhi Jayaraman provided two beneficial paragraphs from her research on baggage handling and processing.

References

Airline Business (2010), Great expectations, vol. 26(8), August, 90.

Air Transport Intelligence (2009), Ryanair expects check-in desk elimination to save €50m, 28 April. Available at: rati.com.

Air Transport World, 2009, the 2009 passenger self-service survey, ATW and SITA Webinar, 8 October.

Baker, C. (2007), Checking in, *Airline Business*, July, 38–40.

Bhadra, D. (2009), You (expect to) get what you pay for: A system approach to delay, fare, and complaints, *Transportation Research Part A: Policy and Practice*, vol. 43(9–10), 829–843.

British Airways Investor Relations Annual Reports (2001; 2004, 2009). Available at: http://www.bashares.com/phoenix.zhtml?c=69499&p=irol-reportsannual.

Buhalis, D. and Law, R. (2008), Progress in information technology and tourism management: 20 years on and 10 years after the Internet – The state of eTourism research, *Journal of Tourism Management*, vol. 29(4), 609–623.

Burka, K., Carrol, W., Quinby, D., Rheem, C., Schetzina, K. and Sileo, L. (2008), *US online travel overview* (8th edn), Sherman, NY: PhoCusWright Inc.

Castillo-Manzano, J.I. and López-Valpuesta, L. (2010), The decline of the traditional travel agent model, *Journal of Transportation Research Part E: Logistics and Transportation Review*, In Press, Corrected Proof.

ComScore (2006), Comsocre Study Finds 35 Percent Increase in Number of Consumers Visiting Travel Sites. Available at: www.comscore.com/press/ release.

Croft, J. (2006), Power to the People, *Air Transport World*, vol. 43(6), June, 30–33.

Davis, F.D., Bagozzi, R.P. and Warshaw, P.R. (1989), User acceptance of computer technology: a comparison of two theoretical models, *Management Science*, 35(8), 982–1003.

Davis, F.D. (1986), Technology acceptance model for empirically testing new end-user information systems: Theory and results, Doctoral Dissertation, Massachusetts Institute of Technology.

Doganis, R. (2006), *The Airline Business*, 2nd edition, Routledge, London.

Eklund, J. (1994), The Reservisor Automated Airline Reservation System: Combining Communications and Computing, *IEEE Annals of the History of Computing*, vol. 16(1), 62–69.

Fortune Magazine (1985), How to keep customers happy captives, September 2nd.

Franke, M. (2007), Innovation: The winning formula to regain profitability in aviation?, *Journal of Air Transport Management*, 13(1), 23–30.

Gursoy, D., Chen, M.-H. and Kim, H.J. (2005), The US airlines relative positioning based on attributes of service quality, *Journal of Tourism Management*, vol. 26 (1), 57–67.

Harison, E. and Boonstra, A. (2008), Reaching new altitudes in e-commerce: Assessing the performance of airline websites, *Journal of Air Transport Management*, vol. 14(2), 92–98.

Hooke, R. (2005), Common Use Self-Service Kosk: How will they benefit the industry?, MSc Thesis, Cranfield University.

Hooper, M. (1990), Rattling SABRE – new ways to compete on information, *Harvard Business Review*, vol. 68(4), July/Aug, 118–123.

IATA (2010), IATA Economic Briefing, Airline Fuel and Labour Cost Share. Available at: www.iata.org/NR/rdonlyres/2C2C38BA-BB3B-4A4E-A8BE-1AC0FF87AC86/0/Airline_Labour_Cost_Share_Feb2010.pdf.

IdeaWorks (2009), Airlines All Over the Globe Post Big Ancillary Revenue Gains. Available at: www.ideaworkscompany.com/press/2009/PressRelease47AncillaryRevenue Report.pdf.

International Telecommunications Union (2008), Worldwide mobile cellular subscribers to reach 4 billion mark late 2008. Available at: www.itu.int/newsroom/press_release/2008/29.html.

Internet World Stats (2010), Usage and population Statistics. Available at:www.internetworldstats.com/emarketing.htm.

Jane's Airport Review (2004), More CUSS, less fuss, November.

Jarach, D. (2002), The digitalization of market relationships in the airline business: the impact and prospects of e-business, *Journal of Air Transport Management*, 8(2), 115–120.

Jenner, G. (2010), IT spend trends, *Airline Business*, July, 44–46.

Jenner, G. (2010), Mobile Working, *Airline Business*, July, 48–49.

Jenner, G. (2009), Self-Service Switch, *Airline Business*, December, 50.

Jonas, D. (2005), Airlines improve airport self-check-in-Kiosk offerings, *Business Travel News*, 22(15), 30–32.

Juniper Research (2008), Juniper Research Forecasts Total Mobile Payments to Grow Nearly Ten Fold by 2013. Available at: http://juniperresearch.com/shop/viewpressrelease.php?pr=106.

Jupiter Research (2007), European Travel Consumer. Available at: www.marketresearch. com/browse.asp per cent3Fcategoryid¼687&g¼1>.

Kim, T.G., Lee, J.H. and Law, R. (2008), An empirical examination of the acceptance behaviour of hotel front office systems: an extended technology acceptance model, *Journal of Tourism Management*, 29(3), 500–513.

Lam, T., Cho, V. and Qu, H. (2007), A study of hotel employee behavior intentions towards adoption of information technology, *International Journal of Hospitality Management*, 26(1), 49–65.

Leopold, E. (2009), the future of mobile check-in, *Journal of Airport Management*, vol. 3(3), 215–222.

Liou and Tzeng (2007), A non-additive model for evaluating airline service quality, *Journal of Air Transport Management*, vol. 13(3), 131–138.

Masters, A. and Michael, K. (2007), Lend me your arms: The use and implications of humancentric RFID, *Journal of Electronic Commerce Research and Applications*, vol. 6(1), 29–39.

Moores, V. (2010), The last drop, *Airline Business*, January, 34–37.

Offutt, B. (2007), *Airlines approach halfway mark online, powered by website bookings growth*. Datapoint. Sherman, NY: PhoCusWright Inc.

Pakdil, F. and Aydın, Ö. (2007), Expectations and perceptions in airline services: An analysis using weighted SERVQUAL scores, *Journal of Air Transport Management*, vol. 13(4), 229–237.

Pilling, M. (2008), Flying off the shelf, *Airline Business*, June, 54–55.

Proctor, J. (2005), The RFID race, *APICS Magazine*, 15 (6), June. Available at: www.apics.org/Resources/Magazine/S.

Ruiz-Mafé, C., Sanz-Blas, S. and Aldás-Manzano, J. (2009), Drivers and barriers to online airline ticket purchasing, *Journal of Air Transport Management*, vol. 15(6), 294–298.

Sigala, M. (2008), Applications and implications of information and communication technology for airports and leisure travellers, Graham, A., Papatheodorou, A. and Forsyth, .P (Eds) *Aviation and tourism: Implications for leisure travel*, Ashgate.

Sigala, M. (2004), Collaborative Supply Chain Management in the airline sector: The role of GDS, *Journal of Advances in Hospitality and Leisure* 1, 103–121.

Singh, J., Brar, N. and Fong, C. (2006), The state of RFID applications in libraries, *Journal of Information Technology and Libraries*, 25(1), 24–32.

SITA (2010), Airline IT Trends Survey 2010. Available at: www.sita.aero/content/airline-it-trends-survey-2010.

SITA (2009), Air Transport World Passenger Self-Service Survey – Highlights. Available at: www.sita.aero/pss2009.

SITA (2009), SITA Baggage Report. Available at: www.sita.aero/content/baggage-report-2009.

Sobie, B. (2010), Attention Deficit, Airline Deficit, *Airline Business*, March, 36–38.

Sobie, B. (2007), Jumping the queue, *Airline Business*, January, 54–55.

Straus, B. (2008), Revenue Window of Opportunity, *Air Transport World*, April, 37–40.

Sullivan, L. and Dunn, D. (2004), Vendors warn of RFID tag shortage in coming months, Information Week, October 11. Available at: www.informationweek.com/thisweek/10–11–2004S.

Surovitskikh, S. and Lubbe, B. (2008), Positioning of selected Middle Eastern airlines in the South African business and leisure travel environment, *Journal of Air Transport Management*, vol. 14(2), 75–81.

Suzuki, Y., Crum, M.R. and Audino, M.J. (2004), Airport leakage and airline pricing strategy in single-airport regions, *Journal of Transportation Research, Part E*, 40, 19–37.

Svendsen, J. (2010), 'Aalborg Airport debuts Baggage-Handling System with High-Memory RFID Tags', RFID Journal accessed on 15 June 2010, at http://www.rfidjournal.com/article/view/7642/4.

The Economist (2005), Change in the air, 12 March, vol. 374 (8417).

UAPT (2010), Maximizing profits and lowering distribution costs – Don't you want this too? Available at: www.uatp.com/files/uploads/PDF/Whitepaper_6.09_Maximizing_Profit.pdf.

Wall Street Journal (2009), Airlines' Expert on Missing Bags Fights Lost Cause, 13 August. Available at: http://online.wsj.com/article/SB125002419177123735.html.

Wessel, R (2009), RFID Journal website accessed on 3rd July 2010, at http://www.rfidjournal.com/article/view/5302/1.

Yu, S.F. (2008), Price perception of online airline ticket shoppers, *Journal of Air Transport Management*, 14(2), 66–69.

Zhang, A. and Zhang, Y. (2003), Airport charges and capacity expansion: Effects of concessions and privatization, *Journal of Urban Economics*, 53, 54–75.

Chapter 17

Aviation Security in the United States

Robert Raffel and Jim Ramsay

17.1 Introduction

The history of civil aviation security can easily be measured in the span of one or two recent generations. As recently as 1970, one needed merely to purchase an airline ticket, walk out onto the airport tarmac, climb up some air stairs, and board the aircraft. There was no screening of either passengers or their baggage. The sophisticated and ubiquitous screening portals of today's airports were unknown less then 40 years ago. What then, has occurred in that span of time to explain the shift? Why is aviation security a subject of worldwide concern and what will the future bring?

As a fundamental principle, it is important to realize that civil aviation security as a discipline was not manufactured out of whole cloth. It is, and has been, largely reactive to events over the span of three-plus decades; rarely innovative and even more rarely successful in interdicting attacks against the infrastructure it was designed to protect. That is why this chapter must include the history and background which follows. Why is civil aviation a target? Why did aircraft and airports require securing well ahead of all other transportation modalities?[1] Part of the answer lies in the nature of aviation itself.

Aircraft have always carried with them a certain cachet and have been the object of some romanticism. Aircraft are large machines; hijacking one has traditionally been a media magnet. Blowing one out of the sky becomes the stuff of tragic legend. The industry is vulnerable. Aviation exists worldwide; most nations treat 'their' air carriers as national treasures. What could be more visible (and thereby successful, from a terrorist's viewpoint) than to strike at a country than through its airlines? Aircraft incidents are spectacular media events. What could be more certain of attracting the world's press, thereby lifting obscure groups and their messages to the level of world consciousness?[2] The attraction of criminals,

---

1   Recent years have seen an upsurge in attacks against subways, trains and shipping, to name but a few. The Transportation Security Administration (TSA), despite its emphasis on and identification with aviation, is in fact charged with protection of all modes of transport.

2   John Testrake – the Captain of a TWA aircraft (flight number 874) – was forced to make a statement with a gun pointed to his head, while the press, who were situated below the pilots' cabin, lifted boom microphones to listen in to the conversation.

terrorists and others to civil aviation has been one of the few constants in the history of civil aviation security.

In 2006, the Transportation Security Administration, or TSA, devoted half of its $6 billion dollar budget to the screening of passengers and their baggage.[3] Today, the energy, time and resources devoted to screening are around one-half of the total spend given over to all other forms of aviation security. In part, this is due to government's tendencies to always fight the last war; to guard the henhouse, so to speak, whether or not the hens are still there. In other ways, the focus on passenger screening is part of a much larger emphasis on all forms of aviation security, and is indicative of the threat posed against that modality. More than two million commercial aviation passengers are screened in the United States each day for weapons and dangerous articles prior to boarding an aircraft (Airports Council International, 2008). Despite the recent focus on passenger screening in civil and commercial aviation by the US Government and the media, there are many areas that comprise the discipline of civil aviation security. Areas of equal importance include security of the airport perimeter, to include fuel farms, flight schools and other off-site facilities, screening of employees, cargo security and access control, to name a few. However, aviation security owes its beginnings to the acts of hijacking (or *skyjacking*, as the worldwide press labelled it) that began in the early 1960s. These acts accelerated quickly and spawned much of the security-related legislation during those two decades. This chapter will examine the origins and evolution of civil aviation security from its beginnings several decades ago to the present day. Understanding the past is usually helpful in determining the future.

This chapter is organized as a history of aviation security legislation and strategies. It will begin with a short history of aviation security legislation and offer several compelling case studies that exemplify the reason(s) behind such legislative responses. We will then conclude with a short discussion on where the future might lead.

17.2 History and Background: Hijackings and International Responses

The evolution of aviation security is not linear; it operates in fits and starts, and is often (mostly) reactive in nature. Aviation security experts have seldom outguessed the threats directed against civil aviation. Nor is aviation security history amenable to neat patterns of development commensurate with and measured by defined timelines. Threats have overlapped, mutated into new areas and have also evolved. The evolution of threat has to some extent mirrored advances in technology – although that is the mantra of agencies empowered to guard against these threats, as well. Above all else, those who would seek to utilize civil aviation assets as weapons of terror or criminal enterprise have time on their side. Development of

---

3   This refers to both carry-on and check-in baggage. Prior to the TSA, only carry-on bags were screened on a regular basis.

aviation security technologies, processes and ideas can never stop, as that would give terrorists more time to better plan how best to exploit holes or disconnects in existing technology or training of security professionals.

It has taken the international community some four decades and numerous Conventions, Treaties, Protocols and Agreements to define and implement measures directed towards the security of civil aviation and against terrorist acts against the global aviation community. The Convention on International Civil Aviation, also known as the Chicago Convention, established the International Civil Aviation Organization (ICAO) in 1944, a specialized agency of the United Nations charged with coordinating and regulating international air travel. One of its main duties was to adopt international standards and recommended practices (SARP's), and incorporate them into the *Convention* as annexes. Annex 17 deals with airport security standards. The European Civil Aviation Conference, or ECAC, works with various governments to develop measures, standards and recommended practices within Europe.

The first threats against aviation were indirect; borne of a desire on the part of a variety of persons to flee from one area to another in the most expeditious way possible. Although aviation historians differ, one of the first hijackings took place in Florida during the flight of a National Airlines twin-engine Convair CV 440 from Miami to Key West, Florida. The plane departed with eight passengers and one of these passengers named dAntillo Ortiz – falsified his name to El Pirata Cofresi and seized the aircraft by using a pistol and a knife threatening the crew and passengers. Thereafter the aircraft landed in Havana.

The string of aircraft hijackings that followed were dubbed 'skyjackings' by the press and led to the US's first air piracy law, passed in September, 1961. Penalties ranged from imprisonment to death. Under the Aircraft Piracy Act[4] any attempted or successful execution of certain actions (for example, damaging an aircraft; damaging or interfering with an air navigation facility, committing an act of violence against or otherwise injuring an individual on an aircraft) was considered hijacking. Internationally, the 'Convention On Offenses and Certain Other Acts committed On Board Aircraft (Tokyo Convention)' was opened for signatures on September 14, 1963. The Act covered '… offenses or acts committed on board any civilian aircraft registered in a State Party, while the aircraft is in flight or … any other area outside the territory of any State.' The Act went on to state that:

A State Party, other than the State of registration of the aircraft, may not exercise criminal jurisdiction except when the offense has a direct impact on its territory, citizens, or residents; security; flight rules and regulations; or when the exercise of jurisdiction is called for under a multilateral international agreement.[5]

---

4   18 USCA Section 32.
5   International Civil Aviation Organization (ICAO), 'Tokyo Convention', p. 1.

As the number of hijackings grew, more legislation was developed to counter the specifics of each hijacking. Hence, and over time, acts of terrorism drove aviation security recursively. For example, as hijackings to Cuba increased, the United States and Cuba entered into an agreement in 1973 regarding extradition of hijackers.[6] Under this agreement (arranged through an exchange of diplomatic notes; the US had no formal diplomatic relations with Cuba), either country could request the extradition of hijackers.[7] In 1970, to counter the growing threat, US President Nixon ordered the creation of a 'sky marshal' force. These individuals were recruited from Federal law enforcement agencies, and placed aboard aircraft incognito to prevent hijack attempts.[8]

Notwithstanding this legislation, hijackings continued, especially in the United States. From 1961 to 1983, there were 225 attempted hijackings of American aircraft, 115 of them were successful. Flights from 71 different US airports have experienced hijack attempts. The breakdown is as follows: 25 times in New York, 23 out of Miami, 14 out of Los Angeles and one from Pellston, Michigan (Bearak, 1983). Worldwide, over 364 aircraft were hijacked between 1968–1972. In 1970 alone, over 90 planes were seized internationally. The concurrent growth of both the civil aviation industry and worldwide terrorism throughout the late 1960s to 1980s created a dangerous mix of motive and opportunity. For example, in 1968, three members of the Popular Front for the Liberation of Palestine (PFLP) hijacked an El Al flight to Rome. The aircraft diverted to Algiers and negotiations extended to over 40 days.

As attacks directed against civil aviation continued, so too did international legislative attempts to curb the growing threat. In December of 1970, The Hague Convention was ratified. This important document was signed at The Hague on 16 December 1970. The Convention for the Suppression of Unlawful Seizure of Aircraft, as it is known, contains 14 articles relating to what constitutes hijacking, and guidelines for what is expected of governments when dealing with hijackings.

In 1973, the issue of sabotage and other unlawful acts against civil aviation was dealt with in the Montreal Convention. The Convention addressed various acts of sabotage – bombings, for example – and in the US it gave the President power to suspend air service to any country where it was deemed that it encouraged hijacking. It further delineated the question of when aircraft are considered to be 'in flight'.[9]

---

6   Inasmuch as the aircraft were being hijacked *both ways,* it was in Cuba's interest to have hijacked aircraft returned.

7   See 12 ILM 370–76, No.2 [March, 1973].

8   The 'Sky marshals' became 'Air marshals' under the Office of FAA Security.

9   The question of whether a civil aircraft is in flight or on the ground is vital in establishing such issues as criminal jurisdiction, command and control of the aircraft and powers of the aircraft captain. This has the effect of rendering the words 'in-flight' more a term of art than a reflection on the status of the aircraft's flight.

On 14 December 1973, the Convention on the 'Prevention and Punishment of Crimes Against Internationally Protected Persons' was enacted as a supplement to the Tokyo Convention. It stated that each signatory state must criminalize the intentional murder, kidnapping or other attack upon the person or property of an internationally protected person. Senior government officials and diplomats were specifically mentioned.

In May of 1986, seven major democracies[10] completed the Tokyo summit on International Terrorism. In that meeting, the seven nations addressed actions by 'rogue nations' that included a prohibition on the export of arms, small diplomatic footprints, denial of entry to the US of all persons suspected of terrorism, improved extradition procedures and employment of stricter immigration and visa requirements.

Despite the promulgation of these three treaties, however, it quickly became clear that they had not ensured the safety of internationally registered aircraft and their passengers. There were no sanctions or enforcement procedures in any of the three treaties. Some countries refused to extradite; others imposed only small penalties. Putting some meat on the bones of international agreements concerning civil aviation had to wait for the other agreements that followed.

The Bonn Agreement of 1978 was the product of urging by Pierre Trudeau, Canadian Prime Minster. It was signed by Britain, Canada, and France. West Germany, Italy, Japan and the US never ratified it. The Bonn Agreement was an effort by a group of nations to impose sanctions on rogue countries that refused to extradite or prosecute hijackers. The ultimate sanction was to cease flights to that country, and to ban incoming flights.

The Montreal Protocol, signed in February of 1988, sought to cover areas which had been overlooked by previous agreements. Unlawful acts against civil aviation at airports, airport facilities and ticket counters were now added to prior prohibitions against violence directed against civil aircraft and crews.

The Diplomatic Conference on Air Law, convened by an ICAO subcommittee in January of 1990, sought to require the addition of taggants to explosives manufactured by contracting states. The proposed treaty was presented to ICAO member states and accepted as a treaty on the Marking of Plastic Explosives for the Purpose of Detection in March, 1991.

The worldwide growth of civil aviation was paralleled by a commensurate growth in terrorism directed against it. In the United States, the 'homesick Cuban' era gave way to the greater threat of terrorism. Terrorist organizations, many of whom were small and marginalized, began to realize that a hijacked airliner was a sure bet in terms of media coverage and international attention.[11]

---

10 These seven democracies comprised of Japan, US, UK, France, West Germany, Italy and Canada.

11 An example of this phenomenon is the PFLP, who were able to generate a disproportionate amount of attention through hijackings, especially if the aircraft were owned by Israel or the United States.

Despite the creation of both domestic and international laws concerning hijacking of aircraft, delineating both offences and punishments, hijackings continued. At least part of this was due to the fact that the airlines – worldwide – continued to operate in a 'business as usual' fashion. The reasons for this are many, but primarily involve the perception of threat and the cost to specific targets (that is, civil aircraft). Hijackings, although growing in number, were relatively rare. The airlines, always operating on a thin margin of profit, seemingly applied basic economic logic, which resulted in a product of low threat and high security costs. Thus, absent an immediate threat, most of the airlines continued to conduct 'business as usual'. There were some exceptions. The Israelis, security conscious in the best of times, and perhaps realizing that the threat to their national air carrier (El Al) was there to stay, proceeded to develop an aviation security system that is still the world's benchmark. They were, however, a decided minority.

17.3 Terrorism and the Global Ramifications of Aviation: The PFLP as a Case Study

As mentioned above, one of the leading terrorist groups targeting civil aviation was the Popular Front for the Liberation of Palestine, known as the PFLP. Representing the Palestinian cause, their message was often ignored or combined with the plethora of organizations utilizing terrorism that emerged in the 1970s and 1980s. Casting about for a platform from which to internationalize their grievances, the PFLP discovered hijackings. The hijackings occurred in the context of the Arab–Israeli conflict, and were exacerbated following the Israeli victory in the so-called Six Day War of 1967. The Popular Front for the Liberation of Palestine, a political/military organization, was founded that same year. Prior to the Dawson's Field hijackings, the PFLP had already achieved notoriety for several similar incidents, including the hijacking of an El Al flight from Rome to London, Israel, on July 23, 1968, in which 21 passengers and 11 crew members were held for 39 days; armed attacks on El Al jets in Athens (December 1968), killing one and wounding two, and Zürich (February 1969), killing the co-pilot and wounding the pilot; and the hijacking of a TWA flight from Los Angeles to Damascus on August 29, 1969, by a PFLP cell led by Leila Khaled, who became the PFLP's most famous recruit. Two Israeli passengers were held for 44 days.

Several months prior to the Dawson's Field hijackings, the PFLP bombed Swissair Flight 330 bound for Israel, killing 47 on February 21, 1970 (Wikipedia, 2009a). Operating out of safe havens in Jordan, PFLP cadres continued to target civil aviation. Their most notorious attempt came on September 6, 1970. On that day, PFLP teams attempted five separate hijackings. TWA Flight 741 and Swissair Flight 100, both bound for New York, were hijacked and forced to land at *Zarqa*, an abandoned British airbase also known as Dawson's Field. An attempted hijack of an El Al flight 219 from Amsterdam was foiled due to passenger involvement and the presence of an Israeli air marshal on board.[12] One would-be hijacker was killed and his partner, the ubiquitous Leila Khaled, was captured. Two members of the team who were prevented from boarding the flight (another example of the good security practices adopted by El AL) were not dissuaded; they promptly hijacked Pan Am Flight 93, diverting the plane to Beirut and then Cairo. The majority of the 310 hostages were sent to Amman, Jordan and released on September 11. However, the PFLP segregated the flight crews and Jewish passengers, and kept 56 hostages in custody. The aircraft were blown up by the PFLP on September 12 (Tugend, 2006).

Reaction to Dawson's Field came quickly. The Kingdom of Jordan, on whose territory much of the drama occurred, moved to expel the PFLP from Jordan. King Hussein declared martial law on September 16 and fought elements of the PFLP until September 27. This nearly ignited a regional war, but did result in the expulsion of the PFLP from Jordan. These events became known as Black September, and eventually spawned a Palestinian militant group by that name. As a postscript, the remaining hostages held by the PFLP were exchanged on September 30 for Leila Khaled and three PFLP members being held in a Swiss jail.

Although not universally recognized at the time, the outcomes of the events surrounding the Dawson's Field incident were widespread and worldwide. By hijacking five planes representing four different countries, terrorists had demonstrated that:

a. The threat to civil aviation was international; no one was safe.
b. Hijackings, as a tactic, worked well.

The international media attention lavished upon the Palestinian militants during September of 1970 was second to none. Obviously, this threat would continue, and continue to grow. The question was, what steps would be taken in response?

17.4 The Growth of Aviation Security

Although the introduction of jet airliners and a series of mid-air collisions spurred the passage of the Federal Aviation Act of 1958, it was the hijacking epidemic of the 1960s that drew the US FAA into the field of aviation security. One of expressions of aviation security, which was implemented by the international community, was the promulgation and ratification of The Hague Convention in 1970, mentioned above. Signed some three months after the events at Dawson's Field, the Convention was an attempt to define hijacking as an internationally recognized criminal act, and to provide for the speedy return of aircraft determined

---

12   The air marshal had become another defence mechanism in securing Israeli aircraft from hijackings.

to have been hijacked.[13] In the United States, attention was finally focused on strengthening aviation security areas. In 1972, the Federal Aviation Administration, part of the US Department of Transportation, required airlines to develop security programmes. These programmes contained descriptions of the airline's screening operations and the security measures necessary to ensure the safety of passengers. This process was accelerated by a hijacking that occurred on November 10, 1972. On that date, three men successfully hijacked a Southern Airways DC-9 from Birmingham to multiple locations in the United States and one Canadian city and finally to Cuba with $2 million dollars in cash and 10 parachutes. The hijackers wounded the co-pilot and threatened to crash the plane into one of the Oak Ridge nuclear installations; at McCoy Air Force Base, Orlando, FBI agents shot out the tyres, at which time the hijackers forced pilot William Haas to take off. The plane finally landed on a foam-covered runway in Havana. Two of the hijackers were sentenced in Cuba to 20 years, one to 15 years, and were returned to the United States to face further charges. This incident led to a brief treaty between the US and Cuba to extradite hijackers, which was not renewed.[14]

After Oak Ridge, the security process accelerated. By December, 1972, law enforcement officers were required at all passenger checkpoints in the United States. By January, 1973, the requirement for a search of all passengers and their carry-on bags was announced.[15] New rules for US carriers dictated that airports of all sizes were to adopt and implement a screening system to detect weapons and explosives in carry-on baggage or on the person of the passenger. Airlines were given until June 5, 1972 to submit their screening programmes to the FAA Administrator.[16] Adding urgency to these endeavours, President Nixon in 1972 issued a presidential decree calling for renewed emphasis on air security. Partly as a result, the new deadline for carrier screening programme implementation was moved up to May 8, 1972. The costs of this new process were borne by the airlines and airports, and passed along to the passengers, thus initiating a long history of security cost handoffs to the travelling public.

These new rules, the *Federal Aviation Regulations* (FARs), were designed to ensure the security of airports serving scheduled air carriers. Airports were responsible for preventing and deterring unauthorized access to the Air Operations Area (AOA), and for law enforcement officer support to the passenger screening

---

13   The refusal of some Middle Eastern governments to return El Al aircraft is a good example of what motivated this part of the Convention.

14   'Cuban Political Violence in the United States' *Disorders and Terrorism, National Advisory Committee, on Criminal Justice Standards and Goals* Washington: 1976. Report of the Task Force on Disorders and Terrorism Appendix 6: Chronology of incidents of terroristic, quasi-terroristic attacks, and political violence in the United States: January 1965 to March 1976 by Marcia McKnight Trick.

15   At this early stage, the search was conducted by airline personnel in the presence of armed guards, who were provided by the airport.

16   See Federal Aviation Regulation (FAR) Part 121, Section 121.538.

points. Their security plans contained a detailed description of the areas of the airport requiring a higher level of security, and the access control systems necessary to effectuate those levels. Air carriers were required to have security programmes that deterred the carriage of weapons and explosives aboard aircraft by potential hijackers. This model formed the baseline for aviation security in the Unites States and, at least conceptually, among international airports and air carriers as well. ICAO issued Annex 17 to the Chicago Convention, in March of 1974. Annex 17 through its Standards and Recommended Practices (SARPs), enunciated the international baseline for airport and air carrier security.[17]

17.5 Terrorism Expands: US and International Responses 1960–1980s

As terrorist groups expanded and grew in sophistication over the 1960s–1980s, more attacks were directed against civil aviation, sometimes with very unclear rationale. For example, in May, 1972, London Airport[18] in Tel Aviv, Israel was attacked. However, the attackers were not Arabs or Palestinians, but members of the 'Japanese Red Army' (JRA), a leftist group with close ties to the PFLP.[19] Twenty-six people were killed and 80 more injured. This attack, one of the first directed against an *airport*, focused attention on the security of an airport terminal, as well as the aircraft flying out of it. Accordingly, the FAA promulgated Federal Aviation Regulation (FAR) Part 107: *Airport Security*.[20] Like the air carriers, airports were given a short time (90 days) in which to prepare and submit to the FAA Administrator their airport security plans (ASPs).

Throughout the 1970s and 1980s, the number of terrorist groups continued to expand. Organizations such as the PFLP, the PFLP-GC,[21] JRA, Black September,[22]

---

17 Known as 'International Standards and Recommended Practices Safeguarding International Civil Aviation Against Acts of Unlawful Interference'.

18 The airport is now called 'Ben Gurion International Airport'.

19 According to the JRA, the attack was conducted in support of the PFLP.

20 The genesis of airport security, found in FAR Part 107, dates back to just before the attacks at Tel Aviv airport. However, the incident gave a sense of urgency to the concept of securing the airports as well as the air carriers.

21 The PFLP-GC was founded in 1968 as a Syrian-backed splinter group from the PFLP. It is led by Secretary-General Ahmed Jibril, a former military officer in the Syrian Army who had been one of the PFLP's early leaders. The PFLP-GC declared that its primary focus would be military, not political, complaining that the PFLP had been devoting too much time and resources to Marxist philosophising.

22 The Black September Organization was a Palestinian militant group, founded in 1970. The group's name from the conflict known as Black September, which began on 16 September 1970 when King Hussein of Jordan declared military rule in response to an attempt by the fedayeen to seize his kingdom, resulted in the deaths or expulsion of thousands of Palestinians from Jordan.

the Baader-Meinhof Gang,[23] and others grew in strength and began to cooperate in their operations as well as philosophically. As before, civil aviation, likely due to its high visibility and relative lack of security became a popular target. From July 1968 to August 1978 the aviation industry suffered 35 hijacks and airport/airline-related attacks. There were 27 hijackings in 1979 alone.

In partial response to the continued attacks against civil aviation assets, the US enacted the Anti-Hijacking Act of 1974.[24] This Act gave the President of the United States broad regulatory power over international air operations – which in practice was easier to legislate than to accomplish – and implemented The Hague Convention for the Suppression of Unlawful Seizure of Aircraft. The Hague Convention added to the Tokyo Convention of 1963 by addressing the issue of punishment of hijackers which was not specifically outlined in the Tokyo Convention.[25]

In the United States, the FAA joined with air carrier industry groups and together developed the Air Carrier Standard Security Program (ACSSP). This effort was the result of a realization that, while airports and airport-related operations were fairly unique (due to airport size, configuration, and so on), air carrier operations were not. The ACSSP sought to standardize and make consistent the commonalities inherent in air carrier operational security.

To monitor air carrier compliance with the ACSSP, the position of Principle Security Inspector (PSI) was established within the FAA's Office of Civil Aviation Security. Following this initiative, every major US carrier had a PSI as a point of contact for security-related issues, concerns and developments. In the airport environment, Part 107 was revised and included a provision to increase the flexibility of the LEO response; under certain specified conditions, the law enforcement officer was no longer required to stand a 'fixed post' at the security screening point, but could respond 'flexibly'. Later refinements included the requirement to, at a minimum, have all persons and their carry-on baggage screened prior to entering an airport departure area. And, all airports and airlines operating under FARs 107 and 108 were required to develop and follow FAA-approved security programmes.

---

23   The Red Army Faction, or RAF in its early stages, was commonly known as Baader-Meinhof Group [or Gang]. It was one of post-war West Germany's most active and prominent militant left-wing groups in the 1970s and 1980s.

24   Public Law 93–366, *also see* 49 USC Sections 40119, 44902.

25   The Convention begins by noting that 'Despite the negotiation of the 1963 Tokyo Convention on Offenses and Certain Other Acts Committed on Board Aircraft, offenses against aircraft continued to occur with increasing violence. Although measures for restraining and taking custody of offenders were established in the 1963 Tokyo Convention, it did not include guidelines for punishment. The Hague Convention was thus developed to address the issue of the punishment of offenders to deter unlawful acts of seizure or exercise of control of aircraft in flight.'

Just as FARs were evolving to match existing threats, terrorists seemed to be evolving their logic, target lists and technologies. For example, in August of 1980, a bomb exploded on Pan American Airlines flight 830 on a flight from Tokyo to Hawaii. The explosive device detonated under a passenger seat and killed a Japanese national, injuring 15 others. Fortunately, the aircraft remained airworthy and made an emergency landing in Honolulu. Ominously, the evolution from hijackings to bombings was noted by the worldwide aviation community.

In June of 1985, Trans World Airways flight 847 from Athens to Rome was hijacked. The organization claiming responsibility was called Islamic Jihad, a Palestine militant group. In a 17-day siege, the aircraft flew from Beirut to Algiers several times. A US Navy diver, Robert Stethem, was murdered by the hijackers and his body dumped on the tarmac at the Beirut airport. Following this event, terror attacks on the civil aviation system came thick and fast, that includes:

- November 1985: Egyptair 737 hijacked by Abu Nidal's (PLO) group and Egyptian forces attempt a rescue, but 57 of 90 passengers perished in the attempt.
- December 1985: Rome and Vienna airports attacked. 19 died, with over 100 are wounded.
- April 1986: EL AL 016, Heathrow Airport. Suitcase bomb was being loaded by Ann-Marie Murphy when it was detected by EL AL security agents.[26]
- April 1986: TWA 727 suffers an explosion while in flight. Four Americans, including a baby, are sucked out of plane.
- October 1986: Pan Am 747 hijacked at Karachi, Pakistan. Pilots escape, but 22 passengers are killed while 125 were wounded, when generator lights were extinguished and Pakistani commandos attempt a rescue. (Also known as the 'Karachi Gate incident').
- From 1983 to1986 there were 45 Middle East-related hijacks.

In terms of aviation security, the 1980s were characterized by several significant terrorist events. For example, Korean Air flight 858 and Pan American flight 103 are perhaps most notable. A description of each event and major lessons learned/ ramifications from each follow.

---

26 'Anne Marie Murphy, a young Irish woman, was planning to take an El Al flight from London to Tel Aviv to meet the parents of her fiancé, a Jordanian. Murphy, who was pregnant, had no idea that the man she was planning to marry had hidden plastic explosives and a detonator in one of her suitcases. Israeli profilers interviewing Murphy found out about her boyfriend, got suspicious, and then discovered the bomb before the jumbo jet took off' (Israel Security Agency, 2009).

Korean Air Flight 858

In November of 1987, Korean Air flight 858, flying from Baghdad to Seoul disappeared over the Andaman Sea near Burma. Subsequent investigation revealed that two North Korean agents had placed a radio containing high explosive in an overhead rack in the passenger cabin of the aircraft. The resulting explosion killed all 115 passengers.

A month later, Pacific Southwest Airlines (PSA) flight 1771, en route from Los Angeles to San Francisco, crashed in a rural area north of Los Angeles moments after the pilot reported hearing gunfire in the aircraft. Investigation led to a disgruntled employee, recently fired, who had purchased a ticket for the same flight taken by his supervisor. The employee was able to bypass security screening by displaying his ID badge, which he had not been returned nor was confiscated.

As a direct result of the PSA incident, emergency rulemaking was initiated by the FAA requiring all airport and airline employees to pass through screening prior to boarding a flight.[27] Although unpopular with flight crews, the rule is still in effect today, and spawned other – albeit equally unpopular – rules involving access to secure airport areas.[28]

Pan American Flight 103

On December 21, 1988, an explosion shook Pan American Airways flight 103, en route to New York from London. The aircraft blew apart over Lockerbie, Scotland, killing all 243 passengers, 16 crew members and 11 residents of the town. Investigation led to Libyan intelligence agents. It was found that the agents had placed about 1 lb of high explosive in the aircraft's forward cargo hold. Winds of 100 knots aloft scattered bodies and debris over an area of 845 square miles. The ensuing investigation became the largest criminal investigation in British history.

The ramifications from the Lockerbie disaster were quick to follow. American aviation security agents immediately deployed worldwide, establishing what came to be known as 'extraordinary security measures' over carriers at every airport serving the US. In November of 1989, President Bush created the Commission on

---

27   The new rule also required the 'immediate seizure of all airline employee credentials' following termination of a position with any airline. See 48508 Federal Register, vol. 52, No. 245, 22 December 1987.

28   See regulation 14 CFR Part 107.14, which in February 1989 required all airports to … [install] or use … a system, method, or procedure for controlling access to secured areas of airports.' This rule, promulgated in the relative infancy of the digital age, required US airports to spend millions on proprietary access control equipment which promptly became obsolete or, even worse, non-proprietary. The passage of this rule cast doubt on much of the proposed rulemaking that followed, making it even more difficult for the embattled Office of Civil Aviation Security to create a proactive, innovative approach to aviation security.

Aviation Security and Terrorism, which was charged with evaluating the bombing and recommending improvements to the aviation security system.[29] On May 15 of 1990, the President's Commission released its report on the incident and the recommendations put forth by the Commission would significantly alter and improve aviation security functions in the United States, and worldwide.

The provisions of Public Law 101–604 were enacted on November 16, 1990. In its report, the Commission found that '… the safety and security of passengers of US carriers against terrorists' threats should be given the highest priority …'. It went on to state, in a damning indictment, that 'the report (of 15 May) found that current aviation security systems are inadequate to provide such protection'. In the report, the Commission's recommendations included the following. Inasmuch as the Commission found that communication between FAA security operations and airports was confused and subject to a bureaucratic alignment of security offices, the position of Federal Security Manager (FSM) was created. The FSM's were each assigned to each 'Category of'[30] airport, and were to be the direct representatives of FAA Headquarters.[31] The Civil Aviation Security Liaison Officer (CASLO) Program was established. Under this Program, a CASLO was assigned as an FAA Security representative to airports throughout the world. As this programme matured, the CASLO provided coordination and facilitation for the FAA's Foreign Airport Assessment Program.

In addition, the FAA Act of 1958 was amended to create the position of Assistant Administrator of Civil Aviation Security. This had the effect of elevating the head of the Office of Civil Aviation Security and, presumably, carried with it more authority. Furthermore, no employee could receive an airport ID badge without a background check. Last, research and development was accelerated as the means to interdict new and emerging threats using technology, rather than improving human factors (that is, human skills, behaviours and competencies), and inter-jurisdictional training and communications.

The overall result of the Pan Am 103 disaster was an attempt to streamline communication, emphasize and facilitate the collection, analysis and dissemination of information and increase cooperation among agencies involved in the civil

---

29   The Aviation Security Improvement Act of 1990 (Public Law 101–604) would become the most significant piece of aviation security-related legislation prior to the attacks of September 11, 2001, over a decade later.

30   Within the FAA, airports were categorized by a series of numbers ranging from four (being the smallest) to one (being the largest). Some airports, however, were clearly in a class by themselves in terms of total enplanements, presence of international flights and/ or were considered high threat. These were the Cat X airports which rated assignment of an FSM.

31   The FSM cadre was in fact deployed to Cat X airports throughout the country. As such, they represented not only a headquarters function, but also a highly-graded (i.e. high-level) FAA aviation security agent working in the midst of the responsible FAA Security Division. The tension inherent in this situation impeded the FSM function at times, as the Security Division managers tended to accept the FSM's with varying degrees of comfort.

aviation industry. It tightened rules governing the issuance of airport ID, and sought to provide an international presence to the aviation security system. It was a bold and almost unprecedented effort, which met with some limited success. It did not, however, prove to be enough to identify and meet the emerging threat.

17.6 US Responses

The Reagan administration, in partial response to the surge in terrorism directed against civil aviation worldwide, announced the enactment of Public Law 99–83, the International Security and Development cooperation Act of 1985.[32] Among other initiatives, the Act formalized the creation of the FAA's Foreign Airport Assessment Program. This programme began assessments of all foreign airports by either:

a. Airports served by a US carrier.
b. An airport that was served as a last point of departure by any carrier entering into the United States.

Airports were assessed according to the Standards and Recommended Practices of ICAO's Annex 17, the international baseline. Airports failing inspections had immediate security enhancements placed on US carriers operating out of them, as well as any foreign carrier operating into the US. Repeated failures resulted in action taken by the FAA's Office of Civil Aviation Security that, in the most extreme form, could curtail air service from that airport into the US This programme addressed many of the loopholes through which attacks could be made upon the aviation industry. In time, other developed countries – the UK, Canada and France, to name a few – reciprocated with inspection visits to US airports.

TWA 800 and the Gore Commission

On July 17, 1996, Trans World Airlines flight 800 took off from John F. Kennedy International Airport en route to Rome, Italy. Shortly after takeoff, the aircraft exploded in mid-air over the Atlantic Ocean. The investigation which ensued was intense and conflicted. The National Transportation Safety Board (NTSB), following its mandate to investigate all civil aviation accidents, deployed its investigators to the scene. The Federal Bureau of Investigation (FBI), under the reasonable assumption that the disaster may have been the result of a criminal act, also deployed. What followed was a careful, yet tension-ridden dance between these two agencies over lead agency status. Some four months later, the FBI

---

32   Enacted August 1985. For an early report on the efficacy of the Program, see US Government Accounting Office, *Aviation Security: FAA's Assessments of Foreign Airports,* GAO/RCED-89–45, December, 1988.

announced that it could find no evidence of criminal activity in the crash, at which time the NTSB assumed sole control over the investigation.

As a result of the crash, but before the final verdict was in, President Clinton asked Vice-President Gore and a commission of aviation experts to '... recommend improvements in our aviation security practices to protect against terrorist or criminal attacks' (The American Presidential Project, 1996). The Commission on Aviation Security and Safety had been convened shortly before the TWA 800 incident, but the President took advantage of its' presence to enlarge the Commissions' mandate. It was popularly called 'The Gore Commission'. The Commission's work resulted in the Federal Aviation Reauthorization Act of 1996. In that Act, Commission members examined the allocation of security responsibilities between airlines, airports and Federal authorities. They concluded that a system of shared responsibilities worked best, and further concluded that security costs were best borne by the user – the traveller. These findings would provide the basis for a model cost sharing and resource allocation across federal agencies in the future.

September 11, 2001, and the Aftermath

The attacks of September 11, 2001, forever changed the face of civil aviation security. Aspects of the security system, notably screening of passengers and their carry-on baggage, changed dramatically. Interest in security technology was moved to the forefront of policy and planning initiatives and areas that had received scant attention in the pre 9/11 security environment, such as screening of airport and air carrier employees, was now considered more seriously. In sum, the face of aviation security was changed forever. These changes consisted of legislative reactions, improvements in human factors, technology and procedures. Of the many changes initiated after the attacks, the major ones follow:

- Legislation and the Air Transportation Security Act of 2001.[33] The 'ATSA', as it came to be known, created that Transportation Security Administration, or TSA. It was signed by President Bush on November 19, 2001. As a result of the changes made by the ATSA, the entire FAA Office of Civil Aviation Security was moved into the TSA, which itself was made part of the new Department of Homeland Security, a new agency containing 180,000 employees. As such, it represented the largest formation of a Federal Agency in the United States since the creation of the Pentagon in 1944. Along with personnel, all pertinent security regulations were moved in February of 2002. TSA amended the regulations and moved them from Title 14 (FAA) to TSA's part of the Code of Federal Regulations (CFR),

---

33 Public Law 107–71 (Transportation Security Administration, 2001).

chapter XII of Title 49.[34]

- The ATSA was a far-ranging document. It created a new position, the Federal Security Director (FSD), based upon the FAA's FSM Program. The new position carried with it a good deal of Federal authority and oversight, as the FSD cadre took over responsibilities for security at most of the airports in the United States.

- Human factors and the addition of the Federal Air Marshal (FAM) Program. Federal Air Marshals had undergone several modifications in strength, tactics and concept since being formed in the late 1960s. Just prior to 9/11, they were a small (double-digit) cadre assigned to 'high-threat' international flights. After the 9/11 attacks, this cadre underwent exponential growth, eventually numbering in the thousands.[35]

- Technology. On a more tactical level, cockpit doors were armoured and locked while in flight. Pilots could also avail themselves of the Federal Flight Deck Officer's Program, which would train civil aviation pilots along the same lines as the Federal Air Marshals and permit them to be armed during flights. This programme was controversial, both within and without the United States, but has proceeded nonetheless.

- Procedural changes and screening techniques and strategies, post-9/11. Perhaps no other aspect of civil aviation security was affected more than screening of passengers and their carry-on baggage. Moving from a model in which the airlines contracted with private security companies to screen passengers and baggage, the TSA was given responsibility for this activity. The Act attempted to settle the long-standing argument over responsibility for airport security, decreeing that the United States Government, represented by the TSA, would begin screening of passengers and their carry-on baggage. It also promised to begin to screen *all* baggage (for example, passenger checked baggage) within 60 days.[36] The Act further mandated that all federal screeners be in place within one year of enactment.[37] With reference to training standards, the ATSA ordered the undersecretary to establish qualification standards for the new, federalized screening force.[38] These screeners – later to be known as 'Transportation

---

34   As it exists today, Part 1540 covers Civil Aviation Security, Part 1542 covers Airport Security, and Part 1544 deals with Aircraft Operator Security.

35   The actual number of Federal Air Marshals is classified by the TSA, but is thought to number less than 5,000.

36   ATSA, Section 110.

37   Ibid, Section 110.

38   Section 111: screeners must pass a federal security screening personnel selection exam; be a US citizen; pass a criminal background check; and be proficient in English. They were also to be tested annually and have at least 40 hours of screening instruction plus an additional 60 hours of on-the-job training. Veterans had preference; however, the Federal force was not permitted to strike.

Security Officers'[39], or TSOs, were to be a different breed than their private-sector predecessors; they would be held to higher standards in hiring, training and expertise; poor performance would not be tolerated; any screener could be dismissed by his or her supervisor.[40] At the screening point itself, new rules and procedures changed the model drastically, with sometimes serious ramifications for airports and airlines. The TSA decision to allow only ticketed passengers past the screening point, for example, rendered some airports; 'sky malls' largely unvisited and empty.[41] New requirements for showing identification were also levied. Importantly, the TSA also effected a change in public perception of the screening function. By refusing to adopt a totally 'user friendly' attitude towards the travelling public, commensurate with a no-nonsense attitude towards jokes and overt displays of anger, the TSA has created an overall attitude of healthy respect towards screeners and their functions. As to whether this new attitude is worth the price in terms of public attitude, only time will tell.

• Screening models in the US and Europe. For decades, most major European airports have operated under a performance-contract model in which the government sets policy, provides robust inspection oversight of the screening force, and contracts with private-sector security firms to actually provide the hands-on screening. This system was in place, by and large, throughout Europe prior to 9/11. A 2001 United States General Accounting Office (GAO) report examined airport screening operations in several European countries. The report noted that:

Screening operations in Belgium, Canada, France, the Netherlands, and the United Kingdom – countries whose systems we have examined – differ from this country's in some significant ways. Their screening operations require more extensive qualifications and training for screeners, include higher pay and better benefits, and often include different screening techniques, such as 'pat-downs' of some passengers. Another significant difference is that most of these countries place responsibility for screening with airport authorities or the government instead of air carriers. The countries we visited had significantly lower screener turnover, and there is some evidence they may have better screener performance ... (United States General Accounting Office, 2001)

---

39   The latest available statistics from the Transportation Security Administration indicated that during 2006, the Transportation Security Officers (TSOs) screened over 535 million pieces of checked luggage and opened 16 per cent of the checked bags. They intercepted 13.7million prohibited items at security checkpoints, of which 11.6 million were lighters and 1.6 million were knives (Transportation Security Administration, 2006).

40   ATSA, Section 110.

41   Pittsburgh International Airport is a classic example of such sky malls where spacious stores and shopping areas are found 'downstream' of the passenger screening point.

- Finally, it has been noted that, in the aftermath of 9/11, not a single European country has opted to return to a centralized, government-controlled model (Poole and Carafano, 2006).

Together with the screening process, equipment played a large part in the transition from private to government screening. Although check-in baggage had been screened on a random or as-needed basis for some time, the ATSA mandated 100 per cent screening of such baggage prior to its introduction into the cargo hold. This requirement necessitated the placement of large, outsized screening equipment throughout airports. Although monies have been allocated for construction of more 'in-line' conveyor systems, much needed airport space is still occupied with housing the check-in baggage screening machines. Added to the equipment mix are trace detection units, updated X-ray machines and the introduction of new-generation devices such as backscatter X-rays, 'puffer' trace detectors and advanced closed-circuit television (CCTV) systems.

17.7 Aviation Security Today: Threat and Response

Post-9/11 aviation security threats are arguably more lethal than ever. The advent of the suicide bomber means, among other things, that the September 11 attacks were not anomalies but a next step along the spectrum towards greater destruction and growing body counts. What began in the 1960s with hijackings as a form of political discourse (albeit a criminal one) has morphed into the statement of the deed itself, almost reminiscent of the Anarchist movement in the last century. Many groups now look towards explosives as the means by which statements should be made. This has complicated efforts to secure the aviation system. As a result, policy and law have attempted to keep pace with the evolving and dynamic nature of the threat. So, too, has the logic and process of aviation security countermeasures. The next section details a few of such countermeasures.

Aviation Security Countermeasures: A New Era

With the advent of TSA, and a commensurate growth of technologically advanced security initiatives, civil aviation security today is a quantum leap away from its humble origins in the late 1960s. Pushed by the technological advances of terrorist organizations that are better organized and better funded than their predecessors, especially in the digital age, and based on learned experiences and best practices, aviation security is attempting to meet the dynamic and complex challenges of the post-9/11 world. Aside from the screening function, addressed above, there are other, perhaps equally important aspects of securing airports and aircraft to be considered. Among them are:

- *Access control systems:* access control has been one of the primary beneficiaries of modern digital technology and innovation. Now relatively inexpensive and cost-effective, many airport access systems require the use of biometric identification. The 'lock and key' control systems of the past have evolved into access control technologies utilizing an array of biometrics. From digital fingerprints (cutting-edge just a few years ago; now utilized to some extent everywhere) to facial recognition and iris scan technologies, access has now been rendered nearly 'spoof-proof'. Another benefit of the new technology is that choices abound; information may be imbedded in and combined with airport and/or air carrier identification cards, serving as both visual ID and access media. Conversely, access may be denied instantly and upon demand. As an important adjunct to digitally-controlled access, global positioning systems (GPS) can now trace the movements of employees and equipment. However, the advances in access control systems beg the need for continued improvements to the following six systems:

- *Employee background screening systems*: the most advanced access control system can easily be defeated by a rogue employee. Although the advent of digital fingerprinting has greatly increased the speed by which employees may be vetted through government systems, the results are only as good as the input. Poorly constructed or erroneous databases create a 'garbage-in, garbage-out' phenomenon. Another major problem with employee background checks is simply that, to a great extent, the check is dependant upon factors external to the airport, and beyond their control. Even the best systems may fail due to human nature – how many of the 9/11 hijackers would have passed undetected if they had been responsibly screened for airport or airline employment? This issue gives rise to the need for better airport employee screening.

- *Employee screening*: employee screening in this sense entails security challenges and checkpoints for employees while on the job, as opposed to pre-employment procedures. Employee screening is one of the Achilles heels of modern civil aviation security. However, conventional wisdom indicates that relatively few airports seem to adequately screen their employees; and worse, that most do not seem to screen them at all. This is due to a host of factors, to include the large numbers of total employees and the commensurate plethora of organizations employing them; the number of employees employed by more than one company doing business with the airport;[42] and the almost limitless number of portals through which employees access the secured portions of the airport.

- *Cargo security and screening systems*: is yet another area of neglect and concern. The amount of worldwide cargo that is carried by air is immense; no current system, technology or human-factors approach could conceivably screen it all. An acceptable alternative has been selective screening of cargo

---

42   This renders ID badge recovery in the case of termination more problematic.

and, in the United States, regulations requiring use of a 'known shipper' programme to lessen the opportunity for introduction of an explosive device on cargo or passenger aircraft.[43] Despite calls by the US Congress for improvements, security improvements in this area remain marginal. This may change, however. The Transportation Security Administration is currently conducting a pilot test in nine US cities, a programme that allows certain private sector facilities to screen air cargo that originates in the US and is loaded onto passenger planes. The Certified Cargo Screening Program (CCSP) is designed to help the TSA meet a statutory requirement to implement a system to screen 100 per cent of such cargo by August 2010. Phase one of the CCSP is now underway in San Francisco, Chicago, Philadelphia, Atlanta, Dallas, Los Angeles, Miami, New York and Seattle.[44]

- *Perimeter Security*: central to the security of the airport is the control and oversight of its perimeter. This may not be a contiguous line, but may be broken up into discrete areas, each surrounded by a barrier to unauthorized and easy entry (airport fuel farms are often examples of this type of perimeter). As a general rule, airport perimeters encircle the secure portions of the airport and are mostly composed of fencing.[45] As a general rule, the larger the airport, the more problematic perimeter security becomes. Perimeter patrols are generally a shared responsibility of law enforcement and airport operations. Breaks in and damage to the perimeter barrier constitutes not only a security issue, but often a security violation, and must be addressed immediately. Although still primarily utilized by government and/or military organizations, intrusion detection systems have been utilized by some airports. A common form of detection is Closed-Circuit Camera Systems. Although not built expressly for or utilized only by airports, CCTV systems have been ubiquitous in airports throughout the world. The image of clusters of TV monitors as a synonym for good security is commonplace.

- *Challenges in General Aviation*: general aviation refers to all flights other than military and scheduled airline flights. Although the absolute threat to civil aviation posed by General Aviation is debatable, the security issues

---

43   It is important to note that most cargo is carried aboard passenger aircraft, thus elevating the threat in this area.

44   HR1. Title: to provide for the implementation of the recommendations of the National Commission on Terrorist Attacks upon the United States. Title XVI: Aviation - (Sec. 1602) Requires the Secretary to: (1) establish a system to screen 100 per cent of cargo transported on passenger aircraft, phased in over a three-year period; and (2) submit to Congress and the Comptroller General a report regarding an assessment of each exemption granted and an analysis to assess the risk of maintaining such exemption.

45   There are some exceptions as some airports are partially enclosed by: walls (Beijing Capital International Airport); water (Orlando International Airport); or other types of barriers. Annex 17 to the Convention on International Civil Aviation also makes note of the existence of perimeter barriers other than fencing.

surrounding this mode of aviation are daunting. Most general aviation (for example, privately-owned) aircraft are small and not useful as weapons such as demonstrated on 9/11/2001. However, the size and numbers of larger aircraft, the onset of potentially thousands more of the very light jet, the growth of 'fractional' ownership, air taxis, and so on, are each growing concerns.[46] Additionally, there are an estimated 5,124 general aviation airports in the United States (AirNav.com, 2009).

• There are few state or federal regulations involving security baselines at these airports, and even fewer ways of ensuring compliance, even if such baselines existed. A notable exception is the Airport Watch programme through the Airplane Owners and Pilots Association (AOPA). AOPA has partnered with the US Transportation Security Administration to encourage pilots to be the eyes and ears of security and to teach pilots and airport employees to enhance security at their airports. However, even though the general aviation norm has been to encourage self-compliance, paired with a random inspection protocol governed and managed by the TSA, General Aviation remains largely unchecked, relatively easy to exploit and a wide open target.

17.8 Screening of Passengers and Baggage

This area has undergone significant change over the past decade. Following the 9/11 attacks, the US adopted elements of the UK model and federalized the passenger screening function, which had been accomplished by private sector security organizations. Commensurate with this effort, all check-in baggage also became subject to screening, and improved equipment was soon fielded to meet the new requirement.[47] Although handling and managing a workforce of tens of thousands of screeners has been a difficult task, TSA continues to improve screener performance and the process continues to evolve. Bomb Appraisal Officers (BAO's) now augment the screener force, and the TSA bomb dog programme, inherited from the FAA, has grown. Screeners as well as Air Marshals have undergone behaviour recognition training in addition to their regular duties. New screening equipment and techniques, such as vapour trace analysis ('puffers') and backscatter, whole-body imaging, have immeasurably improved passenger screening capabilities. With the improvements come new concerns, however, especially regarding whole body scanning. Employing either millimetre wave or backscatter technology, the

---

46 Fractional ownership is a business arrangement whereby ownership of an aircraft is shared among parties. For more information, refer to 14 CFR Parts 21, 61, 91, et al., Regulation of Fractional Aircraft Ownership Programs and On-Demand Operations, September 17, 2003.

47 Prior to the establishment of the TSA – and this requirement – such screening was done on a random basis utilizing large and expensive equipment.

whole body scanners permit the screener to detect weapons, explosives and other prohibited items hidden beneath clothing or inserted into body cavities without the need for pat-down or strip-searches. Screener personnel are not visible to the person being scanned, which serves to minimize privacy issues.

Air Carrier Screening Efforts

Utilization of the so-called 'no-fly' watchlists has been the responsibility of the airlines since 2001, when the FBI gave the lists to TSA to administer (Hawley, 2008). Since then, airlines have checked passenger data against the watchlists to identify persons either subject to enhanced screening procedures or enjoined from boarding an aircraft. The host of issues that this process has engendered, for example, false positives, obsolete and erroneous data, privacy right concerns – have forced the US Congress to mandate that TSA take over this responsibility from the airlines. The new programme, called 'Secure Flight', requires airlines to collect the full name, date of birth, and gender, and Redress Number[48] (if available) as of August 15, 2009 for domestic flights and as of October 31, 2009 for international flights (Transportation Security Administration, 2009). It is expected that the transfer from the air carriers to TSA will streamline the process while improving accuracy and objectivity.

Registered Traveler Programs, also known as 'Trusted Traveler', seek to subject airline passengers to security vetting prior to booking a flight. Utilizing powerful search engines and confidential criteria, the vetted traveller would – in theory – be able to avoid some of the more onerous aspects of screening. To register for this programme, travellers agree to undergo a background check, provide biographical and biometric data (fingerprints), allow themselves to be photographed and pay a non-refundable fee (US$100 or so). In return for this the programme provides an expedited process that allows them to enter the screening process through a dedicated lane.[49] These programmes have had mixed success, for a number of reasons. First, the theory that a person's trustworthiness can be determined through any sort of vetting is questionable. Secondly, the programmes never offered more than a quick trip through security screening, a marginal benefit at airports where TSA had improved its processes to the point where dwell times were short. In fact, 'Clear' was the first of these programmes to operate in US airports; however, in June 2009, 'Clear' ceased operations.[50]

---

48   The Department of Homeland Security Travel Redress Inquiry Program (DHS TRIP) is a single point of contact for individuals who have inquiries or seek resolution regarding difficulties they experienced during their travel screening at transportation hubs – like airports and train stations or while crossing US borders.

49   US Customs and Border Protection has its own version of this program, which permits passengers to bypass the regular Customs control line.

50   On July 26, 2008, a laptop containing the names, addresses, birth dates, driver's license numbers, and passport information of 33,000 Clear customers was reported stolen

In-flight Security

The 9/11 attacks brought about almost immediate and fundamental changes in airline flight security. Reacting to the attack strategies, cockpit doors were armoured and locked. Under the 'Federal Flight Deck Officer's Program', pilots meeting certain criteria and completing a course run by the TSA are permitted to carry guns in the cockpit during flight (Transportation Security Administration, 2009b).

Significantly, the US Air Marshal programme exploded in size, growing almost overnight from a two-digit to a four-digit cadre of Air Marshals. No longer would a small group pick and choose flights on which to place robust teams. After 9/11, air marshals appeared on hundreds of flights, foreign and domestic, in widely varying numbers (Transportation Security Administration, 2009c). Although the sudden growth and relatively large numbers of new marshals have given rise to problems with training, retention and career pathways, the Air Marshal Service continues to grow (CNN, 2008). Taken together, these measures – reinforced cockpit doors, armed law enforcement and pilots aboard greater numbers of aircraft, along with an unquantifiable yet undeniable growth in passenger security awareness[51] – together provided the quantum leap in aviation security that had been missing prior to that tragic day.

Perhaps more than any other, the advances in biometric technologies have adapted to civil aviation security applications. Biometrics – including fingerprints and retinal scans – are utilized routinely for airport-based access control systems. Trusted traveller programmes also utilize fingerprints as the identifier of choice. Newer applications – facial recognition systems, for example – will permit continuous identification of larger groups of people, which is a condition normal in the airport and aircraft environment. Teamed with 'smart camera' systems, which recognize programmed biometrics, the ability to undertake surveillance of large spaces and numbers effectively make this a growth area in civil aviation security.

17.9 Summary: Now and Future Security

Civil aviation has evolved constantly since its inception some 40 years ago. As terrorists evolve in both ideological and technological sophistication, trans-nationalism, and financial prowess, faster and more proactive legislative responses are necessary as is better surveillance, imaging and data processing and information

---

from a secured room in San Francisco International Airport. The information was on an unencrypted laptop, in contravention of TSA rules (*San Jose Mercury News*, 2008; Wikipedia, 2009b).

51   Brought about in large measure by the heroic actions of the passengers aboard United Airlines flight 93, where passengers apparently overpowered their hijackers and caused the aircraft to crash into a field, miles from its intended target.

management systems. Indeed, although a historical review tends to demonstrate a predominately reactive mode of development, much has been accomplished worldwide to guard against the threats that continue to be directed against the aviation industry. The sheer size and economic contribution to the nation of the aviation industry, as well as its many components – air carriers, airports, cargo operations, general aviation – give rise to a sobering challenge in terms of security. Although the TSA continues to stress technology as the most desirable means to counter emerging threats, it is, and always has been, the human factors which make a difference between success and failure.

The future of aviation security is far from clear. Having acted quickly to secure the system immediately following the September 11th 2001 attacks, the US was faced with the enormous challenge of managing this huge and unwieldy system that it had established with the Department of Homeland Security (DHS). Some of these greatest challenges included: managing a workforce of airport screeners numbering in the tens of thousands; identifying appropriate organizational positions and roles for air marshals; inspectors; developing a career pathway model that makes sense and enhances retention. Oftentimes, these obstacles affect the strategic aspect of aviation security. The future becomes uncertain; a moving target tied to a myriad of objectives.

There are hopeful signs, however. TSA has continually emphasized the growing role of technology as the tool of choice for securing the civil aviation infrastructure. As noted earlier in this chapter, existing technologies, such as biometrics, have been improved and adapted to civil aviation requirements. Interagency and international cooperation have also improved and is crucial in an era of transnational terrorism. Communications technology will mimic the global revolution and usher in an unprecedented period of security monitoring and surveillance capabilities. In the area of human factors, large federal workforces will streamline, gain focus and become more technologically proficient. To a large extent, advances in technology will continue to drive up the security baseline. It is probably safe to say that future security initiatives will take place in areas not yet in existence. Whether all of this is enough to anticipate, interdict and defeat commensurate changes in terrorist tactics and strategy, remains to be seen.

References

Airports Council International (2008), Annual traffic data. Available at: www.aci. aero/cda/aci_common/display/main.

AirNav.com (2009), Browse Airports USA. Available at: www.airnav.com/ airports/browse.html.

Bearak, B. (1983), Hijackers – They're Still Flying High, *The Los Angeles Times*, August 4.

CNN (2008), Ex-Marshal: Air Marshal training a 'national disgrace', April 17, 2008, retrieved from: http://www.cnn.com/2008/US/04/16/griffin.marshal.training/index.html.

Hawley, K. (2008), United States Department of Homeland Security Transportation Security Administration, September 9th. Available at: www.tsa.gov/assets/pdf/090908_wellen_secureflight_watchlists.pdf.

Israel Security Agency (2009), Anne-Marie Murphy Case (1986). Available at: www.shabak.gov.il/english/history/affairs/pages/anne-mariemurphycase.aspx.

Poole, R.W. and Carafano, J.J. (2006), Time to Rethink Airport Security, No. 1955, the Heritage Foundation, July 26. Available at: www.policyarchive.org/bitstream/handle/10207/8451/bg_1955.pdf.

San Jose Mercury News (2008), Laptop reported stolen from San Francisco airport found. 8th August. Available at: www.mercurynews.com/breakingnews/ci_10103913.

The American Presidential Project (1996), William J. Clinton Statement on Signing the Federal Aviation Reauthorization Act of 1996, October 9, 1996, p. 1. Accessed at www.presidency.ucsb.edu/ws/index.php?pid=52077.

Transportation Security Administration (2001), an Act to improve aviation security, Public Law 107–71, 107th Congress. Available at: www.tsa.gov/assets/pdf/Aviation_and_Transportation_Security_Act_ATSA_Public_Law_107_1771.pdf.

Transportation Security Administration (2006), Screening statistics e facts and figures for 2006. Available at: www.tsa.gov/research/screening_statistics.shtm.

Transportation Security Administration (2009a), TSA: Secure Flight Program, retrieved from www.tsa.gov/what_we_do/layers/secureflight/index.shtm.

Transportation Security Administration (2009b), Federal Flight Deck Officers, Office of Law Enforcement/Federal Air Marshal Service. Available at: www.tsa.gov/lawenforcement/programs/ffdo.shtm.

Transportation Security Administration (2009c), Federal Air Marshals, Office of Law Enforcement/Federal Air Marshal Service. Available at: www.tsa.gov/lawenforcement/programs/fams.shtm.

Tugend, T. (2006), 'The Day a New Terrorism Was Born'. *The Jewish Journal of Greater Los Angeles*, Los Angeles, California: Jewish Publications, February, 24.

United States General Accounting Office (2001), Aviation Security Terrorist Acts. Demonstrate Urgent Need to Improve Security at the Nation's Airports, GAO-01–1162T. Available at: www.gao.gov/new.items/d011162t.pdf.

Wikipedia (2009a), 'Dawson's Field Hijackings'. Available at: http://en.W?ikipedia.org/wiki/Dawson's_Field_hijackings.

Wikipedia (2009b). Registered Traveler. Available at: http://en.W?ikipedia.org/wiki/Registered_Traveler#FLO.

Chapter 18

An Examination of the World's Most Profitable Airline in 2009/10: The Emirates Business Model

John F. O'Connell

18.1 Introduction

It is fitting to conclude this book with an in-depth examination of the world's most profitable airline in 2009/10.[1] Emirates carved out $963 million in net profit in 2009/10, ahead of Air China, TAM and Cathay Pacific. Its all widebody fleet of 124 aircraft carried almost 27.5 million passengers in 2009/10, which represented a 21 per cent increase over the previous year achieved with an impressive 78 per cent load factor. It also transported 1.5 million tons of freight (Emirates Group Annual Report 2009/10). While many carriers throughout the world struggle for survival, Emirates has dazzled the aviation world by placing huge orders for widebody aircraft. By mid 2010 the carrier had placed orders for 90 A380s, together with 101 B777–300ER aircraft making the airline the world's largest operator of such airplanes and shock waves rippled through the aviation world when it also ordered 70 new generation A350s. *The Economist* (2010) reported that Emirates expects to have 400 widebody aircraft in place by 2020, dwarfing the long-haul capacity of any other airline in the world and by which time it will be carrying almost 80 million passengers per year. In terms of revenues, it is now the world's 11th largest carrier and is poised to overtake British Airways in 2010.

Many factors have contributed to Emirates' ascent to the top, among them: visionary leadership and highly competent management[2] and staff who have created a first-class airline; an ideal geographical location that is mid way between Asia and Europe; the rise to geopolitical prominence of the Persian Gulf region; the development of extremely efficient mid-size and long-range aircraft, which perfectly suit its business model; and the ability to establish a carrier from a clean

---

1 Year ending March 2010.

2 Many airlines throughout the world continuously restructure their senior management teams. When new management comes to the helm of an airline, they give it a different direction, not allowing the existing strategies that are in place time to meet their objectives. However, Emirates has had the same management team in place since its foundation, which gives its strategies a solid direction and a one-way roadmap.

sheet of paper, without decades of embedded legacy costs. Its Dubai home base creates a fertile pro business environment by providing first rate airport facilities and a no tax domain which allows staff to keep all of their earnings boosting morale and productivity while at the same time allowing the incumbent to retain more profits for reinvestment in its product. In addition, it has one of the highest aircraft utilization rates in the world, with aircraft operating about 18 hours a day, an endeavour that is facilitated by Dubai International airport which is opened 24 hours a day.

There is no doubt but the Persian Gulf is changing the dynamics of global aviation. Over recent years, there has been a major shift in the global air transport market as the large Arabian Gulf based airlines[3] are having a significant impact on the industry. Passenger demand (measured in RPKs) between 2008 and 2009 increased by over 11 per cent in the Middle East, while North America and Asia both fell by 5.6 per cent, with European traffic falling by five per cent, which indicates that disruptive forces are clearly evident in the Middle East region which are positively impacting traffic growth (IATA 2010).

This chapter examines the relentless growth of Emirates and it investigates the airline's core competencies and underpinning strategies that have been inherently responsible for its 22 years of continuous profitability. The chapter begins by describing the masterplan that is being formulated to synchronously grow airline and airport capacity at Dubai; it then describes how Emirates has been expanding its footprint across the globe; and it then concentrates primarily on the key drivers that have enabled it to generate sustained profitability for the last 22 years, which is highly unique in today's hypercompetitive industry.

18.2 The Unfolding of an Airline and Airport Masterplan for Emirates and Dubai International Airport

Emirates is 100 per cent owned by the Government of Dubai and rose from humble beginnings in 1985 with just two aircraft leased from Pakistan International Airlines. For the next 15 years it added two aircraft per year and has doubled in size every 3–4 years. By mid 2010 it had an all widebody fleet of 151 aircraft serving over 100 cities in more than 60 countries throughout Europe, North America, South America, the Middle East, Africa, the Indian subcontinent and the Asia-Pacific region. It is currently the world's only carrier that connects all the continents and is set to take delivery of two large widebody aircraft each month for the next six years, allowing it to connect to other new long-haul destinations and increase its frequency on existing long-haul routes. In the summer of 2010, Emirates continued to surprise the global aviation world by ordering 30 Boeing 777–300ER aircraft valued at $9.1 billion and 32 Airbus A380s valued at $11 billion during one of the worst aviation downturns in aviation history. It shows

---

3   These include: Emirates, Etihad Airways and Qatar Airways.

a pattern of acquiring large blocks of production capacity from both Boeing and Airbus, and this strategic positioning enables the airline to leverage the list price of the aircraft when negotiating between the manufacturers.

It is also an early buyer of new generation aircraft, whose new technology and unproven economics creates risk – Bloomberg (2007) stated that early buyers of the A380 received as much as a 40 per cent discount, with additional discounts given for bulk orders. By mid 2010, Emirates had a total of 217 aircraft on order, roughly equal to the current fleet size of Cathay Pacific and Iberia combined, while it has further options to purchase an additional 117. Figure 18.1 illustrates the number of widebody aircraft on order (in terms of seats) by mid 2010 from Emirates, the 35 member carriers that belong to the Association of European Airlines[4] (AEA), and the 17 carriers that represent the Association of Asia Pacific Airlines[5] (AAPA). Surprisingly, Emirates has 20 per cent more long-haul seat capacity on order than the entire 35 members of the Association of European Airlines, and it has 55 per cent of the total seat capacity on order when compared to the 17 carriers that represent the Association of Asia Pacific Airlines. In fact, the 22 members of the Arab Air Carriers Organization (AACO) have now captured about eight per cent of global traffic and they have ordered 23 per cent of widebody aircraft that are currently backlogged from the two aircraft manufacturers – the majority of this stemming from Emirates, Etihad Airways and Qatar Airways.

Emirates' capacity represents a major threat to both Asian and European carriers as it is increasingly encroaching on the primary hubs of their competitors' core cities by adding frequencies, while at the same time starting new routes to secondary cities.

The Emirate state has formulated a master plan to prepare for the post-oil era as the rapid increase in airline seat capacity will be catered for by a similar growth in

---

4   The member airlines that make up the Association of European Airlines include: Adria Airways, Aegean Airlines, AeroSvit, airBaltic, Air France, Air Malta, Alitalia, Austrian, BMI, British Airways, brussels airlines, Cargolux, Croatia Airlines, Czech Airlines, Lufthansa, DHL, Finnair, Iberia, Icelandair, Jat Airways, KLM, LOT Polish Airlines, Luxair, Malev, Montenegro Airlines, Olympic, SAS, Swiss, TAP Portugal, TAROM, TNT, Turkish Airlines, Ukraine International Airlines and Virgin Atlantic. Collectively, these airlines operate 11,585 flights a day to 662 destinations in 162 countries and collectively carry 366 million passengers together with 7 million tonnes of cargo. They operate 2,617 aircraft and employ 394,000 personnel and generated a total turnover of €79.5 billion in 2009 (Association of European Airlines, 2010).

5   The member airlines that make up the Association of Asia Pacific Airlines include: Air New Zealand, All Nippon Airways, Asiana Airlines, Cathay Pacific Airways, China Airlines, Dragonair, EVA Airways, Garuda Indonesia, Japan Airlines, Korean Air, Malaysia Airlines, Philippine Airlines, Qantas Airways, Royal Brunei Airlines, Singapore Airlines, Thai Airways International and Vietnam Airlines. Collectively, these airlines carry 520 million passengers and 15 million tonnes of cargo, representing one-quarter of global passenger traffic and two-fifths of global air cargo traffic respectively (Association of Asia Pacific Airlines, 2010).

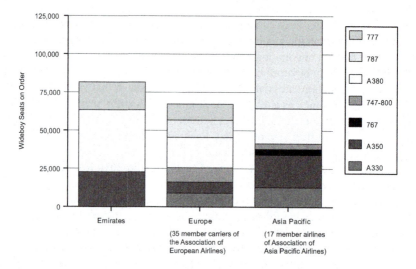

Figure 18.1   Wide body seats on order for Emirates, for the 35 members of the Association of European Airlines and for the 17 members of the Association of Asia Pacific Airlines (September 2010 data)

Source: Analysis from ACAS data.

airport capacity. Dubai International airport[6] had a passenger throughput of almost 41 million passengers in 2009. In August 2010, Dubai International was served by around 130 airlines[7] with scheduled airlines connecting 162 destinations[8] from Dubai (Air Transport Intelligence, 2010). OAG analysis reveals that Emirates[9] provided almost 50 per cent of the flights and 60 per cent of the seat capacity at Dubai International in August 2010, while its low-cost carrier subsidiary flydubai[10] contributed an additional five per cent, which shows the dominance of the

---

6   As of May 2010, Dubai International was the fourth busiest airport in the world by international passenger traffic, 13th busiest airport in the world by passenger traffic, and the sixth busiest airport in the world by cargo traffic (Airports Council International, 2010).

7   This includes around 32 cargo airlines.

8   Dubai International airport has services to 162 destinations worldwide which comprise of 25 in Africa, 54 in Asia, 34 in Europe, 37 in the Middle East, seven in North America, four in the South Pacific and one in South America (Air Transport Intelligence, 2010). This illustrates the geographical centricity of Dubai and provides the perfect formula for the creation of a megahub.

9   Emirates itself serves 99 destinations from Dubai which comprise of 19 in Africa, 29 in Asia, 25 in Europe, 14 in the Middle East, five in North America, six in the South Pacific and one in South America (Air Transport Intelligence, 2010).

10   flydubai is a low-cost carrier subsidiary of Emirates, which commenced services in June 2009. By mid 2010, it had 9 737–800 aircraft in operation, each with 189 economy class seats and had a further 48 on order. It is 100 per cent owned by the Emirates Group.

incumbent at its hub. In 1997, the Dubai Department of Civil Aviation launched a US$4.1 billion expansion plan to upgrade the two existing terminals and to create a new third terminal[11] (T3) totally dedicated to Emirates. The terminal increases the airport's maximum passenger capacity annually by 43 million, bringing the total annual capacity of the airport up to 70 million passengers. Figure 18.2 shows the traffic growth at Frankfurt, Singapore and Dubai airports from 1991 to 2009 and it clearly illustrates the exponential growth of passenger traffic at Dubai. Over the 11 year period (1999–2009) passenger traffic at Dubai has increased fourfold, while traffic at Singapore Changi airport grew by 43 per cent, whereas Frankfurt airport encountered only marginal growth. Econometric models[12] conducted by the author using historical data on: origin and destination passengers; transfer passengers; United Arab Emirates passengers (residents including expatriates); and GDP; calculated that around 75 million passengers will use Dubai International airport by 2020, which will exceed its overall capacity – inciting the need to further expand the existing airport or to build a new one. A sensitivity test[13] revealed that on more optimistic assumptions, the number of passengers passing through Dubai International could reach as many as 86 million passengers by 2020.

Some 40 km away, another first for the aviation world is unfolding. A newly opened[14] airport called Dubai World Central (54 square miles in surface area), costing $10 billion, is set to become the world's largest airport. It will be comparable (in terms of number of passengers) to the combined size of Chicago O'Hare, New York JFK and Los Angeles International (LAX), handling 160 million passengers per year when fully operational. It will have five parallel runways, which will allow up to four aircraft to land simultaneously 24 hours a day and there will be four terminal buildings. It will also have an annual cargo capacity of 12 million tons, more than three times that of Memphis International Airport – today's largest cargo hub. This joint airline/airport master plan will enable Emirates/Dubai to become a global challenger within the next decade and equal its peers in the US, Asia and Europe.

18.3 Emirates: Expanding its Footprint Across the Globe

Emirates push to expand is territorial advantage is evident from Table 18.1, with it relentlessly increasing its presence in the majority of the countries that it serves. International liberalization across global markets is increasing and Emirates will be well positioned to take full advantage because of the huge volume of aircraft that is joining its fleet. The UAE and the US, for example, initiated an 'Open Skies' agreement in 1999 and the Arab incumbent has quickly sought to capitalize

---

11   T3 is single largest airport building in the world by floor space.
12   A value of $R^2 = 0.995$ was obtained confirming the good fit of the model.
13   The sensitivity test was performed by using a linear program model.
14   Dubai World Central opened in mid 2010.

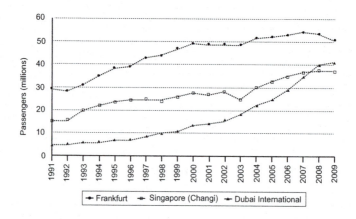

Figure 18.2   Passenger traffic at Singapore, Frankfurt and Dubai airports (1991–2009)

Source: Airport Council International.

on this opportunity. It was serving 4 US destinations by mid 2010, with a double daily service to New York,[15] Houston and Los Angeles, while San Francisco was served daily. In the world's most populous and economically prosperous countries, notably India and China, Emirates has made enormous inroads into capturing traffic by significantly increasing its frequency over the years. Table 18.1 shows that Emirates operated just 25 flights a week to India in January 2000, but by 2010 it was operating a whopping 184 flights a week. Similarly for China, the incumbent has doubled its flights over the period 2000–2005 and then tripled the number of weekly flights over the corresponding period 2005–2010. In the popular Australian market, Emirates is significantly impacting the market as it operated 97 flights a week[16] in 2010, while 10 years earlier it had just a daily flight.

Table 18.2 shows that Emirates has a very widespread geographical dispersion of its global sales, which indicates that a large number of passengers from different continents are being attracted to this carrier as a result of its strong marketing

---

15   The Open Skies agreement between the US and UAE allows fifth freedom traffic rights and fares are based on the understanding of 'double' disapproval pricing. The Open Skies agreement triggered Emirates to operate a third daily flight between Dubai and New York via Hamburg, which impacted Lufthansa's capacity on the lucrative North Atlantic market, however the route terminated in March 2008 after 15 months of operation. Based on 2010 schedules, the US carriers notably Continental, Delta and United each have less than two per cent of their total capacity scheduled on the US–Middle East market, which clearly favours Middle East based carriers like Emirates.

16   In January 2010, Emirates operated 48 direct flights a week from Dubai to Australia and exercises its fifth freedom traffic rights by also connecting Australia with New Zealand (four flights a day), Singapore (double daily), together with a daily flight to Thailand.

Table 18.1   Emirates weekly departures from each country in 2000, 2005 and 2010

	2000	2005	2010
India	25	78	184
UK	35	78	98
Australia	7	63	97
Germany	14	35	49
China	8	16	49
Thailand	14	24	42
Pakistan	32	36	37
South Africa	7	14	35
Qatar	18	28	35
US	0	7	35
Italy	6	7	34
Singapore	22	36	32
New Zealand[†]	0	28	28
Kuwait	10	11	28
Saudi Arabia	9	15	23
Sri Lanka	15	22	22
Bahrain	14	14	21
France	3	7	21
Iran	7	17	21
Lebanon	5	12	18
Bangladesh	13	13	17
Switzerland	6	7	14
Oman	12	14	14
Kenya	7	14	14

[†] Emirates operates only from New Zealand to Australia.

Note 1: Traffic data taken for January 1-7, 2000, 2005 and 2010.

Note 2: This data also includes all fifth freedom traffic.

Source: OAG Max.

Table 18.2   Group revenue by geographical region, originating point of sale for 2007/08

	Europe	The Americas	Africa and Middle East	Indian subcontinent	Asia Pacific and Australia
British Airways	63.7%	19.3%	9.4%	Included in Africa & Middle East	7.6%
Lufthansa[1]	47.2%	26.0%	6.7%	Included in Asia Pacific	20.1%
Air France–KLM	68.6%[2]	15.5%	5.7%	Included in Asia Pacific	10.1%
Emirates	35.9%[3]	Included in Europe	25.4%[4]	8.9%	29.8%
Singapore Airlines	17.3%	8.3%	Included in Indian sub[5]	7.8%	66.6%

Notes:

[1] Lufthansa's financials include Swiss and are for the financial year ending December 2007, while the all the other carriers have their financial accounts ending March 31, 2008.

[2] Includes North Africa.

[3] Includes Europe and the Americas.

[4] 14.8 per cent of Emirates revenues comes from its Middle East operations and 10.6 per cent comes from Africa.

[5] Singapore Airline includes Africa, Middle East and Indian subcontinent as West Asia.

programmes. It sells almost 36 per cent of its tickets in Europe and the America's; Asia Pacific and Australia are responsible for 30 per cent of its sales; while Africa and the Middle East account for over 25 per cent; with India producing almost nine per cent. In contrast, almost 70 per cent of Air France/KLM's ticket sales originate in Europe, while almost 67 per cent of sales for Singapore Airlines emanate in Asia. Emirates has tactically engineered a well balanced and geographical distribution of sales worldwide and this formula creates the perfect platform for an airline to develop a strong megahub, as its aim is to collect and redistribute large volumes of traffic over its hub. British Airways and KLM/Air France generate a large proportion of their sales in Europe, while Singapore Airlines does the same in Asia – and this exposes these carriers to risk if there is a regional catastrophe such as the Asian financial crisis or Severe Acute Respiratory Syndrome (SARS). Emirates has been one of the few carriers between 2001 and 2002 that remained profitable, while at the same time increasing its passenger base by 27 per cent as it was in a better positioned geographically to spread the risk and focus on regions where the downturn was less pronounced.

Cargo has become an integral component of its successful business model with it comprising around 16 per cent of its transport revenues in 2009/10. An advantage of having an all widebody fleet is that Emirates can provide freight forward and logistics companies with a large volumetric capacity. Around 65 per cent of all Emirates cargo is carried in the bellyhold of its aircraft, while the remainder is carried on its dedicated freighters.[17] Its custom-designed cargo mega terminal is a fully automated facility that contains a 43,600-sq metre processing area (including 6,000 sq meters for temperature-sensitive cargo) and the facility has an annual throughput capacity of 1.6 million tones.

18.4 The Accusation of Emirates' Subsidies

There has been a notable media presence concerning the 'dumping' of so much seat capacity. Forbes (2005) reported that Qantas had strongly objected to Emirates' bid to double its flights to Australia in 2005. Lufthansa appealed to its government to restrain further liberalization between Germany and the UAE as the competition between the two nations has been severely imbalanced[18] (Air Transport Intelligence, 2007).

There have also been major concerns raised over state subsidy. Evidence from press interviews reveals that some Middle East governments do subsidize their respective airlines. Airline Business interviewed the CEO of Saudi Arabian Airlines, Khalid Almolhem, in August 2009 and he claimed that the carrier enjoys sudsidised fuel, which helped to counterbalance the low domestic fare cap (Pilling, 2009). In addition Gulf Air's CEO Samer Majali stated that the Bahrain Government has propped up the carriers' finances over the years and he stated that 'We cannot expect to continue to receive government financial support and subsidy indefinitely ... Gulf Air is not sustainable and is losing public money' (Emirates, 2010 and UBS, 2010). However, Emirates has reconfirmed on several occasions that it does not receive subsidies and constant allegations by European, Canadian[19] and Asian airlines had concerned the carrier so much that it published a detailed document on its website pertaining to the issue (www.emirates.com/us/english/about/public_affairs/subsidy_myths_facts.aspx). Research by the author reveals that there is no jet fuel refining capacity in the Persian Gulf, which

---

17   By mid 2010, Emirates operated 6 747–400 Freighters and 2 777–200 Long Range Freighters. In addition it has 15 747–800F and 6 777–200LRF on order.

18   In the summer of 2010, Emirates operated 49 flights a week to Germany from the UAE, while Etihad operated trice daily. Meanwhile Lufthansa conducted 20 flights a week.

19   The Canada–UAE bilateral, which was last expanded in June 2003, permits three weekly flights from Dubai and three weekly flights from Abu Dhabi. Transport Canada has turned down multiple requests to give UAE carriers more rights, claiming the current rights are sufficient to meet the demand of travellers whose origin or destination is either Canada or the UAE.

forces Emirates to source fuel on international markets. Emirates funds its aircraft purchases through the following mechanisms: 25 per cent through equity; 10 per cent Bonds; 18 per cent Finance leases; and 46 per cent through operating leases, with the remaining one per cent via other sources (UBS, 2010). It has received a total injection of $98 million[20] – which has all been paid back in full through dividends, and it continues to pay dividends each year to its government (Pilling, 2005). Its financial accounts are independently audited each year by PricewaterhouseCoopers to disclaim the suspicions over hidden subsidies.

18.5 The Core Competencies of Emirates

Emirates' core competencies are now examined to determine the underlying formula for its continuous profitability.

18.5.1 The Hub and Spoke Operation of Emirates

The hub and spoke mechanism allows a number of cities (spokes) to be linked to a central hub, with each additional spoke that is added magnifying the linkage benefits and through services. By combining spoke-to-hub traffic with transfer traffic at a central hub, airlines are able to offer a wider variety of destinations to consumers, with high frequencies as consolidated traffic at the hub allows the carrier to operate synchronized banks or waves of flights. Burghouwt and de Wit (2005) argue that a connection wave is a complex set of incoming and outgoing flights, structured such that all incoming flights connect to all outgoing flights. The interplay of economies of traffic density occur resulting in the average unit cost of production declining, as the amount of traffic increases between any given set of points served. Button (2002) also argued that a hub and spoke network can ensure profit maximization and can also act as an important entry barrier. Hub-and-spoke networks generally consolidate short-haul traffic into long-haul operations; however, Emirates primarily concentrates on long-haul to long-haul traffic flows transferring long-haul traffic between Europe, Asia, India and Australasia via its Middle East hub. Like Swiss and KLM, Emirates does not have a natural catchment area to underpin traffic volumes so it is forced to develop a strong network of connecting services to underpin growth.

Franke (2004) argued that passengers accept transfers on intercontinental rather than continental trips and that most airlines that use an intercontinental hub and spoke operation are profitable. Emirates capitalizes on its hub's unique geographical position, as it is perfectly located, being equidistant between Europe's northern hemisphere and Asia's southern hemisphere where an estimated

---

20   It received $10 million from the Government of Dubai in start-up seed capital in 1985 and $88 million which was invested into infrastructure, which included two Boeing 727 aircraft and the construction of the Emirates Training College (Emirates, 2010).

4.5 billion people reside within an eight-hour flight radius of Dubai. The range of A380s and B777 will enable the carrier to reach 98 per cent of the world's population from Dubai. Airbus (2009) researched that 86 per cent of the world's population together with 63 per cent of the World's GDP is within a 4,500 nautical mile radius of Dubai. When compared to its European counterparts, a key difference is Dubai's geographical positioning with Emirates well placed to serve much of the European, Asian and African market, without an expensive short haul operation that is saturated with low-cost carriers.

Emirates' strategy is to serve both primary and regional airports. The sixth freedom network of Emirates offers 22 European gateways from Dubai, giving it a competitive advantage with passengers who wish to travel to secondary cities in Europe. In the UK for example, Emirates carried around 1 million passengers from UK regional airports (that is, Manchester, Birmingham and Glasgow) in 2006, up 4,400 per cent from 10 years earlier, and it is now the largest foreign carrier serving these UK regional airports. Around 70 per cent of passengers travelling on Emirates from Birmingham to Dubai were connecting for onward journeys, while the number transferring from flights originating in Glasgow and Manchester were equally as impressive, with 72 per cent and 79 per cent respectively in 2005–06 (UK CAA, 2006). Clarke (2007) stated that 50 per cent of Emirates traffic is presently transiting through Dubai, down from 75 per cent a decade earlier as more passengers are terminating at the base airport because of its developing tourism, conference and business facilities.

Emirates' hub configuration at Dubai is shown below in Figure 18.3: it shows the coordination of aircraft arrivals and departures over 24-hours for the period of one week. Two major waves are evident, and the timings of these are influenced by curfews and flight restrictions at the destination airports. There are also a number of smaller waves, but these are influenced by the meteorological conditions at Dubai airport as high temperatures (40 degrees Celsius and 82 per cent humidity in the summer) during the day impact the takeoff and climb performance of aircraft between noon and 15.00. The wave configuration maximizes the number of destination permutations, while it also gives passengers more flexibility when choosing their departure times as there are a greater range of frequencies to each destination. The first large wave of arrivals from Europe, Africa and the Middle East occurs between 23.00 and 02.00, and is immediately followed by a wave of departures toward Asia and Australia between 02.00 and 04.00. The next large wave of arrivals from Asia, Australia and Africa occurs between 04.00 and 07.00, followed by a wave of departures mainly toward Europe, the Middle East and America until noon. Day operations involve smaller banks that connect all the continents, and there is enormous potential for additional connections during this period, especially from China, India and Africa whose airports also operate on a 24-hour basis. The geographical orientation of the inbound and outbound flights is clearly a mix of East-West and North-South traffic.

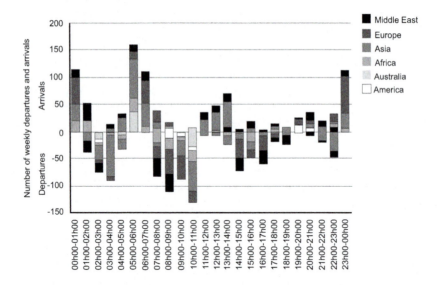

Figure 18.3   Hub configuration for Emirates at Dubai, during one week in May 2009

Source: Analysis from OAG Data.

A description of the different types of traffic flows through Emirates' hub in Dubai follows, which highlights the dynamics of its operation.

(i) UK–India

There are around 300 million citizens that are classified as 'middle class' in India, and around 7 million new mobile phones are sold every month, which shows its growing prosperity. Emirates Sky Cargo takes advantage of India's prosperous economic growth and transports around 2,500 tones of cargo a week from Dubai to India. There are over 2 million passengers travelling between India and the UK. The most recent bilateral air services agreement between the UK and India caped the number of services for UK registered airlines operating from London Heathrow to India's two major gateways of Mumbai and New Delhi at 112 weekly services. This was very restrictive as around 70 per cent of India's domestic and international passenger traffic goes through these two major cities. In addition, there are double daily frequencies available for British carriers from the UK to Chennai and Bangalore, and a daily service is allowed to any other city within India, while Indian carriers can operate on any route and have no capacity limitations. However, Indian carriers are unable to fill their bilateral quotas to the UK market and are also facing unprecedented challenges such as: an inadequate aviation infrastructure; excessive aviation taxes that are curtailing the industry's competitiveness; tight restrictions on foreign ownership; and mass consolidation among Indian carriers as the domiciled carriers collectively lost $2 billion both in 2008 and in 2009. This provides a significant opportunity for the Gulf-based carriers to capitalize on their sixth freedom traffic rights and move Indian traffic through their respective hubs to the UK market. MIDT data for 2008 shows that 62 per cent of the traffic departing from India toward the UK was carried on direct flights shared between Jet Airways (22 per cent), British Airways (16 per cent), Air India (15 per cent) and Virgin Atlantic (nine per cent). Emirates has been continuously growing its share of the UK – India market and has now captured 13 per cent, as it connects 10 cities in India and five cities in the UK from its hub at Dubai. However, India is steadily liberalizing its skies which will trigger more airlines to offer direct routings. This could severely impact Emirates' ambitions in gaining additional sixth freedom traffic as passengers prefer direct routings rather than extending their journey time by travelling to their final destination via an external hub.[21] The average connection time for passengers transferring between UK and Indian flights is more than three hours, but Dubai's immigration policy gives it a competitive advantage, as passengers are not subject to any investigation or visa requirement when transiting between aircraft at the airport.

(ii) Africa–Rest of the World

Africa – an impoverished continent reputed for its social and political instability, has a combined population of around 1 billion and has been largely unconnected to the global air transport network. The UNTWO (2009) researched that inbound tourism to Africa has increased from 20 million international tourist arrivals in 1995 to 47 million by 2008, while the continent's extensive mineral and oil wealth is triggering high yield business traffic. The 31 members of the Association of European Airlines (AEA) reported that the Sub Saharan African market was the second most profitable region after the North Atlantic in 2006 with recorded net profits of €486 million (Association of European Airlines, 2007). Many African carriers are banned from operating to the EU (Regulation No. 2111/2005) because of safety concerns, and this provides Emirates with an opportunity as it serves 14 African destinations from where it derived 10.6 per cent of its revenues in 2007/08 (Emirates Annual Report 2007–2008). O'Connell (2006) showed that almost 11 per cent of the European traffic that is transiting through Dubai on Emirates is connecting onwards to Africa. It is increasingly pulling more traffic away from the closely linked colonial powers of Britain and France. Gebremariam (2008) explained that Ethiopian Airlines and Kenya Airways have developed strong East–West African links at their respective hubs at Addis Ababa and Nairobi, and around 50 per cent of their traffic from West Africa is onward connecting at these hubs to international destinations such as the Far East and Asia. The long-haul international networks that are operated by these small African airlines are under increasing threat from the rapidly rising Gulf based carriers. MIDT data shows

---

21   This could be counter measured if Emirates significantly undercuts the fares of its competitors.

that Emirates has captured 20 per cent of the Nigeria–China traffic and 40 per cent of the Nigeria–India traffic.

(iii) Australia–Europe

Australian airports handled 122 million passengers in 2008/09,[22] of which 23.5 million were international passengers, and a total of 53 airlines operate international services to/from Australia (BITRE, 2010). Knibb (2008) indicated that 75 per cent of all Emirates passengers on flights to/from Australia are transiting through its hub. To date the carrier has carried over six million passengers to Australia. On the Australia–UK market, Emirates increased its market share from nine per cent in 2003 to 19 per cent by 2007, while Qantas retained its one-third share over the period, with both British Airways and Singapore Airlines losing ground (Tourism Australia, 2008). In an effort to claw back market share, Singapore Airlines deployed its A380s between London and Sydney via Singapore in early 2008. The new UK–Australia bilateral agreement signed in mid 2006 removed all restrictions for end point carriers from both countries – however, the route still requires a stopover, which removes any advantage that might be gained.

The Australian Government has decided to further loosen its regulatory restrictions in order to boost tourism receipts and international trade, and this opportunity was immediately seized on by Emirates operating 97 flights[23] a week to Australia by mid 2010. Thomas (2008) revealed that Emirates considers Australia to be a lucrative market and claims that it has spent $37 million in promoting the country in Europe and the Middle East, thereby pressurising the Australian flag carrier. OAG data for July 2010 shows that Emirates was the fourth largest carrier serving Australia with just over nine per cent of the international market share as against 27 per cent for Qantas/Jetstar, down considerably from 41 per cent 10 years earlier. In response to falling market share, Qantas will use its long-haul low-cost carrier subsidiary Jetstar to operate to several European cities via an Asian hub. Around 60 per cent of the seat capacity out of New Zealand is destined for Australia, and Emirates is also capitalizing on this important market by operating 28 weekly flights across the Tasman Sea.

18.5.2 The Competitive Cost Structure of Emirates

Emirates' cost structure is compared to British Airways and Singapore Airlines in Table 18.3. These two leading long-haul flag carriers are also very dependent on their hub airports.

---

22   The data was collected from April 2008 to March 2009.

23   A breakdown of the 97 flights per week were as follows: 42 flights per week from the United Arab Emirates, 28 from New Zealand, 14 from Singapore, seven from Malaysia, and seven from Thailand.

Table 18.3   Emirates cost comparison against British Airways and Singapore Airlines (€ Eurocents), year ending March, 2008

	Emirates	British Airways	Singapore Airlines	Emirates v British Airways (%)	Emirates v Singapore Airlines (%)
Fuel/ATK	8.12	11.40	9.71	-29%	-16%
Labour/ATK	4.36	12.01	5.89	-64%	-26%
Landing and Navigation/ATK	1.45	2.93	1.28	-51%	+13%
Handling/ATK	1.69	5.42	1.13	-69%	+50%
Aircraft Maintenance/ATK	0.50	2.50	0.83	-80%	-40%
Depreciation & Amortization/ATK	1.34	3.84	2.96	-65%	-55%
Distribution and Sales/ATK	2.80	1.99	1.34	+41%	+109%
Operating Leases/ATK	2.83	0.38	0.74	+645%	+282%
Total Cost/ATK	26.56	43.69	26.75	-39%	-0.7%
Total Revenue/ATK	28.78	48.55	30.86	-41%	-6.7%

Note: Available tonne kilometres (ATK) is the overall capacity, measured in tonnes available for the carriage of passengers, excess baggage, cargo and mail on each sector multiplied by the sector distance. All currencies were converted to euros on 1 May 2008 through bank of Canada's currency converter. Available at: http://www.bankofcanada.ca/en/rates/exchform.

Source: Analysis from Emirates Annual Report (2007/08); British Airways Annual Report and Accounts (2007/08) and Singapore Airlines Annual Report (2007/08).

Fuel has replaced labour costs as the largest expense of running an airline, and it was responsible for 28 per cent of airline costs in 2007, rising to 32 per cent in 2008. Fuel constituted 30.6 per cent of Emirates' costs in 2007/08, up by $745 million over the previous year. Reports confirm that the carrier has saved over $1 billion in fuel cost since the start of the millennium through hedging policies, with $242 million in savings in the financial year 2007/08 (Jain, 2008; Emirates Annual Report 2007/08). The carrier closely monitors its yield and its unit cost on a route by route basis, and subsequently suspended its Dubai to Alexandria, Egypt, service in 2008 as the high fuel costs made the route unprofitable. The region's aviation fuel is marginally cheaper because of its proximity to oil production and refining facilities, which has ultimately reduced the supply chain costs. Emirates has also been very aggressive in investing in technologies that reduce fuel costs – it was one of the first to use technologies such as a cruise flight speed optimizer and a sophisticated flight routing technology called Flextrack that incorporates tailwinds into its route planning while avoiding headwinds in real time. Emirates' competitive advantage in lower fuel costs is primarily due to its young fleet whose average age was 5.5 years in 2007/08, compared to 6.5 years for Singapore Airlines and 11.4 for their British counterpart.

Labour is a big cost for British Airways as it operates out of one of the most expensive cities in the world, which in turn mandates higher salaries. It represented 27.5 per cent of British Airways' costs in 2007/08, and ICAO data for 2007 indicated that the average salary for each employee was $73,082. The legacy carrier has to make large payments to its pension scheme as well as servicing its existing pension deficit that has already ballooned to £3.7 billion (*The Independent*, 2010). Emirates has a two-tier, tax-free salary system. Labour intensive tasks such as ground handling, maintenance, catering, call centres, and so on, are sourced from the cheap labour markets of India, Pakistan, Sri Lanka, Bangladesh and Nepal. Al-Kibsi et al. (2007) state that unskilled labour receives about $500 per month in the Gulf states. The majority of its revenue accounting and IT requirements are outsourced to India. Professionals, on the other hand, are generously rewarded and are provided with free housing, but expectations of their productivity are very high. Labour laws in the UAE forbid strikes and there are no trade unions, so workers are unable to leverage companies for higher salaries. Emirates' labour costs are on average 64 per cent lower when compared to British Airways, and 16 per cent lower when set against Singapore Airlines.

Worldwide, airlines and their passengers pay some US$48.8 billion in fees a year for airports and ATC expenses. In the UK for example, the CAA has allowed landing charges to rise by 23.5 per cent at London Heathrow during 2008/09, while 39 per cent of the departures at London Heathrow involved delays of around 32 minutes and over one-third of the arrivals involved delays of over 35 minutes during the latter part of 2007 (BBC news, 2008, DG TREN, 2007). These difficult operating circumstances drive up the costs for British Airways being 50 per cent more expensive than their Middle East rival. Airport landing charges at Dubai are almost 40 per cent cheaper than Singapore's Changi and more than 53 per cent cheaper London Heathrow for a large widebody aircraft. In the UK, British Airways, the Civil Aviation Authority and British Airports Authority are all independent organizations, whereas the United Arab Emirates is in a rare situation: its owners control Emirates, the airport authority and the region's aviation policy, whose activities are overseen by Sheikh Ahmed bin Saeed Al Maktoum, who is both the chairman of the airline and minister in charge of the civil aviation department. The dual management role allows for cost synergies and pressurises airports to act in the interests of airlines. Clearly, the strategy of joint airline-airport ownership has forced the partnership to co-support each others activities and objectives. Dubai airport has developed an extensive duty-free facility and recorded sales of over $1.1 billion ($120 m worth of gold), and accounts for around seven per cent of total global duty free sales. Part of its competitive advantage is that it raffles numerous grand prizes such as luxury cars and million dollar draws, which may influence a passenger's decision on which airport to transit through, which has a knock-on effect for the domiciled airline.

Ground handling represents the interface between an airline and an airport, and is a complex logistical process which ensures that aircraft depart on time. It is a labour intensive industry with staffing costs accounting for some 66 per cent of the total costs, followed by infrastructural costs estimated at 22 per cent (Serpen, 2008). British Airways' ground handling costs have risen by six per cent over the three-year period from 2005 to 2008, indicating the difficulty that the carrier experiences in controlling this cost. Dubai is unique as all the airport's ground handling operations are conducted through an Emirates owned monopoly called Dnata, which creates an enormous revenue opportunity and cost advantage for the incumbent. Dnata is now represented in seven countries across 18 international airports and it handles all the ground functionality for Emirates at these outstations. The Singaporean incumbent also has it own subsidiary, however, known as Singapore Airport Terminal Services (SATS), and competes for business against three other service providers at Changi whose handling costs are 50 per cent lower than Emirates. The cost advantage is primarily due to its technological edge – for example, a total of 11 interfaces such as the Flight Information Processing System, the ULD Management System and the Resource Management System, are co-jointly interlinked in real time to manage logistical processes.

The global Maintenance Repair and Overhaul (MRO) business is a huge complex entity and airlines from around the world pay approximately $45 billion[24] each year to service, maintain, upgrade and modify aircraft. On average, it represents between 10–15 per cent of airline operating costs. However, these costs are significantly reduced if the carrier has a modern and young fleet. New generation aircraft operate for longer time periods between maintenance cycles than their predecessors and are less prone to maintenance related delays. Boeing estimates that the cost of a maintenance related delay for a widebody aircraft to be as much as $20,000 per hour (Airlines International, 2009). Emirates reported that maintenance was responsible for just 1.8 per cent of its costs or $1.5 million per aircraft, while British Airways' costs were almost five times more as its ageing fleet is composed of 737 classics, 757/767 and 747–400s aircraft. Depreciation follows the same general trend as maintenance costs.

Distribution is the one cost that airlines have managed to significantly curtail, as the Internet allows passengers to purchase directly from the airline, thus bypassing the traditional travel agent. British Airways for example was paying £1.3 billion on distribution charges in 2001, but by 2008 this had been reduced to just £359 million as more tickets were sold online. However, Emirates' costs are 41 per cent higher than British Airways and 110 per cent higher than Singapore Airlines because of their reliance on travel agents to sell tickets across their global network. While most carriers worldwide have stopped incentifying agents, Emirates still offers seven per cent commission in Australia and five per cent in India. In addition, it has been steadfast in refusing to join a global alliance, which has prohibited it from leveraging its distribution network to partner airlines. Also, part of the high cost stems from the fact that Emirates derives over one-third of its

---

24   Globally airlines spend around $14 billion on modifications, $10.9 billion on the airframe, $10.1 billion on components, $5.4 billion on line maintenance and $4.6 billion on engine maintenance (MRO Management, 2010).

revenues from the Middle East, Africa and West Asia, which generally have a low internet penetration coupled with low credit card usage.

However, Emirates' financing costs are very concerning. Repayments for its existing fleet and for the financing of an additional aircraft place a significant burden on the Arab incumbent. *Airfinance Journal* (2008) reports that all pre-delivery payments are financed from its $3.1 billion cash reserve, while it purchases 15–25 per cent equity in each aircraft. UBS (2010) indicates that it finances the remainder through bonds, 10 per cent, finance leases 18 per cent, and 46 per cent through operating leases.

18.5.3 The Strengthening Brand of Emirates

Aaker (1996), the leading academic in branding, states that a company's brand is the primary source of its competitive advantage and a valuable strategic asset. Dennis and Denton (2004) pointed out that airlines, such as British Airways and Lufthansa, have developed strong brands which are associated with quality and recognized worldwide. Interbrand publishes a list of the top 100 global brands each year, where unassuming brands such as Durecell and Nivea are included, which were valued at $3.4 and $3.6 billion respectively in 2008 – yet there are no airlines within the top 100 global rankings (Interbrand, 2009). The United States' leading airline branding company, Aerobrand, confirmed that there is very little product differentiation between carriers – thus, marketing efforts to strengthen the brand become paramount (Arnoult, 2004). Teece (2000) argued that strong brands are key value creating resources, and that high-value customers place great importance on brands when making their travel related choices compared to more price-sensitive, lower-value customer groups. Mercer Consulting (2001) stated that customers were four times more likely to choose an airline with the strongest brand than the airline with the weakest. Emirates spends around four per cent of its revenues each year on marketing, which equated to around $380 million in 2008, with this split evenly between sponsorship and advertising (Airline Business, 2006).

Sponsorship is an important marketing communications tool that seeks to achieve favourable publicity for a company within a certain target audience via the support of an activity not directly linked to the company's normal business. Emirates is one of the world's most proactive airlines in sports sponsorship, and Stockhaus (2008) researched that Emirates will sponsor a sport depending on the level of coverage and the popularity of the sport. The chairman of Emirates, Sheikh Ahmed bin Saeed Al-Maktoum, maintains that sponsorship is a vital part of the airline's marketing strategy and states that 'Sponsorships are one of the best ways to connect with our passengers. They allow us to share and support their interests and to build a closer relationship with them' (Al-Maktoum, 2009). Sponsorship appears to be an integral component of Emirates' brand strategy and is leveraged to develop brand affiliation and loyalty. It allows them to take quantum leaps in promoting their brand in new markets. While airlines worldwide cut costs, Emirates has persisted in strengthening its brand throughout the world by sponsoring sporting events, as shown in Table 18.4 below.

The diversity of these sporting events is reflective of the different segments of its passenger's profiles. All these sporting events display the 'Fly Emirates' logo on the athletes' clothing which the television cameras transmit the games to millions of people, stretching and strengthening its brand awareness. In terms of global television coverage alone, sponsorships generated over US$500 million in media exposure for the Emirates brand in 2007/8. It is the first-ever airline to become an Official Partner of the FIFA World Cup, and in 2006 the final between Italy and France attracted 715.1 million viewers, making its brand visible to a huge audience spread across the globe. The 2010 world cup games in South Africa were expected to be the most-watched television event in history[25] (FIFA, 2010). The UK is one of the Emirates' most important market which accounts for 13 per cent of all its seat capacity – the highest proportion of any country. Football is the nation's most popular sport and Mintel (2004) calculated that around 44 per cent of the adult population ranked soccer as their most popular sport. Emirates sponsored a £100 million ($143 million) contract with London's premier soccer team, Arsenal, where its stadium was renamed the 'Emirates Stadium' for 15 years, this being the largest sponsorship agreement ever established in British football. It will also sponsor the 2011 rugby world cup which will take place in New Zealand in association with two other iconic global brands of Heineken and Mastercard. It also supports 12 international golf tournaments – a sport played by many business executives, thereby allowing it to target this specific passenger segment. Horse racing is another sport that is highly targeted. It appeals to a wide audience and is big business – in the US for example, the equine industry has a $112 billion direct and indirect impact on the economy, supporting 1.4 million jobs and involving seven million people (Keaveney, 2008). Emirates invested $19 million in sponsoring the US breeders championship, and its inaugural flight to Los Angeles in 2008 coincided with the event bring hosted in that city. It is apparent that Emirates views sponsorship as an influential platform for brand strategy. In order to support and strengthen its brand, it engages over 120 agencies comprising of consultancies, designers, publishers, copywriters, ad agencies and production houses, involving over 275 staff dedicated full time to the Emirates advertising account. Over 1,600 campaigns were developed in 2008 in over 100 countries.

---

25   It is estimated that a cumulative audience of 26 billion people watched the world cup soccer games in South Africa in 2010, which is an average of approximately 400 million viewers per match (Wikipedia, 2010).

Table 18.4   Sponsorship activities of Emirates

Football	Rugby	Golf	Cricket	Horse racing
FIFA 2006, 2010 and 2014 World Cup	World Cup 2011	Dubai Desert Classic	ICC Umpires	National Thoroughbred Racing Association (US)
Arsenal FC and Emirates stadium, UK	IRB Referees and Match Officials	Dubai Ladies Masters	Cricket Australia	Dubai World Cup
AC Milan, Italy	Dubai Rugby Sevens	Malaysian Open	Lord's Taverners	Melbourne Cup, Australia
The Emirates Cup	South African Rugby Sevens	Hong Kong Open	Pro Arch Tournament	Champion Stakes, Newmarket, UK
Paris Saint Germain	London Sevens	BMW Open		Yorkshire Cup, York UK
Hamburg SV	Edinburgh Sevens	Austrian Open		Singapore Derby
Olympiacos CFP, Greece	World Cup Sevens	Volvo Masters of Asia		Godolphin (Dubai)
Asian Football Confederation (AFC)	International Sevens England & Somoa	Hero Honda Open		Australian Jockey Club
	Emirates Western Force	Australian PGA Championship		Dubai Intl Racing Carnival
		Africa Open		Melbourne Cup Carnival
		Volvo China Open		Australian Jockey Club Autumn & Spring Carnival
		HSBC Champion, China		
Yacht racing	**Powerboat racing**	**Tennis**	**Auto Racing**	
Team New Zealand	UIM Class 1 World Powerboat Championship Dubai	Dubai Tennis Championship	Dubai Grand Racing	

Source: Compiled from Emirates website.

18.6 Concluding Comments

The Middle East is rapidly becoming an important component of the global air transport market. The region's airlines are capitalizing on its unique geographical position half way between Asia and Europe, and an estimated 4.5 billion people reside within an eight hour flight radius of the Middle East. However, it is the prolific growth of Emirates, that is reshaping the competitive dynamics of the industry as it is growing traffic by cannibalizing the traditional traffic flows between Asian and European hubs, and by connecting secondary cities as a result of exercising their sixth freedom traffic rights. An airport master plan to create a corresponding mega-hub is also unfolding in order to handle this huge traffic growth. By mid 2010, Emirates had 217 widebody aircraft on order and it has been relentlessly pushing into new markets while continuously expanding its existing operations. As liberalization increases its footprint across global markets, Emirates is poised to take full advantage, and this represents a major threat to European and Asian incumbents. An investigation into Emirates' core competencies reveals three underpinning strategies that are responsible for its continued success. Firstly its creation of a mega-hub at Dubai enables the carrier to collect traffic from the six continents that it operates to and then redistribute this traffic over its hub. Secondly, its low cost structure enables it to offer a low fare which in turn triggers traffic – it is very focused on controlling its costs and, as the Internet penetration across the Middle East, Africa and West Asia increases, it will produce a very competitive cost base for the incumbent. Thirdly, Emirates invests very heavily in developing its brand and sports sponsorship has become an integral component of its marketing mix. However, there are also dangers facing Emirates as its aggressive expansion is stirring the concerns of both airlines and governments in some of the countries that its serves. As the skies continue to become liberated, more airlines will offer direct routings which are more preferable to passengers, which will impact Emirates. Dubai's debt is another burden that may offset the growth of Emirates as they are intrinsically interlinked. However, Emirates has been resilient and steadfast in its climb to success and its strategies that are in place will provide it with a solid roadmap to become a global challenger.

18.7 References

Aaker, D. 1996, *Building Strong Brands*, The Free Press.

Al-Kibsi, G., Benkert, C. and Schubert, J. 2007, Getting labor policy to work in the Gulf, *McKinsey Quarterly* special edition: Reappraising the Gulf States, 19–29.

Al-Maktoum (2009), Emirates Sport Sponsorship. Available at: http://www.emirates.com/au/english/about/sponsorships/sponsorships.aspx.

Airbus (2009), Airbus and the Middle East – a story of history and future, p. 22, presented by Fouad Attar, head of Commercial, Airbus Middle East, Muscat 21st October.

Airline Business 2006, The Airline Strategy Awards – Marketing, Airline Business, 43, August.

Airfinance Journal 2008, The new order, June, 22–26.

Airlines International 2009, Right Place, Right Time, *IATA Publication*, Volume 19, April–May, 26–30.

Airports Council International (2010), Year to date traffic data. Available at: www. airports.org/cda/aci_common/display/main/aci_content07_c.jsp?zn=aci& cp=1-5-212–218–222_666_2__.

Air Transport Intelligence 2010, Airport database for Dubai International, accessed on www.rati.com.

Air Transport Intelligence 2007, Lufthansa urges restraint on further Middle East liberalization, 19 December.

Association of Asia Pacific Airlines (2010), 2010 Press releases. Available at: www.aapairlines.org/2010_Press_Releases.aspx.

Association of European Airlines (2010), Press releases. Available at: www.aea. be/press/releases/index.html.

Association of European Airlines 2007, Operating Economy of AEA Airlines. Available at: http://files.aea.be/RIG/Economics/DL/SumRep07.pdf.

Arnoult, S. 2004, Selling the airline, *Air Transport World*, November, 32–37.

BBC news 2008, BAA to raise airport landing fees, 11 March. Available at: http:// news.bbc.co.uk/1/hi/business/7288937.stm.

BITRE 2010, Airport Traffic Data 1985–86 to 2008–09. Available at: www.btre. gov.au/info.aspx?ResourceId=191&NodeId=96.

Bloomberg 2007, Airbus hands over A380 as delay, losses irk investors (Update2), October. Available at: www.bloomberg.com/apps/ news?pid=20601085&sid=adjAi_ZE0m2o&refer=europe.

Burghouwt, G. and de Wit, J. 2005, Temporal configurations of European airline networks, *Journal of Air Transport Management*, vol. 11, no. 3, 185–198.

Button, K. 2002, 'Debunking some common myths about airport hubs', *Journal of Air Transport Management*, vol. 8, 177–188.

Clarke, T. 2007, The Lindbergh Lecture, twenty-first century Civil Aviation – Raising the Game, Royal Aeronautical Society, 13 March, London.

Dennis, N. and Denton, N. 2004, Airline franchising in Europe: benefits and disbenefits to airlines and consumers, *Journal of Air Transport Management*, vol. 6(4), 179–190.

DG TREN 2007, Air Transport: Quarterly Report No. 17, 4th Quarterly 2007 (October to December). Available at: http://ec.europa.eu/transport/air_portal/ observatory/doc/vademecum/atv_q42007_17.pdf.

DG TREN 2008, Air Transport: Quarterly Report No. 18, 1st Quarterly. Avaiable at: http://ec.europa.eu/transport/air/observatory_market/doc/atv_q12008_18. pdf.

Doganis, R. 2006, *The Airline Business*, 2nd edn, Routledge, London.

Emirates 2010, Subsidy. The myths and facts about Emirates and our industry. Available at: www.emirates.com/us/english/images/Subsidy per cent20-per cent20Myths per cent20and per cent20Facts per cent20August per cent20FINAL_tcm272–557688.pdf.

Emirates Group Annual Report (2009/10), Annual report. Available at: www.theemiratesgroup.com/english/facts-figures/annual-report.aspx.

Emirates Annual Report 2007–2008, Annual Report. Available at: www.ekgroup.com/Annualreports/2007–2008/PDF.asp.

Emirates Operating Statistics 2007, Operating statistics. Available at: http://www.ekgroup.com/Annualreports/2006–2007/OperatingStatistics.asp.

FIFA 2010, Beaming 2010 to the world. Available at: www.fifa.com/worldcup/news/newsid=1223134/index.html.

FIFA 2007, 2006 FIFA World Cup™ broadcast wider, longer and farther than ever before. Available at: www.fifa.com/aboutfifa/marketingtv/news/newsid=111247.html.

Forbes 2005, Emirates Air criticizes Australia's Qantas for 'protectionism'. Available at: http://www.forbes.com/markets/feeds/afx/2005/11/07/afx2320603.html#.

Franke, M. 2004, 'Competition between network carriers and low-cost carriers – retreat battle or breakthrough to a new level of efficiency?', *Journal of Air Transport Management*, vol. 10, 15–21.

Gebremariam, T. 2008, Examining the potential of an African hub, 16th Annual Conference of the Future of Air Transport, Radisson SAS Portman Hotel, London, 3 December.

IATA 2010, 2009: Worst Demand Decline in History – Encouraging Year-End Improvements, 27 January 2010. Available at: www.iata.org/pressroom/facts_figures/traffic_results/Pages/2010–01–27–01.aspx.

Interbrand 2009, Best Global Brands, 2008 Rankings. Available at: www.interbrand.com/best_global_brands.aspx.

Jain, S. 2008, Emirates saves $1bn by hedging fuel costs. Available at: http://www.iag-inc.com/news/shweta8.pdf.

Keaveney, S. 2008, Equines and their human companions, *Journal of Business Research*, vol. 61, no. 5, May 2008, 444–454.

Knibb, D. 2008, Emirates leads from the front, *Airline Business*, January, 20.

Mercer Consulting 2001, Leveraging brand strategy in the travel industry, *Mercer report*, vol. VIII, no. 2, Spring/Summer.

Mintel 2004, *Football Business*, UK, December.

MRO Management 2010, *Taking a dip*, vol. 12, 2, 38–40.

O'Connell, J.F. 2006, The changing dynamics of the Arab Gulf based airlines and an investigation into the strategies that are making Emirates into a global player. *World Review of Intermodal Transportation Research*, 1(1), 94–114.

Pilling, M. 2009, The quiet type, *Airline Business*, August, 28–32.

Pilling, M. 2005, Flanagan: the elder statesman of Emirates. Available at: http://www.flightglobal.com/articles/2005/11/16/203634/flanagan-the-elder-statesman-of-emirates.html.

Serpen, E. 2008, Airline Productivity Improvement, IATA /IGHC Ground Operations Symposium, Malaysia, May 12–14. Available at: www.sh-e.com/presentations/eserpen_12_may_08.pdf.

Stockhaus, L. 2008, An assessment of sports sponsorship as an integrated component of the corporate communications mix in the airline industry, MSc thesis, Cranfield University.

Teece, D. 2000, Strategies for managing knowledge assets: The role of firm structure and industrial context, *Long Range Planning*, 33, 35–54.

The Independent 2010, British Airways' pension deficit move agreed, 16 March. Available at: www.independent.co.uk/news/business/news/british-airways-pension-deficit-move-agreed-1922171.html.

The Economist 2010, Rulers of the Silk World, 3 June.

Thomas, G. 2008, Pirates or Pioneers? *Air Transport World*, February, 80–82.

Tourism Australia 2008, United Kingdom Aviation Profile, understanding the UK to Australia Aviation Environment. Available at: http://www.tourism.australia.com/content/UK/profiles_2008/Aviation per cent20profile per cent202008 per cent20- per cent20UK per cent20 per cent5BCompatibility per cent20Mode per cent5D.pdf.

UBS 2010, UBS Investment Research, Who is most at risk from Middle Eastern Airline Expansion, 7th June.

UK CAA 2006, Air Services at UK Regional Airports, an update on Developments, CAP 775, Civil Aviation Authority, November.

UNTWO 2009, *World Tourism Barometer*, vol. 7, no. 1, January.

Wikipedia, 2010, 2010 FIFA World Cup, section 14.1 – Broadcasting. Available at: http://en.W?ikipedia.org/wiki/2010_FIFA_World_Cup#Broadcasting.

Index